15

The CHARLES ELIOT NORTON LECTURES for 1938-1939

SIGFRIED GIEDION

SPACE, TIME

AND ARCHITECTURE

the growth of a new tradition

CAMBRIDGE, MASSACHUSETTS
HARVARD UNIVERSITY PRESS
FIFTH EDITION, REVISED AND ENLARGED

Library of Congress Catalog Card Number 67-17310
ISBN 0-674-83040-7
Printed in the United States of America

FOREWORD TO THE FIFTH EDITION

In preparing the fifth edition (sixteenth printing) of this work I have attempted to bring this history of the contemporary tradition up to date. I have included many new works, such as Gropius' American Embassy at Athens; Le Corbusier's Carpenter Center for Visual Arts at Harvard University and his Priory of La Tourette; the Bacardi Administration Building in Mexico by Mies van der Rohe; and several community centers by Alvar Aalto. A discussion of "The Legacy of Le Corbusier" has been added together with a presentation of some of his latest works, including the Le Corbusier Center in Zurich.

I have added a new chapter on the Danish architect Jørn Utzon, "Jørn Utzon and the Third Generation," as well as a short chapter on the International Congresses for Modern Architecture (CIAM).

It was thought necessary to supplement the section on "Space-Time in City Planning" with a new chapter, "Changing Notions of the City," in view of various present-day tendencies, such as those manifested in the works of Kenzo Tange and Fumihiko Maki, and in J. L. Sert's Harvard dormitories for married students, Peabody Terrace.

I should like to thank Professor Jaqueline Tyrwhitt for translating the new material and for her invaluable assistance in preparing this edition for the press.

ROME, AMERICAN ACADEMY, SEPTEMBER 1966   S.G.

FOREWORD TO THE FIRST EDITION

Space, Time and Architecture is intended for those who are alarmed by the present state of our culture and anxious to find a way out of the apparent chaos of its contradictory tendencies.

I have attempted to establish, both by argument and by objective evidence, that in spite of the seeming confusion there is nevertheless a true, if hidden, unity, a secret synthesis, in our present civilization. To point out *why* this synthesis has *not* become *a conscious and active reality* has been one of my chief aims.

My interest has been particularly concentrated on the growth of the new tradition in architecture, for the purpose of showing its interrelations with other human activities and the similarity of methods that are in use today in architecture, construction, painting, city planning, and science.

I have found it preferable, in order to arrive at a true and complete understanding of the growth of the new tradition, to select from the vast body of available historical material only relatively few facts. *History is not a compilation of facts, but an insight into a moving process of life.* Moreover, such insight is obtained not by the exclusive use of the panoramic survey, the bird's-eye view, but by isolating and examining certain specific events intensively, penetrating and exploring them in the manner of the close-up. This procedure makes it possible to evaluate a culture from within as well as from without.

In keeping with this approach, the bibliographical apparatus has been reduced to a minimum. For those interested in further study and research in the subject, the necessary information is given in footnotes. No general bibliography has been provided. Its addition, in view of the theme and design of the book, would simply have swollen the volume by some fifty extra pages without at the same time affording scientific completeness.

Space, Time and Architecture was written in stimulating association with young Americans — an outgrowth of lectures and seminars which I gave as Charles Eliot Norton Professor at Harvard University. The problem of its composition was to transmute the spoken word of lecture and discussion into the quite different medium of the printed page. For the lectures the English version was prepared by Mr. *R. Bottomley*. Mr. *W. J. Callaghan* and Mr. *Erwart Matthews* made the English translation of the book, which was completed at Cambridge, Massachusetts, in the Spring of 1940. . . .

ZÜRICH, DOLDERTAL, JUNE 1940   S. G.

FOREWORD TO THE THIRD EDITION

Jacob Burckhardt and Heinrich Woefflin never touched their books once they were written; they let others "improve" later editions. Jacob Burckhardt, in reference to a late printing of his *Cicerone*, once remarked to his students, "I can really recommend this book to you; nine tenths of it have been rewritten by others."

Indeed, books are born of a particular moment; it does no good to revise them later. For the eighth printing (second edition) of *Space, Time and Architecture* we have merely added some new illustrations, scattered here and there throughout the book; some pages on "Gustave Eiffel and His Tower"; some additional notes on the works of Robert Maillart; and a chapter on Alvar Aalto.

Since for the tenth printing (third edition) *Space, Time and Architecture* had to be reset, we have had an opportunity to add some new chapters, particularly in Part II. The chapter on "Perspective and Urban Planning" outlines the formation of urban elements during the Renaissance, including some of the contributions of the great masters, such as Bramante's Court of the Belvedere in the Vatican, Michelangelo's Capitol, Leonardo's preludes to regional planning. The chapter on "Sixtus V and the Planning of Baroque Rome" evaluates the work of the first modern town planner, as it grows out of Rome's medieval and Renaissance background.

A chapter on "Mies van der Rohe and the Integrity of Form," one on "Gropius in America," and some indispensable remarks on "Le Corbusier's Development since 1938" have been added in Part VI.

ZÜRICH, DOLDERTAL, JUNE 1953   S. G.

FOREWORD TO THE THIRTEENTH PRINTING
(FOURTH EDITION)

On the occasion of this thirteenth printing the question arose whether a second volume, concerned with developments during the last twenty years should not be added. More than enough material is available. But I have abstained from following this suggestion. One reason was that I feel *Space, Time and Architecture* is an entity in itself which, with all its shortcomings, should not be disturbed.

Instead, I have permitted myself to add a short introduction. I have never ceased to be interested in the formation of the man of today, nor have I ever lost contact with contemporary architecture and planning, and from time to time I have given accounts of it: *A Decade of Contemporary Architecture* (Zürich, 1954), showed — in the form of an anthology — what happened to architecture during the disturbed years between 1937 and 1947. In 1954, when Walter Gropius was awarded the international prize for architecture at the Biennale of São Paolo, Brazilian officials asked me to recount his life's work. *Walter Gropius, Work and Teamwork* (1954) is to some extent a record of the beginnings of contemporary architecture in Germany. *Architecture, You and Me* (Cambridge, Massachusetts, 1958), subtitled "a diary of a development" gives an account of my attitude towards evolving problems since 1937.

To these publications may be added the anonymous activity of teaching in Zürich and Harvard where — in addition to other courses — a long series of seminars on "The Human Scale" has been closely connected with contemporary urban and architectural development.

To gain insight into contemporary man and contemporary architecture the most direct methods have not always proved the most rewarding. The frame has had to be constantly enlarged. I have never had a preconceived plan. I have followed problems as they developed. Only when looking backwards, can I see how each was foreshadowed by the previous one. I let myself be led by the evolving problems just as a sculptor is led by his material.

Space, Time and Architecture was concerned with contemporary man's separation between thinking and feeling — with his split personality — and with the unconscious parallelism of methods employed in art and science.

In *Mechanization Takes Command* (New York, 1948) I tried to show how this break between thinking and feeling came about, and how every generation has to find its own solution to the same problem: how to bridge the gap between inner and outer reality by reestablishing the dynamic equilibrium that governs their relationships.

This still seemed too small a frame to encompass the psychic structure of the man of today. The question which at present comes everywhere to the fore and which cuts increasingly deeper into the marrow of this century, is the relation between constancy and change. In other words — as a result of bitter experiences — we are concerned to know what can be changed and what can not be changed in human nature without disturbing its equipoise. I have been closely concerned with this problem for more than a decade. Contemporary art was born out of an urge to go back to elemental expression. The artist plunges into the depths of human experience, just like the psychologist. The artist shows that an inner affinity exists between the expressions of primeval man and contemporary man with his longings to become aware of his buried depths. This led me to the third step of my research, to the problem of *Constancy and Change* in primeval art and in the architecture of the first high civilizations, which is to be issued in two volumes of the Bollingen Series: *The Eternal Present: The Beginnings of Art* and *The Eternal Present: The Beginnings of Architecture.*

Zürich, Doldertal, December 1961   S.G.

CONTENTS

xii

ILLUSTRATIONS

xviii

INTRODUCTION **ARCHITECTURE IN THE 1960'S:
HOPES AND FEARS**

CONFUSION AND BOREDOM

In the sixties a certain confusion exists in contemporary architecture, as in painting; a kind of pause, even a kind of exhaustion. Everyone is aware of it. Fatigue is normally accompanied by uncertainty, what to do and where to go. Fatigue is the mother of indecision, opening the door to escapism, to superficialities of all kinds.

A symposium at the Metropolitan Museum of New York in the spring of 1961 discussed the question, "Modern Architecture, Death or Metamorphosis?" As this topic indicates, contemporary architecture is regarded by some as a fashion and — as an American architect expressed it — many designers who had adopted the fashionable aspects of the "International Style," now found the fashion had worn thin and were engaged in a romantic orgy. This fashion, with its historical fragments picked at random, unfortunately infected many gifted architects. By the sixties its results could be seen everywhere: in smallbreasted, gothic-styled colleges, in a lacework of glittering details inside and outside, in the toothpick stilts and assembly of isolated buildings of the largest cultural center.

A kind of playboy-architecture became *en vogue:* an architecture treated as playboys treat life, jumping from one sensation to another and quickly bored with everything.

I have no doubt that this fashion born out of an inner uncertainty will soon be obsolete; but its effects can be rather dangerous, because of the world-wide influence of the United States.

We are still in the formation period of a new tradition, still at its beginning. In *Architecture, You and Me* I pointed out the difference between the nineteenth- and twentieth-century approach to architecture. There is a word we should refrain from using to describe contemporary architecture — "style." The moment we fence architecture within a notion of "style," we open the door to a formalistic approach. The contemporary movement is not a "style" in the nineteenth-century meaning of form characterization. It is an approach to the life that slumbers unconsciously within all of us.

In architecture the word "style" has often been combined with the epithet "international," though this epithet has never been accepted in Europe. The term "international style" quickly became harmful, implying something hovering in mid-air, with no roots anywhere: cardboard architecture. Contemporary architecture worthy of the name sees its main task as the interpretation of a way of life valid for our period. There can be no question of "Death or Metamorphosis," there can only be the question of evolving a new tradition, and many signs show that this is in the doing.

SIGNS OF THE EVOLVING TRADITION

An easy pandering to popular taste in architecture has been tried several times since the optical revolution around 1910. These trends came and went. And the playboy attitude of the sixties will vanish too. There are definite signs that the process of developing a new tradition is continuing in spite of temporary disturbances.

A period terrified that mankind may destroy itself at any moment is simultaneously impelled by a frantic desire to found new cities such as has not occurred since the thirteenth century.

Another phenomenon is that contemporary architecture has become enriched, both in architecture and urbanism, by contributions from countries on the rims of Western civilization, first from Finland and Brazil and lately from Japan.

The directions in which architecture will develop have become increasingly clearer: strengthening of its plastic tendencies and strengthening of conditions for its further evolution.

There is universal agreement that the values lost to our period must be restored: the human scale, the rights of the individual, the most primitive security of movement within the city. Behind this desire stands the unchanging constancy of human life which demands fulfillment. In earlier periods it was relatively simple to create settlements in which man was not too far removed from his need for contact with the soil. Today nothing is harder than to fulfill the simplest needs of life. The heavy weight of mechanization and all that follows in its train have entailed enormous complications that make it almost impossible to adopt any simple lines of direction.

As a result the questions which preoccupy us today tend to demand a global solution. Large-scale planning has long since moved from making plans for an individual city or region to the realm of mass production.

But despite the complicated situation of the present day, the unchanging values of life remain. Despite obstructions which impede its fulfillment, the uppermost question is: *How do we wish to live?* The present state of urban planning indicates the current trends.

URBAN DEVELOPMENT

The future way of life consists in the recovery of the intimacy of life. An increase in urban population from ten thousand to ten million gives one an almost physical revulsion. The enormous heaping up of human beings induces a horror of mankind. Crowded cities have perforce led to a bankruptcy of life. An irrepressible desire for more concentration is again perceptible, despite all decentralization.

Formerly poets and painters retired into isolation. Today research laboratories and the offices of large organizations or insurance companies flee from the great metropolitan cities to barricade themselves with an undisturbed green belt of privacy.

A feeling of uneasiness and dissatisfaction with the urban situation has crept over the whole earth: schemes to displant urban centers, so that the city can expand without strangling its ancient compact center, exist for nearly every major city, from Helsinki to Athens in Europe and in the old and new capitals of the developing areas — Baghdad, Khartoum, Islamabad, Chandigarh, Brasilia.

Chandigarh is paramount among newly founded capitals for placing its government center at the head of its urban body and not in its womb as was the custom in the medieval walled towns. Brasilia solves the same problem by placing the government center — the plaza of "the three powers" (legislative, executive, and judiciary) — at the tail of its airplanelike plan (*fig.* **III**).

The idea of placing a government center at the head of a city is not new, but it had to be re-invented. In another form it was inherent in the Château de Versailles. The constituent fact embodied in Versailles is the direct confrontation of a large building complex — including government ministries — with nature. Today I would also stress that the city behind it could have expanded at will. If the urbanists of the nineteenth and twentieth centuries could have understood early enough the new message of Versailles, the situation today would be radically different; but, because of the inertia of human decisions, the world waited till it stood before a nearly insoluble situation.

The center within the city is by no means moribund. It is being renewed or even newly created, depending on the circumstances. As early as 1953, several university professors planned a new center over an old railroad yard in Boston (*fig.* **306**). If built, it would have been a prototype for the whole country. As far as the placing of volumes in space is concerned, the much earlier Rockefeller Center still remains the most impressive, though a farsighted scheme for Penn Center in Philadelphia was developed as far as circumstances permitted.

In the fifties nobody would have expected an urban renewal boom in the United States. A decade later, it is proceding much more quickly than the knowledge of how to accomplish it architecturally.

New ideas for urban development are coming from Japan. To diminish the overcrowding and the congestion within Tokyo, proposals have been made to create new land by building out over the bay. The horrifying growth of Tokyo during twenty years to an agglomeration of over ten million provided the incentive for this idea. Different schemes used different modern techniques. In one project ferroconcrete pillars, anchored at the bottom of the sea, were proposed as foundations for high-rise buildings; another proposed enormous ferroconcrete rafts upon which the buildings would be placed. Kenzo Tange's plan, 1960 (*fig.* **524**), is the most comprehensive. His structures, built on stilts, were in the Venetian tradition and, if one likes, could be traced back even to primeval lake-dwellings. It is astonishing that it has taken such a long time for modern construction methods to be proposed for this purpose.

Everything becomes clearer by comparison. If we confront the amount of urban exploration of the last twenty years with what was done in the preceding century, the results are remarkable.

In the first edition of *Space, Time and Architecture* we posed the question: Destruction or transformation of the city? Frank Lloyd Wright's desire to see the complete destruction of the city has not been followed up. The city will not disappear. It has been an ineradicable phenomenon since the very beginning of higher civilization. But its form is changing. Today all development moves in the direction of making the aspect of major cities more rural and smaller rural agglomerations more urban. We now see the way before us, though it still has to be implemented: the reconquering of intimate life, the human scale, the planning for growth. There are many other problems. But we can see the way.

UNIVERSAL ARCHITECTURE

In the last quarter of a century Europe has not been the only source of breezes freshening the development of contemporary architecture. A universal civilization is in the making but it is by no means developing in every country at the same pace.

It has in common a space conception, which is as much a part of its emotional as of its spiritual attitude. It is not the independent unrelated form that is the goal of architecture today but the organization of forms in space: space conception. This has been true for all creative periods, including the present. The present space-time conception — the way volumes are placed in space and relate to one another, the way interior space is separated from exterior space or is perforated by it to bring about an interpenetration — is a universal attribute which is at the basis of all contemporary architecture.

To this can be added another factor which is of no little importance and which lies at the basis of the best contemporary architecture. Its emanating force is generated by the respect it has given to the eternal cosmic and terrestrial conditions of a particular region. Instead of being regarded as hindrances these have served as springboards for the artistic imagination. It has often been remarked that the painting of this century has again and again driven boreholes into the past, both to renew contact with spiritual forebears and to draw new strength from these contacts. As in architecture, this is not achieved by adopting the forms of the past but by developing a spiritual bond.

This penetrating into the cosmic and terrestrial elements of a region I have elsewhere called the "new regionalism." The contemporary space conception and contemporary means of expression can reopen a dialogue with these unchanging elements.

The manner in which the new regionalism is expressed by a creatively oriented architect depends entirely upon his actual tasks and their specific needs. These are different in the Near East and in the Far East, in Finland and in Brazil. Beneath the general shelter of the contemporary space conception a polyphonic architecture can develop.

Individual differences in architectural structures together with a similar over-all approach provide hopeful signs for future development.

UNIVERSAL ARCHITECTURE AND REGIONAL DEVELOPMENT

Structures imbued with creative force suddenly arose, first in Finland and then in Brazil. Each country made its own regional contribution. Strongly democratic Finland showed how contemporary architecture can be simultaneously relaxed, regional, and universal. Brazil, constantly menaced by Latin American upheavals, introduced a grandeur of line and form in a series of glittering façades and astonishingly impressive projects.

The entry of Japan into the main stream of contemporary architecture announced for the first time the voice of the Far East. Before this moment traditional China and Japan had provided incentives for the West during the eighteenth century — Rococo — and, more profoundly, during the nineteenth century when Japanese woodcuts helped to release the imagination of the Impressionists.

But in the sixties the situation is quite different. The Japanese contribution is no longer confined to work in an age-old tradition. When, in 1953, I wrote a foreword for the Japanese translation of *Space, Time and Architecture* I felt it in some way a duty to point out that we of the West no longer adhere to a creed of production for production's sake and that the civilization which is now in the making may lead to a cross-fertilization of West and East. The West is again becoming conscious of something the Japanese civilization never forgot: the continuity of human experience. The rejuvenation of Japanese architecture is nurtured by elements which have persisted throughout its own tradition. The creative impulse for this rejuvenation came from certain young Japanese architects who found their inspiration when working in the atelier of Le Corbusier at 35 Rue de Sèvres.

The emergence of contemporary architecture in Japan came later than one might expect. It might seem that Frank Lloyd Wright's Imperial Hotel in Tokyo (1917–22) would have released the new movement. But it was not so. The Imperial Hotel was not conceived in a contemporary Japanese spirit. It was closer to the Chinese influence in Japan. Though this hotel survived so marvelously the earthquake of 1923, it could not — with its lavish ornamentation — give the necessary impetus for a new move forward.

The means bringing Western and Eastern spirits together were different. The key lay in the hands of young Japanese architects — Maekawa, Sakakura and others — who had found their way to Le Corbusier's atelier. Here they discovered what they needed. Le Corbusier was more closely connected than others to that Eternal Present which lives in the creative artifacts of all periods.

Except for a short interlude, the Japanese — in contrast to Western man — have never severed themselves from times past. They have had no incentive to imitate former "styles," since the past is constantly alive. The simplicity of their homes, despite all refinements, remains primeval. Their contemporary use of concrete beams and stilts appears simultaneously age-old and new-born.

There are now a number of young Japanese architects, of whom Kenzo Tange, who once worked in the office of Maekawa, is the best known. Their secret is a close contact with the living past and an eagerness to reach out into the future.

CONSTRUCTION AND ITS SPATIAL IMPLICATIONS

In the nineteenth century, structural engineering gave expression to desires which lay slumbering in the subconscious of the architecture of that period. In this century things are different. Architecture is now in the forefront and often asks more from the engineer than he can yet accomplish.

Structural engineering grew out of new methods of calculation and new developments in the manufacture of ferrous metals. For purposes of calculation, all structural parts were conceived as linear elements — forces obliged to follow and act in a prescribed direction — so that their behavior could be measured and controlled in advance. These forces were guided through beams, trusses, and arches as through a pipe line. Prefabrication and standardization naturally followed this linear procedure. The Eiffel Tower is the most famous example of its early application.

A peak of development was reached just before 1890 with brilliant bridges spun in mid air, the Eiffel Tower, and the Palais des Machines of 1889. Simultaneously the modern skyscraper was born in Chicago. Its construction, based on prefabricated linear elements, has been continually perfected up to the present day. The highly complicated procedures for calculating pre-stressed concrete beams also, to some extent, follow nineteenth-century linear methods.

Twentieth-century structural engineering is moving along a different path. The tendency to activate every part of a structural system instead of concentrating the flow of forces into single lines or channels continues to grow. Such systems can expand with full liberty in all directions. This results in certain difficulties. The forces cannot be easily controlled: often they evade precise calculation. Only tests by means of models and mock-ups can help. Construction merges with the irrational and sculptural.

This development required a more flexible material than straight-line steel trusses. About 1900 reinforced concrete was sufficiently developed for shell construction to be possible. In this book we show the bridges of Robert Maillart because they have a pure beauty to eyes trained by contemporary art. This beauty was not arbitrary. Maillart was one of the first to conceive and to develop the idea of using surface tension in the flat or curved slabs of his bridges and mushroom ceilings, eliminating all linear elements. Freyssinnet and Maillart built their eggshell vaults about 1930.

Maillart once said he had got his inspiration from a steam boiler. The directive of a spatial distribution of forces throughout an entire structure has now been extended in many fields. E. Y. Galantay, one of my former Zürich students, who has taught architecture at Harvard and Columbia, has prepared an approximate record of these tendencies: in the design of automobiles and railroad rolling stock, the chassis and the body have been replaced by a single stressed-skin structure. A move from open-truss to stressed-skin bodies in airplane construction presents the most spectacular development, but shell construction also occurs in shipbuilding. Large-scale thin-shell dams (first developed in France) are slowly replacing the heavy arch and buttress types. Even furniture design follows this trend. The single-legged chairs of Eero Saarinen, who died so prematurely, are pure shell structures.

Since the death of Maillart in 1941, shell structures and space frames have continued to develop an astonishing richness and versatility and to offer more and more possibilities to kindle architectural imagination.

Shapes formerly possible only with the use of the lightest materials can now be made in shell concrete. The earliest forms of shelter reappear: the nomad's tent, the hanging roof used in prehistoric Russian settlements, the baldachin and other canopies. Even the principle of the hammock is employed in a network of concave roofing, and the principle of the drum appears in pre-stressed concrete.

A bewildering multitude of possibilities can arise from combinations of rotational shells with a single or double curvature or complicated spatial forms such as hyperbolic paraboloids arising from straight-line generators. Cables — the most flexible of building materials — acquire symptomatic importance for prefabricated concrete.

The lightness and great flexibility of form offered by shells are now, for the first time in the history of vaulting, accompanied by no lateral stress. The structural system is equilibrated within itself. Shell construction appears ever more strongly to be the starting point for the solution of the vaulting problem for our period.

This does not mean that linear structural elements have been discarded. They continue to be used both in large and in small constructions. They have been developed further by great engineers, such as Pier Luigi Nervi, who uses prefabricated linear elements in spanning his large vaults and domes. In his Turin Exhibition Hall of 1961 — one of Nervi's most daring experiments — he strives for a more complicated spatial organization by the use of huge free-standing columns of different heights, which radiate fanlike structural fingers. A certain dichotomy arises between the form of these individual structural members and the total boxlike enclosure with its flat ceiling. It may be that this building represents both the peak and the end of a long development.

The way ahead lies with a freer use of shell construction such as has been developed by Candela in Mexico, the architect-engineer Catalano, now at Massachusetts Institue of Technology, and, above all, Torroja in Spain. Eduard Torroja, who died in June 1961, was a profound theoretician as well as a great artist who sometimes, as in the structure of the Madrid Racecourse (1943), seemed to reach the point where construction acquires the organic power of nature. The Tachira Club of Caracas, Venezuela (1957), one of his latest works with S. Vivas, has the lightness and overwhelming grace of a moving sail.

Jørn Utzon solved the vaulting problem in yet another way in his use of a sequence of ten great shells, rising up to sixty meters over the Sydney Opera House (*fig.* **I**). The folding

I. JØRN UTZON. Sydney Opera House, Australia, 1957. *View from west. A sequence of great shells rises from the stepped platform, each growing out from a steel shoe.*

wings of each of these giant shells (erected without use of scaffolding) tilt over a single section of the complex, each closed by a concave glass wall designed to be spatially sucked up into the vault (*fig.* **436**). It is clear from the form of these shells that they have been built up from prefabricated elements of a heavy material. It is quite otherwise with Kenzo Tange's hall for the Olympic games in Tokyo, 1964. In its interior the primeval form of the tent takes on a fantastic new dimension, and its exterior has the dynamic tension of a seashell. Its construction — which presented some difficulties — depends from a single great steel cable (*fig.* **V**).

Solutions to the vaulting problem of our period show a marvelous symbiosis: they make full use of the most advanced methods of construction and simultaneously come ever closer to organic forms.

DIFFERENT APPROACHES TO THE PAST

I have always regarded the past as something not dead but an integral part of existence, coming to understand more and more the wisdom of the Bergsonian saying that the past gnaws incessantly into the future. It all depends on how one approaches the past. One way is to regard it as a useful dictionary from which one can select forms and shapes. The nineteenth century did this, using the past as a means of escape from its own time by masking itself with the shells of bygone periods.

The fashion of the sixties is more refined. It only flirts with the past, nibbling at random details — pointed arches, renaissance porticoes, cupolas — giving them a surrealistic flavoring, so as to achieve a "poetic" expression.

The creative artists of this period — poets, painters, sculptors, and architects — have taken another way. In their work, past, present, and future merge together as the indivisible wholeness of human destiny.

Early in this century the paintings of the great masters used means of expression — abstraction, transparency, simultaneity — which are close to those of primeval art. This did not represent a sudden, quickly devaluated, fashion. It was the outcome of an unconscious parallelism, arising from an urge to probe into the elemental, the irrational, the sources of symbolic expression. It was born of a desire to counteract the damages of mechanization. This can only be noted briefly here but is treated extensively in my book *The Beginnings of Art* (*The Eternal Present*, volume I).

This attitude toward the past emerges in the work of leading architects, not in the adoption of shapes but in the expression of inner affinities. In the priory of La Tourette by Le Corbusier, 1960 (*fig.* **337**), the customary placement of everything seems radically changed: the cloister, the church, and the plastic thrust of the tower are all welded with the monastic buildings. Yet La Tourette was inspired by French monasteries of the twelfth century. In it their spirit continues to live.

Another example of this approach is the reintroduction of the patio in contemporary architecture. The patio, the inner court, the secluded part of a dwelling, has been known since the private houses of Ur, built around 2000 B.C. Roman country houses had a whole series of interior courts, serving specific functions. In 1949 José Luis Sert reintroduced the patio for workers' settlements in Chimbote, Peru, to give the people some needed privacy and distance from their neighbors (*fig.* **527**). By this means, Sert — with some memories of Moorish-Spanish patios — achieved a spatial generosity despite a highly condensed plan. This is perhaps best shown in his own house in Cambridge, Massachusetts, built in 1958, where the interior patio gives a spatial magnificence to a compact house plan.

A new chapter in this edition, "Jørn Utzon and the Third Generation," deals with this changing approach to past history and the relations of his architectural generation to the founders of the modern movement.

The approach to the past only becomes creative when the architect is able to enter into its inner meaning and content. It degenerates into a dangerous pastime when one is merely hunting for forms: playboy architecture.

THE PRESENT STATE OF ARCHITECTURE

Many architects are disturbed by the sculptural tendencies evinced in much of today's architecture: the Ronchamps

Pilgrimage Chapel (1955) by Le Corbusier; the Sydney Opera House (1957) by Jorn Utzon; the Tokyo Festival Hall (1961) by Kunio Maekawa; and the National Indoor Stadium in Tokyo (1964) by Kenzo Tange. Architecture is approaching sculpture and sculpture approaches architecture. What do these symptoms mean?

To recognize and evaluate what is happening today and where we now stand needs a longer perspective than the immediate historical past. It may be advisable to project the present happenings against the large screen of historical developments. We see them in the light of the prejudices we were born with. Among these is a belief that architectural space is synonymous with hollowed-out space, with interior space. This belief is based on the development of the last two thousand years. Since the days of Imperial Rome, the formation of interior space has been the major problem of the art of building. This experience of architectural space is so familiar that it requires a very considerable effort for us to become aware of its relative nature, as I have said in *Architecture, You and Me* (p. 119) and elsewhere.

Volumes in Space

But another space conception exists which has an equal right to recognition. This persisted throughout the first high civilizations — Egypt, Sumer, and even Greece. In all of these, the shaping of interior space was not regarded as of great importance. From the point of view of later times it could even be said that their builders neglected or disregarded it. They remained beginners in finding solutions to the vaulting problem because they never gave it the high symbolic importance it acquired in later periods.

It was the masters of modern painting who sharpened our eyes so that we could recognize that these Archaic high civilizations had their own conception of space. This conception led them to such supreme achievements as the placement of the triad of pyramids at Giza and the assemblage of temples upon the Acropolis at Athens.

II. KUNIO MAEKAWA. Festival Hall, Tokyo, 1961.

At the dawn of history, man's relations with the cosmos had not yet been severed. One of the expressions of this relation was a setting of volumes in boundless space. Interior space received little light. It signified darkness, the motherly womb of the earth. This situation, basic for what is happening in architecture today, is developed in *The Beginnings of Architecture* (*The Eternal Present*, volume II).

Forms are not bounded by their physical limits. Forms emanate and model space. Today we are again becoming aware that shapes, surfaces and planes do not merely model interior space. They operate just as strongly, far beyond the confines of their actual measured dimensions, as constituent elements of volumes standing freely in the open. It is not just the size of the pyramids or the never-surpassed perfection of the Parthenon that is significant. It is the interaction between volumes which gives full orchestration to the first architectural space conception.

Today we have again become sensitive to the space-emanating powers of volumes, thus awakening to an emotional affinity with the earliest origins of architecture. We again realize that volumes affect space just as an enclosure gives shape to an interior space. We can turn to the work of a sculptor for an expression of this contemporary awareness of the relations between volumes of different form, height, and position. For twenty years Alberto Giacometti experimented with the interplay of primitive forms: from his *Pour une Place* of 1930 and the *Palace at 4 a.m.* of 1932 until he designed a small bronze group, *Passers-by on a Square*, in 1948. The bodies of these passers-by are dematerialized to the utmost, yet they are so formed and placed that they fill the space between and beyond them.

In contemporary architecture I think the first planned relations of volumes in space can be found in Le Corbusier's project for the City Center of Saint Dié (1945). Here the different buildings are designed and placed in such a way that each emanates and fills its own spatial atmosphere and simultaneously each bears an intimate relationship with the whole. Today architects constantly face the task of placing volumes of different height and form in mutual relationship. But the

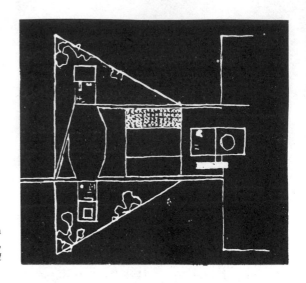

III. LUCIO COSTA. Plaza of the Three Powers, Brasilia, 1957. *Sketch from the pilot plan.*

talent to do this has become rare, perhaps because the shaping of interior space has for so long been regarded as architecture's supreme task. Even the marvelous urban courts and squares of the late baroque, with their surrounding walls, were a form of interior space, roofed by the open sky.

Our situation is fundamentally different. The enclosing walls have disappeared. High towers must be related with low buildings. Squares without walls are developing. One of the first plans of this type is the triangular Plaza of the Three Powers in Brasilia (1957–60; *fig.* **III**), where the dominating complex of senate, congress and administration buildings enter into a free relation with lower structures — the presidential palace and the high court of justice — at the corners of the triangle. There are no walls: "le jeu savant des volumes dans l'espace."

Architecture and Sculpture

That architecture is approaching sculpture and sculpture is approaching architecture is no deviation from the development of contemporary architecture.

One of the features of this evolving tradition is the simultaneity of freedom and involvement. Through this volumes have reacquired the significance they possessed at the dawn

IV. LUCIO COSTA.   Plaza of the Three Powers, Brasilia, 1957–60.

of civilization.   They have again become active emanating bodies.   This is one of the reasons why buildings like the Ronchamps Chapel, the Tokyo Festival Hall, and the Sydney Opera House are so strongly modeled.   The shaping of Ronchamps constantly reminds one of the interconnection between inner and outer space that Le Corbusier calls "acoustic space."

At the beginning of the present development painting stood in the foreground.   Now it is sculpture.

With good reason, warnings have come from many sides that a building like Ronchamps could be a disaster in the hands of a mediocre architect.   The secret of Le Corbusier's work is that he is an architect, a painter, and a sculptor.   These gifts are normally divided today between different personalities. The average architect rarely knows how to place volumes and even less how to sculpture them.   Sculptors, on the other hand, have developed this sensitivity. But there is no connecting bridge between them and the architects. Normally it is only when everything about a building has already been decided that an artist is called in and offered some spot to "decorate."

Following this principle, even the best and most carefully selected artists can never achieve more than a museum display. An integration is impossible. After several such bitter experiences most of the best sculptors have given up hope and returned to their workshops. There is but a faint hope that the necessary humility will develop so that architect and artist can work together from the very beginning. Yet this presents the only way forward.

The Vaulting Problem

During the last two millenia, each period has created its own form of vaulting interior space: the Roman, Byzantine, Romanesque, Gothic, Renaissance, Baroque. Each specific form of vaulting has almost become the symbol of its age.

We are still at the beginning of a period. It is far too early to make any definite statement in view of the multitude of different vaulting possibilities offered to architects by the engineers of our time. It is possible, in contrast to earlier periods, that many forms may develop simultaneously.

One possibility is that ceiling and floor may mirror one another like mussel shells, as in Naum Gabo's early design for the assembly halls of the Palace of the Soviets (1931). Le Corbusier's outstanding proposal for the assembly hall of the United Nations in New York (1947), which would have created one of the most exciting interior spaces of our period, also moves in this direction.

The greatest possibilities are offered by shell concrete vaults. Up to now the center of a vaulted ceiling has always been indicated by its point of highest elevation. But now ceilings are able to become concave and their center can occur at the lowest point: Le Corbusier's Ronchamps Chapel (1955), Berlin Conference Hall (Stubbins and Severud, 1957). This is

1

psychologically significant. The interpenetration of inner and outer space, fundamental at the beginning of the new tradition, has become transposed into a more refined form. The concave ceiling rises to the encompassing walls, indicating that it does not stop there but extends further. At Ronchamps a narrow rim of glass separating ceiling and wall underscores this intention. The ceiling rests upon the walls like a descending bird.

The hyperparaboloid space frame offers a new starting point for the spatial imagination. Whether of wood or of shell concrete its balance is always contained within itself and its hovering impression derives from its inner constitution.

The Revitalization of the Wall

To become a constituent element of a volume, the wall had first to be cleansed of all decorative eruptions of the nineteenth century. There had to be a rediscovery of the aesthetic values of the pure surface plane whose expressive power had been lost since Egyptian times.

In terms of space conception this rediscovery tore the massive traditional house apart. It was in the early twenties that Doesburg, van Eesteren, Rietveldt and Mies van der Rohe achieved this transformation. The house became dissected into flat rectangular planes.

This rediscovery of the surface plane was fundamental. It formed the basis on which a second phase could be developed. This second phase also embodied the plane as an inherent element. It was diametrically opposed to the use of the wall as a backdrop for the attachment of reliefs: an attitude which finds its prototype in late Hellenistic, almost free-standing, reliefs (Altar at Pergamon). What concerns us in this second phase is the plastic integration of surface and modeling. This is the hallmark both of reliefs and of architectural-sculptural treatment of the wall. The nature of primeval reliefs, embedded in the rock, and of the sunken reliefs of Egypt, embedded in stone, is given new life.

Contemporary interest in sculpture and in the plastic possibilities of architecture results in an increasing interest in mural

V.   LE CORBUSIER.   Pilgrimage Chapel of Notre Dame du Haut, Ronchamps, 1955.

VI.   KENZO TANGE.   Annex to National Indoor Stadium, Tokyo, 1964.

VII. LE CORBUSIER. The Secretariat, Chandigarh, 1952–56. *In the foreground is the entrance to the Parliament Building.*

reliefs on the part of the sculptor and in the revitalization of the wall on the part of the architect. Artists pioneering in this field, even before 1920, included Lipschitz, Duchamp-Villon, Marcel Duchamp. A big impetus was given in the early fifties by Mirko's beautiful relief portals in the Fosse Ardeatine, Rome (1953), a monument to murdered prisoners of war; by Henry Moore's brick reliefs growing out of a brick wall, Rotterdam (1955); and by the entire work of Etienne Hajdu.

The architectural revitalization of the wall, like Ronchamps, can be dangerous. It has already thrown a beguiling cloak over the playboy fashions of the 1960's. One can observe everywhere a tendency to degrade the wall with new decorative elements. This is not the basic purpose. Architecture is fundamentally concerned with the revitalization of the wall from within. Le Corbusier must again be cited as the pathfinder. In his Unité d'Habitation, Marseille (1947–52), a plastic modeling of the wall was already accomplished. Its surfaces are interwoven with large-scale rhythms of horizontality and verticality. The glass walls of the apartments retire behind a perforated screen.

In his Chandigarh Secretariat (1952–56; *fig.* **VII**) the revitalization of the wall acquired the strongest expression it had yet received. This results from a sculptural use of construction elements, such as vertical parapets and vertical and horizontal *brise-soleils*. The delicate vertical expansion joints which separate the Secretariat's four divisions, subtly articulate the entire 254-meter building. The section for the Minister acquires an especial charm through the plastic differentiation and variation of its massive and perforated elements. But the most daring feature of this structure is the building housing the 40-meter high ramp, with its great unbroken plane surfaces, which shoots forward at a sharp angle, like a pointing finger. The contrast of a filigree-like articulation of the walls with the large planes of this slender ramp structure brings the wall surfaces of this building into an inspirited tension.

Organic and Geometric

Usually in architecture the organic and the geometric are strictly separated; they may run parallel to one another but they never meet. The notion of organic architecture is closely linked with the work of certain architects: Antoni Gaudi (1852–1926), Hugo Haring (1882–1958), and Hans Scharoun (1893——).

Rational geometric forms were characteristic of the early period of contemporary architecture. They were developed especially in the Stijl movement and had great influence over the whole later development.

The trend to the organic again asserted its right in the buildings of Alvar Aalto, in the late work of Le Corbusier, in Kenzo Tange's National Indoor Stadium for the Olympic Games, 1964 (*fig.* **VI**), as well as in the work of Jørn Utzon, to mention but a few. All faced a common problem of linking a geometric structure to organic forms.

A very direct confrontation of these opposites — geometric and organic — can be found in the work of Le Corbusier. It existed quite early, as in the roof structures of the Villa Savoie, 1928–30 (*fig.* **315**), where curving and rectangular forms stand side by side. The same principle — the emergence of the organic next to the geometric — appears on the roof of the Unité d'Habitation at Marseille, 1947–52 (*fig.* **326**).

In the House of Parliament at Chandigarh (1957) an organic hyperbolic form is the main element of the entire interior. It thrusts its mighty curve upward through the roof. In the Pilgrimage Chapel at Ronchamps, 1955 (*fig.* **V**), the organic principle permeates the whole building. In the crypt of the church of La Tourette (1960) Le Corbusier achieved an interplay between progressive geometric elements and an organically undulating curve (*fig.* **344**).

We have only referred to a few examples, but the synthesis between the rational-geometric and the mystic-organic principle runs through all the late work of Le Corbusier. He made no clear separation between purely geometric and purely organic forms, as can also be seen in his paintings. It was an integral part of his being that he knew how to reconcile these seemingly so divergent realms, and finally he allowed neither the insistence of the rational nor the insistence of the organic to prevail.

THREE SPACE CONCEPTIONS

It is easier to understand what is happening in architecture today when it is set into a wider frame of architectural reference. To summarize briefly: There are three stages of architectural development. During the first stage — the first space conception — space was brought into being by the interplay between volumes. This stage encompassed the architecture of Egypt, Sumer, and Greece. Interior space was disregarded.

The second space conception began in the midst of the Roman period when interior space and with it the vaulting problem started to become the highest aim of architecture. The Roman Pantheon with its forerunners marks its beginning. During the second space conception, the formation of interior space became synonymous with hollowed-out interior space. Alois Riegl was the first to recognize this. Despite several profound differentiations, this second space conception persisted throughout the period from the Roman Pantheon to the end of the eighteenth century.

The nineteenth century forms an intermediary link. A spatial analysis of its buildings indicates that elements of all the different phases of the second stage are simultaneously intermingled (Paul Frankl). But the earlier spatial unity vanished more and more. Buildings which most truly represented the period were ignored by the public.

The third space conception set in at the beginning of this century with the optical revolution that abolished the single viewpoint of perspective. This had fundamental consequences for man's conception of architecture and the urban scene. The space-emanating qualities of free-standing buildings could again be appreciated. We recognize an affinity with the first space conception. Just as at its beginning, architecture is again approaching sculpture and sculpture is approaching architecture. At the same time the supreme preoccupation of the second space conception — the hollowing out of interior space — is continued, though there is a profoundly different approach to the vaulting problem. New elements have been introduced: a hitherto unknown interpenetration of inner and outer space and an interpenetration of different levels (largely an effect of the automobile), which has forced the incorporation of movement as an inseparable element of architecture. All these have contributed to the space conception of the present day and underlie its evolving tradition.

PART I HISTORY A PART OF LIFE

INTRODUCTION

Unknown in the United States and using a language that is foreign to me, I must seek the shortest way to direct contact with an American public. The way of personal contact is always the shortest route to understanding, not merely in personal but in general matters. Let me begin then by saying a few words about where I come from and where I intend to go — for these facts have a bearing upon the discussion that follows.

Heinrich Wölf-flin: contrasting periods

As an art historian I am a disciple of Heinrich Wölfflin. In our personal contacts with him as well as through his distinguished lectures, we, his pupils, learned to grasp the spirit of an epoch. Wölfflin's incisive analysis made clear to us the true meaning and significance of a painting or a piece of sculpture.

He delighted in contrasting one period with another. He employed this method most effectively both in his teaching and in his books — in his *Renaissance and Baroque* (1889), in *Classical Art* (1899), in which the fifteenth century is opposed to the sixteenth, and even in his *Principles of Art* (*Kunstgeschichtliche Grundbegriffe*, 1915), which had just appeared when I studied under him at Munich. Many of his pupils have tried to emulate this method of contrasting styles, but none have achieved the same depth and directness.

Late Baroque and Romantic Classicism

In my own first book, *Late Baroque and Romantic Classicism* (Munich, 1922, written as a thesis), I tried to follow Wölfflin's method. The periods contrasted were the end of the eighteenth century and the beginning of the nineteenth, both periods of classicism. The Louis XVI style formed in shape and structure the end of late baroque tendencies, with classicism serving as its framework. The classicism of the beginning of the nineteenth century found its most significant outlet in that country of romantics, Germany. In the architecture of the time the trend toward an individualistic isolation of rooms from each other was nowhere so strongly marked as it was in Germany — in the work of K. F. Schinkel, for example. This was the true architectural equivalent of the individualism of the romantic poets.

I called this period one of romantic classicism. Classicism in both periods was only a coloring — a transitory fact, as I would

2

say now. The essential characteristic of this time was that, beneath the classic exterior, the baroque inheritance had begun to disintegrate and nineteenth-century tendencies had begun to appear.

The problem which fascinated me was how our epoch had been formed, where the roots of present-day thought lay buried. This problem has fascinated me from the time I first became capable of reasoning about it until today.

Heinrich Wölfflin was the pupil of Jakob Burckhardt, and succeeded him as professor at the University of Basle when he was only twenty-seven years old. He later taught with great success at Berlin and Munich. Wölfflin always laid stress on the wide view taken by Jakob Burckhardt and often quoted Burckhardt's words not only in his lectures but also in conversation. Thus the Swiss historical tradition formed the basis of our instruction in the science of art. But I am afraid that many of us did not grasp the significance of Burckhardt — a significance which reached beyond his *métier* — until much later.

Jakob Burckhardt (1818–1897) was the great discoverer of the age of the Renaissance. He first showed how a period should be treated in its entirety, with regard not only for its painting, sculpture, and architecture but for the social institutions of its daily life as well.

Jakob Burckhardt: the integral treatment of a period

I shall mention only one book in this connection, his *Civilization of the Renaissance*, which first appeared in 1860. The English translation was produced in 1878. An extremely well-informed review of it appeared in the *New York Herald* for October 20, 1880. Burckhardt, who normally shrank from praise, was so pleased with this review that he wrote "Bravo!" at the bottom.

In *Civilization of the Renaissance* Burckhardt emphasized sources and records rather than his own opinions. He treated only fragments of the life of the period but treated them so skillfully that a picture of the whole forms in his readers' minds. Jakob Burckhardt had no love for his own time: he saw during the forties an artificially constituted Europe which was on the verge of being overwhelmed by a flood of brutal forces. The

3

South at that time appeared to have withdrawn from history; for Burckhardt it had the quiet of a tomb. So it was to the South, to Italy, that he turned for refuge from all those things for which he felt hatred and disgust. But Burckhardt was a man of great vitality, and a man of vitality cannot entirely desert his own time. His flight to Italy produced the finest traveler's guide that has ever been written, his *Cicerone* (1855) — a book which has opened the eyes of four generations to the unique qualities of the Italian scene. His *Civilization of the Renaissance* aimed at an objective ordering of factual material, but in it his greatest efforts are devoted to uncovering the origins of the man of today. John Ruskin, Burckhardt's immediate contemporary, also hated the age and sought to draw the means for its regeneration from other periods (though not those which preoccupied the Swiss historian).

Contemporary artists: significance for historical method

But I owe as large a debt to the artists of today as to these guides of my youth. It is they who have taught me to observe seriously objects which seemed unworthy of interest, or of interest only to specialists. Modern artists have shown that mere fragments lifted from the life of a period can reveal its habits and feelings; that one must have the courage to take small things and raise them to large dimensions.

These artists have shown in their pictures that the furniture of daily life, the unnoticed articles that result from mass production — spoons, bottles, glasses, all the things we look at hourly without seeing — have become parts of our natures. They have welded themselves into our lives without our knowing it.

My activities have brought me into friendly contact with the architects of our day. We have sat together in small groups about many tables in Europe, from Stockholm to Athens — not to discuss problems in art or matters of specialized detail but to determine as clearly as possible what directions housing, town planning, or regional planning had to take. As secretary to CIAM (Congrès Internationaux d'Architecture Moderne) during its entire existence (1928–1956), I acquired an insight into the problems of contemporary architecture from its inception.

THE HISTORIAN'S RELATION TO HIS AGE

The historian, the historian of architecture especially, must be in close contact with contemporary conceptions.

The historian and contemporary conceptions

Only when he is permeated by the spirit of his own time is he prepared to detect those tracts of the past which previous generations have overlooked.

History is not static but dynamic. No generation is privileged to grasp a work of art from all sides; each actively living generation discovers new aspects of it. But these new aspects will not be discovered unless the historian shows in his field the courage and energy which artists have displayed in their use of methods developed in their own epoch.

History dynamic rather than static

Architects have imitated other periods, taken over their special shapes and techniques, in the hope of escaping from transitory work and achieving a timeless rightness. And after a short time their buildings have become lifeless masses of stone, in spite of the incorporation into them of details from works of eternal beauty. These men possessed the exact contrary of the "Midas touch" — everything they put their hands on turned to dust rather than to gold. Today we can see why. History is not simply the repository of unchanging facts, but a process, a pattern of living and changing attitudes and interpretations. As such, it is deeply a part of our own natures. To turn backward to a past age is not just to inspect it, to find a pattern which will be the same for all comers. The backward look transforms its object; every spectator at every period — at every moment, indeed — inevitably transforms the past according to his own nature. Absolute points of reference are no more open to the historian than they are to the physicist; both produce descriptions relative to a particular situation.

History is changed when touched

Likewise there are no absolute standards in the arts: the nineteenth-century painters and architects who thought certain forms were valid for every age were mistaken. History cannot be touched without changing it.

The painters of our period have formulated a different attitude: *lo spettatore nel centro del quadro*. The observer must be placed in the middle of the painting, not at some isolated observation point outside. Modern art, like modern science, recognizes the fact that observation and what is observed form one complex situation — to observe something is to act upon and alter it.

The historian's relation to the present Historians quite generally distrust absorption into contemporary ways of thinking and feeling as a menace to their scientific detachment, dignity, and breadth of outlook. But one can be thoroughly the creature of one's own period, embued with its methods, without sacrificing these qualities. Indeed, the historian in every field must be united with his own time by as widespread a system of roots as possible. The world of history, like the world of nature, explains itself only to those who ask the right questions, raise the right problems. The historian must be intimately a part of his own period to know what questions concerning the past are significant to it. Apart from this approach, history remains a wilderness of blank happenings in which no creative work is possible. Only dead chronologies and limited special studies will be produced. The historian detached from the life of his own time writes irrelevant history, deals in frozen facts. But it is his unique and nontransferable task to uncover for his own age its vital interrelationships with the past.

The historian cannot in actual fact detach himself from the life about him; he, too, stands in the stream. The ideal historian — out of the press of affairs, *au-dessus de la mêlée*, surveying all time and all existence from a lofty pedestal — is a fiction.

The historian, like every other man, is the creature of his time and draws from it both his powers and his weaknesses. By virtue of his calling he may survey a larger circle of events than his average contemporary, but this does not lift him out of his own historical setting. It is even to his advantage to be forced from his academic chair occasionally and made to participate in the common struggles of the moment. For direct contact with life and its necessities sharpens his abilities to penetrate the jungle of printed records to the unfalsified voices of the real actors.

Unfortunately the historian has often used his office to proclaim the eternal right of a static past. Ever since man recognized the impossibility of making objective judgments, such an attitude has been discredited. Today we consciously examine the past from the point of view of the present to place the present in a wider dimension of time, so that it can be enriched by those aspects of the past that are still vital. This is a matter concerning continuity but not imitation.

THE DEMAND FOR CONTINUITY

For planning of any sort our knowledge must go beyond the state of affairs that actually prevails. To plan we must know what has gone on in the past and feel what is coming in the future. This is not an invitation to prophecy but a demand for a universal outlook upon the world.

The need for a universal outlook

At the present time the difficult field of town planning seems to resist all handling. In times when a universal viewpoint existed no genius was required to produce urban treatments of high quality whose influence long outlasted the period of their creation. Achievements brought about for a specific purpose and a specific social class proved serviceable in a quite different period for different purposes and different groups. This was possible simply because the original creation came out of a universal point of view.

Today the urge toward such universality is deeply felt by everyone. It is the reaction against a whole century spent in living from day to day. What we see around us is the reckoning that this shortsightedness has piled up.

This living from day to day, from hour to hour, with no feeling for relationships, does not merely lack dignity; it is neither natural nor human. It leads to a perception of events as isolated points rather than as parts of a process with dimensions reaching out into history. The demand for a closer contact with history is the natural outcome of this condition. To have a closer contact with history: in other words, to carry on our lives in a wider time-dimension. Present-day happenings are simply the most conspicuous sections of a continuum; they are like that small series of wave lengths between ultra-violet and infra-red which translate themselves into colors visible to the human eye.

7

The destructive confusion of events in the world at large today is so great that the movement toward universality is clearly visible in the field of science and scholarship. The desire for similarity of methods in the separate sciences — including the social sciences — in philosophy, and in art, becomes more and more definite. Already the demand for a universal outlook upon the world has made itself felt in the college: intellectual connections between the various faculties are consciously being developed.

Everybody knows that we have far more means of bringing change under farsighted control than any of the peoples of earlier times. It is the new potentialities at our disposal which are the key to a new and balanced life for enormous numbers of men.

The desire for universality is an expression of the need we feel to master and coördinate these new potentialities.

It is always dangerous to assume that one's own time has an exceptional importance. Even so, the years through which we are living seem to constitute a test period for mankind, a test of man's ability to organize his own life.

CONTEMPORARY HISTORY

The need for a historical background

A wider survey of the whole domain of human activity is the unmistakable need of the century. It is in this connection that history can play an important role. One of the functions of history is to help us to live in a larger sense, in wider dimensions. This does not mean that we should copy the forms and attitudes of bygone periods, as the nineteenth century did, but that we should conduct our lives against a much wider historical background.

Consequences of living from day to day

In the part of contemporary history we shall be concerned with, the most important developments are the changes that have come about in daily life.

The eternal complaint of the nineteenth century was that all the dignity had gone out of ordinary life. And ordinary life did lose its dignity from the moment it was put on an exclusively day-to-day basis. People lost all sense of playing a part in history; they were either indifferent to the period in which they lived or they hated it. When they compared themselves with the people of other periods their activities seemed unimportant and without significance, either good or bad.

The same feeling produced an extreme disregard for the immediate past — for contemporary history, that is. Unconsciously, in their matter-of-fact constructions, the men of the nineteenth century were producing the constituent facts from which the future was to take its structure. They did not see this, however; indeed, it is sometimes not recognized today. The result was not merely the neglect of contemporary history but something still worse — the wanton destruction of the objects and the records which were essential to its understanding. Later periods will be forced to leave great gaps in their accounts of the modes of existence of the nineteenth and twentieth centuries and the origin of these.

Indifference to the immediate past; its effects

On every hand we hear the complaint that essential documents have been lost through sheer indifference to our own tradition. The town planner, for example, cannot find the detailed accounts of the evolution of great cities which he needs in his researches. The virtues and defects of the various types of cities — governmental centers, sea ports, factory towns — cannot be compared, simply because there has been no steady and unified research. The fact that research has been so irregular means that the historian anxious to complete a survey such as this one must sometimes fall back on his own investigations. The danger of overemphasis is, of course, always present.

On town planning

The history of nineteenth-century industry has suffered heavily from our indifference to our own tradition and is full of gaps. The extremely interesting development of tools, for example, can be seen only from the few surviving nineteenth-century hardware catalogues. For the most part these catalogues of the thirties, fifties, and seventies have been lost. There are only a few places where these irreplaceable documents have been preserved; the library of the Victoria and Albert Museum in London is one of them.

On the history of nineteenth-century industry

The period in America when complicated trades abandoned handwork and changed over to machine production is a unique one, without counterpart elsewhere in the world. I myself visited a great factory outside Boston where clocks and watches were first assembled from standardized parts shortly after 1850. (This principle later found its most extensive use in the manufacture of automobiles.) The early products of this factory were mentioned by some European observers of the seventies. I wanted to see examples of them and to study the early catalogues of the company. There were no old catalogues at all — the company destroyed them, on principle, when they were three years old — and the only old watches were those which had come in for repairs. There was, on the other hand, a large, valuable, but historically unimportant collection of European watches.

The oldest mail-order house in the country, with an annual business of $500,000,000, is located in Chicago. I went there to see what changes had been made in articles of daily life since Civil War times. The company possessed some material — incomplete, however — and very properly kept it in a safe. The Otis Elevator Company in New York had comparatively full records of their products — and the literature dealing with elevators is none too precise — but even here material dealing with the earliest beginnings had not been preserved.

On architecture In the 1880's, when European architecture seemed given over to a future of muddle, indecision, and despair, a new architecture was growing up on the American prairies. From 1880 to the time of the Columbian Exposition of 1893 the "Loop" area in Chicago (its business quarter, that is) was the center of architectural development not merely for the United States but for the whole world.

It may be that after a few decades the skyscraper automatically becomes a sort of blighted area and must be torn down. It may be that the Marshall Field wholesale store — one of Chicago's finest buildings and Henry Hobson Richardson's best work — had to be destroyed to create a parking lot. It may be that there was no other direction for a highway except one that will eventually lead over the site of the Adler and Sullivan Auditorium, with its unique theater interior. In 1962 the building was still standing, but several other valuable witnesses of this period, such as Sullivan's Garrick Theater, have been destroyed.

10

It does concern us, however, that there is no particular feeling for what is being destroyed. Chicago seems quite unaware of the significance of the Chicago school. I went searching in Chicago for pictures of the interiors of its great hotels and apartment houses in the eighties, buildings which in their whole organization foreshadowed many present-day developments. One photographer told me that he had destroyed thousands of plates picturing these interiors; he needed the space, and was aware of no reason why they should be preserved. For the past few years several institutions in Chicago have been endeavoring to preserve material of this sort. It is doubtful, however, whether their endeavors are enough to stop the losses that constantly occur.

These remarks have been made simply to indicate the widespread indifference to the immediate past, to the century out of which our period grows and derives the basic elements for its own life. Chicago has been used as an example, but the fanatical destruction of objects from the past is not limited to Chicago, or to America. It has descended like an ever-growing plague upon the old cities of Europe.

THE IDENTITY OF METHODS

Our period is a period of transition. The tangle of different tendencies continuing from the past or pointing to the future, tendencies which mix confusedly and interpenetrate at every point, makes our period seem to lack any definite line of advance. To some it presents the appearance of a chaos of contradictory impulses. An eminent French sociologist wrote recently that "we see around us nothing save tumult, aimless agitation, hesitant opinions, vacillating thoughts."

Our period one of transition

We must not forget, however, that this particular transition period has lasted for a whole century. It has made itself felt in each country at the same rate and in the same proportion as the disorder which the process of industrialization produced everywhere.

Ever since the opening of this transitional period, our mental life has been without equilibrium. Our inner being has undergone division. This state of the contemporary spirit has been recognized often enough, but its consequences have not been drawn.

If chaos had for its only definition the coexistence of tendencies contradictory to one another, our period would certainly deserve to be called chaotic. But we believe that these contradictions are merely surface ones.

There is this remarkable circumstance which we can observe today: sciences which differ widely in their objects are beginning to resemble each other in their methods. A continued and extensive search for exact knowledge is at the bottom of this growing resemblance. It is being recognized in all quarters that the ideas which we have taken over from the past are both too complex and too crude.

A transition period may affect two observers in very different ways. One may see only the chaos of contradictory traits and mutually destructive principles; the other may see beneath all this confusion those elements which are working together to open the way for new solutions. It is not a simple thing to decide between two such judgments, to determine which has emphasized the essential marks of the time. We need some objective guide to what is going on in the depths of the period, some sign by which we can determine whether or not its dispersed energies are being brought into united action. A comparison of the methods which govern its major activities, its thinking and feeling, may afford us such an objective criterion.

Have science and art anything in common?

John Dewey, in his *Art as Experience*, points out that "compartmentalization of occupations and interests brings about separation of that mode of activity commonly called 'practise' from insight, of imagination from executive doing, of significant purpose from work, of emotion from thought and doing." Each of these activities is then assigned "its own place in which it must abide. Those who write the anatomy of experience then suppose that these divisions inhere in the very constitution of human nature."

It is just such an evolution which lies behind the doubt as to whether science and art have anything in common. The question would not be raised except in a period where thinking and

12

feeling proceed on different levels in opposition to each other. In such a period, people no longer expect a scientific discovery to have any repercussions in the realm of feeling. It seems unnatural for a theory in mathematical physics to meet with an equivalent in the arts. But this is to forget that the two are formulated by men living in the same period, exposed to the same general influences, and moved by similar impulses. Thought and feeling could be entirely separated only by cutting men in two.

We have behind us a period in which thinking and feeling were separated. This schism produced individuals whose inner development was uneven, who lacked inner equilibrium: split personalities. The split personality as a psychopathic case does not concern us here; we are speaking of the inner disharmony which is found in the structure of the normal personality of this period.

Separation of thinking and feeling

What are the effects of this inner division? Only very rarely do we encounter a master in one field who is capable of recognizing workers of the same stature and tendency in another. Contemporary artists and scientists have lost contact with each other; they speak the language of their time in their own work, but they cannot even understand it as it is expressed in work of a different character. The great physicist may lack all understanding of a painting which presents the artistic equivalent of his own ideas. A great painter may fail entirely to grasp architecture which has developed out of his own principles. Men who produce poetry which is purely an expression of this time are indifferent to the music which is contemporary in the same sense and to the same degree. This is our inheritance from the nineteenth century, during which the different departments of human activity steadily lost touch with one another. The principles of *laissez-faire* and *laissez-aller* were extended to the life of the spirit.

The split personality

Throughout the nineteenth century the natural sciences went splendidly ahead, impelled by the great tradition which the previous two hundred years had established, and sustained by problems which had a direction and momentum of their own. The real spirit of the age came out in these researches — in the realm of thinking, that is. But these achievements

The split civilization

were regarded as emotionally neutral, as having no relation to the realm of feeling. Feeling could not keep up with the swift advances made in science and the techniques. The century's genuine strength and special accomplishments remained largely irrelevant to man's inner life.

This orientation of the vital energies of the period is reflected in the make-up of the man of today. Scarcely anyone can escape the unbalanced development which it encourages. The split personality, the unevenly adjusted man, is symptomatic of our period.

Unconscious parallelisms of method in science and art

But behind these disintegrating forces in our period tendencies leading toward unity can be observed. From the first decade of this century on, we encounter curious parallelisms of method in the separate realms of thought and feeling, science and art. Problems whose roots lie entirely in our time are being treated in similar ways, even when their subject matter is very different and their solutions are arrived at independently.

In 1908 the great mathematician Hermann Minkowski first conceived a world in four dimensions, with space and time coming together to form an indivisible continuum. His *Space and Time* of that year begins with the celebrated statement, "Henceforth space by itself, and time by itself, are doomed to fade away into mere shadows, and only a kind of union of the two will preserve an independent reality." It was just at this time that in France and in Italy cubist and futurist painters developed the artistic equivalent of space-time in their search for means of expressing purely contemporaneous feelings.

Some less spectacular duplications of methods in the fields of thought and feeling also date from this period. Thus new basic elements designed to permit the solving of problems that had just been recognized were introduced in construction and painting around 1908. The basic identity of these elements will be discussed in Part VI, "Space-Time in Art, Architecture, and Construction."

Nineteenth-century popularization of the sciences: emphasis on results

Only a small part of the full range of the sciences can be mastered by a single man. Their specialized inquiries and complicated techniques of research make any far-reaching competency impossible. But, even apart from this impossibility, we move in a different direction today in seeking to arrive at a general outlook. It is no longer specific scientific facts and achievements that call for popularization, as was the case in the nineteenth century. Then even the greatest scientists felt it necessary to acquaint the public with what was being done in their fields. In the thirties of the nineteenth century Michael Faraday in England and François Arago in France were greatly concerned with increasing popular knowledge of the sciences. Faraday's chair during his lifetime was associated with the Royal Institution in London, a society founded in 1799 for "the promotion and the diffusion and extension of useful knowledge." To the present day the weekly evening meetings of this rather exclusive society are attended by members only (white ties obligatory) in Faraday's old lecture theater in Albemarle Street, London. Faraday himself introduced in 1826 a special course for juvenile auditors which until the present day has been delivered every year at Christmas time.

François Arago, the well-known physicist who discovered fundamental laws of electricity and who was a pioneer in the undulatory theory of light, was most celebrated for his gift for treating difficult subjects — such as astronomy — in a popular manner. In his courses at the observatory in Paris, he spoke to an audience unacquainted with mathematics. The larger part of the fourteen volumes embracing his work is devoted to such popularizing.

University extension in the modern sense, introduced in the seventies of the nineteenth century at Oxford and Cambridge, grew out of these efforts to popularize scientific results.

Today a leading scientist — a "Secrétaire perpétuel de l'Académie," such as Arago was, for example — would not make the popularization of scientific research one of his chief concerns. Other problems are more important today. The methods of science are of more concern to us now than any of their separate results.

The problem of today is not to popularize science. What our period needs much more than this is to gain an understanding and a general view of the dominant methods in different fields of human activity, recognizing their differences and their likenesses.

The scientific education of our day is designed to produce extreme specialists. That there is, on the other hand, an urge toward interrelation cannot be denied. Yet there is no institution to help us understand the interrelations that exist between the different sciences or between the sciences and the realm of feeling.

Knowledge of scientific method more important today

A general contemporary understanding of scientific method is more important for our culture as a whole than widespread knowledge of scientific facts. It is through their increasing similarity of method that the various activities of our times are drawing together to constitute one culture. Some grasp of the way in which different sciences resemble each other in the employment of similar methods is needed for insight into contemporary life as a whole.

But science is not an activity which goes on independently of all others. Each period lives in a realm of feeling as well as in a realm of thought, and changes in each realm affect the changes in the other. Each period finds outlets for its emotions through different means of expression. Emotions and expressive means vary concomitantly with the concepts that dominate the epoch. Thus in the Renaissance the dominant space conceptions found their proper frame in perspective, while in our period the conception of space-time leads the artist to adopt very different means.

Economics and politics have been taken as points of departure for explanations of the structure of a period in all its aspects. The influence of feeling upon reality, its constant permeation of all human activities, has been largely disregarded or felt to be of negligible importance. In tracing the interrelated developments in art, architecture, and construction through the period we have selected, it is precisely the influence of feeling which we shall emphasize.

Cosmological background of the baroque period

Our culture has a structure different in many of its aspects from the cultures that grew up in pre-industrial periods. In the baroque period, for example, Leibnitz arrived at the discovery of the calculus from a starting point in philosophy. He moved from a general — one might say a cosmological — outlook to this particular discovery.

16

With our inheritance from preceding generations, we are obliged to adopt a different starting point and follow another route. We must take our departure from a large number of specialized disciplines and go on from there toward a coherent general outlook on our world. It is beside the point whether or not this route is more difficult, more precarious, and less certain to end in success than the path that lay open to Leibnitz. It is the route that present realities force us to take. Unity, for us, will have to come about through the unintended parallelisms in method that are springing up in the specialized sciences and the equally specialized arts. These are the indications that we are nearing a spontaneously established harmony of emotional and intellectual activities.

In both contemporary science and contemporary art it is possible to detect elements of the general pattern which our culture will embody. The situation is a curious one: our culture is like an orchestra where the instruments lie ready tuned but where every musician is cut off from his fellows by a sound-proof wall. It is impossible to foretell the events that will have to come before these barriers are broken down. The only service the historian can perform is to point out this situation, to bring it into consciousness.

The degree to which its methods of thinking and of feeling coincide determines the equilibrium of an epoch. When these methods move apart from each other there is no possibility of a culture and a tradition. These are not deliberations remote from our subject: we shall soon see that it was just this unfortunate schism between its thought and feeling which struck down the magnificent power of the nineteenth century. Out of such a schism come split personalities and split civilizations.

TRANSITORY AND CONSTITUENT FACTS

It is not the historian's task to tell the public what pleases or displeases him personally. That is a private affair which loses all its interest in the telling. The historian is not required to correct an epoch in the light of his own opinions. He has to explain it, to show why history took a certain direction. The

Fact and interpretation in history

people who lived in a period can best tell us, out of their own inner feelings, whether its development was happy or unhappy.

The voices which come to us out of the fortunes or misfortunes of an age furnish indispensable testimony. No man of a later time, however great the impartiality which distance from the events has brought, can approach the direct and certain feeling for a period which belonged to those in the midst of the struggle — a struggle which involved their destiny. Words uttered out of the needs of the time are the historian's real guides, and it is from them that he must draw his explanation of the period. The true critique of an age can only be taken from the testimony of that age.

Entirely objective judgment with no trace of personal bias is, on the face of things, quite impossible. Nevertheless, the infiltration of the personal must be reduced to a minimum. The historian is not solely a cataloguer of facts; it is his right, and indeed his duty, to pass judgment. His judgments must, however, spring directly from his facts.

The historian cannot speak with the direct authority of a contemporary, but he has a breadth of outlook which the contemporary inevitably lacks. He sees facts which were hidden from the people of the time he studies. He can tell more or less short-lived novelties from genuinely new trends. The facts of history fall into one or the other of these classes, and it is the business of the historian to distinguish accurately between them.

Constituent facts: recurrent and cumulative tendencies

Constituent facts are those tendencies which, when they are suppressed, inevitably reappear. Their recurrence makes us aware that these are elements which, all together, are producing a *new tradition*. Constituent facts in architecture, for example, are the undulation of the wall, the juxtaposition of nature and the human dwelling, the open ground-plan. Constituent facts in the nineteenth century are the new potentialities in construction, the use of mass production in industry, the changed organization of society.

Transitory facts: sporadic trends

Facts of the other sort — equally the work of the forces moving in a period — lack the stuff of permanence and fail to attach themselves to a new tradition. At first appearance they may have all the éclat and brilliance of a firework display, but they

18

have no greater durability. Sometimes they are interlaced with every refinement of fashion — the furniture of the Second Empire in France is an instance. These we shall call transitory facts.

Transitory facts in their dash and glitter often succeed in taking over the center of the stage. This was the case with the experiments in historical styles that went on — with infinite changes of direction — throughout the whole nineteenth century. The entire output of official painting was a transitory fact of that period, almost wholly without significance to the present day.

A period may be dominated by transitory or by constituent facts; both alternatives are open. There is, however, no doubt which of these two classes of trends is the more likely to produce a solution of the real problems of the age.

It is in this field that the historian is not only free to use his judgment but obliged to. To make the not always obvious distinction between transitory and constituent facts is his own personal responsibility.

ARCHITECTURE AS AN ORGANISM

We are looking for the reflection in architecture of the progress our own period has made toward consciousness of itself — of its special limitations and potentialities, needs, and aims. Architecture can give us an insight into this process just because it is so bound up with the life of a period as a whole. Everything in it, from its fondness for certain shapes to the approaches to specific building problems which it finds most natural, reflects the conditions of the age from which it springs. It is the product of all sorts of factors — social, economic, scientific, technical, ethnological.

However much a period may try to disguise itself, its real nature will still show through in its architecture, whether this uses original forms of expression or attempts to copy bygone epochs. We recognize the character of the age as easily as we identify a friend's handwriting beneath attempted disguises. It is as an unmistakable index to what was really going on in

Architecture as an index to a period

a period that architecture is indispensable when we are seeking to evaluate that period.

In the great architectural masterpieces, as in every great work of art, the human shortcomings which every period exhibits so liberally fall away. This is why these works are true monuments of their epochs; with the overlay of recurrent human weaknesses removed, the central drives of the time of their creation show plainly.

But if architecture is the result of so many conditions, is it either proper or possible to examine it out of its context, as a finite organism in its own right?

Architecture as an independent organism

An architecture may be called into being by all sorts of external conditions, but once it appears it constitutes an organism in itself, with its own character and its own continuing life. Its value cannot be stated in the sociological or economic terms by which we explain its origin, and its influence may continue after its original environment has altered or disappeared. Architecture can reach out beyond the period of its birth, beyond the social class that called it into being, beyond the style to which it belongs.

Continuing tendencies

When a Roman baroque architect of the late seventeenth century invents the undulating church façade we can account for the invention in various ways. This was the time of the Counter Reformation; means were demanded of focusing all the attention of the people upon the Church. Or we might invoke economic factors and attribute the undulation of the wall to the constricted streets of Rome and the economy of front which they made necessary.

Both factors were no doubt involved. The undulating wall, however, was used later on, when these factors were no longer operative, in the great dwelling complexes of the eighteenth and early nineteenth centuries. The undulating wall, once invented, became a constituent fact in architecture, and continued to work in the realm of architectural knowledge after the Counter Reformation and Roman late baroque had both come to an end.

The château of Versailles admits of a purely sociological explanation. Or, again, the shapes that compose it and the planning of its rooms can be analyzed in the light of the historical styles from which they derive. The Italian and Dutch influences in the great gardens can be disentangled. All these studies result in a picture of the time, taken from various angles, which is certainly informative and interesting. They overlook, however, the constituent facts, the lasting tendencies, which made their first appearance at Versailles.

In a modern work of art it is the relationships between the elements in the composition that are decisive in determining its character. Modern science likewise seeks to fit the objects of its study into a relational scheme. It is not the qualities which make these objects unique among others that are of interest but rather the ways in which they function in their environment. History is always the last of the sciences to develop a method in harmony with its own period. Nevertheless, a modern history seems to be taking form which is following the direction art and science have already adopted. The historian nowadays seems more concerned with the links between periods, the lines of force which persist and develop through several periods, than with those special aspects which separate each period from every other.

Search for historical interrelations

In the arts, periods are differentiated by the "styles" which became fixed and definite in each stage of development. And the study of the history of styles was the special work of nineteenth-century historians, a work most skillfully carried through. But it may be that the links and associations between periods — the constituent facts — are more important to us than self-enclosed entities such as styles.

When we consider the château of Versailles, for example, what we find most interesting in it is that here, for the first time, a great dwelling complex (equal to a small town in size) was placed in direct contact with nature. This had never been done before on such a large scale. The juxtaposition of residences with nature was one of the constituent facts that grew out of the period of Louis XIV. A century later, this pattern for living was adopted in town planning for a completely different social class in another country.

The associations and interrelations of events are what matter most to us. We know that there are no isolated or spontaneous happenings, and we look always for the connections between them.

Parallel between the history of art and the history of science

Even though architecture is inseparable from life as a whole, it is still possible to write a history of architecture in which it is regarded as an independent organism. The case is no different from that of mathematics or physical science. The evolution of mathematical knowledge is discussed ordinarily without reference to the social background against which it took place — this in spite of the fact that there is a baroque mathematics, as well as a baroque physics. The integral calculus is a perfectly consistent outgrowth of the baroque universalistic point of view. It is no coincidence that in this period two investigators hit upon it simultaneously, though the most promising of previous efforts in this direction invariably stopped short of a solution. And the two discoverers developed distinctively baroque schemes in other fields — Newton in his universally active laws of gravitation, Leibnitz in the monad's internal relationships to the entire universe. But it would not occur to anyone to stress the baroque origin of the integral calculus. It is independently a part of the whole body of mathematical knowledge, and its most significant aspect is the role it played in the evolution of mathematics.

The human factor obviously plays a much larger part in architecture than it does in science; the two are not entirely comparable. Nevertheless there is a history of architecture, and there are developments which are influenced by architectural considerations alone and can be evaluated solely in architectural terms. This history from baroque to nineteenth-century times has its stormy moments and its full share of dramatic episodes.

Lessened importance of stylistic variation

If it is the general line of evolution which interests us — the development which runs through different periods, social orders, and races — then the formal and stylistic variations which mark the separate stages will lose some of their importance. Our attention will shift to the history of architecture as an enterprise with a continuous and independent growth of its own, apart from questions of economics, class interests, race, or other issues.

Architecture is not exclusively an affair of styles and forms, nor is it completely determined by sociological or economic conditions. It has a life of its own, grows or dwindles, finds new potentialities and forgets them again. The view of architecture as a growing organism is particularly useful in the study of American architecture. In this field concentration on styles, on particular outlets or manifestations of the life of architecture, leads us nowhere. The fundamental line of development that runs through the different periods, ignoring stylistic fashions, is the only way of escape from complete confusion. Styles and their variations form a baffling maze, with all its alleys stopped.

From the beginning, styles in America were imported. They were not developed in the country but came here full-grown. None of them in the nineteenth century — romantic, Victorian, Tudor, Gothic revival—is representative of the American spirit, whose adventures and changes went on outside their narrow limits. The manor houses of the romantics, the Victorian villas, even the doorways and columns of colonial dwellings — charming as they are — mislead rather than inform us about that spirit. The elements of American architecture have their sources elsewhere.

PROCEDURE

We intend to see how our period has come to consciousness of itself in one field, architecture. To do this we must understand the architectural inheritance of our period, the knowledge which had been continuously evolved in the preceding periods. These periods do not have to be examined in their entirety. We shall touch lightly on space conception — the enveloping force of all architecture — and note how the early Renaissance was absorbed in a passion for the newly discovered optical perspective, which in the late baroque led to a new boldness and flexibility in space conception.

The architectural inheritance

Our next concern will be the ways in which outer space was organized, first in the South and then (in the seventeenth century) in northern countries — France and England. These developments, employing the architectural experience which had accumulated since the Renaissance, raised town planning and the organization of space on a large scale to new heights. Throughout the eighteenth century this tradition in urbanism spread and developed. All over Europe we encounter examples of its ability to bring separate and often already existent elements into splendid, coherent, and surprising unity. At that time, just before industrialization set in, town planning was advancing toward solutions which artists of our day are once more attempting — with the changed approach which new needs and new knowledge dictate.

Importance of construction and town planning

The fact that we are considering architecture as an organism makes it natural for us to examine both its beginning and its end, construction and town planning. And it will be easier for us to deal with our subject if we can, so to speak, use two handles to pick it up by. At all events, it will be necessary for us to give more attention to construction and town planning than would be the case if we were writing a history of styles.

Construction as the subconsciousness of architecture

It would be a mistake to look at modern engineering constructions only through the eyes of the engineer or to see in them only efficient adjustments to useful purposes. Their technical aspects will not concern us so much as the general methods that appear in them and their content of feeling — prophetic of architectonic expressions which come later.

In the nineteenth century, as in all periods when methods of production are changing, construction was particularly important for the architectural knowledge which lay hidden in it. The new potentialities of the period are shown much more clearly in its engineering constructions than in its strictly architectural works. For a hundred years architecture lay smothered in a dead, eclectic atmosphere in spite of its continual attempts at escape. All that while, construction played the part of architecture's subconsciousness, contained things which it prophesied and half revealed long before they could become realities. The constituent facts in the nineteenth century can often be found in construction when the ruling architecture gives no clue to them. It is construction and not architecture which offers the best guideposts through the century.

24

Architecture has caught up with construction very gradually. Our own period has been slowly finding the ability to express in architecture what construction has for a long while been mutely signifying in its abstract language. This process moved so slowly that around 1900 on the Continent most of the buildings from which the modern development stems lacked all connection with human residence. They were factories, stock exchanges, warehouses, and the like. The building schemes which represent the first solutions in the manner of the present day were set forward in a neutral atmosphere, one far removed from the range of intimate personal feelings.

Architects today are perfectly aware that the future of architecture is inseparably bound up with town planning. A single beautiful house or a single fine residential development accomplishes very little. Everything depends on the unified organization of life. The interrelations between house, town, and country, or residence, labor, and leisure, can no longer be left to chance. Conscious planning is demanded.

Town planning the index of architectural knowledge

In a single building something extraordinary may be sought after and achieved. The whole body of a city, however, shows beyond dispute the state of the architectural knowledge of a period. It shows the extent to which the period was capable of organizing its own life.

In Europe during the nineties a demand for morality in architecture arose in many different countries. As van de Velde puts it, people saw that the reigning architecture was a "lie," all posturing and no truth, and that greater purity of expression was needed. This means that, besides the urge to find new ways of expression suitable to the times, there was the more general urge to bring artistic expression into harmony with the new potentialities born of the age. Or we might say that the desire grew up to reconcile methods of feeling with methods of thinking.

Demand for morality in architecture during the nineties

We shall observe the development which the demand for morality set under way through some close-ups of a few of its critical stages. The whole process is bound up with the progressive awakening to the potentialities inherent in modern construction: with the iron-skeleton building in Belgium of the nineties, for example, and with the ferroconcrete skeleton in France around 1900.

Significance of the Chicago school of the eighties	Architecture gradually threw off its confusion and indecision in the face of the new building tasks of the century. It saw its way clearly first as regards those buildings which stood half-way between "neutral" industrial constructions and the human residence, with its inescapable associations of feeling. Thus the gap between bare construction and architecture in the grand manner is first bridged in the Chicago business buildings of the 1880's. The architecture of the Chicago school shows with astonishing clarity the urge to use constructional discoveries expressively that is a keynote in this period.
Frank Lloyd Wright	It was the Chicago atmosphere that made it possible for a phenomenon like Frank Lloyd Wright to appear during the nineties. During his stay in Chicago, Wright reached solutions of the dwelling problem which furnished the basis for further developments in Europe at the hands of the post-war generation. These men resumed the problem at the point where Wright had left off.
The new space conception in painting and architecture	Up to 1910 architects tried many ways of arriving at a new feeling for space — the basis and the strongest impulse for original architectonic creation. They could never quite break through. Only the narrow gates of "fitness for purpose" and "rejection of historical styles" were open to such endeavors.

Around 1910 an event of decisive importance occurred: the discovery of a new space conception in the arts. Working in their studios as though in laboratories, painters and sculptors investigated the ways in which space, volumes, and materials existed for feeling.

The speculations of the mathematical physicists seem very far removed from reality and from practical affairs, but they have led to profound alterations in the human environment. In the same way the experiments of the cubists seemed to have little significance for any kind of practice — even for architecture. Actually, however, it was just such work which gave the architects the hints they needed to master reality in their particular sphere. These discoveries offered architecture the objective means of organizing space in ways that gave form to contemporary feelings.

Our interest is confined to the reflection in architecture of the process by which the period has moved toward self-consciousness. We shall follow the development to that point when architecture achieves a clear mastery of means of expression natural to our time. This point was reached before 1930, and we shall attempt to observe its subsequent development.

Stages in nine-teenth-century town planning

In the field of town planning we shall consider only those places where the furthest advance was made at a given period. The London squares (1800–50) illustrate the continuation into the nineteenth century of late baroque urban forms. The *rue corridor*, an outstanding fact of nineteenth-century urbanism, has its first large-scale development in Haussmann's transformation of Paris (1850–70). The evolution to the city of today is summarized in the step-by-step development of Amsterdam that has continued from 1900 until the present time.

Contemporary tendencies in town planning

In town planning we cannot ignore the developments that are still in progress. Town planning, always the last branch of architecture to reach full growth, has begun to arrive at new conceptions only quite recently — since about 1925. We shall try to assemble the fragmentary and dispersed work that has been done and derive from it some insight into the tendencies which are still evolving.

Choice of events and figures

The history of architecture could be treated by sketching, in very broad strokes, all the great variety of movements and the masses of facts connected with them. But in attempting to determine the extent and the nature of our period's consciousness of itself, it is more helpful to examine rather carefully cross sections of decisive stages in the history of architecture. We prefer to deal with fewer events more penetratingly, in close-up view. A few facts seen clearly enough may lead to a knowledge of something more important than the isolated facts themselves: the inner structure of architecture at the stage of growth which it has reached in our time.

There are some individual artists whom we shall also scrutinize at close range, men in whom the spirit of an age crystallizes. In each case we shall examine only those of their works which are most helpful in understanding the period.

Often we can learn more about the way in which nineteenth-century life developed from forgotten and unsuccessful figures of the period than we can from its great official celebrities. Simple utilitarian structures reveal more of its essential spirit than magnificent edifices intended to have an immortal appeal. The anonymous products of industry, unpretentious articles of daily use, often show more creative force than luxurious and immensely expensive furnishings.

Significance for
history of objects
of daily use

Picasso once wrote, "The artist is a receptacle for emotions, regardless of whether they spring from heaven, from earth, from a scrap of paper, from a passing face, or from a spider's web. That is why he must not distinguish between things. *Quartiers de noblesse* do not exist among objects." The historian has to take the same attitude toward his material: he wants to know the truth about life, and he must take it where he finds it. It will not do for him to study only the highest artistic realizations of a period. Often he can learn more about the forces that shape its life from the common objects and utensils which are the undisguised products of its industry.

These considerations formed the stepping stones to my later investigation of the Janus-headed influence of mechanization, which I developed in *Mechanization Takes Command* (Oxford University Press, 1948).

PART II OUR ARCHITECTURAL INHERITANCE

Why a knowledge
of our architectural
inheritance is
necessary

With no clear perception of the relation in which it stands to the past or of the route by which it must advance into the future, the life of any period will be lived on an aimless, day-to-day basis. Our time has suffered severely from this short-sighted, *laissez-faire* attitude, and from the complete lack of planning that is its result.

But it is plain that a revolt against this myopic outlook is under way, in science, art, and industry. There is a growing demand for a wider survey of all realms of human activity.

It is in this connection that history has an important role to play. History can reveal to our period the forgotten elements of its being, just as our parents can recover for us those childhood and ancestral peculiarities which continue to determine our natures though they are not to be found in our memories. A connection with the past is a prerequisite for the appearance of a new and self-confident tradition.

THE NEW SPACE CONCEPTION: PERSPECTIVE

Florence as the
workshop of the
modern spirit

Jakob Burckhardt in *The Civilization of the Renaissance* asserts that "the most elevated political thought and the most varied forms of human development are found united in the history of Florence, which in this sense deserves the name of the first modern state in the world. . . . That wondrous Florentine spirit, at once keenly critical and artistically creative, was incessantly transforming the social and political condition of the state, and as incessantly describing and judging the change." But Florence around 1400, at the beginning of the *quattrocento*, was important not merely as the home of political and social experiments; it was also the place where the *esprit nouveau* of the Renaissance broke through most strongly. It was this peculiarly Florentine temper that made it the "unique city — the most important workshop of the Italian and, indeed, of the modern European spirit."

The Renaissance ferment which was working in Florence showed itself under the widest variety of forms. We shall consider only one of the new developments in which it resulted: a new conception of space. At the start of the fifteenth century,

30

in Florence, this conception was translated into artistic terms through the discovery of perspective. Throughout the following five centuries perspective was to be one of the constituent facts in the history of art, the unchallenged canon to which every artistic representation had to conform.

In linear "perspective" — etymologically "clear-seeing" — objects are depicted upon a plane surface in conformity with the way they are seen, without reference to their absolute shapes or relations. The whole picture or design is calculated to be valid for one station or observation point only. To the fifteenth century the principle of perspective came as a complete revolution, involving an extreme and violent break with the medieval conception of space, and with the flat, floating arrangements which were its artistic expression.

With the invention of perspective the modern notion of individualism found its artistic counterpart. Every element in a perspective representation is related to the unique point of view of the individual spectator.

This principle came as an entirely new invention, but seldom has a new invention been so much in harmony with a basic feeling of an epoch. From the time of its discovery no hesitation can be observed in its application; it was used at once with complete confidence and sureness. Artists and scientists elaborated its secrets with a readily understandable excitement and pride. Their feeling toward it appears in the enthusiastic exclamation of the painter Paolo Uccello, "How sweet is perspective!"

Perspective was not the discovery of any one person; it was the expression of the whole era. We shall encounter a similar situation later, when we come to discuss cubism. There, too, we shall find a whole movement arising in response to the new space conception developed in our time, rather than a single inventor. In both cases the significant thing is the mixture of art with science, but the two worked together far more closely in the development of perspective. Indeed, one rarely sees so complete a unity of thinking and feeling — art and science — as is to be found in the early fifteenth century. There was not only the important identity of method in these two spheres, but a complete union of artist and scientist in the same person.

Linear perspective and the growth of modern individualism

No single inventor of perspective

31

Unity of thinking
and feeling in the
Renaissance:
Brunelleschi

Brunelleschi (1377–1446), one of the great initiators of perspective, was just such a figure. He began his career as a goldsmith and a student of ancient languages, and went on to become at the same time a great architect, sculptor, engineer, and mathematician. We have no right to say that such extreme versatility was possible only in earlier times. In a certain sense, it is possible in any time when specialists do not rule independently, but are included within a unified conception of life. It is, in fact, one of the secrets of the high degree of perfection of Renaissance work that it was not divided among limited specialists. Thus Brunelleschi, when he undertook the task of building the dome of the cathedral at Florence, could set about it as, simultaneously, a daring architect and a bold constructor. He projected a cupola which was double-shelled, like earlier Oriental constructions. The vault was erected without scaffolding, built freely up into the air to a height of around ninety feet. In its boldness as an engineering work this dome is comparable to the bridges of the French engineer, Eiffel, which were constructed straight out into space.

Do we realize, in comparing our own period with this one, what it means to find a single man uniting the capacities needed for executing both the most audacious engineering works and the finest sculpture? Yet such a union of talents is to be seen in nearly all the great artists of the Renaissance. Leonardo da Vinci represents a type, not an exception. And the tradition that the scientist and the creative artist are combined in the same person persists throughout the seventeenth and eighteenth centuries.

In the Renaissance the longest step forward was taken during the ten years between 1420 and 1430.

Masaccio, the painter, was the youngest of the great Renaissance masters, and the most advanced. Born with the new century — in 1401 — he was a true incarnation of the Renaissance spirit. The history of painting in this period would certainly have been different but for his early death at the age of twenty-seven. Brunelleschi, the architect, was nearly twenty-five years older than Masaccio, and to a great extent shared the Gothic spirit of the fourteenth century. Donatello, the sculptor, was eighteen years older than Masaccio; he too had to break away from Gothic ways of feeling, and succeeded in doing so through his astonishing naturalistic genius. The fact that, among these three, the painter was the first to attain to the new vision of his time is by no means unparalleled. We shall see, further on, that modern painting anticipated modern architecture in much the same way.

Masaccio's "Fresco of the Trinity" (*fig.* 1) in Santa Maria Novella at Florence was executed when he was about twenty-five years old. Painted during the twenties of the *quattrocento*, it was rediscovered in the late nineteenth century and exists today in a badly damaged condition. The Trinity fresco has long been famous for its naturalistic portraits of the founders of the church that contains it. It is the first example of an endless series of paintings of this type. But it is of much more significance to us that the whole composition is encircled by a majestic barrel vault. The point of origin from which its perspective is calculated is taken very low, so that the vault may be seen in all its grandeur. This fresco, painted at a time before any Renaissance interior had been completed, represents what seems to be the first successful expression, in architectonic terms, of the Renaissance feeling that underlay the development of perspective. It reveals a surprising use of the newly discovered elements in combination with absolutely circumscribed tectonic surroundings. Its impressiveness was undeniable; even Vasari — familiar with daring perspective treatments of space — admired the way in which this painted vault pierced the flat surface of the wall.

Masaccio's "Fresco of the Trinity"

It is possible that Masaccio was taught perspective by Brunelleschi; it has even been argued that Brunelleschi himself may have executed the perspective architecture of the Trinity fresco. It was quite common in the *quattrocento* for painters and sculptors to employ qualified specialists for this part of their work. But Masaccio's barrel vault is not a part incidental to the whole composition; it is not a simple background. Instead it dominates the entire picture. At the time it was painted Brunelleschi was occupied with the building of the portico of the Innocenti and with the sacristy of San Lorenzo. Not even in his last works did he ever use the vault in this way; he always kept some attachment to medieval modes. The

34

2. LEON BATTISTA ALBERTI. S. Andrea, Mantua, 1472–1514. *Almost five decades after the Trinity fresco, the longitudinal barrel vault was used in the interior of this church. Even in the exterior, the desire to use the receding barrel vault led to its employment at the most unexpected points.*

Trinity fresco with its heavy coffered vault has the greatness of a triumphal arch. The cheerful expression beloved by early Renaissance taste and present in all the works of Brunelleschi is absent. In its place there is the Roman gravity of a later age.

The barrel vault from the Trinity fresco to St. Peter's

The longitudinal barrel vault that Masaccio painted was to prove the great solution to the vaulting problem that confronted the architects of the full Renaissance and baroque periods. It does not appear in concrete form before the church of San Andrea at Mantua (*fig.* **2**), in 1472 — nearly forty-five years after Masaccio's death. This church, with its severe vaulting, is the architectural realization of the ideal prefigured in Masaccio's painting. It is likewise significant that San Andrea was designed by a member of Masaccio's generation, by

←

1. MASACCIO. Fresco of the Trinity, Santa Maria Novella, Florence, c. 1425. *The longitudinal barrel vault which Masaccio painted not only fulfilled the aim of perspective by receding deeply into space but also anticipated the chief vaulting problem of the Renaissance builders.*

another man born just as the *quattrocento* began: the Florentine humanist and architect, Leon Battista Alberti (1404–1472). Even in the exterior the desire to use the receding barrel vault led to its employment at the most unexpected points.

Bramante's "illusionistic" choir in Milan — a work of small size but great influence — is one of the steps leading from Masaccio's fresco to St. Peter's in Rome. A continuous line of development connects the Trinity fresco, Bramante's choir, and the immense baroque nave of St. Peter's — its culminating point.

Bramante's illusionistic choir (*fig.* **3**) in the church of Santa Maria presso San Satiro (1479–1514) is actually only a small niche. It was half built up and half painted, in order to produce the greatest possible effect of depth with the space at the artist's disposal. For us it has importance as one of the steps leading from Masaccio's fresco to St. Peter's.

Carlo Maderno executed the central nave of St. Peter's (*fig.* **4**), along with its side chapels and façade, during the ten years

3. BRAMANTE. Illusionistic choir in Santa Maria presso S. Satiro, Milan, 1479–1514.

36

4. CARLO MADERNO. Nave of St. Peter's, Rome, 1607–17. *The most majestic solution of the Renaissance vaulting problem. Earlier stages leading up to this solution appear in the San Gesù and many other Roman churches.*

between 1607 and 1617. Following the orders of a new pope, he altered Michelangelo's scheme for its ground plan, changing it from a Greek into a Latin cross. We are told that the change was made to afford more room for the congregation and to take up the entire site of the Early Christian basilica and some additional space as well.

Nevertheless, the scale for this enterprise had already been set by Michelangelo in the height of the pillars for the central dome which he had built. Michelangelo had envisaged a concentration in one place of all the artistic energies represented in the cathedral: they came together in his cupola in one great explosion. The later generation of Maderno and his pope enlarged this conception longitudinally, in accordance with late baroque desires for a long and unbroken expanse. The impression that the spectator receives on entering St. Peter's derives from the superhuman dimensions of this new nave.

Its height exceeds a hundred and fifty feet — equal to that of the early skyscrapers. Its width is relatively small, but Maderno knew how to keep the onlooker from becoming conscious of this. The fully developed art of the baroque period and its control over space appear in the way this is done: the side chapels, almost imperceptibly, expand the actual dimensions of the nave and impart a new power to it.

Masaccio's Trinity fresco marks the discovery of the majesty and strength which can be expressed through simple and grand elements. Carlo Maderno's nave in St. Peter's differs from Masaccio's painted vault both in its dimensions and its complexity. But these differences only sum up the possibilities that were latent in the vision which had come to the fifteenth-century master.

The generation which immediately followed Carlo Maderno carried this unfolding to further and more special results. But before we deal with these we shall turn to some of the architectural works already executed in which the spirit of the early Renaissance first showed through.

The new feeling in early Renaissance buildings

The first building in which the Renaissance spirit appears is Brunelleschi's loggia on the front of the Spedale degli Innocenti at Florence. The Spedale degli Innocenti, or the Foundling Hospital, was built at the order of the silk-weavers' guild, of which Brunelleschi, as a goldsmith, was also a member. Between 1419 and 1424 he constructed the nine arches in the center of the building.

The Spedale degli Innocenti

Since this first Renaissance building was intended for a practical community service, it did not have to conform in its appearance to the dignified and impressive standards that held for edifices of state — buildings which are often found to reflect the taste of the previous period. Thus Florentine palaces preserved their resemblance to Gothic closed fortresses up to the middle of the fifteenth century. In the Foundling Hospital Brunelleschi had an opportunity to open up the closed, fortress-like block of the house. He did this by means of a round-arched porch, pleasant in its graceful lightness.

The upper wall of the Innocenti is not rusticated, but is kept a flat surface, with sparsely distributed windows. A Renaissance preference is revealed on the outside by the entablature which bisects the whole surface of the wall horizontally.

But the hospital's chief distinction is the portico, and the most interesting feature of the latter is the manner in which the vault is treated. The diagonal Gothic cross ribs have disappeared; a light coved vault, resembling wind-filled sails, replaces them. Binding arches are used for marking distinctly the boundaries between each vault and the one next it, thereby enforcing the Renaissance demand for the complete independence of every section of a design.

Relation to Byzantine architecture

There is no direct connection between classical architecture and Brunelleschi's Foundling Hospital. It has often been remarked that the chief features of Brunelleschi's architectural style are closely related to buildings which he saw every day in Florence — to the Baptistery, to San Miniato, and to the Badia of Fiesole. All these are in the tradition of medieval architecture from the eighth to the twelfth century. The coved or hemispherical vault which Brunelleschi used with such great sureness in his churches and in the Innocenti — and which was always the vaulting motif he preferred — was likewise unusual in antiquity. It was, however, quite common in Byzantine architecture, especially for loggias and the entrance halls of ecclesiastical structures. There was a comparatively close connection between Florence and Byzantium in Brunelleschi's time. Recent researches have also made it plain that some other early Renaissance treatments of the vaulting problem owe more to the Middle Ages and to Byzantium than they do to classical antiquity.

The Pazzi Chapel, Florence

Brunelleschi's Pazzi Chapel (*fig.* 5) is the first Renaissance structure in which the interior as well as the exterior is of monumental size and character. It was begun in 1430, some ten years after the Innocenti, and when Masaccio was already dead. The chapel itself was finished in 1442; its decoration was not completed until 1469. Brunelleschi replaced the spherical vaults used in the Foundling Hospital with barrel vaults arranged transversely, instead of receding as they do in Masaccio's Trinity fresco. (Transverse barrel vaults are to be found in

5. BRUNELLESCHI. **Pazzi** Chapel, Florence, begun in 1430. *The barrel vaults are placed transversely, not receding as in Masaccio's Trinity fresco. Bold display of the wall as a flat surface.*

Byzantine and Syrian architecture.) These vaults, together with the dome over their place of intersection in the middle, produce a flat impression rather than the depth-penetrating perspective which was sought by Masaccio and the later Renaissance.

The interior; difficulty in working with a new space conception

The interior of the Pazzi Chapel forms the starting point for all Renaissance churches of the centralized type. It is developed by the addition of compartments whose geometrical form can readily be grasped, all clearly marked off by stone framework in contrasting colors. It has all the inimitable freshness of a new birth, but the two small barrel vaults, in their cautious dimensions, show that confidence in the new vision had not yet been attained. When contrasted with Masaccio's Trinity fresco, for example, the handling of the vaulting problem shows — in all that involves the newly introduced shapes — a noticeable timidity. It is from cases such as this that we learn how difficult it is for the human spirit to plunge into a new conception of space. The Brunelleschi who shows hesitancy here is the same man who, as long as he was working within the familiar Gothic tradition, threw himself into the most daring enterprises. A complete confidence appears in his design for the Cathedral of Santa Maria del Fiore in Florence, with its immense dome over a system of radial ribs.

One feature of the exterior of the Pazzi Chapel requires mention here: the bold manner of displaying the wall as a flat surface. (Its present small roof is a later addition.) This wall, with its delicate subdivisions, has nothing to support; it is like a screen that masks the end of the barrel vault. The emancipation of the wall that appears here is important for the whole future. The wall taken simply as a surface will soon be the subject of important architectural innovations.

The flat surface of the outer wall

PERSPECTIVE AND URBANISM

Prerequisites for the Growth of Cities

Like plants, human settlements require certain conditions for growth; but human community life depends upon far more intricate conditions than the plant. What is common to both is that there are periods which favor growth and other periods which hinder growth.

A city is the expression of the diversity of social relationships which have become fused into a single organism.

The conditions that influence its growth can be of a widely dissimilar nature. Cities have arisen in periods of dictatorship, when the despot has power to compel everyone to build in conformity with a single design. They have also arisen in periods of purposeful communal energy.

The despot has the advantage of his capacity for rapid and ruthless action; but since his sovereign will is bound to ignore the imponderable laws which stimulate human coöperation, a city built under a dictatorship can never acquire the essential quality of organic diversity.

41

In cities that have been developed by the united efforts of their citizens, everything — even to the last detail — is permeated with a wonderful strength. Never since the democratic way of life first found expression in Greece in the fifth century B.C. has so much loving care been lavished on the development of cities, or space been so amply provided for gatherings of the populace; nor has the spot where the people's decisions were enunciated and carried into effect ever dominated the town's physical and moral structure so effectively as did the agora in these early Greek cities. Perhaps the only later towns which could sustain comparison with them in such respects are some of those founded in the midst of Europe in the twelfth to fourteenth centuries, whose dogged struggles against temporal or spiritual feudal overlords laid the foundations of modern democracy.

At the dawn of the Renaissance, the principal city-republics of Italy — Venice, Siena, and above all Florence — already had their struggles for democracy behind them. But exaltation of the individual ego now began to supersede the old team spirit of the Middle Ages, and paved the way for the absolutism of the seventeenth century. An age so imbued with the supreme importance of personality was not likely to be one known for the building of new towns.

The Star–Shaped City

It is not easy to arrive at a definite conclusion regarding the nature of urban planning in the Renaissance town. Compared with the immense creative urge manifested in every other field, city planning seems at first sight strangely devoid of that vigorous and imaginative grasp of the subject which is so overwhelmingly evident in painting and sculpture.

How can this be explained?

In contrast to the collective spirit of the Gothic period, the complex organism of a city with its manifold social indentations was foreign to the Renaissance — to the period in which perspective was invented, where the whole picture is calculated from a single focal point, from the viewpoint of a single static observer.

The Renaissance was hypnotized by one city type which for a century and a half — from Filarete to Scamozzi — was impressed upon all utopian schemes: this is the star-shaped city. From a symmetrical fortified polygon, radial streets lead to a main center. This is the basic diagram. The central area is either left open, as in the completed city of Palmanova (1593), or contains a central tower — a central observation post — from which the radiating streets are seen in shortened perspective.

Certainly the sharply faceted conformation of these six-, eight-, nine-, and twelve-pointed stars was decisively influenced by the introduction of gunpowder. In the Middle Ages a close circuit of protecting walls with towers rising above the battlements at appropriate intervals had been adequate. Now the encircling wall is transformed into a series of regularly indented bastions (*fig.* **6**) from which flanking fire can be directed upon the attacker.

The influence
of firearms

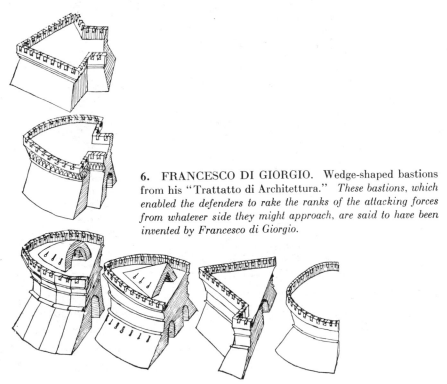

6. FRANCESCO DI GIORGIO. Wedge-shaped bastions from his "Trattatto di Architettura." *These bastions, which enabled the defenders to rake the ranks of the attacking forces from whatever side they might approach, are said to have been invented by Francesco di Giorgio.*

The centralized
building and the
star-shaped city

The polygon and star shapes of the *città ideale* result from the fortification system of the Renaissance: but this is not the decisive influence. In the background of the star-shaped city stands the Renaissance theory of the centrally organized building. This conception dominated Bramante throughout his life, and it is known that the combination of a domed structure with radiating chapels was the architectural problem which more than all others piqued the interest of Leonardo

7. VITTORE CARPACCIO. S. George and the Dragon, between 1502 and 1507. *As is so often the case in Venetian pictures, the most important part of the composition is not the subject matter but the display of a large spatial expanse. The centralized church in the background is more dominant than the main actors in the foreground. No piazza of such grandiose conception and dimensions was ever built by Carpaccio's contemporaries.*

da Vinci. The central building in the midst of a star-shaped city fulfills the same role — that of a symbolic observer standing at the focal point. The central building recurs persistently in the painting of the period. We need only to mention a well-known early work of Raphael in the Brera, the "Sposalizio" or "Marriage of the Virgin" (1504), where a polygonal temple soars right up to the top of the frame and dominates the whole composition, while from the short flights of steps surrounding the temple wide expanses of dark marble paving radiate into perspective distance on every side. The drawing of Vittore Carpaccio (*fig.* 7) may serve as one of many other possible examples.

Medieval origins

The star-shaped *città ideale* of the Renaissance is really the rationalization of a medieval type [1] in which the castle, cathedral, or main square forming the core of the town is encircled by anything from one to four irregular belts.[2] The tree-like plan of Bagnocavallo in Italy (*fig.* 8) shows the organic manner in which a similar situation was handled in the Middle Ages. The difference is that what the Middle Ages brought about organically in a number of different ways the Renaissance proceeded to freeze into a rigid formal pattern from the outset. The medieval city is characterized by expanding belts of streets; the Renaissance, by streets that radiate directly from the center.

Filarete (1400–69)

The star-shaped town is the creation of the *quattrocento.* It was first elaborated soon after the middle of the fifteenth century by the Florentine Filarete (Antonio di Pietro Averlino), who was followed some twenty years later by the Sienese architect, sculptor, and painter Francesco di Giorgio Martini.

Although that great animater Leone Battista Alberti had discussed the possibility of building an "ideal city" in the tenth book of his "De Re Aedificatoria," written about 1450, it was left to Filarete to fill in the details and work out a definite scheme. Filarete wrote his "Trattato d'Architettura"[3] between 1451 and 1464, when he was in the service of Francesco Sforza and while he was engaged in building the large Ospedale Maggiore in Milan which was badly damaged in the Second World War. Since this treatise was intended as propaganda,

---

[1] Information about other still earlier examples of this type of town will be found in L. Piccinato, "Origini dello Schemo Urbano Circolare nel Medioevo," *Palladio,* vol. V. no. 3 (Rome, 1941); and in *Urbanistica,* XVI (Rome, 1947), 124–136.

[2] Various examples are given under "Urbanistica Medioevale" in L. Piccinato's *Urbanistica dall' Antichita ad Oggi* (Florence, 1943), and on p. 298 and following of the second edition of G. Giovannoni's *Saggi sulla Architettura del Rinascimento* (Milan, 1935).

[3] This was first published in Vienna in 1890 by W. von Oettingen, in *Quellenschriften für Kunstgeschichte und Kunsttechnik,* under the title "Antonio Averlino Filarete's Tractat über die Baukunst." There is also an illustrated edition published under the title *Filarete, Scultore e Architetto del Secolo XV,* edited by M. Lazzaroni and A. Muñoz (Rome, 1908). See also Peter Tigler, *Die Architekturtheorie des Filarete* (Berlin, 1963).

8. Bagnocavallo, a medieval town of Roman origin. *The streets grow like the annular rings of a tree and not on the radial system of the ideal cities of the Renaissance. Their irregularities are caused by the natural formation of the ground.*

9. FILARETE. The site of the star-shaped city "Sforzinda" about 1460–64. *The geometrical pattern for this city is placed in a mild Italian "valley surrounded by hills through which the river 'Inda' flows," described by Filarete in his second book.*

Il fiume sforzindo
Laualle inda

lita didetta ualle domandai come sichiamaua quello fiume chedxorreua
perlomezzo didetta ualle & lui disse chesichiamaua sforzindo & laualle
sichiamaua inda ilperche molto mipiacque & acceptai laproferta chedeñ
gentile huomo maueua fatta & cosi insua compagnia andai uedendo qª
sto sito & questa ualle mella quale non era gia terre grosse mamolte uille

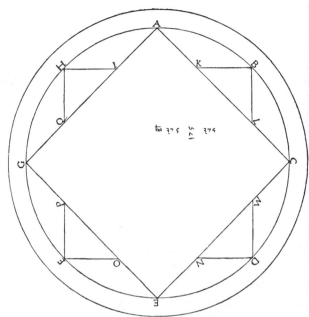

Come to detto lo rimostrerò questo plaiamento ilquale o riquadrato in
quadri piccholi ruglipotresti intendere grandi & piccholi arivo fermo maio
clinrendo diquesta misura cioe diquattro stadij paraschetto quadro che fare
to almodo nostro mezzo miglio pquadro Sicbe uedendo questo tupuoi fa
pere quanto mene aessere grande per lacum o uuoi dire migha o uuoi
due stadij ouuoi dure braccio tu sai quanti stadij o uno migho &sai
quanto braccio eloftadio molupricha & saperai quanto ella arcunda
è quanto elle perogni uerso Co cosi allamgione diqueste misure massor

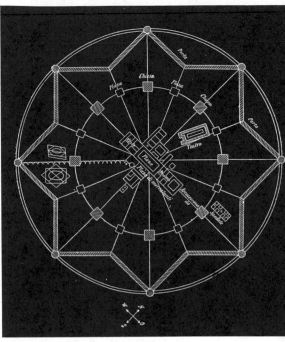

11. FILARETE. "Sforzinda," the star-shaped
city with its radial road pattern. *Sixteen main
streets radiate from the central piazza to the eight city
gates and the eight corner towers. Midway, each street
crosses an open square, eight of which have a church in
the center.*

it took the form of a dialogue between a Tuscan architect
(Antonio Filarete) and a Renaissance prince (Francesco
Sforza). The building of an ideal city, to be called "Sforzinda," was proposed and described in great detail, from the
prince's palace and the cathedral down to the quarters to be
alloted to merchants and artisans, and not forgetting the pris-
ons. In plan Sforzinda was to be a symmetrical eight-pointed
star: "The outer walls should form a sixteen-sided figure and
their height be four times their depth. The streets should
lead from the gates to the center of the town where I would
place the main square, which ought to be twice as long as it
is wide. In the middle of it I would build a tower high enough
to overlook the whole surrounding district" (*figs.* **9–11**).

The idea of the *città ideale* was probably received by Filarete
from Leone Battista Alberti, but it first took on a plastic form
in the hands of that consummate all-round artist Francesco di

Francesco di
Giorgio Martini
(1439–1502)

47

Giorgio Martini (1439–1502). In the third book of his treatise on architecture [4] he is preoccupied with the development of the star-shaped city. The original star plan has already become altered to a regular star-shaped polygon with a projecting bastion at each of its exterior angles. Francesco di Giorgio, being a Sienese, had been familiar from birth with a town built on a steep hill, and for that kind of site he suggested a second plan resembling a clerical skullcap, with spiral roads corkscrewing up to the summit. In a third and most important type of plan — a type adopted by most of his successors and one which influenced Evelyn's plan for rebuilding London after the Great Fire of 1666 — he compressed a severely rectangular pattern of streets opening out of a number of big public squares into yet another polygonal mold. Francesco di Giorgio was at pains to make plans for the *città ideale* suitable for widely varied conditions. He was, moreover, quite clear in his own mind that the city planner need only establish the main lines of the plan and leave it to life itself to make adjustments where necessary.

Vigevano:
Piazza Ducale
(1493–95)

The time at the disposal of Italian despots of the late fifteenth century was far too limited for them to become involved in such long-term ventures as the erection of an ideal city. One of the few cases before 1500 where there is a faint reflection of Filarete's "Sforzinda" is in the little town of Vigevano, which lies with its medieval castle twenty miles southwest of Milan. Here, in 1452, Ludovico Sforza ("il Moro") was born, the great Maecenas to whose court came Leonardo da Vinci and Bramante. Long before he had become Duke of Milan, Ludovico Sforza decided to embellish his birthplace by modernizing its towering medieval stronghold into a Renaissance palace — partly by Bramante himself — and by building a wide and regular open square, approximately to the dimensions 1:2 advocated by Filarete. In this way Vigevano's Piazza Ducale came into being, built as it were at one stroke within the shortest possible time, 1493–95.

---

[4] The *Trattato di Architettura Civile e Militare di Giorgio di Martini* was first published in Turin in 1841. See also R. Papini, *Francesco di Giorgio, Architetto*, 3 vols. (Florence n.d., circa 1946). Volume II contains good illustrations from the whole field of his work, and also an index to the contents of the *Trattato*.

12. Vigevano: Piazza del Duomo, 1493–95. *A rare example of an early and rapidly completed Renaissance square. It is surrounded by arcades as in the new towns built in the thirteenth century. The fourth side is occupied by the baroque façade of the cathedral. The tall "Tower of Bramante" overlooks law buildings that surround the square, which was created by Ludovico il Moro rather as an approach to his castle than as a center of local activity. It is interesting that, despite the contemporary Renaissance theories of the square as a focusing point for radial streets, this square looks more like an enclosed courtyard.*

13. Vigevano: Main Entrance to the Piazza del Duomo. *The picture shows the arches through which the main street enters the square surmounted by a sham façade to maintain the continuity of the wall surfaces. This view is of the entrance from the outside looking toward the cathedral: in the former illustration the entrance arches and sham façade can be seen in the center.*

The whole program is certainly reminiscent of Filarete: there is a tower "high enough to overlook the surrounding district," the palace of the prince, and even the rudiments of some radiating streets. But the 180-foot tower and the dominating palace (now crumbling away as a barracks) stand apart from the arcaded square, which contains only the medieval church with a seventeenth-century façade along its fourth side. Ludovico expropriated and scrapped, under severe legislation,[5] the buildings that had formerly occupied this area. It was a good instinct that obliged him to work so quickly, for he had little time to enjoy the results of his endeavor. Within a few years he was defeated by Francis I and became a prisoner in France, and never returned.

Ludovico Sforza considered the Piazza Ducale as part of a grandiose access to his palatial castle. Yet the square remains strictly isolated, and the great tower (the so-called Tower of Bramante) looms up strangely behind the regular arcaded wall of the square, only two and a half stories high.

It seems that one of the secrets of a good public square or gathering place is the simplicity of its architectonic elements. This simplicity is evident in the stoa, the *Wandelhalle*, and the agora as well as in the heavy arcades of medieval cities such as the thirteenth-century squares of the fortified towns in Southern France and, here, on the verge of the early Renaissance, the lightly swinging arcades of the Piazza Ducale. Above these distinctly articulated arches the walls are broken by sparsely distributed, round-headed window openings. At one time the entire wall surface was overlaid by playful Lombardesque frescoes, but now only a few faded fragments remain of this colorful mockery of architecture. The square itself still holds its reposeful human dignity even though its role has become that of a car park, flooded incessantly with cycles, motor scooters, and tourists.

The many-sidedness of Renaissance man

One of the most convincing explanations of the immense creative energy of the Renaissance is that it consciously developed the whole man instead of training him as a specialist in a single field. Universality is the secret of its wealth of all-round talent and the glowing fullness of life which confronts us in its works.

---

[5] *L'Arte*, V (1902), 249.

Francesco di Giorgio was certainly a man of this sort. In the treatise on which he worked throughout a generation, while dealing with the wide scope of his own experience he refers also to the Greek philosophers. These are not superficial quotations, for he consciously followed the Aristotelian method of proceeding from the general to the particular.

Francesco di Giorgio was a celebrated fortress engineer; for the Duke of Urbino alone he built nearly seventy strongholds. His versatility as an architect is well known. He ended his career as the master builder of Siena Cathedral. The extent of his experience is reflected in some of the building schemes in his treatise which are well in advance of the development of his time. These designs provide a refreshing contrast both to the sixty-odd dreary projects which the younger Vasari (Vasari *il giovane*) worked into stillborn plans for ideal towns a century later and to those produced somewhere about the same time by that otherwise rather interesting architect Bartolomeo Ammanati.[6]

How natural it was for the painter Francesco di Giorgio to blend imagination and reality is shown by several of his *cassone* paintings (paintings on wooden chests) of ideal squares and streets. These pictures not only express the subtlety of a Sienese painter but also contain new architectural concepts. There is a narrow picture of a "Piazza Ideale" now in the Walters Collection at Baltimore (*fig.* 22) in which there is a very interesting treatment of different levels; the surprisingly modern spatial setting of the plastic elements reveals the experience of a practiced sculptor. It is to Francesco di Giorgio, incidentally, that we owe the delicately modeled bronze angels on the high altar of Siena Cathedral, which rank among the most distinguished sculptures of the period immediately before Michelangelo.

---

[6] The rich and largely still unstudied collection of architectural drawings in the Uffizi includes the "Città Ideale del Cavaliere Giorgio Vasari Inventato" as well as Bartolomeo Ammanati's frigid designs. It is only fair to add that among the latter's endless repetitions of columned courtyards he at least shows some interest in making provision for various crafts. No hint can be found in any of these designs that the great development of Baroque was close at hand, or that they are the designs of the man who was at this very time building the florid Palazzo Ruspoli on the Corso in Rome.

This Sienese painter of delicate annunciations and madonnas became a stern rationalist as soon as he took up his T square and set about the plan of a town. When he presupposed a special case, such as a town with a river running through the middle of it, the river would be forced into a straight channel and crossed by bridges at mathematically regular intervals (*fig.* 14). In the Windsor Castle collection there is a very sketchy plan of Florence drawn by Leonardo da Vinci in which he remodels Florence upon a chessboard pattern: the River Arno — as in the Francesco di Giorgio drawings — becomes as straight as a bowstring (*fig.* 15). These two artists stood close to one another in point of age. They met in 1490 at Milan, where they had been called in to give expert advice on the construction of the dome of the cathedral. We know that Leonardo felt that he had much in common with Francesco di Giorgio and held him in esteem.

The Renaissance did not envisage the complete overall replanning of towns, but it took a passionate interest in the development of certain urban architectural elements.[7]

The origin of Renaissance porticoes

Most of the piazzas built during the Renaissance were surrounded by arcades. Although of Roman origin (as may be seen at Ostia), it is probable that they were reintroduced into Italy, by way of Venice, from Byzantium, whose streets, often arcaded on two stories, had long been famous. But, even if not with historical accuracy, arcaded piazzas have been chiefly identified with the Renaissance. Michelangelo himself proposed to arcade both the Piazza della Signoria at Florence and the square in front of St. Peter's.

The stately open squares of the Renaissance often took hundreds of years to complete, and the noblest of all — the Piazza di San Marco with the Piazzetta in Venice — remained unfinished for nearly five centuries.

The rigidity of the star-shaped city

As has already been pointed out, the *città ideale* merely systematized a preëxisting medieval type. Both were based on the exigencies of defense. In Italy, towns with elected municipalities had usually been sovereign city-states, and a wall-girded city was a symbol of political independence. Since the princi-

---

[7] Volume X of the *Enciclopedia Italiana* contains a good selection of illustrations of the *città ideale* on page 490.

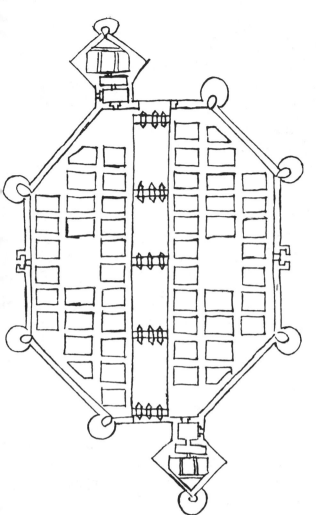

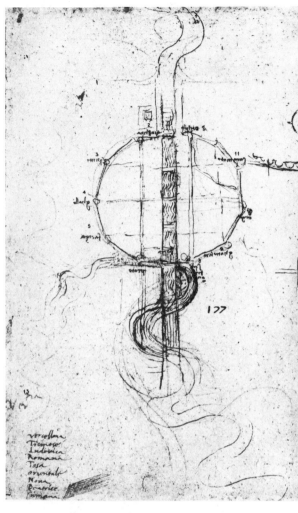

14. FRANCESCO DI GIORGIO. Polygonal city crossed by a river, c. 1490. *The river is forced into a rigidly straight channel crossed by bridges at mathematically regular intervals.*

15. LEONARDO DA VINCI. The city of Florence changed into an "ideal city." *Florence is remodeled upon a chess-board pattern and the River Arno becomes as straight as a bow string.*

ple of self-government broke down during the Renaissance, it is clear that the star-shaped towns were only meant to serve as fortresses.[8] The frontier stronghold of Palmanova, some sixty miles northwest of Venice, was famous as the classic example of regularity until well into the Baroque period: nine-pointed ground plan, hexagonal central piazza as the meeting

---

[8] It is significant that in a more northern country Vauban should have adopted a star-shaped plan for the fortress-town of Saarlouis as late as 1681.

place of six radial roads. It was built by Vincenzo Scamozzi, the architect of the Procuratie on the south side of the Piazza di San Marco, of which he built several bays. Scamozzi is the last of the Renaissance theorists, with his *Idea dell' Architettura Universale*, published in Venice in 1615, just before his death.[9]

The hundred and fifty years which elapsed between Filarete's *Trattato* and Scamozzi's *Idea* saw no notable changes, for the polygonal town was far too rigid a type to lend itself to progressive evolution.

Town planning and the conception of space

From the particular visual angle of that age the star-shaped town was a perfectly logical concept, for Renaissance perspective is based on a strictly limited range of distance and demands a measurable point of optical arrest. In Francesco di Giorgio's Piazza Ideale (*fig.* **22**) an arch of one of the town gates is set in the extreme background as a sort of ultimate target for the eye. No one gave nobler expression or grander scale to this sort of design than Michelangelo, in a work of his later years, the Porta Pia at Rome.

Baroque perspective, on the other hand, was based on a limitless field of vision. Hence typical towns of the late Baroque period, such as Versailles (second half of the seventeenth century) and Karlsruhe (about a hundred years later), have nothing to do with the star-shaped plan. The palace of the ruler stands boldly between town and country, dominating — at least in the optical sense — limitless space.

---

[9] Scamozzi described his own *città ideale* in his second book. Julius von Schlosser's *Materialen zur Quellenkunde der Kunstgeschichte* — more particularly Part II, "Frührenaissance" (Vienna, 1915) and Part VI, "Die Kunstliteratur des Manierismus" (Vienna, 1919) — is an invaluable source of information on the architectural theorists of this period.

PERSPECTIVE AND THE CONSTITUENT ELEMENTS OF THE CITY

It would be misleading to judge Renaissance town planning simply by these successive versions of the *città ideale*. The idea of the town as an entity in which the interactions of thousands of separate existences can be coördinated was foreign to the temper of that era. None of the great Renaissance artists has left us a plan for a new kind of town — neither Bramante, nor Michelangelo, nor even Leonardo, from whose vision, which so often leapt forward centuries in time, it might almost have been expected.[1]

What was new in Renaissance civic design must be sought elsewhere, in the thorough mastery of some of a town's constituent elements. In that field Bramante and Michelangelo opened up hitherto unknown possibilities. Intermediate between the fruitful age of Gothic, with its communal ethos, and the absolutism of Baroque, in the realm of town planning the Renaissance is a preparatory period. The fifteenth century in northern countries was still wholly Gothic, but in Italy the position is complicated. Although perspective was creating a new attitude of mind, the Gothic tradition lived on in many ways and influenced the implementation of city improvements, particularly in the public squares.[2] In a sociological sense Italy and the northern countries by no means stood in such marked contrast to one another during this transitional period.

---

[1] In a celebrated letter to Ludovico il Moro, Duke of Milan, which probably dates from the plague of 1485–86 in that city, Leonardo da Vinci expressed a desire to see towns made more sanitary, so that their inhabitants would no longer have to live "packed together like goats and polluting the air for one another." He proposed building ten towns for the Duke, each for a population of five thousand. These were to be "situated on rivers regulated by locks. . . Within them light, air and cleanliness shall prevail." Among Leonardo's drawings preserved at Windsor Castle there are plans of existing towns but none of any *città ideale* (*I Disegni Geografici, conservati nel Castello di Windsor*, edited by M. Baratta (Rome, 1941).

[2] Evidence of the persistence of the Gothic tradition in major civic undertakings can be found in a large number of the many public squares that were laid out in North-Italian towns during the *quattrocento* — the Piazza del Santo in Padua, the Piazza Grande in Parma, the realignment of the Piazza del Campo in Siena (fig. 21), the Piazza Principale in Piacenza, and so on. A good selection of these are illustrated on pages 268–280 of the second edition of G. Giovannoni's *Saggi sulla Architettura del Rinascimento* (Milan, 1935).

The modeling of
large volumes

The Renaissance learned to handle large volumes and to shape them into new forms. Palaces often thrust aside the homes of the townsfolk, streets, and squares. But their builders discovered how great expanses of wall could be opened on to the street. This was something antiquity had never achieved, though here and there it sometimes allowed glimpses of the street from one or two windows. These Renaissance palaces gazed wide-eyed upon the world without as if they were seeking to appraise it just as with the new medium of perspective. Although Gothic elevations are often loopholed by fenestration to a considerable extent, the windows remain islanded, lost in a vast expanse of walling, as in the thirteenth-century Palazzo della Signoria at Florence.

At the zenith of the Renaissance, however, about 1500, we find windows ranged upon windows, each treated as a separate feature and accentuated by a pediment, pilasters, or columns, yet rhythmically articulated to one another.

The Palazzo
Farnese

Nowhere can the changes undergone by the wall surfaces be more plainly perceived than in the Farnese Palace at Rome, which Cardinal Alessandro Farnese began in 1514. Antonio Sangallo the younger designed this building and carried it out up to the roof cornice, but Michelangelo, among others, added to it after Sangallo's death in 1546 — that is to say, at the very end of the late Renaissance. Sangallo's volumes overwhelm the capacity of the site, exemplifying the exaggerated individualism of the Renaissance mind. The incredibly pretentious magnificence of this residence for a single man points to the imminence of Baroque.

Alessandro Farnese started to build himself a palace as a cardinal, and finished it as Pope Paul III. He portrays the transition from individualism to absolutism. Michelangelo knew how to express this sculpturally. Sangallo had already emphasized the central window with two concentric arches,[3] but Michelangelo set to work in quite a different manner. In

---

[3] As illustrated by C. de Tolnay in his "Beiträge zu den späten architektonischen Projekten Michelangelos," *Jahrbuch der Preussischen Kunstsammlungen*, vol. 51 (1930).

salient contrast to the alternating triangular and segmental pediments over the windows on either side, he placed an architrave over the dominant central window where the whole emphasis could be concentrated on a huge shield carved with the Farnese coat of arms and surmounted by the papal tiara. This monumental window seems to await the arrival of the great overlord who is about to show himself to the populace.

On the garden front the Palazzo Farnese faces the Via Giulia, which Bramante had traced, and the Tiber. Michelangelo felt there was need for more open space round the huge bulk of the palace. He proposed a bridge across the river so as to include the Villa Farnesina and the Trastevere quarter in the way that was later adopted for the approaches to many French châteaux.

The Renaissance did not treat the street as a unity even where it would have been quite easy to do so. Scenically, the Renaissance street consisted of a number of individual buildings set down at random on separate sites; and this holds good from the late *quattrocento* up to the sixteenth century. Francesco di Giorgio's fine paintings of streets and squares (*figs.* **16, 22**) show no two houses alike. Even the porticoes of the houses which so clearly call for uniform treatment are not continuous; each house has its separate arcade. Even much later, as can be seen in the frequently reproduced stage set of Sebastiano Serlio about 1550 — which is not designed simply to produce a perspective effect — the street is still an agglomeration of heterogeneous buildings.

The street in the Renaissance

Thus when Donato Bramante (1444–1514) laid down the alignment for the first new street in Rome, the kilometer-long Via Giulia,[4] at the behest of Pope Julius II, he did not envisage continuous frontages, for he intended to place his Palace of Justice, with its massive quoins and corner towers, foursquare along part of this street. The Palace of Justice was begun in 1506, but after the death of Pope Julius II the work stopped. A few Cyclopean blocks of stone built into some nearby houses

Bramante's Via Giulia in Rome

---

[4] Ceccarius, *Strada Giulia* (Rome, 1941). Straight and still broader streets were not uncommon in newly founded twelfth- and thirteenth-century towns north of the Alps, e.g., Berne.

give an idea of the extent to which this building would have disrupted the Via Giulia.[5]

Giorgio Vasari and the Uffizi

All the more surprising, therefore, is the architectural uniformity of the short street in Florence originally known as the Piazza degli Uffizi on which Giorgio Vasari erected administrative buildings for the Medici between 1560 and 1574. The continuous, lightly bracketed triple cornice seen with the sym-

16. FRANCESCO DI GIORGIO. Piazza and Street of an Ideal City, Detail. *The Renaissance did not treat the street as an architectural unit, even when it would seem almost obvious to do so. In Francesco di Giorgio's fine painting no two adjacent houses are alike.*

metrical outline of the roof above make this a masterpiece of perspective in depth (*fig. 17*). This regular planning of the

[5] Domenico Gnoli, "Il Palazzo di Giustizia di Bramante," *Nuova Antologia*, April 16, 1914.

58

Uffizi would have been almost inconceivable but for the example Vasari's master, Michelangelo, had given him in the group of buildings then under construction on the Capitoline hill in Rome.

Vasari's indebtedness to Michelangelo appears even in details, such as the use of alternating piers and pairs of columns, but instead of being dynamically backed against the piers, as on the Capitol, Vasari's columns are spaced out at regular intervals. It is known that Vasari showed his designs to his master in Rome, so Michelangelo had his hand in the design.

Bramante and the Open Stairway

Besides their bold handling of the surfaces of walls facing streets and squares, Renaissance builders went to great pains

17. GIORGIO DI VASARI. The Uffizi, Florence, 1560–74. *In the latest development of the Renaissance, the Mannerist painter Vasari achieved a masterpiece of perspective in depth in the short street of the Uffizi by means of continuous horizontal lines: the projecting roof, the three cornices, the steps. This view is taken from the arch of the loggia which closes the vista toward the Arno.*

to bring horizontal surfaces lying on different planes into spatial relation with one another. This they achieved by the device of imposing monumental stairways left open to the sky.

18. JACOPO BELLINI. The presentation of the Virgin in the Temple, c. 1440.
The subject-matter and the figure of the Virgin Mary are only a pretext for the artist's real intentions. From the stone floor in the foreground, where the observer is placed, up to the immense barrel vault of the spacious church, numerous figures are dotted about at different levels, in a supreme effort to conquer perspective in depth. The stairway zigzagging backward and forward is the early attempt of a painter to convey perspective in depth in terms of architecture.

19. ÉTIENNE DU PÉRAC. Tournament in Bramante's Cortile del Belvedere, 1565.
This engraving was executed shortly after Pirro Ligorio had finished the building of the
Belvedere Court by the addition of the Nicchione and left-hand corridors. A few years later,
Bramante's conception, already altered by Ligorio, was annihilated by Sixtus V, whose high
library wing cut the court in two. From then on worldly feasts were forever banished from
the Vatican. In contrast to Jacopo Bellini's drawing, the observer has chosen here an all-
embracing viewpoint high in the air, revealing the High Renaissance control of perspective in
depth and creating a setting particularly suited to worldly pleasures in festivities.

Bramante used these flights of steps as a means of incorporating expanses of outlying space within his composition, and thereby introduced a new element into urban architecture.

Terraced buildings and monumental stairways go back almost to the beginning of architecture. The monumental stairway appeared for the first time in the ziggurats of Sumer around 2000 B.C. Pyramidal flights of steps which formed the plinths of temples and processional approaches to sunken courts are a conspicuous feature of pre-Columbian Mexican architecture. Renaissance builders, however, used terrace formations and monumental stairways in an entirely different manner.

Jacopo Bellini
(c. 1440)

A silverpoint drawing in Jacopo Bellini's sketchbook, which dates from about 1440, shows the purpose that a stairway was intended to serve (*fig.* **18**). A barrel-vaulted church crowns the highest of three successive terraces ascended by a stairway which zigzags back and forth from one level to another up to the open church front. These terraces, like the numerous figures dotted about the foreground and background, reveal the designer's object: to produce an impression of perspective in depth.

Bramante's stairways in the forecourt of the Belvedere

Donato Bramante of Urbino was the first architect to introduce monumental stairways as a formative element through which space could, as it were, be embodied in the design of buildings; and the place where he first realized this embodiment was the garden forecourt of the Belvedere at the Vatican (1506–13). The buildings of Bramante around 1500 display for the first time the new grandeur which the atmosphere of Rome and the patronage of the humanist Pope Julius II brought into the work of the artists. These influences are seen in Raphael, and even to some extent in the towering genius Michelangelo himself. Bramante evinces a new sense of power in his control of the unprecedented dimensions he was called upon to handle at St. Peter's after 1506. Though less ambitious, his handling of the Belvedere's forecourt is no less masterly.

[6] P. Kelemen, *Medieval American Art* (New York, 1943), vol. II, plates 4 and 7.

[7] To the best of my belief no investigation into the treatment of stairways in the Middle Ages (notably in Italy) has yet been undertaken.

The Belvedere is a small papal summer residence which stands on an eminence some three hundred meters distant from the Vatican Palace. In 1506 Julius II entrusted Bramante with the task of combining these two buildings in a comprehensive architectural vista. The Pope had already set up some classical sculpture in the forecourt. He now directed that the whole intervening area be remodeled in the new majestic Roman manner. As the culminating point of his vista at the upper

20. The Cortile del Belvedere after Bramante's death. Detail of a fresco in the Castello S. Angelo, Rome, 1537–41, attributed to the Mannerist painter, Perino del Vaga. *This fresco shows the grandeur of Bramante's modeling of exterior space better than any of the well-known representations of the Cortile. The unfinished architecture helps one to understand how, in Bramante's hands, the open stairway and ramps, the working with levels on different planes, became a new element of urban design.*

end, on the front of the Belvedere, Bramante erected a monumental screen with a huge niche in the middle after the manner sometimes adopted in villas under the Caesars; and at the lower end, in front of the Vatican, a semicircular arena. Terracing enabled him to establish a formal relation between the new buildings with their triple tier of loggias.

Here we are concerned with this stairway as an agency by means of which spatial areas have been articulated and woven into a spatial unit.[8]   A wide flight of steps leads from the first to the second level, where it divides into two branches under the retaining wall to gain the topmost garden and with it the Belvedere (*fig.* **20**).   As secluded as the garden of an immense medieval cloister, everything was here devised for courtly pleasures.   Nearly fifty years after Bramante's death, when the vast ensemble had been finally completed, the marriage of one of Pius IV's nephews provided a fitting occasion for inaugurating the Cortile del Belvedere.   Étienne du Pérac's engravings have perpetuated the splendor of those sumptuous feasts and tournaments (*fig.* **19**).   But the Cortile was not destined to remain for long as Bramante had remodeled it. In 1589, Sixtus V wrecked the unity of the design by building a new library athwart the middle of its parterres.   That great town planner destroyed many monuments of ancient Rome, but this was his most destructive act.

Later on, the monumental stairway, of which Bramante's stately ascent to the platform of the Belvedere had been the prototype, became the noblest pediment that could be added to a church (S. Maria Maggiore).   Eventually the monumental stairway became an almost independent structure whose role was to merge planes lying at different levels into a single field of space (the Scala di Spagna, 1721–25, which connects S. Trinità dei Monti with the Piazza di Spagna).   In late Baroque interiors we find large staircases — the symbol of movement — used to create cavernous voids which have no parallel in the history of architecture.

Michelangelo and the Modeling of Outer Space

Michelangelo's "Capitolina" in Rome

In the Area Capitolina, the great square in which stood the Roman Capitol, Michelangelo showed how to achieve a balance between carefully molded masses — the spatial relationship of great volumes.   When he took this work in hand in 1536,

---

[8] There is a good detailed description in M. L. Gothein, *A History of Garden Art* (London, 1928), I, 227–231.   See also James S. Ackerman, " The Belvedere as a Classical Villa," *Journal of the Warburg and Courtauld Institutes*, XIV, Nos. 1–2 (January–June 1951). I am indebted to Professor Ackerman for fig. 20.

toward the end of the Renaissance, he had already reached the zenith of his fame as a painter and sculptor: the ceiling of the Sistine Chapel, the tomb of Pope Julius, and the Medici Chapel in Florence all lay behind him. Thus his architecture is the fruit of his ripest years. Giovanni Lorenzo Bernini, whose colonnade in front of St. Peter's so marvelously completes Michelangelo's conception and who seldom spoke good of others, said, "Michelangelo was great both as sculptor and painter: but divine as an architect." Bernini's closing words find an eternal echo in the Area Capitolina, where Michelangelo's plastic genius created a sublime spatial symphony out of a jumble of medieval remains.

This square, now called the Piazza del Campidoglio, occupies the cliff-top site of the ancient Capitol which overhung the Forum Romanum. It is a complex consisting of three buildings, the square itself, and a broad-ramped stairway called "la Cordonata" which leads down to the town. The whole complex faces toward the medieval city, and closing the approach is the modest town hall, the Senatorial Palace, flanked on the right by the Palace of the Conservatori and on the left by the Capitoline Museum, the world's oldest collection of antiquities.

Michelangelo lived to see only a part of his great branching stairway finished in front of the Senatorial Palace. Both the other buildings were begun after his death. Yet in spite of certain modifications introduced during the course of their construction, which continued until well into the seventeenth century, the plans and dispositions Michelangelo had got out in 1546 (reproduced in the engravings of Du Pérac, 1568 and 1569) were adhered to in essentials.

The great stairway was not yet built when Charles V made his triumphal entry into Rome in 1536. He had to clamber up to the Capitol from the other side — from the Forum — to which the Area Capitolina was oriented in Roman times. "La Cordonata" is a ramped stairway — an inclined plane built up of sloping treads. Those mounting the wide, shallow steps to the platform above are constrained to a slow and measured ascent. The bronze equestrian statue of Marcus Aurelius which Michelangelo transferred from the Lateran

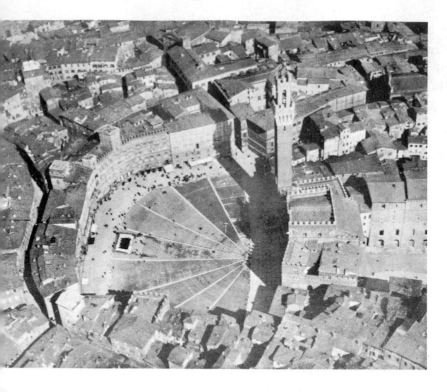

21. Siena: Piazza del Campo, paved in 1413. *The huge, shell-shaped public square in the center of Siena is set between the three hills upon which the city is built. Admirable use is made of the natural slope to give the Public Palace its dominating position. Eleven streets run out from the square, and the white marble stripes of the pavement shoot out like rays from a lighthouse at the focal point of the community.*

22. FRANCESCO DI GIORGIO. Piazza of an ideal city. *The interesting treatment of different levels, and the surprisingly modern spatial setting reveal the experience of a practiced sculptor. The human figures scattered here and there show that he saw columns in space, varied planes, and sculptures, all in relation to moving people. These are problems that in our period are again coming to the fore, as can be seen in certain aspects of the work of Alberto Giacometti.*

66

23. MICHELANGELO. The Capitol, Rome, begun 1536. *This photograph, taken from the height of the Senatorial Palace, gives some idea of Michelangelo's spatial conception: the sunken oval; the equestrian statue in the center of a twelve-pointed star that explodes like a firework; the majestic Cordinata, which leads down to the medieval city. The three buildings that surround the square give evidence of its trapezoidal form, even though they are seen only as fragments.*

comes into sight in the center of the square. As an effigy it is as nobly simple in its disdain of all heroic gesticulations (as Stendhal remarked) as the unassuming pedestal Michelangelo designed for it.

None the less its lonely sky-girt position commanding the axis of the stairway from the very center of the square proves that the master who confidently handled such unprecedented voids as the dome of St. Peter's could treat the nicest graduations in plane with the same unerring sureness.

The wedge-shaped piazza of the Area Capitolina narrows toward the balustrade where the stairway debouches. No particle of the ground is left unconsidered. Michelangelo places an oval within the wedge-shaped square. This oval is slightly recessed and is ringed around by two steps, whose curving shadows define the formal ambit of the statue's emplacement. The ground itself swells gently upwards toward the pedestal. This spot is called the *caput mundi*, and its curving surface has been likened to a segment of the terrestrial globe.[9]

What an excitement has now infected those quiet stripes of marble which in the *quattrocento* used to cover the surfaces of the most distinguished squares, such as the rounded piazza at Siena! Now the stripes radiate out in fingerlike beams from Marcus Aurelius on his pedestal to form a twelve-pointed star of flattened intersecting curves.[10] Their fantastic pattern enflames the whole frenzied interplay of contrasts: oval, trapezoid, the background of Roman and medieval tradition, the subtly shifting interplay of Baroque light and shadow that models the walls,[11] the grandiose gesture of the great stairway — all combine to form a single all-embracing harmony, for the relation of each to each and of the whole to its parts has

---

[9] C. de Tolnay, "Beiträge zu den späten architektonischen Projekten Michelangelos," *Jahrbuch der Preussischen Kunstsammlungen*, vol. 51 (1930), p. 26. This statement may be compared with H. Sedlmayr's prompt attack on it which will be found on pages 176–181 of the same publication for 1931.

[10] In 1940, over 400 years after Michelangelo had designed it, the original star-shaped paving at last replaced the meager pattern which was substituted after his death.

[11] None of the photographs so far published bring out the extraordinary dynamic quality of this composition, but the reader may be referred to Plates 50–75 in Armando Schiavo's *Michelangelo Architetto* (Rome, 1949) and to the magnificent volume by Paolo Portoghesi and Bruno Zevi, *Michelangiolo Architetto* (Rome, 1964).

been consummately affined. One understands Vasari's statement: "Whatever he set his hand to, Michelangelo worked miracles." [12]

In the "Last Judgment" and the tomb of Julius II Michelangelo had already replaced the static emptiness of *quattrocento* space with a dynamic space of his own. This he also achieved in the Capitol.

Our mental picture of the Renaissance begins to evaporate. That "extremely divergent opinions as to Michelangelo's precise historic significance" [13] should have prevailed among scholars ever since Jakob Burckhardt is understandable enough, for Michelangelo was one of those infrequent geniuses who bridge periods in art which do not necessarily succeed one another chronologically. John Constable and J. M. W. Turner, if of minor stature, belong to this same exceptional order of men in that they form the link between the painting of the late Baroque and that of nineteenth-century France. Michelangelo was an admixture of Gothic and Baroque. He connects the worldly universality of the Baroque with the spirituality of the Gothic. Life and death to him were one and the same: from the day of his birth every man is doomed to carry the seed of death hidden within him. In 1555 he wrote to Vasari, "I have never expressed an idea which was not molded in the lineaments of death." [14] That is the utterance of a medieval craftsman, not of a Renaissance artist. Yet he was always powerfully attracted to the problems of movement,[15] had the urge to experiment with its artistic and physical potentialities, which, being inherent in Western man, permeates the Gothic just as it does the Baroque.

The architectural significance of the Capitol can be rapidly summarized. It is a development of Bramante's use of terraces at the Belvedere into an element of urbanism. It is a comprehensive composition in depth — piazza, stairway, city — and

Michelangelo as a bridger of styles

The architectural significance of the Capitol

---

[12] C. de Tolnay, *Werk und Weltbild des Michelangelo* (Zürich, 1949), p. 90.

[13] C. de Tolnay, "Beiträge zu den späten architektonischen Projekten Michelangelos," p. 47.

[14] C. de Tolnay, *Werk und Weltbild des Michelangelo*, p. 59.

[15] Cf. my *Mechanization Takes Command* (New York, 1948), pp. 14–30, in the chapter on Movement.

at the same time a preparation for the great axis emanating from a single building, the Senatorial Palace: something the ancient world had never sought to realize. In the Area Capitolina, Michelangelo was able to carry out some, though not all, that he had vainly planned for the Palazzo Farnese. Later, in the hands of the French, the axial vista was studied with assiduity and, proudly termed "le culte de l'axe," became the vertebrate principle of eighteenth-century town planning.

What Is the Real Significance of the Area Capitolina?

None of Michelangelo's notes about the Capitol exist, so there is free scope for conjecture as to what was in his mind when he planned this proud civic monument to the purely nominal remnant of autonomy which the citizens of Rome could still lay claim to. What could his private feelings have been when he built it?

In 1530 the city-republic of Florence lost its former independence to the Medici despot Cosimo I. Michelangelo had taken an active part in the defense of his native city against the Medici Pope Clement VII. Following the death of the Pope, who was his personal enemy, Michelangelo left Florence in profound antagonism to the new regime in 1534 and spent the last thirty years of his life as a voluntary exile in Rome. After the death of Antonio Sangallo the younger in 1546, he became the city's master builder. Although he was then over seventy, every important building was entrusted to him: the dome of St. Peter's, the Farnese Palace, the whole comprehensive layout and design for the Capitol.

Charles De Tolnay, whose *Michelangelos politische Anschauungen* shows profound insight into the master's political beliefs, quotes a sonnet [16] which reveals all the gnawing bitterness he felt even so late as 1545. That sonnet makes his own statue of Night in the Medici Chapel say:

> *Non veder, non sentir, m'è gran ventura;*
> *Però, non mi destar, deh! parla basso!*

(*Speak softly that I wake not, for this one sovereign boon I crave: to see and feel no more!*)

---

[16] On page 32.

The significance of the Capitol would appear to be analogous to that of this sonnet. In neither does Michelangelo express himself directly, but deliberately chooses to speak through a seemingly impersonalized mouthpiece. Could he really have raised the Capitol to glorify a shadowy vestige of power? Should we not rather see in it a passionate longing to retrieve the lost freedom of his native Florence, a dream wrought out and made manifest in stone?

The whole of Michelangelo's work reflects his own tragic conception of life. Even in planning his layout he knew how to give succinct expression to the conflicting motives that actuate every human being and every true democracy — the need to preserve the rights of the individual while safeguarding those of the community. What he had derived from his youthful experience in Florence was brought to reality in the Rome of the Counter Reformation, a Rome in which there was no freedom and no democracy. So his Capitol is both a symbol of the vanished liberties of the medieval city-republics and a memorial to the tragic dream of its creator.

Sociological and esthetic reality

The supine imagination evinced by our contemporary attempts to devise new features in town planning, such as civic centers, is invariably condoned on the plea that we no longer have a manner of life it would be possible to express. What Michelangelo has mirrored in the Area Capitolina is the baffling irrationality of historical events and the enigmatic omission of any direct relation between effect and cause. Once more we realize that a great artist is able to create the artistic form for a phase of social history long before that phase has begun to take tangible shape.

71

LEONARDO DA VINCI AND THE DAWN OF REGIONAL PLANNING

The sketches Leonardo used to make of his observations, whether they concern mechanical spinning devices, helicopters, proposals concerning traffic regulations, or surveys for regional planning, all appear today as distant glimpses into ages yet unborn. In a manuscript now in possession of the Institut

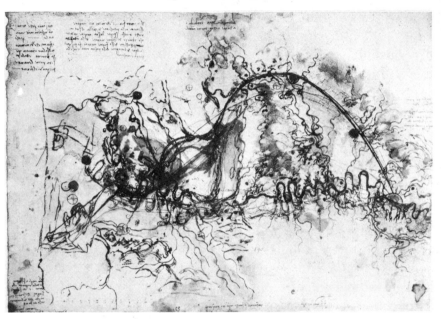

24. LEONARDO DA VINCI. The River Arno and its regulation by a canal. *Bold proposal to make the Arno navigable by building a broad canal in a curving sweep over all differences of level, to link Florence with Pistoia. Reproduced by gracious permission of H.M., The Queen, Windsor Castle.*

de France,[1] proposals for separating pedestrian from wheeled traffic at different levels and a scheme for delivering produce to householders by barges along canals controlled by locks have been interpolated between hydrodynamic studies and drawings of cranes, engines of war, and systems of fortification.

These are flashes of insight into technical possibilities, but little more; there is no trace of comprehensive town planning in any of them. The fragmentary scheme for Florence now

[1] *I Manoscritti e i Disegni di Leonardo da Vinci*, vol. V, "Il Codice B. (2173) nell' Instituto di Francia" (Rome, 1941).

in the collection at Windsor Castle is merely a project for regularizing the River Arno so as to make it flow in a dead straight line through the middle of the town — a plan which treats Florence as if it were yet another *città ideale*. No buildings are shown, and the streets bordering the river are ruled out into chessboard squares (*fig.* **15**). Leonardo's interests lay in other directions.

25. LEONARDO DA VINCI. Scheme for draining the Pontine Marshes, 1514. *This project has never been completely carried out to this day, though, seventy years later, part was begun by Sixtus V, on the lines planned by Leonardo. Reproduced by gracious permission of H.M., The Queen, Windsor Castle.*

His hydrodynamic studies deal with scientific problems that for the most part were not solved until centuries later. For instance, he investigated the conditions which cause whirlpools; he had realized that water moves faster on the surface than at lower levels. At eighteen he was already concerned with representing the whirlpools in the river in the landscape which he had to paint for his master Verrocchio's picture "Baptism of Christ." [2] Leonardo always tried to investigate

---

[2] L. H. Heydenreich, *Leonardo* (Berlin, 1943), p. 267. Heydenreich's broad outlook with its inseparable interrelation of the artistic and the scientific work of Leonardo offers perhaps the best introduction to Leonardo's work.

the hidden, dynamic, forces in the inorganic and organic sphere, in the microcosm and in the macrocosm. As no one else, he could fill his drawings of plants with a feeling of dynamic growth.

Of all the natural forces, however, Leonardo was most interested, as he himself expressed it, "in the nature and movement of water," which was the only motive power available at the time. From his hydrodynamic studies he is led step by step to formulate definite plans based on a comprehension of the physical structure of a region — a rationalized standpoint characteristic of Renaissance enlightenment. To these belong his accurately surveyed projects for irrigating the Po valley and for building a network of canals between Milan and the North Italian lakes, of which he actually had trial sections excavated. During the time he lived in Rome under Pope Leo X and did not paint a single picture (1513–14), Leonardo drew up an impressive hydrographic plan for draining the Pontine marshes, an undertaking that was only partly carried out by Sixtus V at the very end of his reign (*fig.* **25**). The boldness of another proposal of his to make a river navigable by building a broad canal in a curving sweep eighty kilometers long over all differences of level is, so far as we know, unsurpassed even by the canals constructed during the nineteenth century. In a sepia pen-and-ink drawing as arresting as any of his pictures, Leonardo plotted out the line of a canal that would bypass the Arno, link Florence with Pistoia, and rejoin the river lower down its course (*fig.* **24**).[3]

Regional planning must have an insight into the conditions of a certain area in order to permit coördinated planning of the use of land and organization of human activities. The detailed inquiries necessary today are far removed from the cosmological approach of Leonardo, who tried to survey and organize the natural forces of a whole region so as to serve human purposes. Nevertheless, all of Leonardo's plans were

[3] Mario Baratta, *I Disegni Geografici*, pl. 5 on right; Mario Baratta, "Leonardo da Vinci negli Studi per la Navigazione dell'Arno," *Bolletino della Società Geografica Italiana*, serie V, vol. VI (1905), pp. 739–761 and 893–919; Kenneth M. Clark, *A Catalogue of the Drawings of Leonardo da Vinci in the Collection of His Majesty the King at Windsor Castle* (2 vols., 1935).

the fruit of painstaking analysis of each of the various problems he had to contend with. For all its volcanic turbulence, his was a zealously inquiring age. Out of its tumultuous urge to leave no field of knowledge unexplored there emerged the first conscious attempts at regional planning: seed which, though foredoomed to fall on stony ground, held more latent promise than all those geometric plans for ideal new cities that never looked beyond the immediate orbit of their own day.

SIXTUS V (1585–1590) AND THE PLANNING OF BAROQUE ROME

Rome, Paris, and London — the most important foci of western civilization — created the prototypes of the large cities of to-day. Rome, however, is unique. There had been cities in earlier periods with a million or more inhabitants, focusing points of vast empires and cultures. But when these fell, their nerve centers disintegrated completely. They had never a chance to rise again. Even Rome — after its name had been given to a world-wide empire — sank for a thousand years after its overthrow into a languishing decline.

Rome: the unique city

But by 1500 Rome had risen anew, and for the next one and a half centuries it became the center, first of artistic developments, then of town planning. It was on Roman soil that the Renaissance reached its zenith and it was here that the Baroque means of expression were formulated, which penetrated the whole of western culture, halting neither at territorial nor at religious frontiers.[1]

To anticipate: In Rome the urban scale of the Renaissance was shattered once and for all. In place of the limited, wall-girded, star-shaped city, a new development of great importance was heralded during the five years' reign of Sixtus V.

---

[1] Christopher Wren's St. Paul's Cathedral in London (1675–1716) has been shown by recent research in England to have been based on a good grounding in Baroque architecture. George Baehr's protestant Frauenkirche in Dresden, which was unfortunately destroyed by bombs in the Second World War, was one of the finest of the Baroque churches.

It was in Rome that the lines of the traffic web of a modern city were first formulated, and were carried out with absolute assurance.

The development of Rome by non-Roman artists

There are other reasons also why Rome is unique among cities — reasons which are perhaps less easily grasped. The Holy See is supported by no world empire. The Papacy is an international religious power. The citizens of Rome, being subject to the papal dictatorship, had little say in the development of their city. Nevertheless here was created one of the most sumptuous achievements of civic design, Baroque Rome, which, even today, dominates the entire face of the City.[2]

From the Renaissance onwards, the development of Rome was almost entirely the work of men who came in from outside — artists, bankers, merchants and manufacturers. When the Popes moved from the Lateran to the Vatican, the district around the Basilica of St. Peter was gradually built up as the *Borgo Nuovo*, and in the middle of the fifteenth century Pope Nicholas V (1447–1455) was struck with the idea of creating here a huge isolated and impressive ecclesiastical residence. This scheme, which was never carried out, was planned by the Florentine, Leone Battista Alberti.

About 1500, when rebuilding started in earnest and the Popes became the greatest builders in the world, Julius II, a Rovere from Urbino, and Leo X, a Medici from Florence, called in their compatriots — Bramante and Raphael from Urbino and Michelangelo from Florence — to carry out their grandiose schemes: and the employment of designers from other cities continued even in the time of Baroque Rome.

There is no clear reason for this curious state of affairs. It can only be said that Rome itself did not produce many outstanding artists either during the Renaissance or during the Baroque period. But there is no doubt that the atmosphere of the Eternal City and the vast scale of the Papal undertakings kindled the imagination of the visiting artists and inspired them to create works of such majesty as exist in no other city of that period.

---

[2] Naturally this is bound up with the pervading presence of antiquity. Before the "hollow luxury" (as J.J.P. Oud once described buildings of the late nineteenth century) it is better simply to close the eyes.

Rome, like Paris in recent times, became a gathering place for contemporary talent. A continual process of interchange took place. The talent of the outsiders — the foreigners — was heightened by the atmosphere of the city: in turn their creations gave the city a new polyphonic expression.

Within the Roman phenomenon there lies a hope for a still intangible future, for a time when it may become indispensable for the existence of the western world to create a new form of central administration inspired by spiritual principles. Baroque Rome shows that this does not necessarily result in a deadening of all achievement to a colorless monotone, a drab international gray. On the contrary it demonstrates that the interaction of a diversity of forces can produce a new vitality.

The Medieval and the Renaissance City

It is not possible to see Sixtus V's master plan for Rome in its true setting without at least a glance at the legacy he had received from the Middle Ages and the Renaissance. Sixtus did not tinker with fragmentary remedies. He left medieval Rome untouched and concentrated his energy, from the very first, upon new adventures.

The reawakening of Rome from its lethargy of the Middle Ages is as much a historic marvel as the rest of its destiny. In other parts of Europe (and in the north of Italy since the eleventh century) there had been a remarkable resurgence of city life. Rome still slept. Though the spiritual might of the Pope was never more powerful than during the Middle Ages, the city of Rome led but the existence of a shadow. In Baroque Rome churches sprang up like mushrooms, but in Medieval Rome there were no new cathedrals that could stand even a distant comparison with those of the self-governing cities of the north. It was the same with the population.

The comparison often made of Rome's thirteenth-century population — estimated at 17,000 — with that of Venice or London or Paris shows its immense shrinkage.

26. GIOVANNI BATTISTA FALDA. Medieval Rome, from the Castello S. Angelo to the Bridge of Sixtus IV (detail from map, 1676). *Falda's map shows very distinctly how the principal part of medieval Rome lay cramped within a fold of the Tiber dominated by the Castello S. Angelo with its new wedge-shaped bastions. Falda even depicts the sub-terranean corridor which connected this papal treasure-house. prison, and place of refuge with the Vatican. The Ponte S. Angelo, which since the days of Hadrian had crossed the river on the axis of the fortress, and the Piazza di Ponte at the bridgehead now became the hub of the main arteries of the medieval city. The radiating pattern of streets emanating from this square, which was completed under Paul III (1534–49), is the first of its kind.*

→

27. The Planning of Baroque Rome by Sixtus V. *This diagrammatic map attempts to show the plans of Sixtus V in relation to what existed before his time. Streets laid out for Sixtus V are marked by heavier lines; the limit of medieval Rome is shown by shading, and the outline of Rome under Marcus Aurelius by the line of the Aurelian wall. It becomes obvious that Sixtus V planned his streets as organically as a spine, strengthened by structural connections wherever these were demanded by the Roman topography.*

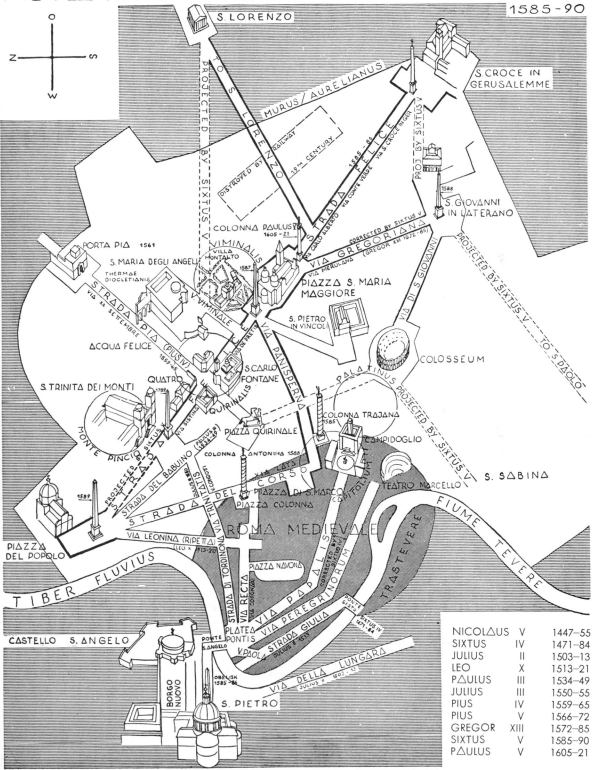

The situation changed slowly with the return of the Popes from their exile in Avignon, their new settlement in the Vatican, and the rise to the papacy of the worldly-wise Medicis and members of other mercantile families, or of descendants of *condottieri* such as Julius II.

The scarcely usable medieval kernel of Rome was a district wedged into a fold of the Tiber opposite the Castello S. Angelo. It was noted for its insalubrious climate and, for this reason, had been left undeveloped throughout the period of the ancient Roman Empire. Medieval Rome had spread out from this center slowly and chaotically in the directions of the Capitol and of the Theater of Marcellus,[3] near the Tiber.

Transformation of the city began outside the medieval kernel in the Borgo Nuovo, the area that connected the Vatican with the Castello S. Angelo. This castle served the Popes as treasure house, prison, and place of refuge in times of invasion or revolt. Its dominating position is obvious in Giovanni Battista Falda's map (*fig.* **26**), which also shows the parallel Renaissance streets of the Borgo Nuovo.

The Ponte S. Angelo — the bridge on the axis of the castle — now became the most important entry into the central area and gave its name to the Renaissance business center. Here was the papal mint and here assembled the foreign banking houses and great mercantile organizations such as the Chigi, the Medici, and the Fuggers from Augsburg. Here, in fact, was the Wall Street of Renaissance Rome, and in this small district decisions were made that sometimes affected the monetary, diplomatic, and ecclesiastical fate of the whole of Europe.

From the time of Nicholas V, the Popes were occupied with the formation of the piazza at the bridgehead — called the "Forum Pontis" in Bufalini's map of Rome (1551) and "Piazza di Ponte" in Falda's map of 1676.[4] At the time of the Renais-

---

[3] Piero Tomei, *L'Architettura a Roma nel Quattrocento* (Rome, 1942).

[4] The best introduction to the study of the development of Rome is afforded by the excellent reproductions, published by the Vatican Library, of the principal sixteenth-, seventeenth-, and eighteenth-century maps of the city. These are, for the time of Julius III, the map by Leonardo Bufalini (1551); for Rome before Sixtus V, Du Pérac–Lafréry (1577); for Rome after Sixtus V, Antonio Tempesta (1593); for Rome during

sance this square becomes a focal point from which, directly or indirectly, radiate the main arteries through the medieval city. These streets bear proud names. The Via Peregrinorum,[5] by piecing together a number of short lengths of irregular medieval lanes, finally led to the Theater of Marcellus. The Via Papalis, which carries an even more splendid name, makes an equally tortuous connection with the Capitol and further on with the Lateran. A third important through connection is the Via Recta — in part of ancient origin — [6] which, not without some difficulty, makes a connection with the later-formed Piazza Colonna and the Corso or Via Lata (*fig.* **27**).

The Via Peregrinorum, Via Papalis, and Via dei Coronari were all partly of medieval origin and partly composed of fifteenth-century improvements. In his Papal Edict of 1480, Sixtus IV, the *Restaurator Urbis*, commanded that all building projections and street obstructions be cleared away. This was the most important single act of improvement in the urban condition of the city.

It was during the late Renaissance that the Popes, in especial Paul III (1534–1549), successfully completed their work around the Piazza di Ponte by establishing short and direct connecting streets from the piazza to the medieval and Renaissance roads across the city. This pattern of short but radiating streets is the first of its kind. It included the Via Paolo, leading to Bramante's Via Giulia, and the Via di Panico, which, a short way along its route, connects with the Via dei Coronari.

The streets of the Renaissance city

Finally one of the most important through routes of Renaissance Rome, the Via Trinitatis, had its source at the Piazza di

---

the Baroque, Giovanni Maggi (1625) and G. B. Falda (1676); for Papal Rome before its decline, G. B. Nolli (1748). Bufalini's map, a woodcut, is the first drawn on the basis of a precise pattern of streets; Tempesta and Falda are outstanding for their clarity of presentation; Nolli, like Bufalini, uses the modern method of depicting streets and the delightful handicraft of this engraving approaches a work of art. For more detailed information see C. Scaccia-Scarafoni, *Le Piante di Roma* (Rome, 1939).

[5] Piero Tomei, "Le Strade di Roma e l'Opera di Sisto Quarto," *L'Urbe*, II (1937), July, pp. 12–20.

[6] Its most famous section, the Via dei Coronari, named after the sellers of rose wreaths, is today almost a slum. Anyone who retraces Ludwig von Pastor's walk, after a lapse of little more than a generation, cannot but be shocked at the speed with which decay has followed upon neglect and disfigurement of the buildings. See L. von Pastor, *Die Stadt Rom zu Ende der Renaissance*, 3rd edition (Freiburg, 1916). This little book describes in great detail the condition of Rome before the time of Sixtus V.

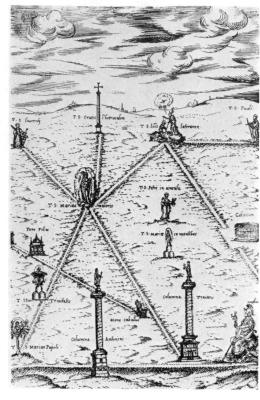

28. G. F. BORDINO. Sketch plan of the streets of Sixtus V, 1588. *This contemporary sketch plan of the work of Sixtus V reduces his street planning to a simple system of connections between holy places.*

Ponte by means of the northbound Strada di Tor di Nona. The Via Trinitatis was begun by Paul III and continued by Julius III (1550–1555). It is shown on Leonardo Bufalini's map of 1551 as a long straight line, traversing for the most part still unbuilt sections of Renaissance Rome, and terminating near the Renaissance church of S. Trinità dei Monti at the foot of the Pincio hill, where it enters into the sphere of activity of Sixtus V.

Sixtus V and his Pontificate

The papal throne

Only members of the nobility and the ruling houses of Italy were usually elected to the papal throne. There were, however, exceptions, even in a period such as the end of the sixteenth century, when the steadily increasing privileges of the nobility had usurped the medieval rights of the populace. Hence it was possible for Sixtus V, a man from the lowest stratum of society, to be invested with the highest dignity of

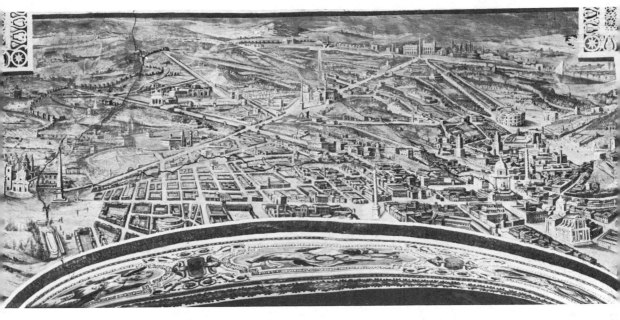

29. Sixtus V's Master Plan of Rome, 1589. *This fresco in the Vatican Library is oriented from northwest to southeast. Medieval Rome and the Vatican are both cut away by the arch of the Library door, so that the view is concentrated upon the undertakings of Sixtus V. The picture is dominated by the straight line of the Strada Felice which runs from the Piazza del Popolo on the left, past S. Trinità dei Monti to S. Maria Maggiore and then further on to the Lateran. Obelisks and columns project from their squares, and the fountains of the Acqua Felice can also be seen in the middle distance to the left, on the Strada Pia.*

spiritual and temporal power to which a mortal could aspire. It says much for the inner strength, vitality, and instinct of the Catholic Counter Reformation that it had the courage at this very dangerous moment to elevate a man such as Sixtus V to this office — a man who, regardless of his ancestry, was clearly born for action.

Sixtus V, as the Franciscan mendicant friar was known, had been admitted to the order at the age of twelve. He was the son of a peasant of Dalmatian stock. His family name is unknown and he was called after the first name of his cousin, Peretti. Filled with visions of the future destiny of his son, his father had christened the boy Felice (Felix). This name, Sixtus V, in contrast to other Popes, never laid entirely aside. He bestowed it upon two of the projects that lay nearest his heart: the Strada Felice, Rome's grandiose northwest–southeast highway, and the Acqua Felice, the water system which brought life to the hills of the southeast.

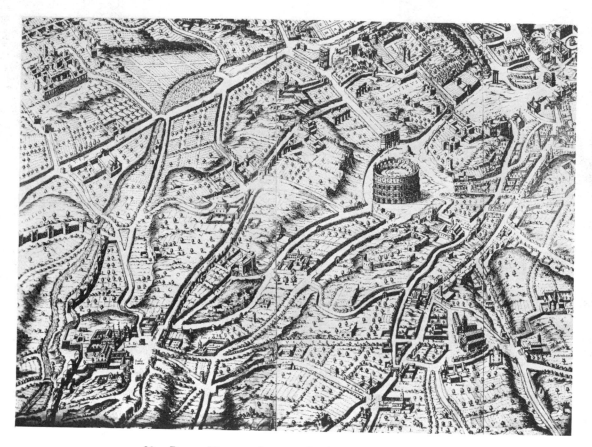

30. Rome: The area between the Coliseum and the Lateran, from the map of Du Pérac Lafréry, 1577. *The country-like character of the hill districts shortly before the time of Sixtus V is clearly shown, as well as the haphazardly winding roads. In the map the Lateran is to the left and S. Maria Maggiore, in its country setting, can be seen on the right. It is also clear that the Via Gregoriana, built by Gregory XIII, consisted of one short straight stretch between the two churches. The difficulties faced by Sixtus V in forming the Strada Felice between S. Maria Maggiore and the Pincio can be well understood from this map.*

The unusual human situation in which a Pope of the Counter Reformation found himself suited Sixtus V well. For a short period he was given the highest power over thought and state. To be spiritual sovereign and worldly sovereign simultaneously was a tremendous stimulus to him to accomplish things that could never otherwise be accomplished. However, a Pope should not reign too long. He should be wise but he should also be aged. This requirement gave rise to a tragic conflict for each of the great Popes, between his desire to carry out his schemes and the limits imposed by death. The life of Sixtus V illustrates this tragic situation.

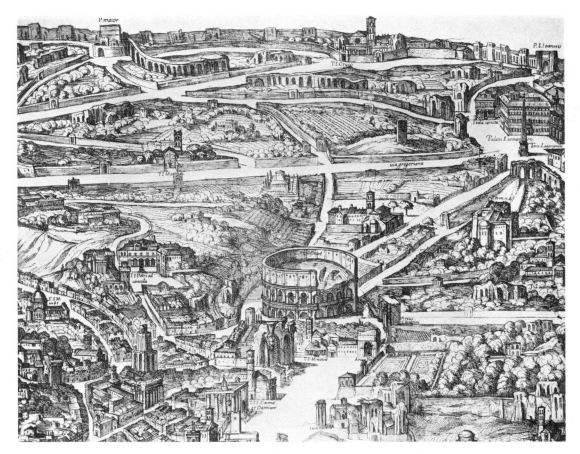

31. Rome: The area between the Coliseum and the Lateran, from the map of Antonio Tempesta, 1593. *This map, made shortly after the time of Sixtus V, cannot easily be compared with the other because of their different orientation. Even so, it is at once apparent that immense changes had occurred within these few years. A straight road now leads from the Coliseum to the obelisk before the Lateran Palace and from there a straight line (the improved Via Gregoriana) runs right across the map to S. Maria Maggiore (off the map to the left). This, Sixtus V's favorite church, was also connected by a straight route (part of the Strada Felice) to S. Croce (at the top of the map). Close to the Coliseum great building activity can be observed as the countryside becomes covered with houses.*

Felix Peretti (1521–1590) had to wait long, the most painful period being the thirteen years when he was coldly ignored by his papal predecessor, Gregory XIII. At thirty he was called to Rome as Lenten preacher. At thirty-five he was the pitiless inquisitor of the Republic of Venice. At forty-eight he became Cardinal, taking the name of Montalto, a village close to his birthplace, Grottammare. At sixty-four he was elevated to the papal throne. At sixty-nine he succumbed to malaria in his unfinished palace on the Quirinal.

Life of Sixtus V

85

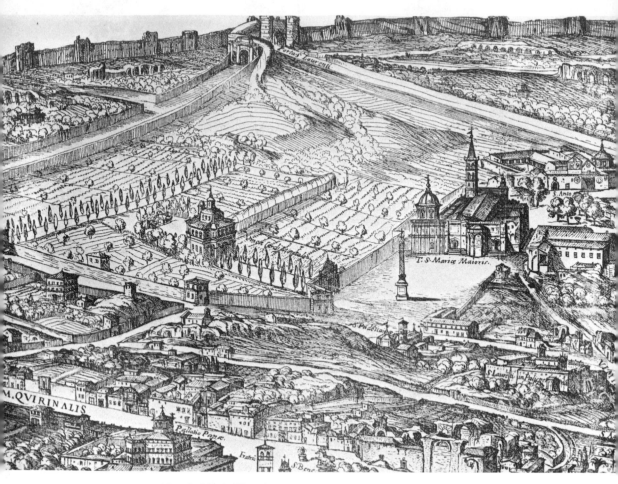

32. S. Maria Maggiore and the Villa Montalto, from the map of Antonio Tempesta, *1593. S. Maria Maggiore with its monastic buildings stood alone upon a deserted and waterless spot on the Esquiline Hill when the Cardinal Montalto (later Sixtus V) purchased the site for his Villa Montalto in 1581.   In Tempesta's map the wall-girdled estate with its "palazzotto" and tower and two avenues of cypress trees is clearly shown, as well as the newly created square and the obelisk before S. Maria Maggiore, while, behind the church, Sixtus V's new road to S. Lorenzo pierces through the Aurelian wall.   The Strada Felice is not easy to discern, since Tempesta felt obliged to curve it to depict the rugged nature of the land.*

When, as a high dignitary, he was freed from the vow of poverty, and when, as Cardinal, comparatively large revenues fell his way, early peasant instincts reawoke in him and he purchased an estate in an area completely deserted except for the church of S. Maria Maggiore with its convent.[7]   There, despite financial difficulties and enemies, he built a country

---

[7] A. von Hübner, *The Life and Times of Sixtus V* (London, 1872), I, 225 ff.

33. S. Maria Maggiore and its obelisk, 1587, from the fresco now in the Collegio Massimo. *This fresco once decorated the buildings that Sixtus V erected along the outer wall of his estate for his household staff. In the foreground is an early high-wheeled carriage, and to the left the young trees bordering his estate, in all their tender fragility, planted by his own hands.*

34. The obelisk today, from the opposite side. *This view of the obelisk, taken from S. Maria Maggiore, looks down the Strada Felice toward the Pincio.*

house surmounted by a tower and called it the Palazetto Felice (*fig.* **32**).

He engaged the young and unknown Domenico Fontana[8] to build his Palazetto and, what was much more important to the peasant's son, to lay out his garden. Its interesting plan,

---

[8] Domenico Fontana was one of the first architects who came to Rome from the far north — from Melide on the Swiss side of the frontier lake of Lugano. It is interesting to note that Fontana's nephew, Carlo Maderno, builder of the nave of St. Peter's, and Francesco Borromini, a nephew of Maderno, all came from nearby villages and belonged to the same clan. See Ugo Donati, *Artisti Ticinesi a Roma* (Bellinzona, 1942).

as well as Fontana's later plan for the renewal of Rome, shows that Pope and architect, client and constructor, worked together in a happy and rare cooperation.

In the Villa Montalto, as he named his estate, the cardinal lived in retirement through the long years when he was in disfavor with Gregory XIII. He busied himself with the writings of the fathers of the church and with new plans; he also awak-

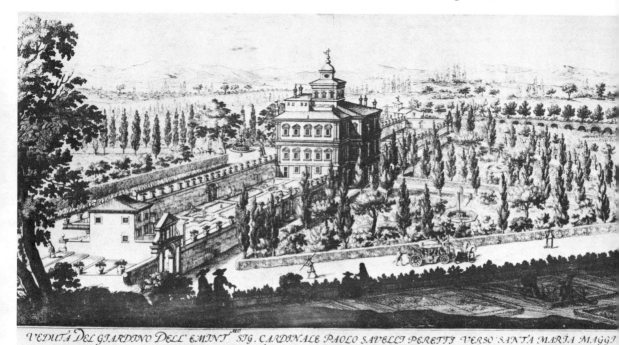

VEDUTA DEL GIARDINO DELL' EMINT.^{MO} SIG. CARDINALE PAOLO SAVELLI PERETTI VERSO SANTA MARIA MAGGI
1. Aspetto del Palazzetto felice . 2. Giardini secreti . Architettura del Caual.^r Domenico Fontana . 3 Teatro è fontane auanti il Palazzo felice . 4 Fontane de le ...

35. The Villa Montalto in the late seventeenth century. *The gardens with their directional vistas as they were laid out by Sixtus V, a century ahead of the square parterres of the Renaissance. The avenues of cypress stood until they were devoured in the railway age by the growth of the city planned by Sixtus himself.*

ened his passion for building. The wrath of Gregory XIII, who deprived him of the financial support given to poor cardinals after seeing the unusually large dimensions of the funerary chapel that Sixtus had started to build as an annex to S. Maria Maggiore, is perhaps not entirely incomprehensible. In this chapel Sixtus, bareheaded, without his crown, his hair combed forward over his forehead, his heavy peasant hands folded, kneels before the invisible sacred crib that Do-

36. DOMENICO FONTANA. *The Transportation of the Chapel of the Sacred Crib. The removal of the entire chapel, which contains the remains of the Sacred Crib, from its former place within S. Maria Maggiore to the new chapel that Sixtus V built for his own tomb and that of his benefactor, Pius IV, was a most precarious undertaking and revealed Fontana's great capacity for feats of engineering.*

menico Fontana, as his first act of bravura, had transported there and sunk below the floor together with its enclosing chapel (*fig. 36*).

Fontana belonged to the artistically mediocre generation of architects between Michelangelo and the rise of Roman Baroque. His taste was as flavorless as that of his client. The Lateran, the Quirinal, and the wing he built of the Vatican are among the dullest palaces of Rome, but the collective interaction of his work produced an urbanism that had no parallel at that period.

Fontana's Palazetto on the Montalto estate was equally insignificant, but the layout of the garden (*fig.* **35**) with its long vistas was a century ahead of the square-patterned gardens of the Renaissance. At Montalto the son of a tenant farmer had found a piece of land that was entirely his own, and here his long-suppressed yearning for contact with the soil came to the fore. As Cardinal and Pope he gave the utmost care to the cultivation of his property, planting cypress and olive trees with his own hands. On one of the frescoes, in a new wing that he added later, now preserved at the Collegio Romano, these new young trees appear behind a wall in all their fragility (*fig.* **33**).

Simultaneous planning

Perhaps the most impressive aspect of his activity as Pope is the simultaneity with which Sixtus V carried out his great works, from the very day of his appointment. The power to accomplish his master plan in so limited a period was acquired during the years of contemplation he spent upon the very spot on which he started. The synchronization of the work was carried out with the unfailing surety of a general staff plan. Baron Haussmann effected the transformation of Paris step by step, *réseau* by *réseau;* Sixtus V began everywhere at once, with an astonishing simultaneity.

Just five years and four months were allotted to this great organizer for the immense tasks he desired to accomplish — in politics, in administration, in town planning. Nowhere is his race with death more apparent than in the incredible rapidity with which he carried through his building program. Again and again his architect, Domenico Fontana, remarks that nothing could be accomplished quickly enough to please his beloved lord.

At the outset of his reign, Sixtus V completed the Strada Felice in less than a year (1585–86), and at the end his enormous determination enabled the cupola of St. Peter's (which had hardly been touched for a quarter of a century) to rise within twenty-two months (1588–90). Giacomo della Porta and Domenico Fontana, who were responsible for carrying out Michelangelo's designs, had eight hundred workmen on the job, day and night, weekdays and holidays.

90

A scrupulously kept notebook is still preserved recording the minute transactions of the mendicant friar Felix Peretti. The Pope Sixtus V determined to introduce the same order into the social and financial affairs of the Papal State. He was successful in both. In a short time he had broken up the gangs of bandits and aristocrats which had worked together to terrorize the people both within and outside the city,[9] and during his short reign the papal treasury at the Castel S. Angelo increased twentyfold. The measures he took, in every field, touched the fringe of cruelty. He combined the rigid morality of his puritan contemporaries with the pitilessness of the Catholic inquisitors. In the words of the Grand Duke of Tuscany, construction was handled as recklessly as men.

At the same time that he was establishing order in the country, Sixtus V was carrying through his *magnanime imprese*, his "grandiose enterprises" as Domenico Fontana called them. In the first year of his reign, work was started upon the Strada Felice and completed the same year; the task of moving the obelisk in front of St. Peter's was begun; a beginning was made upon the viaducts and canals for the Acqua Felice, the Lateran Palace and Basilica, the clearing of the Trajan column, and the drainage of the Pontine marshes (with two thousand workers). Besides all this, work was proceeding at a frantic pace on the development of his own estate and of the sumptuous chapel of S. Maria Maggiore. This account may serve as sufficient illustration of the simultaneity of his urban planning.

The Master Plan

In the domain of town planning, Sixtus V was one of those rare men who are able to organize, assemble the facts, and execute the scheme. He allowed nothing to stand in the way of the realization of his plans. Only death itself could check — all too soon — his unbridled energy.

Already, before the time of Sixtus, a strange phenomenon had taken place in Rome. Instead of developing, as most cities do, from east to west, modern Rome had grown from west to east

Rome grows from West to East

---

[9] Hübner, *Sixtus V*, gives details of this struggle, I, 275, 284, 293.

— or, more exactly, from northwest (the Vatican) toward the more salubrious hill regions of the southeast.

Between 1503 and 1513, Julius II had laid out two straight streets on either side of the river Tiber: the Lungara on the right bank, the Via Giulia on the left. His successor, Leo X (1513–1521), planned the Strada Leonina (Via Ripetta), the most easterly of the three streets that radiate from the Piazza del Popolo. Paul III (1534–1549) was responsible for its counterpart, the Via Babuino; while the central, axial, street, the Via Lata (today the Corso) was already in existence as the ancient entry into Rome from the north. It is typical that two of the few Renaissance churches of Rome that stand here — S. Maria del Popolo and, on the summit of the Pincio, S. Trinità dei Monti — were completed under Sixtus V.

Now the development takes an energetic leap toward the southeast. From the deserted Quirinal hill Pius IV (1559–1565) shot a straight line across two kilometers to Michelangelo's unexcelled Porta Pia (1561). This street was named after him the Strada Pia. Here we are already amidst the sphere of Sixtus V's scheme. Lastly, the immediate predecessor (and opponent) of Sixtus V, Gregory XIII (1572–1585), straightened out rather fragmentarily, the old road that connected S. Maria Maggiore with the basilica of S. Giovanni in Laterano (*fig.* **30**).

Ecclesiastical impulse for Sixtus V's planning

At his accession to power, the Franciscan Pope, Sixtus V, thus found a series of fragmentary developments extending, in chronological order, from west to east. He was able to bring all of them together into a unified scheme — his master plan. The first impulse for this new transformation was, naturally, an ecclesiastical one. Road connections should link all the seven main churches and holy shrines which had to be visited by the faithful during the course of a day's pilgrimage. Behind this enterprise can be seen the Counter Reformation and the newly awakened vitality of the Church. The desire of Sixtus — as expressed by Pastor — was to make the whole of Rome into "a single holy shrine."

To the clergy and pilgrims, Sixtus' plan appeared as a simple street connection between the holy places. There is a poem of praise to the works of Sixtus V, written by the oratory monk, Bordino, in Latin hexameters (1588) [10] — at a time when the work was still under way. It is illustrated by a rudimentary sketch-plan (*fig.* **23**) in which only the main churches and their connecting streets are shown. These streets form a star radiating from the basilica of S. Maria Maggiore to the various churches, *in syderis formam*. The star-like plan has given rise to misunderstandings concerning the real purpose of the scheme — which was, in fact, of an entirely different nature from that of the star-shaped city of the Renaissance.

Unfortunately our search for the architect's original plans has been without success. Maybe they never existed. In Domenico Fontana's work on the projects he carried out under Sixtus V, he makes only a few brief remarks "on the streets opened by our lord." Yet these are the first expressions of the point of view which has determined the layout of the streets of a modern city. This is sufficient reason for some of Fontana's passages [11] to be included here. He begins by describing the general problem:

First observations on the modern layout of streets by Domenico Fontana, 1589

"Our lord, now wishing to ease the way for those who, prompted by devotion or by vows, are accustomed to visit frequently the most holy places of the City of Rome, and in particular the seven churches so celebrated for their great indulgences and relics; opened many most commodious and straight streets in many places. Thus one can by foot, by horse, or in a carriage, start from whatever place in Rome one may wish, and continue virtually in a straight line to the most famous devotions."

The lines of the roads were carried through, regardless of the many difficulties that were encountered, overcoming all natural obstacles and tearing down whatever was in the way. At the same time, Sixtus was well aware of the marvelous diversity of the Roman topography, and he made use of its "various and divers perspectives . . . to charm the senses of the body."

---

[10] Giovanni Francesco Bordino, *De rebus praeclare gestis a Sixto V* (Rome, 1588). This book is very rare; there are however copies in the Library of the Palazzo Venezia in Rome, in the British Museum, and in the Bibliothèque Nationale.

[11] The following quotations from *Della Trasportatione dell' Obelisco Vaticano et delle Fabriche di Nostro Signore Papa Sisto V, fatto dal Cav. Domenico Fontana, Architetto di Sua Santita*, Libro Primo (Rome, 1590), have been kindly translated by Dr. James S. Ackerman.

"Now at a truly incredible cost, and in conformity with the spirit of so great a prince [Sixtus], has extended these streets from one end of the city to the other, without concern for either the hills or the valleys which they crossed; but, causing the former to be leveled and the latter filled, has reduced them to most gentle plains, and charming sites, revealing in several places which they pass, the lowest portions of the city with various and diverse perspectives; so that, aside from the devotions, they also nourish with their charm the senses of the body."

In a few words Fontana presents the basic intentions of Sixtus. Two thirds of the city of Rome lay within the Aurelian walls. Of this portion the hill areas, which had the best climate, were practically uninhabited, and, indeed, barely habitable. Nothing was there except "some church towers, dating from the Middle Ages, projecting from among some anciently revered basilicas. The whole deserted region seemed destined forever to be the abode of prayers and silence. The only habitations were cloisters and a few scattered hovels." [12]

It was these hills of ancient Rome, open to the winds of the Campagna, and stretching from the Pincio in the northeast to the Esquiline, Quirinal, Viminal, and Caelius, that Sixtus wanted again to make accessible. To accomplish this, he immediately set to work to change a simple assembly of roads into a multiple urban transport system.

"The wish is now serving to refill the City, because, these streets being frequented by the crowd, houses and shops are being built there in the greatest profusion, where formerly one was impeded by the many turnings of the road."

Following the practice of the Middle Ages when founding new cities, Sixtus encouraged building activity by granting various privileges. One of his biographers [13] records that Sixtus' own sister, Donna Camila, who was shrewdly aware of commercial advantage, built some shops which she rented profitably on a part of the Esquiline near S. Maria Maggiore.

---

[12] Pastor, *Die Stadt Rom zu Ende der Renaissance*, p. 102.
[13] Hübner, *Sixtus V*, II, 137 f.

The change in the city was so great and so rapid that a priest on returning to Rome after the death of Sixtus remarked that he could hardly recognize it any more: "Everything seems to be new, edifices, streets, squares, fountains, aqueducts, obelisks." [14]

The greatest pride of Fontana was the Strada Felice, which bore the name of the Pope, and which was started and completed within one year, 1585–86. This great street (now the Via Agostino Depretis and the Via Quattro Fontane) slopes down hill from the obelisk before S. Maria Maggiore, then climbs up to the summit of the Pincio and the church of S. Trinità dei Monti, which Sixtus dedicated in 1585,[15] and which thus becomes linked to S. Maria Maggiore upon the Esquiline hill. The final stretch, which was never completed, was intended to lead downwards again to the obelisk in the Piazza del Popolo. This is clearly shown in the fresco in the Vatican (*fig.* **29**). The Spanish Steps, planned by Sixtus as a link between the lofty S. Trinità dei Monti and the heart of the city — by means of the Via Trinitatis (today Via Condotti) — had to wait until the eighteenth century to be built.

On the far side of S. Maria Maggiore, the Strada Felice continues in an undeviating straight line to the church of S. Croce in Gerusalemme. In the second half of the nineteenth century this stretch of the road was to serve as the backbone of one of the most wearisomely dull districts of Rome, and various names were then given to different sections of the road. Fontana speaks of the Strada Felice as follows:

"The most celebrated is the street called Felice, which originates at the church of Santa Croce in Gerusalemme, passes the church of Santa Maria Maggiore, and then continues on to the Trinità dei Monti from where one descends to the Porta di Popolo: which in all comprises a distance of two miles and a half, and throughout straight as a plumb line and wide enough to allow five carriages to ride abreast."

---

[14] "Lettere di Angelo Grillo, Venezia, 1612," quoted by Antonio Muñoz, *Domenico Fontana* (Rome, 1944), p. 39.

[15] The obelisk before this church was erected in 1789 by the classistic Pope Pius VII.

A road along which five carriages could drive abreast — in other words, a five-lane road — must have seemed somewhat extreme to the Romans, for this was at the beginning of the change-over from horse and sedan chair to coach and carriage.[16] Sixtus scarcely ever forgets to include in his frescoes one of the primitive carriages of the period, with open front and back, as a reminder of the improvements he had brought about in such a short span of time.

Sixtus' plan not star-shaped Fond as Sixtus V was of the area around S. Maria Maggiore, he never thought of making the Basilica the center of a star-shaped street pattern, as in the "ideal cities" of the Renaissance. His was no paper plan. Sixtus V had Rome, as it were, in his bones. He himself trudged the streets the pilgrims had to follow and experienced the distances between points, and when, in March 1588, he opened the new road from the Coliseum to the Lateran, he walked with his cardinals all the way to the Lateran Palace, then under construction.

Integration of new and old Sixtus V spread out his streets organically, wherever they were demanded by the topographical structure of Rome. He was also wise enough to incorporate with great care whatever he could of the work of his predecessors. Sometimes he improved upon their work, as in the straightening of Gregory XIII's Via Gregoriana (*fig.* **28**) or the raising and leveling of the Strada Pia. He traced his own Strada Felice to form a most happy conjunction with the Strada Pia.[17] The angle at which they cross is not quite a right angle, but Domenico Fontana placed four fountains here, fed by the waters of the Acqua Felice, so that the deviation disappeared and the importance of the crossing was emphasized. The spot has added interest from the vistas afforded in each direction: Michelangelo's Porta Pia; the obelisk of S. Maria Maggiore; the giant late-Roman statues of the Two Horse Tamers at the Quirinal near by; and, continuing the perspective of the Strada Felice, up hill and down dale to S. Trinità dei Monti and the Pincio.

---

[16] L. von Pastor, *Sisto V, il Creatore della Nuova Roma* (Rome, 1922), p. 15.

[17] This junction proved extremely valuable after 1870, when the building up of this quarter came into full swing following the confinement of the papal authority to the Vatican and the sequestration of the papal lands.

Sixtus V integrated his new web of streets not only with stretches of existing roads, but also with the needs of the city itself. The fresco that he had painted on the ceiling of the Vatican Library in 1589 is far from exact either in scale or completeness, but, by giving an indication of what Sixtus V would have done if time had given him the chance, it conveys the idea of his master plan better than the maps of what was actually carried out (*fig.* **29**).

On the left-hand side of the fresco is the obelisk at the Piazza del Popolo. The straight line of the Strada Felice runs up to the obelisk of S. Maria Maggiore and continues on to S. Giovanni in Laterano. From here a connection is outlined to the distant church of S. Paolo fuori le Mura (St. Paul's Outside the Walls) and, in the opposite direction, to the nearby S. Croce in Gerusalemme. The stretch connecting the Lateran and the Coliseum has already been mentioned.

Returning to S. Maria Maggiore, we find another road leading directly to S. Croce in Gerusalemme, and — particularly interesting for this period — a connection to S. Lorenzo fuori le Mura which would not have stopped at the old Roman town wall. Finally, contact with the old city is secured by the Via Panisperna, leading directly to Trajan's Column and the Piazza S. Marco (Venezia). A web of cross streets interconnects these main arteries.[18] If time had permitted, Sixtus V would have redeveloped the whole of Rome with streets, squares, water supply, and buildings.

Rome had been unable to create proud civic cores expressing civic spirit in monumental terms such as were built in Florence, Siena, and Venice. The squares of Rome were off back streets, such as the Piazza Navona which followed the outline of Domitian's stadium. These squares were used for markets or carnivals, but they possessed no buildings of social signifi-. cance. Even the Capitol, for all its architectural grandeur, occupied a rather isolated site. Sixtus V gave a far more energetic impulse than any Pope before or since to the creation

[18] Excellent information on the realization of some of the work of Sixtus V can be found in the *Avvisi di Roma*, some of which were published by L. von Pastor, *Geschichte der Päpste*, X (Freiburg, 1926), 591–609, and in I. A. F. Orbaan, *Sixtine Rome* (London, 1910).

37. G. F. BORDINO. The Antonine Column and the beginning of the Piazza Colonna, 1588. *Sixtus V placed his obelisks as though with a divining rod at points where marvelous squares would later grow up. Here he cleared the Antonine Column and the space around it from the debris of centuries, fixing the boundaries that achieved their architectural form only in the late seventeenth century. In Bordino's engraving the primitive character of the contemporary buildings can be seen more clearly than in the Vatican fresco. Even at the present day the Piazza Colonna holds its position as the center of Rome.*

of squares all over the city. Many of these were related to churches, but not by any means all.

In front of his buildings — the Lateran and Quirinal — and wherever his streets joined, Sixtus V made provision for ample open space, sufficient for much later development. An example is the large area he reserved in front of the Diocletian Thermae and bordering his own estate of Montalto which developed into the Piazza delle Terme, the square of the nineteenth-century railway terminal. By clearing around the Antonine Column and tracing the outline of the Piazza Colonna (1588) he created the present-day center of the city (*fig.* **38a**). Trajan's Column near the Coliseum with its enlarged surrounding square was a link between the old city and the new.

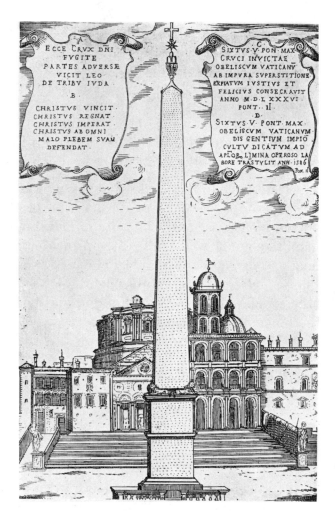

ECCE CRVX DNI
FVGITE
PARTES ADVERSÆ
VICIT LEO
DE TRIBV IVDA

B
CHRISTVS VINCIT·
CHRISTVS REGNAT·
CHRISTVS IMPERAT·
CHRISTVS AB OMNI
MALO PLEBEM SVAM
DEFENDAT·

C
SIXTVS·V·PON·MAX·
CRVCI INVICTÆ
OBELISCVM VATICANV
AB IMPVRA SVPERSTITIONE
EXPIATVM IVSTIVS ET
FELICIVS CONSECRAVIT
ANNO M·D·L XXXVI
PONT·II·

D·
SIXTVS·V· PONT·MAX·
OBELISCVM VATICANVM
DIS GENTIVM IMPIO
CVLTV DICATVM AD
APLOB. LIMINA OPEROSO LA
BORE TRASTVLIT ANN·1586
Pon·II

38. G. F. BORDINO. The obelisk before St. Peter's shortly after its erection, 1588. *The transportation of this obelisk, as well as the removal of the Sacred Crib in S. Maria Maggiore, are typical of the virtuosity and great interest shown in difficult mechanical exploits during the late sixteenth century, and foreshadow the later work of Galileo.*

Like a man with a divining rod, Sixtus V placed his obelisks at points where, during the coming centuries, the most marvelous squares would develop. Of all his enterprises, the most sensational and spectacular for more than a century was the dismantling, transportation, and reërection of the obelisk before St. Peter's (1585–86). It was the only obelisk that still stood upright where the Emperor Caligula had placed it at the *spina* of Nero's circus. Since Nicholas V, the Popes, and especially Gregory XIII, had considered moving and reërecting the obelisk, but nobody dared to attack the problem of taking it down and transporting it.

Italy at the end of the sixteenth century had a highly developed technology and interest in machines and mechanics, and Sixtus V had the necessary daring. Yet much more important than the sensational reërection of the obelisk is the new artistic significance Sixtus V gave to the Egyptian symbol of sun rays as a space-absorbing medium. The instinct for civic design of the Pope and his architect is demonstrated again in their selection of a new site for the obelisk at just the right distance from the unfinished cathedral: it was as though Bernini himself had pre-selected it as the magical center for his colonnades.

The last of the four obelisks that Sixtus was able to set up was given perhaps the most subtle position of all. Placed at the northern entrance to the city, it marked the confluence of three main streets (as well as the often projected but never executed final extension of the Strada Felice). Two centuries later the Piazza del Popolo crystallized around this spot. The only other obelisk to occupy such a dominating position is that in the Place de la Concorde in Paris, set up in 1836. That came from the temple of Luxor, where, like all other obelisks, it stood directly against the great pylon walls. No Egyptian obelisk was ever placed out in the open as a free-standing sculpture.

The Social Aspect

Sixtus V was the first of the modern town planners. From the beginning he was aware of the city as a complex organism, and knew that the beauty of open squares and wide streets had to be buttressed by social implementation.

The Acqua Felice   The very day that he entered the Lateran as master, he made the decision, we are told by Domenico Fontana,[19] that he would provide a water supply — the Acqua Felice — for the hill areas of the city, which had lain deserted since the destruction of the Roman aqueducts built by Alexander Severus (A.D. 222–235). Sixtus V intended to conduct water to the very highest points of the Roman hills — the Esquiline, Caelius, Viminal, Capitoline, and Pincio. The main difficulty was that there was only a very small fall from the springs that he had purchased near Palestrina, sixteen miles away; and the topography

---

[19] Muñoz, *Domenico Fontana*, p. 42.

38a. The Piazza Colonna at the time of Sixtus V. Fresco in the Vatican Library. *Here one can clearly see how Sixtus V positioned his landmarks, his obelisks and fountains, as focal points in a chaotic setting.*

seemed to make it impossible for the conduit to be laid in a straight line. The problem was solved by carrying the conduit for seven miles along a high arched aqueduct and for seven miles under ground. Within eighteen months the work was successfully accomplished. It was an exciting moment for Sixtus V, wondering whether the flow of water would reach the Quirinal and other places. But by October 1586 water was running in the gardens of the Villa Montalto, and in 1589 it gushed from all the twenty-seven public fountains.[20]

Other Popes had restored the aqueducts that served the lower parts of the city, and Gregory XIII had had the intention of carrying out the same venture as Sixtus V, but he had been frightened by the technical difficulties and the high costs and had never got further than preliminary negotiations.

On the fresco at the Vatican Library, the monumental entry of the Acqua Felice into the city is marked by the three-arched

Social establishments

[20] Pastor, *Päpste*, X, 426–433; A. D. Tani, *Le Acque e le Fontane di Roma* (Rome, 1926), p. 49 ff.

40. Basins of the Moses Fountain. *Even today the basins of the fountain are in constant use by the local inhabitants.*

41. Drinking-water fountain. *The Egyptian lions still spit water for the thirsty passers-by.*

39. The Moses Fountain, 1587. *This three-arched fountain with Moses in the center symbolizes the triumphal entry of the Acqua Felice into the hill areas of Rome, which had been without a water supply for more than a thousand years. The large basins of the fountain were designed for practical use as a water reservoir for the local people, while a special trough was provided on the right for the use of animals.*

Moses Fountain (1587) which juts out, very white and out of proportion, on the Strada Pia (*fig.* **39**). Even in the seventeenth century this fountain was considered as being in very bad style (*pessimo stile*) [21] and it is scarcely conceivable that such mediocrity was possible only two decades after the death of Michelangelo. The real purpose of this fountain can be seen in another of the Vatican Library frescoes (*fig.* **42**); it is not intended as a show piece. It is a reminder that this part

---

[21] See the biography of Domenico Fontana in G. Baglione, *Le Vite de' Pittori, Scultori, et Architetti* (Rome, 1642).

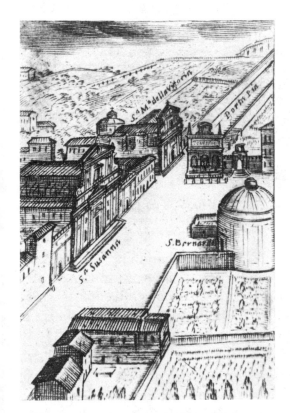

42. The Moses Fountain beside the Strada Pia, 1616. *Here, too, Sixtus V provided a square which, under the special circumstances, served both a practical and a social function.*

43. The Moses Fountain today. *This square, created almost entirely by Sixtus V, retains its original character.*

QVA·LAVET·IMMVND OS·MVLIER·PAVPERCVLA·PANNOS
FELICEM·SIXTVS·SVPPEDITAVIT·AQVAM

44. The wash house at the Piazza delle Terme, fresco in the Collegio Massimo. *Here two long basins were installed for the use of all who wished to clean their linen. Covered wash houses for bad weather and greater privacy were also provided.*

of Rome had had no water for over a millennium, but above all it is a social institution.   The Egyptian lions are spitting water for the use of the passers by; the three large basins serve as water reservoirs for the local inhabitants; the marble barriers are there to protect them from pollution by animals, while to the right is a special basin for the use of horses and cattle.

Near to the Moses Fountain, on what is now the Piazza delle Terme, Sixtus V installed a public washing place with two long basins (*fig.* 44) "for everbody who wanted to clean dirty laundry."   He further provided an enclosed space containing a covered wash house "for bad weather and where women could

104

stay without danger of being bothered by anybody (*alcuna sorte di persone*)." [22] This sixteenth-century establishment reminds us of the hesitating experiments at erecting public laundries in England around 1830 and in France under Napoleon III.

The largest basin of water that Sixtus offered to the people of Rome was a basin for the rinsing of wool, planned as an encouragement to the woolen industry. It was made over in the eighteenth century into the theatrical Fontana di Trevi.

When Sixtus V came to power, he found the treasury exhausted and the city full of beggars and unemployed. He dealt with this problem by building poorhouses and by employing thousands of workers upon his program of public works. But these measures did not prove sufficient, and he decided to develop export trade by reviving (of course by foreigners) the old

---

[22] Fontana, *Della Trasportatione dell' Obelisco Vaticano* (2d ed., Naples, 1604), pt. I, fol. 88.

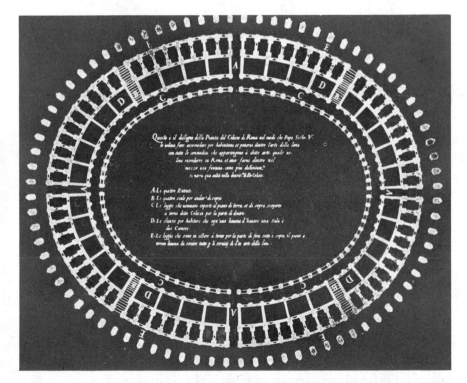

45. DOMENICO FONTANA. Sixtus V's plan transforming the Coliseum into a factory for wool spinning, 1590. *During the last year of his reign Sixtus V made plans to transform the Coliseum into a colony of workshops for wool spinners, where they could have their living quarters in the upper stories and working areas on the ground floor.*

Roman wool and silk industries. He made a law that mulberry trees must be planted everywhere, and one of his last schemes was for the transformation of the Coliseum into a wool-spinning establishment. There were to be workshops on the ground floor and dwelling apartments for the workers in the upper story (*fig.* **45**). "He had already begun to excavate the earth and to level the street, working with seventy wagons and a hundred laborers, so that if the Pope had lived only one year more" [23] the Coliseum would have become the first worker's settlement and large-scale unit of manufacture.

The greatness
of Sixtus V

There is no doubt that Sixtus V's extraordinary passion for town planning stands out spectacularly from among his other achievements. In other ways than in the somewhat naive inscriptions upon obelisks and slabs of marble his name is deeply engraved upon the face of Rome.

Sixtus V was clearly aware of the great complexity of modern urban planning. This is the reason for the striking assurance with which he attacked the most diverse urban problems at one and the same moment, but this simultaneity in urban planning is only one of the facets of this great organizer. There were not many quiet hours during the pontificate of Sixtus V. The church was again in danger, and the disturbing political background could not be ignored. Germany was divided and in disorder; France was on the verge of becoming Protestant; Mary, Queen of Scots, had been decapitated, the Spanish Armada destroyed, and England lost forever to the faith. Most wearisome of all were the never-ending controversies with the arrogant and ambitious Philip of Spain, which, Pastor believed, Sixtus V paid for with his life.

Against this uncertain political background, Sixtus V attempted to fashion Rome as a world capital where the Pope would reside as eternal arbitrator of the balance of power between temporal states. This did not happen. Rationalism forced development into another direction. But the religious faith of Sixtus V had inspired him with an optimism that enabled him to accomplish the seemingly impossible. One cannot plan cities if one does not believe in life.

[23] Fontana, *Della Trasportatione* . . . (2d ed., Naples, 1604), pt. II, fol. 18.

46. FRANCESCO BORROMINI. San Carlo alle Quattro Fontane, Rome, 1662–67. Exterior. *The whole wall translated into undulating movement. The undulating wall — first used by Borromini in S. Filippo Neri, Rome — is one of the constituent facts in late baroque architecture.*

THE LATE BAROQUE

The manner in which Renaissance modes shaded off into baroque, the way in which the new shapes became more and more evident until they were wholly transformed by the architects of the late seventeenth century — all this is quite familiar.

Universal outlook of the baroque period

In the hands of the baroque builders, the Renaissance shapes were no more than the primitive elements of architectural composition. In just the way that Bach would transpose a simple melody into a great new harmony, elaborate and subtle, these architects transmuted the forms developed in the Renaissance. The interiors they produced are marked by an inseparable union of two kinds of interests usually encountered separately: they are at once the products of purely mathematical speculations of a high order of complexity, and completely visionary or mystical imaginative creations. The same union of two such different spirits appears in the work of a baroque master of another medium, Blaise Pascal (1623–1662). At sixteen he had written a classic work on conic sections; he went on to study the cycloid curve, to develop the theory of probability, and to do pioneer work in physical science. Pascal's religious mysticism had its roots in such speculations. "The eternal silence of these infinite spaces terrifies me" comes out of his work on the mathematical implications of infinity, and leads up to his feeling for the insignificance of man without God.

The last phases of the baroque development are the true inheritance of the epoch out of which we grow. We shall have to consider first the Italian products of the baroque era, and then go on to see what the north of Europe adds to these results.

"Baroque" indicates a period rather than special shapes

It may perhaps be advisable — in view of the history of the term — to offer the prefatory comment that "baroque" does not apply exclusively to an overdecorated building in Mexico or Spain. For more than fifty years the history of art has used "baroque" to designate the period beginning with Michelangelo and continuing until the eighteenth century, and even beyond in some fields — town planning, for example. "Late baroque" would date a work as after 1660. The baroque age lasted therefore about as long as the Gothic. Its name, curiously enough, has had much the same fate — thus "Gothic" up to the nineteenth century remained a synonym for the barbarous or the uncouth. In some contemporary English histories of architecture, baroque is still taken to mean a "debased" form of art. But the work of Heinrich Wölfflin had taught us, even before 1890, to appreciate the early Roman baroque that begins with Michelangelo. The German archi-

108

tect, Cornelius Gurlitt, soon performed the same service for the late baroque of nearly all countries. More recently, the excellent Viennese school of history has covered the late period with great thoroughness. "Baroque" has by now an accepted meaning in the field of art history, as referring not to a special shape but to a whole period.

The distinguishing mark of the baroque age is the method of thinking and of feeling that prevails in it; its outstanding feature is the development of a specific kind of universality. In our field, this manifests itself as a new power to mold space, and to produce an astonishing and unified whole from the most various parts. But it is worthy of note that, in all departments, baroque methods and ways of feeling survive until the disintegration produced by the industrial age sets in and brings with it a temporary destruction of the universal point of view.

In the late seventeenth century we find the baroque universality working with the infinite in the field of mathematics as a basis for practical calculations. In painting and in architecture the impression of infinity — the infinite in a linear sense, as an indefinitely extended perspective — is being used as a means for artistic effect. Thus, early in the century, the Dutch landscape painters introduce an "atmospheric infinity" into their works; somewhat later the Roman architects succeed in realizing the same mystical feeling of endlessness — often in astonishingly small churches — through a simultaneous exploitation of all the resources of painting, sculpture, architecture, and optical theory. With the French landscape architects of the late seventeenth century there appears the artistic employment of the infinity of nature (although much the same kind of thing had been done previously, on a smaller scale, in Italy and in Holland). For the first time in history their gardens incorporated great highways as essential parts of an architectonic expression, and were placed by this means in direct and obvious relation with the unending extension of space. Versailles, with the impressive open road leading from it to Paris, is the great example of such creations. These gardens, in their total effect, stood as models of the baroque universe, and retained its aspect of infinity.

Perspective and baroque notions of infinity

109

THE UNDULATING WALL AND THE FLEXIBLE GROUND PLAN

Francesco Borromini, 1599–1667 [1]

Borromini's San Carlo alle Quattro Fontane

There is an interval of nearly two hundred and fifty years between the flat surface of the entrance wall of the Pazzi Chapel and the last work of Francesco Borromini: the façade of San Carlo alle Quattro Fontane (St. Charles of the Four Fountains) in Rome, 1662–67 (*figs.* **46** and **82**).

The flat surface of the outer wall of the Pazzi Chapel represents a clear succession of equal compartments, each of them closed within itself. The wall of Borromini's San Carlo alle Quattro Fontane expresses movement. The individual compartments are no longer marked off from each other; a continuous chain of interrelations runs through them all and comes to a focus in the center of the structure to produce the impression of an upward straining.

The statue of San Carlo Borromeo, to whom the church is dedicated, stands in a niche above the central porch. An angel is placed on each side of the statue; their wings arched over its head help to accentuate the figure's upward gaze. This ascending motif is continued through the whole façade until, above the vertically elongated medallion, even the surmounting balustrade melts away into a molded gable, which focuses and concludes the upward-surging impulse.

The undulating wall

Rome at this time was a medieval town, with narrow streets and little space between its buildings. The façade of San Carlo alle Quattro Fontane, in its extraordinary concentration, is no larger than a single pier of St. Peter's. But the façade of this church embodies a conception which was of great influence on the time that followed. Not merely a single form but the whole wall has been translated into undulating movement; the wavelike surface that resulted was Borromini's great invention. It is an invention which did not reappear merely as a means of

---

[1] The work of Francesco Borromini embraces problems which are among the most complicated in the history of architecture. We treat it only in so far as it concerns our architectural inheritance.

attracting the attention of passers-by in the small Roman streets. It is present again, in astonishing form, in the English "crescents" of the late eighteenth century, and it persists, in a somewhat altered way, in contemporary architecture.

If the intentions behind this undulation of the wall were simply decorative, they would not demand our attention. Such an attitude toward it might even justify the opinion of Jakob Burckhardt, who angrily observed that the façade of San Carlo looked like something that had been dried in an oven. But our present-day point of view springs out of conditions very different from those that operated in 1855,[2] when Burckhardt wrote his *Cicerone* — which still remains unexcelled as a guidebook to Italy. Nowadays it is easy for us to see the force that appears in the whole structure, in the stressing of the progression and regression of the wall through the hollowing out of niches and the building up of contradistinguished parts. There is to be seen here a real molding of space, a swelling and receding that causes the light to leap over the front of the church. Francesco Borromini succeeded in creating, through purely architectonic means, and in the open air, something which is equivalent to the mild chiaroscuro of his contemporary, Rembrandt, at work on his own last paintings at this same time.

Several historians have found sources for Borromini's treatment of the wall in antiquity. It is possible, but by no means certain, that Borromini knew a contemporary etching of the

Does the undulating wall appear in antiquity?

---

[2] The rediscovery of Francesco Borromini began with Cornelius Gurlitt's *Geschichte des Barockstils in Italien* (Stuttgart, 1887): "All who have still not lost courage for the invention of new means of expression to meet the new tasks . . . in construction will find a congenial spirit in Borromini" (pp. 365–366).

The systematic study of Borromini was first undertaken by the "Vienna School" after 1900. Its leader, Max Dvořák, published a short article on Borromini's work on the restoration of St. John Lateran in 1907: "Francesco Borromini als Restaurator," *Beiblatt zum Kunstgesch.*, Jahrb. der K. K. Zentralkommission (Vienna, 1907), I, 89ff. Oscar Pollak, one of Dvořák's circle, published a biographical study of Borromini in Thieme-Becker, *Allg. Lex. d. bild. Künstler* (Leipzig, 1910), vol. IV. The influence of Borromini's work was pointed out by A. E. Brinckmann, *Die Baukunst des 17. und 18. Jhdts. in den romanischen Ländern* (Berlin, 1915). The standard biography is Eberhard Hempel's *Francesco Borromini* (Vienna, 1924), which contains a full bibliography. Hans Sedlmayr's *Die Architectur Borrominis* (Berlin, 1930) contains complicated "structural analyses" of his work — sometimes very instructive, sometimes overpointed.

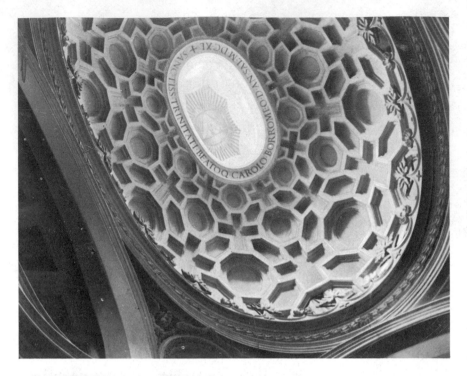

47. FRANCESCO BORROMINI. San
Carlo alle Quattro Fontane. Interior: the
dome, 1634–41.

rock temples at Petra in Asia Minor.[3] But these temples (El
Chasne is the best known) are cut into the stone face of a
mountain, the wall does not undulate, and all of their elements
— the columns, the broken gables, the "sentry boxes" — are
isolated one from the other. It seems much more natural to
suppose that Borromini started with the flat church façade
used since Alberti's Florentine Santa Maria Novella and
that he molded all its parts into conformity with his vision.

The comparison with the *Kuppelsaal* of the Piazza d'Oro at
Hadrian's villa near Tivoli is more interesting.[4] This late
Roman Empire interior has a ground plan determined by
eight segments of a circle, with columnal screens alternately
convex and concave. The entire hall is set down in the middle
of a great square chamber. But here as in other ancient build-

[3] Sedlmayr suggests that Borromini knew these second-century temples through this
source, and that he was also familiar with Roman painted wall decorations (*op. cit.*, p. 59).
[4] Sedlmayr, *op. cit.*, pp. 56–57.

112

ings there is no undulation of the wall in the sense of an un-broken flow of movement that carries through its length. In the Piazza d'Oro there is no continuity of movement: there are breaks where the wall sections meet. Its treatment is the reverse of that appearing in the Temple of Venus at Baalbek, where concave entablatures were built onto a circular central part.

The undulating wall of Borromini's invention gave flexibility to stone, changed the stone wall into an elastic material. The undulating wall is the natural accompaniment to the flowing spaces of the flexible ground plan.

San Carlo was built for the Spanish order of Discalced Trini-tarians out of their small means, and was the property of their monastery. Borromini does not achieve his effect through ornament and decoration. On the contrary, he is very sparing with both, as a glance at the small cloister would show.[5] This court with its severe forms is an example of creation through purely architectonic means. Its out-curving edges offer an-other instance of Borromini's power of infusing new life into all forms, even into the Palladian motif.

Treatment of traditional forms: the court of San Carlo

Borromini built the cloister and the interior of the church nearly thirty years before he completed the façade — in the interval between 1634 and 1641. The interior is thus one of his earliest productions. It is left almost entirely dark; on this account the way in which the light bursts into it through the lantern is all the more effective. The light shimmers over the curious combination of geometrical forms which are cut into the underside of the dome. As Borromini handles them, these forms give the dome an appearance that suggests the cellular structure of a plant (*fig.* 47).

The interior: the dome

Borromini's treatment of an interior space is best shown in Sant' Ivo (*fig.* 48), the church which he built for the Sapienza (the University of Rome). He began work on the church in 1642, one year after finishing the interior of San Carlo, but it was not completed until twenty years later. Sant' Ivo is situated at the back of the Renaissance court of the Sapienza. Bor-romini knew perfectly how to fuse together into an integral whole the loggia of the Renaissance court and the receding

Borromini's Sant' Ivo, Rome

[5] Cf. Hempel, *op. cit.*, Pl. 13.

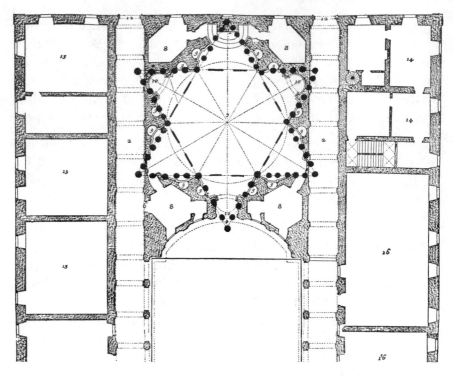

48. FRANCESCO BORROMINI. Sant' Ivo, Rome, 1642–62. Ground plan. *Built within the Renaissance court of the Sapienza, Sant' Ivo is fused with it into an integral whole.*

façade of his own church. His addition to it brings a new and vital movement into the quiet Renaissance enclosure. Even the sensation of movement achieved through the unusually formed cupola, one full of new invention, is not in any way disturbing.

Its union of geometry and imagination

The interior of Sant' Ivo exhibits in its wall the same flexibility that marks the outer wall of San Carlo alle Quattro Fontane. Every motif that is introduced is continued throughout the entire building, to the very topmost part of the dome. But the average onlooker probably notes only the wonderful animation and movement. The artistic impulse of its creator can be grasped without analysis of the complicated space conception involved; indeed, the eye cannot pick out the simple mathematical basis of the ground plan. A six-pointed star — Borromini's favorite motif — is the invisible kernel from which the plan grows. But this governing form is hardly more obvious on the plan than the skeleton is in a healthy animal: one can only detect it by a sort of X-ray examination. (The reproduc-

114

tion of Borromini's plan given here has had some of its lines strengthened to reveal the star basis more distinctly.) [6] The star is formed by the intersection of two equilateral triangles. Berlage, the well-known Dutch architect, and some other investigators have shown that many medieval buildings are also based on this pattern. The six points where the sides of his pair of triangles intersect each other are used by Borromini as the master coördinates in his design. From the ideal hexagon which they bound he molds the six niches that transfer the movement of the main elements of his composition upward into the shell of the golden-starred dome. In this way the dome is intimately bound up with the whole interior (*fig.* **49**).

Up to that time, domes had always been round or oval. To cut out sections along the perfect circle of the dome, to continue the movement of a design by treating it as though it were flexible, must have had the same stunning effect upon Borromini's contemporaries that Picasso's disintegration of the human face produced around 1910 (*fig.* **50**). A cross section of Sant' Ivo (*fig.* **53**) reveals what such treatment accomplished in its case: the movement of the whole pattern made up by its design flows without interruption from the ground to the lantern, without entirely ending even there. Borromini, of course, did not have at his disposal the means that enabled Eiffel to bring about the complete interpenetration of inner and outer space achieved in his great tower at Paris. But Borromini, by leading the movement which penetrates every division of the building's inner space on and out through its topmost spiral, is making an approach to the same problem.

Flexibility in the modeling of the interior

The lantern which surmounts the church,[7] with its coupled columns, boldly curved cornice, and the fantastic spiral which replaces the usual cupola cap, resembles some organic growth. The culminating spiral carries a narrow pathway which leads to its top (*fig.* **51**).

Motion transmitted to architecture

---

[6] The complicated organization of the interior space of Sant' Ivo has received various explanations. Some authorities hold that the interior was developed out of a simple prism with an equilateral triangle for its base — other volumes being added on to this in the manner of Peruzzi's early Renaissance plan. Others hold that it was developed through the interpenetration of two such prisms, which together would form a six-pointed star. Cf. Sedlmayr, *op. cit.*, p. 70.

[7] It has been compared to the Temple of Venus at Baalbek.

115

Now, in our day, when the transition between inner and outer space can be completely effected, it is no wonder that projects appear which spring from the same spirit as that toward which Borromini groped. A clear expression of the same kind of feeling appears in a monument projected by the Russian constructivist painter, Tatlin, in 1920. Like Borromini, he employed the spiral form, with its inherent movement (*fig.* **52**).

Relation to our period

Borromini, like most of the great baroque artists in Rome, came from the far north of Italy. He began as a stonemason employed in the work on St. Peter's. This was his calling for many years, and throughout his life he remained in personal contact with the actual working of materials. But he was also a sculptor, and one of the greatest of the baroque age, although he produced neither brilliant portrait busts nor figures of saints melting away in mystical-erotic ecstasy. Indeed, he did no sculpture at all in the normal sense of the word. He expressed himself — like some modern masters — in abstract spirals, in the wire sculptures on the tops of his churches. But he was, above all, a sculptor of buildings, expressing himself

Borromini as a sculptor

←
49. FRANCESCO BOR-ROMINI. Sant' Ivo, Rome. Interior of dome. *The continuous inner surface of the dome is broken up. It is made to transmit the movement which runs throughout the whole elevation.*

50. PICASSO. Head. Sculpture, c. 1910. *Borromini's intersection of the continuous inner surface of the dome must have had the same stunning effect upon his contemporaries that Picasso's disintegration of the human face produced.*

118

52. TATLIN. Project for a monument in Moscow, 1920. *This, like the Eiffel Tower and some other monuments of our time, is a contemporary realization of the urge toward the interpenetration of inner and outer space.*

53. FRANCESCO BORROMINI. Sant' Ivo, Rome. Section through interior.

←

51. FRANCESCO BORROMINI. Sant' Ivo, Rome. Lantern with coupled columns and spiral. *Culminating point for the movement that penetrates the whole design.*

most fully through an inseparable union of mathematically elaborated ground plans with fantastically hollowed spaces, in structures of which it is hard to say where architecture stops and sculpture begins.

Borromini's chief interest was always the molding of space. He worked with wavelike lines and surfaces, with the sphere (*fig. 54*), with the spiral, and with still more unusual shapes in the wire sculptures on the points of his towers. In his hands all the inherited forms took on a new flexibility. He took nothing for granted, and almost from the beginning of his work he was accused of cultivating the bizarre and allowing himself too great liberties.

Significance of the undulating wall

By his treatment of the wall and the ground plan Borromini gave a new flexibility to architecture. He infused movement into the whole body of architecture. The undulating wall, the sections cut out of the dome of Sant' Ivo, the cupola ending in a spiral toward the sky, are all means working toward the same end.

54. FRANCESCO BORROMINI. Sant' Ivo, Rome. Detail. (Pantheon in the background.) *These cement-like globes are of marble dust molded over an iron armature.*

Borromini's influence spread all over Europe and was absorbed into architectural knowledge even in that part dealing with town planning — this in spite of its condemnation by French and English academicians all through the eighteenth century and far into the nineteenth.

For two centuries Borromini figured as a man who had no feeling for the majestic simplicity of antiquity, but in actual fact he was intimately related to the past. He was not an imitator of shapes or façades and did not use history as a substitute for imagination. This revolutionary made careful studies of Gothic frescoes — drawings which still survive. Max Dvořák, who did some of the earliest research on his restoration of St. John Lateran, was astonished at the pains Borromini took to preserve fragments of the old church wherever it was possible, incorporating them into his own work.

Like every great creator, Borromini preserved connections with the past. He did not imitate the shapes of bygone epochs; he made them part of his own creations. Much as we try to do today, he found in his relations with history a source of power for further development.

Guarino Guarini, 1624–1683

The last phase of late baroque development appears at Turin in the northwest of Italy in the work of Guarino Guarini. Guarini, a Theatine monk and a distinguished savant, was born at Modena just a quarter-century after Borromini and Bernini. He first came to Rome at the time Borromini was at work on the interior of his San Carlo alle Quattro Fontane. The normal course of his calling as a Theatine monk later brought him to Messina in Sicily as professor of philosophy. He designed several churches here, all of them destroyed in the last earthquake. In 1662 he was transferred to Paris, where he taught theology. He began to build another church in this city. This effort was even more unfortunate than his Sicilian enterprises; gutted by fire while it was under construction, the building was never finished.

Guarini's travels brought him into contact with the Gothic churches of France and the Moorish mosques of Cordova in Spain. He was a complete cosmopolitan. Although he never lost touch with his own country and his own time, he had an awareness of history in all its aesthetic manifestations.

Nothing is more characteristic of this late baroque period than the frequency with which it displays mathematician, empirical scientist, and artist combined in one person. There is an astonishing unity subsisting between methods of thought and of feeling; more precisely, there is a direct connection between artistic and mathematical knowledge. Whenever a new conception appears in mathematics it at once finds an artistic counterpart. Thus the integral calculus, taking definite shape at the end of the seventeenth century, found its architectural equivalent in the complicated treatments of space that appeared at the same time. Guarini's own career is a perfect illustration of the intimate relation between art and mathematics in the late baroque. He was not only an architect and a scholar; he was likewise an eminently talented mathematician. His published work reveals him as anticipating, to a considerable extent, the discovery of descriptive geometry made a century later by Gaspard Monge (1746–1818).

Palazzo Carignano: undulating wall and flexible ground plan

Guarini's most important work was done at Turin, where he lived from 1666 until his death. He was a *prepositus* or abbot of the Theatine order and, at the same time, an engineer in the service of the Duke of Savoy. It was at Turin that he built his finest churches and palaces. One of the latter, his Palazzo Carignano (1680), is an example of the way in which his architectural creations took on a flexibility that was nearly equal to that of Borromini's work. This palace, with its convoluted front and the molding of its staircases, certainly influenced palace architecture of a later period in southern Germany. The large, vaulted entrance hall, elliptical in shape, forms the kernel of the design for the Palazzo Carignano. The elliptical movement of the hall is communicated to the two wings of the staircases on its right and left, and is carried from them into all parts of the undulating outer wall. But, in spite of the architectonic vigor Guarini shows in this work, the arrangement of the interior of the building makes no approach to a

122

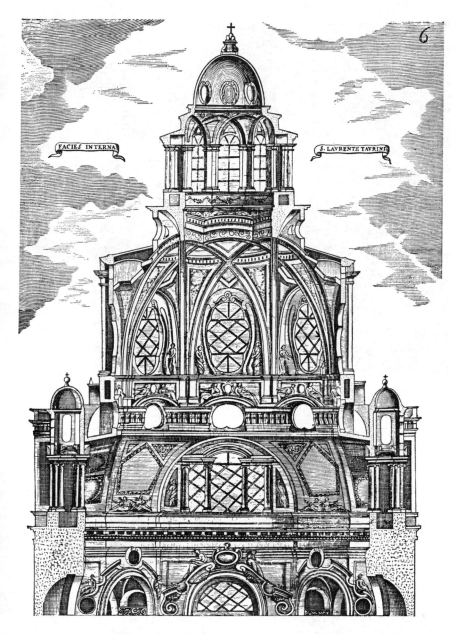

55. GUARINO GUARINI. San Lorenzo, Turin, 1668–87. Section through the cupola and the lantern, with intersecting binding arches.

solution of those strictly residential problems confronting architects of the time. All the force of Italian architecture in this period was being expended upon the interiors of churches. To put it rather more technically, all this unbounded imagination was given over to the molding of huge interior spaces. The

56. GUARINO GUARINI. San Lorenzo, Turin. Cupola with intersecting binding arches. *Architectural vision pushes to the limit of constructional resources in striving to produce the impression of infinity.*

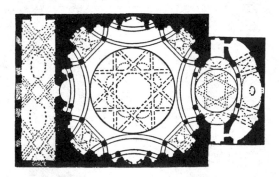

57. GUARINO GUARINI. San Lorenzo, Turin. Ground plan.

generalization holds true in Guarini's own case; he produced his masterpiece in the church of San Lorenzo (*figs.* **55** and **57**), at Turin (1668–87).

San Lorenzo: infinity expressed through architectural means

San Lorenzo was built for Guarini's own order. The basic form of the church is that of a solidly walled square. The dome is circular. Between the ground floor and the cupola there is inserted an octagon with its sides bent alternately in and out in

124

58. Mosque al Hakem, Cordova, 965. Dome of one of the Mih'rabs. *First use of the binding arch as a constructional device.*

a complicated manner which serves to make the transition to the upper elements. The intention of Guarini was to satisfy by architectonic means the baroque feeling for mystery and infinity. The baroque period felt strongly attracted to constructions which seemed to defy the force of gravity. All the arts — including even the use of colored lights — were exploited to produce this exciting impression. In Bernini's San Andrea on the Via Flaminia the lantern appears to be raised aloft by an angel. In San Lorenzo, Guarini uses purely architectonic means to put gravity at defiance. He proceeds conventionally until the ring of the cupola is reached; there he plunges at once into the realm of fantasy. Intersecting binding arches are carried from one point to another on the ring like a network woven by some giant spider. They cross each other to form a kind of filigree-work star with an octagon-shaped opening in its center. In this way the impression is produced that the lantern above the arches is magically suspended in mid-air. In reality it rests on the octagon formed by their intersection (*fig.* **56**).

The impression of unlimited space has been achieved not through the employment of perspective illusions or of a painted sky but through exclusively architectural means. The dazzling light that penetrates the star-shaped filigree has the effect of dematerializing its surroundings. This is one of the rare cases where a feeling of infiniteness is produced by architectonic means alone.

Relation to tenth-century works: the mosque at Cordova

It is safe to assume that the dome of San Lorenzo would never have been conceived had Guarini not seen the domes of the Mih'rab — the praying niche — of the mosque Al Hakem in Cordova (*fig.* **58**). These domes were constructed toward the end of the tenth century — to be exact, in 965. The same method of construction was employed in the domes that Guarini used in San Lorenzo. They, too, were built on a square base, with a system of binding arches intersecting overhead to form an eight-pointed star, on which the suspended lantern rests.

The cupolas of the praying niches in the mosque at Cordova are the earliest known specimens in which the binding arch is given a constructional function. It has even been asserted by some French historians that it was this Moorish invention which suggested to Gothic builders of a century and a half later the possibility of replacing the solid vault by a framework of ribs in stone. But the dimensions of these Moorish domes are humble in comparison with Guarini's daring masterpiece. As far as I could ascertain, the binding arches of San Lorenzo are composed of long, massive stone beams, a dangerous and laborious method. In fact, the architect of San Lorenzo asked from construction almost more than it was prepared, at that date, to give. No later architect dared to follow the precedent Guarini set in this church. With San Lorenzo the technical possibilities of the age were exhausted, just at the moment when the vision of further architectural advances was beginning to dawn. We find ourselves quite spontaneously driven to think how easy the solution of such a problem would be with the means available to modern construction. But we must

126

reject such reflections as absolutely unhistorical. The dome of San Lorenzo presents the case of an architectural vision that goes to the very end of constructional resources. The situation today is just the reverse. There are available to us constructional possibilities which we have not been able to exploit to anything like their full extent.

South Germany: Vierzehnheiligen

Of the northern countries, only South Germany and Austria, including Bohemia, adopted the complicated space conceptions of Borromini and Guarini. Germany has always been known architecturally as the land of late phases — of late Gothic, late Renaissance, late baroque. In southern Germany especially, the best examples of these periods are to be found.

Belated development in Germany

The late baroque of South Germany in the eighteenth century [8] does not possess the constituent force which Borromini's work spread far beyond his own time. It arose in a country cut up into small principalities, many of them ecclesiastical. It marks the close of a development reaching back to roots in Italy and France, to which it gave a new and exciting expression. It flowered throughout the Catholic lands of South Germany — Franconia, Baden, Bavaria — Austria, Bohemia, and parts of Switzerland. Its largest outgrowth is to be found in Franconia and Bavaria, and also its ripest solutions. These are like full-grown fruits just before they drop from the tree, with all the charm and flavor of a perfect maturity, that final ripening before the beginning of decay. They fulfilled, all unconsciously, their task of closing the period. Instinct with the joy of life, finding expression therefore in terms of spatial imagination, utilizing at the same time the whole orchestra of the arts, they were ultimate and crowning masterpieces.

---

[8] The rediscovery of the German baroque may be credited to Cornelius Gurlitt, whose *Geschichte des Barockstils und des Rokoko in Deutschland* (Stuttgart, 1889), prepared the way for an understanding of this period. The small booklet by Wilhelm Pinder, *Deutscher Barock* (Leipzig, 1911), with excellent introduction and choice of illustrative materials, helped much to popularize it on a large scale (more than 100,000 copies were sold). That the baroque is not characterized simply by superficial ornament but has its own spatial and artistic qualities was recognized in England only in the thirties.

59. BALTHASAR NEUMANN. Vierzehnheiligen (Church of the Fourteen Saints), 1743–72. Façade. *Influence of secular architecture visible in the rows of windows; continuation of Borromini's undulating wall.*

In the fifteenth and sixteenth centuries Franconia had already shown its artistic power by producing such figures as Albrecht Dürer and Veit Stoss. At that time the social background was one of free cities and free citizens, as in Nuremberg. In the eighteenth century the background was an ecclesiastical one, the Counts of Schönborn, who at this time were for the most

60. BALTHASAR NEUMANN. Vierzehnheiligen. *Detail of the undulating wall of the façade.*

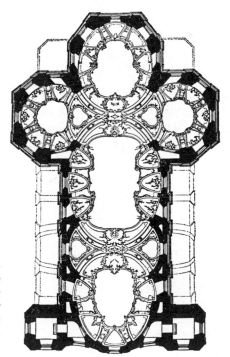

61. BALTHASAR NEUMANN. Vierzehnheiligen. Horizontal section. *The usual dome has been done away with. Its place is taken by the space in which the four variously shaped (spherical and ellipsoidal) vaultings meet: those of the nave, the choir, and the two short transepts.*

129

62. BALTHASAR NEUMANN. Vierzehnheiligen. Interior. *The altar is pushed forward into the nave of the church. Light pours in from all sides through great windows of clear glass.*

part the ruling bishops or archbishops of the ecclesiastical principalities of Mainz, Speyer, Bamberg, and Würzburg, being throughout the century the influence under which churches, cloisters, and residences were built.

We shall take from this late period the late work of a late master — Balthasar Neumann (1687–1753) and his Pilgrim's Church of the Fourteen Saints, known as the Vierzehnheiligen.[9] Neumann was in the service of the Schönborns, for whom he built the castle of Würzburg, with the great spatial refinement of its interior evident in every detail from the wide Italian staircase to the concentrated chapel like a jewel transmuted

---

[9] Richard Teufel, *Die Wallfahrtskirche Vierzehnheiligen* (Berlin, 1936); Hans Eckstein, *Vierzehnheiligen* (Leipzig, 1939).

63. BALTHASAR NEUMANN. Vierzehnheiligen. *Warped-plane binding arches.*

into space.   He grew up in the German part of Bohemia,
where he became familiar with the Italian baroque churches.
He also traveled in France, and we know that he had in his
library Guarini's *Architettura civile* (first edition, Turin, 1686;
second edition, 1737), which contained Guarini's principal
buildings.   Late baroque architecture had made its way north
through the work of German, Italian-influenced architects,
such as Lucas von Hildebrandt, who built the Belvedere in
Vienna, and Christoph Dientzenhofer (1655–1722), the direct
precursor of Balthasar Neumann.

The Church of the Vierzehnheiligen, standing high on a mountain top overlooking the broad valley of the river Main, is the
quintessence of Neumann's architectural experience (*figs.* **59–
61**).   Construction began at the very end of baroque ecclesiastical architecture, in 1743, and was not completed until 1772,

Influence of palace
architecture

131

long after Neumann's death. The church has a comparatively simple exterior in the shape of a cruciform basilica and a slender façade with two towers of the sort that are so familiar in northern countries, though not in Italy. An Italian visitor would likewise be astonished to find this front pierced by many large windows in story formation, testimony to the influence upon church design of the northern châteaux, both French and German. Here, in other words, is an instance of a secular influence upon an ecclesiastical building. The statues in niches are almost wholly eliminated in this limestone front, and instead large windows are cut through the undulating wall.

Interior The *interior* (*fig.* **62**), however, follows more closely the late Italian baroque. It does not continue the complicated constructional treatment of Guarini's domes, nor has it Borromini's plastic intensity. All is lighter and without tragic notes. Yet there is also the use of intersecting and interpenetrating spaces. The ground plan (*fig.* **61**) is worked out on a basis of intersecting circles and ovals. In a church of this cruciform type, the central crossing is customarily covered by the dome. Here, however, the dome, the most important part of the church, has been completely done away with. Its place is taken by the space in which four variously shaped (spherical and ellipsoidal) vaultings meet: the nave, the choir, and the two short transepts. The interpenetration of the complicated volumes of these vaults requires the use of binding arches formed in warped planes. Their unusual curves reveal the systematic way in which the different spaces are blended into one another. No single particle of space remains separable from the others. The necessity of passing on from each subdivision to the other parts of the scheme that includes it produces the final impression that the whole interior is in motion. The warped-plane binding arches (*fig.* **63**) that establish these relations consist of curves of the third degree — that is, of curves developed in three dimensions, not capable of being embraced in a flat surface, as circles are. It is interesting to note that in this period such three-dimensional curves could be calculated by the aid of the integral calculus.

In the late baroque churches of Italy, the cupola was often left in semidarkness, but here, in this white Church of the

132

Fourteen Saints, light is permitted to pour in from all directions. Certainly in no earlier period had light been allowed to flow into an ecclesiastical building in such dazzling effulgence. Plain glass, without any decoration, was used for the large windows, so that they might carry out their function — the letting in of light — entirely without hindrance.

The principal force at work in this church is not preëminently architecture — as in the constructions of Borromini and Guarini — but rather a magnificent balance between architecture, sculpture, and painting. In the atmosphere in which Neumann worked, the different arts had grown up in perfect association. Indeed, the secret of this late eighteenth century was the production of a most effective unification of all the arts. The architects of the eighteenth century knew all the hidden secrets of architectural effect. Despite their letting in of light as never before, because of this perfect unity of the arts they kept the mystic power to impress. The forms were so modeled that the natural light never became dimmed but always filled the space, like torches in the night.

It should perhaps be remembered that these magnificent churches were created just at the time when the Protestant workmen of Birmingham and Manchester were inventing their first cotton-spinning machine.

THE ORGANIZATION OF OUTER SPACE

The Residential Group and Nature

The work of the baroque architects was both continued and supplemented in France during the late seventeenth century. French contributions appear especially in two fields: in the development of more highly refined types of human residence, and in the organization of outer space.

The role of France

The decisive influence upon developments in France, which had just become the leading European country, was the complete supremacy of a secular government. Absolutism was in

Influence of
secular absolutism

133

the saddle, and, as a corollary, the personal life of the monarch had become the center of all social life.

The feminine influence

But in addition a new power was making itself felt, a power of the greatest importance and one which did not affect the Roman baroque: the feminine influence. The growing demand for a better organization of human residences, for greater comfort, *commodité*, was intensified by the novel importance of women in French society. These two factors, of course, worked together. In 1665, for example, Louis XIV asked the Pope to permit Lorenzo Bernini, his greatest architect, to come to Paris and draw up a plan for the new Louvre. Bernini's design was rejected — with all possible politeness, of course, but not because it was too theatrical, as the usual explanation has it. An eighteenth-century architect gives us the real reason: "Bernini ne pouvait se prêter à entrer dans tous les details de ces distributions, de ces commodités qui rendent le service d'un palais commode." In other words, Bernini failed to show a grasp of the complicated problems set by a palace building where women played an important role; he quite lost sight of the ladies. The part that women play in the development of French architecture from this period onward is a very important one.

Court ceremonies

The elaborate routine of court ceremonies is another major conditioning circumstance. These changes in French social life dictated a more complicated arrangement of rooms in great houses. A new delicacy and refinement appears in their treatment. At the same time changes are made in the designs of furniture, especially as concerns such pieces as are intended for sitting and lying: these become better accommodated to women, and to love-making.

Refinements in residences of the nobility

At this period in France the general type of dwelling was being transformed; the château was replacing the villa of Italian style. The town mansions of the nobility and of high state officials, buildings like the Hôtel Lambert which Louis Le Vau built at Paris in 1650, showed a highly developed dwelling culture that had arisen out of the special requirements of French life. But very soon the growth of this culture was to be impeded. The importance of the great nobles, the wealthy financiers, and the chief state functionaries alike was eclipsed by the demands of an absolute king.

134

In keeping with this change, the royal château — placed outside the city — became both the social and the architectural
center. It dominated the town behind it and the natural terrain that spread out before it. The idea of locating the château
midway between town and country had originated in Italy
considerably earlier. Michelangelo, for example, when building the Palazzo Farnese in Rome, had conceived the fantastic
notion of throwing a bridge across the Tiber as a means of
prolonging the axis of the palace far beyond the other side of
the river.

Emergence of
the château

It was not the French king, however, but Fouquet, the greatest financier of his time, who was the first to carry this open
style of château construction to its logical conclusion, in the
château of Vaux-le-Vicomte. This château was built by the
architect Louis Le Vau just past the middle of the seventeenth
century, 1655–61 (*fig.* **64**). It was comparatively modest in
size, but it faced an immense park, the work of André Le
Nôtre. The château is built on the principle of the French
pavilion. The steep roofs with their tall chimneys are reminiscent of Gothic tower-caps; they are in abrupt contrast with
the cupola and its lantern of the middle pavilion. We can well
imagine the kind of impression this mixture of building styles
must have made on Lorenzo Bernini, who was in Paris at the
time the château was erected. Nevertheless, Vaux-le-Vicomte
was the first instance of a dwelling designed in close unity with
nature, with a park on a grand scale. It embodied this great
experiment years before it was adopted, and carried much
further, at Versailles. But, as is well known, Fouquet paid a
heavy price for his daring. His château and park excited the
envy of the King, who would not tolerate rivalry in any direction. Louis XIV accordingly commanded the architect Le
Vau and the park designer Le Nôtre to build the palace
at Versailles, in all its vaunting splendor — and he put
Fouquet in prison for the rest of his life. The incident is not
an isolated fact; it represents one stage on the way to absolute rule. The power and prestige of great nobles and the
great financiers had to be broken to make Louis an absolute
monarch.

Vaux-le-Vicomte

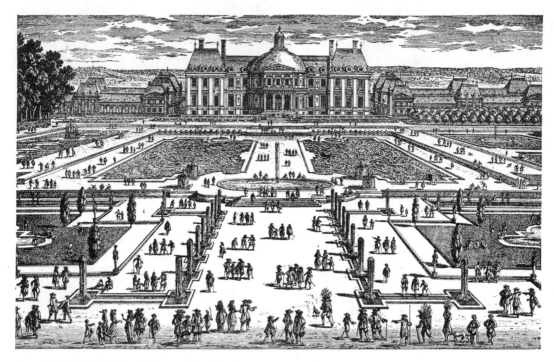

64. LOUIS LE VAU. Château Vaux-le-Vicomte, 1655–61.

65. LOUIS LE VAU and JULES HARDOUIN–MANSARD. Versailles. *The château, the garden, and the boulevard.*

136

The château of Versailles symbolizes the supplanting of the ecclesiastical authority of a pope by the secular absolutism of a king. It took Louis XIV nearly half a century (1661–1708) to erect Versailles in all its magnificence. He began the work when he was twenty-two, firmly rejecting the suggestions of his minister Colbert, who advised him to complete the residence of his ancestors, the Louvre in Paris. Of another generation than Colbert, Louis cared neither for the old palace nor for his capital city of Paris. Bernini, then nearly seventy years old, had been brought all the way from Rome to Paris and had been presented by Colbert with a complete list of the requirements for a royal residence. But all this was quite in vain; Louis XIV had other ideas.

Versailles

In particular, the notion of mastering nature, *forcer la nature*, fascinated the King. Louis XIV detested the narrow streets of Paris. A dislike of large cities was, indeed, one of the characteristics of baroque absolutism everywhere. Even when new towns were founded in connection with the new palaces, they failed to prosper. This was to prove true in the case of Versailles, as well as in those of Mannheim and Karlsruhe. But, in any event, Versailles and the idea of creating a new mode of life that would be unrestricted by the confines of a city preoccupied Louis intensely for more than thirty years — this in spite of the fact that it was an unprecedented thing for a ruling monarch to desert and neglect the capital of his country.

Absolutism's dislike of large cities: *forcer la nature*

The Versailles of Louis XIII's day had been a mere hunting-seat, built on a low hill which was surrounded by woods. It was at first merely enlarged. But these alterations — carried through by the architect of Vaux-le-Vicomte, Louis Le Vau — did not suffice; larger dimensions were necessary. During the years 1668–74 a new conception took shape, a conception gigantic in scale (*fig.* 65). The great U-shaped, central block faces the park. Jules Hardouin-Mansard elongated the front of the palace by building a long wing at right angles to each end of the U. The left wing (1679–82) was built for the royal princes; the right wing (begun in 1684) was built as an office building for the various French ministries. (It was in 1683, when he decided to house the administration of France in his

The hunting-seat of Louis XIII the center of France, 1668–74

own palace, that Louis XIV proclaimed Versailles as his official residence. The proclamation almost caused a revolt in Paris.)

The two long wings combined with the U of the central block resulted in an open style of construction that had been hitherto unknown. The whole structure, complex and enormous, served three functions: it housed the King, the royal family, and the ministries of France. Building activity on these immense residential quarters was carried on at its greatest intensity in the years from 1668 to 1684; thirty thousand men were employed on the work. The interval in question corresponds exactly to the rise of the absolute monarchy. At the same time, Roman baroque architecture underwent the last phase of its development in the work of Borromini and Guarini.

Juxtaposition with nature

What is the significance of Versailles? What is the important constituent fact it embodies? It is the close contact it effects with nature. An immense complex of buildings, more than two thousand feet long, has been directly confronted with nature; the grounds are a real part of the structure itself, and form with it a whole of great power and grandeur.

The constituent facts in Versailles

Lorenzo Bernini had not been permitted to carry out his project for the Louvre; nevertheless, when Louis XIV began the new enlargement of Versailles in 1668, Roman grandeur, *grandezza*, scored a success. Straight lines and flat roofs replaced the crabbed medieval silhouette. In the simplicity of a long straight line, used without deviation, there lies a tremendous courage and self-assertiveness. The whole edifice is the architectural response to a new sociological demand: the demand for a new setting for the personal, the ceremonial, and the governmental life of an absolute king. The major functions combined under its one roof have already been noted. Less important ones were likewise provided for; the salons, for example, for all their mythological names, were actually intended for gambling, dancing, and musical entertainments.

The form for a new mode of living

But the interesting thing is still the manner in which great complex buildings for social, residential, and administrative purposes have been welded together and closely juxtaposed with nature (*fig.* **67**). Versailles is important not because of

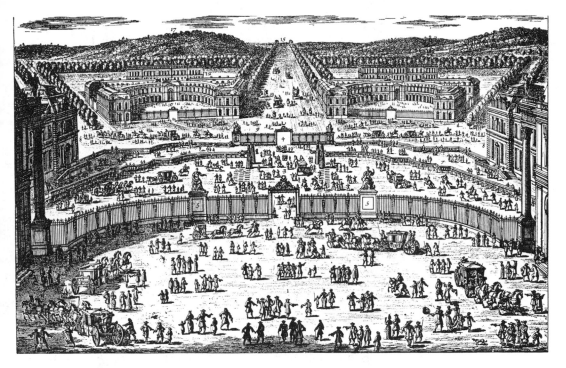

66. Versailles. Great court, stables, and highway to Paris. *Engraving by Perelle.*

67. Versailles. The gardens, the "Tapis verts," the Grand Canal, and the terraces. *Engraving by Perelle.*

its royal splendor but because it clearly reveals the solution to a problem of living. Nature had been mastered before by man's will, but never before had so large a community been housed under one roof, in open country, away from any big town.

<table>
<tr><td>

The highway as an architectonic means

</td><td>

Versailles has a highway linking it with Paris (*fig.* **66**). It starts from between two buildings overlooked by the great court; it ends in Paris in the Champs-Élysées and the Louvre. The beautiful curving constructions which give its commencement at Versailles such power and dignity are — almost incredibly — the royal stables. The accentuation of the highway by means of these stables emphasizes the approach to the château. The highway, in other words, has been incorporated into an architectonic expression, is an essential part of it.

</td></tr>
</table>

The highway as an architectonic means

Versailles has a highway linking it with Paris (*fig.* **66**). It starts from between two buildings overlooked by the great court; it ends in Paris in the Champs-Élysées and the Louvre. The beautiful curving constructions which give its commencement at Versailles such power and dignity are — almost incredibly — the royal stables. The accentuation of the highway by means of these stables emphasizes the approach to the château. The highway, in other words, has been incorporated into an architectonic expression, is an essential part of it.

The plan of the gardens anticipates later town planning

The baroque will to master the illimitable is best shown by the other side of the palace. The ground slowly declines from the terrace with its ornamental pools. The eye is led by the long lawns — the *tapis verts* — to the Grand Canal, cruciform in shape, with a length of one mile (*fig.* **67**). In the time of Louis XIV it was graced by gondolas and other luxury craft. Beyond the Grand Canal, the view fades into an endless countryside. The woods and shrubbery of the enormous park — its area is one-fourth the area of all Paris — spread out to the right and to the left. Provision was made here for every sort of leisure activity, for sports, for hunting, for festivals, for lovemaking. The woods are dotted with round clearings from which paths emerge like the rays of a searchlight. These circular areas with their radiating pathways or roads will find a place in eighteenth-century town planning.

Louis XIV as "the open-air king"

The extensive and carefully ordered natural setting for the château of Versailles was the background not only of these great new buildings but of the new kind of living that had been developed there. The old myth that Versailles was a kind of vast and sumptuous mausoleum in which Louis XIV was confined like a royal mummy has been destroyed by history. Louis Bertrand, one of his biographers, presents a picture which contradicts the old, familiar, and inaccurate one. He calls Louis "the open-air king" and tells us of those hunts on which he went alone, twice every week, into the forests of

Versailles, making hunting his excuse for solitude. From the windows of his bedchamber in the palace he had an unbroken vista of forests and green meadows — a view which, of course, is spoiled today. The constituent facts that are presented by Versailles, the trends that were to be continued in later periods, were not bound up in its royal splendor. They lie in the new ways of living for which it provided a form. An enormous structure, almost a small town in itself, had — together with the life that went on within it — been brought into close contact with nature.

Single Squares

At the time when baroque architecture flourished in Rome, cities all over the world were crowded and lacked space within the walls that surrounded them. The first large open space within a city — in contrast to the enclosed Renaissance square — was the Piazza Obliqua (the "Oval Place") of St. Peter's in Rome (*fig.* **68**). It was built just after the middle of the seventeenth century. Its graduated areas are embraced within the fourfold colonnades of St. Peter's as though by a giant pair of pincers, and linked by them with the portico. Three elements are combined here: the oval plaza, the rectangular plaza, and the body of the church with the dome that crowns it. Bernini had intended to close the opening of the Piazza Obliqua with another colonnade, leaving two narrow entrances. The plan was never executed, however.

Bernini: the Piazza Obliqua, Rome

André Le Nôtre had designed Vaux-le-Vicomte five years before the appearance of Bernini's colonnades for St. Peter's. The work of both men sprang from an urge to dominate wide spaces that manifested itself all over Europe at this time. But Bernini's colonnade is unique in the precision of its modeling, which is calculated to the last inch. The exactitude involved can be fully appreciated only during those church festivals when the Oval Place is filled by the crowds awaiting the papal benediction. The plaza slopes gently downward to the obelisk in its center; it then rises, in slightly inclined terraces and long steps, to the enormous portico. Bernini's architectural mastery

141

68. LORENZO BERNINI. Piazza Obliqua, St. Peter's, Rome. *Lithograph, 1870.*
Crowds awaiting the papal benediction.

is revealed when the onlooker, awaiting the blessing, discovers
that he can overlook all the great congregation, in addition
to seeing everything that takes place on the terraces immediately in front of the church.

Paris under Louis XIV: late start in building squares

What did the north have to offer in comparison with work like
this? Paris had the *grands boulevards* with which Vauban, the
great engineer of Louis XIV, replaced the city walls when he
tore them down. Grass-covered earthworks, more suited to
"modern" defensive needs, were thrown up farther outside the
city. The first great square of Paris was the Renaissance
Place des Vosges (1612). Louis XIV did not build his first
square until thirty years after Bernini's colonnades of St.
Peter's, and twenty-five years after the beginning of his reign.
This was the Place des Victoires (1685–87). It had the form of
a circle flattened on one side, and was quite modest in its
dimensions. But it was the first circular *place* in Paris intended
as a meeting point for streets.

142

The first really large public square built in the Paris of this period was the Place Vendôme, constructed at the beginning of the eighteenth century. It is worthy of note that the Place Vendôme was not built until after the completion of Versailles. The architect of Versailles, Jules Hardouin-Mansard, now had time for work on the important *places* in Paris itself. His first plan in 1699 provided for a simple rectangle; later its corners were cut off, and the new sides that were thus developed were bent outward. Seventy years earlier, Borromini had used the same treatment in the small cloister-court of San Carlo alle Quattro Fontane. But the most significant development in Paris, one which could not be valued truly at the time, was the highroad that was carried directly across the countryside to connect the axis of the château of Versailles with the axis of the Château du Louvre. To this day, the Champs-Élysées follow exactly the plan originally laid down by Louis XIV and continue to provide the only sufficiently broad exit from Paris.

The Place Vendôme

The eighteenth century is a century remarkable for the laying-out of squares. Just as the name of Louis XIV is associated with the building of palaces and gardens, so the name of Louis XV, who succeeded him, is linked with the construction of new town squares and public places. The plan of Paris drawn by Patte in 1748 (*fig.* **69**), which shows all the *places* of the city, both those already in existence and those merely projected, shows at a glance the great amount of such construction under Louis XV. Probably the best-known single example is the Place de la Concorde, designed by Jacques-Ange Gabriel and constructed in 1763.

Series of Interrelated Squares

In many towns series of squares or plazas were laid out, not as a mere succession of mutually independent units but in such a way that all together they constituted a rhythmical progression. A compelling and thoroughly self-conscious desire for unity governed their location and the manner in which streets

Interrelated squares character-ize the mid-eight-eenth century

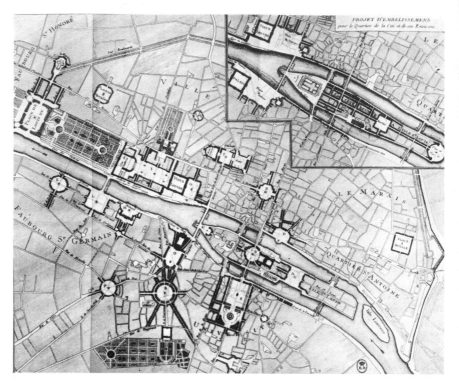

69. PATTE. Plan of Paris, 1748, with projected and executed squares. *This plan clearly demonstrates the mid-eighteenth century endeavor to organize open spaces — squares — of every shape in all possible locations. Very few of them were ever executed.*

were made to radiate from them. Often whole towns were made to conform to a predetermined scheme of this sort. Karlsruhe, Germany, which was founded in 1715, is one instance. When whole towns were treated in this fashion as architectural units, already existing buildings frequently had additions made to them so that they would fit harmoniously into the system of relations the new scheme established.

The three *places* of Nancy

Among all such series of squares, the most pleasing is that formed by the three *places* of Nancy, the capital of Lorraine. Nancy was at one time the residence of Louis XV's father-in-law, the exiled king of Poland, Stanislas Leszinski. Its three *places* (*fig.* **71**) were built by Héré de Corny between 1752 and 1755, just one century later than Bernini's colonnades. The first *place* (Place Stanislas) — with the Hôtel de Ville (*fig.* **70**), which antedates it — is connected through a triumphal arch with the oblong Place Carrière. The charming rococo wrought-iron work of Lamour forms a transparent screen between the

144

70. HÉRÉ DE CORNY.
Three interrelated squares at
Nancy, Place Stanislas, 1752–55.
View.

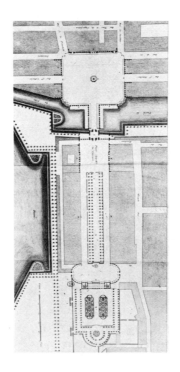

71. HÉRÉ DE CORNY.
Three interrelated squares at
Nancy. *Plan. New elements
were used in these squares to bring
already existing features into a
new, inspiring, and vital spatial
unity.*

72. HÉRÉ DE CORNY. Palais du Gouvernement with oval colonnades, Nancy.

two. Avenues of trees and symmetrical rows of houses lead on to the third of these squares, the Place Royale. The Palace of Government which faces the Place Royale is another building that was already in existence when the plan for these *places* was being made. The building was made to fit into the whole new composition by the addition of an elegant colonnade to the square. This colonnade around the *place* repeated the motif already present in the arches of the Palace of Government (*fig.* **72**).

Synthesis of separate elements

An immense fund of architectural knowledge is revealed in each one of these squares. It appears equally in the way the heights and proportions of the buildings are regulated and in the handling of the materials used. Walls, transparent ironwork, fountains, trees, colonnades — all these materials are used with instinctive correctness. It is in this that we find the

146

secret of the architecture of the middle eighteenth century: each element is coördinated with all the others; isolated phenomena are synthesized to form the most effective whole.

At the same time that the three squares at Nancy were being constructed, a small town existed in England which was the product of an equal wealth of architectural knowledge, although it had grown up to meet quite different purposes — Bath. In eighteenth-century England, to "take the waters" at Bath's hot springs was a fixed part of social routine; Bath was "the rallying place of good company and social intercourse." There was no church or castle to which the town had to conform. Bath was built for the entertainment of an anonymous and mixed society. It attracted the aristocracy, artists, men of letters, and — as Oliver Goldsmith relates — types still more various: "Clerks and factors from the East-Indies, loaded with the spoils of plundered provinces, planters, negrodrivers from our American Plantations, agents who have fattened in two successive wars, brokers and jobbers of every kind, *men of low birth*." This sketch might have been written in the late nineteenth century, rather than in the eighteenth.

73. JOHN WOOD THE YOUNGER. The Circus, 1764, and the Royal Crescent, 1769, Bath. *Air view.*

74. JACQUES–ANGE GABRIEL. Place Louis XV — Place de la Concorde, Paris, 1763. *Here nature and an open square are juxtaposed, the same principle as that involved in the Royal Crescent, Bath.*

The Circus and the Royal Crescent

Bath was built for the new bourgeois society by a man who was "at once architect, builder, speculator and an artist" — John Wood. His son and successor, John Wood the younger, completed the Circus in 1764, and in 1769 built the famous Royal Crescent, in which thirty houses are joined together in the shape of an open ellipse (*fig.* **73**).

The Royal Crescent is comparable, in many respects, to Jacques-Ange Gabriel's Place Louis XV (Place de la Concorde), completed six years earlier (*fig.* **74**). The latter remains, despite all changes, the most beautiful of Parisian *places*. It owes its charm to the fact that its single boundary wall permits a country view in the midst of a city: the gardens of the Tuileries are to the left, the Champs-Élysées lie on the right, and the Seine is directly in front. Here is the opinion of a contemporary, the Abbé Laugier, who was already capable of discerning the intention behind this highly developed piece of town planning: "Entourée de jardins et de bosquets, elle ne presente que l'image d'une esplanade embellie au milieu d'une campagne riante. . . ." Quite simply, this *place* is made an integral part of the outlying landscape.

148

75. JOHN WOOD THE YOUNGER. The Royal Crescent, Bath, 1769. *The broad lawn in front of the Royal Crescent slopes down toward the floor of a valley.*

The single boundary wall of the Place de la Concorde is left open in the center. In this manner the street — the Rue Royale — which leads from this opening (to terminate in a church built at a later date) becomes the axis of the *place* itself.

The Royal Crescent at Bath (*fig.* **75**) has no axis and no central opening leading out to a church or a château. Nothing blocks the view from it; there is no building, whether representative of secular or ecclesiastical authority, to which it stands in a servile or dependent relationship. There is only a broad lawn which slopes gently toward the town, and the countryside beyond lies at its front. A completely open view has been attained through a concentration of many individual lodgings. Thirty small standardized houses have been fused into a single unit to produce the Crescent, and its monumental impressiveness derives from the fact that these standardized units are added together without any separations. Not until our own time do we encounter similar undertakings. For example, Gropius' 1937 scheme for eight-story apartment houses to be erected at St. Leonard's Hill — a park near Windsor — tends in the same direction. The wide expanse of the grounds, with their trees and meadows, is retained unbroken by concentrat-

The Royal Crescent: a self-sufficient residential complex

149

ing individual apartments into three eight-story buildings. In this way there is an open view for each tenant. Contrasted with such schemes as the Royal Crescent and that of Gropius, the health and holiday resorts of the nineteenth century, with their rambling hotels and private houses, present the chaotic appearance of a mining camp.

Building speculators of the eighteenth and early nineteenth centuries

Eighteenth-century Bath was built on speculation; the elder John Wood began building there in 1727. The Place Vendôme in Paris (1701) likewise was the work of speculators for the major part, as were the London squares and crescents with their high architectural standards. Many of the best English architects in the eighteenth century and at the beginning of the nineteenth — men like the Adams, John Nash, Soane, and others — were at one and the same time builders, artists, and speculators. For all that, this architecture manifests discipline and the working of a vigorous tradition. There is only a fragmentary knowledge of the part speculation has played in the development of architecture. And yet the extent of that influence would be worth knowing, not merely for architectural reasons but also for the sake of discovering both the initiative and the destructive roles of the speculator.

Assured town planning in the eighteenth century: Piazza del Popolo, Rome

Nancy and Bath were not the only towns, nor Paris the only great city, in which town planning attained such astonishing proficiency. The same expertness was displayed throughout eighteenth-century Europe. Thus the basic principle common to the Place de la Concorde and the English crescents and terraces — the blending together of residences with their natural surroundings — likewise governed Valadier's adaptation of the Piazza del Popolo in Rome. Giuseppe Valadier (1762–1839) was, according to the *Enciclopedia italiana*, "the first figure in modern Italian architecture who carried out town planning, together with the preservation of green spaces, as a science." Valadier's choice of forms certainly makes him an architect of the classical revival, but the scheme for this great square, with regard to the space conception on which it rests, follows the late baroque tradition in town planning.

Some knowledge of the condition of the Piazza before Valadier began his alterations is necessary if his work is to be appreciated. The test of the town planner is his ability to instill

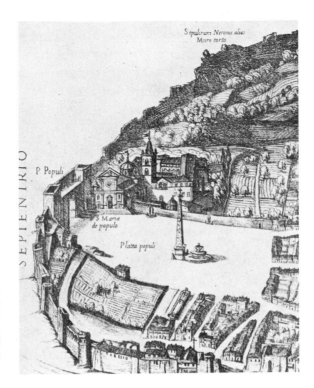

76. Piazza del Popolo, Rome. *Engraving by Tempesta, 1593. The Porta del Popolo, the Renaissance church of Santa Maria del Popolo, the obelisk, and the gardens of the Pincio.*

77. Piazza del Popolo, Rome. *View toward the twin churches of Rainaldi.*

order into the diversified complex that confronts him at the start.

Until the age of railroads, the Piazza del Popolo (*fig. 76*) was the main entrance to Rome for all visitors coming from the north. It was here that the stranger received his first impressions of the papal city. He entered the square through the

The Piazza del Popolo in the seventeenth and eighteenth centuries

151

Porta del Popolo, which had been restored and redecorated during the seventeenth century on the occasion of the visit of Queen Christina of Sweden to Rome. Facing him on the far side of the *piazza* there appeared — as the first symbols of Rome's special importance — Carlo Rainaldi's twin churches of 1662 (*fig.* **77**). With their identical cupolas and porticos, they were like ecclesiastical sentries guarding the three main arteries of the city, which since antiquity have radiated from this spot. Isolated in the center of the *piazza* stood the Egyptian obelisk which had been placed there at the end of the sixteenth century. On the left there was only the simple Renaissance façade of Santa Maria del Popolo, the church attached to the Augustinian monastery where Martin Luther once stayed. The gardens of the monastery rose to the heights of the Pincio. On both sides of the square there was the same combination of high walls and insignificant buildings. These, together with the plain drinking troughs for animals that were placed in it, gave the whole *piazza* the air of being a suburb. This was the situation that Valadier faced in 1794 when his first scheme for the *piazza* was prepared and published. The final scheme, however, was actually carried out between 1816 and 1820, the years when building activity in the squares of Bloomsbury was at its height [10] (*fig.* **78**).

Valadier's scheme (executed 1816–20)

Valadier touched none of the monumental buildings in or around the square; he tore down, however, all walls and buildings that had no importance. He transformed the greater part of the gardens of the Augustinian monastery into a public park, giving access to the Pincio. Through this park he led a winding ramp which provided for the passage of vehicular traffic between the *piazza* and the Pincio. Upon the heights of the Pincio itself, Valadier built a terrace, giving it a large substructure whose proportions were related to his other buildings lower down (*fig.* **80**). Thus, despite its being on a much higher level, it fits within and makes a unity of his whole spatial composition. It is possible to see from figures **79** and **80** how successful Valadier was in bringing together into a new relationship buildings of quite different styles and periods.

[10] An excellent study of the Piazza del Popolo, by Rowland Pierce and Thomas Ashby, is contained in *Town Planning Review*, vol. XI, December 1924.

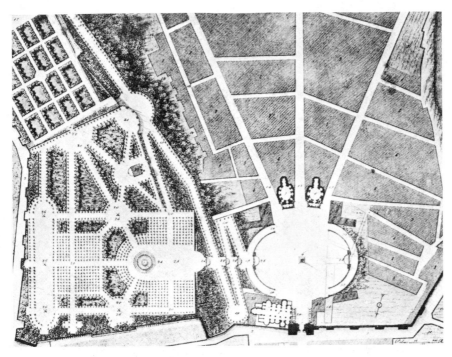

78. GIUSEPPE VALADIER. Scheme of the Piazza del Popolo, Rome, 1816. *This is the final scheme followed in the actual rebuilding.*

79. Piazza del Popolo, Rome. Section through the different levels and ramps. *Drawing by Edward W. Armstrong, 1924.*

In addition to these works, Valadier erected a few residential units bordering the *piazza* and built two elegant hemicycles which served — as they still do — to guide traffic. Beyond this, he provided very carefully for the introduction of landscaped areas into the whole design. This careful infiltration of greenery is characteristic of all such work at this time. He further planned to leave the west side of the square permanently unenclosed and free of buildings so that the

Innovations by Valadier: infiltration of greenery, regulation of traffic, relation of different levels

153

80. Piazza del Popolo, Rome. *View from the Pincio terrace, showing the different horizontal levels involved and their relations to the vertical planes in the Piazza. Valadier here touches upon a fundamental conception of our time: the relation between horizontal and vertical planes as a basis for aesthetic response.*

view might lead out upon a wide green area as it does in the Place de la Concorde and in the Royal Crescent at Bath. Today this area is occupied by broad avenues and tall houses and defaced by advertising signs.

The Piazza del Popolo has remained to this day one of the most "modern" in appearance of all the great squares. To a certain extent this is due to the thoroughgoing fusion of buildings and park. Its air of modernity is owing much more, however, to the way in which different levels are brought within the same composition. The series of *places* built at Nancy in the middle of the eighteenth century had exploited the relations that can be made to hold among the vertical surfaces of buildings of different heights. In the Piazza del Popolo, Valadier embodies

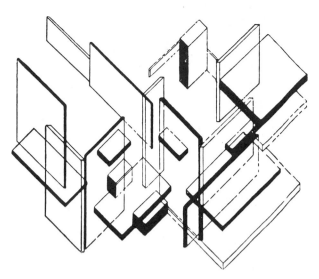

81. THEO VAN DOESBURG. Relation of horizontal and vertical planes. c. 1920.

a hovering sensation in the total effect produced by his design by bringing into relation with each other two horizontal areas of different levels: the terrace on the Pincio, and the *piazza* proper. A proportion in three dimensions — not merely in two, as at Nancy — is developed.

We have seen how Borromini, in striving to lead the movement of a design through the space of the interior into outer space, anticipated a concern of modern architecture. Valadier's *piazza* touches upon another fundamental conception of our time: the relation between horizontal and vertical surfaces as a basis for aesthetic responses of a special sort. That this is one of the constituent facts in modern architecture, one of the tendencies determining its character, cannot be doubted. A drawing made about 1922 by the Dutch painter, poet, and architect, Theo van Doesburg, founder of the "Stijl" group, shows a conscious recognition of this conception (*fig.* **81**). It depicts the interacting relations of hovering and transparent vertical and horizontal plane surfaces of a house.

To avoid misunderstanding, it may be worth repeating that neither Borromini nor Valadier worked with space con-

Interrelated horizontal and vertical surfaces

ceptions identical with those of today. The exact ways in which they differ will be discussed later. But the historian always finds it both interesting and important to note early beginnings of movements that only much later come to a full realization.

82. FRANCESCO BORROMINI. Undulating wall of San Carlo alle Quattro Fontane, 1662–67. *This late baroque invention, the undulating wall, reappears in English town planning toward the end of the eighteenth century.*

Previous to the turbulent and overwhelming onset of industrialization, a high standard existed for housing on both simple and luxurious scales. The principles of town planning were a matter of common knowledge to everyone connected with architecture. When a period succeeds in developing its natural culture, and when this culture is supported by a long tradition, works of the highest quality can be produced by anonymous

156

artists as well as by distinguished ones. For example, it happens that we do know the name of the architect who built the Lansdowne Crescent at Bath toward the beginning of the nineteenth century, but it is a name of no importance for history.

83.   Lansdowne Crescent, Bath, 1794. *Its serpentine windings follow the contours of the site.*

Lansdowne Crescent lies high above the town of Bath (*fig.* **83**). Its three serpent-like windings give it an organic aspect which is strengthened by the way in which they follow the accidental rise and fall of ground to catch as much light and sun as possible. This crescent embodies two of the constituent facts of the preceding centuries. Borromini's use of undulating walls (*fig.* **82**) to bring an unexpected movement and flexibility into

The constituent facts in Lansdowne Crescent, Bath (1794)

the narrow Roman streets reappears in the serpentine curves
of its outline. Its second predecessor was Versailles, the first
great building to be set at the front of an immense park instead
of in the midst of a city's narrow streets. The manner in
which this great residential group was placed in direct contact
with nature, and the effect of unhampered freedom that resulted, made it the guide for all later experiments. A similar
freedom characterizes Lansdowne Crescent. The combination
of movement, surprise, and openness makes its houses exactly

84. Bath and its crescents. *Air view. Near the center are the Royal Crescent and the
Circus; below and to the left is Lansdowne Crescent.*

what every residence should be: the adequate background for
leisure. Lansdowne Crescent was not an isolated phenomenon. Its flexible planning survived into the early nineteenth century, though too seldom, and can be found in the
layouts of South Kensington and Edinburgh.

During the last few decades, endeavors have been made to
reconquer and to extend the lost knowledge of town planning
displayed in schemes like Lansdowne Crescent. The task is
difficult, what with all the complications attendant upon new
technical developments. Nevertheless it cannot be evaded.

The sort of solution to this problem that is possible to us today can be seen — to take only one example — in Le Corbusier's scheme (1930–1934) for the improvement of Algiers (*fig.* **85**). Le Corbusier makes use of skyscrapers which have the "organic" outlines of the crescents at Bath. Like the latter, they are adjusted to the rise and fall of the ground, although the variations of level are much more extreme than those encountered in the English town. The individual apartments in these skyscrapers each take up two stories, and are so arranged that

Relation to the present: Le Corbusier's undulating skyscrapers

85. LE CORBUSIER. Scheme for skyscrapers in Algiers, 1931. *Late baroque space conceptions came very near to contemporary solutions like this one.*

their tenants have considerable control over the interior layout. The plan provides for access to terraces and hanging gardens from every apartment, and all of them would command a magnificent view of the city, the sea, and the sky. This plan was an immensely bold project for its time. The new residential area on a mountainside high above the town and two distant community centers were linked by a highway built over the roofs of a continuous apartment house. Although too much dominated by technological possibilities, the urbanistic imagination received a tremendous impetus. In Le

Corbusier's later master plan (1942) the massive concentration of dwelling complexes was greatly loosened.

Late eighteenth-century town planning; long tradition

Town planning is always the last department of architecture to reach full development. It frequently attains maturity only when a period is nearing its close; this was the case in the late baroque. Late baroque town planning brings together the artistic inheritance of four centuries, but it was not at once applied to residences of all classes. Versailles, the first great experiment in placing a large residential and administrative block in contiguity with nature, was built for the use of court society and the ministerial staff. Bath marks the point when a middle-class development is given the same treatment; Charles Dickens, for example, lodges Mr. Pickwick in the Royal Crescent at Bath. At the end of the century this type of residential development had become a general mode of expression in architecture. By the early nineteenth century the squares and crescents of London extended the baroque tradition of a juxtaposition of nature and human residences to the housing of still lower classes, and made it no longer the exclusive privilege of wealthy people.

Sudden break

But just at this time there came a sudden break. The kind of town planning that was summed up in contemporary architectural knowledge and concretely exemplified in Bath did not suit the new conditions created by industry. With its demands for dignity and proportion it represented only an obstacle to a time of chaotic expansion, when towns and industrial centers were growing up with uncontrolled speed. Factory towns like Manchester and Birmingham have been scenes of architectural disorder from the day of their inception. From the first onset of the new forces of industry, the knowledge upon which town planning rests was lost with terrifying rapidity.

This disorganization spread from the industrial towns to the old capital cities. A new and deadly influence was at work; the pursuit of wealth through the new increase in the power of production became an end in itself. This led on the one hand to the appearance of slums, and on the other to the building of large and formless mansions. Leisure vanished; no one had the time to live gracefully; life lost its equilibrium. The result was a deep spiritual uncertainty — and the more uncertain of himself man became, the more he tried to bolster up belief in

160

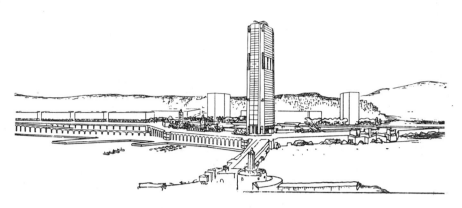

85a. LE CORBUSIER. Plan for the Marine Sector of Algiers, 1938–1942. *The setting of the skyscraper was above all a forceful space-creating focal point. Equally important was Le Corbusier's urbanistic, differentiated site planning, which others had not achieved at that time. The realm of the pedestrian was carefully organized and vehicles moved on raised and subterranean roads and parked in underground garages, ideas which only decades later became a general ideal.*

the rightness and stability of things through the creation of buildings in the grand, pseudo-monumental manner. But there is one branch of architecture where deceit is impossible, and that is town planning. Town planning can spring only from the full life; it is possible only when the different levels of human activity have attained a certain unity and equilibrium.

A sudden rift at the onset of industrialization is a phenemenon that can be frequently observed in history. Again and again man lights on a development that is stymied by certain outside influences: seeds that fail to grow, but that later, under quite other conditions, spring up again into consciousness. So it was that the desire of the artists of our century to rediscover age-old phenomena long dormant in man brought their work into an inner relation with prehistoric art.

In the field of architecture something similar can be observed. Right at the beginning, in Sumer, the earliest temples have an astonishingly well elaborated interior space with several entrances, to enable the people to make direct contact with the invisible powers. This situation changed when the first great conqueror absorbed the small priestly towns into a single empire. Henceforth it was no longer possible either for the great lord, who had become divine, or for the people, to enter the cella of the god. At one stroke the development of interior space was broken off. Only in the Roman period did it rise again to become the highest expression of architectural skill.

161

85b. LE CORBUSIER. Skyscraper for the Marine Sector of Algiers, 1938–1942.
*Again and again Le Corbusier worked on the planning of Algiers, the plans always growing
in ripeness. The Marine Sector, the administrative center of the city, would have been
dominated by this skyscraper, 150 meters high. The skyscraper would have stood on a projecting spit of land, with its narrow side toward the sea, looking like a huge magnetic needle.
Its vertical surfaces were sculpturally treated, their faces meeting at an obtuse angle. About
a quarter of a century later, this architectural solution arose in several countries in several
buildings. It had first appeared in 1932 in a modest building by Le Corbusier for a Zurich
assurance company (model in the Museum of Modern Art, New York).*

PART **III** **THE EVOLUTION OF NEW POTENTIALITIES**

Destiny of our cul-
ture determines the
evaluation of the
nineteenth century
We have hardly the right to compare our century with the nineteenth so far as boldness and urge toward the unknown are concerned. But what will the final judgment on this period be?

Here the historian comes up against questions of destiny. The final judgment on the nineteenth century cannot be passed today. The main outlines are not settled; transitory and constituent facts are confusingly intermingled.

Some think that we stand at the beginning of a great tradition. Others, seeing the disaster around them, think that we are at the utmost end of an age. The evaluation of the nineteenth century depends upon which of these is right.

If our culture should be destroyed by brutal forces — or even if it should continue to be terrorized by them — then the nineteenth century will have to be judged as having misused men, materials, and human thought, as one of the most wretched of periods. If we prove capable of putting to their right use the potentialities which were handed down to us, then the nineteenth century, in spite of the human disorder it created and in spite of the consequences which are still developing out of it, will grow into new and heroic dimensions.

For these reasons the evaluation of the nineteenth century is inextricably connected with the destiny of our culture — that is to say, with our own destiny.

In treating the nineteenth century we should arrive at unsatisfactory results if we adopted the approach we used for the previous period. A sufficiently comprehensive insight into the period could not be derived from nineteenth-century monumental architecture — which remains, moreover, an incompletely explored subject. The sorting-out of good buildings is still to be done; the history even of transitory developments is not understood. We shall concern ourselves instead with the evolution, during this period, of new architectural potentialities, an evolution that proceeded anonymously and was born out of the depths of the age.

Industrialization as a Fundamental Event

The Industrial Revolution, the abrupt increase in production brought about during the eighteenth century by the introduction of the factory system and the machine, changed the whole appearance of the world, far more so than the social revolution in France. Its effect upon thought and feeling was so profound that even today we cannot estimate how deeply it has penetrated into man's very nature, what great changes it has made there. Certainly there is no one who has escaped these effects, for the Industrial Revolution was not a political upheaval, necessarily limited in its consequences. Rather, it took possession of the whole man and of his whole world. Again, political revolutions subside, after a certain time, into a new social equilibrium, but the equilibrium that went out of human life with the coming of the Industrial Revolution has not been restored to this day. The destruction of man's inner quiet and security has remained the most conspicuous effect of the Industrial Revolution. The individual goes under before the march of production; he is devoured by it.

Effect of the Industrial Revolution

The heyday of the machine and of unlimited production is heralded in the eighteenth century by the sudden appearance of a widespread urge toward invention. In the England of 1760 this urge had gripped people in all strata of society. Everyone was inventing, from unemployed weavers, small hand workers, farmers' and shepherds' sons like the bridge-builder Telford, to manufacturers like Wedgwood and members of the nobility such as the Duke of Bridgewater (whose tenacious labor was responsible for the creation of the English canal system). Many of these inventors did not even take the trouble to protect their discoveries by taking out patents on them. Many, far from drawing profit from their inventions, were even persecuted because of them. Profit-making and unfair exploitation belong to a later period.

The eighteenth-century urge toward invention

England

We must, in fact, take care to avoid the delusion that this activity had its source only in material ambitions or in the desire to shine. Its actual source lay much deeper and was one that had for a long time been artificially denied outlet. But at this date the urge to invent could no longer be stemmed. When,

165

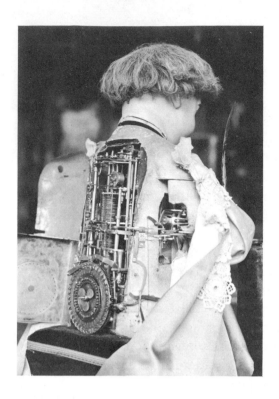

France   as in France, it was kept from entering into important regions of practical activity, it was only diverted, not destroyed. It manifested itself then in the creation of odd mechanical contrivances and of marvelous automatons, lifelike mechanical dolls capable of performing the most amazing feats, from walking to playing musical instruments and drawing pictures. Some of these automatons, in the ingenuity and precision of their workmanship, even succeeded in anticipating the principle of the modern automatic telephone — for example, the "writing doll" made at Neuchâtel about 1770 by Pierre Jaquet-Droz. This doll (*fig.* **86**) still exists in a perfectly workable condition.

Invention, carried on in this way by men of all nations and all walks of life, led to the industrialization of almost every human pursuit. But this movement which was to give the nineteenth century its essential character is scarcely reflected at all in its official architecture. We should never be able to perceive the real nature of the period from a study of public buildings, state residences, or great monuments. We must turn instead to an

166

examination of humbler structures. It was in routine and entirely practical construction, and not in the Gothic or classical revivals of the early nineteenth century, that the decisive events occurred, the events that led to the evolution of new potentialities.

But life is complex and irrational. When its evolution is blocked in one direction it seeks another (and often an entirely unexpected) outlet. The development of modern industry is essentially material. Nevertheless, in following its material urge, industry unconsciously creates new powers of expression and new possibilities of experience. These possibilities at first remain bound up in quite matter-of-fact enterprises that do not in any way enter into the intimate and personal lives of men. But, slowly and gradually, the new potentialities become a part of private and individual life. Thus a devious line of development leads from innovations in industrial buildings of all kinds — mines, warehouses, railroads and factories — to the private home and personal life. The history of this metamorphosis is, in large measure, the history of the nineteenth century. Finally these potentialities come to be realized for what they are in themselves, apart from considerations of utility. The architecture of today stands at the end of such a process. Consequently, to understand it, we are obliged to survey in considerable detail developments in regions which seem far removed from aesthetic feeling.

Industry and private life

IRON

Iron, as everyone knows, is far from being a new material; its use dates back to prehistoric times. It was employed only sparingly, however, in the great buildings of classical antiquity. Both the Greeks and the Romans preferred bronze, because of its greater resistance to weather. Neither had the Renaissance much faith in iron as a building material. Thus we find Leon Battista Alberti, the Florentine architect and theorist of the *quattrocento*, recommending materials which are ready for use in their natural state in preference to those which must be prepared by the hand and art of man — *hominum manu et*

Iron before industrialization

167

arte. Even the iron rings which Michelangelo used to hold together the cupola of St. Peter's must be considered merely as fastenings. Even as late as the Victorian period, iron was still regarded as suitable only for fastenings by those men who — like John Ruskin — hated industry. Poor resistance to exposure and lack of classical precedents in its use were not the only reasons why iron played such a small part in construction of every kind. There was also the difficulty that it could not be produced except in relatively small quantities.

Iron as a new material

The moment its production was industrialized, iron took on an entirely new importance. In order to produce the metal industrially, an understanding of its molecular arrangement was requisite. But neither the equipment nor the knowledge essential to the study of the molecular structure of materials was available before the last quarter of the eighteenth century. The history of iron as a substance in wide use is accordingly a part of the history of chemistry, physics, and research into the comparative strengths of materials. Such studies, in making the industrial production of iron possible, converted it into what amounted to a new natural material. And the availability of iron furthered in turn the sciences responsible for it.

Initial setbacks to industrialization in France

England was the birthplace of the whole Industrial Revolution. The desire to advance from manual to industrialized production existed in other countries as well — in France, for example. But the preliminary experiments undertaken in these countries were all singularly unsuccessful, whether they concerned the building of bridges or the industrialization of silk weaving. An instance in point is the failure of the attempt that was made in 1755 to build a cast-iron bridge across the Rhone. It was more than twenty years later that the first cast-iron bridge in England was finally erected over the river Severn. The French effort proved premature and had to be given up simply because it was impossible to cast iron into members of the requisite dimensions.

Conditions in England

Conditions in England were quite different from those prevailing elsewhere. At the end of the seventeenth century the wooded areas of England had been seriously diminished. As a result, attention turned to pit coal as a fuel that might possibly make up for the increasing scarcity of wood and charcoal.

Mineral fuel had already supplanted wood to some extent. By the end of the seventeenth century it had become the normal fuel for heating the home, and had even come into pretty general use by tradespeople, bakers, brewers, sugar refiners, cloth weavers, and coppersmiths. During the century its use was increased fourteen-fold. And of course in the eighteenth century demand for it was still further increased by its employment in the iron industry. By this time the use of mineral fuel had come to be regarded by everybody as the natural and ordinary thing. When Abraham Darby in the first half of the eighteenth century began experimenting with the blast furnace in the production of iron, he used coke and not charcoal.

Early Iron Construction in England

It often happens in England that one family dominates a certain trade or industry for several generations. The Darbys occupy this position in the opening stages of the industrialized production of iron. The first Abraham Darby leased an old furnace at Coalbrookdale in 1709, and it was here that the Darby family later succeeded in smelting iron ore with coke instead of charcoal for fuel. The first printed account of these operations appeared in 1747. About 1750 he turned to the use of coal, employing it to turn out pig iron of a quality that could be forged into bar iron. Mass production of iron was now possible, and this advance from manual production of the metal was to change the face of the whole world.

The production of iron industrialized

The new material was at first employed only in making machines. When John Smeaton, the great engineer who was one of James Watt's antagonists, used cast-iron utensils for the first time (in 1755), he spoke of this application of cast iron as "a totally new subject." But with Abraham Darby the third, the time had come when cast iron could be used for a variety of entirely new purposes. In 1767 the first iron rails were cast, and at the beginning of the third quarter of the century the first cast-iron bridge was erected over the Severn.[1]

---

[1] John L. and Barbara Hammond, *The Rise of Modern Industry* (London, 1925), p. 136.

The Severn Bridge
(1775–79)

The Severn Bridge (*fig.* **87**) represents one of the boldest experiments in the use of the newly available material. The idea for it seems to have originated in the year 1773 with John Wilkinson, "the ingenious iron-master" (who also invented the cylinder-boring machine which made it possible for James Watt to build a really efficient steam engine), and with the third Abraham Darby. The bridge, executed during the years 1775–

87. ABRAHAM DARBY. The first cast-iron bridge over the river Severn, 1775–79. *Span, one hundred feet; height, forty feet.*

79, consists of a single arch, with a span of 100.5 feet and a rise of 45 feet, made up of five cast-iron ribs. The whole arch is nearly a semicircle in shape. Since the Severn is subject to floods, the bridge had to be very strong. It was manufactured at Darby's Coalbrookdale works, the only plant which was capable of casting arches of such large dimensions and composed of only two members.[2]

[2] William Fairbairn, *On the Application of Cast and Wrought Iron to Building Purposes* (London, 1854), p. 201.

No artistic ambitions were involved in the design of this bridge, and, as architecture, it represents no very great achievement. In these respects it admits of no comparison with the Church of the Fourteen Saints, which had been completed only a few years earlier. But if the church stands on the highest level reached by architecture in its period, it also stands at the end of that architectural tradition. None of its features points

88. Sunderland Bridge, 1793–96. *Single arch of 236 feet. This comparatively large span was achieved by adapting methods of stone construction to work in iron.*

ahead into the future. This simply constructed bridge, for all its lack of interest as a work of art and even as a problem in architecture, opens a path for developments of great importance.

The Sunderland Bridge

The Sunderland Bridge (1793–96) was one of the most daring experiments in construction of its time (*fig.* **88**). As early as

Thomas Paine as inventor

171

1786 Thomas Paine, the famous American political writer, showed Benjamin Franklin the model of a bridge built on a novel system of his own. Franklin, seeing the difficulty of carrying out work on such a system in America, where industry had hardly begun to develop, advised Paine to take it to Eng-

89. HUMPHRY REPTON. Fneasantry for the Royal Pavilion, Brighton, 1808.

land and provided him with recommendations.[3] But in England, as everywhere else, Paine had no luck. His experimental bridge at Paddington (London) left him badly in debt. His name fell into disrepute — and no doubt his political opinions contributed something to this process. Finally his patents

[3] Richard Blunck, *Thomas Paine* (Berlin, 1936), p. 115 et seq.

were unscrupulously appropriated by a company directed by Rowland Burdon. Using Paine's plans, Burdon built the Sunderland Bridge and took to himself all the credit for its construction.[4]

This bridge at Sunderland had a single arch of a span of 236 feet. (The Severn Bridge had been only 100 feet.) The six ribs forming the arch were composed of cast-iron panels which acted as voussoirs. A series of 105 such panels made up each rib. In this manner stone vaulting was adapted to iron construction. To make a continuous girder of this span was beyond the capabilities of the time.

90. JOHN NASH. Royal Pavilion at Brighton, 1818–21.

Robert Stephenson's verdict on this bridge, delivered in 1856, is so much to the point that we shall quote it. Stephenson was the constructor of the Britannia Tubular Bridge (1849), the most famous bridge of its time and the outcome of three years of laboratory research. Stephenson has this to say of Paine's work: "About the year 1790, Thomas Paine proposed to construct cast iron arches in the form of voussoirs, and with characteristic energy put his views to the test by constructing an experimental arch of 88 feet span . . . at Paddington. . . . His daring in engineering does full justice to the fervour of his political career — for successful as the result has proved . . . we are led rather to wonder at, than to admire a structure

Robert Stephenson on the Severn Bridge

[4] Blunck, p. 22.

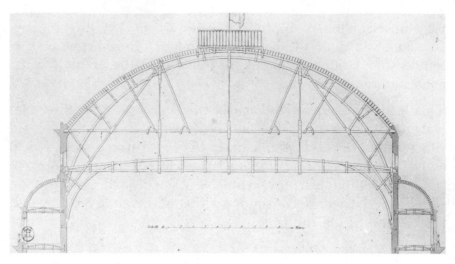

91. VICTOR LOUIS. Théâtre-Français. *Iron roofing, 1786. The form of the girders reveals an instinctive knowledge of the moment of inertia, which had not as yet been given scientific formulation.*

which, as regards its proportions and the small quantity of materials employed . . . will probably remain unrivalled." [5]

The fascination of cast iron

In this period cast iron — like chromium plate around 1930 — was a new and fascinating material which could not be employed too much. Its unexplored possibilities quickened everybody's imagination. It was such an attitude that led John Wilkinson to want a cast-iron mausoleum, and even a cast-iron coffin. The imaginative possibilities in this technical advance were soon seen to affect architecture also. The association of the new material with exotic birds that appears in a design for a pheasantry with a cast-iron frame shows the imaginative flights that ironwork suggested (*fig.* **89**). Humphry Repton, a famous English landscape gardener, included this aviary in a proposed design for the Royal Pavilion of Prince Regent George at Brighton which he submitted in 1808. It was John Nash, the architect of Regent's Park and Regent Street in London, who finally built this royal pavilion in 1818. A fantastic creation in Indian style, it had a great bulbous cupola over the middle section. The cupola was built over a cast-iron framework that weighed sixty tons [6] (*fig.* **90**).

[5] Robert Stephenson, in *Encyclopaedia Britannica* (Boston, 1856).

[6] John Summerson, *John Nash* (London, 1935), p. 162.

92. The Granary, Paris, 1811. *Bellangé and Brunet used methods of wood construction here, just as the English used methods of stone construction in their first cast-iron bridges. One of the first buildings in which the architect and the engineer were separate persons.*

Early Iron Construction on the Continent

On the Continent iron was first used for building purposes as a roofing material. The timberwork roofs of theaters and warehouses were continually catching fire and burning like tinder. As soon as hand-wrought iron became available in sufficient quantities, attempts were made to prevent such fires by its use. An early effort of this kind came in 1786 with the construction of a wrought-iron roof for the Théâtre-Français in Paris (*fig.* **91**), by the celebrated theater builder, Victor Louis.[7] The elegance and boldness required in the use of iron in a building of this type was to remain continuously characteristic of iron construction in France. The same qualities are exhibited by French work for more than a century after, until iron construction reaches its classic height in the Paris exhibition of 1889.[8]

Elegance of first French uses: Théâtre-Français (1786)

[7] Some years before this, Victor Louis produced the last great theater of the *ancien régime* at Bordeaux, one in which spatial relations of the different parts are handled with masterly skill. Victor Louis had some excellent etchings made of this theater. Cf. S. Giedion, *Spätbarocker und romantischer Klassisismus* (Munich, 1922), p. 184.

[8] The elegance of this construction has long been admired; cf. Charles L. Eck, *Traité de l'application du fer, du fonte, et de la tôle* (Paris, 1841), p. 50.

The iron roofing of the Théâtre-Français deserves notice for a more specific reason. The entire construction is counterbalanced in such a way that it needs only comparatively thin walls for its support. As some French theorists have pointed out, the form of its girders reveals an instinctive knowledge of

93. MARC SEGUIN. First French suspension bridge, of wire rope, over the Rhone, near Tournon, 1824.

the moment of inertia, which had not as yet been given scientific formulation.

Cast-iron cupola of the Granary, Paris (1811)

The wooden cupola of the Granary at Paris — covering the circular court — was destroyed by fire in 1802. In 1811 it was replaced by an elaborate construction in iron and copper (*fig.* **92**). The architect Bellangé and the engineer Brunet collaborated in its erection. This was one of the first works in which the architect and the constructor were not the same person. The building shows little more than an adaptation of old constructional methods to the new material, a clever sub-

176

stitution of iron ribs for the woodwork normally used. Nevertheless, the Granary was much admired when it was completed. Napoleon I even found time to assist in its opening. Drastically altered, it survives as a part of the present Bourse de Commerce.

94. Golden Gate Bridge, San Francisco, 1933–37. *The longest single-span suspension bridge. Dimensions: over-all length, 9,200 feet; length of main span, 4,200 feet; width of roadway, 60 feet.*

It was not until about 1850, in the cast-iron cupola of the rotunda of the British Museum, that cast-iron ribs extending from the ground to the top were used in the construction of a large building. In this example papier-mâché was employed in covering the interior of the dome. About this same period — in 1855–63 — the old wooden dome of the United States Capitol in Washington was replaced by a dome with cast-iron ribs. Its peristyle rests on an octagonal base and was interlaced with complicated iron constructional members. Truss girders

Use of the cast-iron cupola in England and the United States

177

were required in the peristyle and the dome to help support the intricate marble profiles on the outside of the whole structure. It is interesting to note how the conventions of the period led, in the case of this important American building, to a mantling of the iron construction by the architecture of the exterior surface.

Seguin's suspension
bridge over the
Rhone (1824)

The wire-cable suspension bridge goes back to the early nineteenth century. The first French example was built over the Rhone, near Tournon, in 1824 (*fig.* **93**). Marc Seguin, its constructor, was a nephew of Montgolfier and had already invented the tubular boiler which made long railway runs possible. The North American suspension bridges provided models for Seguin's work at Tournon. These bridges were suspended on hemp or rawhide ropes; Seguin used wire cables instead. This was the first time wire rope had been employed for such a purpose in Europe, and Seguin made careful scientific tests of its strength before starting his project. The new material made possible constructions of an extreme elegance and lightness. More than four hundred bridges of this type were eventually erected.

Later examples

In America, Seguin's principles were applied on a larger scale by John Augustus Roebling in his bridges over the Monongahela River at Pittsburgh, 1846, and the Niagara River, 1851–55, and in the Brooklyn Bridge, on which the preliminary work was begun in 1868. And this principle — the transmission of all stresses to a continuous, elastic cable running the length of the structure — still forms the basis for the most daring bridges built today. Seguin's bridge, incidentally, is still in use, although only pedestrian traffic is permitted on it nowadays.

The suspension bridge was continuously developed throughout the nineteenth century as wider spans were demanded and traffic volumes increased. More elaborate constructional applications of this apparently limited principle of elastic suspension were made, until fantastic spans were attained and voids were bridged that had hitherto seemed outside the range of human powers.

Often these bridges are set amidst landscapes of almost cosmic dimensions, and constitute with them new wholes on a more

95. FONTAINE. Galerie d'Orléans, Palais Royal, Paris, 1829–31. *A gathering place for elegant society and the precursor not only of such large galleries as the Galleria Vittorio Emmanuele, Milan (1865–67), but also of the glass and iron halls of the great exhibitions. Destroyed in 1935.*

than human scale. The Golden Gate Bridge (*fig.* **94**), the longest single-span suspension bridge in the world, crosses San Francisco Bay against an overwhelming background of sea and rock.[9]

Golden Gate Bridge, San Francisco

Iron and glass are the two materials whose conjunction in nineteenth-century architecture led it to new solutions. They were first brought together in any considerable structure by Fontaine, some five years after the wire-cable bridge was developed. Fontaine (who, with Percier, founded the Empire style) in his later years (1829–31) used wrought iron to construct the glass roof of the Galerie d'Orléans, a part of the Palais Royal in Paris (*fig.* **95**).

Galerie d'Orléans (1829–31)

[9] Erected during the years 1933–37, it has the following dimensions: length over all, 9,200 feet; length of main span, 4,200 feet; width of roadway, 60 feet (accommodating six auto lanes). The capacity of the two cables is 430,000,000 pounds.

96. ROUHAULT. Greenhouses of the Botanical Gardens, Paris, 1833. *The prototype of all the large iron-framed conservatories. In contrast to Paxton's English conservatories of the period, the rigidity of these high pavilions is derived solely from the use of cast-iron columns and beams.*

Earlier examples of such galleries in London made an altogether different use of glass. The Royal Opera Arcade, built in 1790 in conjunction with the old Her Majesty's Theatre, has circular openings cut into the vaulting. The light from the hidden glass roof pours into the building through these apertures. A distinctly different impression was created by the Galerie d'Orléans, an impression of freedom and openness as though one were out-of-doors, yet shielded from the elements.

Situated at the end of the inner garden of the Palais Royal, the Galerie d'Orléans was the gathering place of elegant society. It was destroyed in 1935, when the Palais was remodeled, and an open colonnade was put in its place. With its destruction, one of the most charming specimens of early nineteenth-century architecture disappeared, the precursor not only of such large

180

galleries as the Galleria Vittorio Emanuele, Milan (1865–67), but also of the glass and iron halls of the great exhibitions.

The first large structure consisting simply of an iron framework and glass panes was a French conservatory, *les serres des jardins du Musée d'histoire naturelle* (*fig.* **96**), the greenhouse of the botanical gardens at Paris. Built by Rouhault in 1833, this greenhouse was the prototype of all large, iron-framed conservatories. The unusually large panes of glass, combined with the unrestricted influx of light that the elimination of wood made possible, caused this building to be named "the glass gardens," the *jardins de verre*. Rouhault's conservatory, which is still standing, has an interior volume of nine thousand cubic meters. It is made up of two superimposed quarter-section barrel vaults (where the lower temperatures are maintained), situated between two pavilions fifteen meters high which house the tropical plants. In an article written in 1849 a contemporary — the architect Gottfried Semper — tells of a much more ambitious plan for these gardens. Prior to the overthrow of Louis-Philippe in 1848, there existed a fantastic scheme for completely covering the Botanical Gardens with an immense portable glass roof which could be removed during the summer.

Conservatory of the Jardin des Plantes

FROM THE IRON COLUMN TO THE STEEL FRAME

Perhaps the most characteristic feature of nineteenth-century architecture is its addiction to "period pieces." All the important buildings, all those edifices from which the spectator imagined himself to gain a serious aesthetic impression, appeared in elaborate historical dress. The theoretical issues which received most attention at the time were those raised by the various "revivals" — now classical, now Gothic. Advances in building technique seem to have brought with them only the practical problems involved in using new methods to produce old effects. But even at that early date there were people who saw that no genuine and distinctive tradition could emerge from the medley of inherited forms that overlaid the architecture of the period. A hundred years ago critics spoke

"Period pieces" in nineteenth-century architecture

of "the Harlequin dress of architecture," and indicated with that phrase a disease which is still malignant in our day.

Submerged tendencies

Nevertheless, beneath all the masquerade, tendencies of lasting importance lay hidden and were slowly gathering strength. The architecture of the present is a continuation of these tendencies: it is the product of a great stream of development that has covered a whole century. The common opinion that contemporary architecture owes its foundation to a few innovators appearing around 1900 is both mistaken and superficial. The seeds of this new architecture were planted at the moment when handwork gave place to industrialized production. Like so many other aspects of our civilization, it owes its distinctive character to influences stemming from the Industrial Revolution.

Isolation of architecture from technological advances

But why is it that these tendencies, so important to the future, are to be discovered almost nowhere except in the utilitarian structures of the nineteenth century? Why was their effect upon its official architecture so slight? We should of course expect technological advances to make themselves felt first in the field of industrial construction, but this is not a complete explanation. The Industrial Revolution may have begun in science and technology; that is no reason why it should not have acted upon the arts as well. We have already seen how, in baroque days, new scientific discoveries — even the most abstract and mathematical ones — immediately found their counterparts in the realm of feeling and were translated into artistic terms. In the nineteenth century the paths of science and the arts diverged; the connection between methods of thinking and methods of feeling was broken. The mutual isolation of these two kinds of enterprise, far from being a consequence of their different natures, is a phenomenon peculiar to the nineteenth century and responsible for much about its culture that is otherwise incomprehensible.

The historical posturing of nineteenth-century architecture is simply a special case of this separation, manifested in this field in the schism between the architect and the engineer. The architects of Gothic times did not merely employ the new engineering knowledge; they saw in it possibilities for expressing the aims, emotions, and outlook peculiar to their age. Similarly, the progress of mathematics brought something more into baroque architecture than new instruments of calculation. In both cases new inventions were, so to speak, humanized; emotional and intellectual advances paralleled each other. The situation with regard to those nineteenth-century buildings which were expressly meant to symbolize the spirit of the century is exactly the opposite. Structural iron, for example, was simply a new tool enabling one to erect pseudo-monumental exteriors in the old modes. The new tool, of course, by its very employment reduced these "revived" forms to the status of false fronts.

But as long as scientific and technological advances were used in architecture without being absorbed by it, the engineer remained subordinate to and detached from the architect. The architect, on the other hand, was left isolated from the most important movements going on in the world about him. Until he succeeded in coming to terms with the changed environment, until he recognized the architectonic possibilities in modern constructional methods, no new tradition relevant to the age could develop. It was out of those technical innovations which appear only behind the scenes in nineteenth-century architecture that the architecture of the future had to grow. Construction was, as it were, the subconsciousness of architecture; there lay dormant in it impulses that only much later found explicit theoretical statement.

Hence the interest these apparently trivial developments, these timid introductions of new materials and new methods, have for the historian. Tendencies still living and active in our day, the constituent facts of contemporary architecture, trace back to just such unpretentious beginnings. The advent of the structural engineer with speedier, industrialized form-giving components broke up the artistic bombast and shattered the privileged position of the architect and provided the basis for present-day developments. The nineteenth-century engineer unconsciously assumed the role of guardian of the new elements he was continually delivering to the architects. He was developing forms that were both anonymous and universal.

The Cast-Iron Column

The cast-iron column was the first structural material produced by the new industrial methods to be used in building. As early as 1780 — even before the introduction of steam power — such columns replaced wooden posts as roof supports in the first English cotton mills. The size of the new machines demanded large rooms with a minimum of obstructions.

The history of these mills has not yet been thoroughly investigated. One of the rare reports on such buildings — the source of the illustration we shall discuss next — confesses that "the buildings have been treated merely as structures, no attempt being made to probe into their fascinating history. The 'dates' of the various factories have been reduced to an average 'period' rather than a conclusive and accurate date of actual erection." [1] A typical late eighteenth-century factory at Bolton shows how the attic stories of existent buildings were converted to house the newly invented cotton-spinning machines (fig. 97). This factory had been erected with the kind of heavy wooden framework that had been in use since Gothic times. At first the machinery was installed only in the attic; the timber roof trusses — soon to be replaced by trusses of cast iron — left enough space down the center for the installation of the long spinning frames. Later on, the use of cast-iron pillars made it possible to install machinery on all the floors.

These masonry buildings (a type which reappeared in Massachusetts when New England began to be industrialized) had the wide windows of late baroque structures. Standing amidst unspoiled rural surroundings near the rivers from which they drew their power, they present an appearance quite different from factory districts of the steam age. A factory near Manchester, built in 1783, illustrates this stage in the development. This particular mill was among the first to have iron pillars in its interior. It is still in operation, and still uses auxiliary water power.

---

[1] *Official Record of the Annual Conference of the Textile Institute* (Bolton, 1927), pp. 41 ff.

97. Wooden attic of factory, Bolton, England, c. 1800. *The heavy wooden roof trusses left the whole center line of the attic clear for the long spinning machines.*

98. Attic story with cast-iron roof framework, c. 1835. *The cast-iron roof framework represents a later advance; its invention has been credited to J. B. Papworth in 1821. We mention Papworth later as one of the earliest designers of "garden cities" (about 1827).*

The attic of a cotton-spinning factory about 1835 (*fig.* **98**), with its cast-iron roof trusses, shows how room was made for the newly invented self-acting mule spinning frames. The necessity for rooms of very large dimensions is apparent. In this case the spinning frame had to be set up parallel with the long axis of the loft.

Combination with other materials; widespread use

Iron pillars were used in combination with stone, brick, and timber alike. Somewhat later, the cast-iron girder and the brick-arch floor were used in mill construction. But for more than a century the cast-iron column played a major role in building of every sort, in all parts of the world. It was used

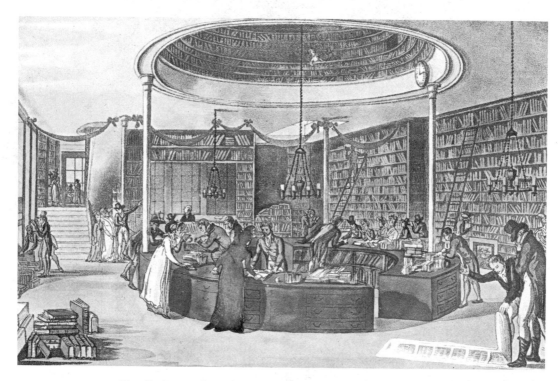

99. Early use of cast-iron columns, London bookshop, 1794. *Lackington's " Temple of the Muses," Finsbury Square: " The internal arrangement of the building is perfectly novel, . . . the capaciousness of which may be readily conceived from the circumstance of the Weymouth mail, with four horses, having actually been driven around it at . . . its first opening. This room . . . is supported by pillars of iron." (" Ackerman's Repository of Arts," April 1, 1809; courtesy of Mrs. Albert C. Koch, Cambridge, Mass.)*

for a countless variety of architectural purposes during the entire nineteenth century. In the Crystal Palace and in thoroughly workaday market halls, in libraries and in greenhouses — even in the first skyscrapers built in Chicago — the cast-iron pillar furnished the principal means of support. To some extent in England but much more often in America, the cast-iron column was used, during the forties, to form the façades of buildings and to erect structures from prefabricated parts.

As a new material which still had something of the fabulous about it, cast iron even found a place in the Royal Pavilion at Brighton. It was used liberally in this extraordinary edifice, sometimes for purposes of display. John Nash, the Royal Architect, was not one to hesitate in delegating to others the

Use in the Royal Pavilion, Brighton

100.   JOHN NASH. Royal Pavilion, Brighton, 1818–21. *Red drawing-room.*

work of designing, but, according to Summerson, he personally designed the "intricate carpentry and ironwork which supports the ceiling"[2] (*fig.* **100**). This was in 1818. So far as I know, it was the first time that cast-iron columns had been used in a formal interior. Nash leads these columns freely through the space of the drawing room. Twenty-five years later Henri Labrouste made a similar undisguised use of iron columns in the small reading room (*La Reserve*) of the Bibliothèque Sainte-Geneviève in Paris. When some contemporary

Undisguised use by Labrouste

[2] *John Nash*, p. 162.

architects — around 1925 — proposed doing the same thing, they met with great opposition.

The Royal Pavilion at Brighton was the center of great festivals; in it cast iron as a material for the architect found a setting very remote from labor or affairs. The enormous kitchen (*fig.* **101**) had in its center four slender cast-iron supporting columns, each fantastically elongated and bearing a palm-leaf

101. JOHN NASH. Royal Pavilion, Brighton. *The kitchen.*

Use in the oval garden of the Paris Exhibition of 1867

capital at its top. The unusual slenderness of cast-iron pillars and columns opened up the possibility of new and strange proportions in architecture. Almost fifty years later, in the oval garden in the middle of the main building of the Paris exhibition of 1867, just such exotically slender cast-iron columns were placed in direct association with the palm trees of the South (*fig.* **102**).

Miscellaneous new uses

We can easily find important witnesses to testify that cast iron soon came to be an approved material for everything from steam engines to churches. Thus Thomas Tredgold, one of the first scientists to interest himself in the possibilities of this material, writes in 1823 that "it is used for the principal supports of churches, theatres, manufacturies, warehouses, and for the main parts of engines." And Tredgold goes on to give some of the reasons for this popularity: "improvements in the processes of its manufacture had made it cheap even in comparison with timber, and . . . it gave a certain protection against fire such as wooden beams could not offer." Thus the reign of cast iron in the nineteenth century was founded upon its fire-resistant qualities, its cheapness, simplicity of manufacture, and resistance to heavy loads. These advantages were

102. Paris Exhibition, 1867. *Oval garden in the center of the main building. Cast-iron columns figure throughout the century, but their use reached its high-water mark around this period. Catalogues of Paris hardware manufacturers offered them in every imaginable shape for Haussmann's great works of transformation.*

enough to assure the domination of the cast-iron pillar until the eighties of the last century, when the steel frame was developed in Chicago.

But there was another reason for the use — and misuse — of cast iron: it is a material which can easily be given any desired shape. The catalogue of a French hardware manufacturer of about 1860 has hundreds of pages devoted to cast iron used for all sorts of purposes. It was even employed in quite abominable imitations of sculptures by the great masters. The

Protean character of cast iron: misuse in mass production

189

cast-iron pillars, columns, and balustrades for which Haussmann's rebuilding of Paris created a demand were available in
finished condition in every conceivable shape. Indeed, the
cast-iron column — used without precision or restraint —
became one of the symbols of the nineteenth century. As late
as 1889 Vierendeel, the great Belgian engineer, still had reason
to write, referring to the Paris exhibition, that "the enormous
danger of this sort of support lies in its revolting vulgarity."
The charm that lay in the proper use of the material was lost
in a hopelessly misdirected mass production.

103.   Aquatint of Telford's proposed cast-iron bridge over the Thames, London, 1801.

TOWARD THE STEEL FRAME

Telford's project
for London Bridge
(1801)

Two other early examples of the use of cast iron in construction must be mentioned. Both date from the very beginning
of the nineteenth century. The first, the Telford and Douglas
design for London Bridge, was made in 1801 but never executed (*fig.* **103**). This elegant and well-known design is for a
really colossal work in cast iron, a bridge with a rise of 65 feet
and a single span of 600 feet. Even five decades later Robert
Stephenson's Britannia bridge fell short of this span. Nevertheless the design for London Bridge could have been carried out
at the time it was made, since Telford, adopting the system
proposed by Thomas Paine in 1783, suggested building it like
a stone arch out of a number of small wedge-shaped sections.

190

The cotton mill of Philip and Lee, built at Salford, Manchester, in 1801, is the second example (*fig.* **104**). This mill surpasses all others of its time in the boldness of its design. It represents the first experiment in the use of iron pillars and beams for the whole interior framework of a building. The erection of this factory was an event of the first importance in the history of modern construction. This truly extraordinary feat for builders of that date — a feat which in time came to be almost forgotten — was accomplished by Boulton and Watt's Soho foundry. The inventor of the steam engine was then concentrating most of his attention upon a machine for making portrait statuary, and was meditating retirement from active business.

The original drawings for this mill, which have never before been published, are in the Boulton and Watt Collection of the Birmingham Reference Library. The plate shows the ground plan and the elevation of the Salford mill. The building is a large one, about 140 feet long and 42 feet wide; its height of seven stories is extraordinary for this early date. As the ground plan shows, there are two ranges of iron pillars set on each floor. For the first time, iron beams are used in combination with these iron columns. These beams, the first of the I-section type, extend across the building from wall to wall at regular distances. The Scottish engineer, William Fairbairn, praises this first employment of the I beam as an example of intuitive recognition of the most efficient shape in advance of the calculations that would prove it to be such. (A similar instance of the instinctively correct solution of an engineering problem has already been encountered in the iron roof of the Théâtre-Français of 1786. Its wrought-iron girders were adjusted to the moment of inertia, even though the theoretical basis for such an adjustment did not exist until much later.) The drawing also shows how the floors of the mill were built up from brick arches, brought to a level surface by a layer of rough concrete.

The second drawing gives a cross-section (*fig.* **105**) of the width of the building. It shows the special foundations provided for the iron columns of the ground floor, and the junctions between the cast-iron columns and beams of the first two floors.

Precision of detail

The third drawing shows the construction of the hollow cast-iron pillars, each of which had an outside diameter of nine inches. This extremely careful treatment reflects the experience acquired by Boulton and Watt in the making of steam-engines (*fig.* **106**). The details of the assembly of pillar and socket (on the right-hand side of the plan) show a precision that had been learned in machinery construction.

Fairbairn
on the
Salford mill

As Fairbairn remarked in 1854, this experiment at Salford was "the pioneer of that system of fireproof structure which now distinguishes the manufacturing districts of this country. For a quarter of a century this mill was a model for similar buildings. From 1801 until 1824 little or no variation took place in the form of beams." The reason for this was that time was

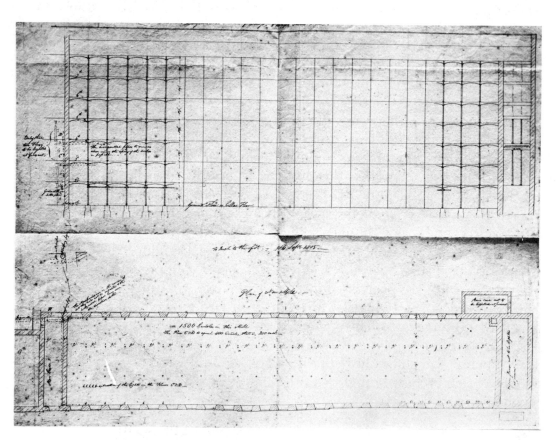

104. WATT and BOULTON. Working drawings for the first seven-story mill with cast-iron beams and columns, Salford, Manchester, 1801. *The first building ever designed or executed with a metal skeleton — cast-iron columns and beams — enclosed in the outer masonry walls like the works of a watch in its case.*

192

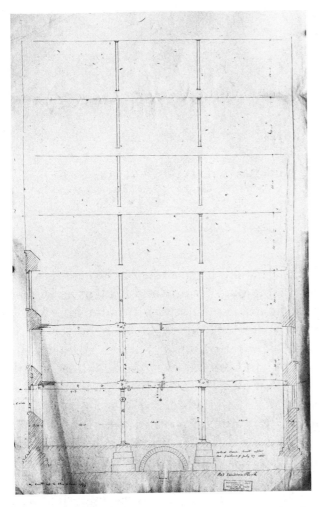

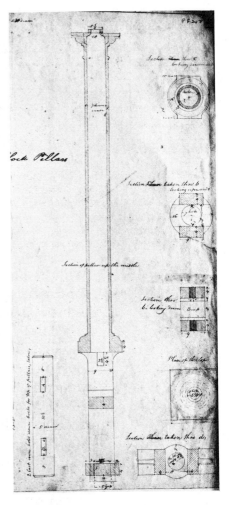

105. WATT and BOULTON. Working drawings for the first seven-story mill with cast-iron beams and columns.

106. WATT and BOULTON. Working drawings for the first seven-story mill with cast-iron beams and columns. *Sections of a cast-iron column.*

needed to enable experiment and calculation to overtake Watt's astonishingly farsighted structure. The type of building represented by this seven-story mill of 1801 with its cast-iron skeleton surrounded by outer walls of masonry became the standard for warehouses throughout the century and was adopted for some advanced public buildings as well. Watt's Salford experiment was the first step in the development of the steel frame which was finally to appear in Chicago during the eighties.

193

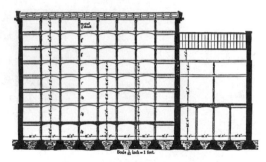

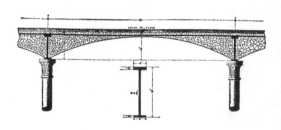

107. WILLIAM FAIRBAIRN. English refinery, c. 1845. *Cross section. Developments moved
very slowly during the first half of the century, with
no important changes in the methods used by Boulton and Watt. In this Fairbairn refinery there
are simply certain technical refinements.*

108. WILLIAM FAIRBAIRN. English refinery,
c. 1845. *Ceiling construction.*

Fairbairn im-
proves on Watt's
construction
in the forties

William Fairbairn himself laid a large share of the groundwork
for further advance. A builder of ships and bridges as well as
industrial structures, the experiments with tubular iron which
he completed in 1846 at his laboratory in Manchester made
possible the building of the Britannia Tubular Bridge, the
most famous of its time, and encouraged the building of still
larger spans later on. The decisive change in methods of industrial construction that is to be observed shortly before the
middle of the century owes much to other experiments conducted by this able engineer. Before this time, as he writes,
"we had little or no knowledge of the superior resisting powers
of wrought iron in the shape of beams: . . . our knowledge of
[its] properties may be considered as still very imperfect and
confined within exceedingly narrow compass." [1]

In his attempts to make his buildings fireproof Fairbairn was
led to employ a remarkable principle of construction. The
eight-story, flat-roofed refinery which he built during the middle forties introduces wrought-iron as well as cast-iron members (*fig.* 107). Wrought-iron I-section girders joined with iron
tie bars are here supported by cast-iron pillars. Instead of the
brick-arch floor, thin wrought-iron plates are used; running
from column to column, they are bent in the segmental form
of an arch and then filled to floor level with concrete (*fig.* 108).
The jump from such a building to the building of ferroconcrete

[1] William Fairbairn, *The Application of Cast and Wrought Iron to Building Purposes,*
p. 152.

194

is not very great; the time had not yet arrived, however, for this suggestion to be taken up.

The use of iron as a structural material was further increased by the invention of machinery for producing rolled iron and steel joists. The American railroad builder, Robert Stevens of Hoboken, went to England in 1830 to buy locomotives. During his visit he tried to make rolled-iron railroad tracks, finally succeeding in this endeavor, despite its many difficulties, in a South Wales rolling mill. Rolled-iron I beams did not come into use until much later, however. The architect Boileau wrote in 1871 that a combination of exceptional circumstances led to the introduction of rolled-iron beams in France. This was in 1845 at Paris; a strike of masons, the high price of timber, the fear of fire, and the demand for wider spans led a foundryman named Zorès to roll the first wrought-iron joist sections produced in France. They did not appear in England until still later.

Important preliminary work for later construction was carried out in the show windows of stores, where, as industrialization continued, ever-larger glassed surfaces were needed. The manuals of iron construction that were published from the fifties to the nineties are filled with instructions for supporting the brickwork of the upper stories on iron girders. These iron columns were the only structural elements of the building visible behind the wide display windows. In view of the fact that the set-back pillar is used in so many modern buildings, a continuous account of the evolution of this practice would be most interesting. It was from these store windows that we first learned how to use large glass areas in dwelling houses.

James Bogardus

The beginnings of the skeleton construction of the present day are met with as early as 1848 in the home of the skyscraper, the United States. The decisive step was the substitution of iron columns for the masonry of the outer walls as a means of support for the floors of a building. An early example of this type of construction is a five-story factory that was erected in New York in 1848. Its builder was the man who invented this

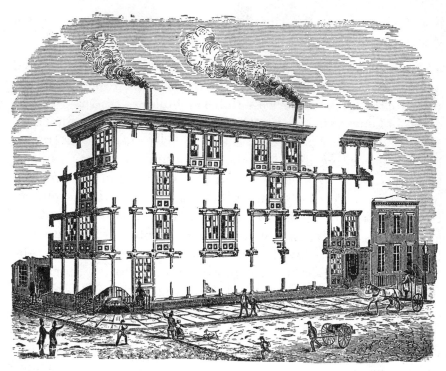

109. JAMES BOGARDUS. Design for a factory, 1856, showing the resistance of cast iron.

method of construction, James Bogardus (1800–74). American department stores, warehouses, and office buildings of the period between 1850 and 1880 were based on this system of building. Using prefabricated parts, Bogardus erected these buildings in every section of the United States. According to the *New York Herald* of April 14, 1874, he even delivered an immense building to Santa Catalina, near Havana, Cuba. Excellent examples of these buildings still exist in most American cities. Some particularly fine specimens (warehouses and office buildings) are to be found in the river-front area of St. Louis. One of them, located at 7911 North First Street, is particularly interesting for the uncompromising way in which large areas of glass are introduced into the front wall. All have value as monuments not merely for the step forward in construction which they represent but for the restrained and sober quality of their architecture. This type of building is undoubtedly one of the chief sources of a specifically American architectural style. But in spite of its contemporary importance and its very real merit the work of Bogardus is almost unknown today.

James Bogardus' best-known building was executed in Franklin Square on Pearl Street in New York for the famous publishing house of Harper and Brothers, in 1854 (*fig.* **110**). A single glance reveals the way in which Bogardus transformed the outer wall into a surface almost entirely of glass. The combination of wide expanses of glass with iron columns and arches in the Venetian Renaissance style is a perfect illustration of the spirit of his time. Bogardus himself gives a quite explicit statement of that spirit. In a booklet bearing the title, *Cast Iron Buildings: Their Construction and Advantages*, by James Bogardus, "Architect in Iron" (New York, 1858), he impersonally relates that "Mr. Bogardus first conceived the idea of emulating [the rich architectural designs of antiquity] in modern times, by the aid of cast-iron." This was in the year 1840. (This small but important publication has fallen into such obscurity that it is not mentioned in the sketch of Bogardus in the *Dictionary of American Biography*.)

Harper and Brothers Building (1854)

Like many of his eighteenth-century precursors, Bogardus believed cast iron to be a material capable of satisfying all the demands of both the engineer and the artist. He would have liked to apply his system to the building of dwelling houses as well as commercial structures (*fig.* **109**). He apparently felt

Projected cast-iron dwelling houses

110. JAMES BOGARDUS. Harper & Brothers' Building, New York, 1854.

111. JAMES BOGARDUS. Project for the New York World's Fair, 1853. *The amphi-theater was twelve hundred feet in diameter. The three-hundred-foot tower was intended to house a passenger elevator. In a circle of this size, straight girders — capable of resale afterwards — could be employed.*

that the exclusion of his methods from the residential field was due to mere chance. "Mr. Bogardus firmly believes," we read on page 14 of the booklet, "that had his necessities required him to construct a dwelling house rather than a factory [this method] would be now as popular for this purpose, as it is for stores." And he planned fantastic houses so designed that even "with the greater part of their ironwork removed . . . or destroyed by violence . . . they will yet remain firm."

Bogardus' unexe-cuted scheme for the New York World's Fair of 1853: original and farsighted

James Bogardus' most imaginative work was the project which he submitted for the first of the American world's fairs, held at New York in 1853 (*fig.* 111). He advanced as the chief recommendation for his scheme its great economy — the total cost would be only two hundred thousand dollars — and "expressed a conviction that the whole structure would be worth very considerably more when dissected, for ordinary purposes, than in its present form, owing to the economy in reproducing so large a number of identical parts from the same pattern." With future dissections in mind, Bogardus proposed building a great circular amphitheater twelve hundred feet in diameter.

198

A circle as huge as this could be assembled from straight girders, easily disposed of afterwards.[2]

Bogardus' plan called for an immense coliseum in cast iron. The exterior wall was sixty feet high, with arches and columns running in series about it to mark off the separate stories. A three-hundred-foot tower rose in the center of the enclosure "to serve the double purpose of a support for the hanging roof of sheet-iron suspended from it by rods in a catenary curve, and also as a grand observatory."[3] Such supporting rods of catenary curvature were standard practice in suspension bridges. Bogardus planned to install an elevator in this tower to carry spectators to its top.

The shapes that figure in this design were borrowings from traditional styles, but the structure as a whole was amazingly advanced, a daring prevision of future developments. This building would have been as original a document for the fifties as the French exhibitions from 1867 on were for their period.

The building actually erected for this fair had no historical importance, and the other plans entered in the competition were either undistinguished in quality or inappropriate to the site. This includes even the scheme submitted by Joseph Paxton.[4]

The career of James Bogardus was a most interesting one. He began his active life as a watchmaker and an inventor of great fertility. He had to his credit a new kind of pencil, the lead of which was always sharp, the engraving machine that produced the first English postage stamps, a deep-sea sounding machine, and a variety of other devices. He was, in fact, a classical exemplar of a type of inventor peculiar to the beginning of the nineteenth century, when men were trying to invent, in one great rush, everything that had *not* been invented in the past.

Bogardus as a type of inventor

---

[2] The main building at the Paris exhibition of 1867 had two hemicycles built on at its ends. When the building was torn down at the close of the exhibition, it was very difficult to find a market for the curved ironwork used in these hemicycles. The American foresaw this situation, but his project had been forgotten by that time, and remained so until the present day.

[3] B. Silliman, Jr., and C. R. Goodrich, *The World of Science, Art, and Industry* (New York, 1854), p. 4.

[4] *Ibid.*, pp. 1–3.

It was a time when it was common to find a single person conducting experiments in the most widely separated departments of industry. The contrast with the Renaissance is striking. Then the ideal figure was the "Universal man," the person who could unite in his own life the greatest number of different *kinds* of activity, the man who was at once artist, scientist, engineer. In the early nineteenth century the ideal was the man who could do all things in one field of industry, the watchmaker-ironworker-engineer type represented by Bogardus.[5]

The St. Louis River Front

Anonymous commercial buildings of the fifties

Commercial buildings with cast-iron fronts, and often with cast-iron skeletons as well, sprang up all over the United States between 1850 and 1880 — the so-called "cast-iron age." Many similar buildings can be found in England, especially in Liverpool. Whether Bogardus was the first to introduce this type of structure cannot be determined at present. The lack of documents makes even a general survey of these buildings impossible — and many of them were astonishingly fresh and straightforward in their design, showing a direct grasp of the functions that had to be fulfilled. They were often erected by the foundries which produced their parts, with no architect taking a share in the work. The owners of these foundries, unlike James Bogardus, had no Italian travels behind them and no desire to inaugurate a Renaissance revival in cast iron.

St. Louis during the fifties

From this anonymous development we select a complete district comprising about five hundred buildings — the central river front of St. Louis. For more than a century after its founding in 1764 as a headquarters for the fur trade, St. Louis was the leading trading center for the entire trans-Mississippi West. Its most prosperous decade came in the 1850's: steamboat traffic was at its height; the gold rushes to California and Colorado were under way; and new lands in the Missouri Valley had just been opened. At this time St. Louis is believed to have been the third steam port of the country, and by 1870 it

Decline after the Civil War

was the fourth largest city in the United States. The river front was the city's old business area, and most of it was built

---

[5] James Watt and the Brummels are other instances of this same type.

200

up during this flourishing period.[6]   Building began after the great fire of 1849 (the year of the California gold rush, for which St. Louis was one of the crossroads) and continued until the outbreak of the Civil War.   During the post-war years St. Louis steadily fell off in importance, while Chicago went on to take its place as the great mid-western market and railroad junction.   Finally, "with the entry of the eastern railroads over Ead's Bridge in 1874 and the decline of the steamboat, the commercial center of the city shifted and left the old river front in decline." [7]

The half-deserted river front survived as a witness to one of the most exciting periods in the development of America. Some of its commercial buildings — fur and china warehouses, Pony Express offices, ordinary business blocks — exhibited an architecture far in advance of the ordinary standards at the time of their erection.[8]

[6] I owe these data to Mr. Charles E. Peterson, Senior Landscape Architect in the National Park Service.

[7] *The Old St. Louis Riverfront, An Exhibition of Architectural Studies in the Historic Area of the Jefferson National Expansion Memorial* (St. Louis Public Library, 1938), p. 17.

[8] The importance of preserving nineteenth-century documents leads us to mention the history of the St. Louis river front.

Forty blocks of the St. Louis river front were taken over by the United States government as the site for a Jefferson National Expansion Memorial which will extend along the bank of the Mississippi.   The first step in the work was the razing of this historic quarter.   In connection with this, research was made into the dates of erection of these buildings and they were systematically photographed — unusual happenings at this date.

The National Park Service decided to preserve the fronts of some of the most important of these buildings.   The proposal was made to set up these façades in the courtyard of a new building.   However, the entire section was completely destroyed.

I visited St. Louis in August 1939 on the kind invitation of Mr. Peterson and inspected the district just before the pickaxes went to work on it.   It seemed to me that the building at 523–529 North First Street at the extreme northern end of the site, could be preserved intact.   (Cf. *St. Louis Post-Dispatch, St. Louis Star-Times, St. Louis Daily Globe-Democrat,* Aug. 10, 1939.)   The best examples from elsewhere in the section could be moved into this block.   All of them could be fitted out as they were when the river front was at its peak — complete with Pony Express office, stock in the warehouses, and the typical stuffed animals under glass domes that stood in the windows of the old fur-trading establishments.

Some one of these buildings could even be used as a museum of the history of the Mississippi region.   It would be possible to display its relations with the past and the present, and with the whole United States — north and south, east and west.   George Henri Rivière of the Musée du Trocadéro produced a similar re-creation of a Burgundian village for the Paris exhibition of 1937.   It told the story of a community in a manner which was full of life.   Is it actually so very difficult to realize that commercial buildings of the nineteenth-century are as important witnesses to a period as any seventeenth-century château?

These commercial buildings are of various architectural types, but even when they adapt motifs of stone architecture to cast iron they are not without a certain French elegance, as in the building at 523–529 North First Street (*c.* 1870–71, *fig.* **112**), at the very end of the Memorial area. Another fine specimen is the five-story brick warehouse at 7–9–11 North First Street. Its upper stories are bound together into two pairs by slim columns. Its flat surfaces are reminiscent of the shapes of the simplified Romanesque style which later became so celebrated at the hands of Henry Hobson Richardson. Beyond this there are such simple constructions as the building at 109–111 North First Street, which we shall later find occasion to compare with one of the first modern dwellings in Europe, the Horta house in the Rue de Turin of 1893 (*fig.* **177**). These structures carry the simplification of the front so far that the iron columns and lintels become scarcely more than the crosspieces in a great casement window spread across the whole façade. For this treatment, and for its excellent proportions as well, the Gantt Building (1877) at 219–221 Chestnut Street (*fig.* **113**) deserves to be known as one of the finest in the whole period. In vain I

202

tried to convince the authorities that the best buildings in this section were forerunners of the Chicago skyscrapers. But the indifference of the Americans to their own architectural heritage resulted in the complete destruction of the entire section, which, for nearly twenty years, was used as a parking lot for trucks until work started in 1964 on Eero Saarinen's tall, parabolic Jefferson Memorial arch.

Early Skeleton Buildings

First building
of skeleton
construction:
France, 1871

The first building of true skeleton type was the chocolate works constructed in 1871–72 by Jules Saulnier at Noisiel-sur-Marne, near Paris (*fig.* 114). The factory rests on four piers set into the bed of the Marne, whose current supplied the power for its machinery. The building itself is erected upon four hollow iron girders, each square in section. The building whose base these girders constitute is the first to employ the principles of skeleton construction, the first, that is, in which an iron skeleton is made to carry the whole weight. This skeleton can be seen on the surfaces of the walls; the latter, made of hollow brick, function merely as filling. The diagonal iron stiffeners show clearly that Saulnier derived a part of his inspiration from methods used in wood construction.

Plane surfaces and
the new structural
means coincide

All contemporary buildings intended to have any formal or stately character had their walls overloaded with decoration. The walls of this chocolate works are plane surfaces. As Saulnier himself explains, the construction was responsible for this: "The system of construction used for the façades produced a surface entirely plane from top to bottom, with no projections either horizontal or vertical."[9] European taste in the early seventies nevertheless required some concessions on Saulnier's part. Although he preserved the flat surfaces that followed from the logic of his method, the brickwork defining them embodies a pattern in varicolored tiles.

We can see in this building how the flat and unornamented surfaces of present-day architecture appeared simultaneously with the new structural means (*fig.* 115). And it is not the case

[9] *Encyclopédie d'architecture*, 1877, p. 92.

204

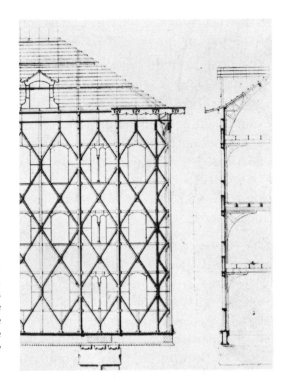

114. JULES SAULNIER. Menier Chocolate Works, Noisiel-sur-Marne, 1871–72. *Iron skeleton. So far as we know, the first skeleton building in the modern sense of the word, with the outer walls reduced to functioning simply as curtains.*

115. JULES SAULNIER. Menier Chocolate Works, Noisiel-sur-Marne, 1871–72. *This factory is built over the river Marne, on four great iron floor girders supported by stone piers set into the river bed.*

that a desire to build cheaply was responsible for the simplicity of the factory at Noisiel. Saulnier's type of construction was considerably more expensive than any other.

No influence on the development of the American skyscraper

The plans of this chocolate mill were published several times in great detail by the best-known French reviews — all of them available in American libraries. It is very curious, accordingly, that Saulnier's work should have remained completely unknown in the United States, as it seems to have done. One would have expected this first example of skeleton construction to have played a considerable part in the development of the skyscraper.

L. S. Buffington as the inventor of the skyscraper

The stages leading up to the American skyscraper are not known with any exactitude. As E. M. Upjohn remarks, "At least three cities — New York, Chicago, and Minneapolis — have sought the honor of being the birthplace of the skyscraper, and several architects have laid claim to distinction as its inventor."[10] The claims of the Minneapolis architect, Leroy S. Buffington, have been advanced more often than any others. They were certainly urged quite strongly by Buffington himself, who claims to have invented the skyscraper in 1880, deriving his inspiration from Viollet-le-Duc's *Lectures on Architecture*, which appeared in translation at about that time. The passage that aroused his interest occurs in volume II of the *Lectures*, on pages 1–2, where Viollet-le-Duc remarks that "a practical architect might not unnaturally conceive the idea of erecting a vast edifice whose frame should be entirely of iron, . . . preserving [that frame] by means of a casing of stone." The possibilities of a building with a "frame of iron . . . clothed with masonry" having been suggested to him, Buffington — so he relates — looked through all the material available in public libraries for an account of such a structure, but without finding any. That being the case, he was quite justified in supposing the system of skeleton construction which he finally developed to be entirely original.[11]

---

[10] E. M. Upjohn, "Buffington and the Skyscraper," *Art Bulletin*, XVII (March 1935), 48–70.

[11] The late William B. Mundie's opinion on Buffington's claim may be of interest. Mr. Mundie was a younger partner of William Le Baron Jenney. I am indebted to Mr. E. C. Jensen of the architectural firm of Mundie, Jensen, Bourke & Havens for the opportunity of quoting these excerpts from one of Mundie's unpublished papers:

116. WILLIAM LE BARON JENNEY. Home Insurance Company, Chicago, 1883–85. *The first skyscraper actually erected upon modern principles of construction. Ten stories high and fireproof, it permitted the maximum amount of light in every office.*

Nevertheless, although Saulnier's methods differ in several respects from those which Buffington proposed, the French constructor had anticipated him in one essential point: he had erected, almost a decade earlier, a building whose outer walls were supported *exclusively* by wrought-iron girders. The mill at Noisiel was, essentially, an iron frame clothed in masonry.

"I feel at a loss just how to approach this claim of Mr. Buffington's for himself as inventor, and the City of Minneapolis as the birthplace of skeleton construction. From my viewpoint it should be ignored, but it has been given such widespread publicity and the Patent Office did issue letters patent calling it an 'invention,' under the name of 'Iron Building Construction,' Patent No. 383,170. Inventor L. S. Buffington. Date May 22, 1888. That cannot be ignored, but it can be controverted."

After some details of the legal controversies between Jenney and Buffington, Mr. Mundie goes on to observe, "All he patented was the use of said construction (which was then well-known) in connection with his laminated steel plate column, composed of plates of steel riveted together side by side, and breaking joints, thus forming a solid steel column from bottom to top. This column being solid was so extravagant that no one ever had a desire to use it. Parties who called to interview Mr. Jenney about the patent, who afterwards proved to be Buffington's attorneys, were told by him that if they could find anyone using that extravagant column, they certainly could be prosecuted for using it, but no architect or engineer of any scientific knowledge would be guilty of using it; in skeleton construction it was worthless."

William Le Baron
Jenney's Home
Insurance Building
(1883)

It is well known that the first skyscraper actually built (and not merely planned) along modern principles of construction was the ten-story building of the Home Insurance Company (*fig.* **116**) of Chicago (1883–85). The commission for its design was given to William Le Baron Jenney in 1883. The Home Insurance Company demanded a new type of office building which would be fireproof and offer the maximum amount of light for every room.[12]

To summarize: a period of slightly more than eight decades lies between James Watt's seven-story cotton factory of 1801 with its iron columns and iron beams and the first iron-framed skyscraper. It is a curious fact that a similar eighty-year interval between the discovery of an important new principle and its assimilation into everyday life is to be encountered in other fields. For example, just this length of time intervened between Volta's discovery of galvanic electricity in 1800 and the first transmission of electric power in the eighties.

Elevators

The first elevators

At the time when James Bogardus was proclaiming that his new cast-iron buildings could "be raised to a height vastly greater than by any other known means . . . and the greater their height, the firmer they would be," [13] the first mechanical elevators were being invented in Boston and New York. Like nearly all inventions of this period, elevators were first intended to serve industrial purposes only.

James Bogardus proposed to install "a mechanism for hoisting observers to the top by steam power," [14] in the three-hundred-foot central tower of his projected building for the New York World's Fair of 1853. Though the very word had

---

[12] Its construction is noteworthy for the fact that it includes not only cast-iron columns but also a few of the first Bessemer steel girders ever used in a building. This was thirty years after Bessemer had made public the process of making steel which he had invented. Other branches of industry had adopted it almost at once; thus it came very soon to be used in the manufacture of railroad tracks and the armor plate for battleships. Further details of this celebrated building can be found in any history of the skyscraper.

[13] James Bogardus, *Cast Iron Buildings.*

[14] Silliman and Goodrich, *The World of Science, Art, and Industry*, p. 4.

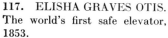

117. ELISHA GRAVES OTIS. The world's first safe elevator, 1853.

118. ELISHA GRAVES OTIS. Passenger elevator at the time of the Civil War.

not yet come into use, Bogardus here proposed what would have been the first passenger elevator in the world.

The first completely satisfactory elevator was the work of Elisha Graves Otis of New York (*fig.* **117**). The world's first safe elevator was produced when he attached a safety device to the ordinary hoisting platform. This elevator received its initial showing and demonstration at the Crystal Palace Exposition in New York in 1853. In each demonstration Mr. Otis stepped onto the platform, which was then hoisted above the ground. As the hoisting rope was cut, the elevator came to a stop, whereupon Mr. Otis made the historical remark: "All safe, gentlemen!" A recent check of the archives of the Otis Company revealed that there are no surviving designs of this first elevator. We know only its approximate type from sketches of machines of a slightly later period.

119. Eiffel Tower, elevator to the first platform, 1889.

First passenger elevator: New York, 1857

What is considered to have been the first passenger elevator was installed by Otis in a department store on the corner of Broadway and Broome Street, New York, in 1857.[15] The next passenger elevator was installed in the old Fifth Avenue Hotel in 1859. Its inventor was a Mr. Tufts of Boston, and the device bore the name of "Vertical Screw Railway." Contemporary pictures of these "railways" are also lacking; sketches from about the period of the Civil War survive, however, to give an idea of the principles employed in their design (*fig.* **118**).

First European elevator: Paris Exposition of 1867

The first European elevator, so far as we know now, was not built until 1867, when one was installed at the great Paris exhibition of that year. A hydraulic elevator exhibiting all the ungainliness of some primordial monster, it transported visitors from the grandiose Galerie des Machines to the corrugated iron roof of that immense hall. From these roof terraces the visitors saw spread out below them not only the great city of Paris but a whole new world of glass and iron.

---

[15] I am indebted to Mr. G. C. Bebb, advertising manager of the Otis Elevator Company, for this date, which corrects a common error.

210

It is pleasant to relate that the first elevator for a structure of modern skyscraper proportions was built to serve no commercial or narrowly practical purposes. It was destined for a structure which sprang out of the vision rather than the daily needs of man — the Eiffel Tower. The Eiffel Tower, indeed, falls outside the usual connotations of the word "building": it might better be regarded as at once the manifesto and the monument of that Iron Age which embraced the second half of the nineteenth century. An unusual traffic problem was solved by constructing a whole system of elevators. Four large, double-decked elevators ran from the ground to the first platform (*fig.* **119**), a height equal to that of Notre Dame; two more ran from the terrace to the second platform, a height equal to that of the dome of St. Peter's; the rest of the ascent was made in two stages by means of a pair of hydraulic elevators operating on a sort of shuttle system. The total ascent to a height of a thousand feet took only seven minutes, and 2,350 passengers could be transported to the summit every hour.[16] This was achieved in 1889.

THE SCHISM BETWEEN ARCHITECTURE AND TECHNOLOGY

We have already spoken in somewhat general terms of the gap that opened in the course of the nineteenth century between science and its techniques on the one hand and the arts on the other, and hence between architecture and construction. The previous chapter should lend support to the contention we made then that the seeds of the architecture of our day were to be found in technical developments little regarded at the time of their appearance. The present chapter will handle this topic in more detail. We shall deal with the question of the time at which this schism became evident, and the manner in which recognition of its existence led to the demand for a new architecture. Contemporary utterances will enable us to show that from this situation developed many questions the answers

---

[16] These details are to be found in a contemporary pamphlet of great interest: Gaston Tissandier, *La Tour Eiffel de 300 m.* (Paris, 1889), p. 68.

to which are still being sought today. Finally, in separating the constituent facts from the episodic trends of the nineteenth century, we shall be able to fill in many of the gaps in the history of our own development, gaps of whose existence we have often been unconscious.

Effect of the revival of the École des Beaux-Arts (1806)

In the year 1806 Napoleon founded the École des Beaux-Arts, thereby reviving an institution of the *ancien régime*. The program of the École, covering the whole field of the plastic arts, maintained that unity of architecture with the other arts which had been both complete and spontaneous during the baroque period. Unfortunately, the school was administered in such a way that bad results soon followed. It fostered a constantly increasing isolation of the arts from the conditions of ordinary life. From the beginning of the century two opposed attitudes, each extreme and each represented by an official institute, face each other in France; the École des Beaux-Arts is confronted by the École Polytechnique.

École Polytechnique (1794), the gathering point for new forces

The École Polytechnique had been founded during the French Revolution, in 1794 — three years after the *Proclamation de la liberté du travail*, the document which abolished the legal hindrances to the growth of modern industry in France. The École Polytechnique was an *école spéciale*; it offered a uniform scientific preparation for the higher technical schools — *l'école des ponts et chaussées, l'école des mines, l'école de l'artillerie*, etc. The great mathematicians, physicists, and chemists of France acted as instructors, men like Monge, Lagrange, Berthollet, Chaptal. The École Polytechnique had the important function of combining theoretical and practical science. That it directly influenced industry is beyond question. In the first decades of the century it became a center for those interested in political economy and sociology and above all for the Saint-Simonists, whose membership included the creators of the large-scale industries and the railroad systems built up in France around the 1850's.

Discussions

The separate existence of an École des Beaux-Arts and an École Polytechnique in itself points to the schism between architecture and construction. A survey of the architectural journals of the nineteenth century will reveal that the two questions most debated at the time grew out of the dissension between these schools. These questions can be stated as follows:

1. Along what lines should the training of an architect proceed?
2. What is the relation of the engineer to the architect? What special functions are proper to each? Are they one and the same?

All the other controversies and discussions regarding architectural form are of secondary importance.

École Polytechnique: the Connection between Science and Life

The immense influence of the École Polytechnique in the first three decades of the nineteenth century can be attributed to the fact that it quite consciously set itself an enormous task; in it, for the first time, the attempt was made to establish a connection between science and life, to bring out the practical applications to industry of discoveries in the mathematical and physical sciences. Jean-Antoine Chaptal, the great chemist and industrialist who was minister of the interior under Napoleon I, laid down this aim for the École at the beginning of the nineteenth century. He insisted that science must climb down from its pedestal and lend a hand in the work of creating a new world.

The architect and the constructor

It was Rondelet — the theorist whose work on the Panthéon in Paris prevented its collapse — who first insisted that scientific techniques had an important role to play in architecture. His *Discours pour l'ouverture du cours de construction à l'école spéciale d'architecture* (1816) argued that constructional methods had to be allowed much more influence upon the character of a building design than had hitherto been given them. From this time on, the engineer slowly encroaches more and more upon the province of the architect. All unconsciously, the constructor during the nineteenth century played the role of scout for the architect. The new expedients which he kept pressing upon the architect continually forced the latter to

Unconscious influence of construction

venture upon unexplored paths. He broke down the architect's ritualistic and artificial formalism, hammered brusquely upon the door of his ivory tower. And it remains one of the chief functions of construction to furnish architecture with the stimulus and incentive for new growth.

The Demand for a New Architecture

Demand for a new architecture in contemporary utterances

With the quickening of the advance of industry in the middle of the nineteenth century there becomes evident a feeling on the part of the architect that his privileged position is menaced and the traditions of his art outmoded. That anxiety grew in intensity with the progress of industrialization. But contemporary statements of this feeling are of more interest than any abstract deductions we might make concerning it. Let us first quote some evidence of the hopes for a new architecture that the appearance of the new potentialities aroused.

1849: "A new architecture which will take us out of the sterility of the past and the servility of copying is what everybody demands, and what the public waits for." [1]

1849: "The new architecture is architecture in iron. Architectural revolutions always follow social revolutions. In the interim periods few changes are to be seen, no matter how long these periods may be. Men insist upon remolding the old forms until a radical upset wipes the slate clean of banal schools and ideas.

"There are great periods in architecture just as there are great geological periods: a new race of plants or animals only appears after the disappearance of the old. In architecture it is the same: The race of old authorities in architecture had to be superseded — just as the mastodons were superseded — in order to make room for new kinds of artists who will not preserve the traditional prejudices of the old schools.

"But, you may say, where shall we find masters clever enough? We should not tell you to seek these people among old masons whose hands have been so long occupied with stone and mortar that it is safe to presume that their brains also move in an

---

[1] César Daly, *Revue générale de l'architecture*, 1849, p. 26.

214

equally restricted orbit. To create what is new, you must have young people." [2]

1850: "Mankind will produce a completely new architecture out of its period exactly at the moment when the new methods created by recently born industry are made use of. The application of cast iron allows and enforces the use of many new forms, as can be seen in railway stations, suspension bridges, and the arches of conservatories." [3]

1867: Toward the end of the Second Empire, César Daly once more laments the continued influence of old traditions: "One perceives the eclectic atmosphere enveloping the world; all organs of respiration absorb it and, mixed with our blood, it acts on heart and brain." [4]

1889: Two decades later the situation had scarcely improved. Every time new and unusual constructions appeared to stimulate the imagination by their boldness, the old cries went up again. Even the novelist Octave Mirbeau — not in general given to urge on the march into the future — realized after seeing the Eiffel Tower and the Galerie des Machines that "while art cultivates *l'intimisme* or attaches itself to the old formulas with its gaze still fixed on the past, industry moves forward and explores the unknown. It is not in the studios of the painters and sculptors that the revolution so long awaited is preparing — it is in the factories!" [5]

The Interrelations of Architecture and Engineering

There grew up before the eyes of the world in the years after 1850 the iron constructions of the great exhibitions. In them the methods of engineering entered the field of architecture; with that entrance the question of the relation between archi-

---

[2] Jobard, "L'Architecture de l'avenir," *Revue générale d'architecture*, 1849, p. 27.

Jobard was an engineer, the first director of the Musée de l'Industrie at Brussels, and one of those scientists most interested in the new processes and materials developed in industry. Jobard did not confine himself simply to invoking the appearance of a new architecture of iron and glass. For example, he suggested a type of structure with double walls filled with glass panes which would permit air-conditioning of the interior. The space between the panes was to be filled with hot air in the winter, cold air in the summer.

[3] The romantic poet Théophile Gautier, in the newspaper *La Presse*.

[4] *Revue générale d'architecture*, 1867, p. 6.

[5] Octave Mirbeau in *Figaro*, 1889; cf. also *Encyclopédie d'architecture*, 1889/90, p. 92.

tect and engineer was raised and became ever more vexing and urgent. For more than sixty years that question was agitated by various theorists.

1852: "Far be it from me to pretend that the style pointed out by our mechanics is what is sometimes miscalled an economical, a cheap style. No! It is the dearest of all the styles! It costs the thought of men, much, very much thought, untiring investigation, ceaseless experiment. Its simplicity is that of justness; I had almost said, of justice.

". . . the mechanics of the United States have already outstripped the artists, and have, by their bold and unflinching adaptation, entered the true track and hold up the light for all who operate for American wants, be they what they will.

"By beauty I mean the promise of function.

"By action I mean the presence of function.

"By character I mean the record of function." [6]

1867: "Is it the fate of architecture to give way to the art of engineering? Will the architect be eclipsed by the engineer?" [7]

1877: In this year the question entered the Académie, when a prize was offered for the best paper discussing "the union or the separation of engineer and architect." Davioud, one of the architects of the Trocadéro, won the prize with this answer: "The accord will never become real, complete, and fruitful until the day that the engineer, the artist, and the scientist are fused together in the same person. We have for a long time lived under the foolish persuasion that art is a kind of activity distinct from all other forms of human intelligence, having its sole source and origin in the personality of the artist himself, and in his capricious fancy." [8]

1889: "A long time ago the influence of the architect declined, and the engineer, *l'homme moderne par excellence*, is beginning to replace him. . . . It will not be [arbitrarily chosen] shapes

---

[6] Horatio Greenough, the American sculptor, in *The Travels, Observations, and Experiences of a Yankee Stonecutter*; cited by Nancy Wynne and Beaumont Newhall, "Horatio Greenough: Herald of Functionalism," *Magazine of Art*, XXXII (January 1939), 15.

[7] César Daly, *Revue générale d'architecture*, 1867, p. 6.

[8] *Encyclopédie d'architecture*, 1878, p. 67.

216

which will form the basis of the new architecture: in urban planning, in the real application of modern construction, the taking into account of the new situations which must be reckoned with will lead us to the shapes so long sought in vain. But, you will say, what you propose are the methods of engineering today. I do not deny it, for these are correct." [9]

1899: Thirty years after César Daly's anxiety with regard to the future of architecture one of the founders of the *art nouveau* sees quite clearly that "there is a class of men from whom the title of artist can no longer be withheld. These artists, the creators of new architecture, are the engineers.

"The extraordinary beauty innate in the work of engineers has its basis in their unconsciousness of its artistic possibilities — much as the creators of the beauty of the cathedrals were unaware of the magnificence of their achievements." [10]

Van de Velde already recognized that the engineer promised the regeneration of architecture and not its destruction. It is still the case — as much so as when van de Velde wrote — that the latest works of the engineers embody possibilities of aesthetic experience not as yet exploited, which have still to find their place in architectonic expression. There are, for example, those fantastic, single-columned shelters built in France to protect freight while it is being transshipped, those curving Swiss bridges which are formed out of thin slabs of ferroconcrete, and various other strikingly original constructions elsewhere, which embody unexplored potentialities for architecture.

1924: "The century of the machine awakened the architect. New tasks and new possibilities produced him. He is at work now everywhere." [11]

Such an opinion — one that is shared by the whole generation of architects to which Le Corbusier belongs — marks the solution of the break between the architect and the engineer.

[9] Anatole de Baudot, at the first International Congress of Architects in Paris, 1889.
[10] Henri van de Velde, "Die Rolle der Ingenieure in der modernen Architektur," in *Die Renaissance im modernen Kunstgewerbe* (Berlin, 1901).
[11] Le Corbusier in *L'Esprit nouveau* (Paris, 1924), no. 25.

On the whole it is true that contemporary architects have succeeded at the end of a century of struggle in drawing abreast of construction. New tasks await architecture today. It must now meet needs other than the strictly rational, other than those which are pragmatically determined. A living architecture must also succeed in satisfying those subrational, emotional demands which are deeply rooted in our age.

HENRI LABROUSTE, ARCHITECT–CONSTRUCTOR, 1801–1875

Labrouste born with the new century

Until now we have had to dissect practically anonymous constructions to find the first signs of the new developments which life, almost unconsciously, was bringing about. Toward the middle of the nineteenth century, we encounter for the first time in this period a man who unites the abilities of both the engineer and the architect: the architect-constructor Henri Labrouste. Henri Labrouste was born in Paris in 1801. In the same year Telford offered his project for London Bridge, a plan calling for a colossal structure in cast iron. It was also in 1801 that James Watt's Soho foundry built the first cotton mill to embody cast-iron beams and pillars in its interior construction.

Wins *grand prix de Rome;* sees stay in Italy as an estrangement from life

Labrouste was educated at the Académie des Beaux-Arts and was one of its outstanding pupils. When he was twenty-three, he was awarded the *grand prix de Rome*, which made it possible for him to spend five years at the Villa Medici in Rome. During those five years he came to see antique Rome as something more than a monument or an arsenal of beautiful forms on which a student might draw. He took toward it very nearly the attitude of an onlooker of today; what astonished him was the skill in construction everywhere visible in these works. When, as *pensionnaire de l'Académie* in Rome, he was studying Roman aqueducts and examining the temples at Paestum, he sought always to grasp the spirit behind each construction, *l'organisme de chaque construction.*[1]

---

[1] Labrouste did not make the usual picturesque reproductions of ancient monuments. He approached them with the sharp eyes of an engineer or an archaeologist. His draw-

For all that, he ended by regarding his stay in Italy — meant as the highest reward to talent — as a systematic estrangement from life. He preferred studies dealing with problems arising out of his own time. Significantly enough, the last project which he sent to the Academy from Rome was a design for a bridge, one appropriate to stand on the frontiers of two friendly countries.

Labrouste, belonging to that generation which arrived at its maturity around 1830 and seemed to include among its members the most vigorous characters in the century, shared its feeling that social, moral, and intellectual life all alike demanded renewal. In the summer of 1830, when he returned to Paris, he found the routine of the Academy unchanged. He wrote to his brother Theodore on July 12, 1830: "What should I say to you about the École? Its programs of courses are always uninteresting and badly organized; its pupils lack enthusiasm. And even the master of an *atelier* would exhaust himself through futile efforts on programs like these. . . . Architecture must not be circumscribed within studies like those actually pursued at the École des Beaux-Arts. Reforms are called for — what master will have the courage to make the pressing cause of our art his own?" [2]

During this same summer he opened his own *atelier*, a school of design opposed to the principles of the Academy, in which he instructed the progressive youth of France. Once again a letter to his brother (written in November 1830) will give some insight into his methods of instruction:

"I am working prodigiously and — what is harder — I am making my pupils work.

"I have drawn up several schedules of study to drill the beginners in something useful: I want them to learn to compose with very simple means. It is necessary for them from the

---

ings of the temples at Paestum were the source of much controversy at the French Academy. He was among the first to discover traces of the colors which had originally overlaid the buildings and attempted reconstructions of them. During the late fifties the questions raised by the use of polychromy in ancient art occupied many architects in various countries — Schinkel, Hittorf, Gottfried Semper, and others.

[2] *Souvenirs d'Henri Labrouste, Notes recueillies et classées par ses enfants* (Paris, 1928; privately printed), p. 24.

start to see the direction of their work so that they may arrange its parts according to the importance which they can reasonably be given. Then I explain to them that solidity depends more on the way materials are put together than upon their mass, and — as soon as they know the first principles of construction — I tell them that they must derive from the construction itself an ornamentation which is reasoned and expressive.

"I often repeat to them that the arts have the power of making everything beautiful, but I insist that they understand that in architecture form must always be appropriate to the function for which it is intended.

"Finally, I am happy to find myself in the midst of these young comrades, who are attentive, full of good-will, and resolved to continue along the path which we are following together." [3]

First large commission when he had passed forty

The Academy waged a bitter war against the so-called "rationalistic school" which Labrouste headed. This official opposition had its consequences. On the occasions when Labrouste set foot on a building plot it was to inspect the work of other architects. The winner of the *grand prix de Rome* had to wait more than twelve years for a chance to show his talents in an executed work of importance. It was not until he was past forty that Labrouste was commissioned to build the Bibliothèque Sainte-Geneviève in Paris (1843–50).

Bibliothèque Sainte-Geneviève, Paris

In the library of Sainte-Geneviève he made the first attempt to use cast- and wrought-iron construction in an important public building from the foundations to the roof. Sainte-Geneviève was, in addition, the first library building in France designed to be a complete and independent unit. As in the English mills and warehouses, the iron construction is enclosed in the stonework of the exterior like the works of a watch in its case. Thick masonry outer walls still remain, but all structural members — columns, beams, and roofing — are of iron (*figs.* **120, 121**).

Iron skeleton in the interior

The framework of the long, double-naved reading room forms, with that of the roof, a single structure. Labrouste achieved an

---

[3] *Ibid.*

220

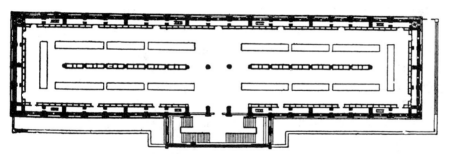

120. HENRI LABROUSTE. Library of Sainte-Geneviève, Paris, 1843–50. *Section through the reading room and the wrought-iron framework of the roof.*

121. HENRI LABROUSTE. Library of Sainte-Geneviève, Paris, 1843–50. *Plan.*

astonishing thinness in the barrel vaults by extending an iron network along them; this network at the same time afforded a base for the plaster covering of the vault. This construction recalls the eggshell-like reinforced concrete vaults in the dock buildings at Casablanca which the French architect Perret constructed in 1916. But Labrouste's chief accomplishment in this library rests in the manner in which the iron construction is balanced in itself, so that it puts no stress on the walls. The achievement of just such a hovering equilibrium became the chief task for engineers in the second half of the nineteenth century.

Labrouste reached his full development with the building of
the Bibliothèque Nationale in Paris, begun in 1858 and completed after his death.[4] The increase in the production of
books during the nineteenth century made the provision of
sufficient space the main problem in library building. The
stacks took up more and more room. In earlier times, stack
and reading rooms had been identical; now they had to be
separated. There is no library which solved the problem this
situation created so elegantly as Labrouste's Bibliothèque
Nationale.

Difference from
British Museum

In it Labrouste departed from the example set by his English
contemporary in the same field, Sydney Smirke (1798–1877).
Smirke designed the monumental and frequently imitated
circular reading room in the quadrangle of the British Museum.
But the circular outline of this room left only the remnants of
the quadrangular space whose center it occupied available for
the stack rooms. The inspiration for such an arrangement
came not from the architect but from Sir Anthony Panizzi, the
principal librarian of the British Museum and the creative
force behind much of its development. Panizzi was also responsible for having the reading desks placed along lines
radiating from a central observation point. The library of the
British Museum is worthy of note in another respect; its circular dome is constructed from top to bottom of iron and was
the first of its kind.

Sydney Smirke, its designer, remains an interesting figure in
the architecture of the time. Though overshadowed by his
brother, Robert, he did important work in the design and
equipment of club buildings. His work on English club
interiors is one of the points from which the evolution
of modern furniture proceeds. He also designed those
chairs in the British Museum reading room which are still
unique, in point of comfort, among the great libraries of
the world.

The reading room
in the Bibliothèque
Nationale

The reading room (*figs.* **122, 123**) which Labrouste designed
for the Bibliothèque Nationale was square and contained
sixteen cast-iron pillars. Immediately behind it was the

---

[4] Cf. Michel Roux-Spitz, "La Bibliothèque nationale de Paris," *L'Architecture d'aujourd'hui,* vol. IX, no. 3 (March 1938).

122. HENRI LABROUSTE. Bibliothèque Nationale, Paris, 1858–68. *Reading room. Sixteen slim cast-iron columns; spherical vaults, each with a round opening at the top so that all the desks are equally well-lighted. It is typically nineteenth-century in the way its architectural shapes are borrowed from a variety of earlier periods.*

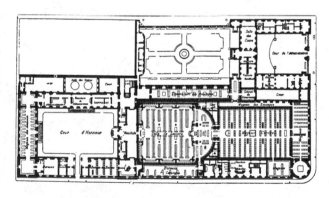

123. HENRI LA-BROUSTE. Bibliothèque Nationale, Paris, 1858–68. *Ground plan.*

large stack room known as the *magasin central*. He thus set the example of giving the stack room, the real heart of a modern library, the important position which it deserves. The reading room in its construction follows the line Labrouste had already taken in the library of Sainte-Geneviève: the iron construction is enclosed by the massive walls. The tall, slender columns (one foot in diameter

124. HENRI LABROUSTE. Bibliothèque Nationale, Paris, 1858–68. *The stacks (magasin central). Four stories above ground and one below, all surmounted by a glass ceiling. The gridiron floor plates permit the light to penetrate to all parts of the stacks.*

125. HENRI LABROUSTE. Bibliothèque Nationale, Paris, 1858–68. *The stacks (magasin central). Light pouring through the gridiron floor. Floor plates of this open design seem to have been used first in the engine rooms of steamships. Here they serve a purely utilitarian function, but at the same time they contain the germ of new artistic possibilities.*

126. HENRI LABROUSTE. Bibliothèque Nationale, Paris, 1858–68. *The stacks (magasin central). Detail of gridiron floor and banisters.*

and thirty-two feet high) impart an airy lightness to the room.

The columns are connected with each other by means of semi-circular girders which come together to form nine light, covered vaults reminiscent of those in Brunelleschi's Foundling Hospital at Florence. Labrouste's spherical vaults are built up of thin plates of faïence earthenware; there is a round opening in the top of each after the manner of the Roman Pantheon. In this way excellent lighting for every reading desk is assured. These details are mentioned only to show how the space conceptions of all periods are mixed together in nineteenth-century architecture.

But Labrouste's masterpiece is the *grand magasin* or stack room (*fig. 124*) built along the same axis. The *magasin central* has four stories above ground and one below, and was built to accommodate 900,000 volumes. In the recent renovation of the library Labrouste's excellent work in its construction was adjudged to be in perfect condition, and was left completely undisturbed. The whole area was covered with a glass ceiling. Cast-iron floor plates in a gridiron pattern permit the daylight to penetrate the stacks from top to bottom.[5] Floor plates of this open design (*fig.* **126**) seem to have been used first in the engine rooms of steamships. No doubt they were introduced into library buildings with purely practical ends in view. Nevertheless, observing them in our day, we recognize in the manner in which light penetrates the grillwork of the iron floor the germ of new artistic possibilities (*fig.* **125**). This hovering play of light and shadow appears as an artistic means in certain works of modern sculpture as well as in contemporary architecture.

Labrouste took great care to provide for efficient communication between all parts of the *magasin central*. The different stories are connected by bridges so that one can go from one section to another by the shortest route. These bridges, quite apart from their obvious utility, give a certain effect of power

---

[5] Labrouste had been anticipated in this feature of his design. Panizzi not only conceived the plan for the circular reading room of the British Museum but also the idea of using gridiron floor plates in its stack rooms. This was in 1852. Cf. Arundal Esdaile, *National Libraries of the World* (London, 1934), pp. 10, 27.

to the room. Light stairways with gridiron treads permit easy access to all the books. Except for the bookshelves, all the construction is of iron.

In view of the fact that the stack rooms were not open to the general public, Labrouste could proceed quite freely in their design and was not impeded by popular taste. He made good use of this freedom. He dispensed with all applied decoration. There is in its stead an astonishing sureness of expression, resulting from a perfect fitness for purpose which only the hand of an artist could achieve.[6]

In this room — one never meant for public display — a great artist unfolded new possibilities for architecture. It is true that the Crystal Palace of some years before was a much more spectacular and imaginative structure. In the *magasin central*, however, Labrouste had been set a problem in architecture that was detailed and specific. Using the means possible to an architect of his day, Labrouste solved it in a manner that bears the stamp of a timeless rightness. If there is a Pazzi Chapel to be found anywhere in contemporary architecture, it is here.

The *magasin central* connects with the main reading room through a large arched opening (*fig.* **127**). Labrouste had the audacity that was needed in his day to erect a large glass screen in this opening, so that the magazine of books stored in the stacks could be glimpsed from the reading room. This was an early use on a large scale of the transparent areas so dear to modern architects (*fig.* **128**).[7] Labrouste, afraid of his own daring, partially covered his glass screen with heavy red-velvet drapery, unfortunately "modernized" in later renovations.

Henri Labrouste is without doubt the architect of the middle nineteenth century whose work possessed the most significance for the future. His time, of course, dictated the use of Renaissance or classical shapes, and he used them with the greatest artistic distinction.

---

[6] The stack rooms behind the circular reading room of the British Museum used similar gridiron floor plates (as we have just seen), but nothing was achieved by their use beyond an efficient organization of this part of the library.

[7] John Nash had used a glass partition to shut off the south end of the principal corridor of Buckingham Palace. But he interlaced this glass partition with ornaments, in the baroque manner. Cf. Henry D. Roberts, *A History of the Pavilion at Brighton* (London, 1939), Fig. 25.

127. HENRI LABROUSTE. Bibliothèque Nationale, Paris, 1858–68. *Glass wall between the stacks (magasin central) and reading room. Early use of large areas of glass in the interior of a permanent public building. The heavy velvet drapery suggests that Labrouste was somewhat alarmed by his own daring.*

128. Glass wall of the Garage Rue Marbœuf, Paris, 1929. *After Labrouste's early recognition of the possibilities of glass, it came increasingly into use throughout the century, ending in immense panes like these whose framework has to be suspended from overhead bridge girders.*

But it was in his methods, in the way he analyzed and executed a task in building, that he stood far in advance of his times and of his colleagues. In spite of this, no studies of this architect have appeared since his death. We have no precise knowledge of the wearisome struggle with the Académie in which he was involved after 1830, or of the resistance he encountered that made a full realization of his ideas impossible. Perhaps the details still lie buried in the archives of the Académie. Some years ago I tried to learn more about the planning and development of Labrouste's most important work, the Bibliothèque Nationale. A search of the Building Department of the Bibliothèque Nationale itself disclosed that Labrouste's plans had been lost.

NEW BUILDING PROBLEMS — NEW SOLUTIONS

In the nineteenth century, buildings which owe nothing to the past begin to appear. Their new lines originate in the new demands presented by big towns, multiplied means of communication, and an ever-expanding industry. All these buildings have one thing in common: they are intended solely for a periodic use that involves rapid distribution of large volumes of merchandise. It is no accident that this type of construction should embody the solutions to the main architectural problems of the century. Because these unpretentious buildings contain the seeds of so much that followed, we must treat them at considerable length.

Market Halls

One of the new problems that were arising first finds a solution in the great public markets, three examples of which will be given. The earliest of such structures to require discussion here was the market hall of the Madeleine, built in Paris in 1824 (*fig.* **129**). The grace of its slender cast-iron columns is reminiscent of Pompeian mural paintings. The lightness of the construction is unbroken by any purely decorative additions. This is one of the earliest examples of the attempts nineteenth-century engineers were making to develop methods of construction which would combine elegance with economy of material.

Hall of the Madeleine, Paris, 1824

The market which was built in London in 1835 to replace the old Hungerford Fish Market represents a somewhat greater advance, so far as construction alone is concerned. A detailed description of the new Hungerford Fish Market (*fig.* **130**) appeared in the *Transactions* cf the Institute of British Architects in 1836.[1] On sanitary grounds, the use of lumber in this building had been forbidden. The cast-iron construction dictated by this provision is particularly noteworthy for the wide roof span of thirty-two feet, with its straight line. It has all the elegance of a much later period. "The chief particularity in the construction," according to the report of 1836, "is

Hungerford Fish Market, London, 1835

[1] I (1836), 44–46.

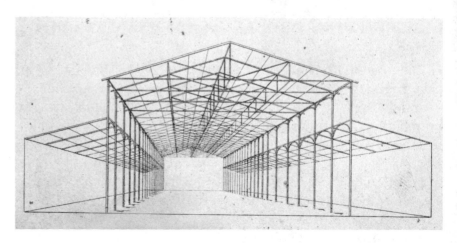

129. Market Hall of the Madeleine, Paris, 1824. *One of the earliest examples of the attempts of nineteenth-century engineers to combine elegance with economy of materials.*

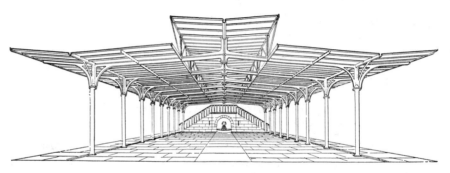

130. Hungerford Fish Market, London. *Metal roof, 1835. Particularly noteworthy for its wide roof span (thirty-two feet) with its straight line.*

the absence of any tie or lateral abutment." Already we find the planes of the roof given an inward slope, so that rain water might be carried away through the central columns.

Les Grandes Halles, Paris, 1855

The Grandes Halles of Paris, begun in 1853, had both a more interesting origin and a greater future influence than either of the structures we have just discussed. This market, the first designed to serve a population in the millions, was a part of Haussmann's great transformation of Paris. The Grandes Halles consist of two groups of pavilions connected by covered passageways. Their designer, Victor Baltard, is not by any means to be regarded as one of the great architects. His initial attempt — a stone pavilion that was built in 1851 — aroused a public disapproval so clamorous that Haussmann, then newly appointed prefect, ordered it pulled down.

131. VICTOR BALTARD. Halles Centrales, Paris. *Interior. Begun 1853. Baltard had to be forced to use iron in his second attempt (the first — in stone — was a disastrous failure). "Du fer! Du fer! Rien que du fer!" Haussmann insisted.*

It was only direct commands by Napoleon III and Haussmann that induced the academic Baltard to turn to iron construction in his second attempt (*fig.* 131). Napoleon III, greatly impressed by the recently built Gare de l'Est, had decided that a similar umbrella-like shelter was all that was required in the projected market hall. "Ce sont de vastes parapluies qu'il me faut, rien de plus!" And the prefect Haussmann thundered at Baltard. "Du fer! Du fer! Rien que du fer!" The final design that Baltard produced under this pressure was a derivative patchwork of other men's plans; for all that, it had an important influence on future work.

The new version, all iron and glass, once again amazed Napoleon III when Haussmann brought it to him — this time for different reasons. "Is it possible," he asked, "that the same architect designed two such contradictory buildings?" Haussmann replied, "The architect is the same, but the prefect is different."

The project actually realized in the Grandes Halles is less interesting than two designs which were rejected. The first was the work of Hector Horeau (1801–1872). Hector Horeau was one of those architects who never know the satisfaction of

Unexecuted projects: Hector Horeau

231

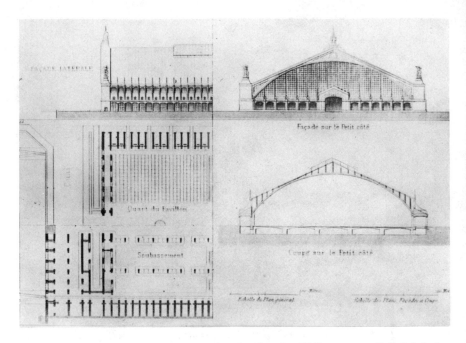

132. HECTOR HOREAU. Project for the Grandes Halles, 1849. *Rejected designs were much more advanced. The three-hundred-foot span in Horeau's project was not practicable until decades later. The principle used here was employed in the main building at the Paris exposition of 1855.*

fulfillment. His projects — all on a grand scale — could not be executed. The theory of statics had not yet progressed to a point where the calculations required for such buildings could be carried through; it was still impossible to build spans as large as those included in his plans without using tie bars, or to turn out such large iron trusses. His plan for the Grandes Halles (1849) shows an immense hall with a span of three hundred feet, calling for enormously thick walls to take the heavy lateral thrust. It was not until decades later that such an intention could be achieved. Nevertheless, figures like Horeau — men who see the right way before it can be trodden — are not useless; they give the first impulse to what later becomes reality.[2]

Eugène Flachat

The second rejected design was the work of Eugène Flachat (1802–1872), a contemporary of Horeau and of Labrouste.

---

[2] A plan submitted in the Crystal Palace competition in 1850 won first prize for Hector Horeau. It was a sort of basilica with five naves (fig. 147), not to be compared with Paxton's later design.

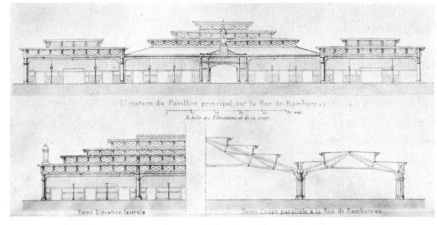

Élévation du Pavillon principal sur la Rue de Rambuteau

Échelle des Élévations et de la Coupe

Demi Élévation latérale

Demi Coupe parallèle à la Rue de Rambuteau

133. EUGÈNE FLACHAT.   Project for the Grandes Halles, 1849.   *This project, using the Polonceau tie system in a span of 260 feet, could have been executed at the time.   It was a most pleasing and functional solution to the problem.*

Flachat belonged to the most forceful generation of the nineteenth century, that of 1830, which included De Lesseps, the builder of the Suez Canal, Victor Hugo, the painter Eugène Delacroix, and Auguste Comte, the prophet of the scientific era.   It was Flachat who, overcoming widespread resistance, built the first French railroad in 1837.   He designed docks, warehouses, ports and canals, projected transatlantic steamship companies, and planned a tunnel through the Alps.

That Flachat was a follower of Saint-Simon is by no means irrelevant to this recital.   The Saint-Simonists took it as axiomatic that "la Société toute entière repose sur l'industrie," and were almost alone in foreseeing the scale and the extent of the progress that industry was embarking upon.   The Grandes Halles (*fig.* **133**), in its magnitude and social function, was a typical part of that new age the Saint-Simonists felt themselves destined to call forth.   In submitting a plan for it, Flachat was animated by the same spirit that stood behind his other more grandiose proposals.

The design itself, like Horeau's, features a very wide span — one of 260 feet.   It could, nevertheless, have been executed with the means available at the time.   The Polonceau tie system is employed, and, with its minimum of support and widely spread horizontal lines, the plan achieves a most pleasing and functional solution to the problem posed.

Products of
industrialization

The department store is a product of the industrial age; it results from the development of mass production and from the loss of direct contact between producer and consumer that was one of its consequences. The department store has no equally large forerunner in the past. In this respect it is like the market halls, railway stations, and exhibition buildings of the nineteenth century, and the object it serves is the same: the rapid handling of business activities involving huge crowds of pedestrians. Like these other buildings, the department store arises out of the growth in the population of cities, the heightened tempo of living, and the demand for cheaper goods.

The name "store" rather than "shop" points to the conditions of its origin; it is more a storage place in the normal sense of that word. The early stores in Paris during the sixties, for example, were known as *docks à bon marché*; they were simply places where goods were kept in quantity for cheap retail sale. To be fit for such a purpose, a department store — like a library stack room or a market hall — must offer a clear view of the articles it contains, a maximum of light, and ample facilities for communication. All these requirements could be met with the new means open to the builder.

Uncertainty as to
their beginnings

The economists tell us that "it is fairly certain that the department store originated in Europe, probably in Paris, and antedated American department stores by several years. The Bon Marché has often been credited with being the first department store in the world." [3] Lack of interest in research work into the origins of such contemporary institutions makes it impossible to speak more exactly than this. The origins of the American department store are particularly obscure; no one has definitely determined when and where the first store of this kind was opened. We can only outline the general types out of which this important institution of our economic life has evolved.

Origin as a
building-type

Even previous to the forties "commercial buildings," as they were called, were erected in such business centers as Boston,

---

[3] R. H. Nystrom, *Economics of Retailing*, 3rd ed. (New York, 1932), pp. 1–7.

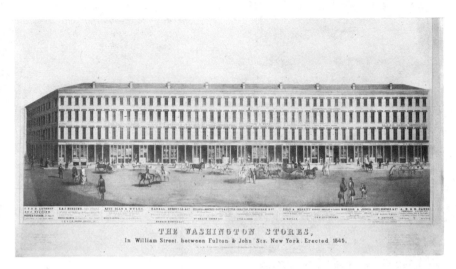

THE WASHINGTON STORES,
In William Street between Fulton & John Sts. New York. Erected 1845.

134. Washington Stores, New York City, 1845. *A row of stores all under one roof; separate units could be thrown together to house a single establishment.*

St. Louis, and New York. These buildings comprised a row of stores all under one roof and so arranged that two or more units could be thrown together to house a single establishment. Most of them were built on speculation, and the builders rented the individual stores to both retail and wholesale dealers. The "Boston Commercial Buildings," the St. Louis river front warehouses and wholesale places, and the "Washington Stores" (1845) in New York (*fig.* 134) are all typical of this stage in the development. The department store as a building type traces back to these "commercial buildings."

As a business institution the American department store evolved from those establishments which first made cheap ready-to-wear clothing available to the masses. In the forties Boston — flourishing trading-center for the New England area — had one of the largest of these enterprises. This was Oak Hall (*fig.* 135), a concern whose annual turnover was about five hundred thousand dollars.

Origin as a business institution: the ready-made clothing trade

The American stores which grew up from beginnings like these took on a character very different from that of the early European concerns. European stores specialized in dry goods; they did not deal in ready-made clothing.

Difference between American and European department stores

235

OAK HALL CLOTHING HOUSE,

UNRIVALLED EMPORIUM FOR
GENTLEMEN'S, YOUTHS' AND LITTLE CHILDREN'S

READY-MADE CLOTHING,

FURNISHING GOODS, HATS, CAPS, &C.,
WHOLESALE AND RETAIL.

GEO. W. SIMMONS, PIPER & CO.,

OAK HALL,

32, 34, 36 and 38 North Street,
BOSTON, MASS.

135. Oak Hall, Boston, c. 1850. *Ready-made clothing. One of the ready-made clothing concerns which were precursors of the department store in America.*

The majority opinion among economists is that genuine department stores do not appear before the sixties.[4] It seems to me likely that they started at an earlier date. We know — and this is one of the few exact dates available in these matters — that the first installation of a passenger elevator in a department store was made in 1857, in a building on the corner of Broadway and Broome Street, New York City [5] (*fig.* **136**).

The American department store building derives from the big seven- or eight-story warehouses which were so common during the second half of the nineteenth century. The many-storied English warehouse which the Manchester engineer, William Fairbairn, built in 1845 was an early example of such a building.[6]

Somewhat later, James Bogardus used a system of construction in cast iron which made it possible to erect relatively

---

[4] Nystrom, *op. cit.*, p. 134.

[5] Cf. p. 210.

[6] Cf. p. 194.

236

136. Broome Street, New York, 1857. *The first department store to house a passenger elevator. The building is typical of these early establishments.*

137. John Wanamaker Store, Philadelphia, 1876. *A freight shelter transformed into an immense, single-story dry goods store.*

tall buildings of the warehouse type from prefabricated parts. The A. T. Stewart store in New York — believed to be the first large department store — is a structure of this kind. The original building, now a part of the Wanamaker establishment, is still in existence. Completed and first occupied in 1863, it had two stories in the basement, five stories above ground, an attic, and six elevators.

The immense stores erected in Chicago in the late eighties, with their great unbroken areas of floor space, continued to follow the warehouse type. Examples from this period in Chicago are the Leiter Building of 1889 (built originally for single offices and now owned by Sears, Roebuck & Company) and "The Fair" of 1891 — both by William Le Baron Jenney.[7]

A peculiar solution in Philadelphia (1876)

One large store departed from the warehouse pattern — John Wanamaker's "Grand Depot" at Thirteenth and Market streets, in Philadelphia — but even this building was another type of storage place (*fig.* **137**). The Grand Depot, opened as a department store in 1876 (the year of Eiffel and Boileau's Magasin au Bon Marché), was originally a freight depot of the Pennsylvania Railroad. It had served as a freight shelter for over twenty years before Wanamaker hit upon the daring idea of transforming it into an immense, single-story dry goods store.[8]

The Grand Depot had more than two acres of floor space. A circular counter ninety feet around occupied the center of the building. From this counter there radiated a series of aisles which were intersected by other aisles and counters that were concentric with the big counter in the middle.[9] The layout resembles that used for the Paris exhibition of 1867.

The Magasin au Bon Marché, Paris, 1876: constructed by Eiffel

The first modern glass and iron department store with a free influx of natural light throughout was the Magasin au Bon Marché in Paris. It was in complete contrast to the warehouse type with its superimposed, artificially lighted stories. At the time of its building in 1876, it was regarded as a model of elegance.[10]

The Bon Marché was the work of the engineer Eiffel (later to construct his famous tower) and the architect L. A. Boileau (the son of one of the great French pioneers in the use of iron in architecture).

---

[7] Cf. pp. 370–374.

[8] J. H. Appel, "Reminiscences of Retailing," *Bulletin of the Business Historical Society,* vol. XII, no. 6 (December 1938).

[9] Cf. *The Golden Book of the Wanamaker Store* (Philadelphia, 1911), p. 52.

[10] There were many older department stores in Paris; the Magasin au Bon Marché itself had been founded a quarter-century earlier, in 1852.

Boileau felt that thick walls were unsuited to buildings of this type; "only pillars of small diameter are permissible." And he goes on to remark that these pillars "should be no more than the hors d'œuvre of the construction."[11] The ground floor of the building already shows the use of large glass surfaces set in unbroken series. A glass shelter is carried in a continuous line along the whole front of the store above the show windows and reinforces the impression produced by the areas of glass they contain.

The corner of the store is built out, like a pavilion, reminding one of the round towers of the French châteaux. Later examples were unable to break away from this precedent. A similar treatment appears in Paul Sédille's Magasin Printemps, Paris, of 1881–89. Even Louis Sullivan's Carson, Pirie, Scott store in Chicago, built around 1900, reflects in the shape of its corner the persistent memory of the pavilion.[12]

Corner of store
built out like a
pavilion

The mark of the great constructor Eiffel is visible in the treatment of the interior of the Bon Marché. Its area of more than thirty thousand square feet is divided into a series of courts of various shapes, each covered by a large glass skylight. The passage from court to court is simplified by the presence of lofty iron bridges or *passerelles* like those Labrouste had used, nearly two decades earlier, in the stack room of the Bibliothèque Nationale (*fig.* **138**).

Never before had light flowed into a store in such bright streams. A true glass architecture had been erected over the framework of the building (*fig.* **140**). The creative fantasy of the nineteenth century can be felt in its combination of glass skylights, aerial bridges in iron, slim iron columns, and the curious ornamental shapes so characteristic of the period. For all this variety, there is a seriousness and simplicity about the Magasin au Bon Marché taken as a whole. The architectonic pomp and boastfulness later called upon to attract and seduce the masses is avoided here.

Seriousness and
simplicity

The great masses of light which enter the building through its refined and even airy construction anticipate one of the chief

Relation to con-
temporary work

---

[11] L. A. Boileau, *fils*, "Les Magasins au Bon Marché," *Encyclopédie d'architecture*, 1880, p. 184.   [12] Cf. pp. 388–390.

138. EIFFEL and BOILEAU. Bon Marché, Paris, 1876. *Iron bridges in the interior. The creative fantasy of the nineteenth century can be felt in this combination of glass skylights, aerial bridges in iron, slim iron columns, and the curious ornamental shapes so characteristic of the period.*

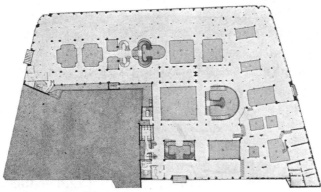

139. EIFFEL and BOILEAU. Bon Marché, Paris, 1876. *Ground plan. Area, thirty thousand square feet. The "perforated" interior space is typical of French buildings.*

concerns of contemporary architects. Five decades after Eiffel's construction of the Bon Marché, the same joy in the play of light through space perforations is to be found in Le Corbusier's interiors and exteriors and in the way he makes the two interpenetrate.

140. EIFFEL and BOILEAU. Bon Marché, Paris, 1876. *Glass roof over skylight.*
This glass architecture was invisible from the street. The moment the nineteenth century
feels itself unobserved and has no longer to make a show, then it is truly bold.

Eiffel's imaginative approach to technical problems can be seen in the exterior forms of the high glass roof which is built over the skylights of the courts. The ordinary spectator never sees this part of the building. The communicating *passerelles* are fantastically balanced over the inclined planes of this tent-like glass roof.[13] The moment the nineteenth century feels itself unobserved and is no longer conscious of any need for making a show — then it is truly bold!

Boldness of the nineteenth century where it is unobserved

From this time onward the undisguised shapes with their natural content of feeling that mark the rear and unobserved portions of railroad stations and factories begin to make themselves felt in the front walls of buildings.

---

[13] The very early photograph made at the time of the erection of the building shows that even then people felt something unusual had been accomplished here.

141. Winter Garden and Assembly Room, Paris, 1847. *Joseph Paxton may well have been inspired for the idea of his Crystal Palace by this once celebrated cross-shaped building, which, standing between Rond Pont and the present Avenue Marbœuf, changed the simple glass house into a social meeting place containing ballroom, café, reading room, and paintings on sale along the high glass walls. "The magnificent building," observed Loudon's En-clopaedia of Gardening in 1850 (pp. 93–94), "is supposed to be one of the largest and finest in Europe . . . extreme length 300 feet, extreme breadth 180 feet, extreme height 60 feet."*

Different ways
to solve a new
building
problem

Comparing nineteenth-century department stores in France and America we may observe how a new building problem — apparently governed solely by practical considerations — is brought to a different solution in different countries.

In America, as we have just seen, the department store followed the warehouse type: one unbroken floor area was built on top of another. In France the light court and "perforated" interior space appear even before Eiffel in department stores of wooden construction (*fig.* **139**). The Eiffel and Boileau Magasin au Bon Marché reveals very clearly a tendency in-

242

herent in French architecture. The urge to hollow out interior spaces to the greatest extent possible appears in French buildings from Romanesque times onward. It is visible in those daring Gothic choirs which seem to have been left almost too fragile to stand, and in the latest works of our own day. The audacity of French engineering is only a modified expression of this same trend.

142. First Industrial Exposition, Champ-de-Mars, Paris, 1798.

THE GREAT EXHIBITIONS

In the second half of the nineteenth century, with industry undergoing its greatest expansion, industrial exhibitions afforded truly creative architecture its best opportunities. Toward the end of the century, when industry had come to be taken as a matter of course and was no longer looked upon as new and marvelous, they lost their creative force. New problems had emerged in the meantime which demanded new solutions.

The exhibitions

The exhibitions were born almost simultaneously with modern industry; they appeared at the time when the shift from handwork to machine production made itself obvious. Throughout that period people in many countries were working feverishly to invent new machines and new processes. The chief purpose

Facilitated comparison of products

of the early exhibitions was to bring together the results of this work, to display the new discoveries side by side, and thus to facilitate their comparison and adoption. The development of industry in all its branches was accelerated by these exhibitions, in which every sphere of human activity was represented: the implements, methods, and products of mines, mills, machine shops, and farms were on display, together with work in the fine and the applied arts.

The industrial exhibition embodied a synthesis of the as yet unformulated aims of the nineteenth century. It foretold the transformation that was to be effected in man as well as in industry, in human feelings as well as in human surroundings. The exhibitions were a part of the march of industry and were bound up in its destiny.

Two periods in the history of the exhibitions

The history of the exhibition is divided into two periods. The earlier of these periods opens and closes in Paris; it begins with the first industrial exhibition ever held — that of 1798 — and ends with the Paris exhibition of 1849. The exhibitions of this initial period were made possible by the collapse of the guilds in 1791, and were all purely national in character.

The first period, national exhibitions: Paris, 1798

The *première exposition des produits de l'industrie française* was opened on the Champ-de-Mars in Paris in September 1798 (*fig.* **142**). It inaugurated an exhibition movement which was to lead to some of the outstanding achievements of the nineteenth century. The start made at Paris in 1798 was a very modest one. There were some luxury articles displayed, but the precedent for nearly all future exhibitions was set by the central position given to articles of daily use: watches, wall paper, cloth, and cotton yarn — yarn which "was carded and spun by means of machinery," as the catalogue was careful to state.

There were only a hundred and ten exhibitors at this first exposition, but this does not detract from its importance. It was primarily intended as a sort of people's festival, in celebration of the freedom from guild restrictions that the Revolution had brought. This festive motive accounted for its location in the Champ-de-Mars, the scene of all national celebrations since the fall of the monarchy. It was the *proclamation de la liberté du travail* in 1791 that first gave every citizen the right to follow whatever trade he desired. What was more important, this proclamation, in according a new liberty to production, gave official encouragement to a progress of industry and invention from which everyone expected great things. "Ces arts n'avaient pas pu encore se developper à cause des entraves sans nombre. Mais la liberté les vengerait. . . . Sous l'égide de la liberté, les arts utiles étaient appelés à un brilliant avenir."

The second period, international exhibitions: motives

The second period occupies the latter half of the nineteenth century and owes its force to the principle of free trade. In this period the exhibition takes on a new character; it becomes international in its scope. The national exhibitions of industry during the first half of the century had followed upon the abolition of the legal obligation to belong to a guild. Something else was demanded for an international exhibition; there was no reason to bring together products from all over the world unless there existed at the same time the possibility of selling to the whole world. An international exhibition could have value only in a world where trade restrictions of all kinds had been reduced to a minimum. These great exhibitions were the product of the liberal conception of economy: free trade, free communication, and improvement in production and performance through free competition.

The exhibitions also fostered a spirit of rivalry, a desire to equal or improve upon the last exhibition. Thus risks were taken in many departments, not least of all in architecture. Such a spirit of rivalry, together with the efficiency it promoted, is visible in the Crystal Palace world exhibition of 1851.

Advances in construction fostered by exhibitions

The history of exhibitions during the latter half of the nineteenth century constitutes at the same time a history of iron construction. Exhibition buildings were planned for rapid erection and dismantling: both were facilitated by the use of iron. Again, iron parts for such buildings could be fabricated in widely separated workshops. Finally, iron was everywhere regarded at this date as the medium of expression most truly appropriate to the period. But exhibition buildings did not simply call for the use of iron; the fact that they appeared at short intervals and were meant to be only temporary encouraged the experimental employment of iron in their construction. The exhibition became the trial ground for new methods. In all the great international exhibitions — from the first at Crystal Palace, London, in 1851 to the last at the end of the century — constructors attempted tasks that had never been faced before. When their experiments succeeded in this special field they became a part of standard building practice. It was in this way that the Eiffel Tower came to be erected in 1889, despite the most doleful prophecies of disaster.

New constructions demanded new aesthetic responses

The history of the exhibition shows not only the developments in iron construction during the period but also important changes in habits of aesthetic response. The new structural treatments of load and support demanded new aesthetic reactions. In the past people had grown to expect the basis of the equilibrium between load and support in a building to be visible at a glance, to lie open to inspection. But with the introduction of new methods of iron construction it became more and more difficult to differentiate between load and support: a new poised equilibrium of all the parts of a structure began to appear.

What the exhibitions symbolized

The optimism of the nineteenth century and its faith in the possibilities of industry are reflected in the great exhibitions. Industry would "unite the human race" — or so Prince Consort Albert dreamt in 1850. There seemed no limit to what industry could achieve at the start of its period of greatest expansion; people confidently expected it to solve all the problems of the world.

Unparalleled concentration of human activities

The exhibitions sprang from and symbolize the urge to master the earth's resources and draw out all its wealth. In a manner which is unparalleled in earlier periods they served as a concentration point for human activities of every sort, the emphasis always falling on industry and its latest inventions. These exhibitions mark the points where the nineteenth century drew aside from the rush of production in which it was caught to survey the progress that had been made.

The concentration of the activities of the century in a single place attracted interested representatives from all over the world. The exhibitions became, naturally, the scene of all

246

sorts of international congresses — of science, industry, finance, and labor. Beyond this, they attracted official observers from all those countries which were anxious to learn of and adopt the new developments. There are reports by Spanish, Italian, and Turkish observers which fill many volumes. The report of the United States Commissioner to the Paris exhibition of 1867 takes up six volumes, each of about three hundred and fifty pages.

The very complete surveys published by the countries where the exhibitions were held show a contemporary realization of their unique importance. They were edited with great care; later generations will find them the most satisfactory sources for a knowledge of what actually went on during the nineteenth century. These reports were often made under the supervision of men who possessed real foresightedness and initiative. Henry Cole was responsible for the first of these large-scale surveys — the *Official Descriptive and Illustrative Catalogue of the Great Exhibition* (London, 1851), in four big blue volumes. The thirteen-volume report on the Paris exhibition of 1867 was prepared under Michel Chevalier, a former Saint-Simonist. As an exile, Chevalier had traveled in the United States during the thirties; after his return to France he worked continually to promote industry.

Official reports: scope, and historical value

Exhibitions grew out of the old fairs, familiar to every century. The first French exhibition in 1798 was essentially a kind of people's festival, and all later exhibitions retained this festival motif.

The nineteenth century marks the point when leisure vanished from daily life. The ability to develop an original form for festivals vanished with it. During the second half of the nineteenth century the exhibitions remained the great festivals in the life of nations. Warehouses, department stores, and office buildings remained closely bound up with immediate practical needs. The exhibitions had their practical function to fulfill also, but they operated in an atmosphere far removed from the rush of everyday life and were able to sustain a festive character. There was always a sharp contrast between their festive and their practical or official aspects. The sureness which appears in the construction of their great halls is not

The great exhibitions, the nineteenth century's original form for festivals

carried over into the social arrangements in the interiors of the halls, for example. But, even so, they represent the closest approach of the period to an original form of group celebration.

Even in the nineteenth century, when architecture was rooted in the background of industrial development, it was in these buildings of a certain festive intent that the great solutions of the period to the vaulting problem were made.

Significance of the vaulting problem during the Renaissance, the baroque period, and the nineteenth century

From the beginning of architecture the vaulting problem has always brought forth the highest architectural expressions of every epoch. Thus the barrel vault painted by Masaccio during the early Renaissance was developed into a ceremonious expression of the full Renaissance and early baroque world. In the late baroque, changes in vaulting once again accompanied changes in the outlook of the age.

Solutions to the vaulting problem played the same important role in the nineteenth century. The *haut goût* of the nineteenth-century style in architecture requires — as we have already noted more than once — more careful study than it has yet been given. But, whatever results such a study may lead to, the constituent facts of architectural development will be found to be those original solutions of the vaulting problem which first took shape in the large halls of great exhibitions.

New vaulting problems of the nineteenth century solved in industrial buildings

Objections to this view could readily be advanced. It might be said that these exhibition buildings represented nothing but the answers to very sober practical needs, while the vaulting problem had possessed an almost metaphysical significance in earlier periods.

These objections cannot be ignored. Furthermore, it is obvious that such exhibition buildings were out of direct contact with human needs. But in a certain sense this remark applies to the period as a whole. Their indifference to human needs makes these constructions a true — if harsh — expression of the times. Nevertheless we may succeed in showing that behind this indifference a new feeling lies hidden.

The two most beautiful buildings of the period of the great exhibitions — the Crystal Palace of 1851 and the Galerie des

Machines of 1889 — have disappeared. The first was destroyed by fire in 1937; the second was senselessly torn down in 1910. Their loss is a typical consequence of the day-to-day mood that governs our period. Only photographs and etchings remain as witness that the overcoming of gravity in apparently floating constructions (which is the essence of any solution to the problem of vaulting) was achieved in magnificent form during the nineteenth century.

The Great Exhibition, London, 1851

The Crystal Palace (*fig.* 143) had the impact of a fairy story on all those who saw it opened in London in 1851. Industry, after all the blight and disorder it had brought about, now displayed another and a gentler side, aroused feelings that seemed to belong only to the world of dreams.

The Crystal Palace housed an exhibition that was the first of its kind, one that reflected the courage and enterprise of the early Victorian period. The Prince Consort, Albert, and Sir Henry Cole [1] were its leading spirits, and it was the former who gave it a central theme. Cole relates a conversation he had with Prince Albert at Buckingham Palace on June 29, 1849: "I asked the Prince if he had considered [whether] the exhibition should be a national or an international exhibition. The French had discussed whether their own exhibition should be international, and had preferred that it should be national only. The Prince reflected for a minute and then said, 'It must embrace foreign productions' — to use his words — and added emphatically, 'International, certainly. . . . Where do you think it should be?' I answered, 'In Hyde Park.'" The prince's decision was by no means a casual reply. In 1850 he declared: "None will doubt that we are living in a most remarkable period of transition, laboring forcefully toward that great

The great exhibition initiated by the Prince Consort and Sir Henry Cole

---

[1] Sir Henry Cole (1808–1882) was an active influence upon English industry from 1845 on. Unlike the members of the movement begun by William Morris in the sixties, Cole tried to work with industry rather than to revive hand crafts. As he said in 1845, his aim was to develop "'art manufactures,' meaning fine art or beauty applied to mechanical production." His program included the founding of schools of design intended to raise the level of popular taste. As a part of this program he founded the first museum of decorative art, the Victoria and Albert Museum in South Kensington. For further information see S. Giedion, *Mechanization Takes Command* (Oxford University Press, 1948).

143.　Crystal Palace, London, 1851.　*General view.　Lithograph.*

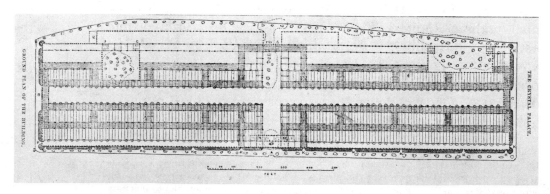

144.　Crystal Palace, London, 1851.　*Plan.　Ground area, eight hundred thousand square feet.　The Crystal Palace made no real contribution to the nineteenth-century problem of vaulting in iron, but it marks the first use on a grand scale of prefabricated parts, and it arrives at a new artistic expression through the use of the new material, plate glass.*

250

aim indicated everywhere by history: the union of the human race. . . . Gentlemen, the exhibition of 1851 shall give a vivid picture of the stage at which industry has arrived in the solution of that great task." [2]

The Crystal Palace had behind it the highly developed industry of England and is an application of the most simple and rational system of manufacturing — that of serial production. Its builder, Joseph Paxton, used the "ridge and furrow" construction employed in the greenhouses which were used to protect the tropical plants at Chatsworth in 1837. The design of the whole building was planned around the largest standard sheet of glass, which was only four feet long. Larger panes could not be made at this time. The panes used in the Palace were the work of the Chance Brothers' Birmingham plant. (The furnace used in this work is still in service.)

Crystal Palace based on prefabricated parts

It is astonishing to find Paxton able at this early date to dissect the whole building into a simple system of small prefabricated units. There are the wooden ridge and furrow frames for the glass, the iron lattice girders on which the panes rested, and the cast-iron supporting pillars — bolted together floor by floor. The wood and iron structural members were manufactured in various shops in Birmingham and fitted together on the site at London. In this manner a building with a ground area of some eight hundred thousand square feet — about four times that of St. Peter's, as contemporaries remarked with pride — arose within six months. Its length was 1,851 feet — to correspond with the date of its erection. But for all its architectural beauty, the Crystal Palace makes no contribution to the problem of vaulting as it concerns iron construction. The barrel vault in its transept had a wooden framework, and its span of seventy-two feet was less than that of many medieval buildings (*fig.* **144**).

Small span

The Crystal Palace was the realization of a new conception of building, one for which there was no precedent. It was, in addition, the first building of such dimensions constructed of glass, iron, and timber over a framework of cast- and wrought-

"A revolution in architecture"

---

[2] Sir Henry Cole, *Fifty Years of Public Service* (London, 1884), I, 124–125.

145. Crystal Palace, Sydenham. *Interior. Photograph of the transplanted Crystal Palace, taken in 1935, shortly before its destruction by fire.*

iron girders accurately bolted together. The possibilities dormant in modern industrial civilization have never since, to my knowledge, been so clearly expressed. It was recognized at the time that this combination of wood, glass, and iron — incidentally a combination resulting in an admirably practical exhibition technique — had evoked a new kind of imagination which sprang directly from the spirit of the age. Only thus can we explain the confident prediction of contemporaries, since justified in all essentials, that "the Crystal Palace is a revolution in architecture from which a new style will date."[3]

---

[3] Lothar Bucher, *Kulturhistorische Skizzen aus der Industrieausstellung aller Völker* (Frankfort, 1851), p. 174.

Lothar Bucher wrote in 1851 that "the building encountered no opposition, and the impression it produced on those who saw it was one of such romantic beauty that reproductions of it were soon hanging on the cottage walls of remote German villages. In contemplating the first great building which was not of solid masonry construction spectators were not slow to realize that here the standards by which architecture had hitherto been judged no longer held good." [4]

An opinion
of 1851

Bucher, a democratic political exile who was later to become Bismarck's right-hand man in the Wilhelmstrasse, then goes on to describe the interior (*figs.* **145, 148**). The description reads almost exactly like a present-day analysis of architecture: "We see a delicate network of lines without any clue by means of which we might judge their distance from the eye or the real size. The side walls are too far apart to be embraced in a single glance. Instead of moving from the wall at one end to

"All materiality
blends into the
atmosphere"

146. "The Favorites": popular sculpture of 1851. *It is important not to lose sight of what was really admired in the nineteenth century by officials, critics, and the public. A contemporary opinion of "The Favorites": "One of the most charming groups of the British Sculpture Court . . . lifelike, interesting and beautiful . . ."*

[4] Bucher, *ibid.*

253

that at the other, the eye sweeps along an unending perspective which fades into the horizon. We cannot tell if this structure towers a hundred or a thousand feet above us, or whether the roof is a flat platform or is built up from a succession of ridges, for there is no play of shadows to enable our optic nerves to gauge the measurements.

"If we let our gaze travel downward it encounters the blue-painted lattice girders. At first these occur only at wide intervals; then they range closer and closer together until they are interrupted by a dazzling band of light — the transept — which dissolves into a distant background where all materiality is blended into the atmosphere. . . . It is sober economy of

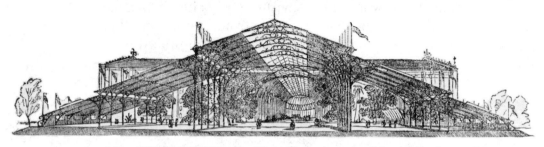

147. HECTOR HOREAU. First prize in the competition for the Crystal Palace, 1850. *Hector Horeau (whose project for the Grandes Halles we remember) won the first prize with a light iron construction of the basilica type. It may to some extent have influenced the committee's decision not to erect a monumental edifice, their original intention.*

language if I call the spectacle incomparable and fairylike. It is a Midsummer Night's Dream seen in the clear light of midday."

Counterparts in painting: the landscapes of Turner

Are there counterparts of the Crystal Palace among the paintings of the period — any paintings, that is, which give "no idea of the actual size or distance involved," and where "all materiality blends into the atmosphere"? There are none to be found outside the orbit of English painting. J. M. W. Turner's study of the Simplon Pass,[5] painted c. 1840 (*fig.* **149**), uses a humid atmosphere to dematerialize landscape and dissolve it into infinity. The Crystal Palace realizes the same intention through the agency of transparent glass surfaces and iron structural members. In the Turner picture the means employed are less abstract, but an equivalent insubstantial and hovering effect is produced. The deep hollows in the

[5] In the Fogg Art Museum, Cambridge, Massachusetts.

mountains — done in gray, brown, and blue — and the yellowish-brown road that winds up to the peaks in the background combine to eliminate every naturalistic feature: they seem precisely to make up parts of a dream landscape, "seen in the clear light of midday."

In the Crystal Palace an artistic conception outdistances the technical possibilities of the era — something which is very rare in the nineteenth century. The whole building reflects the careful hand of its builder, the landscape gardener Joseph Paxton, who was more accustomed to work with plants than with machinery. The curious association of an unmistakable grandeur with a certain gentleness was never again to be achieved.[6] From now on, development will come for decades at the hands of the engineer. He will achieve the new solutions.

The Crystal Palace: association of gentleness with grandeur

The Universal Exhibition, Paris, 1855

The exhibition was inaugurated in France as a national festival in 1798 and continued to develop along such lines throughout the first half of the nineteenth century. In 1849 the French Minister of Commerce proposed making the Paris exhibition of that year an international one. The French chambers of commerce, however, lacked sufficient courage to open their frontiers to foreign industry. It was not until 1855, four years after the international exhibition at the Crystal Palace, that the first "exposition universelle des produits de l'industrie" was held in France. But from 1855 on, all the great exhibitions, all those that had any historical importance, were held in France. During this period, as in Gothic times, France was the scene of the most audacious constructions. Both the public and the press adopted a certain waiting attitude toward the exhibition of 1855 which disappears with later French exhibi-

France the center of exhibitions after 1850

[6] During the fifties several attempts were made to construct a building exclusively of glass and iron — as in the New York exhibition of 1853, for example. The plan executed at New York in 1853 was a mediocre one which grafted a monumental dome upon Paxton's ideas. Paxton himself submitted a design, but it was unsatisfactory. The plan of James Bogardus — an original and genuinely American solution to the problem — was also rejected (cf. Fig. 111). The beginnings Paxton had made in the Crystal Palace suffered another setback in the London World's Fair of 1862. Its pseudo-monumental domes and triumphal arches followed in the path of the Palais de l'Industrie, Paris, 1855, but without equalling its constructive hardihood. For further details, cf. "Record of the Great Exhibition," *Practical Mechanic's Journal* (London, 1862).

148.   Crystal Palace, Interior.   *"We see a delicate network of lines without any clue by means of which we might judge their distance from the eye, or the real size"* (*Lothar Bucher, 1851*).

tions.   At first people were anxious not to commit themselves; finally new applications for exhibition space were made in such numbers that the area originally fixed upon proved too small. The exhibition consequently ended by showing numerous additions.

Scheme for the exhibition of 1855

Ground plan (*fig.* **151**): The Palais de l'Industrie was a rectangular structure with a high center aisle which was surrounded by a double row of galleries.   The low side aisles were supported by numerous cast-iron pillars.   The center aisle connected with one of those circular panoramas so popular at the time and with the twelve-hundred-meter Galerie des Machines which extended along the Seine.   The Galerie des Machines (*fig.* **152**), in spite of the narrow barrel vault which seems to link it with Fontaine's gallery in the Palais d'Orléans, was the starting point for that succession of *halles des machines*

149. J. M. W. TURNER. Simplon Pass. *Water color, c. 1840. Fogg Museum, Cambridge, Mass. The unsubstantial and hovering effect of the Crystal Palace is achieved here through a humid atmosphere which dematerializes the landscape and dissolves it into infinity.*

which produced the most daring solutions to the vaulting problem.

Span: The Palais de l'Industrie had a span of forty-eight meters. This was the widest vaulting attempted in the period. It represents a great advance over what was achieved in the Crystal Palace, with its span of about twenty-two meters.[7] Wrought-iron lattice girders, partially hand-forged, were used. It was the first time they had been employed for vaulting. The enormous areas of glass introduced into the vaulting almost blinded contemporary spectators, who were unaccustomed to the amount of light that was admitted. The form of the vaulting recalls the manner in which great halls and staircases were covered during the first and second empires. Even

Widest vaulting of the period

---

[7] Long before this, Gothic builders had attained a span of twenty-nine meters in the wooden vaulting of the Salone at Padua.

150. International Exhibition, Paris, 1855. *Interior of the main building. Span of forty-eight meters very great for the period. No tie bars were used, but they were avoided artificially, through the use of heavy buttresses.*

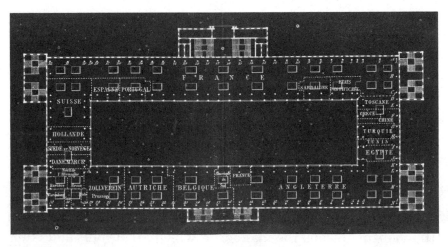

151. International Exhibition, Paris, 1855. *Plan.*

152. The Hall of Machines, Paris, 1855. *A gallery twelve hundred meters long paralleling the Seine, the starting point for those Galeries des Machines which became more and more the pivotal points of the industrial exhibitions.*

at this early stage, the meaning of the new materials had been grasped; emphasis rests upon the opening-up of space rather than the walling-in of a volume (*fig.* **150**).

Construction: The round, high-swung arches of the center aisle show how much progress had been made. No tie bars encroach upon the free space, in spite of the bold span of nearly fifty meters. Still, one feels that the construction lacks a certain lightness which is familiar to us from present-day work. In order to counteract the lateral stress there was still no alternative to the imitation of Gothic principles of construction. The immense blocks of lead that were used as abutments were as expensive as they were wasteful of space. Hector Horeau had used the same principle in his unexecuted design for the Grandes Halles (1849).[8]

No tie bars; use of buttresses instead

In this exhibition a combination of a wide span with a light construction was attempted before the appropriate methods had been discovered. But there is also a dangerous retrogres-

Use of stone

---

[8] Cf. pp. 231–232.

sion from the advance which the Crystal Palace represents. The main building, the Palais de l'Industrie, was completely encased in heavy stone walls and included an immense triumphal arch. This monumental stonework was unhappily taken as a pattern for later exhibitions in London (1862) and in Chicago (1893).[9]

The Palais de l'Industrie stood in the Champs-Élysées — during the whole Second Empire a central point in Haussmann's project for building a new Paris. It was used for society gatherings and for shows of various kinds until 1897, when it was pulled down to make room for the exhibition of 1900.

Paris Exhibition of 1867

Ground plan symbolized the globe; director an economist

Ground plan: The external contour of the exhibition building was intended to symbolize the globe (*fig.* **154**). When the Champ-de-Mars was chosen as a site it became impossible to give the building a circular outline, and it was designed as an ellipse instead. The long axis was 490 meters (1,608 feet) and the short axis 386 meters (1,266 feet). Frédéric Le Play — the distinguished engineer, economist, and expert on European labor conditions whom Napoleon III appointed director of the exhibition — was responsible for the outline of its ground plan, and for its general program as well. From this time on, the Champ-de-Mars, the site in 1798 of the first of the small national exhibitions, was the accepted site for the great world exhibitions.

With regard to the ground plan, the question arose: How should the separate sections be arranged so as to give the spectator an ordered and undisturbed insight into the industry of all nations?

Organization of the elliptical exhibition building

Within the elliptical main exhibition building seven concentric galleries were placed, each conforming to the main outline of the grounds (*fig.* **156**). A garden was laid out inside the central ellipse of this *colisée du travail*. The galleries increased in size as one moved outwards from the center. The outermost

---

[9] Cf. pp. 275–277, 380–382.

gallery — the Galerie des Machines — was twice the height and width of the others (*fig.* **157**). Industrial machinery was exhibited here. Clothing, furniture, and raw materials were displayed, in that order, in the next three galleries, counting toward the center. The two innermost and smallest galleries contained exhibits which concerned, respectively, *l'histoire du travail* and the fine arts. A palm garden with statues occupied the innermost oval (*fig.* **102**).[10]

Transverse walks divided this building into separate segments. From each segment a spectator could trace without effort the developments within a single country and compare them with the displays of other countries occupying adjacent segments. This was an attempt at "living" statistics.

The aim of the exhibition can be gathered from a quotation taken from an official publication of 1867. "To make the circuit of this palace, circular, like the equator, is literally to go around the world. All peoples are here, enemies live in peace side by side. As in the beginning of things on the globe of waters, the divine spirit now floats on this globe of iron." The flowery language, somewhat reminiscent of Second Empire decoration, nevertheless reveals the essential motive.

LES AMOURS DES ANGES, d'après de M. Bouguet

153. Popular sculpture, "The Love of the Angels," 1867.

Construction: The iron skeleton of the Galerie des Machines — span thirty-five meters, height twenty-five meters — consisted of pillars twenty-eight meters high. The arches of the vault girders reached twenty-five meters into the air.

Projecting pillars replace the bars

The pillars did not stop at the level of the vaulting but were allowed to continue straight up into the air. The chief constructor, J. B. Krantz, did this to avoid the use of tie bars, and because the lateral stress could only be supported by girders built out from the pillars to the basket arches. These pillars extending into the air were considered hideous, and an attempt was made to disguise them as flag poles.

Hydraulic lifts with all the clumsiness of newborn monsters afforded communication between the ground floor and the roof,

---

[10] Cf. *L'Exposition universelle de 1867, illustrée, publication internationale autorisée par la commission impériale* (Paris, 1867).

around which there ran a platform giving a striking view of this city of galleries in corrugated iron and glass.

Behind the chief constructor stood the young Eiffel, who had founded his own factory a short time before. It was from him that the real inspiration for the Galerie des Machines came. In all sorts of ways — by the extensive use of new materials, by the employment of new devices like the elevator, by the provision of walks along the transparent glass surfaces of the *promenoirs* — the public was introduced not only to the new technical achievements but also to completely new aesthetic values.

154. International Exhibition, Paris, 1867. *Air view.*

155. MANET. View of the Exhibition of 1867. *Oil painting. Manet, whose pictures were denied entry to this exhibition, showed his whole output on the Pont de l'Alma. Manet has not only grasped externally the actuality of this building; he has set it forth in an adequate artistic language. The thing that is important here is dynamic relation between the masses of color.*

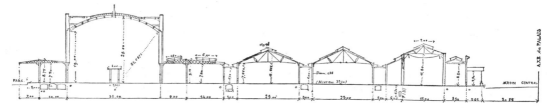

156. International Exhibition, Paris, 1867. *Section of the galleries of the main building. Seven concentric galleries were placed within the elliptical main building; the Galerie des Machines was twice the height and width of the others.*

157. International Exhibition, Paris, 1867. *Galerie des Machines. The entire span of thirty-five meters was achieved without visible tie bars.*

Paris Exhibition of 1878 [11]

Scheme   The exhibition of 1878 was intended to show the world that France had recovered from its defeat in 1870. The success of the exhibition of 1867 had been so great that in planning its successor a larger area was fixed upon. The exhibition was

---

[11] The Philadelphia exhibition of 1876 is of interest as the first example of the use of the pavilion system. This system was used again at Chicago in 1893 and at Paris in 1900. By the end of the century it had become the accepted method of organizing an exhibition. The increasing scope and complexity of industry made it necessary to segregate its different aspects in separate buildings. But all this falls outside the scope of our research. The Philadelphia exhibition brought no new solutions to the vaulting problem which was just on the verge of being solved in France.

158. International Exhibition, Paris, 1878. *The main entrance. The inflated sheet-metal architecture is of no importance as compared with the glass wall and the marquise vitrée. The latter so intersects the vertical elements that the relation between load and support can no longer be grasped at sight.*

divided into two sections: one devoted to a monumental building in stone, the other to temporary exhibition structures. On the far side of the Seine Davioud and Bourdais had been building the stone palace of the Trocadéro since 1876.

The main exhibition building follows the rectangular outline of the Champ-de-Mars. The ellipsoidal shape was abandoned because it had proved very difficult, after an exhibition ended, to find a use for the curved girders such a shape dictated.

Main building rectangular

A series of galleries in parallel formation extended over the length of the site, all of them flanked and dominated by the

Galerie des Machines. Along the shorter sides of the grounds ran two vestibules constructed by Eiffel facing the Seine.

Transitory
facts conceal
constituent
phenomena

The inflated sheet-metal architecture of the main entrance (*fig.* **158**) and of the pavilions on both sides is a transitory fact of little consequence. Even at the time it was regarded as of questionable merit, *fort discutable*. But if we carry our attention beyond the temporarily favored shapes it embodied, we shall find that the building exemplifies many constituent elements of architecture after 1900. The courage shown by the glass façade was an augury of the future. Beside this glass wall of 1878 we could place the glass walls of the Bauhaus in Dessau and the Hallieday warehouse in San Francisco (1918).[12]

The glass
wall and the
marquise vitrée

Another constituent fact of later architecture appears in the projecting glass canopy, or *marquise vitrée* which is carried the length of the glass front wall. This *marquise vitrée*, constitutes a hovering, horizontal plane surface, intersecting the vertical elements in such a way that the relations between load and support can no longer be grasped at sight.[13] Next to this continuous glass skylight of 1878 we could place the skylight of a 1926 shopping street in Amsterdam which constituted a similar hovering element.

From the very beginnings of architecture, a visible relation between load and support had been one of its outstanding facts. This sort of construction marks the beginning of a different kind of aesthetic feeling.

Construction: The main building of the exhibition of 1878 was flanked on both sides by the imposing Galerie des Machines (*fig.* **159**). The barrel vault had disappeared. The Galerie resembled in form the hull of an overturned ship. Its framework girders, meeting in the roof, were built up of separate parts, which showed already that construction was no longer dependent on rigid continuous supports running right through the building.

---

[12] An intermediate step is to be found in a ferroconcrete loft building on Sutter Street, San Francisco where a glass surface, covering the whole front, is suspended, cantilever fashion, in front of the supporting pillars.

[13] Eiffel seems to have been fond of this device. He used another canopy of plain glass and iron on the front of his Magasin au Bon Marché in Paris (1876). This canopy remained unchanged until very recently. (Cf. p. 241.)

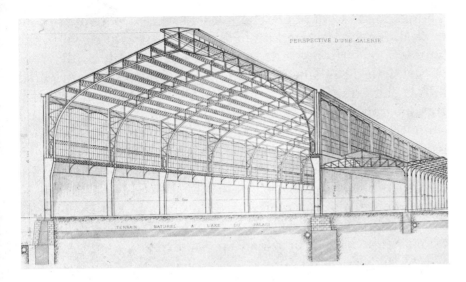

PERSPECTIVE D'UNE GALERIE

159. International Exhibition, Paris, 1878. *Section and perspective of the Galerie des Machines. Span, thirty-five meters; height, twenty-five meters. Thanks to the engineer De Dion, it had become possible to lead all the forces at work on a building directly into the foundations, without employing tie bars.*

Girders: The girders used are of the De Dion type. The engineer Henry De Dion was the real creator of girders fit for large spans. From a careful study of the tensile strength of materials he arrived at the proper form for a built-up girder capable of withstanding the various stresses put upon it without the assistance of tie bars. De Dion died shortly before the opening of the 1878 exhibition, while he was still engaged upon these calculations. (The arrangement of the framework girders shows a certain inner elasticity consequent upon the researches into the essential laws of materials.)

Stepped roof joists ran through the lattice girders and joined them into a continuous structure expressing a tranquil precision that had never been possible before. On both sides, from the halfway point up, the walls were filled in with glass. Such a union of glass and iron demands by its nature an extensive dematerialization of a building, which can be felt when one studies the Galerie des Machines. The contemporary architect Boileau defines with perfect precision the impression produced by this union: "The spectator is not aware of the weight of transparent surfaces. These surfaces are to him air and light, that is to say, an imponderable fluidity." [14]

Toward new solutions of the vaulting problem

Glass walls: an "imponderable fluidity"

[14] *Encyclopédie d'architecture*, 1887–88, p. 97.

Thanks to the work of De Dion, it had become possible to conduct all the forces bound up in a building straight down to the foundations. However, this foundation was still rigidly connected with the pillars and framework. The pillars are riveted into U-shaped iron sockets which are sunk in the foundations. But an iron skeleton is subject to temperature changes and cannot be rigidly bound together in the manner of a stone palace. De Dion was a pioneer in the study of the problems that follow from this fact. The matter was dealt with quite directly in the 1878 Galerie des Machines. Every sixty meters along the ridge of the roof where the pairs of lattice columns met, there was a complicated system of bolts set in oval holes which automatically provided for the expansion and contraction of the whole skeleton.

The rigid connection with the ground that is still maintained, together with the box-section girders and the canopy that rests on them like a capital, suggests that memory of the ancient column and its simple relation of load and support still lingered. But from this time on, with the rise of the truss girder, a new system sets in, a system that in the iron skeleton demands a hovering balance of the forces acting upon it.

Paris Exhibition of 1889

Climax of the development

The exhibition of 1889 marked at once the climax and the conclusion of a long development. In it great engineers like Eiffel reached the height of their powers. New conceptions in construction and new advances in industry united to give this exhibition expressive brilliance and an enormous influence. The long but humble Galerie des Machines of 1855, the huge circular Galerie which Krantz and Eiffel built in 1867, and the two great aisles of De Dion's Halle des Machines of 1878 are steps in a development which culminates in the Palais des Machines of 1889.

The exhibition of 1889 centered around the Eiffel Tower, which Eiffel and his engineers had raised on the bank of the Seine in the short space of seventeen months. The exhibition buildings were spread out behind the tower. There were two

160. International Exhibition, Paris, 1889. *Galerie des Machines. Span, 115 meters; length, 420 meters. The first time a span of such size had ever been bridged. It embodies constructional experience accumulated during almost a whole century. This building was wantonly destroyed.*

wings, one housing the *beaux-arts*, the other the *arts liberaux*, which were joined together by a section devoted to general exhibits. The immense metal bulk of the Galerie des Machines rose in the background to dominate the whole complex.

A kind of traveling crane — *les ponts roulants* — was erected within the Galerie des Machines (*fig.* **160**). It transported spectators over the length of the immense hall and enabled them to inspect all the machinery (much of it in operation) which was displayed on the floor below. On good days as many as a hundred thousand passengers rode on this crane.

269

For the last time industry aroused some of the wonder with which it was viewed at the time of its birth. Four years later at the Chicago World's Fair a display of machinery on view from *ponts roulants* could not have had this degree of success. But the progress made between 1878 and 1889 was so tremendous that visitors were stirred to the point of excitement by the boldness of the Galerie des Machines and the Eiffel Tower. The sculptor Raymond Duchamp-Villon (1876–1918) wrote of his impressions as a thirteen-year-old boy: "Public opinion had so long ignored the art of iron construction [that people were not prepared to recognize or evaluate a work of the strength and boldness of the Galerie des Machines]. I remember very clearly a hallucinatory passage through the brightness of the nave in a traveling crane, above whirlpools of twisting reptilean belts, creakings, whistles, sirens, and black caverns containing circles, pyramids, and cubes." [14a]

Unprecedented dimensions

The constructor of the "Galerie des Machines" (actually named the "Palais des Machines") [15] was Cottancin; the architect, Dutert. The dimensions of the Galerie exceeded anything previously known. The largest vaulting attempted up to this time had been that of the St. Pancras Station in London, 1868: span of 73 meters, height of 25 meters. The Palais des Machines spanned 115 meters and was 45 meters high. Its skeleton was composed of twenty trusses. Its length was 420 meters. Huge glass walls enclosed the sides.[16]

A building not bounded by its structural limits

The volume of free space included by the 1889 Galerie des Machines represented an entirely unprecedented conquest of matter. There is no earlier example that is comparable to it in this respect. But the glass end walls do not, strictly, close up the building; they constitute only a thin transparent membrane between the interior and outer space. And it is not as

---

[14a] "L'Architecture et le fer," in *Poème et Drame* (Paris), January–March, 1914.

[15] This building, one of the high points reached in the evolution of construction, was torn down in 1910 — out of "artistic sadism," as Frantz Jourdain correctly says.

[16] Somewhat earlier, and in a more unassuming way, J. W. Schwedler had attempted a similar *Auflagerung* in his Central Railway Station, Frankfort on Main (opened in 1888). This, however, did not break away from the barrel shape, which is ruled out in the Galerie des Machines by the very nature of the triply articulated girders used. Dimensions of the Frankfort Station: length 186 m., width 56 m., height 29 m.

a building circumscribed within definite limits that the Galerie des Machines is important. The girders in its skeleton could have been either more or less numerous without thereby effecting any distinctive alteration. The aesthetic meaning of this hall is contained in the union and interpenetration of the building and outer space, out of which there grows a completely new limitlessness and movement in keeping with the machines it contains.

Each arched truss is made up of two segments. A pin unites them at a pivotal point high above the center line of the hall. Moving downward, the trusses become increasingly attenuated until they appear scarcely to touch the ground; moving upward, they spread and gain weight and power (*fig.* **161**). The usual proportions seem to be exactly reversed. These triply articulated arches disturb, or rather disrupt, traditional static feelings with regard to the rational relations of support and load. Elongated like immensely drawn-out cantilevers, the trusses embody movement in all their parts. Nothing remains of the quiet stone architecture of the barrel vault. A new sort of movement, penetrating space — as new in kind as that achieved in Borromini's cupolas — is created here.

Traditional static feelings disrupted

There is a further distortion of scale which must be noted: a section of these trusses would be about five times as deep as it was wide (three and a half meters deep by seventy-five centimeters wide). This is felt as a distortion, since the eye tends to take the dimensions of the stone architrave as its standard of comparison.

When trusses were enlarged to such proportions there seemed to be a lack of filling material. In addition these girders were unusually light, since this was the first time steel framework had been used to such an extent. The eye of the contemporary onlooker was confused by these strange dimensions. Even Anatole de Baudot, one of the first to open a path for contemporary architecture, declares that the proportions are a failure, and the Belgian constructer Vierendeel complains that "this lack of proportion produces a bad effect; the girder is not balanced; it has no base . . . it starts too low. . . . The eye is not reassured. . . . The supports of the Galerie des Machines show another fault: they are too empty."

Contemporary criticisms

161. International Exhibition, Paris, 1889. *Base of three-hinged arch.*

162. EDGAR DE–GAS. "The Dancer." *Degas, the most daring experimentalist among the painters of the period and the exact contemporary of Eiffel, projects his dancers stripped of all erotic façade. He shows their distended nostrils and all the tenseness of straining effort. Max Liebermann remarks (in "Pan," the most "precious" of the German avant-garde reviews, p. 195) that "he seems to disguise his models and to see the nascent prostitute in the young dancer: no other painter has so completely subdued the novelistic element." This painting exhibits in its field the impersonal, precise, and objective spirit which produced constructions like the Galerie des Machines.*

It is precisely the features that are criticized which pointed to later developments. Here construction is unconsciously moving toward aesthetic feelings which did not find their equivalents in art and architecture until decades later.

Construction moves unconsciously toward new aesthetic feelings

In this hall the light pouring in from above swallowed up the thin latticework. So far as the optical impression is concerned, the vault attains a floating or hovering state.

The last hint of the antique column has disappeared. It is impossible to separate load and support.

Bent as though in the act of leaping, the vaulting starts at a very low level to take up its load. If we wish, we may regard this vaulting as our equivalent of the caryatid. It does not

273

163. Popular painting, "The Kiss of the Wave," 1889. *An immense woodcut filling two pages in no. 2 of "Le Courrier de l'Exposition," special edition, April 14, 1889. With its facile histrionics and its full share of erotic façade it met all the demands of its day.*

carry its burden with the dignity of the maidens of the Erechtheum nor does it break down under it like the nude giants on baroque portals. It springs up against its load to unite with it.

The ends of the girders, narrowing as they approach the floor (*fig.* **161**), are no longer rigidly connected with the ground but are left free to move. The girders transmit their own weight, plus the horizontal stress of 120,000 kilograms, directly through a hinged joint. With this system of support, even foundation movements could take place without setting up internal stresses.[17] This was the only means whereby the play of forces at all points of the system could be controlled.[18]

---

[17] This is an example of the way in which during the nineteenth century important results followed from the application to building of discoveries made in purely technological fields. Hinged joints were used in bridges around 1870 by Eiffel and others. (Cf. Erving Matheson, *Works in Iron*, London, 1873, p. 145.) The outstanding example is Eiffel's bridge over the Douro, in Portugal.

[18] "A single method of construction produced a mathematical determination of the distribution of the forces in different sections of the arch. This was the articulation at base and apex. The system ensured a rational and completely exact distribution of the stresses and of the materials used" (Alphand, p. 46).

The division between load and support which was still indicated in De Dion's halls of 1878 is here obliterated. Iron vaulting has found its true form. The play of enormous forces is held in an equilibrium that is floating rather than rigid.

It is the equilibrium of a balance beam daringly poised against continually varying forces.

A new oscillating harmony is created.

An elastic counterpoise is achieved which absorbs changes in the interior, the exterior, and the foundation.

This counterpoise adjusts itself to fluctuations of the ground.

An equilibrium is achieved against changes in the molecular structure of the building itself.

An equilibrium is achieved against external pressure, wind, and snow.

Construction passes over into expression.

Construction becomes the form giver.

Chicago, 1893

It is a curious illustration of the complex character of the nineteenth century that the great exhibitions should have begun their decline in Chicago. At this period Chicago was the place where the most daring and original work with office buildings and apartment houses was being done. While the Paris exhibitions — and especially that of 1889 — produced structures that opened up new ranges of feeling, the World's Columbian Exhibition at Chicago was the beginning of "mercantile classicism." The influence of its plaster architecture was widespread and tenacious. This was foreseen at the time by Louis Sullivan, who in his *Autobiography of an Idea* predicted that "the damage wrought to this country by the Chicago World's Fair will last half a century."

Chicago: advanced office buildings and "mercantile classicism"

Louis Sullivan's prediction

It is true that there were good things at Chicago in 1893: Louis Sullivan's own Transportation Building (his one contribution to the fair) and the covered piers that ran out into Lake Michigan. The contemporary Belgian constructor Vierendeel

275

was nevertheless quite justified in saying that "the constructions were only imitations of what we have known in Europe
for a long time. We expected better, much better, from the
well-known audacity, initiative, and originality of the Americans. We have been profoundly deceived." The staff architecture enveloping the metal framework also lacked originality.
"In a new world they dared no innovations. They had doubts
of themselves." [19]

It was not the pure curves of the piers extending out into the
lake that delighted the public but rather the gondolas and
gondoliers that had been especially imported from Venice
(*fig.* **164**). Louis Sullivan's building also failed to achieve a
popular success, which went instead to those "marble"
colonnades that were born out of the spirit of the French academicians — the very men who had done everything in their
power to prevent the erection of the Eiffel Tower. At the
Chicago World's Fair the architects believed that they were

[19] *La Construction architecturale en fer et acier* (Brussels, 1902), p. 249.

164. World's Fair, Chicago,
1893. *Venetian gondoliers.*

reviving the creative spirit of Medicean times and the public fancied that the radiance of Florence was being recalled for them to live in. These attitudes are easily understood; they represent only another one of those frequent and futile attempts to escape from the actual present, which — like financial crises — recur constantly throughout the industrial era.

It would have been very interesting — had space permitted — to deal in some detail with the immense influence of the "Great Exhibitions" on the industry and life of nations. The manner in which the "theme" of each exhibition found expression certainly merits some discussion also. Ultimately, "the industry of all nations" came to be the inevitable theme for any great exposition — and also came to be accepted without any of the wonder and excitement that had attached to it in the beginning. At that moment the exhibition as a problem in building lost all its creative force. It became simply an organized show like many others, and its success or failure was a matter of no historical importance. Since the opening of this century world fairs have been transitory occurrences that have fallen ever further into commercial advertising, although here and there an interesting building has appeared, such as Le Corbusier's Electricity Pavilion at the Brussels World's Fair in 1958. Today's fairs can give no impetus to such themes as "A Formulation of the Needs and Desires of Mankind" (Brussels). These can only find their expression in the real world: in new towns and in the renewal of community life.

Decline of the great exhibitions

GUSTAVE EIFFEL AND HIS TOWER

No other century in the history of the western world developed such hypertrophic building activity as the nineteenth, and none produced such a small number of creative architects. We do not think that this is due to any lack of talent, but rather believe the society gradually killed any creative impulse with the poison of its ruling taste.

Fate of architects and engineers

165. International Exhibition, Paris, 1867. *Iron skeleton. Probably the first pure skeleton construction was the elliptical main exhibition building of this world's fair. Behind the chief engineer stood the young Eiffel, the real inspirer. He calculated and verified the construction of the pillars and the wide span of 35 meters. The modulus of elasticity in a large construction was tested for the first time.*

When revolutionary architects such as Henri Labrouste were finally admitted to the French Academy, it was already recognized by their contemporaries that they had left behind them "la passion et l'espoir de confesser leur temps." [1] Architecture must stand up to wind and weather that it may have a chance to have its impact on man. Unlike painting, architecture that never leaves the paper fades away like an old photograph.

Sheltered in the shadow of industry and protected by the authority of science, engineers were not hampered in their development, for they did not have to play up to the ruling taste. Although their names were unknown in their day, they are noted in history and will not be forgotten. In the same way most of their work remained anonymous, like

[1] Émile Trélat, in *Encyclopédie d'Architecture* (Paris), 1880, p. 45.

Gustave Eiffel's elegant skeleton (1886) that carries the hammered copper skin of the Statue of Liberty at the entrance of New York Harbor. That Eiffel's name is familiar to the public is due only to the fact that the Eiffel Tower bore his name from the very beginning.

Gustave Eiffel (1832–1923) [2] came from Burgundy, the birthplace of many great constructors. He got the best training available, at the École Polytéchnique and the École Centrale. We encountered his name earlier in connection with his calculations for the arches of the Galerie des Machines (1867), the glass walls of the large entrance hall for the international exhibition of 1878, and the marvelously lit Bon Marché department store in Paris (1876), now deprived of its original charm through hopeless "modernization."

Gustave Eiffel

In the daring construction of bridges over deep rivers in Europe and Africa, and also over the enormous streams of Indo-China, he learned to master the elements of weather, water, and wind. By means of hydraulic pressure the piles of his first bridge near Bordeaux (1858), were driven twenty-five meters below the surface of the water. Later, when he had to span deep gorges, he erected columns (pylons) in the shape of slender pyramids, tapering toward the traffic-way they support. The large spans and the lofty heights of these latticed supports, designed according to the newest methods and with the greatest elegance, made him and his engineers familiar with the impact of the wind. Early he was interested in meteorological research, and in his later days he was one of the first to found — at his own expense — an aerodynamic laboratory. From the platform of his tower he dropped an apparatus he had invented for registering the influence of wind pressure on plane surfaces. Later, in his laboratory at Auteuil, he had a large wind tunnel built for experiments in the field of aviation. The action of moving air on rigid bodies continuously preoccupied him — an interest carefully registered in many of his publications.

Eiffel's foremost interest

Gustave Eiffel is the master of elegantly constructed iron towers — pylons — and airy two-hinged arches, which formed, connected by horizontal traffic-ways, bridges like that over

Arched bridges

---

[2] See Jean Prevost's small biography, *Eiffel* (Paris, 1929).

the Douro or the Garabit Viaduct. The grandiose display of equipoise which they offered had never been surpassed.

The river Douro [3] in northern Portugal, with its strong and changing currents, its depth varying between forty-five and sixty feet, in addition to a very unstable soil, made the use of piles in the river bed not possible. Eiffel bridged it in a single span of about five hundred feet — 160 meters — the longest at that time (*fig.* **166**), with exception, of course, of suspension bridges. Eiffel built the two-hinged arch from the

166. G. EIFFEL. Bridge over the Douro, 1875. *Span, 160 meters; height, 61 meters above the level of the water. In erecting the high pylons and assembling the arches in midair, Eiffel gained the necessary precision and experience to build the thousand-foot tower.*

high iron pylons without scaffolding, by means of suspended cables (1876–77). The Americans in bridging the Mississippi River at St. Louis used a similar procedure.

The most daring of Eiffel's bridges remains the Garabit Viaduct (1880–84).[4] Its total length is nearly half a kilo-

---

[3] G. Eiffel, *Notice sur le Pont Douro* (Clichy, 1879). Good descriptions, drawings and woodcuts.

[4] G. Eiffel, *Mémoire présenté à l'appui du projet définitif du Viaduc de Garabit* (Paris, 1889). The importance of this bridge is shown in a large portfolio with all stages of the calculation, the procedures of assembly, and photographs.

280

meter; it crosses the gorge 122.5 meters over the river Thuyère with an arch span of 165 meters (*figs.* **167, 168**). He used every possible graphic, analytic, and experimental means to design his parabolic arches, which touch the ground in point supports.

It was here that Eiffel and his engineers learned to master the difficulties of assembling precisely dimensioned parts, so that later the rivet holes of the factory-made members of the Eiffel Tower could coincide to the tenth of a millimeter when being erected on the site.

The Eiffel Tower

The one-thousand-foot Eiffel Tower, erected for the Paris exhibition of 1889, embodied in one single work all his experience with foundations and supports, against the intricacies of earth and wind.[5] Even Eiffel himself was at first afraid to shock the ruling taste with the erection of an uncompromising bare structure in the heart of Paris, but he was urged on by the head of his "Bureau d'études," the young Swiss engineer Maurice Koechlin (1856–1946), who had made calculations for the Garabit Viaduct.

In his artistic taste Eiffel was a true son of his time. His own residence was filled with "a mess of heteroclite and unbelievably ugly works of art." [6] As is well known, even the creative personalities of our time still suffer from the split between the methods of feeling and the methods of thinking. Eiffel does not differ in this respect from other great constructors, like Freyssinet and Maillart.

Viewed from the standpoint of construction, the whole tower is an adaptation of the lofty supports of iron bridges, increased to cosmic dimensions. It springs in three stages to its full height. Its large dimensions made it necessary to compose the structure of four members meeting asymptotically at the top and embracing an enormous space. The four pylons are anchored to separate foundations, for which

---

[5] In 1900 Eiffel published *La Tour de trois cents mètres* in two monumental folio volumes, describing the structure which will stand forever as a personification of "l'art de l'ingénieur moderne et le siècle d'industrie et de science." These are the words with which in 1885 he introduced his "Tower in iron" before the Society of Civil Engineers in Paris.

[6] Blaise Cendrars, *Aujourd'hui* (Paris, 1931), p. 148.

167. G. EIFFEL. Garabit Viaduct, 1880–84. *The most daring of Eiffel's bridges. Span, 165 meters; total length, almost half a kilometer; height above the water, 122.5 meters. A perfect example of coördination of vision, calculation, and experiment.*

168. G. EIFFEL. Garabit Viaduct. *Detail of abutment. In the late nineteenth century, pure forms — as far as structures are concerned — are found in the works of the great engineers. The plastic form of arch, hinged joint, and abutment transcend the realm of construction.*

169. G. EIFFEL. Decorative arch of the Eiffel Tower, 1889. *The arch is merely a decorative link, somehow a distraction for the eye from the heavy horizontal girders which connect the four pylons.*

170. G. EIFFEL. A pier of the Eiffel Tower. *Viewed from the angle of construction the Eiffel Tower is formed of four immense pylons, merging asymptotically together.*

Eiffel used, of course, the hydraulic press, as he had done for his bridges since 1858. Elevators run in the interior of the supports as far as the second platform. Another elevator runs within the core of the structure from the second to the third platform, 904 feet above the ground. The four arches which connect the supports (*fig.* **169**) are mainly decorative, reminiscent nevertheless of Eiffel's original intention of carrying the tower on four bridge arches.

The airiness one experiences when at the top of the tower makes it the terrestrial sister of the aeroplane. It is interesting that revenue from the entrance fees declined after the enormous success of the exhibition in 1889, to rise again steadily from 1904,[7] which corresponds with the time when the interest in flying machines began to arouse public curiosity. It was no accident that Santos-Dumont chose to circle about this tower on his spectacular flight in his airship.

To a previously unknown extent, outer and inner space are interpenetrating (*fig.* **171**). This effect can only be experienced in descending the spiral stairs from the top, when the soaring lines of the structure intersect with the trees, houses, churches, and the serpentine windings of the Seine. The interpenetration of continuously changing viewpoints creates, in the eyes of the moving spectator, a glimpse into four-dimensional experience.

Emotional content of the tower

The emotional content of the tower remained veiled during the next decades. The tower, which "stood up from Paris like a hatpin" for the generation coming to the fore around 1910, was of course for the representatives of the ruling taste a menace, a disgrace. In February 1887, a month after Gustave Eiffel had signed the contract with the French government and the city of Paris, the famous protest against the erection of the tower was handed to the chairman of the exhibition committee: "We, the writers, painters, sculptors, and architects come in the name of French good taste and of this menace to French history to express our deep indignation that there should stand in the heart of our Capital this unnecessary and monstrous Tour Eiffel." But, fortu-

---

[7] *Journal du Crédit Public*, April 25, 1929.

nately, the chairman was the farsighted engineer and landscape architect Alphand, the same man who had created, under Haussmann, the great parks of Paris.

Two decades later, an optical revolution shattered the static viewpoint of the Renaissance, and suddenly the hidden emotional content of the tower was revealed. It now became the symbol of the "Grande Ville." "Such was Paris, with her great tower from which every night streamed the blue tresses of the wireless telegraph."[8]

It was now that the great tower found its artistic revelation. The Parisian painter, Robert Delauney (1885–1947), found in its structure a possibility of showing what was going on below in the changing apprehension of the outer world (*fig. 173*). Indeed since 1910 the tower, portrayed in all its multi-sidedness, accompanied Delauney through all the different stages of his life. The poet Blaise Cendrars in his *Aujourd'hui* gives us insight into the new approach of this young generation.

No longer is the tower a hideous monster. It grows in its emotional significance, and its contemporary, the Sacré Cœur of Montmartre, with its white cupolas, becomes degraded to a sugarplum in the eye of the poet.

"I saw through my window the Eiffel Tower like a flask of clear water, the domes of the Invalides and the Pantheon as a teapot and sugar basin, and the Sacré Cœur a pink and white sugarplum. Delauney came almost every day to visit me. He was always haunted by the tower."[9]

"At that time there was no artistic formula that could claim to express the plasticity of the Eiffel Tower. Under the laws of realism it crumbled, and the laws of Italian perspective could not catch it. . . . But Delauney wanted to find a plastic interpretation. He dismembered the tower so that he might enter within its frame; he truncated it and inclined it to make it express the vertigo of its full three hundred meters; he took ten standpoints, fifteen outlooks; he looked at this part from

[8] For this and other quotations from contemporary poets, see C. Giedion-Welcker, "Robert Delauney," in *Das Werk* (Zurich), No. 8 (1946).
[9] Blaise Cendrars, *Aujourd'hui*, p. 136.

171. G. EIFFEL. Spiral staircases between first and second floors of the Eiffel Tower. *Ever-changing viewpoints and interpenetration of inner and outer space were experienced here decades before architects or painters realized the new conception of space.*

173. ROBERT DELAUNEY.
Eiffel Tower, 1910. →

172. G. EIFFEL. Eiffel Tower. *View from the second platform to the first. The photo is made in the elevator shaft. Right and left, the elevator tracks which penetrate into the ground floor.*

174. ARNODIN. Ferry Bridge in the "Vieux Port" of Marseilles, 1905. *Iron structure and stone architecture blend well together.*

176. ARNODIN. Ferry Bridge, Marseilles, 1905. *Height, 54 meters; length of carriage-way, 240 meters.* →

175. ARNODIN. Ferry Bridge, Marseilles. *View from upper platform to suspended ferry. Relation between fixed and moving parts. Slender steel construction. Observe platforms of staircase, jutting boldly out into space. (Cf. Bauhaus balconies, 1926.)*

below, that from above, the surrounding houses from the right, from the left, from the wings of a bird and from the bed of the earth." [10]

Of the Eiffel Tower, Duchamp-Villon said, "This masterpiece of mathematical energy rose from its scientific conception into the unconscious realm of beauty. It is more than a mere cipher, for it contains a vital element; our spirit surrenders to it as when it is emotionally moved by the art of sculpture or architecture." [11]

No doubt, in this hovering tower some of the spirit has materialized of the technical Utopianism of Jules Verne, who belonged to Eiffel's generation.

The rapid evolution from James Bogardus' unexecuted cast-iron tower for the New York World's Fair of 1853 (*fig.* **111**) to the Eiffel Tower, conceived only three decades later, when viewed in historic dimension is indeed fantastic. After reaching this peak, the evolution slowed down and turned in other directions. During the following half-century the steel skeleton of the skyscraper developed in America. In France, nearest to the airy sensitivity of the Eiffel Tower were the elegant ferry bridges, especially that of the Vieux Port at Marseille, 1905 (*figs.* **174, 175, 176**), which was heavily damaged toward the end of the second world war and later destroyed.

The engineer, Arnodin, was a specialist in these elegant structures, which he knew how to place excellently in French river ports as in Rouen (1889) or in Nantes, the latest having been erected in the late twenties in Bordeaux.

The ferry bridge at Marseille, the Pont Transporteur, which had to transport vehicles across the river without hindering the passage of tall-masted ships, consisted of two pairs of slender pylons touching the earth at two points. They supported at a lofty height a carriage-way for the traveling crane from which the ferry, hovering over the water, was suspended by cables.

---

[10] *Ibid.*, pp. 145–148, translated by J.T.

[11] "L'Architecture et le fer," in *Poème et Drame* (Paris), January–March, 1914.

PART **IV** **THE DEMAND FOR MORALITY IN ARCHITECTURE**

THE NINETIES: PRECURSORS OF CONTEMPORARY ARCHITECTURE

There are whole decades in the second half of the nineteenth century in which no architectural work of any significance is encountered. Eclecticism smothered all creative energy. Here and there — especially as the century wore on — voices were raised in protest, but they could do nothing to alter conditions.

It was just at this time that an unprecedented wave of building activity swept over Europe. Its cities took on the shapes from which we still suffer today.

The painter was able to withdraw from this overpowering environment. The men who did the important work at this period gave up all prospects of fame and an audience and practiced their art in seclusion. Cézanne and Van Gogh, for example, buried themselves in the solitude of Provence. The architect had no such course open to him; not a single one managed to escape from the atmosphere of eclecticism.

Dissatisfaction with this almost universal state of affairs reached its peak around 1890. Toward the end of the century H. P. Berlage was to produce a building which would serve to purify architecture all over Europe, his Amsterdam Stock Exchange. In the nineties he was already denouncing the prevailing architecture as "Scheinarchitektur, d.h. Imitation, d.h. Lüge" ("Sham architecture; i.e., imitation; i.e., lying"). "Our parents and grandparents as well as ourselves," Berlage wrote, "have lived and still live in surroundings more hideous than any known before. . . . Lying is the rule, truth is the exception."

The smoldering hatred of eclecticism came to a head in Europe with startling suddenness. In the same way, a fish net can be hauled for a long time quite uneventfully and then, in a single moment, the whole catch shows up all bunched together. This moment in the history of architecture did not arrive by accident: industry had at length reached its full development and the time was ripe for great changes. In the earlier part of the century decades go by with nothing achieved in architecture; toward the close of the century almost every year has importance. Ambition revives and brings with it courage and strength to oppose those forces which had kept life from finding its true forms. Developments come in one surge after another. The diversity of movements with their variety of experimental gropings indicates the vitality of the period. Individual failures and the mixture of transitory with constituent facts are of little importance. These are traits of every transitional period. Much of what was attempted between 1890 and 1930 remained fragmentary and incomplete. This period, however, found the courage to undertake the building up of a tradition of its own.

According to the easy explanation that was advanced later, the movement developed as the application of two principles: the abandonment of historical styles, and — consequent upon this — the use of "fitness for purpose" as a criterion. The explanation is correct, inasmuch as both these factors were involved, but it does not go far enough. The movement took its strength from the moral demands which were its real source. The cry went up, "Away with this infected atmosphere!"

Moral demands behind the new movement

The young painter Henri van de Velde was among those who attacked the "infected atmosphere" most vigorously. In the late nineties he took the lead in the fight for *l'art moderne*. He campaigned for it first in his native Belgium, next in France, and then in a country which, at the time, lay wide open to any new movement — Germany. When he showed his furniture to an art dealer in Paris on his first journey abroad, it was rejected; a year later in Germany both the critics and the public were highly receptive. This was the start of his international fame. I met van de Velde in 1938 when he had just returned from laying the cornerstone of the Belgian Pavilion at the New York World's Fair. Knowing that he had begun his career as a painter, I asked him how he had come to turn to architecture. He answered by describing the situation that prevailed around 1890: "The real forms of things were covered over. In this period the revolt against the falsification of forms and against the past was a moral revolt." [1]

Van de Velde: what drove him into architecture

He went on to tell how a nervous breakdown had left him incapable of work. At this point he met his future wife, who

[1] "Toutes les formes étaient cachées. À cette époque la révolte contre les mensonges des formes et le passé était une révolte morale."

gave him renewed courage to face life. "I told myself — this was in 1892 — that I would never allow my wife and family to find themselves in 'immoral' surroundings." [2] But at that date everything that one could buy on the open market was smothered under the *mensonge des formes* which van de Velde hated. He had to design for himself everything in his house, from cutlery to doorknobs. Then — since these articles demanded a setting which would "ward off ugliness" — he was led to build his first house. It showed a remarkable freedom in the treatment of the roof and in the way in which the windows were cut out to meet the special requirements of each room. The revolution this house provoked when it was completed in 1896 derived from its pronounced simplicity, in strong contrast with the over-fanciful façades to which people were accustomed. In this respect van de Velde's earliest house in Uccle, near Brussels, pointed further into the future than Horta's house in the Rue de Turin, Paris.

Henri van de Velde spent his last years in Switzerland in a house built by Alfred Roth on the Aegerisee. The interest of the old master in contemporary problems remained undiminished and he always turned the conversation to the question: What can actually be realized? Once he weighed the balance between the nineties and the present day: "At first, in the revolution against the falsification of forms, we had ourselves to design every detail, down to the door latches and the tableware. Then came the time when interiors had to be designed by Professor So-and-so. Now we can assemble together completely anonymous objects. This is definitely an advance."

Parallel case of William Morris (1859)

A generation earlier the same disgust with the falsification of forms in all objects of trade had led William Morris to create and equip his "Red House" at Upton in Kent, England. According to one of Morris' biographers, Red House had much the same history as van de Velde's house in Uccle: "During the year 1858, William Morris plodded on as a painter with a

[2] "Je me disais — c'était en 1892 — jamais je ne veux pas admettre que ma femme et ma famille se trouvent dans un milieu qui est immorale."

[3] There are some excellent illustrations of this house in a book by van de Velde's biographer and Maecenas, Karl Ernest Osthaus: *Van de Velde* (Hagen i. W, 1920) and in van de Velde's memoirs, *Geschichte meines Lebens* (published and edited by Hans Curjel, Munich, 1962), which, in the chapter "Epilog in Oberaegeri, 1947–1957," give an insight into van de Velde's last years.

growing dejection over the work accomplished despite the fact that he sold one picture for £70. But Morris' wedding, in April 1859, turned his mind again and more intensely to those domestic arts which had attracted him at Red Lion Square. He now set his heart on building a home that should fulfill his conception of the 'house beautiful,' and secured Webb's services as architect. . . . The name of the house, which is built of red brick and tiles, expressed a revolt against the prevailing and tyrannous formula of stucco walls and slate roofs." [4]

Does this parallel mean that van de Velde simply followed the example Morris had already set? We do not think so. The parallel springs from the fact that the disorder introduced into human life by industry made itself felt in England more than thirty years earlier than on the Continent. Identical conditions led to identical reactions.

Brussels the Center of Contemporary Art, 1880–1890

Why was Belgium, rather than some other country on the Continent, the starting point of the new movement?

The pioneering spirit of Henri van de Velde can only be understood in relation to the background provided for it by Belgium in the eighties. Belgium was the first country on the Continent to become heavily industrialized. The problems that grow out of industrialization thus showed themselves first and most intensely in Belgium.

But there was another reason — at least as important as this one — why it was in Belgium that *l'art nouveau* first began to affect architecture and the industrial arts. Brussels between 1880 and 1890 was the one city in the entire cultural world which gave a welcome and a hearing to those creative artists who were despised or ignored by the great public. Painters like Seurat, Cézanne, and van Gogh, sculptors like Rodin and Meunier, musicians like Debussy and Vincent d'Indy, and poets like Verhaeren were invited to Brussels to present their work for exhibition and discussion. The courage and

---

[4] Montague Weekley, *William Morris* (London, 1934), p. 53. It was at Red Lion Square that Morris had established his first workshop, in conjunction with Burne-Jones.

artistic instinct required to establish such a policy cannot be overestimated. These exhibitions, lectures, and concerts represented the first systematic attack upon a public taste that for decades had been corrupted by the productions of an art entirely out of touch with life. The pseudo-monumental façades of the period and its *peinture à la mode* were both alike examples of the *mensonge des formes*.

The work of education in Belgium was carried on by two men who loved the arts, and who themselves wrote, painted, and composed in the time allowed them by their professions: Octave Maus (1856–1919) and Edmond Picard (1836–1924). Both were well-to-do lawyers who entertained extensively.[5]

L'Art moderne
(1881)

In 1881 Maus, Picard, and some others founded the weekly periodical, *L'Art moderne*. Each number contained only a few printed sheets; there were no illustrations, and the articles published were usually unsigned. One of these anonymous essays in the first issue of the magazine (dated March 6, 1881) announces a program directed not only against academic art but against fixed conceptions of all kinds:

"Art is for us the contrary of every recipe and formula. Art is the eternally spontaneous and free action of man on his environment for the purpose of transforming it and making it conform to a new idea."

L'Art moderne appeared regularly for over thirty years — extraordinary longevity in a review of this type — and served as a model for many of the later periodicals that took up the cause of the *avant-garde*. Its files offer a still unexplored mine of information to the historian of the period. It was this review that soon after its foundation brought together the group of young Belgian artists known as "Les XX" ("The Twenty"). Among its members were Ferdinand Knopff and A. W. Finch (who, according to Henri van de Velde, made the bridge between Morris and his circle and the Belgian *art nouveau*).

---

[5] Picard was perhaps the more versatile of the two. In his youth he interrupted his studies for some time to become a sailor. Later he studied philosophy and law and became a valued advocate at court. Over and above his professional work he was active as a critic. In his review, *L'Art moderne*, he defended the victims of popular disapproval, the impressionists and all the rest. Octave Maus was an initiator with a great range of interests. He had both the instinct and the tireless energy needed for organizing endeavors on a large scale.

Another member was James Ensor. Ensor was already prominent as a painter when the first exhibition in 1884 showed a large number of his pictures. (Most of these now hang in the Musées Royaux des Beaux Arts in Brussels.)

Maus was the secretary and the leading spirit of Les XX for as long as the society existed, from 1884 to 1893. He went on to found La Libre Esthétique, the association which replaced Les XX in 1894. The Libre Esthétique showed the work of William Morris and gave the young Henri van de Velde a chance to put his ideas before the public. In a lecture on the "déblaiement d'art" van de Velde told of what had been done in England and France and pointed to America as the land of the future.

Maus discerned in all countries the hidden forces that were at work, quite ignored by the public. He sought to persuade all those artists who — like Cézanne — were unwilling to show their work to exhibit at Brussels. At the first exhibition in 1884 the Frenchman Rodin (who exhibited his bust of Victor Hugo), the American Whistler, and the German Max Liebermann were represented. As year followed year, new names appeared on the list: in 1886 Auguste Renoir, in 1887 Georges Seurat (who showed one of his principal works, "Un Après-midi de Dimanche sur l'île de la Grande Jatte," now in the Chicago Art Institute). Pissarro and Berthe Morisot were also included in the 1887 exhibition. *Avant-garde exhibitions*

This huge Seurat picture, arriving fresh from the artist's studio with its flat treatment of landscape and figures and all its *poésie aérienne*, caused a terrific uproar. This picture — whose value is no longer a subject for controversy — was attacked with umbrellas at its first showing, so van de Velde told me.

In 1889 van Gogh made his debut at Brussels. His feverish colors made the greatest impression on the young artists. Cézanne, who exhibited at the same time, was almost overlooked.

We have mentioned only one phase of the activity that went on in Brussels during these years and have noted only the high points in that phase. Even so, there is no need for further explanation of the sudden emergence there of so many talents. Henri van de Velde is one instance; Victor Horta and Paul Hankar are others.

The English
arts and crafts
associations of
the eighties

In Brussels between 1884 and 1894 the works of great contemporary painters and sculptors found display. In England during the same period a different kind of contribution to the arts was made. It was at this time that the work of Morris and his circle began to bear fruit, and that a serious attempt was made to reform public taste in the field of household furnishings. Meanwhile a younger generation of artists had grown up — men like Arthur H. Mackmurdo, Cobden-Sanderson, and C. R. Ashbee — who did not share Morris' hatred of modern techniques and business methods. The social point of view of Morris and Ruskin, however, was carried even further by this younger generation.

Numerous associations, like Mackmurdo's Art Workers' Guild of 1884, rallied together the artists and architects who were interested in art and handicrafts. Even the dilettantes joined together in the same year to form the Home Arts and Industries Association. The Arts and Crafts Exhibition Society organized great shows intended to prove that the so-called "minor arts" occupied as high a level as painting. This belief was — as is well known — taken up on the Continent about a decade later by the *art nouveau* movement, and vigorously argued by them.

As early as 1892 the Brussels exhibition had included examples of industrial art, specimen pieces of stained glass and ceramic work. In 1894, the year La Libre Esthétique was founded, there appeared the creations of the Morris group, as well as a typical contribution from a French artist — a studio interior.

So once more it was Brussels which was the starting point from which the arts and crafts movement spread over the Continent. Henri van de Velde — tireless both as an artist and as the evangelist of the *art nouveau* — carried his version of the findings arrived at in Brussels first to Paris (1896) and then to Dresden (1897). The few interiors which he exhibited created a sensation such as was rarely aroused at the time by work of this nature. The demonstration stirred to full consciousness talents in both countries which had hitherto been uncertain in what direction to turn for an outlet. The impact of the arts and crafts movement upon the all-too-long dormant Continent dates from this time.

Victor Horta's Contribution

Considering the receptivity of Brussels to new work in the arts, it is not surprising that the first really daring Continental residence should have been built there. This was Victor Horta's house at 12 Rue de Turin (*fig.* **177**). Completed in 1893, before there were any signs of a new European architecture, the Horta house marked a turning point in the treatment of the private home. From that time on, new artistic principles were to be applied to the problem of the dwelling, and new human needs were to be allowed to affect its design. This house roused Continental architecture from its lethargy at one blow.

House in the Rue de Turin (1893): a starting point for new developments

Number 12 Rue de Turin stands in a row of conventional Brussels residences. Since it had to conform to the same conditions, it resembles them in being long and very narrow: the front is a bare twenty-three feet across. The ground plan developed within these predetermined proportions, however, is entirely original. In the typical Brussels house, Horta tells me, the whole extent of the ground floor is visible from the entry. Horta avoided this by breaking the floor up into different levels. Thus the drawing room is half a story higher than the entrance hall which leads into it. Differences in level represent only one of the devices which Horta employed to give new flexibility to the ground plan. He hollowed out the massive body of the house, introducing light-wells that provided new and unusual sources of illumination in so narrow an exterior. The photographs do not reveal the surprising interrelations into which these rooms at their different levels are brought. And all this was done within the smallest compass imaginable (*fig.* **178**).

Flexible treatment of the ground plan

Horta's house was soon famous in every European circle interested in restoring the vitality of architecture. It was ad-

Contemporary opinion

177. VICTOR HORTA. 12 Rue de Turin, Brussels, 1893.

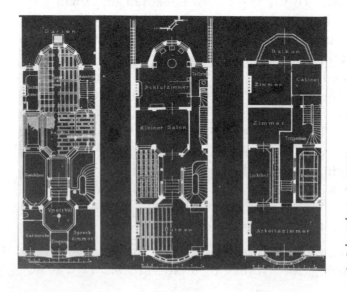

178. VICTOR HORTA. 12 Rue de Turin, Brussels. *Plan. Horta achieves flexibility and some independence between floors through the use of the internal iron skeleton.*

300

179. St. Louis river front, 109–111 North First Street, 1849 or 1850. *An earlier American combination of those elements developed for industrial buildings which Horta translates into residential terms.*

mired chiefly for two things: its perfect adjustment to its owner (a Mr. Tassel), and its freedom from any trace of historical styles. Five years after it was built, the Austrian critic, Ludwig Hevesi, published an article which shows the value his contemporaries placed on Horta's work.

"There lives in Brussels now, in 1898, the most inspired of the modern architects, Victor Horta. . . . His fame is exactly six years old, and dates from the residence of Mr. Tassel in the Rue de Turin. This is the first of these famous modern dwellings which fit their owners like faultlessly cut coats. It houses the man for whom it was built in the most perfect manner conceivable — as perfectly as the mussel shell does the mussel. It is most simple and logical . . . altogether new and just as delightful. But — and note this — there is in it not the faintest echo of any of the historical styles. . . . No detail derives from anything at all in existence. It has the pure charm of lines, curves, and surfaces — and it is quite personal, as personal as if Horta, instead of simply drawing the parts, had handed them to the workmen all modeled in advance." [6]

John Nash, in the drawing room of the Royal Pavilion at Brighton (1818), had openly displayed the ornate cast-iron columns and girders that entered into its construction. No one before Horta had dared to follow this example and permit construction to intrude upon the intimacy of a private house. In Horta's house the staircase clearly reveals pillars and girders, which hold the eye by their shape and ornamentation (*fig.* **180**). The drawing room is even more notable in this respect; an I-section support is carried across its free space without any attempt at disguise.

The visitor receives his first impression of the interior of the house from the cast-iron column that rises from the elevated main floor next the staircase. Curved iron tendrils spring out of its vase-shaped capital. Their forms are partly like those of primitive plants, partly arbitrary creations. Their lines are freely continued on the smooth surfaces of the walls and vaulting and on the mosaics of the floor in wild and swirling curvilinear patterns.

The house in the Rue de Turin marks the first appearance of the *art nouveau* in the field of architecture. It is for this reason — not merely because of the qualities Hevesi admired in it — that it finds a place in all histories of art. In Horta's house the aims of the *art nouveau* were fully carried out in architectural terms at the very first attempt. There are no earlier examples in architecture of this transitional style. Indeed its best representative, Aubrey Beardsley, did not arrive at his own artistic language until 1893 — the date of the Rue de Turin residence.[7]

One source of the *art nouveau*

In Horta's house the point of origin of the *art nouveau* becomes patent: it is iron construction. What are these lines but the *unrolled* curls and rosettes that are to be found under the eaves of so many Belgian railway stations? They have simply stripped off their Gothic or Renaissance clothing (*fig.* **181**).

---

[6] *Wiener Tageblatt*, November 11, 1898.

[7] His drawings were included in the first volume of *Studio*, 1893.

180. VICTOR HORTA. 12 Rue de Turin, Brussels. *Iron column and staircase. At the end of the cast-iron period, the cast-iron column is once more introduced into the house — and brings the art nouveau with it.*

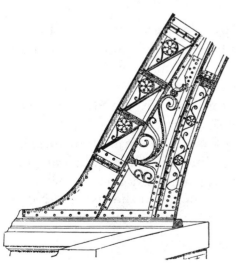

181. ALPHONSE BALAT. Strap-iron ornaments on the conservatory, Laeken, 1879. *One source of the art nouveau.*

The *art nouveau* was an interesting intermezzo between the nineteenth and twentieth centuries. It would be a digression, however, to go into the various theories of its origin.[8] In spite of the revolutionary intentions behind its fight against the use of historical styles, it succeeded only in matching shape against shape. It was in truth an "anti-movement." It should however be noted that the flat, unmodulated surfaces of painters like Gustav Klimt, and the fantastic sculptural modeling of the architecture of Antonio Gaudi were important for the future.

Significance of the façade

The front of the Tassel house is as original in its modeling as the interior. The bow window — a standard feature of every house in Brussels — is preserved, but Horta transforms it into a curved, glassed-in surface. The smoothly treated wall is blended into this undulating section. For all its fresh modeling, the façade is quite conservative in construction for the date it was built: it is simply the ordinary type of massive stone wall. Where a series of windows has been let in, horizontal supporting girders of wrought iron are introduced. These second-story windows run downward from the supporting girders to a point level with the floor. They are based on the principle of the display windows developed in the second half of the nineteenth century. The rivets in the girders are accentuated with the same fondness Otto Wagner shows in his handling of the aluminum bolts on the front of the Vienna Postal Savings Bank (1904).

The revolutionary aspect of Horta's work consists in this: he took over elements which had appeared in business and industrial buildings of the fifties and incorporated them in a private house. Purely utilitarian structures erected in America between 1850 and 1870 — for example, the St. Louis river front commercial buildings with their cast-iron fronts — are based on a principle which Horta uses. There are the same slim iron columns erected in front of a continuous range of glass windows. These earlier buildings make an even simpler and more convincing use of this principle, as in the 109–111 North First Street establishment of 1849–50 (*fig.* **179**).[9]

---

[8] Cf. Fritz Schmalenbach, *Jugendstil* (Würzburg, 1935).

[9] Cf. also figs. 112, 113.

What remains of importance in the house at 12 Rue de Turin? From our later point of view, it is neither its perfect adjustment to its owner nor the first appearance in it of the *art nouveau*. It is rather the flexible ground plan in which the consequences of the new materials were drawn — the free disposition of the rooms at different levels, and the independence of the partitions one from another. This is one of the European beginnings of what Le Corbusier was later to call *le plan libre*.

In 1897 Horta built his Maison du Peuple at Brussels. Its curved glass and iron façade is one of the boldest achievements of the period (*figs.* **182, 183**). The youthful freshness of his house in the Rue de Turin reappears in it; in this building Horta really is the *chercheur* that one of his contemporaries named him.[10]

The Maison du Peuple (1897); glass and iron front, imaginative layout

The interior shows all the independence of his earlier work. Without waste of either space or time, one is brought immediately into the great dining hall, with its wide opening and its freely outspread iron structure. Horta did not hesitate to place the lecture hall — so seldom called into use — in the upper story. The Maison du Peuple reveals in its every detail the hand of a trained architect who is at the same time an ingenious inventor. It is typical that in 1963 this milestone was threatened with destruction.

Horta (1861–1947) had a brilliant career. He was made head of the Academy at Brussels in 1913; later he became Baron Horta. He built many important structures. But comparatively soon he lost contact with youth and with the movement which continued his own efforts. This will concern us again when we speak of the competition for the League of Nations Palace (1927),[11] in which Horta played a decisive role as a juror.

Horta's later conservatism

During the summer of 1938, when I was in Brussels, I asked Baron Horta how he had come to build such a revolutionary structure as the house in the Rue de Turin.

When he was a young man, he explained, an architect at the beginning of his career had three courses open to him: he could

---

[10] *L'Émulation* (Brussels, 1895), p. 187.
[11] Cf. pp. 530–531.

establish himself as a specialist in Renaissance, classic, or Gothic modes. Horta found these restrictions illogical. "I asked myself why architects could not be as independent and daring as painters were." With that he pointed to a faded photograph which stood on his table: "This is my teacher, Balat, a classicist and a revolutionary — as well as the best Belgian architect of the nineteenth century.[12] I drew my youthful inspiration from his teaching."

Horta went on to explain the real individuality of Balat's work. His museum in Brussels was an entirely independent masterpiece in spite of its classical façade. It was this building which determined Horta to follow his own bent.

"Its fine ground plan — thoroughly organic and independent of conventional formulae — was entirely of Balat's creation. Why then did he have to copy the classic in its façade? Why not make a modern elevation, too, and be as independent and individual as the painters were?"

Paul Hankar and the Belgian movement

Victor Horta did not work alone; he was simply the outstanding member of a group. "En Belgique," as a Parisian critic wrote at the time, "on a toutes les témérités." In the Rue de Facque, not far from the Rue de Turin, Paul Hankar also built a house in the year 1893. While he does not show Horta's imagination, Hankar was working in the same direction.[13]

But Hankar's masterpiece was the installation of the colonial exhibition at Tervueren (1897), where the perfect unity of the spirit behind the iron construction and the interior aroused the interest of artistic Europe. Finished two years before the opening of Horta's Maison du Peuple, the exposition was entirely the product of the younger generation in Belgium. At this exposition, intended by Leopold II to render the Congo problem more attractive (its motto was "New State, New Woods, and New Shapes"), the young innovators were

---

[12] Alphonse Balat (1818–1905), *architecte du roi.* Besides the Brussels museum, he was famous for his bell-shaped *jardin d'hiver* of the Residence of Laeken (1879). The iron construction here is exceptionally fine. The strap-iron ornaments on the trusses suggest Horta's *art nouveau* ornamentation of his house in the Rue de Turin.

[13] Hankar and Horta were among the first Europeans to attack the design and equipment of department stores as an artistic problem, and Hankar's solutions are sometimes the purer. Hankar had to his credit the Magasins de la Maison Claessen, Rue de l'Écuyer, Brussels (1896), and the Maison de Coumerie, Rue Lebeau, Brussels (1895–96).

182. VICTOR HORTA. Maison du Peuple, Brussels, 1897. *Exterior. The curved glass and iron façade is one of the most advanced productions of the period.*

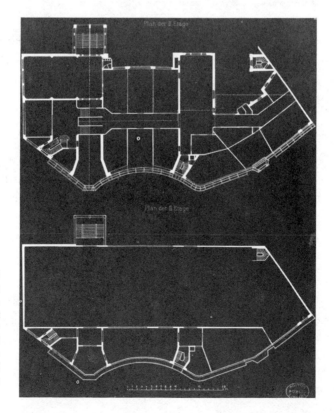

183. VICTOR HORTA. Maison du Peuple, Brussels, 1897. *Second- and third-floor plans. An interior organized with great astuteness and independence, the little-used lecture hall relegated to the upper story.*

184. H. P. BERLAGE. Stock Exchange, Amsterdam, 1898–1903. *Wall treatment. This — the Damrak Street side, which contains the offices of the Exchange — is one of the first European façades to return to the wall as a plane surface.*

given charge of the equipment of the interior. Even in the great Paris exhibitions this had remained the work of the *tapissiers.* This unity in design of interior and exterior had a decisive influence upon later developments.[14]

Berlage's Stock Exchange and the Demand for Morality

Dutch architecture in the nineteenth century

Dutch painting and architecture in the nineteenth century exhibited considerable moderation. The cities of Holland succeeded in escaping much of the disfigurement that other Continental cities experienced. The Rijks Museum and Cuyper's railway station are examples of the mild eclecticism that governed large buildings in Amsterdam.

On the other hand, Holland failed to take effective part in the developments going on (under French leadership) in painting and construction, or in the arts and crafts movement which

---

[14] For a more extended discussion of Hankar, cf. Charles Courady and Raymond Thibaut "Paul Hankar, 1859–1901," *Revue la Cité* (Brussels, 1923).

185. H. H. RICHARDSON. Sever Hall, Harvard University, Cambridge, Mass., 1878.

grew up in England. The Dutch stood aside from this activity; they never quite lost sight of the great tradition they had to preserve. And the seventeenth- and eighteenth-century mansions that stood alongside their canals served as quiet and constant reminders of that past.

One man and a single building announced a new vitality in Holland — Hendrik Petrus Berlage (1856–1934) and his Amsterdam Stock Exchange of 1898. Even in his own lifetime Berlage's contemporaries recognized what his unique achievement had been. It was he who first succeeded in realizing, in an actual building, the demand for a purified architecture. Others had seen the need for morality in architecture, but his Amsterdam Exchange actually embodied the thoroughgoing honesty they had only called for.

New vitality introduced by one building

Berlage's career as an architect was a curious one. Like another leader of his generation, Chicago's Louis Sullivan, his early work in the middle eighties was confined to office buildings of various types. They were in the mixed style — half

186. H. P. BERLAGE. Stock Exchange, Amsterdam, 1898–1903. *Drawing.*

Romanesque, half Renaissance — which was favored at this period.

Berlage was always very cautious in the use of new forms. He received first prize in a competition for the Amsterdam Stock Exchange as early as 1885.[15] If this plan for a quite conventional structure in Dutch Renaissance style had been followed, the Exchange would have failed entirely to influence later architecture.

In his final version Berlage used forms slightly suggestive of the Romanesque (*fig.* **186**). The Romanesque fascinated Berlage, as it had Henry Hobson Richardson some twenty years earlier. Berlage had carefully examined medieval buildings and knew their laws of proportion. We shall soon see, however, that Berlage's approach to the Romanesque differs from the transitory imitation of historical shapes.

Conservative methods of construction

We should not expect to find Berlage's treatment of the construction of the exchange embodying any revolutionary advances. Holland did not possess the great tradition in constructional matters which stood behind French architects, for example. It is nevertheless surprising that he did not avoid visible tie bars in the great hall of his Amsterdam Exchange by using the triply articulated girder. He is likewise very sparing

---

[15] He was not awarded the building contract until 1897, however. Cf. Jan Gratama, *Dr. H. P. Berlage* (Rotterdam, 1925), p. 28.

in his use of glass and iron. All this just before the turn of the century, when elegance in iron construction had been taken for granted for several decades. The construction of the Amsterdam Stock Exchange does not go a significant step beyond Henri Labrouste's work in the Bibliothèque Sainte-Geneviève of 1843. There too the iron work had been enclosed in a self-supporting masonry shell which was quite independent of it structurally.

Much greater daring in this respect was shown at this time by Victor Horta, in his Maison du Peuple at Brussels (1897–99).[16] Horta broke the façade wide open, and filled it with glass and iron. It was Berlage's work, however, which had the deeper and the more widespread effect. By their own testimony, it acted upon his contemporaries like a revelation.

Comparison with Horta's Maison du Peuple, Brussels

The Amsterdam Stock Exchange is a brick building without stucco surfacing on either the interior or the exterior. Its ground plan, which includes three glass-roofed halls, is very compact. The largest of the halls is occupied by the Commodity Exchange and dominates the whole building (*fig. 188*). Through the open arcades which lead to the brokerage and committee rooms the actual exchange in the center of the hall can be seen.

The exterior is the final result of many separate designs. In the earliest schemes everything was in a state of turbulence. In the final plan all the sections have been cleanly fused into the flat surface of the outer wall; not even the tower is allowed to project. It is only at the monumentally treated corner of the building where the main entrance and the tower come together that a trace of the restlessness of European architecture appears. There is nothing restless in the treatment of the side that fronts on Damrak Street (*fig. 184*).[17] This wall of the Exchange has the aspect of a simple office building — and that is just what it is on that side. The windows are flush with the wall, which is held to a flat surface, broken only by the square fall-pipes and the window sills.

Flat surfaces outstanding in Berlage's treatment of its exterior

---

[16] Cf. p. 303.

[17] In the design of this front Berlage used as a module the Egyptian triangle with its sides in the ratio 5:8.

187.　H. P. BERLAGE.　Stock Exchange, Amsterdam, 1898–1903.　*Interior.*

The brick walls of the loggias enclosing the Commodity Exchange also form a flat surface, from top to bottom (*fig.* **187**). Berlage, working with great discretion and smoothness, introduced several different materials into these walls: majolica, granite (in the square pillars), and various bright stones in the capitals of the pillars. But these capitals do not protrude in the usual way; they are level with the wall, as though cut off with a razor.

This feature is by no means a casual one. In a lecture on style in architecture Berlage explains what he was aiming at: "Above all we should show the naked wall in all its sleek beauty. . . . Pillars and columns should have no projecting capitals: the joint should be fused with the flat surface of the wall."[18]

What is the source of the great influence exerted by the building? The secret lies in the unshakeable consistency with which Berlage strives for sincerity and purity in its architecture. The granite steps of the staircase are only coarsely chiseled out; they are still rough today. The brick arches of the ceilings in the committee rooms are shown entirely without disguise. The iron girders of the framework are emphasized with paint. The clean white joints of the brickwork in the unplastered walls stand out sharply. Used this way — as though for the very first time — these materials act as unexpected decoration.

Source of Berlage's influence

As he himself points out, Berlage sought to impart to this building something of "the quality which distinguishes old monuments from the buildings of today: quiet!" With the least compromise possible at the time, he gave the wall — until then either chaotically dismembered or deceptively patched together — the reconquered unity of the flat surface.

The reconquest of the flat surface

The wall as a flat surface was soon to become the starting point for new principles in architecture, not merely in Holland but everywhere.

Berlage's conscious asceticism — called barbarism by some of his contemporaries — joined with his fanatical zeal for truth at any price to produce in the Amsterdam Stock Exchange a building which served as a guidepost to many. He gave an example of the honorable treatment of a problem in building. No other building accords so well with the demand that lay behind the movement in architecture at that time — the demand for morality.

In Europe, where the entire previous generation had taken an altogether different line, the purity of the wall came with the

---

[18] H. P. Berlage, *Gedanken über Stil in der Baukunst* (Leipzig, 1905), pp. 52–53.

impact of a revelation. It is improbable that it would have had the same revolutionary effect in America at that time — for reasons that we shall discuss later in some detail. At this point, however, some related work by an American architect may be mentioned.

Berlage and Richardson: their leaning toward Romanesque forms not mere historical imitation

Henry Hobson Richardson was one of the first Americans in this period consciously to practice architecture as a fine art. His Sever Hall of 1878 (one of the Harvard College buildings, Cambridge, Massachusetts) has much in common with Berlage's work (*fig.* **185**). Berlage and Richardson both tend toward simplified Romanesque forms, forms which from the time of their inception have been bound up with the treatment of the wall as a flat surface.

It might seem that these two men, in taking over Romanesque forms, simply differ from others among their contemporaries in the direction of their choice. The majority of these eclectics appropriated classical and Gothic shapes. And certainly their followers — those of Richardson particularly — returned to the familiar path of historical imitation. The rows of little houses, each like a tiny Romanesque castle, which sprang up some years later in America and Europe demonstrate this.

But the history of the nineteenth century is complicated. The new aims derived from their study of Romanesque buildings, and not the fact that Berlage and Richardson used somewhat Romanesque shapes, are what matter. The time was not ripe for the outright invention of new forms derived from a new space conception, and they turned — very naturally — to history for help. Romanesque methods started them on the way toward the new forms their own period still awaited.

The same relation exists between the Romanesque and their best buildings that links modern painting with primitive art. Picasso did not copy the patterns of African masks; he learned from them a new way of looking at his subjects. There was an affinity between that art and the not fully conscious endeavor of his own period to compose in terms of planes. To a certain extent Berlage and Richardson also found in the Romanesque not simply another transitory fashion but an inner affinity which aided them in moving toward the still-veiled expressions of their own period.

When we penetrate to what is significant in the Amsterdam Stock Exchange we understand why Berlage became the admirer and the European advocate of American architecture, particularly that of Frank Lloyd Wright. Berlage came to America in 1911, after his Stock Exchange had been finished, on the invitation of George E. Elmslie, Louis Sullivan's partner. He found here in American buildings just those things he himself had been fighting for so passionately in complete isolation.

Berlage and the next generation

Berlage's influence upon the rising generation was very great. Even when the younger men took other directions than those he had indicated, they retained all their reverence for his

315

artistic integrity. In Holland his influence and the image of the Amsterdam Stock Exchange appear behind an early project for a swimming pool by J. J. P. Oud (1915). As one of the first to introduce Frank Lloyd Wright's work to Europe, Berlage unconsciously made sure that the generation after him in Holland would be stimulated to production.[19]

In Belgium, too, Berlage made a deep impression on the rising generation. Victor Bourgeois, the Belgian architect whose Brussels garden settlement of 1922 — La Cité Moderne — gave the signal for the present-day movement, told me that around 1914, when he was a student at the Brussels Academy, only two names fascinated young men: those of Berlage and Frank Lloyd Wright.

Berlage was almost a recluse, so far as personal relations were concerned, but he valued objective connections. He was the only representative of the older generation to take part in the founding of the CIAM (*Congrès Internationaux d'Architecture Moderne*) at Château de la Sarraz, Switzerland, in June 1928. At this first international rally of contemporary architects, the younger men discussed nothing except the new points of departure. But Berlage, who, though he was the oldest participant, had not hesitated at the long journey from Holland, was the only one to read a carefully prepared paper, "The Relations between the State and Architecture."[20]

This small man — wearing the inevitable black cravat — sat in the Gothic chapel at La Sarraz quite isolated in the midst of a younger generation, and read his essay with imperturbable earnestness.

Otto Wagner and the Viennese School

Wagner's function as an educator

In the year 1894 Otto Wagner (1841–1918) was made professor of architecture at the Academy of Vienna. The Academy at the time appeared to have lost its attraction for the younger generation, and Wagner seemed the man to restore it. He was

---

[19] Curiously enough, Le Corbusier was first directed to Frank Lloyd Wright by a lecture Berlage delivered in Zurich (published *in extenso* by the *Schweizerische Bauzeitung*, vol. LX, nos. 11–13, 1912).

[20] This paper is preserved in the archives of the C.I.A.M., Zurich.

316

then just past fifty. He was a successful and energetic architect whose buildings in the manner of early Florentine and full Renaissance work were celebrated for their excellent plans. The Academy could expect to gain in luster from his presence. Just at the moment of his election, however, a metamorphosis which had long been preparing showed itself in his work.

It was in that year — 1894 — that he began a small book for his students with the title *Modern Architecture*.[21] Soon translated into many languages, it became the textbook of the new movement. In it Wagner asserted that "our starting point for artistic creation is to be found only in modern life." [22] He goes on to insist that new principles in construction and new materials are not isolated facts, but that they must lead to new forms and be brought into harmony with human needs. The effect of Wagner's writing was increased by the rare mixture of sarcasm with confidence in the future that marks it. In addition, his readers felt that mature experience in architecture stood behind his every word.

In this small book there is condensed the experience that every nineteenth-century artist underwent from the moment he set himself against accepted standards. Wagner makes it plain that he no longer hopes for help from the state in any new developments.[23] His disparagement of the layman's judgment, "which always has been, and is, disastrous in its influence," reflects bitter experience of his own.[24] He holds with Goethe's dictum: the artist must create what the public ought to like, not what it does like.

This book speedily disillusioned the official circles responsible for Wagner's appointment. "A fully developed architect has become a mere experimenter with art — a sensation-monger, a train-bearer of fashion" — this judgment appears in a pamphlet of 1897.

In the year of his election to the Academy, Wagner built the system of elevated and underground railways which encircles Vienna on its outskirts. The elevated stretches were carried on

---

[21] *Moderne Architektur* (Vienna, 1895; 4th edition, 1914). "Architectural education should educate the architect as an artist and not as a mere specialist."

[22] Page 115. [23] Pages 133–134. [24] Page 113.

heavy brick arches like a Roman aqueduct. Wagner carried out all the details involved in this railway, including the stations along the line. He made separate designs for each of these; those built earliest show some classical influence, while the later ones move in the direction of *l'art nouveau.*

Wagner's isolation In Brussels, as we have seen, untiring efforts were made to create an atmosphere favorable to new movements. In Vienna there was no trace of such endeavors. We miss the significance of Wagner's work if we do not realize what it is to work in complete isolation. In 1894 no one in Wagner's country was working along the same lines as he. The Austrians, Josef Hoffmann, Adolf Loos, and Joseph Olbrich, and the German Peter Behrens were of the generation of 1870, and at this date were just starting their activity.

The Karlsplatz station (*fig.* **189**) of the Vienna subway serves to show that Wagner was moving toward modern architecture. Its ornamental ironwork and the hemispherical roof are a prolongation of nineteenth-century usages. They are a further development of French iron architecture as it appeared in the domes and vaults out of which Eiffel formed the front for the main building of the Paris Exhibition of 1878.[25] Wagner's contemporaries seem to have recognized this: in one of the many vicious pamphlets directed against him, we read that Wagner "is an adherent of the brutal Gallic architectural materialism."

Wagner did not merely continue the work of the French: he introduced new elements of his own. In 1894 he prophesied that "the new architecture will be dominated by slablike, tabular surfaces and the prominent use of materials in a pure state." [26] In the Karlsplatz station he himself used thin marble slabs for the outer walls, securing them with angle irons which are left visible. This treatment shows the wall as simply a slablike screen, with no load to carry.

Ten years later in the Vienna Postal Savings Building (1904–06) he stressed still more the function of the wall as a plane surface. The façade of this bank is covered with marble slabs

[25] Cf. Fig. 158.
[26] *Moderne Architektur,* p. 136.

318

attached by massive aluminum bolts whose heads can be seen plainly.

The interior of the Postal Savings Building (*fig.* **190**) reveals an astonishing purity of design. It is without doubt one of the most uncompromising rooms of the first years of the twentieth century. It is very characteristic of the work of Wagner (and of his contemporaries as well) that this purity follows upon the contact with new materials. Wagner gave this bank a glass-roofed interior court. Such courts had been common since the middle of the nineteenth century. Here in the white hall of the Postal Savings Building, however, the glass and iron vaulting does not merely fulfill all functional requirements but also blends into and becomes a part of a whole architectonic expression.

In the pure and abstract forms of this glass and iron hall the touch of the architect is no longer apparent; yet his hand is everywhere present, in its curves, its colors, and the modeling of its space.

The Continental successes of these architectural pioneers were won mainly by surprise attacks. Wagner's experience followed the same pattern. A reaction against his early work in the new directions set in, and his later projects — for museums, public buildings, and towns — exist only on paper. Nevertheless, Wagner's influence on the younger generation in Austria was very strong. Although his students were men of talent, they never achieved work of his standard. One of his students was the architect Josef Hoffmann, who was the founder of the Wiener Werkstätte for handicrafts. Another, who died quite young, was Joseph Olbrich. Wagner showed these young men the direction they should take, but they were all more directly influenced by Charles Rennie Mackintosh and the Glasgow group. This was especially true of Hoffmann and the Werkstätte circle. This meant that in Austria around 1900 the movement was from handicrafts to architecture and not from architecture to handicrafts.

It resulted in the sort of overconcentration on decorative aims which appears also in Joseph Olbrich's "Secession" gallery in Vienna (1898). This was bitterly denounced by Adolf Loos.

Wagner and the Vienna school

189. OTTO WAG-
NER. Karlsplatz Sta-
tion, Vienna, 1894.
Detail. "The new ar-
chitecture will be domi-
nated by slablike tabu-
lar surfaces and the
prominent use of ma-
terials in a pure state"
(Otto Wagner, 1895).

190. OTTO WAGNER. Savings Bank, Vienna. *The hall. In this hall glass and iron*
vaulting not only fulfills all functional requirements but also blends into and becomes a
part of a unified architectonic expression.

This Viennese architect had lived in England and America,
and had learned to recognize the importance of the anonymous
work being done in those countries in the production of

articles of everyday life — from clothing to bathtubs and trunks. As late as 1914 in Hoffmann's Stoclet house, Brussels, the influence of the cabinetmaker and of decorative art is still evident. The flat surfaces of this house are made up of white marble slabs, but they are treated like framed pictures.

The influence of Wagner and his Austrian school can be detected in an entirely unexpected quarter — in the work of Antonio Sant' Elia (1888–1916), the young Italian futurist architect who was killed in the war. Sant' Elia shared the Italian futurists' delight in the artistic expression of dynamic movement. Like them he loved the big city and all its manifestations. Shortly before the outbreak of war he designed

Wagner and
Sant' Elia

191. OTTO WAGNER. Drawing for bridge, subway, and different street levels, Vienna, 1906. *Part of a system of elevated and underground railway lines encircling Vienna along its outskirts.*

192. ANTONIO SANT' ELIA. Project for a subway, 1914. *Different street levels, combined with apartment houses and elevators. Sant' Elia's Nuova Città reflects the futuristic delight in intersecting streams of movement.*

feverishly his visions of the *città nuova*. These sketches were never carried further; they remained architectural ideas. Otto Wagner's drawings for the Vienna railroad station (1894–1906; *fig.* **191**) show his interest in the architectural integration of traffic routes, but what was to Wagner merely an accidental appendage became for the much younger Sant' Elia a flaming manifesto. One of his first designs (*fig.* **192**) was a skyscraper totally integrated with an underground railway, strongly emphasized elevator shafts, and roads on different levels, showing the traffic problem as an actively working ingredient of architecture.[27] These drawings anticipate the present situation, half a century later, when the cancerous growth of automobiles forces the city planner to find ways and means to build in traffic movement as a constituent element of the organism of the city.

FERROCONCRETE AND ITS INFLUENCE UPON ARCHITECTURE

Late appearance of ferroconcrete

The *art noveau*, in architecture at least, had its roots in the tradition of iron construction. At the beginning of the century, when this movement was spreading from Brussels, there appeared a new building material which achieved a surprisingly rapid influence upon architecture: ferroconcrete. It was at this time that architecture tore itself loose from the prejudices which had held it back for so long, and absorbed the new methods that had grown out of the period itself. It was this which promoted the use of ferroconcrete. Hardly had it been developed to the point where mills, silos, and reservoirs could be made from it than it was employed for more purely architectural purposes. Between 1910 and 1920 it became almost the trademark of the new architecture. Although it was very late in reaching maturity, this material with its complicated composition has a past that goes very far back. There is no need to retrace its technical development, since there are many sources of information on the subject. We shall only consider a few matters that have a bearing on architecture.[1]

[27] Design for a "City of the Future," 1913.

[1] See G. Huberti, *Vom Cementum zum Spannbeton* (Wiesbaden, 1963) for a concentrated history of concrete from the Roman rubble concrete to today.

193. JOHN SMEATON. Eddystone Lighthouse, England, 1774. *Etching from Smeaton's report on the lighthouse.*

John Smeaton, one of the great engineers of the eighteenth century, attained a triumph in the construction of the Eddystone Lighthouse (*fig.* **193**) in England. Previous lighthouses on this spot had been destroyed by storms, and the site was exposed to the full strength of the sea. But Smeaton used a system in the construction of his stonework which bound it together into an extremely tenacious whole. He locked the stones into one another, and for the foundations and the binding material he used a mixture of quicklime, clay, sand, and crushed iron-slag — concrete, that is. This occurred in 1774, five years before the first cast-iron bridge — the one over the Severn — was built. This — so far as we know — is the first use of concrete since the Roman period. Smeaton's experiments are described in detail in the magnificent volume, illustrated by etchings, dealing with the lighthouse which he published.[1a] These experiments began in the fifties of the eighteenth century, when he observed that quicklime containing clay would harden under water. As we have

Early rediscovery of concrete; Smeaton, 1774

[1a] *A Narrative of the Building and a Description of the Construction of the Eddystone Lighthouse* (London, 1793).

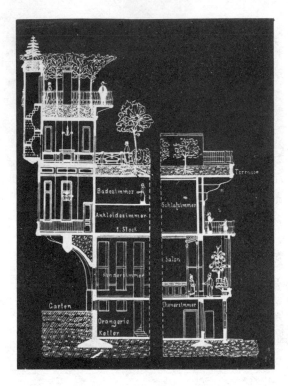

194. HENNEBIQUE. Residence, Bourg-la-Reine. *Hennebique tries to display in one spot all the potentialities of ferroconcrete but finds no architectural language available beyond the common idiom of the late nineties.*

already seen, it was Smeaton again who first dared to use the new material, cast-iron, for pumps and other machinery.

The success of Smeaton's work on the Eddystone light led to numerous further experiments. In 1824 Joseph Aspdin of Leeds produced the first "hydraulic" binding material: Portland cement. (A hydraulic cement is one which hardens in water.) Smeaton had used the constituents as they occur in their natural state; Aspdin regulated the admixture himself.

Five years later, in 1829, a Dr. Fox developed a method of making concrete floors by using the concrete as a filling between iron girders. In 1844 this method came to be protected by patent. As we have seen, it was used (in a developed form) throughout the seven- and eight-story warehouses built by the Manchester engineer, William Fairbairn. This system of construction, using tie bars embedded in concrete, comes very close to true ferroconcrete construction. Nevertheless, fifty years went by before scientific analysis revealed the exact nature of the connections between the two elements in

195. ANATOLE DE BAUDOT. Saint-Jean de Montmartre, Paris. Begun 1894. *The first church to be built with a ferroconcrete skeleton closed in by thin outer walls.*

ferroconcrete.   During this interval all effort and attention were devoted to the development of the great iron constructions.

So far as can be discovered, the first extensive use of concrete was at the Paris Exhibition of 1867, where it was employed for the floors of the sub-basements of the restaurants in the great main building.

Ferroconcrete, taking the term in its strict sense, made its initial appearance in 1868, when the gardener Monnier began to use wire network for the cores of concrete tubs.   This procedure involved nothing new in itself: Labrouste had made the vaulting in his Bibliothèque Sainte-Geneviève of interlaced wires covered with layers of plaster.

Reinforced concrete did not come into common employment on a large scale until the 1890's, when it was so used in America by Ernest Leslie Ransome (born in 1844, in Ipswich, England)[2] and in France by François Hennebique (1842–1921).

First large-scale use of reinforced concrete in the 1890's: François Hennebique

---

[2] The employment of ferroconcrete in America previous to the Leland Stanford Jr. Museum of about 1890 and the building of the Pacific Borax Company deserves more

325

François Hennebique had as his guide preliminary work carried out by a number of constructors. He knew the separate requirements of the iron and of the compressed concrete, how to apportion one to the other, and how to dispose the iron reinforcing rods — all the relevant laws, in short. But, beyond this, he was an excellent contractor and had built in every part of Europe: mills at Nantes, granaries at Genoa, silos at Strasbourg, sanatoria in Switzerland.

Use in residences The villa which he built for himself during the nineties at Bourg-la-Reine (*fig.* **194**) served as a piece of propaganda for the use of ferroconcrete. The villa makes its possibilities obvious at once to any observer. The octagonal tower rests on two cantilevers which project four meters. Not content with this, the tower exhibits other projecting constructions higher up; these enclose a spiral staircase that leads to the uppermost roof garden (which is planted with trees). Roof gardens, terraces, freely projected building elements: a veritable architectural tightrope dance! Done entirely in the architectonic idiom of the nineties, it is a fantastic mixture, one calculated to win the heart of any Surrealist.

Use in a church (1894) French architecture of the nineties is not to be compared with its forceful Belgian counterpart: after reaching its high point in the 1889 Galerie des Machines it entered upon a decline. There are some achievements which are of interest, however, even if they failed of international influence. In 1894 Anatole de Baudot began work on the first church to have a ferroconcrete skeleton enclosed by thin walls, his Saint-Jean de Montmartre in Paris (*fig.* **195**). Anatole de Baudot in his official capacity was the "Protector of Ancient Monuments"; in his lectures, delivered over a period of twenty-five years, he stood for the regeneration of architecture. As soon as the new material, ferroconcrete, appeared, he used it for a church — a marked departure from outworn routine. In his "Architecture and Reinforced Concrete"[3] he informs us that he was

careful study, directed at the progressive stages of this early development. Shortly before this, Ransome had built the Academy of Sciences at San Francisco, using reinforced concrete floors and iron columns. For more details cf. Ernest L. Ransome and Alexis Saurbrey, *Reinforced Concrete Buildings* (New York, 1912), especially the first chapter, "Personal Reminiscences."

[3] *L'Architecture et le ciment armé* (Paris, n.d.).

awarded the contract because by using the new material he was able to underbid all his competitors. The boldness of De Baudot's work was recognized, but for many reasons it failed to equal the great effect produced by Victor Horta's house in the Rue de Turin.[4]

By the first decade of the twentieth century reinforced concrete came into widespread use nearly everywhere. It was used in the Queen Alexandra Sanatorium, built at Davos, Switzerland, in 1907 (*fig.* **196**). Robert Maillart was responsible for its construction; the architects were Pfleghard and Haefeli. The

196. PFLEGHARD, HAEFELI, and MAILLART. Queen Alexandra Sanatorium, Davos, 1907.

Queen Alexandra Sanatorium (today the Thurgauer Health Center) stands on a wide ledge halfway up a mountainside. Its three wings with their wide open terraces are carefully oriented to catch all the available sunlight.

In the same year work was begun in Chicago on a warehouse designed for Montgomery, Ward and Company.[5] Completed

---

[4] Quiet pioneer work was also done by Louis Bonnier, who was responsible for the construction of a civic building at Pas-de-Calais (devoid of the usual decoration). Dutert, who had been in charge of the architectonic part of the Galerie des Machines of 1889, erected a museum of uncovered brick for the Jardin des Plantes in Paris, a building which likewise honestly displayed the iron in its construction wherever it was used.

[5] Cf. Fig. 249.

in 1908, this warehouse was the work of R. E. Schmidt, Garden, and Martin — members of the Chicago school's second generation. Some eight hundred feet long, it has large windows of the horizontally elongated Chicago type and broad horizontal bands running without interruption the full extent of its façade. "It is a huge aggregation of storage lofts, nine stories high, a repetition of units of a monotony truly appalling. . . . It is entirely of reinforced concrete construction — foundations, columns, floors, and walls." [6] Contemporary critics were thoroughly bewildered by this structure, one of the first in the United States, I believe, to use ferroconcrete with a clear recognition of its properties. "It is not intended to be an architectural monument . . . the qualifications are functional, structural, and economical . . . in this building architectural expression was not wanted." But "if it is not in itself beautiful or graceful, it is at least logical." [7] Actually this warehouse is one of the few late buildings in which the spirit of the Chicago school still survives.

The further advance in reinforced concrete construction and in the exploitation of its artistic potentialities took place in France.

A. G. Perret

Auguste Perret (1874–1955) remained an *architecte-ingénieur* throughout his career.[8] Perret came from Burgundy, from a town near the great monastery of Cluny. One might discern connections between the severe engineering art of the Cluniac monks and this architect who was the first to recognize how to employ reinforced concrete as a means of architectural expression.

Rue Franklin apartment

Perret built his 25 *bis* Rue Franklin apartments in Paris in 1903 (*fig.* 197), ten years after Horta's Rue de Turin house. This apartment house by no means embodies the pure forms of the Chicago office buildings, and it fails to match the strength of Frank Lloyd Wright's work of the same period. The familiar European restlessness is still present to a considerable degree.

[6] "On American Architecture," *Architectural Record*, XXII (1908), 115–120.

[7] *Architectural Record*, XXII, 115–120.

[8] See Paul Jamot, *A.-G. Perret et l'architecture du béton armé* (Paris and Brussels, 1927).

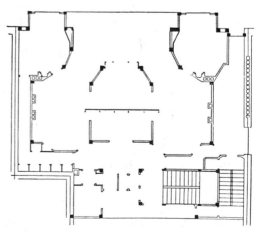

198. AUGUSTE PERRET on the roof of 25 bis Rue Franklin.

199. AUGUSTE PERRET. 25 bis Rue Franklin. *Plan. The flexible planning which the ferroconcrete skeleton makes possible.*

197. AUGUSTE PERRET. 25 bis Rue Franklin, Paris, 1903. *The ferroconcrete skeleton, instead of being disguised, is openly presented as a constituent element.*

329

Nevertheless, it represents the first employment of ferro-concrete as a medium for architectonic expression, and many of its features were to prove seeds for future developments.

The ferroconcrete skeleton is used without disguise; it stands out plainly as one of the constituent elements of the building. Earlier buildings in concrete — Hennebique's Rue Danton apartments, for example — made no architectonic use of the skeleton. But in the Rue Franklin, the use of the façade as a mere support for ornamentation has been abandoned. It is

200. AUGUSTE PERRET. 25 bis Rue Franklin. *Office on ground floor. The street floor has been almost dissolved into pure glass.*

hollowed out, recedes in depth, springs forward. Six projecting stories are allowed to hover in mid air, the sixth one leaving bare the square supporting columns of the concrete skeleton (*fig.* **197**). The whole façade is in movement. The upper part of the building almost seems to float and the ground floor (which at one time housed Perret's office) is almost dissolved into glass. It is roofed with thin, narrow concrete slabs (*fig.* **200**), which project to provide an area of shade surmounted by a balcony

The total effect is reminiscent of some iron structures: everything seems to grow lighter and lighter toward the ground, until finally only a few thin members connect the building with the earth. This impression of fragility had its financial consequences. Banks refused to take a mortgage on the apartment house, since the experts predicted its speedy collapse.

The flat roof, like several in Tony Garnier's projected "Cité Industrielle," exhibits a rudimentary roof garden (*fig.* **198**). The light-well has been done away with, and the walls for the staircase are executed in glass bricks, which leave it entirely open to the daylight. Perret told me that he used these bricks because his neighbors could legally have forbidden the cutting of windows on this side of the building. This does not at all detract from Perret's ingenuity in finding a new use for a familiar material. The same trait appears in his adoption of simple pipe railings to replace the usual elaborate hand-wrought affairs and in his opening up the ground floor with glass walls.

Interior: novel uses of materials and flexible planning

But Perret made his most important contribution to the younger generation of French architects in the flexible treatment of the ground plan (*fig.* **199**). Partitions are set in with complete freedom to connect separate ferroconcrete pillars. Perret was working here in the same spirit as Horta and, later on, Le Corbusier. Each story is planned as an independent unit.

A short time later Perret built what he himself regards as the "première tentative (au monde) de béton armé esthétique." This was his garage in the Rue Ponthieu. Here the reinforced concrete skeleton is given full opportunity to determine the character of the façade.

Garage in the Rue Ponthieu

There are other fine works of Perret's which, unfortunately, we shall be unable to discuss: his Théâtre des Champs-Élysées (1911–14), the source of so much controversy between him and Henri van de Velde; the docks at Casablanca (1916), with their eggshell-thin vaultings; his churches at Rancy (1922) and elsewhere, which exerted such influence upon contemporary church buildings; his private houses; and his latest works. Auguste Perret, with his sense for construction, gave Le Corbusier a decisive impetus toward his own work.

And the next generation of architects as a whole carried Perret's results still further. Perret's buildings follow the best nineteenth-century French tradition in construction. Like the earlier *architectes-ingénieurs*, he drew his inspiration from his materials. Perret did for ferroconcrete what Henri Labrouste had done for iron.

Classical
reminiscences

Like Tony Garnier, Perret preserved some connections with the classic past. But classical canons remained alive and flexible for the best French architects, just as they had for the French masters of baroque days — for Racine, Molière, and Descartes. Perhaps later on we shall come to see that something of the classic spirit is present even in the work of the men who came after Perret; that they too reflect the classic urge toward balance, symmetry, and repose.

201. TONY GARNIER. Central Station, 1901–04. *Project. At a time when railroad stations were customarily executed in the style of huge monuments, Garnier returns to actual functions and exploits the new materials: glass and reinforced concrete.*

Tony Garnier

Ferroconcrete
the basic material
in Garnier's work

The *architecte-constructeur* Auguste Perret was the first to find new architectonic means in the unexplored potentialities of ferroconcrete. This material was, indeed, peculiarly attractive to French builders. Concrete accorded perfectly with their traditional penchant for daring and extensively hollowed out structures.

Tony Garnier (born in 1869) made reinforced concrete the basis of all his work. In his "Cité Industrielle" (1901–04) this new material was used to organize a whole town along original and strikingly farsighted lines. This is a scheme which we shall discuss in some detail later on.[9] The Cité Industrielle, planned when Garnier was only thirty, really laid down the outlines for his whole future output. The "grands travaux de Lyon," carried out under Édouard Herriot in Garnier's native city, were practical outgrowths of his youthful project. These "grands travaux" were very extensive; they included the Lyons stockyard (1909), the city stadium (1915), twenty-two pavilions of the Granges-Blanches hospital (begun in 1911, but erected over a period of some two decades), and part of a residential district — "Quartier des États-Unis" — which was begun in 1920. Garnier's later work included pavilions at several French exhibitions, his own house, and a number of villas along the Riviera. All these buildings can be regarded as developing out of his first serious work, and it is his foresighted planning of this Cité Industrielle which gives Garnier his place in the history of architecture (*fig.* **201**).

We are approaching the moment when European architecture could at last attain a mastery of contemporary problems through the means created by the engineers. By this time people could see that modern techniques offered the only means of expression for feelings stemming from modern life. But we have first to retrace developments in America, whose influence was to become effective only when this European architecture had begun to recover from its own maladies.

---

[9] Cf. pp. 787 ff.

PART **V** **AMERICAN DEVELOPMENT**

The colonial and the republican periods were of great importance to American development; they provided a solid foundation for future advance. But the period between 1850 and
1890 is more important for American influence on the outside
world. The preparations which made that influence possible
were completed during these decades. The years between 1850
and 1890 produced not only the great surge toward the unsettled lands in the West but also strong manifestations of a
new and specifically American spirit. This period has particular significance to foreign eyes. The new forms which grew up
in it had their roots in an organization of labor altogether different from that which prevails in Europe.

The illustrative material published here was often unearthed
with difficulty. Documents from this period are not readily
accessible, just because there is so little interest in it and so
little understanding of its importance. Material showing the
development of the life of the period and the daily habits reflected in it is very difficult to find. What is of more importance, there is the constant danger that it will be lost forever.

Manufacturers simply laugh when asked for specimens of their
early productions and for old catalogues. There is no time for
and — above all — no interest in the sources of the tradition
which governs the life of the man of today. In the future, historians who examine this period will certainly be more interested in uncovering the roots of the great anonymous productions of industry than they will be in the monumental or
official architecture of the time. But what institute tries, out
of a human rather than a technical interest, to collect the
documents dealing with the anonymous beginnings of our
period? We are too unaccustomed to considering interrelations between different realms of human activity to see clearly
the points at which they are connected. The danger is that the
material for reconstructing these relationships may be lost by
the time their importance has been recognized.

Europe Observes American Production

The European public had its initial contact with American
tools and furnishings at the first international exhibition — the

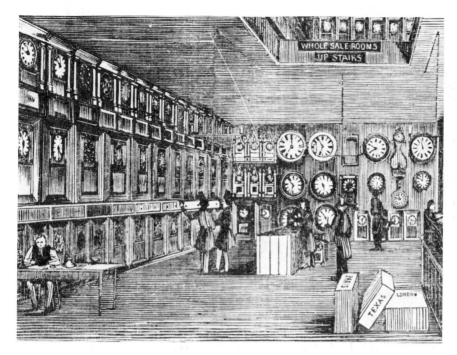

202.   American clocks, c. 1850.

great London Exhibition of 1851.   European observers were astonished by the simplicity, technical correctness, and sureness of shape revealed in American productions.   The astute Lothar Bucher called attention to "the grandfather clocks with their excellently contrived works and simple walnut cases; the chairs — from simple wooden work benches to easy chairs — with their freedom from the gingerbread carving which tears at our hands and clothing, and the absence of the right angles of those currently popular Gothic chairs which are hunching everyone's shoulders.   All that we see of American domestic equipment breathes the spirit of comfort and fitness for purpose" [1] (*fig.* 202).

Similarly, Count Léon de Laborde, a French observer, saw in the Americans "une nation industrielle, qui se fait artiste" — an industrial nation which was becoming artistic.   He added that "America would go her own way." [2]

---

[1] Lothar Bucher, *Kulturhistorische Skizzen aus der Industrieausstellung aller Völker* (Frankfort, 1851), pp. 146 ff.

[2] Léon de Laborde, *De l'union des arts et de l'industrie*, I, 312 ff.

337

The height of the lower part of the top of the desk, is just equal to the highest part of the back of the chair, so as to allow it to pass under.

The front edge of the seat is in a perpendicular line with the edge of the top of the desk, so that the scholar is required to sit erect, when engaged in writing or studying, and the same time that part of his back which requires support is fully in contact with the chair.

203. Standards of American school furniture, 1849.

Gottfried Semper expressed a similar opinion. Semper was a German architect who (like Richard Wagner) had been exiled from his own country for revolutionary activities in Dresden. He was one of the founders of the first English school of design, organized at London in this same year — 1851. Semper writes that "although there is very little evidence of craftsmanship in America, nevertheless a real national art will spring up there first." [3]

American school furniture, c. 1851; advanced functional design

The Americans showed schoolroom furniture with cast-iron supports in which everything was carefully adjusted to the pupil's age, occupation, and anatomical structure (*fig.* 203). This furniture — most of it produced in the New England area, around Boston — was the product of a twenty-year fight for better school equipment that had begun in 1830 with W. J. Adams' lecture, "Schoolhouses and School Apparatus," before the American Institute of Instruction. In 1838 Henry Barnard completed one of the pioneer works in this field, his essay on school architecture, for the Senate's Standing Committee on Education. Barnard was perfectly clear on the functional demands that such furniture had to satisfy: "Every pupil, young or old, should be provided with a chair just high enough to allow, when properly occupied, the feet to rest on the

[3] Gottfried Semper, *Wissenschaft, Industrie und Kunst* (Brunswick, 1852), pp. 73 ff.

338

floor without the muscles of the thigh being pressed hard upon the front edge of the seat. . . . The seats should be provided with a support for the muscles of the back, and, as a general rule, this support should rise above the shoulder blades, and should in all cases incline back as it rises, one inch in every foot." [4]

A quarter of a century later, at the Philadelphia Exposition of 1876, the European observers split into two camps. Those who expected to find European fashions in the American exhibits were disappointed. They found, as Jakob von Falke says, "neither furniture nor furniture covers, neither glassware nor fayence ware, which attracted us by reason of its taste, color-scheme, or beauty." Certain objects of daily use which, according to von Falke, ought to be richly decorated — grandfather clocks, for example — "show the sad state of American taste by their complete absence of ornamentation." [5]

In this instance a European observer condemned the characteristic which gave American industrial art its individuality and significance for the future: simplicity.

On the other hand, those observers who did not judge on the basis of preconceived standards were impressed with "the beauty of form in which the Americans cast their tools and machinery." F. Reuleaux, the well-known scientist who headed the German delegation to the exposition, comments on this in his "Letters from Philadelphia" of 1876: "The axes, hatchets, hoes, hunting knives, hammers, etc., are executed with such variety and beauty as cannot but excite admiration and astonishment. A constraint runs through all of them. They are designed so well for the purpose to be served that they seem actually to anticipate our needs." [6]

The Victoria and Albert Museum at South Kensington has preserved the catalogue of a Chicago hardware firm of the

---

[4] Henry Barnard, *School Architecture, or Contributions to the Improvement of Schoolhouses in the United States*, 5th ed. (New York, 1854), p. 342. The Senate committee refused to publish Barnard's essay, which did not appear until 1841, and then only — as he relates — "through the strenuous effort of a few intelligent friends of school improvements," and with the author bearing a part of the expense.

[5] Jakob von Falke, "Vorbemerkungen zur Weltausstellung in Philadelphia," *Der Gewerbehalle*, XIII (1875), 144 ff.

[6] F. Reuleaux, *Briefe aus Philadelphia* (Brunswick, 1877), pp. 18 ff.

MAYDOLE'S CAST STEEL HAMMERS.

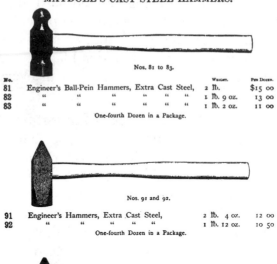

Nos. 81 to 83.

No.		WEIGHT.	PER DOZEN.
81	Engineer's Ball-Pein Hammers, Extra Cast Steel,	2 ℔.	$15 00
82	" " " " " "	1 ℔. 9 oz.	13 00
83	" " " " " "	1 ℔. 2 oz.	11 00

One-fourth Dozen in a Package.

Nos. 91 and 92.

91	Engineer's Hammers, Extra Cast Steel,	2 ℔. 4 oz.	12 00
92	" " " " "	1 ℔. 12 oz.	10 50

One-fourth Dozen in a Package.

Nos. 61 and 62.

61	Blacksmith's Hand Hammers, Extra Cast Steel,	3 ℔.	15 00
62	" " " " " "	2 ℔. 10 oz.	13 50

One-fourth Dozen in a Package.

The Weights given above are for Single Hammers, without the Handles.

204. Ball-peen machinist's hammer; blacksmith's hammers. Chicago catalogue of 1877. *Reuleaux remarked of tools like these that "they are designed so well for the purpose to be served that they seem actually to anticipate our needs"* (*1876*).

seventies.   The precise and sensitive forms of the tools illustrated in it show why Europeans were so astonished by them (*fig.* **204**).   Such articles as the "engineer's machine hammer" and the Yale lock were not even introduced into Europe until comparatively recent years (*fig.* **205**).

Julius Lessing, the first director of the Museum of Industrial Arts in Berlin, when he saw the exhibit of American tools at the Paris World's Fair of 1878, experienced — so he says — as intense an aesthetic pleasure from a display of American axes as from a real work of art.   He remarked the beauty of line which was achieved without any ornamental embellishment, "simply by molding the axe to the human hand and to the movement of the human body as it is used." [7]

Lessing goes a step further.   He points to the surprising parallelism between these tools and the most beautiful of primitive stone and bronze instruments.   At the same time he regards as

[7] Julius Lessing, *Berichte von der Pariser Weltausstellung von 1878* (Berlin, 1878), p. 99.

a "lamentable retrogression every effort of the Americans to imitate European art forms."

The official French report on the exposition at Philadelphia in 1876 includes some comment on American furniture. Particular attention is called to the fact that American furniture, in contrast with European, is marked by its use of flat surfaces, of fewer surface planes. "The moldings are simple, with very little carving. The parts are thus easy to make separately and are easily assembled." [8] The French report argues that a new style has appeared on the other side of the Atlantic, a style which manifests itself in all forms of the industrial arts. To show how typically American these products were in their eyes, they called this the "Pullman car style."

Elaborate and costly furniture appeared at the exhibitions. Thus the Paris Exposition of 1867 featured a French sideboard, valued at twenty thousand dollars, which awed all beholders. Regarded as a museum piece at the time, it now presents a somewhat dreadful appearance. American exhibitors — especially after the seventies — preferred to display what was known as "patent furniture." A page from the official cata-

American "patent furniture" in the sixties

205. Yale lock, Chicago catalogue of 1877. *One early instance of the way machinery came to displace the skilled craftsman — here the locksmith.*

[8] *Exposition internationale et universelle de Philadelphie 1876* (Paris, 1877), pp. 185 ff.

341

206. Folding bed, Philadelphia Exhibition, 1876. *A specimen of the patent combination furniture which came into extensive use about this time.*

logue of American exhibits at Paris in 1878, headed "Cheap and Fancy Furniture, all Series Productions," lists "Perforated Veneer Seats," "Automatic Sofa-Spring Beds," "Folding Chairs" (they folded into a lounge), a "Swing Convertible Cradle," a "Child's Crib," a "Reclining Chair," etc. (*fig.* **206**).[9] All these things were developed just at the period when European photomontages of historical styles were beginning to influence American production.

Innate beauty of American tools

By the time of the Chicago World's Fair of 1893 Lessing found the Americans awarding all the prizes to heavily ornamented European articles. "But we who went over with the will to

[9] Patent furniture had its origin in the early industrialized England of the beginning of the nineteenth century. Thomas Sheraton, known to the public for the style that bears his name, is perhaps more important today as one of the first cabinetmakers to be interested in producing "patent" furniture. (Cf. Sheraton, *Designs for Household Furniture*, third ed., London, 1812: easy and hunting chairs, chairs which may be converted into beds, tables which may be converted into high desks, movable bookcases, etc.) American furniture-makers followed this trend, which nearly disappeared in Europe through the influence of "period" furniture, and consciously developed very original solutions. In 1939 no research seemed to have been done on this important branch of American furniture making. In *Mechanization Takes Command* (Oxford University Press, 1948) America's patent furniture was presented for the first time as the constituent furniture of the nineteenth century. Like other constituent elements of the nineteenth century, such as iron construction, it shows a close similarity to the trends of the twenties of our century.

learn," he writes, "have found other things more important for future development. We are bringing back to Europe smooth wooden chairs, polished doorknobs, and gracefully curved utensils entirely devoid of embellishment.

"Here we saw utensils and tools created in the same spirit as railroads, ships, and wagons. Here we saw objects of daily use developed clearly and without any preconception — objects appealing not so much to the calculating intellect as directly to the senses. They convey to the eye the satisfying sensation which only beauty can give." [10]

As the last of the European observers, Gropius may be quoted. In 1913, just after his completion of the Fagus works, he wrote an essay on the development of modern industrial buildings for one of the publications of the German Werkbund, which did so much to introduce contemporary ideas into Germany. For the first time he gives illustrations and speaks of the unintentional beauty of American industrial architecture:

"In comparison with the other countries of Europe, Germany seems to have gone far ahead in the field of factory design. But in America, the motherland of industry, there are great industrial structures which, in their unconscious majesty, are superior to even our best German buildings of that type. The grain elevators of Canada and South America, the coal conveyors of great railway lines, and the more modern industrial plants of North America are almost as impressive in their monumental power as the buildings of ancient Egypt. They present an architectural composition of such exactness that to the observer their meaning is forcefully and unequivocally clear. The natural integrity of these buildings resides not in the vastness of their physical proportions — herein the quality of a monumental work is certainly not to be sought — but in their designers' independent and clear vision of these grand, impressive forms. They are not obscured by sentimental reverence for tradition nor by other intellectual scruples which prostrate our contemporary European design and bar true artistic originality" [11] (*fig.* **207**).

---

[10] J. Lessing, "Neue Wege," *Kunstgewerbeblatt*, VI (1895), 1 ff.

[11] Walter Gropius, "Die Kunst in Industrie und Handel," *Jahrbuch des Deutschen Werkbundes* (Jena, 1913), pp. 21–22.

207. Grain elevator, Chicago, 1873.

The Structure of American Industry

American industry differs from European industry in its structure. These differences have to be kept in mind if one is to understand clearly the process of evolution which American industry has followed. Such structural differences are also the grounds for the dissimilar attitudes toward the crafts — and later toward the "arts and crafts" — which exist in these two areas.

Industrialization of complicated handicrafts

European industry, springing into existence on English soil in the late eighteenth century, substituted the machine for hand labor in the working of some simple raw materials — iron, and plant and animal fibers. The spinning and weaving machines which were invented in England at this time served as unsurpassed trail-breakers in the mechanization of industry.

American industry became robust at a much later period, around 1850. Naturally, European inventions were adopted

344

and introduced into this country. Divergences appear at the points where problems inherent in a totally different situation demanded new solutions.

About 1850, in America, all these complicated crafts based on skilled labor became industrialized. The change came about partly through new inventions and partly through new methods of organization. The major emphasis, indeed, rested on a new organization. Very early this new organization even penetrated the household. New tools were introduced to lighten hand labor in cooking — the apple parer (1868), for example.

Before 1850 the manufacture of men's and children's clothes had been largely a household industry, but the invention of the sewing machine transferred it to the factories. A team of three to five, or more, persons produced the finished garment.[12] By the 1840's the "Oak Hall" establishment in Boston was supposed to be the largest clothing store in the United States. It was housed in a building of the Gothic Revival style which resembled a medieval tomb.

From an author of the sixties we discover that "few are aware of the vast extent to which the sale of ready-made clothing is carried on at the present day. Probably no branch of business has so rapidly increased.

"But a few years ago it was confined to goods of very inferior quality, style, and make, worn mostly by laborers and seamen." [13]

By 1876 Wanamaker was producing ready-made clothing for men and boys on a great scale, and with all the knowledge of service, advertising, and price policies best calculated to attract the masses.

In the manufacture of boots and shoes, machinery did not come into use until nearly the middle of the century. At

---

[12] Walter W. Jennings, *A History of Economic Progress in the United States* (New York, 1926), p. 430.

[13] C. D. Goyer, *History of Chicago, Its Commercial and Manufacturing Interests* (Chicago, 1862), p. 170.

about the same time butchering was converted into the meat-packing industry, with stockyards, elaborate refrigeration methods, and the modern, endless-chain system of operation — including mechanical hog-scraping apparatus.[14] The first "mechanical bakery" was established in Brooklyn in December 1856. The second mechanical bakery was set up shortly afterwards in Chicago. It had "one oven passing from the basement to the third floor and within the oven . . . three endless chains supporting the cars containing the bread." [15]

To summarize: In America materials were plentiful and skilled labor scarce; in Europe skilled labor was plentiful and materials scarce. It is this difference which accounts for the differences in the structure of American and European industry from the fifties on. In America just about that date, mechanization began to replace skilled labor in all the complicated crafts.

This trend can be observed astonishingly early in the field of housing; mechanized methods appear even before the fifties. In this period James Bogardus was producing cast-iron buildings assembled from prefabricated parts which were forerunners of the skeleton frame. The encroachment of industrialization upon skilled hand trades is shown much more plainly, however, in the introduction of a new type of wooden construction, one used for some 60 to 80 per cent of all the houses in the United States: the balloon frame. The balloon frame in its technical aspects has little interest for us, but a study of its origins may yield us an insight into an important period in the American development.[16]

---

[14] Jennings, *op. cit.*, p. 734; H. T. Warschow, *Representative Industries in the United States* (New York, 1882), pp. 444 ff.

[15] Goyer, *op. cit.*, p. 122.

[16] Some of the quotations in this section are from Heinrich Waentig, *Wirtschaft und Kunst* (Jena, 1909). Waentig, as he remarks in his foreword, "gathered together out of life and the libraries" the materials for one of the few really penetrating studies of the arts and crafts movement in the nineteenth century. Anyone who has done similar research into nineteenth-century developments can understand his remark that he was more than once on the verge of abandoning the whole enterprise.

Waentig goes directly to the constituent facts of the period. He was not an art historian but a political economist — that is, he had been trained to concentrate on the problems of his own age at greater length than a final appendix to a study of some earlier period permits. His book has great value for anyone interested in the nineteenth century.

THE BALLOON FRAME AND INDUSTRIALIZATION

The balloon frame (*fig.* **208**) is closely connected with the level of industrialization which had been reached in America. Its invention practically converted building in wood from a complicated craft, practiced by skilled labor, into an industry.

The principle of the balloon frame involves the substitution of thin plates and studs — running the entire height of the building and held together only by nails — for the ancient and expensive method of construction with mortised and tenoned joints. To put together a house like a box, using only nails — this must have seemed utterly revolutionary to carpenters. Naturally enough, the balloon frame met with attack at the start: "The Balloon Frame has passed through and survived the theory, ridicule, and abuse of all who have seen fit to attack it. . . . Its name was given in contempt by those old fogy mechanics who had been brought up to rob a stick of timber of all its strength and durability, by cutting it full of mortices, tenons and auger holds, and then supposing it to be stronger than a far lighter stick differently applied, and with all its

208. Balloon-frame construction. *From G. E. Woodward, "Woodward's Country Homes" (New York, 1869).*

209. St. Mary's Church, Chicago, 1833. *The first building in balloon frame. Razed and reërected three times during its short life.*

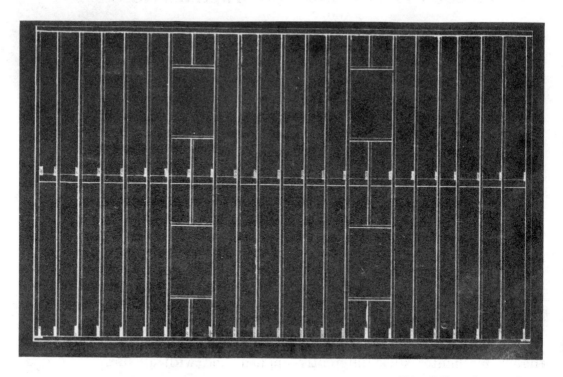

210. Balloon frame. *From W. E. Bell, "Carpentry Made Easy" (1859). "If it had not been for the knowledge of the balloon-frame, Chicago and San Francisco could never have arisen, as they did, from little villages to great cities in a single year" (Solon Robinson, 1855).*

211. Windsor chair. *Parallels the balloon frame both in its use of thin structural parts to produce a light and strong construction, and in its anonymous development.*

348

212. R. J. NEUTRA. House in Texas, 1937. *Modern balloon-frame houses like this one reveal the elegance and lightness which are innate qualities of this type of skeleton construction.*

capabilities unimpaired. . . . The name of 'Basket Frame' would convey a better impression, but the name 'Balloon' has long ago outlived the derision which suggested it.''

The balloon frame marks the point at which industrialization began to penetrate housing. Just as the trades of the watchmaker, the butcher, the baker, the tailor were transformed into industries, so too the balloon frame led to the replacement of the skilled carpenter by the unskilled laborer.

''A man and a boy can now (1865) attain the same results, with ease, that twenty men could on an old-fashioned frame. . . . The principle of Balloon Framing is the true one for strength, as well as for economy. If a mechanic is employed, the Balloon Frame can be put up *for forty per cent less money* than the mortice and tenon frame.'' [1]

---

[1] The quotations are from G. E. Woodward, *Woodward's Country Homes* (New York, 1869), pp. 152–164.

Without machine-made nails the balloon frame would be economic nonsense. It was only when machinery had made nails cheaper, and "cut nails of steel and iron and nails made of wire could be furnished of excellent quality and at a cost much less than old-fashioned wrought-iron nails [that] the comparatively expensive system of house framing with mortise and tenon began to be supplanted by a more economic system dependent entirely upon the efficacy of nailing." [2]

The invention of the balloon frame really coincides with the improvement of sawmill machinery as well as with the mass production of nails (*fig.* **210**).

Several machines for cutting and heading nails were developed in both England and the United States toward the end of the eighteenth century. Thomas Clifford patented such a device in 1790, and about the same time a similar machine was invented by Jacob Perkins of Newburyport. A machine which cut, shaped, and headed tacks in a single operation at the rate of sixty thousand a day was patented by Jesse Reed in 1807. [3]

"When the manufacture of cut nails was first undertaken, wrought nails cost 25c a pound. . . . This made their use for houses and fences difficult." [4] All this changed with the introduction of machinery. The price of nails was suddenly reduced. "In 1828 the production was so brisk that the price was reduced to 8c a pound. . . . In 1833 the rapidity of production had brought prices down to 5c . . . in 1842, 3c." [5]

The Balloon Frame and the Building-up of the West

The balloon frame has an established connection with the conquest of the West from Chicago to the Pacific Coast.

Contemporaries knew quite well that houses would never have sprung up with such incredible rapidity — either on the

[2] Russell Sturgis, *Dictionary of Architecture and Building* (New York, 1902), III, 1125.

[3] *Great Industries of the United States* (Hartford, 1872), p. 1072.

[4] William E. Bell, *Carpentry Made Easy* (Philadelphia, 1859). Bell worked as a carpenter in Ottawa, Michigan. Writing in 1857 he claims (p. 53) to have had fifteen years' experience constructing and repairing balloon frame buildings.

[5] Albert S. Bolles, *Industrial History of the United States* (Norwich, Conn., 1889), p. 220.

350

prairies or within the big cities — had it not been for this construction.

"With the application of machinery, the labor of house building has been greatly lessened, and the western prairies are dotted over with houses which have been *shipped there all made*, and the various pieces numbered." [6] Another observer goes further: "If it had not been for the knowledge of the balloon-frame, Chicago and San Francisco could never have arisen, as they did, from little villages to great cities in a single year." [7]

At the period when the West was being built up, contemporaries called "the method of construction known as 'balloon framing' the most important contribution to our domestic architecture."

To me it seems very characteristic of the negligence with which contemporary history is treated that no dictionary of architecture or construction gives a precise answer to the question of who invented the balloon frame and when it was invented.

The Invention of the Balloon Frame

Even as far back as the fifties and sixties there seems to have been no certainty with regard to the invention of the balloon frame. One early witness, writing in 1872, relates that "when it was first used is not known with any definiteness, but it has within the last fifty years replaced the old method of construction." [8]

Woodward, in 1869, confesses that "the early history of the Balloon Frame, is somewhat obscure, there being no well authenticated statements of its origin. It may, however, be traced back to the early settlement of our prairie countries, where it was impossible to obtain heavy timber and skillful mechanics. . . . The Balloon Frame belongs to no one per-

---

[6] *Great Industries of the United States.*

[7] Solon Robinson in *New York Tribune*, January 18, 1855. Quoted in Woodward, *op. cit.*, p. 151.

[8] *Great Industries of the United States.*

son; nobody claims it as an invention, and yet in the art of construction it is one of the most sensible improvements that has ever been made." [9]

Nevertheless, the balloon frame does seem to have had an inventor and to have emanated from one particular town.

George Washington Snow, 1797–1870

The inventor of the balloon frame was George W. Snow.[10] He was born at Keene, New Hampshire, September 16, 1797, of an old American family which traced back to the *Mayflower*.

He must have been rather a restless spirit, since he first left the family homestead for New York and afterwards went to Detroit with his wife. Under rather primitive conditions he crossed the state of Michigan, and finally, in a canoe paddled by an Indian guide, he reached the mouth of the Chicago River, July 12, 1832. The small community he found there — there were only two hundred and fifty inhabitants — pleased his pioneer temperament. He took an active part in its affairs for many years: in 1833, when Chicago became a city, Snow was appointed its first assessor and surveyor; he was elected alderman in 1849, and made drainage commissioner the same year; he was at one time chief of the pioneer hook and ladder company.

As one of his descendants remarks in a letter, like many of the first settlers Snow was something of a jack-of-all-trades. He was one of the earliest of the Chicago lumber dealers, purchasing "Carver's Lumberyard" in 1835. He owned considerable land and conducted a real estate business. He was a building contractor, as well as a general contractor and financier.

Snow was not merely a surveyor; he had been educated as a civil engineer in his youth. This technical training may have led him to the invention of the balloon frame. How this came

[9] Woodward, *op. cit.*, pp. 151–154.

[10] Until more exact researches have been made it cannot be taken as certain that no other men figured in the development of the balloon frame. Solon Robinson (to whom we have already referred) writes that he was using the balloon frame as early as 1835. Walter Field in a Harvard thesis, "A Reexamination into the Invention of the Balloon Frame," shows how difficult it is to give George Snow full credit for the invention of the balloon frame. Further investigation seems to be necessary.

about and what his struggles were we do not know. The tag, "balloon frame," was a mere nickname, a jocular reference to the lightness of this new type of construction.

There are several confirmations of the tradition in Snow's family that he invented the balloon frame. Its invention is credited to him by Andreas in his *History of Chicago*,[11] and in *Industrial Chicago*, the most important book on the development of Chicago, we read that "the balloon frame is the joint idea of George W. Snow and necessity."[12] Andreas' statement is based on the words of one of Snow's fellow townsmen, the architect J. M. Van Osdel, who arrived in Chicago in 1837. In an article, "The History of Chicago Architecture," published in a Chicago monthly of the early eighties, Van Osdel remarks that "Mr. Snow was the inventor of the 'balloon frame' method of constructing wooden buildings, which in this city completely superseded the old style of framing with posts, girts, beams and braces."[13]

George Snow's name is nearly unknown. There is no portrait of him in any of the local histories, but one was obtained from a family album which reveals a face at once full of puritan energy and of human sensitivity.[14]

The first building in balloon frame was St. Mary's Church in Chicago, the earliest of the Catholic churches of the city (*fig. 209*). "In July 1833 a number of men are found erecting a church on Lake Street near State Street."[15] Old builders prophesied its collapse. In the short term of its existence this church was razed and reërected three times.

Until the seventies the balloon frame was called simply "Chicago construction," as we learn from a report of United States Commissioner H. Bowen, published in Washington in

---

[11] I (Chicago, 1890), 504.

[12] I (Chicago, 1891), 51.

[13] *Inland Architect and Builder*, I, no. 3 (April 1883), 36. This magazine was the organ of the developing Chicago school of architects.

[14] I am indebted for this biographical material to Miss Marion Rawls, librarian of the Burnham Library of the Art Institute of Chicago, and to Mrs. George A. Carpenter of Chicago, Snow's granddaughter, who provided the portrait. I published this portrait in an article in the annual, *New Directions*, 1939.

[15] *Industrial Chicago*, I, 51.

1869. Bowen speaks of the western farmhouse which was forwarded in sections to the Paris Universal Exposition of 1867 as being of "Chicago construction."

The balloon frame, then, is associated with Chicago, like the skyscraper construction which, half a century later, was also called simply "Chicago construction."

The balloon-frame building with its skeleton of thin machine-cut studs and its covering of clapboards grew out of the seventeenth-century farmhouses of the early settlers. Snow was familiar with such houses in his home state of New Hampshire and his wife's home, Connecticut, where they were especially common. In these houses comparatively thin and narrow studs were used as intermediary framing, with the whole construction tied together by the clapboard covering.[16]

George Snow started with these traditional methods, changing and adapting them to meet the new possibilities of production in a way which was as simple as it was ingenious.

The balloon frame has kept its vitality for a whole century and is still used extensively. This simple and efficient construction is thoroughly adapted to the requirements of contemporary architects. Many of Richard J. Neutra's houses in Texas and southern California reveal the elegance and lightness which are innate qualities of the balloon-frame skeleton (*fig.* **212**).

The Balloon Frame and the Windsor Chair

The thin two-inch studs of the balloon frame stick up into the air apparently without weight in comparison with the traditional timber construction. Even today the European observer finds their thinness really daring.

The same idea, the use of thin structural members to produce a most efficient whole construction, had figured a century earlier in the development of the Windsor chair. The Windsor chair is as outstandingly important in the history of American

[16] Cf. J. F. Kelly, *The Early Domestic Architecture of Connecticut* (New Haven, 1935), p. 40. Here the "studs or intermediary framing members" are described as "generally measuring about 2½ × 3 inches in section." Their height, however, was only equal to "the distance between the horizontal members of construction."

furniture as the balloon frame is in the history of American housing.

There is a familiar anecdote attached to the name of this piece of furniture. The Prince of Wales, toward the end of the seventeenth century, is supposed to have seen the original specimen in a peasant's cottage near Windsor Castle, and to have ordered it copied for his own use, though England never gave the artistic consideration to the Windsor chair that America did. Windsor chairs were the strongest type of chair made in the colonies and easily movable. Their construction was of spindles (*fig.* **211**), and the early ones were made by wheelwrights. It is very seldom that the vogue for furniture extends over a century, but that of the Windsor chair lasted from 1725 to 1825. No single chair-maker won individual fame for the design.[17]

For the historian it seems worth while to observe the curious interrelation existing between the development of the balloon frame and the Windsor chair in two different centuries.

There is the same tendency to counteract the American climate — wet and dry in turn — by assembling thin structural parts to produce a light type of construction. There is the same tendency toward anonymous work and toward serial manufacture, with lightness and efficiency achieved by the simplest means.

PLANE SURFACES IN AMERICAN ARCHITECTURE

In speaking earlier of architecture as an organism with its own continuing life, we remarked that nowadays we are chiefly interested in those persisting influences which give this life its continuity. The lines of force which spread and develop throughout several periods concern us more than the history of styles, for styles are those special aspects of periods which mark them off one from the other.

---

[17] See Marta K. Sironen, *A History of American Furniture* (New York, 1936), p. 18.

Historical styles are particularly uninformative with regard to what was actually going on in America. They arrived here fully grown and give little insight into the constituent facts of the native American development.

During the eighties European architecture lost more and more of its dignity. The closer it clung to historical forms in the search for security the more insecure it really became. In barely fifty years the whole architectural inheritance of the eighteenth and early nineteenth centuries was lost in a welter of transitory detail. The inner unrest and uncertainty of the period appears time and again in unbalanced treatments of the wall and of the ground plan. The whole organism of architecture was riddled by a fatal disease.

American independence of Europe showed itself in the development of new and logical forms for tools and furniture, and in the informal and flexible ground plan of the American house. In the same way the wall maintained its unity and balance in America throughout this whole period of European uncertainty and confusion. America produced its share of grotesque work during these years, but — in contrast to Europe — attention never entirely strayed from the basic elements of architecture. These elements always remained dominant in American work, taken as a whole. It may be that this is why new architectural solutions were reached in America earlier than they were abroad.

The plane surface: the brick wall

The plane surface — the flat wall of wood, brick, or stone — has always been a basic element in American architecture. In part this has been due to the simplicity which a scarcity of skilled labor enforced; in part it directly continues late eighteenth-century tendencies. The Georgian manner of treating the brick wall has been carried over into the nineteenth century; wooden houses have kept to traditions established by the first settlers.

The *brick wall*, to be cheap, must be kept flat and simple. All openings are cut very cleanly into the flat surface of the wall.

Such undisguised brick walls (*fig.* **213**) are familiar features of the American scene; they appear in New England mansions

213. Old Larkin Building, Buffalo, 1837. *Specimen brick building of a type omnipresent in the United States, with flat, undisguised walls and clean-cut openings.*

of the late eighteenth century, in small anonymous buildings on the main streets of all the cities, and in the big factories of the Civil War period. The plain brick wall was firmly established as a basic element in architecture when men like Henry Hobson Richardson began their work in the seventies. Richardson's Sever Hall was built in 1878. We found a European example of such scrupulously level surfaces in Berlage's Amsterdam Stock Exchange. But the Stock Exchange was built two decades later; flat brick surfaces, such as Richardson used, were almost unknown in the Europe of the seventies.

Frank Lloyd Wright, too, was able to use the brick wall, taken as a simple surface, from the very start. Unlike van de Velde and Horta, there was no need for him to begin by crusading against the mutilation and overcrowding of the wall, or to invent an *art nouveau* to compete with established modes of ornamentation. He was able to begin his work on a much higher level.

357

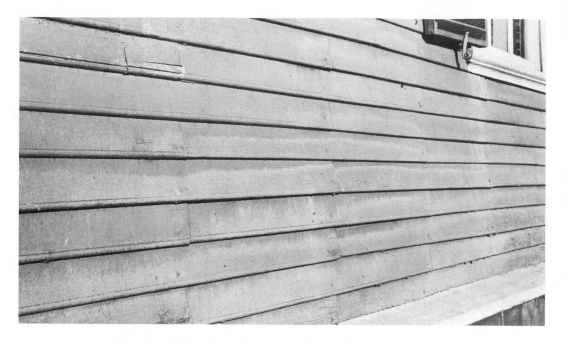

214. Longfellow House, Cambridge, Mass., 1759. *Clapboard wall of the sort which has been used continuously in America for three centuries.*

The
wooden wall

The *wooden wall* has been governed by eighteenth-century American traditions to an even greater extent than the brick. The simple clapboard wall (*fig.* **214**) has remained a constituent element for three centuries, without any interruption, from the time of the first colonists to the present. Clapboards had been used in England, but only for unpretentious farmhouses. In America they dominated the whole field of wooden building. We find them everywhere, from the rudest huts to the finest mansions, churches, and town halls. Such a widespread and enduring authority for one type of wall treatment covering a period of three hundred years is entirely unknown on the other side of the Atlantic.

The use of clapboards automatically tends toward balanced and simple treatments of the wall. They are ill suited to breaks or interruptions in its flat expanse, and they discourage the use of applied ornament.

The stone wall

Stone walls were treated with the same simplicity in states where stone was used as a building material. Excellent workmanship was displayed in the New England states: in the flat

358

215. Stone wall, Union Wharf warehouse, Boston, 1846. *The granite posts and lintels for windows and doors were cut in one piece at the Quincy quarries.*

granite walls of the community houses of the Shakers (*fig.* **216**), in the granite warehouses along the Boston wharves (*fig.* **215**), and in the commercial buildings of Boston of the fifties and sixties (*figs.* **217, 218**).[1]

---

[1] Many of these buildings were designed by Alexander Parris, who also designed Quincy Market (the market buildings around Faneuil Hall, *c.* 1825). The earliest of the waterfront buildings date from the middle twenties; the wharf warehouses were built in the forties; the mercantile blocks on Commercial Street were erected in the fifties; the remainder were mostly completed by 1869, when Franklin Street was opened.

Many of these mercantile buildings are excellent examples of a well-proportioned and logical pre-Richardson architecture which certainly played a larger part in later developments than is generally believed.

In a seminar which I conducted during the summer of 1938 on Boston office buildings between 1830 and 1860 we endeavored to learn more about this work. An account of one of the earliest of the great commercial architects, Gridley J. Fox Bryant, was discovered in a copy of the *New England Magazine* ("An Architect of the Old School," vol. XXV, n.s., November, 1901). Between the fifties and the seventies, Bryant built hundreds of business blocks on the Boston water front, most of them granite buildings. According to the *New England Magazine*, he left all his papers to Henry Turner Bailey. One of my students, Miss Lydia Jones, wrote to Bailey's widow. This material has apparently disappeared, for Mrs. Bailey replied that her husband had "got rid of it one day." By 1960 most of these buildings as well as the granite wharfs had disappeared.

216. Shaker Community House, Concord, Vermont, 1832. *A specimen of the excellent stonework that was produced by this religious sect.*

These commercial buildings with their rusticated walls display typical plane surfaces and economy of detail. Earlier warehouses, dating from the forties, are built of huge plain blocks of rough-hewn granite, but no reminiscences of Florence are involved. Their impressive austerity is easily explained: the granite came from the Quincy quarries near-by, and labor was saved by cutting out the window or door pillars on the spot, in one piece.

Richardson was a student at Harvard in the period when these commercial buildings were erected. Later on he went to Paris and came under European influences. These new buildings along the Boston water front must nevertheless have constituted his earliest architectural impressions.

The Marshall Field Store Richardson's Marshall Field Wholesale Store in Chicago (1885–87) was his best work (*fig.* **219**). This building with its massive stone walls occupies a rather strange position in the Chicago development as a whole. For all that, it furnished a strong incitement to the work of the Chicago school, and something of its character was reflected in other buildings erected in the Loop during the eighties.

Louis Sullivan's criticisms of the architecture of his time were as uniquely severe as they were just. The Marshall Field Store, however, was to him an "oasis" in the midst of a desert of doubtfully sincere edifices. The "young man" to

217. Commercial Block, 140 Commercial Street, Boston, Mass., 1856. *Detail. One example of the well-proportioned and logical pre-Richardson architecture that appeared in Boston during the fifties and sixties.*

218. Commercial Block, 140 Commercial Street, Boston, Mass. *From Boston Almanac, 1856. A contemporary print of the building from which the detail in Fig. 217 was taken.*

219. H. H. RICHARDSON. Marshall Field Wholesale Store, Chicago, 1885. *Richardson here continues the American tradition of the plain and massive stone wall.*

whom he so describes it in his *Kindergarten Chats* interrupts him with ironic astonishment:

"'You mean there is a good piece of architecture for me to look at?'

"'No, I mean, here is a man for you to look at. . . . I mean that stone and mortar here spring into life and are no more material and sordid things . . . wholesomeness is there, the breath of life is there, an elemental urge is there.'" [2]

We break in upon this poetic vision only to ask, What is this building? Romanesque? Florentine Renaissance? [3] But need we go so far back? Would it not be simpler to look for its origin in the rugged stone walls which gave Richardson his first

[2] *Kindergarten Chats* (Lawrence [?], Kansas, 1934), p. 15.

[3] Henry Russell Hitchcock in his biography of Richardson makes a very careful effort to trace the stages by which Richardson arrived at his Romanesque style. The account (inevitably) presents large gaps.

362

architectural impressions? The plain and massive stone wall had been one of the basic elements in American architecture from the very beginning, from the fortifications of the Revolutionary period to the commercial buildings contemporaneous with Richardson's student days at Harvard. The sober impressiveness of this store could be Romanesque and at the same time thoroughly indigenous, an artistic transmutation of elements which had grown out of American life.

The Flexible and Informal Ground Plan

American architecture has been marked by one tendency since the arrival of the earliest settlers: the American house is given a ground plan which can be enlarged whenever new social and economic conditions make it desirable. This contrasts very sharply with European procedure. In Europe a farmhouse is planned as a solid, cubical unit from the very beginning. Sometimes the interior is left unfinished, to be fitted up by later generations when they come to need larger living quarters.

The American and the European farmhouse

The American practice of adding new units to the original one can be seen in those New England houses which survive from the seventeenth century.[4] All these heavily timbered houses began as one and a half or (at most) two-story structures, with a single room on the ground floor. The next generation, with improving circumstances, enlarged this ancestral nucleus both horizontally and vertically. A new roof was spread over all these additions, quite asymmetrically. But the important thing was the addition of wings, which was very general. The L-shaped ground plan, the beginning of the flexible and informal layout, developed from this sort of planning.

Houses were not invariably enlarged. Sometimes — as in the William Pepperell house at Kittery, Maine — they proved too big for a later generation and were cut down. "This family mansion was then much more imposing than at present, being 10 feet longer at each end and surrounded by a beautiful park. It was reduced after the American Revolution when the estate was confiscated in 1779."[5]

[4] For example, the Hancock house, Lexington, Mass. (1698, enlarged in 1734), the Jackson house, Portsmouth, N. H. (c. 1664), and the Whipple house, Ipswich, Mass. (1642).

[5] *The Portsmouth Guide Book* (Portsmouth, N. H., 1876), pp. 145–146.

In the late eighteenth century people did not hesitate to cut through the solid oak framework of a house and divide it into several portions. These were then moved to a new site and reassembled, with whatever changes and enlargements suggested themselves. The house at 34 Chestnut Street, Salem, Massachusetts (*fig.* **220**), is the product of such methods, although no one would ever suspect it. This charming residence, which seems to have been conceived as a unified whole, was really built in three sections. "It is the only house now standing on the street which was not built in its present location but

220. House at 34 Chestnut Street, Salem, Mass., 1824. *The two ends were originally part of another house and were moved on wheels to the Chestnut Street site; there the center portion was built.*

was moved to the street. . . . It was originally a portion of the house on the West Farm at Oak Hill, Danvers [miles away], and was moved on wheels to Chestnut Street, in two parts, about 1824." [6] The architect added the center with its Palladian window, and changed and adapted it to the so-called Palladian or academic ground plan which was in favor at this period.

The flexible treatment of the house which has been common practice in America since colonial days is one of the keys to

[6] Richard Hall Wiswall, *Notes on the Building of Chestnut Street* (Salem, 1939), p. 18.

its domestic architecture. Opinions are supposed to change oftener in America than elsewhere, but this is not true in the field of housing. Here there has been continuous growth. American developments show more continuity than we find in Europe, and more of the power to develop new elements for the future out of the existing architectural inheritance.

American publications of the sixties and seventies show the great variety of foreign influences which were at work in the country. England, Germany, France, Spain, the Orient — fashions from all these quarters came into favor. They remained, however, only the latest fashions at one season or another; they did not permanently infect American architecture. When Wilhelm Bode visited the Chicago World's Fair of 1893 he remarked that "in contrast to Germany, the modern American house is built entirely from the inside out. It not only corresponds to particular individual demands but above all to the peculiarities, customs, and needs of the Americans. That these customs are pronounced and distinctly marked gives domestic architecture in the United States a great advantage over our own German architecture." [7]

American interiors of the nineties

It was precisely the things which still impress European observers that surprised Bode almost fifty years ago. He notes that "rooms along the hallway are fitted with sliding doors or partitions — often half as wide as their walls — and that these doors are nearly always left open.[8] In this way it is possible to look into the various rooms of the house." The Continental apartment houses to which Bode was accustomed, with their ridiculously high ceilings, dark and overcrowded rooms, and luxuriant wall-coverings, were in sharp contrast to American

---

[7] Wilhelm Bode, "Moderne Kunst in der Vereinigten Staaten," *Kunstgewerbeblatt*, V (1894), 115–117.

[8] To this day the European's house remains, more or less, his castle. Its doors are real doors, and they are usually kept closed. Sliding partitions never open upon the hallways; they are used only to connect interior rooms. In American houses there are not only these daringly placed partitions but even a lack of keys for half of the doors within the house, and a lack of locks in the case of closets and wardrobes. European windows are provided with both shades and curtains, and both — usually neither, in America — are drawn after nightfall. The American rarely even fences his house, and lately there are some signs that he may abandon the garage and take to leaving his car under a mere shelter. "A garage is no longer necessary, as cars are made," says Frank Lloyd Wright. "A carport will do, with liberal overhead shelter and walls on two sides" (*Architectural Forum*, January 1938, p. 79).

interiors. In America, Bode remarks, "the rooms, according to our notions, are somewhat low. They are not overcrowded with furniture, *and they have light-colored walls and ceilings.*" [9] (These are features which contemporary architects have finally established in Europe, after considerable struggle.)

Functional planning in the seventies

Bode's report of an advanced American domestic architecture is supported by popular literature on home building published as early as the seventies. Books like Gardner's *Illustrated*

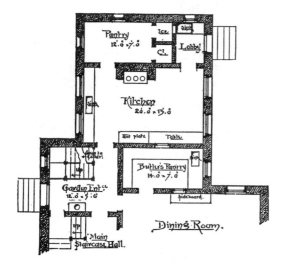

221. E. C. GARDNER. Kitchen, 1882.

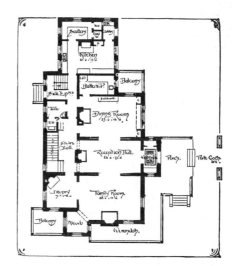

222. E. C. GARDNER. Country house, 1882.

Homes, Describing Real Houses and Real People (Boston, 1875) [10] did much to propagate sound housing. The way in which these books of the seventies approach the problem of the house is surprising, considering the period. Instead of the discussion of details which one might expect, the house is considered as a whole — as a unit which must vary in each special case. Their authors find this attitude so natural that the tone of the discussions is invariably light and easy and sometimes actually playful. They deal with houses planned not in some special style but for some special purpose: with houses for the newly married, doctors' houses, well-to-do business men's houses — even one-room houses for "old maids."

[9] *Op. cit.*, p. 117.

[10] Eugene C. Gardner (1836–1915) was one of the popular authors in this field. He was principal of the Talmadge Academy, at Talmadge, Ohio, and editor of the *Builder* from 1885 to 1887.

The old maid and her house (*figs.* **223, 224**) are particularly interesting. This is a lady who knows precisely what she wants: "I propose to build a house to live in, merely that and nothing more. . . . My house must have one room and of closets four; one for a little dressing room; one for my silk dresses, which will accumulate, as I have no one to give them to except to home missionaries' wives, and they ought not to wear silk; one for my china, and one for my umbrella and

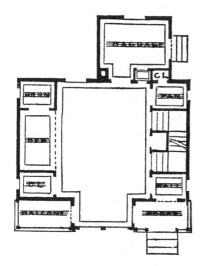

223. E. C. GARDNER. One-room house for an "old maid."

224. The architect and his spinster client. *From Gardner, "Illustrated Homes" (Boston, 1875).*

overshoes." [11] The close-knit unity of the ground plan produced to satisfy these demands and the economy with which its space is put to use recall one of J. J. P. Oud's low-rental apartments of 1920.

The functional spirit which dominated Europe in the twenties is even more clearly apparent in the way the problem of the kitchen is handled. In another of his books Gardner proposes a space-saving treatment strikingly similar to the Frankfort kitchen of about 1920 (*fig.* **221**). The later design was supposed to derive from the space economies effected in the modern dining-car. Gardner achieved his solution through a direct approach to the working problems of the cook and the housewife. The kitchen is made long and narrow "so that it may

---

[11] Gardner, *op. cit.*, p. 114.

have ample wall space and yet keep the distance between the range and the pantry as short as possible." It has windows at opposite sides "to admit plenty of light" and so that "the summer breezes may sweep through it and keep a river of fresh air between the cooking range and the dining room." [12]

The interior of the typical American house is subdivided as little as possible. This urge to unite the various rooms and to open the interior is occasionally reflected in the use of different floor levels, as in certain large Classical Revival houses of the nineties.

An anonymous development

Nineteenth-century Americans who could afford to be stylish had houses whose exterior forms reflected the styles in favor at the time — romantic, Victorian, French Renaissance, Romanesque, or classical. The ground plan, however, generally retained its soundness. The flexible and informal ground plan which was, on the whole, standard in America grew up without any great names being attached to it. Like tools and patent furniture, it remained strictly anonymous. It is the outgrowth both of the urge for comfort in the dwelling and of the American tendency to tackle problems directly. Frank Lloyd Wright found the basic elements of the flexible ground plan ready at hand in its anonymous development. Undoubtedly Richardson gave a new artistic intensity to this sort of planning in his houses of the early eighties — particularly those built around Chicago and in New England. But open planning itself, the flexible and informal ground plan — this is a product of the American development as a whole.

THE CHICAGO SCHOOL

Chicago in the eighties

During the eighties a whole colony of buildings suddenly sprang up in Chicago — to heights of twelve, fourteen, sixteen, and twenty-three stories. These buildings were erected not in

[12] *The House that Jill Built* (New York, 1882), p. 82. Kitchens with a highly differentiated organization and highly developed technical installations are first to be found in England in the forties. Cf. the interesting description of the great kitchen of the Reform Club in London (built by Charles Barry in 1837) in the Larousse *Dictionnaire du XIX siècle*, heading "Club."

368

isolation, as they were in other cities, but in close proximity to each other. Each had its own individual appearance and its own name, and yet the aggregate appearance was not chaotic.

American buildings are commonly so short-lived that in a few decades, perhaps, these buildings will all have disappeared. Many of the best specimens have gone already and many more are destined to go soon.

The strongest growth of the Chicago school is to be found between 1883 and 1893.[1] Two contemporary voices may inform us of the state of development at the beginning and at the end of this period.

"In no period since 1830 has the city experienced such wonderful development in increase of population, trade and building up as . . . in 1882. . . . The character of the buildings are [sic] monstrous and costly. . . . There is such a demand for business and office quarters that the permit to build a block is no sooner obtained than applications are made for renting apartments, and before the building is completed it is all rented and the renters are ready to step in with their implements of trade. Block after block mount up into the clouds overhanging the city from every street and avenue."[2]

---

[1] The works concerned with the Chicago school in its development between 1883 and 1893 are for the most part anonymous. The first two volumes of *Industrial Chicago*, 6 vols. (Chicago, 1891–96), published by the Goodspeed Publishing Company, treat the building interests. These two volumes, rarely found in American libraries, are the Vasari of the Chicago school. The volumes of the *Inland Architect* (Chicago) after 1883 also give some insight into the development of the school.

The best illustrations and plans (besides those in *Industrial Chicago*) are to be found in *Prominent Buildings Erected by the George A. Fuller Company, Chicago* (Chicago? 1893?) and *Fireproof Building Construction: Prominent Buildings Erected by the Geo. A. Fuller Company* (New York and Chicago, 1904), both published by the George A. Fuller Company. George A. Fuller (1851–1900), a Massachusetts man, went into business in Chicago as a builder. He was one of the first building contractors to work with skeleton construction, and he was connected with the erection of many buildings with which we shall deal — the Tacoma, the Monadnock, the Pontiac, the Fair, the Reliance, and the Marquette buildings, the Ashland Block, and the Carson, Pirie, Scott and Company department store as long as Louis Sullivan worked on it.

Not to be overlooked are several guides, such as L. Schick, *Chicago and Its Environs: A Handbook for Travellers* (Chicago, 1891). Others will be mentioned later. For illustrations see *Pictorial Chicago* (Chicago: Rand, McNally, 1893).

For the earlier period see T. A. Andreas, *History of Chicago* (Chicago, 1884), which contains rare statistics and illustrations.

[2] *Stranger's Guide* (Chicago, 1883).

In 1893, shortly before a great crisis affected Chicago and its activities, another contemporary witness traces the end of this period: "many times has it happened in Chicago that the morning papers have come out with accounts of the letting of the contract for the largest office building in the city and the evening papers of the same day have given news of other contracts for buildings far surpassing those told in the morning." [3]

In the eighties the Loop — the business center of the city — became the perfect illustration of American audacity in the direct assault that was made upon its problems. Whole streets were developed in a way that had never been seen before. Walking through the Loop, one is struck by the impression that Chicago is an outpost for the immense areas which are spread out behind it. At the time its great buildings went up, Chicago was the real point of concentration for the products of the West and Middle West, and not merely an enormous stock exchange, like New York. The rapid growth of this great center led to sudden enlargements of its needs. To meet them, the urge grew up to use the new potentialities of construction, potentialities which had hitherto been exploited only in bridges and industrial structures of various kinds.

Large office buildings for business firms and insurance companies were the first to appear. Buildings of equal power soon appeared to meet other demands — immense hotels for the travelers who passed through the city and combination office-theater-hotel buildings like the Adler and Sullivan Auditorium. At the same time the problem of the modern apartment house — which still remains unsolved — was attacked with great consistency and daring.

Office buildings as the starting point of the Chicago school

The Chicago school is bound up with the creation of the modern office building — in other words, with the creation of an administration center (*fig.* **231**). All sorts of engineering problems entered into the solution reached in the Chicago buildings, and the founder of the Chicago school, William Le Baron Jenney (1832–1907),[4] was an engineer before he was an

[3] *World's Fair Souvenirs* (Chicago, 1893).

[4] Cf. Charles B. Jenkins, "W. L. B. Jenney and W. B. Mundie," *Architectural Reviewer* (Chicago), February 1897.

architect. He had received a thorough technical grounding and had been a major in Sherman's corps of engineers. The future architects of Chicago received their training in Jenney's office. William Le Baron Jenny played much the same role in the training of the younger generation of Chicago architects that Peter Behrens did in Germany around 1910, or Auguste Perret in France. He gave young architects the preparation they needed to tackle the new problems for which the schools could offer no solutions.

Today William Le Baron Jenney's imagination and courage are not sufficiently recognized. Even Louis Sullivan describes him as rather a connoisseur than an architect, and in Chicago one of Sullivan's collaborators told me that Jenney had no sense for detail and ornament. Architectonic detail and stylistic remnants play, it is true, a negligible part in Jenney's work. For all that, he was the man whose Leiter Building of 1889 was the earliest solution of the problem of the great building in skeleton construction, a solution whose clarity and freedom from compromise were far above the average.

The role of William Le Baron Jenney

Jenney's background was excellent. He had received the best technical training available in this period at the École Polytechnique and the École Centrale in Paris. In Jenney's studio French engineering combined with the methods of his German specialists in ornament to produce a curious mixture. In 1873, as a young beginner, Louis Sullivan worked in this studio and had his eyes opened to "suppressed functions" in architecture. Besides Sullivan (who stayed here no longer than he did most places) Jenney's staff at one time or other included many of the future builders of Chicago: Martin Roche, Holabird, and even Daniel Burnham — later the partner of John Root.

Jenney's hand first showed itself clearly in a warehouse which he built at 280 West Monroe Street for Leiter in 1879 (*fig.* **225**). This building (which is still in existence) has brick pillars on its outer walls, and wide glass openings similar to the "Chicago windows" of a later date. The interior has the cast-iron columns which were standard during this period.

Jenney's first building of a type new both in respect to its height and its construction was erected for the Home Insur-

225. WILLIAM LE BARON JEN-NEY. First Leiter Building, Chicago, 1879. *Brick pillars on outer walls; cast-iron columns in the interior. The wide glass openings suggest the "Chicago windows" of a later date.*

ance Company in 1884–85.[5] In it a complicated construction was made to produce a thoroughly integrated whole.

Jenney, a leader in construction

Richardson planned the Marshall Field Wholesale Store and Warehouse (*fig.* **219**) while Jenney was at work on his Home Insurance Company building. This store showed Chicago architects how unobtrusively a great volume could be inte-grated. Richardson injected into this building something of the vitality of the rising city, in a treatment which was full of dignity. The dominance of the windows is emphasized, as it is in Jenney's Home Insurance offices, but the construction is rather conservative. Richardson's massive stone walls belong to an earlier period. When Adler and Sullivan came to build their Auditorium, they used similarly massive outer walls, even though the interior iron structure was very daring.

Architects did not at once follow Jenney in his adoption of skeleton construction. In 1889, however, three years after his

---

[5] Cf. p. 207. This building was still sound in 1929 when it was torn down.

226. WILLIAM LE BARON JENNEY. Manhattan Building, Chicago, 1891. *The bay windows of many different forms are intended to catch all the light available on this narrow street. They disappear entirely in the unobstructed upper stories.*

Home Insurance Company, Holabird and Roche put up the Tacoma Building, a twelve-story skeleton structure.[6]

Meanwhile William Le Baron Jenney kept to his own course. He erected his second Leiter Building in 1889. His Manhattan Building (*fig.* **226**) — at this period the highest building of pure skeleton construction — was finished in 1891.[7] The Manhattan is on Dearborn Street, which is comparatively narrow. In order to catch as much sunlight as possible, Jenney — like Holabird and Roche in the Tacoma Building — filled its front

---

[6] In a building of the Tacoma's dimensions, the gain in renting area through the use of skeleton rather than masonry construction was equivalent to the rent on an additional floor. It was for this reason that skeleton construction was used. A certain indecision is still apparent in the design of the Tacoma. The total window area is exceptionally great, but the individual windows themselves are quite small. The Tacoma was torn down in 1929.

[7] "The Manhattan, fronting on Dearborn Street, is the pioneer of the sixteen-story and basement building . . . 204 feet high . . . designed May 1890 and completed in the summer of 1891" (*Industrial Chicago*, vol. I, 1891, p. 69).

with bay windows.[8]   But these windows are very carefully diversified in shape, and they disappear entirely in the unobstructed upper stories.[9]

Jenney built "The Fair," one of Chicago's great department stores, in 1891. With this nine-story building on Dearborn, Adams, and State streets, Jenney returned to his principle of making the skeleton the determining factor in the design. The first two stories of The Fair are almost pure glass (*figs.* **227, 228**). This feature was demanded by the owners of the store, who wanted the largest possible amount of display area.

The new potentialities change the aspect of the city
The spirit of the Chicago school, its impulsion toward the simplest and most self-evident solutions, soon dominated the entire Loop. Its works sprang up one beside another.

Burnham and Root erected their Monadnock Block at the corner of Dearborn and Jackson streets in 1891. This was the last of the high buildings with walls of solid masonry. A contemporary critic — Montgomery Schuyler — called it "the best of all tall office-buildings," [10] but it is not too typical of the Chicago school. Its expression derives more from architectonic refinements than from the new potentialities.[11] And heavy masonry walls were not the solution to the problem of the many-storied building. The rather small dimensions of the windows indicate the extent to which they hampered the architects.

Diagonally across the street from the Monadnock Block is another Burnham and Root building, the Great Northern

---

[8] "Light and space are preferred to any definite style" (*idem*).

[9] The Manhattan was reproduced in *Inland Architect*, vol. XIII (1889), no. 8.

[10] Harriet Monroe, *John Wellborn Root* (New York, 1896), pp. 141–142.

[11] At this period the taste of speculators and investment counselors was sometimes more advanced than that of architects — a rare phenomenon. "The Monadnock — 'Jumbo,' Root used to call it — was the last of the tall buildings to show walls of solid masonry. For this building Mr. Aldis [Owen F. Aldis, of Boston], who controlled the investment, kept urging upon his architects extreme simplicity, rejecting one or two of Root's sketches as too ornate. During Root's absence of a fortnight at the seashore, Mr. Burnham ordered from one of the draughtsmen a design of a straight-up-and-down, uncompromising, unornamented façade. When Root returned, he was indignant at first over this project of a brick box. Gradually, however, he threw himself into the spirit of the thing, and one day he told Mr. Aldis that the heavy sloping lines of an Egyptian pylon had gotten into his mind as the basis of this design, and that he would 'throw the thing up without a single ornament'" (Harriet Monroe, *op. cit.*, p. 141).

227. WILLIAM LE BARON JENNEY. The Fair Building, Chicago, 1891. *The skeleton is made the determining factor in this design.*

228. WILLIAM LE BARON JENNEY. The Fair Building, Chicago, 1891. *Skeleton.*

229. HOLABIRD and ROCHE. Marquette Building, Chicago, 1894. *The front is exceptionally well-proportioned, imposing in its simplicity and its wide expanse of "Chicago windows."*

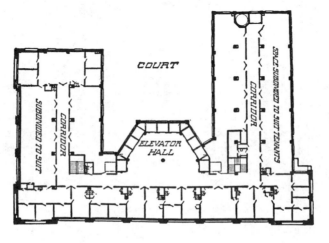

230. HOLABIRD and ROCHE. Marquette Building, Chicago, 1894. *Plan of one story with undivided offices. In most of these buildings large portions of every. floor were left without partitions, so that they could be subdivided later to suit the tenants.*

376

Hotel (1891; *fig.* **232**).   Its clean brick façades carried over to the hotel room the "Chicago windows" used for offices.   The Fair, Jenney's department store, was also built around this time.   Three years later, in 1894, Holabird and Roche constructed their Marquette Building farther down the street (*fig.* **229**).

The front of the Marquette is exceptionally well-proportioned, imposing in its simplicity and its wide expanse of "Chicago windows."   It remains the typical Chicago office building of the nineties.   The demand of the owners that not one inch of the interior be unlighted is exactly satisfied.   From the street the Marquette looks like a closed block, but actually it is cut out at the back somewhat like a letter **E**.   The middle bar of the **E** — relatively the darkest part of the building — is used as an elevator hall, with all the elevators massed together in it.   As in most such buildings, large parts of its floor space were built without partitions so that they could be subdivided later on to suit the tenants (*fig.* **230**).[12]

The Apartment House [13]

In Chicago the problems of large-scale housing, of the hotel and the apartment house, were attacked with the same clear-headedness that appears in the office buildings of the city. During the seventies, just after the great fire, a trend away from the small private home and toward the big many-storied apartment house set in — this on the authority of the anonymous author of *Industrial Chicago*.   As he puts it, "the modern flat is the palace of those who wish to be relieved of house owning and its cares." [14]

The interior organization and the architectonic details of some of these buildings are astonishingly daring and advanced.

[12] J. K. Freitag, *Architectural Engineering, with Special Reference to High Building Construction*, 3rd ed. (New York, 1912), p. 38.   Freitag's book is one of the few technical publications dating from the most flourishing period of the Chicago school.   It contains the ground plans of many important buildings as well as a wealth of technical details.

[13] Cf. *Industrial Chicago*, vol. I, chap. 7, on modern flats and other residences, and illustrations and comments in the following issues of the *Inland Architect:* August 1884, pp. 8, 15; January 1887, p. 101; December 1890, plate (Ricardi apartments); October 1897, plate (Cary apartments); March 1887, p. 28 and plate; February 1893, plate (the "Kenwood"); November 1893, plate (the "Omaha").

[14] *Industrial Chicago*, I, 254.

Solutions which today are still in process of being formulated appeared in outline in these flats and hotels of a generation back — just as contemporary business and civic centers were anticipated by the Chicago office blocks.

The Adler and Sullivan Auditorium marks one of the early stages in this development. This huge and complicated structure housed not only the actual auditorium and an office building but also a large hotel. The hotel is noteworthy in many respects: the staircase is modeled with an impressive strength; the great length of the bar is emphasized by a heavy beam carried along the ceiling parallel to its front edge in a clear span with no vertical supports; the top-floor dining hall (since converted to other uses) is developed as a broad barrel vault, thereby matching the auditorium proper.[15]

The Hyde Park Hotel on the south side of the city was built in 1887–91 by Theodore Starrett and George A. Fuller. Its site on Fifty-first Street, near the lake shore, was then almost rural; it has since been heavily developed. "The hotel has 300 rooms, finished in suites of 2 to 5 apartments, . . . 50 suites are furnished with private baths and incandescent lamps . . . and heated by steam." [16] The building was of eight stories, with broad windows, and — once more according to *Industrial Chicago* — "a very large verandah extending around the building."

Some of these apartment houses had removable partitions so that a suite of five rooms could be thrown together into one. This was the case in the Leander McCormick flats, later the Virginia Hotel, at the northwest corner of Ohio and Rush streets. Its architect was Clinton J. Warren, a product of the Burnham and Root offices.[17]

---

[15] For a detailed description of this theater, the best of the period, with plans, see Hugh Morrison, *Louis Sullivan* (New York, 1935).

[16] *Industrial Chicago*, I, 460.

[17] This building was torn down a few years ago; the site is now used as a parking lot. In its time the Virginia was one of the finest residential hotels in the city, on a par with the Drake. Cf. the illustration in P. T. Gilbert and C. L. Bryson, *Chicago and Its Makers* (Chicago, 1929), p. 529.

231. Chicago in the early nineties: Randolph Street about 1891. *The large buildings here are the Ashland offices, built by Burnham and Root in 1891.* →

232. Great Northern Hotel, Chicago, 1891. *Advances made in Chicago office buildings were taken over to create the type of hotel and apartment house suited to the industrial age.*

The Brewster apartments on Pine Grove Avenue, built during the early nineties, are still in existence. The architect, R. H. Turnock, had done his early work under William Le Baron Jenney. The main staircase has treads of plate glass so that the light can flow through the entire eight stories of the building from the skylight on the roof. As is well known, Le Corbusier came to a similar solution some forty years later in his Clarté apartments in Geneva (1932).

We have been able to do no more here than simply point to a few of the buildings which were included in the field of the Chicago development. It is a field whose importance has been overlooked for too long — so long, in fact, that buildings and documents alike may have disappeared before any real insight into what they represent has been gained. These Chicago apartment houses represent the first steps toward a kind of large-scale housing which is very different from anything we find in Europe. Progress in this direction was largely canceled in the next generation, however. A reaction set in against the big apartment house and the residential hotel, coupled with a fresh concentration of attention on the private, one-family dwelling. Frank Lloyd Wright is the outstanding figure in this later movement.[18]

In 1893 this Chicago architecture impressed a French observer — the novelist Paul Bourget — with "the simple force of need as a principle of beauty. . . . There is so little caprice and fancy in these monuments and these streets that they seem to be the work of some impersonal power, irresistible, unconscious, like a force of nature, in the service of which man has been but a docile instrument. It is this expression of the overpowering immensity of modern commerce which gives to the city something of tragedy, and, to my feeling, a poetry."[19]

The Chicago school has many claims to importance. Its members made the first expressive use of the new technical potentialities in buildings which were permanent and essential parts of the structure of Chicago's daily life. They produced not just a few isolated specimen structures but covered the whole business district with a new architecture. Their work changed the entire face of a great modern city.

TOWARD PURE FORMS

The architects of the Chicago school employed a new type of construction: the iron skeleton. At that time it was called quite simply "Chicago construction."

Innovations of the Chicago school

They invented a new kind of foundation to cope with the problem of the muddy ground of Chicago: the floating foundation. They introduced the horizontally elongated window: the Chicago window.

They created the modern business and administration building.

---

[18] For information concerning its course, cf. Purcell, Feick, and Elmslie, "The Statics and Dynamics of Architecture," *Western Architect*, January 1913, p. 1, and the article on Irving J. Gill's work in California on p. 35 of the issue of April 1913. The issue of August 1913 contains an account by Walter Burley Griffin of some of his own suburban developments (p. 66).

[19] Paul Bourget, *Outre Mer*, vol. I, chap. V, as quoted in Harriet Monroe, *op. cit.*, pp. 136–137.

The importance of the school for the history of architecture lies in this fact: for the first time in the nineteenth century the schism between construction and architecture, between the engineer and the architect, was healed. This schism marked the whole preceding part of the century. With surprising boldness, the Chicago school strove to break through to pure forms, forms which would unite construction and architecture in an identical expression.

Contemporary statement of its aims

These Chicago architects of the eighties were quite conscious of their own boldness. In 1890 John Root — the constructor of the Monadnock Block — said, speaking of modern business buildings, that "to lavish upon them profusion of delicate ornament is worse than useless. . . . Rather should they by their mass and proportion convey in some large elemental sense an idea of the great, stable, conserving forces of modern civilization.

"One result of methods such as I have indicated will be the resolution of our architectural designs into their essential elements. So vital has the underlying structure of these buildings become, that it must dictate absolutely the general departure of external forms; and so imperative are all the commercial and constructive demands, that all architectural detail employed in expressing them must become modified by them. Under these conditions we are compelled to work definitely with definite aims, permeating ourselves with the full spirit of the age, that we may give its architecture true art forms." [1]

The amount of work which came out of the Chicago school in the course of its development was very great. We shall take three buildings, each by a different architect but all showing clearly the inherent urge of the Chicago school toward purity of form.

The Leiter Building, 1889

The first building of pure skeleton type; its aesthetic significance

William Le Baron Jenney not only produced the first example of Chicago construction in his Home Insurance Building of 1884–85, but he also erected the first building in which there was not even one self-supporting wall, the Leiter Building.

---

[1] From a paper read at the Chicago Art Institute and published in the *Inland Architect*, June 1890. Quoted in Monroe, *op. cit.*, p. 107.

With it purity of constructional methods seemed to find its equivalent in architecture; the Leiter Building attains to an expression in which the lingering memories of historical styles play a negligible part.

The Leiter Building, planned in 1889, fills a whole block at Van Buren and State streets (*fig.* **233**).[2] Jenney dealt with and mastered a front four hundred feet long and eight stories high through the use of great and simple units. The skeleton furnishes the dominating accents of the building, appearing in the huge squares into which the outer wall is divided. These panels are filled by plate-glass windows which "are separated only by fireproofed metal columns."[3]

The spirit behind this employment of the skeleton as an architectonic means has received further development in contemporary architecture. Le Corbusier's Maison de Verre, a Geneva apartment house of 1932, represents a later stage in its evolution (*fig.* **234**).

Le Corbusier, 1932

Jenney's contemporaries seem to have recognized the significance of his work. Even the anonymous author of *Industrial Chicago* (1891) momentarily discards his accustomed sobriety in speaking of it: "It has been constructed with the same science and all the careful inspection that would be used in the construction of a steel railroad bridge of the first order. The severely plain exterior is grand in its proportions. The great corner piers are carried upward to a chaste cornice. Designed for space, light, ventilation, and security, the Leiter Building meets the object sought in every particular." With its building, he goes on to exclaim, "a giant structure . . . healthy to look at, lightsome and airy while substantial, was added to the great houses of a great city . . . a commercial pile in a style undreamed of when Buonarroti erected the greatest temple of Christianity."[4]

Contemporary reaction

Although the Leiter Building seems to be the first of the high buildings to exhibit the trend toward the use of pure forms, it

[2] "The building will be located on the East side of State Street and will extend from Van Buren to Congress Street. It will be eight stories; the three street fronts will be of light gray New England granite, the construction a steel skeleton, the masonry protecting the external columns. It is intended that the whole building should be one great retail store" (*Inland Architect*, vol. XIV, no. 1, August 1889, p. 10).

[3] *Industrial Chicago*, I, 205.

[4] *Industrial Chicago*, I, 204–205.

233. WILLIAM LE BARON JENNEY. Leiter Building, Van Buren Street, Chicago, 1889. *The skeleton becomes a means of architectonic expression.*

is today almost unknown, except to a handful of specialists. Its importance consists not in its height — which happens to be of eight, rather than twelve or twenty stories — but in the identity between what is expressed in its construction and in its architecture. The Leiter Building marks a starting point for this kind of architectural purity and should not be ignored in the history of architecture.

234. LE CORBUSIER. Maison Clarté, Geneva, 1930–32. *The properties of the skeleton used in the service of residential needs.*

The Reliance Building, 1894

John Root died in 1891; Daniel Burnham, his partner, swung over into the classical school and took his cues from New York.[5] But in 1894 one more building in the spirit of his dead partner emerged from Burnham's office, the Reliance Building

Experience of the Chicago school summed up in this glass tower

---

[5] Peter B. Wight, "Daniel Hudson Burnham and His Associates," *Architectural Record,* vol. XXXVIII, no. 1 (July 1915).

235. BURNHAM and COMPANY. Reliance Building, Chicago, 1894. *In its airiness and purity of proportion, this building serves to symbolize the spirit of the Chicago school, whose swan song it was.*

236. MIES VAN DER ROHE. Project for a glass tower, 1921. *A modern excursion into the realm of fantasy, something of whose spirit, nevertheless, had been anticipated in the Reliance Building.*

on State Street — the "swan song" of the Chicago school.[6] Speaking in a broader sense, it might perhaps be said to have grown out of the Chicago soil itself, to be a reflection of the high architectural level that has been reached in that city.

The Reliance Building is a glass tower fifteen stories high (*fig.* **235**). The base is formed from some dark and unobtrusive stone, in sharp contrast to the glass and glazed white tile tower which springs up from it. The eaves of the flat roof are only thin slabs, emphasized no more than they must be to serve as protections. There is no overbearing cornice of stone.[7]

Ten years' experience lies behind the understanding treatment of the horizontally proportioned "Chicago windows." In

---

[6] "The Reliance Building was the 'swan song' to the old traditions, based on independence of design, for which were noted the works of Burnham and Root. It stands today a symbol of our inconsistency and an ample proof that no sooner do we approach a common way of working than the promise of a truly expressive style of American architecture is broken by the capricious introduction of a new fashion" (A. N. Rebori, "The Work of Burnham and Root," *Architectural Record*, vol. XXXVIII, no. 1, July 1915, p. 62.

[7] In this respect it differs markedly from Burnham's Flatiron Building in New York (1902), with its immense cornice and its skeleton cluttered with heavy stonework.

earlier office buildings of the Chicago school (the now-destroyed Tacoma Building by Holabird and Roche, for example) the bow windows tend somewhat to be independent and isolated parts of the design. In the Reliance Building they project no more than they are required to in order to pick up light. They are wholly incorporated into the glass body of the building.

This glass tower is still standing, and, although its glazed white tiles have become encrusted with dirt, its airiness and pure proportions make it a symbol of the spirit of the Chicago school. It is curious that this building too has been left unnoticed in the history of architecture. It has its place there as a witness to the best of the spirit of the nineteenth century.

Mies van der Rohe, 1921

Mies van der Rohe's scheme for a skyscraper of glass and iron is the dream of a European architect in the year 1921 (*fig.* **236**). The points of departure for dream projects of this sort should perhaps be sought in works like the Reliance Building of some three decades earlier. But it may be that this Chicago building is something more than an incentive for fantasy: an architectonic anticipation of the future.

Sullivan: The Carson, Pirie, Scott Store, 1899–1906

In 1899 Louis Sullivan began to remodel the Schlesinger & Mayer store at State and Madison streets, on the famous "World's Busiest Corner." The work was done in three sections, in 1899, 1903–04, and 1906.[8] In the summer of 1904 the establishment was taken over by the Carson, Pirie, Scott firm. The third unit was built for it by Daniel Burnham & Company, but Louis Sullivan's scheme for the first two sections was retained, with only a few unimportant changes (*fig.* **237**).

Unsurpassed strength and precision

In spite of its complexity Sullivan's building remains unsurpassed in its expressive strength. The interior is still of the warehouse type, with continuous, unbroken floor areas. The

---

[8] The first unit was nine stories high and three bays (some 60 feet) in width; the second was twelve stories high and 150 feet wide, but otherwise identical in design with the first. The final unit was 105 feet wide. Hugh Morrison (one of the first to recognize the architectural importance of this store) gives a detailed account of its building in his careful study, *Louis Sullivan, Prophet of Modern Architecture* (New York, 1935), pp. 197 ff.

388

237. LOUIS SUL-LIVAN. Carson, Pirie, Scott and Company, department store, Chicago, 1899–1904. *Built in three units on State and Madison streets, the "World's Busiest Corner." The round tower at the corner was included at the insistence of the owners.*

front is designed to fulfill its indispensable function, the admission of light. Its basic elements are the horizontally elongated "Chicago windows," admirably homogeneous and treated to coincide with the framework of the skeleton. The whole front is executed with a strength and precision that is matched by no other building of the period. The slightest differences in proportion can be felt at once against a background of this definiteness. The windows, with their thin metal frames, are sharply cut into the façade (*fig.* **238**). The windows in the lower stories are connected by a narrow line of ornament pressed into the terra cotta. Too thin to be visible in the photograph, this line nevertheless helps to accentuate the horizontal organization of the front.[9]

Even when architects of Sullivan's generation pressed on toward new solutions they sometimes found themselves held back by nineteenth-century traditions. They suffered from the

Intrusion of
the pavilion

[9] George Elmslie, whom we have already mentioned as one of Sullivan's staunchest collaborators, was the designer of most of the ornamentation on his buildings. It was not influenced by the contemporary *art nouveau*.

sort of split personality which we spoke of earlier. The split personality of the nineteenth-century architect makes itself felt in Sullivan's Carson, Pirie, Scott building. The round tower at the corner with its narrow vertical ribs and glass panes suddenly introduces a motif quite out of character with the rest of the building. The owners had asked for this curvilinear addition (which we noted as a stylistic remnant in Eiffel and Boileau's Bon Marché of 1876) as a reminiscence of the pavilion attached to their old store. But this alone would not have affected the work of as strong-minded a man as Sullivan.

Around 1900, on its completion, this store appeared old-fashioned to contemporaries. By this time they had lost their hearts and heads to the "commercial classicism" of the New York architects and its distortion of business buildings into mercantile palaces. For three decades the New York practitioners of the academic architecture ruled the whole country.

The Carson, Pirie, Scott store, one of the late productions of the Chicago school, seems to be molded more by the anonymous spirit which ruled the work of that school than by Louis Sullivan's personal tendencies. In Sullivan's best-known buildings — from the Wainwright in St. Louis (1890–91) to the Prudential in Buffalo (1894–95) and the Bayard Building in New York (1897–98) — he continually increased the stress upon the vertical elements in the design, emphasizing the piers at the corners. He uses narrow pillars and gives the whole building a strictly upward orientation, a movement as marked as that which we encounter in the Gothic cathedrals.

But the skeleton — whether iron or steel or reinforced concrete — is essentially a neutral spatial network. Its "cage construction" bounds a certain volume of space with complete impartiality, and no one intrinsic direction. In his typical buildings Sullivan picks out and emphasizes the vertical lines of force in this network. In the Carson, Pirie, Scott store, however, it is the neutral and impartial equilibrium inherent in the skeleton construction which Sullivan chooses to project upon the façade of the building.

The influence of the Chicago school was cut short by the influx of eclecticism. Louis Sullivan — the great architect of

390

the school — did leave his mark upon the next generation of architects in the Middle West. (Frank Lloyd Wright was to emerge as the outstanding figure in this generation.) And during the first decade of our century, the traditions of the Chicago school survived in works by some of its younger members: George Elmslie, Hugh Garden, George Maher, Griffin, Thomas Tallmadge, and a few others. Some of their buildings might have served as a revelation to the rising generation in Europe. They failed entirely, however, to influence the corresponding groups in their own country. A literary architectural education cut the younger men off from the principles of the Chicago school and destroyed their individuality as well. Left in isolation, the surviving members of the Chicago school grew discouraged, and many of them lost the force which they had shown in a more favorable period.

In the 1922 competition for the Chicago Tribune Building, the plans of a competent American architect — Raymond Hood — won the first prize. By this time, however, the confidence and belief in its own forces which had sustained the Chicago school had completely disappeared. The school might just as well have never existed; its principles were crowded out by the vogue of "Woolworth Gothic." [10]

The Chicago Tribune Tower; nullification of the Chicago tradition

The hundred thousand dollar international competition for the Tribune Building drew entries from everywhere. The projects submitted give an invaluable cross section of the architecture of this period.[11] One of the foreign entrants was Walter Gropius. Both the jury and the public must have considered his scheme quite unstylish and old-fashioned. There is no doubt, however, that it was much closer in spirit to the Chicago school

Foreign projects closer to the Chicago school

---

[10] Stemming from the Woolworth Building in New York, 1911–13.

[11] All these projects, with the exception of K. Lönberg-Holm's entry, were published in *International Competition for a New Administration Building for the Chicago Tribune* (Chicago, 1923), issued by the Tribune Company. The American entries fall tragically short of the level reached in Chicago during the eighties and nineties. Fashionable architects submitted typical specimens of the now dominant "Woolworth Gothic," and all the entries show a secondhand fancifulness instead of a sense for scale and proportion. The competition chiefly inspired an unhappy excursion into romanticism. An equally distressing helplessness appears in the European projects, with the exception of a few entries from the northern countries: Bruno Taut (project # 231), Max Taut (# 229), Bijvoet and Dujker, K. Lönberg-Holm, Walter Gropius, and Adolph Meyer (# 197). (The numbers refer to the plans published in *The International Competition*.) These men produced schemes which represented endeavors to escape from familiar routines.

than the Gothic tower which was executed. When we compare
Gropius' 1922 project and Sullivan's Carson, Pirie, Scott store
they seem like two stages in the development of the same set of
ideas. In both of them the network of the skeleton is the basis
of and inextricable from the architectonic expression. There
are the same hovering and sharply cut surfaces. Gropius even

238. LOUIS SULLIVAN. Carson, Pirie, Scott and Company Department Store,
Chicago, 1899–1904. *Detail. Outstanding for strength and purity of expression even in the
work of Louis Sullivan. The neutral and impartial equilibrium inherent in cage construction is emphasized, rather than its vertical elements.*

employs the "Chicago window," with a fixed glass panel in
the middle and narrow ventilating windows at the sides
(*fig. 239*). The whole plan seems an outgrowth of the Chicago
school, but actually Chicago windows and the Chicago skyscraper were unknown in Europe. This coincidence, the way in
which these two men arrived independently at similar solutions,
shows that the Chicago school really was "permeated by the
spirit of the age," in the phrase of one of its best representatives. It could therefore create constituent facts for architec-

239. WALTER
GROPIUS. Proj-
ect for the compe-
tition on the Trib-
une Tower, Chicago,
1923. *Constituent
facts developed by
the Chicago school
reappear independ-
ently in this Euro-
pean project.*

ture, facts that reappeared in later periods just as Borromini's
undulating wall reappeared in English residential quarters.[12]

The Influence of the Chicago World's Fair, 1893

At the very moment when the Chicago school gained a mastery
of the new means which it had created, its further development
and influence were abruptly choked off. The event which di-

The World's
Fair and the
Chicago school

---

[12] Hood, whose Gothic Tribune Tower was completed in 1925, was himself on the verge
of a change which achieved its full expression about 1930. In that year he built the
McGraw-Hill building in New York, whose architecture recognizes in part the new European developments. He was to arrive at far more impressive solutions later on in the
buildings at Rockefeller Center.

rectly effected this change was the Chicago World's Fair of 1893 (the World's Columbian Exposition), but influences working in this direction had set in long before in another section of the country.

American architecture came under many different influences during the nineteenth century, but none was so strong or came at such a critical moment as the rise to power of the mercantile classicism developed in the East.

Tremendous public success

The 1893 World's Fair elicited a variety of responses. The public and most of the architects were rapturous in their delight. While I was in Chicago, one architect who had worked on it quoted from memory the rather ironical comment of William James: "Everyone says one ought to sell all one has and mortgage one's soul to go there; it is esteemed such a revelation of beauty. People cast away all sin and baseness, burst into tears, and grow religious, etc., under the influence."

Some European observers were more sceptical. The extremely well-informed Belgian constructor Vierendeel found both its staff architecture and the construction it enveloped timid and secondhand — as we saw toward the end of our discussion of the great nineteenth-century exhibitions.

Sullivan's prophecy

The lonely American voices raised against the unexampled seduction of the public taste underlying the Fair's pseudo-splendor went unheard. Louis Sullivan said bitterly that "the damage wrought to this country by the Chicago World's Fair will last half a century." At the time this may have seemed only the exaggerated expression of an outraged artist; it turned out to be a precise prophecy of what was actually to follow.

Influence of the Beaux-Arts

Public, artists, and literary people believed themselves to be witnessing a splendid rebirth of the great traditions of past ages. The immense appeal of this re-created past in "the White City" can only be laid to a quite unnecessary national inferiority complex. It was the same feeling — reinforced by the prestige of the Paris exhibition of 1889 — which gave the French academicians a dominating role at this Chicago fair. The contemporary biographer of John Root expresses it quite clearly: "At that time few hoped to rival Paris; the

394

artistic capacity and experience of the French made us distrustful of ourselves. We should have a great American fair, but in points of grouping and design we must expect inferiority to French taste." [13]   And it was to France that the builders of the Fair turned in their search for beauty. Its beauties were taken out of the preserve jars of the Académie des Beaux-Arts — where they had been laid up during what was certainly its worst period. *Grand prix de Rome* façades were copied, and men like Burnham (who had assisted in raising the Chicago school to a level much higher than the Academy's) acted like docile children in the presence of the French masters. All this is another instance of the split between thought and feeling in the nineteenth century. Only Louis Sullivan had sufficient inner strength to hold fast in the midst of a general surrender. But his Transportation Building for the Chicago fair marked the beginning of his unpopularity as an architect.

Mercantile classicism had been developing and gaining strength in New York since the eighties, but it won its country-wide ascendancy at the World's Columbian Exhibition of 1893.[14]

Eastern mercantile classicism

The spirit behind it had now come to possess authority for American architecture as a whole.[15]   The Fair should, indeed, have stood in New York; it so thoroughly represented the influence of that city. But as soon as a Columbian exposition was proposed, the people of Chicago leaped at the idea. "The enthusiasm of the city was set on its mettle; an aggressive campaign was organized, and five million dollars pledged by private subscription before other cities had begun to act." [16]

The hypnotic spell which mercantile classicism exerted appears from some lines in Frank Lloyd Wright's *Autobiography*. Shortly after the close of the Fair (and after the completion of Wright's Winslow house), Daniel Burnham called on him.

F. L. Wright and the Beaux-Arts

---

[13] Harriet Monroe, *op. cit.*, p. 218.

[14] Immense and thoroughly businesslike New York building firms (McKim, Mead, and White) carried out the greater part of the Fair.

[15] Professor Hamlin observes that "by 1880 there were constantly a dozen or fifteen Americans in the Ecole of Paris. In all the schools, Paris-trained men were in demand as instructors. . . . The Ecole had furnished the model upon which all our American schools were shaping the teaching of design" ("The Influence of the Ecole des Beaux Arts on Our Architectural Education," *Architectural Record*, April 1908, p. 242).

[16] Monroe, *op. cit.*, p. 216.

"To be brief, he would take care of my wife and children if I would go to Paris, four years of the Beaux Arts. Then Rome — two years. Expenses all paid. A job with him when I came back. . . .

"'Another year and it will be too late, Frank,' said Uncle Dan. . . .

"'Yes, too late, Uncle Dan. It's too late now, I'm afraid. I am spoiled already.

"'I've been too close to Mr. Sullivan. He has helped spoil the Beaux Arts for me, or spoiled me for the Beaux Arts, I guess I mean.'

"'. . . The Fair is going to have a great influence in our country. The American people have seen the "Classics" on a grand scale for the first time. . . . I can see all America constructed along the lines of the Fair, in noble "dignified" classic style. The great men of the day all feel that way about it — all of them.'"[17]

FRANK LLOYD WRIGHT

Wright and the American Development

Preëminence as an architect

Of all contemporary architects whose span of work reaches back into the nineteenth century, Frank Lloyd Wright was without doubt the most farsighted, a genius of inexplicably rich and continuing vitality. He ranged the wide expanse of historical interrelations, drawing particularly upon the architecture of the Far East — not, however, in the manner of the last century, as a substitute for creative impulse, but, like Matisse with Negro or Persian art, from an inner sympathetic relationship. At the same time he sprang out of the American soil and the American tradition more directly perhaps than any other of the great American architects. True insight into his work demands a somewhat subtle approach, for Wright's dominating personality, present in every touch of what he did, was not at all simple. He bore in himself the marks of the late

---

[17] F. L. Wright, *An Autobiography* (New York, 1932), pp. 123–124.

nineteenth century; yet isolated and singlehanded, without aid from his contemporaries among painters and sculptors, he introduced the beginnings of a new conception.

When he began work in 1887, he was — in Chicago — at the very center, the fountainhead, of architectural development. He was apprentice in the atelier of two of the best men, Louis Sullivan, "lieber Meister," he called him, and Dankmar Adler, "the grand old chief," at the very time when they were on the ascendant creatively, working on the Auditorium Building. He had as the principal influence of his youth the culmination of the Chicago renascence. And yet when he began to work independently, Wright did not continue directly in the Chicago school; he did not carry over the use of the new materials — the iron skeleton and the great glass surfaces of the office buildings — into his own sphere: housing. Instead he was rather conservative; in many respects he followed Richardson more than Sullivan. It was not until as late as the thirties, when European architects were already utilizing the inherent possibilities of ferroconcrete to the fullest, that Wright, as he said himself, used it for the first time to any great extent for one of his houses.[1] This was due not to any lack of technical ability but to his own will and character.

In Europe Wright was quickly accepted and understood by the generation which was responsible for the modern movement. In 1908 he was visited by Kuno Francke, then a German exchange professor lecturing at Harvard University on aesthetics. The result of this visit was the publication in Germany in 1910 of a monumental work on Wright's architecture.[2] This was supplemented in 1911 by a smaller work on the same subject, which enjoyed a very wide circulation.[3] These two books marked the beginning of Wright's foreign influence; the book published in 1910 has not since been approached in comprehensiveness.

What is the explanation of the fact that Wright was the only architect so far ahead of his own generation, a man who built

---

[1] The Kaufman house, "Falling Water," Bear Run, Pennsylvania, 1937.

[2] *Frank Lloyd Wright, ausgeführte Bauten und Entwürfe* (Berlin, 1910), with a preface in German by Wright.

[3] *Frank Lloyd Wright, ausgeführte Bauten* (Berlin, 1911); foreword by C. R. Ashbee.

240. FRANK LLOYD WRIGHT. Charnley house, Astor Street, Chicago, 1892. *The Charnley house is from Wright's earliest period, designed while he was still an employee of Adler and Sullivan. (The extension of the right wing is of a later date.) In it he uses the flat surfaces of the American tradition, cutting in the windows sharply as if with an axe.*

works of great influence right up to his life's end? The answer is rather simple: he had less debris to clear away than the Europeans. He had been born in the Middle West, within the shadow of the place possessing the greatest architectural vitality of the period: Chicago.

Devotion to housing

From the outset Wright devoted himself to the problem which was to be his life interest — the house as a shelter. He had at his disposal the anonymous American tradition, the example of Sullivan, and the conscious artistry which Richardson had cultivated in home building. The secret of Wright's work is that he saw in the tradition of the American house those elements which could be used as a basis for the future. He took these basic elements and added new ones, enlarging — with all the force of genius — the structure of the house delivered to him.

The objection may be advanced that the English had been working on the problem of the dwelling house since 1860. But the English at this time had no architects of the stature of Sullivan or Richardson. Philip Webb and Norman Shaw are not to be compared with the two Americans. The crux of the difference between the English and American architects lies in their point of departure: the Englishmen began with a reform, through handicraft, of furniture, rugs, wallpaper, and other small household objects which had been debased by industrial production. The Americans, on the other hand, started from the house as a whole, and were not seduced by an overemphasis upon handicraft.

It would not be without interest to make a comparative study of Frank Lloyd Wright and his Scotch contemporary, Charles Rennie Mackintosh,[4] who was born in the same year — to remark their differences and the traits they possess in common; to consider the way in which they treat wall surfaces, how they use and expose wooden posts and beams, and how they conceive their furniture. They both began by working in terms of their own generation, Mackintosh in Glasgow, Wright on this side of the Atlantic. Some of Wright's early peculiarities, especially in his furnishings, persisted until the last phase of his work.

Wright and the English development

The Charnley house on Astor Street, Chicago (*fig.* **240**), with its projecting wings (executed in 1892 while Wright was still in the employ of Adler and Sullivan, and usually attributed to that firm) is not very different from the Mary Ward Settlement in the Bloomsbury district of London.[5] In the final analysis the façades of European buildings cannot avoid restlessness and are to a certain extent split into details. Their architects never dare to use rigorously, as Wright did in the Charnley house, the flat surfaces of the American tradition, cutting in the windows sharply and clearly as if with an axe

---

[4] The Scottish architect, Charles Rennie Mackintosh (1869–1928), noted for his art school in Glasgow and especially for his country houses (e.g., the house of Dr. Blackie, Helensborough, 1902). Mackintosh had a direct influence on the *art decoratif* movement in Vienna, the Wiener Werkstätte. The founder of this institution took his artists to Scotland to show them how household furnishings and architecture should be designed. The influence was a complete one for the moment, but restricted to matters of taste. No new architectural vision came out of it. Nikolaus Pevsner, in his *Pioneers of the Modern Movement* (London and New York, 1937), gives an excellent survey of Mackintosh's work, with a bibliography (pp. 221–222). Pevsner may be consulted also on other questions concerning the British development. A sharply unfavorable attitude toward Mackintosh is taken by his close compatriot, P. M. Shand, in "Glasgow Interlude," *Architectural Review*, LXXVII (January 1935), 23.

[5] Cf. Pevsner, *op. cit.*, p. 157.

and molding the house with few but persistent accents.[6] Yet
as a whole Wright's earliest houses, even the first built on his
own account, are not fundamentally different from the best
English examples. The change, however, was not to be long
in coming. England produced nothing more. Europe was
adrift, seeking solutions. Frank Lloyd Wright went ahead.

The Cruciform and the Elongated Plan

Ground plan and
interior space

Before I had seen any of Wright's houses, I stopped once for a
rest in a hunting lodge in the Vermont hills. It had an immense
stone chimney which stood massively in its center, rising the
entire height from the ground up through the roof. The interior space was undivided, except for a partition which cut
off the kitchen and the sleeping room. There was no ceiling,
but simply open rafters from which hung fox and bear skins.
At that moment I began to understand the way Wright conceived his interior spaces. He worked fundamentally and as
far as possible with the house as one room. Its inner space is
differentiated to meet special needs. As he pointed out, he
"declared the whole . . . floor as one room, cutting off the
kitchen as a laboratory, putting servants' sleeping and living
quarters next to it, semi-detached, on the ground floor, screen-
ing various portions in the big room, for certain domestic purposes — like dining or reading, or receiving a formal caller." [7]

Cruciform plan

In organizing his plans Wright went back to the seventeenth
century in the use of the large chimney in the center of the
house as starting point for the whole layout. He spread out
the different rooms from this massive kernel. What first impressed European architects was his "windmill" plan, so
called because of the way the rooms were extended outward
from the center like the vanes of a windmill (*fig.* **243**). This
"windmill" plan is really cruciform, an interpenetration of
two parts of the house, which cut each other transversely to

[6] Speaking of the Charnley house, Hugh Morrison, in his *Louis Sullivan* (New York,
1935), says that it was "broader in conception than any of Sullivan's other residences,
with more feeling for the organization of plane surfaces, skillfully punctuated by window
voids" (pp. 132–133).

[7] *Modern Architecture* (Princeton, 1931), Princeton Monographs in Art and Archae-
ology, p. 72.

form a cross. Often they are of different heights; then the effect is of one crossbar superimposed upon and penetrating the other.

This early American practice of using a central chimney as the core of the house, as the point about which the whole is organized, was kept alive also through the nineteenth century (*fig.* 241). Again we may cite as evidence one of those unknown writers who reflect the common taste. In one of the small popular books on suburban and country houses in the early seventies, there is proposed a country house built completely around a fourfold, four-sided chimney, with rooms leading off in wings from each of the four sides. The author's reason for this cruciform arrangement is very close to Wright's own intention, both in the stress placed upon light — Wright em-emphasized the fact that rooms in his layout get light from three sides — and in the urge to treat the several rooms as a unit: "The design of this house was made for the purpose of giving each room a sunny southern exposure, and out of ten rooms nine have at least one lookout to the southeast. The principal floor is so managed that the spacious hall with winding staircase presents an attractive feature on entering. The chimney is in the center of the house and sliding doors connect each of the principal rooms so that when occasion requires, hall, parlor, library, and dining room may be thrown together, the octagon form of these rooms adding much to their beauty." [8] As always in this period, the exterior of the house has nothing of the precision of the plan (*fig.* 242). Nevertheless, there are suggestions of the interpenetration of two volumes, for which in his Chicago period Wright was to find artistic solutions.

Most of Wright's houses, especially the smaller ones, are based on the cruciform plan issuing out of and produced by this interpenetration of two volumes of different heights. Such are the Hickox house, Kankakee, Illinois, 1901; the Ward house, Willett Park, Illinois, 1901; the Willitts house, Highland Park, Illinois, 1901; the small country house of Charles Ross at Lake Delavan, Wisconsin, 1902; the Robert Evans house in Long-

[8] George E. Woodward, *Suburban and Country Houses* (New York, copr. 1873), pp. 15–16.

401

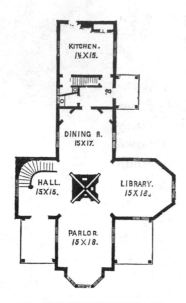

241. G. E. WOODWARD. Plan of a cruciform country house, 1873. *From Woodward, "Suburban and Country Houses" (New York, c. 1873). Built around a fourfold, four-sided chimney with diagonally sliding doors to convert the house, to a certain extent, into a single room.*

242. G. E. WOODWARD. Cruciform country house, 1873. *As always in this period, the exterior has nothing of the precision of the plan. One of Wright's great accomplishments was to find an equivalent for the ground plan in spatial and exterior treatment.*

wood, Illinois, 1904; the Isabel Roberts house, 1907; the Horner house, Birchwood, 1908.

Of these, the Isabel Roberts house in River Forest, Illinois (*figs.* **243, 244**), one of the most charming of Wright's smaller houses, shows an interesting employment of the interpenetration of two volumes of different heights, in which Wright used the higher volume to mold, not the hallway, but the space of the living room from the ground up through the whole height to the inner planes of the roof (*fig.* **245**). It represents an effort to satisfy the feeling of a need for the full height as living space. This feeling finds expression not only in the houses of American settlers of the seventeenth century but in many early civilizations, and it has reappeared in our own period. Wright was one of the first to recognize this feeling, to formulate it and give it expression. In the Isabel Roberts house the living room dominates, rising up to the gently sloping roof,

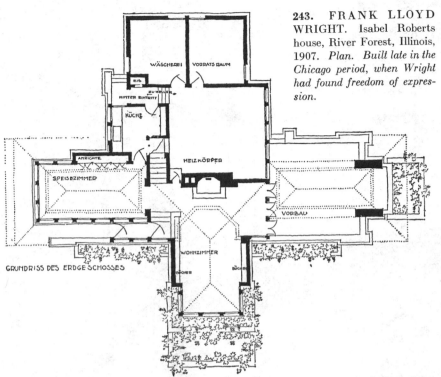

243. FRANK LLOYD WRIGHT. Isabel Roberts house, River Forest, Illinois, 1907. *Plan. Built late in the Chicago period, when Wright had found freedom of expression.*

244. FRANK LLOYD WRIGHT. Isabel Roberts house, River Forest, Illinois, 1907. *The slab roof and the low horizontal extension of the wings are interesting. This exterior shows Wright's clarification and purification of standard material.*

403

245. FRANK LLOYD WRIGHT. Isabel Roberts house, River Forest, Illinois, 1907. *Two-story living room. Wright uses the higher volume to mold the space of the living room from the ground up through the entire height to the inner planes of the roof.*

and divided in height by a gallery, so that there are recessed spaces both above and below. This gives an unaccustomed and new plasticity to the whole room, which is enhanced by the use of various planes in different materials — the brick face of the chimney, the several wall surfaces, and the slope of the roof.

Mies van de Rohe, the German architect — one of the few whose early work reflects Wright's influence without either being absorbed by it or reducing it to a merely decorative use — developed the "windmill" plan in several of his schemes.[9]

Wright himself never abandoned the idea of the house spread out from a central core. When in 1939 he built a low-cost four-family housing unit (Suntop Houses, Ardmore, Pa.; *figs.* **246, 247**),[10] he separated the different apartments by brick walls

[9] Project for a brick house in 1922.
[10] See *Architectural Forum*, August 1939.

404

crossing at right angles. At the central core he put not a chimney but all the utilities — plumbing, heating, electricity, and ventilation — so that they were concentrated in the darkest spot in the building.

When possible, Wright liked to spread his structures out freely over the ground. In the introduction to the study of his work published in Berlin in 1910, he points out that the first floor was often built principally as a cellar. The main living quarters lie in the upper story on one floor, as in the Coonley house (1911), where only the entrance hall and the game room are on the ground floor; in Taliesin, his own house, they are set into and connected with the ground. This led him to the flexible and informal ground plan so deeply embedded in the American architectural development from its beginning. As a consequence of this development Wright now let the different rooms flow out horizontally, just as, in houses like the Isabel Roberts house, he had molded them vertically.

Flexible and informal ground plan

By 1910 Wright had achieved a flexibility of open planning unapproached hitherto. In other countries at that time the flexible ground plan and the flexibly molded interior and exterior were almost unknown. Wright's realization of a flexible treatment of the inner space of a building is probably his greatest service to architecture. It brought life, movement, freedom into the whole rigid and benumbed body of modern architecture.

Plane Surfaces and Structure

The Japanese house impressed Frank Lloyd Wright as "a supreme study in elimination — not only of dirt, but the elimination, too, of the *insignificant*." For the American house he accomplished just such an elimination, a rejection of the confused and the trivial. But he did more than this. He took up those elements lying about everywhere unobserved — elements arising from purely utilitarian solutions — and discovered in this raw material its hidden expressiveness, just as the following generation was to discover the hidden expressiveness in engineering and construction. Wright brought forward these elements and changed them, opened our eyes to their

Use of native elements

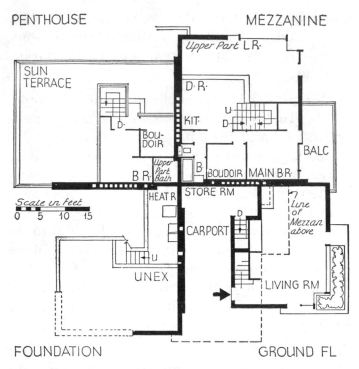

PENTHOUSE

MEZZANINE

SUN TERRACE

Upper Part L.R.

D

BOUDOIR

D.R.

KIT.

U. D.

BALC

B.R.

Upper Part Bath

B.

BOUDOIR

MAIN B.R.

Scale in feet
0 5 10 15

HEAT R

STORE RM

line of Mezzan above

CARPORT

D

U

UNEX

LIVING RM

FOUNDATION

GROUND FL

246. FRANK LLOYD WRIGHT. Suntop Houses, Ardmore, Pennsylvania, 1939. *Plan. In this low-cost, four-family housing unit, Wright separates the different apartments by brick walls crossing at right angles. At the central core he has put all the utilities — plumbing, heating, electricity, and ventilation, so that they are concentrated in the darkest spot in the building.*

247. FRANK LLOYD WRIGHT. Suntop Houses, Ardmore, Pennsylvania, 1939.

secret potentialities and their inherent beauty, revealing their symbolic strength as a poet does in showing forth what inner content of feeling the trees and mountains, the rivers and lakes, of his native land hold for him and for us.[11]

In the treatment of the house as a spatial unit he seized upon these elements wherever he could find them. He also sought to shape the whole house in terms of its own period. The earliest American houses — those of the settlers along the fron-

The porch

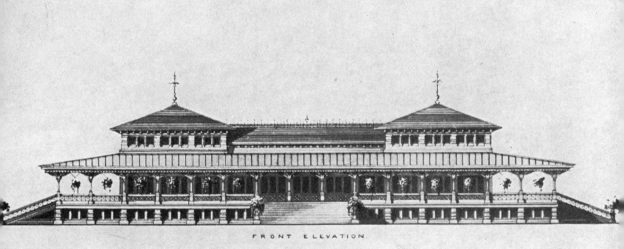

FRONT ELEVATION.

248. Central Park Casino, New York City, 1871.

tier — had to afford protection against attack, and consequently were meagerly supplied with openings on the first floor, being without rows of windows and open galleries like those that have given the peasant houses of Switzerland and southern Germany — at any rate since the early seventeenth century — so distinctive an exterior. Much later, with the

[11] Joseph Hudnut, in the foreword to the catalogue of Wright's first exhibition in New England (Institute of Modern Art, Boston, January–February 1940), emphasizes the fact that to understand Wright "we must think of him . . . as a poet."

appearance of the porch on the houses of southern rice and cotton planters, there was a corresponding opening up of the American house in the southern part of the country. In nineteenth-century America the porch was used much more extensively as the recreation area of the home than the veranda of the European peasant house, even becoming a decisive element in the appearance of suburban and country houses. Sometimes it stretched out in long, unbroken horizontal lines,

249. R. E. SCHMIDT, GARDEN & MARTIN. Warehouse of ferroconcrete for Montgomery, Ward & Co., Chicago, 1908. *Immense warehouse built in the same year as the Robie house. With unbroken horizontal lines.*

covered with a slightly sloping roof. The appearance of the Central Park Casino, New York, 1871 (*fig.* **248**) — one of many anonymous examples — is due to an extension of this peculiarly American employment of the porch. Apparently Americans like a strong and unbroken horizontal line equally in their houses and in the Pullman car.

Wright adopted the porch for his houses — not, however, encircling his buildings with it, but pushing it forward, in keeping with his cruciform or elongated plans, as an extension of the wings. Very often it thrusts out into space as a pure cantilever hovering above the earth. Such a treatment had never been attempted before. True, it is the old element of the porch, but it is not simply something attached to the house; rather it is an essential part of the structure, molded as an inseparable part of it. For several reasons, explained in his writings, Wright used overhanging eaves. He treated them, too, as

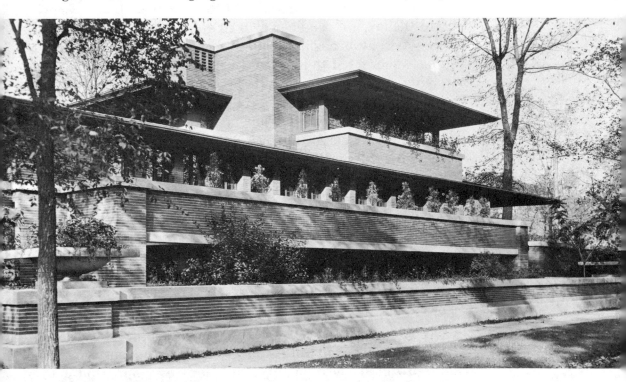

250. FRANK LLOYD WRIGHT. Robie house, Woodlawn Avenue, Chicago, 1908. *In this house, which has had far-reaching influence, Wright has used plane surfaces at different depths, advancing and receding. The Robie house, a town villa, is in close relation to the aims of the Chicago school.*

horizontal planes — "broad protecting roof shelters," as he called them — just as Burnham, before he turned classicist, roofed his Reliance Building (1894) with a thin slab (*fig.* **235**).

To these hovering horizontal elements Wright added the plane of vertical surfaces. When he built the Charnley house in 1892 (*fig.* **240**), he used the clean-cut level surfaces of the American tradition. But soon he became more daring, espe-

Treatment of the walls

409

cially in his elongated schemes, such as the D. D. Martin house in Buffalo (1904), and in the house which has had perhaps the most far-reaching influence of all his works, the Robie house, a town villa on Woodlawn Avenue, Chicago (*fig.* **250**). It is a sad example of the misunderstanding of architectural merit that the University of Chicago wished to pull it down to make room for a student dormitory. It was only saved from destruction at the last minute by a New York realtor. In the nineteenth century the exterior of the American house was not up to the level of the floor plan in quality and artistic expression. Wright brought about a change. He took the plane surfaces presented to him and organized them variously, multiplying them, intersecting them or placing them in different depths one behind another, incorporating the plane of the garden wall with the different advancing and receding planes of the house itself so that often its solid volume is not at all apparent. To speak of these houses as in the "prairie style," as inspired by the long lines of the prairie, does not go to the root of the matter. The forms of the Robie house, the long horizontal bands, the series of windows, the garden walls, are sharply cut as if by a machine. These houses are a pure artistic expression which is deeply connected with the anonymous aims of their period. This handling is not without relation to what was being explored at that time in space conceptions in France.

Chicagoans who did not like the Robie house, who were offended by the novelty of its appearance and its long stretched-out horizontal lines, sought to deride it by comparing it to a steamship, just as later Le Corbusier's critics were to refer similarly to his buildings. Without knowing it, they were implying that the house was built in the spirit of the age out of which it came, that, like the steamship, it had been born naturally out of its period. What is decisive in it is not a superficial and misunderstood similarity to a steamship but its inner relationship with the aims of its time. The warehouse of Montgomery, Ward and Company (*fig.* **249**), with its unbroken front of eight hundred feet and the undisguised expression of its structural body,[12] was built in the same year (1908) as the Robie house.

---

[12] Cf. the section on Ferroconcrete. The warehouse was built by Richard E. Schmidt, Garden, and Martin.

From the beginning Wright treated the inner as well as the Inner space outer wall as a plane surface. It never occurred to him to do what European architects did about 1896 — replace rococo decoration with the serpentine lines of the *art nouveau*. In his interiors, too, there is a constant endeavor to find interrelations between the various separate elements — walls, ceilings, windows, and door openings. Different ceiling heights are sometimes introduced into the same room, a treatment which parallels Wright's use of horizontal planes at different heights, such as cantilevered porches, overhanging eaves, and levels varying according to the grades of the site.

Correlative with the use of abstract plane surfaces is the use of Use of different structures various materials and contrasting structures. The broad brick wall of a chimney and light-colored walls with wooden partitions are often juxtaposed. Very early Wright introduced the rough structure of a rusticated wall into the house, bringing it unbroken from the outside, as in primitive times. In this feeling for different materials and the search to find a new quality of lighting, Wright developed an even greater refinement as he grew older. The buildings of the Johnson Wax Company at Racine, Wisconsin (1937–39), are lighted by means of Pyrex glass tubes (*fig.* **255**). In the winter home of the Taliesin fellowship in the Arizona desert (1939) many contrasting materials are used — desert stone, walls of rubble concrete, wooden trusses, and inclined canvas planes forming in one surface windows and ceilings, creating, as in the Johnson Wax Company buildings, a specific quality in accordance with the existing circumstances.

To use plane surfaces, on the one hand, and to give them force and expression by the frank use of undisguised materials, on the other, is to employ, as we shall soon see, one of the means of painting, which at this time in France was opening the way for our new spatial conceptions.

Wright had around him no painters and sculptors who were Aesthetic directions inspired by the same spirit. He was one of those rare exceptions, the architect who is in advance of the contemporary painter in his optical vision. In Europe, where the new spatial conceptions flowered about 1910, the case was just the opposite; there

411

251. FRANK LLOYD WRIGHT. Larkin Administration Building, Buffalo, 1904. *Details of capitals of pillars. These straight-edged, sharp-cornered forms appear at the top of great piers, occupying the place usually taken by capitals. Though they are decorative, nevertheless, like all Wright's work, they have another impact than the purely ornamental.*

252. FRANK LLOYD WRIGHT. Tennis Club, River Forest, Illinois, 1906. *Bench of concrete slabs. Wright's way of working with slabs and interpenetration of volumes may be observed even in small details, such as this bench, in which concrete slabs are used to elongate one level, pushing through the wall and hovering above the ground.*

412

thc painter showed the way. But Wright had to do his work alone, design his own stained-glass windows, architectural details, and pictorial ornamentation. He did the capitals of the Larkin Building (*fig.* **251**) as "straight-edged and sharp-cornered groups of ornaments at the top of the great piers and directly below the skylights . . . strange masses of square-edge patterning." [13] The fresco of the Midway Gardens, a restaurant in Chicago, now lost with the tearing down of the building, he designed out of interpenetrating circles of different sizes and different colors. In its pictorial intention this fresco stands midway between the designs of the English group around Mackintosh and the new spatial treatments which Wassily Kandinsky was undertaking in Munich at about the same time.

In his houses Wright takes the traditional flat surfaces and dissects them in strips horizontally organized and in a juxtaposed play with solid volumes, his vertical chimneys penetrating the roof in opposition to the horizontal planes of the cantilevered porches and overhanging eaves, thus giving the exterior of the American house an expression synonymous with its plan. He dissects the wall and puts it together again with an unprecedented — after all, we are in the first decade of the twentieth century — keenness of imagination. IIe is impelled unconsciously by the same forces that worked in Europe about ten years later; there, however, the concern was to explore new penetrations of inner and outer space rather than, as with Wright, to treat the house as an enclosed spatial unit.

Wright often used the same elements as the Dutch architects of the "Stijl" group, Mondrian and Doesburg, or the Russian constructivists like Malewitsch — for example, the abstract quadrangle, which remains the hallmark of Wright's work. Malewitsch, however, used it as an absolute form, as a protest against academic *trompe l'œil*. The Dutch organized geometrical forms not for ornamentation but for the expression of pure and undisguised interrelations between surfaces and colors. Behind the European research lies, to a certain extent, another will and another spatial conception.

---

[13] Russell Sturgis, "The Larkin Building, Buffalo, N. Y.," *Architectural Record*, XXII (1908), 320.

The Urge toward the Organic

Throughout history there persist two distinct trends — the one toward the rational and the geometrical, the other toward the irrational and the organic: two different ways of dealing with or of mastering the environment. These contrasting approaches to the problem have been evident in all cultures, both early and late. Since the beginning of civilization there have been cities planned according to regular schemes and cities which have grown up organically like trees. The ancient Greeks put their mathematically proportioned temples on the top of rocky acropolises, outlined against their southern skies; the villages of the Greek islands, whitewashed on the crests of hills, are easily distinguishable far out at sea because of their clearly marked and periodically rewhitened walls.

The difference between organic and geometrical perceptions is present even today in contemporary painting and contemporary architecture. They are constantly recurrent ways of approach; one cannot be considered superior to the other. The artist has the right of choice, of saying according to his own point of view which pleases him and which he will follow. From the beginning Frank Lloyd Wright faced toward an organic perception of the world.

Wright's whole career was an endeavor to express himself in what he called "organic architecture," whatever that may be. He liked to work within the shadow of this feeling. When, on January 25, 1940, he lectured in Jackson Hall, Boston, he devoted his entire discussion to this problem of his life. He tried by a sort of Socratic dialogue, a give-and-take between himself and his audience, to define and explain it. But his effort was futile. It was clear, finally, that no explanation was possible in words, that what he meant by organic architecture could be revealed only in his work.

Around 1900 Louis Sullivan, in his *Kindergarten Chats*,[14] sought to arrive at "the true meaning of the words 'Organic Architec-

---

[14] *Kindergarten Chats*, first published in 1901–02 in *Interstate Architect and Builder*, is the testament of Louis Sullivan to American youth. It is full of prophecies, some of which have already been fulfilled. Others, I believe, will be. The quotations are from the revised edition published in book form by Claude Bragdon (Lawrence [?], Kansas, 1934), pp. 46–49.

ture'" through contrast, by exploring "what the word 'organic' doesn't mean." Organic, he said, means living, means development, and not, as in the reigning American architecture of 1900, "pitiful in its folly, . . . functions without forms, forms without functions; details unrelated to masses, and masses unrelated to anything but folly. . . ." Of this he adds: "Organic it is not. Inorganic it is becoming." "Organic" means for him the "searching for *realities*, — a word

253. FRANK LLOYD WRIGHT. Residence, Taliesin.

I love because I love the sense of life it stands for, the ten-fingered grasp of things it implies. . . ." "Organic," in the sense of Sullivan and of Wright, is a protest against the split personality, against a split culture. It is identical with "the ten-fingered grasp of reality" or with that development in which thinking and feeling approach coincidence.

On a deep blue day in July 1939 we stood on the top of the hill on which is built Wright's own home, Taliesin (*fig.* 253). The dome of the hill was so precise in shape, especially the hill-

Wright's organic treatment

415

crown which became a low-walled garden above the surrounding courts, reached by stone steps walled into the slopes,[15] that I asked if it had been built up in artificial regularity from below. "No, it is the natural soil," Wright said. "I never build houses on the top of a hill. I build them around it, like an eyebrow." And I saw that it was indeed the house itself which brought into consciousness the pure curve of the ground, that in a certain sense its many-layered and unobtrusive forms gave meaning and definition to the contours out of which it rose.

At the time when he was isolated in his profession and without public support, when America had turned against him, Wright even built houses in the folds of the earth, so that they seem to grow into nature and out of it. But even in his earlier houses, like the Coonley house of 1911, with its projecting eaves and its plants growing along and spreading over wooden cantilevers, we may see this tendency of the house to melt into its surroundings, so that it is often impossible to say where it begins. There are also contemporary sculptors, like Hans Arp, who would prefer to set their works in the midst of the forest so that, like a part of nature, they cannot be distinguished from other stones.

This urge toward the organic may partly explain why Wright preferred to use materials taken directly from nature, rugged stone walls, rough granite floors, and heavy unfinished timbers. Throughout his Chicago period he made no use of the skeleton either of iron or ferroconcrete; [16] he was most reticent in the use of glass and of white, and so cautious with openings that it is sometimes difficult even to find the entrance door. Likewise his urge toward the organic accounts for his developing his flexible, open plan — in the age of central heating — from the huge chimneys of the early colonial house.

---

[15] See Wright, *Autobiography*.

[16] When he did employ concrete, it was, as in the Oak Park Temple, in the form of concrete walls without glass surfaces. For his walls and porch pillars Wright preferred brick or small Roman brick such as was used by McIntire in the early and Richardson in the late nineteenth century. He avoided even clapboards and used them — so far as I know — only in a single house in Chicago, designed when he was still working with Sullivan.

The usual criticism of the houses of his Chicago period — the Martin house in Buffalo (1904), for example, and even the Robie house (1908) — is that they are rather dark. They have overhanging eaves and deep, low rooms. It is not completely clear what he was trying to express with them, nor what his real motives were. It may be that, having grown up in Chicago's most vigorous period, he reacted against the big city and its heavily glassed-in areas. In his houses and even his administration buildings he sought to make a spatial unit of the structure, but to seal it rather than to open it up.

Behind this cautiousness in the use of new materials and this hesitation about opening up the house with glass walls, as was done in the Chicago office buildings of the eighties and the European houses of the twenties, seems to lie a special conception of the needs of human nature. Wright bound the human dwelling to the earth as intimately as possible, introducing the earth into the house in the form of rough walls, and attached to it as if, in the words of Louis Sullivan, by "the ten-fingered grasp of reality." For Wright the house was a shelter, a covert into which the human animal can retire as into a cave, protected from rain and wind and — light. There he may crouch, as it were, in complete security and relaxation, like an animal in its lair. Is there back of this the desire for shadowed dimness that prevailed in the late nineteenth century, or is it an urge toward primitive eternal instincts which sooner or later must be satisfied? This we do not know. Always in the study of Wright's personality a distinction must be made between his use of elements belonging to his generation, on the one hand, and, on the other, his own genius, overleaping its natural frontiers.

The European development based on constructive means and the new visual approach had first to clear the atmosphere by pure functionalism. This was necessary, unavoidable, and healthful, but the moment the means of expression had been found, the clearing up accomplished, then again the urge to the organic could be felt. On another level and by other ways than Wright's it is moving toward the organic. In the northern countries the work of the Finnish architect Alvar Aalto indicates this — and not only there.

Office Buildings

Frank Lloyd Wright's distinctively individual feeling for the house as a shelter and his handling of it as an enclosed spatial unit are reflected in his two office buildings — the Larkin Soap

255. FRANK LLOYD WRIGHT. Johnson Wax Company, Administration Building, Racine, Wisconsin, 1938–39. *Interior.*

254. FRANK LLOYD WRIGHT. Larkin Administration Building, Buffalo, 1904. *Nave with surrounding galleries.*

←

Company administration building in Buffalo (1904; *fig.* **254**) and the Johnson Wax Company administration building in Racine, Wisconsin (1939; *fig.* **255**). Though they were erected more than thirty years apart and are very different in appearance, they show the same spirit and give an equal insight into Wright's architectural treatment. Both are treated primarily as *one room;* both are separated from the outdoors; both are enclosed by massive walls and receive their light through skylights and high-placed windows or glass tubing. They are shells shutting out the outer world, isolated and self-contained units, and thus in the strongest contrast, on the one hand, to the buildings of the Chicago school of the eighties with their wide open glass areas and, on the other, to the designs of the European movement of the twenties.

Larkin Building   The Larkin Building stands a resolutely independent mass embraced by the extended wings of the much larger factory building of the company. There is an interplay between the volume of its spatial unit and the square towers at either end and flanking the entrance. These towers, which encase the stairways and rise starkly without interruption upward over a hundred feet, were the despair of contemporary critics, who protested that they thrust up so strongly that there was no play of light and shadow, and who thought that they should be relieved by moldings or softened by glazed tiles in a variety of color patterns.[17] The building itself had for these critics a grimness of aspect which repelled them. It was for them an "accumulation of strange sharp-edged solids, offering no modulation of surface," its features "the square corner, the right angle, the straight edge, the sharp arris, the firm vertical and horizontal lines, unbroken, unmodified, uncompromising in their geometrical precision." [18] Curiously, this is much the same attack which Wright later made upon the right angles, flat surfaces, and triangles of the European architects of the twenties. This uncompromising precision was taken further in 1960 by Louis Kahn's science laboratories for the University of Philadelphia, which seem closely related to the Larkin Building.

---

[17] Cf. Russell Sturgis, "The Larkin Building, Buffalo, N. Y.," *Architectural Record,* XXIII (1908), 319, 321. It is interesting to note how an earnest critic who appreciates the high quality of the plan and organization of the building cannot, however hard he tries, accept it emotionally.

[18] *Ibid.,* p. 319.

420

255a. FRANK LLOYD WRIGHT. Larkin Building, 1904. *The first squared-rod steel office furniture. Desks and chairs for the whole organization were designed by Wright especially for this building. They were completed in 1939, only ten years before the inexcusable destruction of the building. It is doubtful whether any of these chairs or desks were saved for a museum.*

No skeleton was used in the Larkin Building. Just as in his small dwelling-houses, Wright employed brick; the towers are square brick shafts; the walls are a massive brick shell closed above by a flat roof pierced by skylights. The architect himself characterized the structure thus: "Building sealed. . . . Furnishing and filing systems built-in of steel. . . . First air conditioned office building.[19] . . . First metal bound plate glass doors and windows. . . ." (*fig.* **255a**).[20] Its inner core is a large space five stories high surrounded by galleries, form-

---

[19] Buffalo was the birthplace of air-conditioning.

[20] *Architectural Forum*, LXVIII (January 1938), 88.

256. FRANK LLOYD WRIGHT. Johnson Wax Company, Administration Building, 1938–39. *Interior of cornice of glass tubing, outer wall.*

ing a great nave open to the skylight. Square, sand-colored brick piers, rising with a Gothic strength, divide the nave from the galleries. That the owners later on placed an organ in this vast room is an indication of the serenity of the whole. Standing on the uppermost floor and looking down into the nave and the galleries, we can observe how the light falls upon the metal desk tops from high-placed windows. It is hardly believable that this masterpiece of American craftsmanship no longer exists. In 1949 the same firm that built it ordered its destruction.

Johnson Wax
Company Building

The administration building of the Johnson Wax Company (1937–39) is also treated as a spatial unit, but primarily in one story. It soon became famous on account of its unusually formed columns. But the accent here again is on the manner in which the lighting is achieved. I had occasion to see the building just before it was completed, and I should like to give here my first impressions:

"We come to Racine, thirty miles north of Chicago, one of those places which have neither an end nor a beginning. In the middle of the town is the Building Office for which we are looking, and in front of us there is a curved brick wall with strange, long glass strips let into the top, just visible in the winter light. . . . From a dark entrance, we arrive in a big hall filled with mushroom pillars. All the engineers have shaken their heads over these pillars which taper toward their bases and are fitted into steel shoes.[21] At the top there are widespreading circular discs which seem to float like leaves of the *Victoria regia* among the tubes of heat-resisting (Pyrex) glass. Most of the pillars carry nothing but the air above them. This glass is manufactured in small lengths, and it is very difficult to fix. But it does not discolor, and that is what Wright wanted. The pillars are a luxury, and so is the special glass, but why should not an administrative building, which is a work building, for once be based on poetry? The light that shimmers through the tubes is of a marvelous quality. The impression of the hall is magic. We look up into the light, like fish from the bottom of a pond, and the plates seem to swim in the flowing glass. The hall is the most fantastic thing that has been conceived in the architectural imagination for a long time. Its apparent pointlessness irritates many people [22] — one could have spanned the whole space with a single truss. But the magic effect would have been lost.

"This building is said to have cost double the amount originally contemplated, but the firm is able and willing to afford this luxury. There have always existed buildings which satisfied this need for luxury, and they will exist again. The point that matters is what we are to understand by luxury. Luxury

---

[21] This type of column was challenged by the authorities. It "was 22 ft. high, carried about 12 tons, had a base 9 in. in diameter, flagrantly disregarding the code which called for a 30 inch thickness on a column of this height. To demonstrate the soundness of his design Wright poured a test column, let it stand seven days, and watched workmen load it with 60 tons of material. Convinced, doubters piled on no more, pulled it down. On the basis of the test the column would be good for a minimum of 80 tons at 28 days. Secret of its amazing strength is wire mesh, welded into a cone." ("Frank Lloyd Wright Tests a Column," *Architectural Forum*, vol. LXVII, August 1937, p. 10.)

[22] The Johnson Wax Company building has been harshly attacked by the younger architects not only for its streamlined exterior, but also because they say it lacks response to function and is theatrical in effect. Certainly, as in every one of Wright's buildings, there are to be found in the details many reminiscences of a bygone generation, but over against all these objections it seems to us necessary to set into relief the fact that the importance of this building lies in its experimentation with plastic forms and a new quality of light, a new technical means, for broadening the emotional scale. Like a baroque church, the building cannot be judged without being seen, gone through, experienced.

does not simply mean waste of material, but only makes sense when *it broadens emotional experience by means of new discovery*. Only a few can fulfill this. Frank Lloyd Wright achieves in this building by means of silver light and plasticity of form, a new spatial sensation without which it is not possible to think of architecture. He shows us here, after half a century of building, how luxury can still be creative in architecture" (*fig. 256*).[23] The building for the Johnson Wax Company introduced the last twenty years of Wright's work, in which he departed from the right angle and with increasing vigor emphasized circles and curves.

Influence of Frank Lloyd Wright

Wright, the preacher

Frank Lloyd Wright was not only an architect. He belongs among the great preachers of his country; he had by nature the will and the courage to protest, to revolt, and to persevere. He carried on in architecture that tradition of sturdy individualism of which in the middle of the last century Walt Whitman and Henry Thoreau were the literary spokesmen. He regarded this tradition as part of himself. As prophet, preacher, and agrarian individualist, he preached hatred of the city and return to the soil and to the productive, self-sufficient community — in a land where man's relation to the soil is too often remote and impersonal; where at the same moment, according to the varying demands of the economic trend, forests are being changed into farms and acres of growing grain changed back into forests; and where food to a great extent comes to the table out of tins.

American reaction

Frank Lloyd Wright belongs, in one sense of the word, to a sacrificed generation. When he began building, he had every prospect of commercial success; he built more houses in his early period than any of his European precursors. But what he built was only for the individual client. Not that his houses — all of them erected in the Middle West and the West [24] — are purely local, limited by the region and the personal tastes and

[23] S. Giedion, "The Dangers and Advantages of Luxury," *Focus* (London), no. 3, Spring 1939, pp. 34–39.

[24] Not one house was built by Wright in the country's financial center, New York; not one in Boston.

424

requirements of the single client; like any work of art, they embody something that overreaches all restrictions of place and personal ownership. But they have had no influence on the country; they have not become an impelling creative force.

The reason is that Wright began work at the very moment when American architecture was undermined by the most dangerous reaction since the time of its origin. The classic and Gothic fashions which in those years overwhelmed the constituent facts of American architecture had, of course, nothing to do with tradition. They meant nothing more than the giving of an artificial backbone to people who were weak in their emotional structure. Behind the screens of the'r houses — miniature Versailles, Tuscan villa, or medieval manor — or their skyscrapers in sacred Gothic shapes, these people could hide their inner uncertainty. This had its deplorable consequences for the business of architecture. The architect who wished to live by his profession had to conform to the vogue or give up.

During this dominance of classic and Gothic imitations, which became stronger and stronger between 1910 and 1925, Wright and Louis Sullivan had to live almost as exiles in their own country. In the last year of his life, so an older Chicago architect has told me, Sullivan received monetary assistance monthly from some of his colleagues. And Wright in 1940, speaking at his exhibition in Boston, summed it up when he said simply: "They killed Sullivan, and they nearly killed me!"

In this period he and Sullivan became, in the eyes of their contemporaries, the representatives of a lost cause. But actually it was not they who had lost the cause. Rather it was the country which had lost, for later on it was the country, and not Wright, which had to change. At this time, when Europe was beginning to purify architectural means, when the demand for truth appeared in architecture, America had no organ with which to hear what was going on. All that was being expressed abroad was cut off like a silenced radio. The effects are still to be felt today.

The foundation bearing Wright's work is a strong tripod: the American tradition, his urge toward the organic, and his power to find an artistic language for his own period. By the time

Nature of
Wright's influence

the definitive publication of his buildings appeared in Berlin in 1910, all this had been realized. At forty years of age Wright had already achieved a body of work great enough and influential enough to assure him his place in history.

What is to be grasped, what can be observed of his direct influence, is often only superficial and leads to misunderstanding. Whoever as an architect has tried to imitate or even to follow him, whether in Europe or America, has misused his work and misinterpreted his spirit. Much more important perhaps than Wright's direct influence was his significance as an index, as a sort of signpost of new directions, for no equivalent could be found for his work in Europe between 1900 and 1910.

Influence in Europe

After 1910 the best brains of Europe began to understand what he had achieved in America. One of the finest, H. P. Berlage, introduced Wright's work extensively into Europe through his own exhibitions and lectures. By his moral authority he ensured the next Dutch generation a stimulus to their own development.[25] The Dutch people were best prepared to receive help from Wright's impulse. In this connection we are not thinking so much of the work of Dudok in Hilversum, who in the early twenties had a great success with his sentimentalized buildings, but rather with such a sensitive and fine-spirited architect as Robert van t'Hoff, who built two massive concrete houses at Huisterheide in 1914–15. These houses, the only ones van t'Hoff ever built, were a direct reflection of Wright's ideas. Although they stood alone and isolated in Europe, nevertheless they performed a clarifying function there. They were made known to the European advance guard in 1919 by an article of Theo van Doesburg in his review, *Style*.

In the early work of several Dutch architects, and also in some projects of J. J. P. Oud, it was undoubtedly the stimulus that was to be found in Wright's work which helped them to clear a way to self-realization. But it would be completely superficial and wrong to try to find detailed evidence of his influence on them, to refer in their case to models and pictures for similarities to his designs. For there are other elements in European

---

[25] Curiously enough, Le Corbusier was also directed to Wright through an article which appeared in the *Schweizerische Bauzeitung* in 1912, and which was an extensive résumé by Berlage himself of a lecture he had given in Zurich.

architecture — as we shall soon see — which formed their specific character. No. Wright's real influence, his great and educative influence, cannot be shown in a few poor photographs; his real influence is that of his methods and ideas, as they are reflected in his work. We shall see how later on Wright's conception of space, coming into contact with the European movement, was developed and changed in the hands of its leading figures. Wright had always — up to the last — the inspiration of a genius that reached far beyond his own generation.

Frank Lloyd Wright's Late Period

Wright died in 1959. Never before had he had so many commissions and so much adulation. The American press, which ten years earlier had found no space for him, now sometimes overreached itself and labeled him a towering genius and the greatest architect of all time. And all this after he had had for decades to endure great humiliation that would have crushed a less strong nature. In the twenties and early thirties he was pursued by creditors, menaced by legal proceedings, mixed up in scandals (that in a country of puritan opinion usually finish off a man), and almost without work. He was excluded from society and all important activities as a moral outlaw and a man far removed from the ruling taste. The fate of Wright was neither unique to the United States nor limited to his person. All pioneers in our period have met with a similar fate.

The richness of his vision was expressed in immense projects that sometimes got lost in fantasy and eccentricity, such as his scheme for the "Golden Triangle" area in downtown Pittsburgh or his opera house for Baghdad. Both of these, probably to Wright's advantage, were never constructed. At the same time he was busy designing a circular building with spiral ramps inside or outside it. The Morris store in San Francisco (1950) was the first interior space of this kind to be created. The circle and the spiral appear in monumental form in the Guggenheim Museum on Fifth Avenue in New York. The exhibition spaces run alongside the spiral ramp bounded by circular walls that slope together towards the bottom. The difficulties these walls present in mounting an exhibition were apparent in the exhibition of sculpture shown at the Museum's opening shortly after Wright's death.

Frank Lloyd Wright always had the public in mind. Architecturally speaking this meant: the human habitat, the minimum apartment, the single family house, even the mile-high skyscrapers that he designed toward the end of his life. In the single family houses of the Chicago period he had laid the foundations for contemporary architecture. Even in his darkest period, in the twenties, when he was building a few houses of reinforced concrete, the human habitat was his dominant preoccupation. In the final period of his life he was one of the first to abandon the rectangular living room, though, as I stated in *Architecture, You and Me*, "Each of us carries in his mind the results of five thousand years of tradition: a room is a space bounded by four rectangular planes." [26]

Frank Lloyd Wright acknowledged a Japanese influence, and eastern art was the only art he collected and displayed in his home. In his last decade, however, he unconsciously came near to primeval memories. The forms of his houses took on rounded curves following his no longer rectangular living rooms. In them the rounded oval houses of Minoan Crete from around 1500 B.C. or the Mesopotamian houses from the fourth or third millenium B.C. reappear. Wright's house plans in his late years finally took on a sickle-shaped outline (house in Virginia, 1953) with an external surrounding ramp and an internal patio. Wright was probably the first to reincorporate into the house that quiet focal point — the patio — which since then has become more and more an accepted part of a modern dwelling.

---

[26] Harvard University Press, 1958, p. 150.

PART **VI** **SPACE–TIME IN ART, ARCHITECTURE, AND CONSTRUCTION**

THE NEW SPACE CONCEPTION: SPACE–TIME

Social, economic, and functional influences play a vital part in all human activities, from the sciences to the arts. But there are other factors which also have to be taken into account — our feelings and emotions. These factors are often dismissed as trivial, but actually their effect upon men's actions is immense. A good share of the misfortunes of the past century came out of its belief that industry and techniques had only a functional import, with no emotional content. The arts were exiled to an isolated realm of their own, completely insulated from everyday realities. As a result, life lost unity and balance; science and industry made steady advances, but in the now detached realm of feeling there was nothing but a vacillation from one extreme to the other.

The scope and strength of the emotions are both greater than we sometimes suppose. Emotion or feeling enters into all our affairs — speculation is never completely "pure," just as action is never entirely practical. And, of course, we are far from having free choice in this matter of feeling. Large tracts of our emotional life are determined by circumstances over which we have no control: by the fact that we happen to be men, of such or such a kind, living at this or that period. Thus a thoroughly integrated culture produces a marked unity of feeling among its representatives. For example, a recognizable common spirit runs through the whole baroque period. It makes itself felt in activities as distinct from each other as painting and philosophy or architecture and mathematics. This is not particularly surprising. Techniques, sciences, the arts — all these are carried on by men who have grown up together in the same period, exposed to its characteristic influences. The feelings which it is the special concern of the artist to express are also at work within the engineer and the mathematician. This emotional background shared by such otherwise divergent pursuits is what we must try to discover.

Do We Need Artists?

Some people question whether any pervasive unity of feeling is possible in a period like ours. They regard science and industry as inimical to art and feeling: where the former prosper, the latter decline. Or they see science taking over the arts, opening up new means of self-expression which make us independent of them. There is some basis for views like these. Do we, then, really need artists any longer?

In any civilization, feeling continues to filter through every activity and situation. An environment whose chief aspects remain opaque to feeling is as unsatisfying as one which resists practical or intellectual control. But just this sort of emotional frustration has prevailed for a long time past. An official art has turned its back upon the contemporary world and given up the attempt to interpret it emotionally. The feelings which that world elicits have remained formless, have never met with those objects which are at once their symbols and their satisfaction.

Such symbols, however, are vital necessities. Feelings build up within us and form systems; they cannot be discharged through instantaneous animal outcries or grimaces. We need to discover harmonies between our own inner states and our surroundings. And no level of development can be maintained if it remains detached from our emotional life. The whole machinery runs down.

This is the reason why the most familiar and ordinary things have importance for the genuinely creative artists of our generation. Painters like Picasso, Juan Gris, the lyricist of cubism, and Le Corbusier have devoted themselves to the common objects of daily use: bowls, pipes, bottles, glasses, guitars. Natural materials have received the same attention: stones hollowed out by the sea, roots, bits of bark — even weather-bleached bones. Anonymous and unpretentious things like these scarcely figure at all in our normal consciousness, but they attain their true stature and significance under the artist's hand. They become revealed as *objets à réaction poétiques*, to borrow Le Corbusier's phrase. Or, to put it somewhat differently, new parts of the world are made accessible to feeling.

The opening up of such new realms of feeling has always been the artist's chief mission. A great deal of our world would lack all emotional significance if it were not for his work. As recently as the eighteenth century, mountain scenery was felt to exhibit nothing except a formless and alarming confusion. Winckelmann, the discoverer of Greek art, could not bear to look out the windows of his carriage when he crossed the Alps into Italy, around 1760. He found the jumbled granite masses of the St. Gotthard so frightful that he pulled down the blinds and sat back to await the smooth outlines of the Italian countryside. A century later, Ruskin was seeking out the mountains of Chamonix as a refuge from an industrial world that made no kind of aesthetic sense. Ships, bridges, iron constructions — the new artistic potentialities of his period, in short — these were the things Ruskin pulled down the blinds on. Right now there are great areas of our experience which are still waiting to be claimed by feeling. Thus we are no longer limited to seeing objects from the distances normal for earth-bound animals. The bird's-eye view has opened up to us whole new aspects of the world. Such new modes of perception carry with them new feelings which the artist must formulate.

The artist, in fact, functions a great deal like an inventor or a scientific discoverer: all three seek new relations between man and his world. In the artist's case these relations are emotional instead of practical or cognitive. The creative artist does not want to copy his surroundings, on the one hand, or to make us see them through his eyes, on the other. He is a specialist who shows us in his work as if in a mirror something we have not realized for ourselves: the state of our own souls. He finds the outer symbols for the feelings which really possess us but which for us are only chaotic and — therefore — disquieting, obsessive stirrings. This is why we still need artists, however difficult it may be for them to hold their place in the modern world.

Artist and public: how they have lost contact

But if the artist is so necessary to us, how is it that he seems to have lost contact with all but a small number of his contemporaries? Ordinary people make it almost a point of pride to insist that, so far as they are concerned, his vocabulary of forms is totally incomprehensible.

432

This is often said to be a consequence of the revolt against naturalism. Actually, however, it dates from quite another event: the *proclamation de la liberté du travail* of March 17, 1791, which dissolved the guild system. The abolition of all legal restraints upon the choice of a trade was the starting point for the tremendous growth of modern industry and the isolation of the artist.

Cut off from the crafts, the artist was faced with the serious problem of competing with the factory system for his living. One solution was to set himself up in the luxury trades, to cater, quite unashamed, to the lowest common denominator of public taste. Art-to-public-order flooded the world, filled the *salons*, and won the gold medals of all the academies. With no serious aims and no standards of its own, the most such an art could hope for was a financial success, and this it often achieved. The most favored of these cultivated drudges — a Meissonier, for example — sometimes saw their canvases sold at a thousand francs the square inch.

As far as the public and the critics were concerned, this was art — and this the work the artist was meant to do. The half-dozen painters who carried on the artist's real work of invention and research were absolutely ignored. The constituent facts in the painting of our period were developed against the will of the public and almost in secret. And this from the beginning to the end of the century, from Ingres to Cézanne.

The same situation held for architecture. Here too the advances were made surreptitiously, in the department of construction. The architect and the painter were faced with the same long struggle against *trompe l'œil*. Both had to combat entrenched styles by returning to the pure means of expression. For some four decades painter after painter makes the effort to reconquer the plane surface. We have seen how the same struggle arose in architecture as a consequence of the demand for morality. Painters very different in type but sharing a common isolation from the public worked steadily toward a new conception of space. And no one can understand contemporary architecture, become aware of the feelings hidden behind it, unless he has grasped the spirit animating this painting.

The fact that modern painting bewilders the public is not strange: for a full century the public ignored all the developments which led up to it. It would be very surprising if the public had been able to read at sight an artistic language elaborated while its attention was elsewhere, absorbed by the pseudo art of the *salons*.

THE RESEARCH INTO SPACE: CUBISM

In many places, about 1910, a consciousness that the painter's means of expression had lost contact with modern life was beginning to emerge. But it was in Paris, with cubism, that these efforts first attained a visible result. The method of presenting spatial relationships which the cubists developed led up to the form-giving principles of the new space conception.[1]

The half-century previous to the rise of cubism had seen painting flourish almost nowhere outside of France. It was the high culture of painting that grew up in France during this period which formed the fostering soil for our contemporary art. Young people of talent — whether Spanish like Picasso, or Swiss like Le Corbusier — found their inspiration in Paris, in the union of their powers with the artistic tradition of that city. The vitality of French culture served to the advantage of the whole world. Among the general public, however, there was no sympathetic response to this achievement. It was from a form of art which the public despised that nineteenth-century painting drew its positive strength. Cubism, growing up in this soil, absorbed all its vigor.

---

[1] We shall treat contemporary movements in art here only so far as their methods are directly related to the space conceptions of our period, and in order to understand the common background of art, architecture, and construction. For an understanding of these movements the elaborate catalogues of the Museum of Modern Art, New York, are very useful. See Alfred H. Barr, Jr., *Cubism and Abstract Art* (New York, 1936), and Robert Rosenblum, *Cubism and Twentieth Century Art* (New York, 1960). For a short survey with emphasis on historical relations, see J. J. Sweeney, *Plastic Redirections of the Twentieth Century* (Chicago, 1935); for the relation of contemporary art to education, industrial design, and daily life, see L. Moholy-Nagy, *The New Vision* (New York, 1938). The close relation of contemporary sculpture to primitive art, on the one hand, and, on the other, to an enlargement of our outlook into nature is stressed in C. Giedion-Welcker, *Contemporary Sculpture* (New York, 1955).

Picasso has been called the inventor of cubism, but cubism is not the invention of any individual. It is rather the expression of a collective and almost unconscious attitude. A painter who participated in the movement says of its beginnings: "There was no invention. Still more, there could not be one. Soon it was twitching in everybody's fingers. There was a presentiment of what should come, and experiments were made. We avoided one another; a discovery was on the point of being made, and each of us distrusted his neighbors. We were standing at the end of a decadent epoch."

From the Renaissance to the first decade of the present century perspective had been one of the most important constituent facts in painting. It had remained a constant element through all changes of style. The four-century-old habit of seeing the outer world in the Renaissance manner — that is, in terms of three dimensions — rooted itself so deeply in the human mind that no other form of perception could be imagined. This in spite of the fact that the art of different previous cultures had been two-dimensional. When earlier periods established perspective as a constituent fact they were always able to find new expressions for it. In the nineteenth century perspective was misused. This led to its dissolution.

The dissolution of perspective

The three-dimensional space of the Renaissance is the space of Euclidean geometry. But about 1830 a new sort of geometry was created, one which differed from that of Euclid in employing more than three dimensions. Such geometries have continued to be developed, until now a stage has been reached where mathematicians deal with figures and dimensions that cannot be grasped by the imagination.

These considerations interest us only in so far as they affect the sense of space. Like the scientist, the artist has come to recognize that classic conceptions of space and volumes are limited and one-sided. In particular, it has become plain that the aesthetic qualities of space are not limited to its infinity for sight, as in the gardens of Versailles. The essence of space as it is conceived today is its many-sidedness, the infinite potentiality for relations within it. Exhaustive description of an area from one point of reference is, accordingly, impossible; its character changes with the point from which it is viewed. In order to grasp the true nature of space the observer must project himself through it. The stairways in the upper levels of the Eiffel Tower are among the earliest architectural expression of the continuous interpenetration of outer and inner space.

Space in modern physics is conceived of as relative to a moving point of reference, not as the absolute and static entity of the baroque system of Newton. And in modern art, for the first time since the Renaissance, a new conception of space leads to a self-conscious enlargement of our ways of perceiving space. It was in cubism that this was most fully achieved.

Space-Time The cubists did not seek to reproduce the appearance of objects from one vantage point; they went round them, tried to lay hold of their internal constitution. They sought to extend the scale of feeling, just as contemporary science extends its descriptions to cover new levels of material phenomena.

Cubism breaks with Renaissance perspective. It views objects relatively: that is, from several points of view, no one of which has exclusive authority. And in so dissecting objects it sees them simultaneously from all sides — from above and below, from inside and outside. It goes around and into its objects. Thus, to the three dimensions of the Renaissance which have held good as constituent facts throughout so many centuries, there is added a fourth one — time. The poet Guillaume Apollinaire was the first to recognize and express this change, around 1911. The same year saw the first cubist exhibition in the Salon des Indépendants. Considering the history of the principles from which they broke, it can well be understood that the paintings should have been thought a menace to the public peace, and have become the subject of remarks in the Chamber of Deputies.

The presentation of objects from several points of view introduces a principle which is intimately bound up with modern life — simultaneity. It is a temporal coincidence that Einstein should have begun his famous work, *Elektrodynamik bewegter Körper*, in 1905 with a careful definition of simultaneity.

436

The Artistic Means

"Abstract art" is as misleading a term for the different movements which depart from the spatial approach as "cubism" is for the beginnings of the contemporary image. It is not the "abstract," it is not the "cubical," which are significant in their content. What is decisive is the invention of a new approach, of a new spatial representation, and the means by which it is attained.

This new representation of space was accomplished step by step, much as laboratory research gradually arrives at its conclusions through long experimentation; and yet, as always with real art and great science, the results came up out of the subconscious suddenly.

The cubists dissect the object, try to lay hold of its inner composition. They seek to extend the scale of optical vision as contemporary science extends the law of matter. Therefore contemporary spatial approach has to get away from the single point of reference. During the first period (shortly before 1910) this dissection of objects was accomplished, as Alfred Barr expresses it, by breaking up "the surfaces of the natural forms into angular facets." Concentration was entirely upon research into a new representation of space — thus the extreme scarcity of colors in this early period. The pictures are gray-toned or earthen, like the grisaille of the Renaissance or the photographs of the nineteenth century. Fragments of lines hover over the surface, often forming open angles which become the gathering places of darker tones. These angles and lines began to grow, to be extended, and suddenly out of them developed one of the constituent facts of space-time representation — the plane (*fig.* **257**).

The planes

The advancing and retreating planes of cubism, interpenetrating, hovering, often transparent, without anything to fix them in realistic position, are in fundamental contrast to the lines of perspective, which converge to a single focal point.

Hitherto planes in themselves, without naturalistic features, had lacked emotional content. Now they came to the fore as an artistic means, employed in various and very different ways, at times representing fragments of identifiable objects, at

others such things as bottles or pipes flattened out so that interior and exterior could be seen simultaneously, at still others completely irrational forms equivalent only to psychic responses.

Around 1912 new elements entered; the planes were accentuated, assumed strength and dominance, and were given an additional appeal — to the tactile sense — by means of new materials (scraps of paper, sawdust, glass, sand, etc.). And when, though always meagerly, color was employed, it was often corrugated and roughened in order to strengthen the pigment. In such *collages* fragments of newspapers, fabrics, or handwriting, sometimes even single words, achieved the force of new symbols.

The process continued, from the grayish background of the first period through the *collage*, to the reappearance of color, which gradually became stronger and more varied, until its brilliant culmination in Picasso's and Braque's still-lifes toward and at the beginning of the twenties. In this period, perhaps cubism's happiest, color was used in pure strength. At the same time curvilinear forms were introduced, taken from such everyday objects as bowls and guitars, or simply invented. Color no longer had the exclusive function of naturalistic reproduction. Used in a spatial pattern, it was often divorced from any object, asserting a right to existence in itself.

Cubism originated among artists belonging to the oldest cultures of the western world, the French and the Spanish. More and more clearly it appears that this new conception of space was nourished by the elements of bygone periods. Its symbols were not rational, were not to be utilized directly in architecture and the applied arts, but they did give force and direction to artistic imagination in other fields. Following upon the first efforts of the cubists, there came, as has already been said, an awakening in various countries. In France appeared Le Corbusier and Ozenfant; in Russia, Malewitsch; in Hungary, Moholy-Nagy; in Holland, Mondrian and van Doesburg. Common to them was an attempt to rationalize cubism or, as they felt was necessary, to correct its aberrations. The procedure was sometimes very different in different groups, but all moved toward rationalization and into architecture.

When Ozenfant and Jeanneret (Le Corbusier) came together as young painters in 1917, they called their painting *Purisme* (*fig.* **313**). In comparison with the movements preceding it (constructivism in Russia or neo-plasticism in Holland), purism, coming out of French soil, was the closest of all to the aim of cubism and, at the same time, to architecture.

Purism

Two years after the exhibition of the cubists in the Salon des Indépendants, there appeared in Russia an abstract-art movement, fostered by Kasimir Malewitsch, which completely eliminated the object. It was a flight from and a protest against the naturalistic object, with painting reduced to a few signs of symbolic intensity. What its paintings achieve are fundamentally only pure interrelationships. Flatly extended rectangles and strips float in continuous interrelation in space for which there is no true human measure.

Constructivism

Interrelation, hovering, and penetration form the basis of Malewitsch's half-plastic architectural studies, which he calls

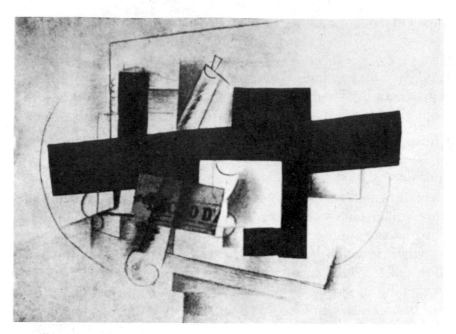

258. BRAQUE. Collage, 1913.

259. MONDRIAN. Composition.

"architectonen." These objects are not intended for a particular purpose but are to be understood simply as spatial research. Interrelations are created between these prisms, slabs, and surfaces when they penetrate or dislodge each other (*fig.* **260**). They come close in spirit to the so-called megastructures of around 1960.

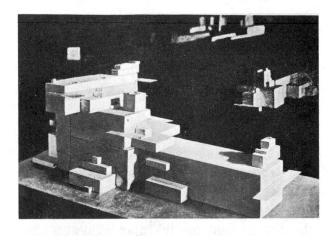

260. MALEWITSCH. Architectonics, c. 1920.

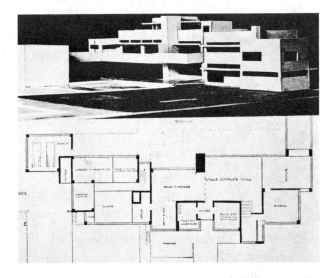

261. THEO VAN DOESBURG and C. VAN EESTEREN. Scheme for a villa, 1923.

262. WALTER GROPIUS. The Bauhaus, 1926.

Neo-plasticism, an expression used by the Dutch painter Mondrian, signifies that three-dimensional volume is reduced to the new element of plasticity, the plane. Mondrian sacrifices every contact with illusionistic reproduction, going back to the fundamental elements of pure color, of planes, their equipoise and interrelations.

The small circle of young artists who gathered around Theo van Doesburg and his periodical, *Stijl*, after 1917 progressed much more radically than the French painters and architects. Van Doesburg and Mondrian sought "pure art" not in any way deflected by external motives. With them everything rests on the distribution and juxtaposition of planes of pure color: blue, red, yellow. To these are added black and various tones of white, all being placed in a network of panels.

The Belgian Vantongerloo, who also belongs to this circle, demonstrated with the prisms, slabs, and hollows of his plastic of 1918 that contemporary sculpture, like painting, was not to be limited to a single point of view.

Van Doesburg, the moving spirit of the circle, was painter, man of letters, and architect. Although he executed few buildings, he cannot be omitted from the history of architecture, since, like Malewitsch, he possessed the gift of recognizing the new extension of the space sense and the ability to present and explain it as though by laboratory experiments.

One of van Doesburg's drawings in which an attempt is made to present "the elementary forms of architecture" (lines, surface, volume, space, time) may very well have appeared to many at that time as so much disjointed nonsense (*fig.* **81**). The present-day observer, who has the advantage of being able to look back upon intervening developments, has a very different attitude toward these mutually penetrating flat surfaces. He sees how the enormous amount of contemporary architecture which has since appeared acknowledges this vision of space.

In 1923 van Doesburg, together with van Eesteren (*fig.* **261**), who later became a town planner of Amsterdam, produced a house that is bolder than any other building executed during the period. The breaking-up of the compact mass of the house,

442

the accessibility of the roof, the horizontal rows of windows — in fact, all the features that were later to be realized in numerous examples were indicated in it. If a *collage* by Georges Braque (*fig.* **258**), produced ten years earlier, consisting of different papers, scraps of newspaper and fragments of planes, is placed alongside a reproduction of this house, no words are necessary to indicate the identity of artistic expression. An architectonic study of Malewitsch might be likened to it equally well. The effect is as if the blind surfaces of the Malewitsch sculpture had suddenly received sight. It is obvious that in the second decade of this century the same spirit emerged in different forms, in different spheres, and in totally different countries.

THE RESEARCH INTO MOVEMENT: FUTURISM

In the first decade of this century the physical sciences were profoundly shaken by an inner change, the most revolutionary perhaps since Aristotle and the Pythagoreans. It concerned, above all, the notion of *time*. Previously time had been regarded in one of two ways: either realistically, as something going on and existing without an observer, independent of the existence of other objects and without any necessary relation to other phenomena; or subjectively, as something having no existence apart from an observer and present only in sense experience. Now came another and new way of regarding time, one involving implications of the greatest significance, the consequences of which cannot today be minimized or ignored.

The notion of time

As was stated at the beginning of this book, it was in 1908 that Hermann Minkowski, the great mathematician, speaking before the Naturforschenden Gesellschaft, proclaimed for the first time with full certainty and precision this fundamental change of conception. "Henceforth," he said, "space alone or time alone is doomed to fade into a mere shadow; only a kind of union of both will preserve their existence."

Concurrently the arts were concerned with the same problem. Artistic movements with inherent constituent facts, such as cubism and futurism, tried to enlarge our optical vision by introducing the new unit of space-time into the language of art. It is one of the indications of a common culture that the same problems should have arisen simultaneously and independently in both the methods of thinking and the methods of feeling.

Beginnings of futurism

During the Renaissance the common artistic perception, perspective, was expressed by one group of artists primarily through lines, and by another primarily through colors. So in our own day the common background of space-time has been explored by the cubists through spatial representation and by the futurists through research into movement.

For Jakob Burckhardt there reigned in Italy "the quiet of the tomb." The futurists were a reaction against this quietness; they felt ashamed that Italy had become simply a refuge for those seeking to escape from the demands and realities of the present. They called upon art to come forth from the twilit caves of the museums, to assert itself in the fullness of modern thought and feeling, to speak out in authentic terms of the moment. *Life* was their cry — explosive life, movement, action, heroism — in every phase of human life, in politics, in war, in art: the discovery of new beauties and a new sensibility through the forces of our period. Not without right did they claim to be "the first Italian youth in centuries." [1]

So, from the beginning, they plunged into the full struggle, and carried their cause militantly to the public. The poet Marinetti, whose apartment in Rome even to this day bears the escutcheon of the "Movimento futurista," proclaimed in the Parisian *Figaro* of February 20, 1909, "We affirm that the splendor of the world has been enriched by a new beauty: the beauty of speed." And later, in 1912, in the "Second Technical Manifesto of Futurist Painting," the futurists developed their principal discovery, that "objects in motion multiply and distort themselves, just as do vibrations, which indeed they are, in passing through space." The most exciting of their paintings realize this artistic principle.

[1] For the literary intentions of futurism cf. the article of its founder, F. T. Marinetti, in *Enciclopedia italiana*, vol. XVI, 1932.

444

The productions of futurist painting, sculpture, and architecture are based on the representation of movement and its correlates: interpenetration and simultaneity. One of the futurists' best minds and without any doubt their best sculptor, Umberto Boccioni, who died much too early, in 1916, has most clearly defined their purposes. In an effort to penetrate more deeply into the very essence of painting, he sought terms for his art, terms which, now obscurely felt, now shining clear and immediate in his increasing creative experience, anticipated those that later appeared in the atomic theory. "We should start," he said, "from the central nucleus of the object wanting to create itself, in order to discover those new forms which connect the object invisibly with the infinite of the apparent plasticity and the infinite of the inner plasticity."

Boccioni tried in these words to circumscribe the sense of a new plasticity which conceives objects (as they are in reality) in a state of movement. This was reflected directly in his sculpture, "Bottle Evolving in Space," 1911–12, with its intersecting spatial planes. One of the few sculptural masterpieces of the epoch, this sculpture expresses the inherent significance of an object of daily use by treating it with new artistic invention. Sometimes, as in this instance, cubistic and futuristic works are closely bound together on a common basis of the same spatial conception.

Futurism and cubism — common traits and differences

The French painter, Marcel Duchamp, who belonged neither to the futurists nor to the cubists, painted at the same time (1912) his "Nude Descending the Staircase," in which the movement is dissected mathematically and yet fully surrounded by the multi-significance of irrational art.

Usually the futurists present movement as such, as subject matter ("Elasticity," Boccioni, 1911; "Dynamisme musculaire, Simultanéité," Carrà, 1912; "Speed," Balla, 1913), or show objects and bodies in motion (Gino Severini's study of the dance as a movement in mass, "The Dance Pan-Pan," 1911; "Walking Dog," Balla, 1913; "Rattling Cab," Carrà, 1913).[2]

---

[2] For illustrations of this first and most important futuristic development cf. Boccioni, *Pittura, scultura futuriste* (Milan, 1914), a volume of over 400 pages, with bibliography of exhibitions, manifestoes, etc.

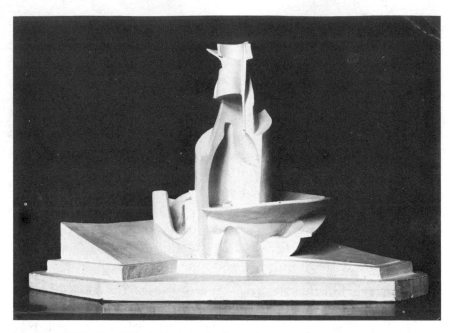

263.   BOCCIONI.   "Bottle Evolving in Space," 1911–12.

In both futurism and cubism this enlargement of the optical was achieved before 1914, before the first world war. The cubists were the more passive and less vocal. Not fighters in the futuristic sense, more purely research men in their work, they kept to their ateliers, preparing quietly and without fanfare the symbols of our artistic language. Braque and Picasso wrote no ponderous tomes expounding their theories. Even the name "cubist" was a label fixed upon them by outsiders. They did not try to paint "movement" itself, or the dynamism of muscles, or the automobile, but through their still lifes of things of daily use sought to find artistic means for our spatial conceptions. This is the reason cubism found extension into so many ramifications. This is why laboratory painters, who had no thought beyond their own artistic problems, could also give an impulse to the expression of the new spatial conceptions in architecture.

Architecture   To try to introduce the principle of movement directly into architecture did not touch the fundamental problem. In his projects for his "Città Nuova," in his skyscraper apartment houses connected with subways, elevators, and traffic lanes at

446

different levels, Antonio Sant' Elia tried to introduce the futuristic love of movement as an artistic element in the contemporary city (*fig.* **192**). Sant' Elia's "Città Nuova," as well as Malewitsch's sculptural studies of the same period, expressed trends that were first implemented in the 1960's when movement in cities came to be recognized as a problem of urban form and obliged different levels to be created for pedestrians and vehicles. We do not know if Sant' Elia's talent would have developed. He died in 1916, at a time when his contemporary, Le Corbusier, was still far from self-realization. Although Sant' Elia's prophetic vision did not direct the way architecture then followed, it did present a new viewpoint in a period when everyone was looking for a signpost. In his manifesto of July 14, 1914, which he published in connection with the exhibition of his schemes in Milan, he demanded an architecture imbued with the utmost elasticity and lightness, utilizing all the newly developed elements of construction from iron and ferroconcrete to composite materials made by chemical processes, including textile fiber and paper. Behind these technical demands loomed his artistic aim: mobility and change. What he wanted to realize he condensed into the few words: "Every generation its own house!"

There are times when the man of the laboratory is compelled to go forth into the street to fight for his work. On occasion Difficulties

264.   BALLA.   "Swifts: Paths of Movement and Dynamic Sequences," 1913.

this may be advisable. But normally he endangers his work by so doing. The futurists were perhaps too much bound up in trying to apply their ideas to all kinds of human activities; the result was that their movement — which our period cannot ignore — had a comparatively short span of volcanic productivity. It was unfortunate in that some of its ablest exponents died too early and that others lapsed into regrettable routine work, bequeathing nothing to the future except the few years of their youth.

265. EDGERTON. Speed photograph of a tennis player, 1939.

Futurism did not have the opportunity of the cubist movement: to accumulate, through all the many-sided stages of modern development, the results of artistic research, until they should appear united and in full power in a single great work — *Guernica*.

PAINTING TODAY

Picasso's "Guernica"

Since the first decade of this century the research into space has broadened through various successive stages, never losing, how-

448

ever, its original and primary concern with the new conception. What it had arrived at in the late thirties may be comprehended in a single painting which in itself sums up the entire experience of three decades — the "Guernica" of Picasso. In it are embodied the principle of simultaneity, the penetration of inner and outer space, the working with curved planes and different textures.[1] Nevertheless, this mural of the Spanish war seems to be the first real historical painting since the beginning of the Renaissance and the work of Paolo Uccello. It is the

266. PICASSO. "Guernica," 1937. *Detail.*

tragedy of a country distilled to its full strength by an artist able to transmute physical suffering and destruction into powerful symbols — a mother with her dead child, a woman falling in a burning house, a spear-transfixed horse, fragments of a mutilated warrior, one severed hand clutching a broken sword, all triumphantly surveyed by a great bull and lit by a lamp held in an outstretched hand. Above the carnage shines

[1] A connection with earlier periods is likewise evident, the figure of the woman falling in the burning house being comparable, as Le Corbusier once remarked, to Raphael's "Fire of Borgo."

449

"the radiant eye of day with the electric bulb of night for a pupil." The picture went through many variations and preliminary studies, but one detail remained almost unchanged — the rush of flight condensed into a symbol of two elongated human heads, hair streaming back, chin and neck in one sweeping line, faces enclosed in spherical triangles (*fig.* **266**). How charged with inner truth this symbol of Picasso's is is revealed by Edgerton's stroboscope, which photographically dissects movement into parts which the human eye is unable to grasp. A study of one of these stroboscopic photographs (*fig.* **265**) makes clear how closely connected are the realizations of the creative artist and those of the scientist. Out of the unknown, an artist like Picasso can produce intuitively symbols for a reality which, as in this instance, is afterwards confirmed by scientific techniques. It should not be forgotten that "Guernica" hung in the pavilion of the legal Spanish government at the Paris World's Fair. Its presence there was largely due to the efforts of José Luis Sert, architect of the pavilion, and a friend of Picasso.

CONSTRUCTION AND AESTHETICS: SLAB AND PLANE

The Bridges of Robert Maillart

We spoke earlier [1] of the way in which the methods of science and the methods of art came unconsciously to parallel each other about 1908. Among other more spectacular instances, we noted that construction and painting arrived at similar basic elements in their search for solutions to problems that had not previously been attempted. With the bridges of the Swiss engineer Robert Maillart we are brought back to this topic. They offer us the chance to compare these basic elements and to investigate the way in which the aesthetic effect produced by a new type of construction arises. [2]

---

[1] Page 443.

[2] This investigation appeared in its original form in *Circle, International Survey of Constructive Art,* edited by J. L. Martin, Ben Nicholson, and N. Gabo (London, 1937), pp. 220–236. It was published there under the title "Construction and Aesthetics" (English version by P. Morton Shand).

Those whose aesthetic sense has been formed or developed by the art of the present age can hardly fail to be stirred by Maillart's bridges, for their appearance may be trusted to arrest such observers before they can even ask themselves why. Maillart's surprising designs, which attract some as much as they repel others,[3] are the product of the uncompromising application of a new method of construction. They have almost as little in common with the solid arches, stout piers, and monumentally emphasized abutments of the usual "massive" type of bridge as an airplane has with a mail coach.

What, then, is the peculiarity of Maillart's methods of building?

In the early days of reinforced concrete the same methods of construction were used as were employed with timber and iron. Timber, being the trunks of trees, has length, just as iron has when rolled into long girders. One dimension always dominates, which is the one that transmits the load. As Maillart himself puts it: "The engineer was so accustomed to using those basic materials which provide only one-dimensional support that they became second nature to him, and restrained him from exploiting other possibilities. This was the state of affairs when reinforced concrete was introduced, and at first no change ensued."

Maillart was a pupil of Hennebique;[4] and Hennebique's reinforced concrete structures had beams and columns like timber-framed buildings. Following the model of timber construction,

---

[3] Although the first of his bridges have stood firmly up to the present day, and their adequacy for their purpose has long since ceased to be questioned, they still continue to arouse antagonism among local bodies, many of which regard them as positively hideous. It happened that most were built across remote Alpine valleys, where they were considerably cheaper to erect than other types and (an equally important consideration) where comparatively few people would see them. The stark, lean assurance of their construction belies the aesthetic lights of a wide section of the public through its elimination of emphasis on means of support and through the taut, weblike appearance of the arch-spans which results. "I am sick of these puff-pastry bridges" was the way the chairman of one of these local bodies expressed his aversion. This remark is worth mentioning, since it shows what an influence aesthetic feelings exercise alike on those who commission the building of bridges and those who merely chance to look at them, and how often these feelings are the secret determining factor of decisions apparently dictated solely by questions of cost and efficiency.

[4] Early in his career Maillart was the engineer in charge of the construction of a sanatorium in ferroconcrete at Davos for which Hennebique was the contractor.

his beams reached from wall to wall and from column to column, the roof stretching across them in the form of a flat, inert slab.

In designing a bridge Maillart began by eliminating all that was nonfunctional; thus everything that remained was an immediate part of the structure. He hid this by improving the reinforced concrete slab until he had turned it into a new structural element. What Maillart achieved after that was based on one idea: that it is possible to reinforce a flat or curved concrete slab in such a manner as to dispense with the need for beams in flooring or solid arches in bridges. It is very difficult to determine the forces present in slabs of this nature by calculation alone. To obtain positive results entails a complicated process which cannot be entered into here, except to say that it is based partly on calculation and partly on experiment. The engineer's adoption of systems incapable of exact calculation is typical of the present day (as in shell concrete structures) and contrasts with the absolute, checked and proven calculations typical of Maillart's period.

Slabs had hitherto played a neutral or passive part in construction. Maillart transformed them into active bearing surfaces capable of absorbing all forms of stress, and he subsequently developed this principle into a comprehensive system of support able to be employed for tasks previously considered impossible for reinforced concrete. Whether engaged in perfecting a new form of flooring or in striking out new principles in bridge construction, he has always adhered to the same basic method of using reinforced concrete slabs as active structural elements.

Mushroom flooring Maillart's experiments with beamless flooring date from 1908. He treated a floor as a concrete slab, converting it into an actively coöperative structural member by distributing the reinforcement throughout its whole area (*fig.* **267**). Since every part of the surface now became self-supporting, beams disappeared, their function being resolved into the floor itself. The heavier the load this homogeneous type of flooring is called upon to bear, the greater the practical inducement to adopt it. Consequently it is usually found in warehouses, factories, and other large, many-storied buildings.

267. MAILLART. Warehouse in Zurich, 1910. *First mushroom ceiling in Europe. The important innovation is the disappearance of the beams: the whole floor is treated like a slab. A new element is the reinforced slab which supports the same amount of weight at each point of its surface.*

The appearance of the branching columns which support this type of flooring somewhat recalls certain traditional styles, for in the basements of warehouses they resemble the heavy pillars of a Romanesque crypt and in the upper stories they suggest the slender palmlike columns of late Gothic. In point of fact, however, mushroom-headed columns have nothing beyond these superficial resemblances in common with either, since the peculiarity of the system resides neither in the formation of the shafts nor in the extruded corbeling of the capitals that crown them, but wholly in forces in the ceiling above, which do not meet the eye.

As floors of this type provide a uniform bearing surface throughout their length and breadth, their ends can be cantilevered out to carry supplementary loads. They are therefore ideal in combination with nonsupporting walls, such as continuous expanses of horizontal fenestration. It is hard to

453

268. MAILLART. Tavanasa Bridge over the Rhine, Grisons, 1905. *Span, 51 meters;
width, 3.60 meters; cost, 28,000 Swiss francs; system, three-hinged arch. Maillart for the
first time achieved here a monolithic construction by integrating arch and roadway into a
structural unit, and the creation of new aesthetic values — transparency and hovering
lightness — by stripping the construction of all disguise. The bridge was destroyed in 1927
by a landslide.*

realize this in the obscurity of a warehouse, for the latent possibilities of mushroom slab construction can only find architectural vindication in buildings which are flooded with the light
of day from all sides.[5]

The American engineer C. A. P. Turner had been experimenting with the mushroom system a year before Maillart, but the
Swiss engineer had employed slabs as basic elements in bridges
since the beginning of the century.[6] American designers have

---

[5] The first specifically architectural endorsements of this principle did not occur until
twenty years after Maillart's initial experiments. Brinckmann and van der Vlugt's
splendid van Nelle factory in Rotterdam (1927–28) is the outstanding example, although
it embodies the ponderous American type of mushroom-headed columns.

[6] Cf. C. A. P. Turner, *Concrete Steel Construction* (Minneapolis, 1909). Turner's article,
"The Mushroom System of Construction" (*Western Architect*, 1908, p. 51), gives an

269. MAILLART.   Salginatobel Bridge, 1929–30. *Span, 92 meters.*

not rid themselves of the idea that a slab is subject to stress
in separate directions, and they embed their rods diagonally
across the floor like intersecting beams.   American practice
has not fully grasped the structural role of the slab; consequently the forms of its mushroom-headed columns manifest a
certain characteristic heavyhandedness.   They can be recognized at the first glance by the presence of an intermediate
slab introduced between the head of the pillar and the ceiling,
as in the Greek Doric order.   To the best of my knowledge,
the Americans have not even yet thought of using the slab as
a basic element in bridge construction.

---

earlier account of his invention: "It was first used in the construction of the Bovey
Building in Minneapolis. . . . The essential feature of this new construction is the formation of a so-called mushroom at the top of each column, by extending its reinforcing rods
laterally, some four feet or more out into the slab in a radial direction and supporting on
these ring rods, which in turn carry the lighter reinforcement for the slab construction.
The top of the column is enlarged, forming a neat capital, which assists in taking the
additional stress, and is advantageous from the fact that there are no ribs to interfere
with light or to reduce the clear story height of the building."

270. MAILLART. Schwandbach-Brücke, Canton Berne, 1933. *Air view. Maillart resolved bridge-building into a system of flat and curved slabs. In Maillart's hands the rigidity of the slab, hitherto an incalculable factor in construction, became an active bearing surface. The torsional strain that would have to be allowed for in a concrete bridge built on a curving alignment can be utilized only by this method of construction.*

271. MAILLART. Schwandbach-Brücke, Canton Berne, 1933. *Slabs.*

457

The slab as a basic element for bridge-building

Maillart had embodied this principle in a bridge as early as 1900; and in that over the Tavanasa (1905) he dared to strip his construction of all disguise. The Tavanasa bridge (span, 51 m.) represented a wholly unprecedented form, for in it Maillart discarded massive beams just as he was also shortly to eliminate the beams from floors. Instead, he employed a shallow, curved, reinforced concrete slab for the arch, which, with the horizontal slab of the platform and a series of stiffened vertical slabs used as ties to articulate them, constituted a monolith.

Thus Maillart resolved bridge-building into a system of flat and curved slabs so juxtaposed as to achieve a positively uncanny counterbalance of all stresses and strains arising between them. The first realization of a stiffened elliptical concrete bridge with

458

273. Rainbow Bridge near Carmel, California. *The same problem — a narrow gorge — as in the Swiss valley. Using the normal construction, the approach had to be built in staggered sections; the alignment of the bridge could not be curved.*

an arch of eggshell thickness (his Valtschiel-Brücke) followed in 1925.

The elimination of all nonfunctional members has led Maillart during the last few years to dispense with the usual separate decking slab. In these later bridges trains and motor cars run directly upon their naked structural framework: that is to say, on the longitudinal slab of the platform itself.

In Maillart's hands the rigidity of the slab, hitherto an incalculable factor in construction, became an active bearing surface, which, being under initial tension, opened up possibilities that had remained a closed book for reinforced concrete engineering. Thus the torsional strains that would have to be allowed for in a concrete bridge built on a curving alignment had previously been deemed to defy calculation.[7] Maillart's Schwandbach-Brücke in the Canton of Berne, opened in 1933 (*figs.* **270, 271**), is the most beautiful example of a road bridge carried out in that material with a sickle-shaped platform.

---

[7] The problem of bridging mountain gorges with curved spans occurs in every mountainous country. When girders and arches are used in the ordinary fashion the bridge must be held to a rigidly straight line. At most, a curve can be produced by building the approaches in staggered sections, as in the Rainbow Bridge near Carmel, California (fig. 273).

459

One of the few large bridges which could pass an inimical jury carries the recently reconstructed main road between Zurich and Saint-Gall over the river Thur (*fig.* **274**) at a point where it traverses broken country with a flat-topped hill in the background. A single arch spans the river bed, flanked on each side by a short approach viaduct supported by remarkably slender pillars.

To appreciate the full plastic beauty of the form of this bridge — the flattened curves of the twin hollow ribs, and the manner

274. MAILLART. Bridge over the river Thur near Saint-Gall, Switzerland, 1933. *Single span, seventy-two meters; cost, $42,000.*

in which they are yoked together; their three-pin articulation on a level with the crown and at the abutments (the slightly ogival pointing of the summit of the arch which results should be noted); the upright slabs that act as vertical ties between the ribs of the arch and the platform, as also the interplay of the pattern of these members with that produced by the unusual section of the columns of the viaducts — it is necessary not only to go and see it, but to clamber down the shingle to the river bank so as to gain a view of the structure from beneath. There are few contemporary buildings in which the solution of the structural problem approaches so closely to pure plastic expression.

Before I throw out the question which underlies this analysis, one or two striking features of Maillart's bridges may be touched on without entering into the technique of his structural methods.

One of the problems in art in which research has not yet made much headway is the relation between sculpture and nature — and, beyond this, the interrelations between sculpture, painting, and architecture. It is easier for the constructor to find a convincing solution than the artist, because physical factors (like the width of the interval to be spanned, the nature of the foundations, etc.) dictate its conditions. All the same, there is something altogether out of the ordinary in the way Maillart succeeds both in expressing and in sublimating the breadth of a chasm cleft between two walls of rock (i.e., in his Salginatobel-Brücke, 1929–30; *fig.* **268**). His shapely bridges spring out of shapeless crags with the serene inevitability of Greek temples. The lithe, elastic resilience with which they leap their chasms, the attenuation of their dimensions, merges into the coördinated rhythms of arch, platform, and the upended slabs between them.

Sculpture and nature

A bridge designed of slabs of various shapes no longer resembles the ordinary kind of bridge either in its form or in its proportions. To eyes that are blind to the vision of our own day, slanting columns with grotesquely splayed-out heads, like those of the approach viaducts of the Thur bridge — a form imposed by purely structural considerations that enabled Maillart to make two columns do the work of four — are bound to appear somewhat ugly; whereas eyes schooled by contemporary art recognize in these shapes an echo of those with which modern painting has already familiarized them.[8]

New forms enforced by the use of the slab

When Picasso paints half-geometric, half-organic plastic images on canvas — forms which in spite of their apparently capricious projection somehow achieve a singular degree of equipoise — and the constructor (proceeding from purely technical premises) arrives at similar absolute forms by sub-

---

[8] Cf. the strangely formed pillars of the Arve bridge (fig. 275).

stituting two vertical supports for four, there is a clear inference that mechanical shapes and the shapes evolved by art as the mirror of a higher reality rank *pari passu* in terms of development.

Parallel methods in painting and construction

It is, of course, easy enough to retort that this is simply the result of chance, and that such resemblances are purely superficial. But we cannot afford to leave the matter there, for what concerns us is the question which must serve as our point of departure: Are the methods which underlie the artist's work related to those of the modern structural engineer? Is there in fact a direct affinity between the principles now current in painting and construction?

We know the great importance which *surface* has acquired in the composition of a picture, and the long road that had to be traversed — starting with Manet's light-fusion of paint, advancing by way of Cézanne's flat coloration and the work of Matisse, and ending with cubism — before this was finally recognized.

Surface, which was formerly held to possess no intrinsic capacity for expression, and so at best could only find decorative utilization, has now become the basis of composition, thereby supplanting perspective, which had triumphed over each successive change of style ever since the Renaissance.

With the cubist's conquest of space, and the abandonment of one predetermined angle of vision which went hand in hand with it, surface acquired a significance it had never known before. Our powers of perception became widened and sharpened in consequence. We discovered the interplay of imponderably floating elements irrationally penetrating or fusing with each other, as also the optical tensions which arise from the contrasts between various textural effects (the handling of color *qua* color, or the use of other media, such as sand, bits of dress fabrics, and scraps of paper, to supplement pigments). The human eye awoke to the spectacle of form, line, and color — that is, the whole grammar of composition — reacting to one another within an orbit of hovering planes, or, as J. J. Sweeney calls it, "the plastic organization of forms suggested by line and colour on a flat surface."

462

If Maillart, speaking as an engineer, could claim to have developed the slab into a basic element of construction, modern painters can answer with equal justice that they have made surface an essential factor in the compostion of a picture. The slab long remained unheeded and unmastered: an inert inadaptable thing which defied calculation and so utilization.

275.   MAILLART.   Bridge over the river Arve near Geneva, 1936–37.   *Span, fifty-six meters; width, ten meters; cost, 80,000 Swiss francs.   This bridge on the outskirts of Geneva was built mainly by the private means of the landed proprietors.   It had to serve for heavy loads and yet be built at minimum cost.   This was a case where Maillart could realize unprecedented construction ideas.   The triple box-like arches as well as the rows of elastic supports are evident here.*

But just as a great constructor transformed it into a medium for solving structural problems that had always been considered insuperable, so the development of surface into a basic principle of composition in painting resulted in opening up untapped fields of optical expression.

This is no longer a fortuitous optical coincidence, as might be objected, but a definite parallelism of methods. By what mental processes the constructor and the painter arrived at it defies analysis. We can only authenticate a particular phenomenon in a particular case: a new method of construction found its simultaneous echo in a parallel method in art. But this proves that underlying the special power of visualization im-

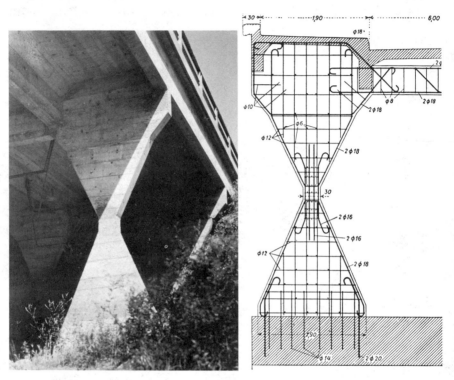

276. MAILLART. Arve Bridge, 1936–37. *Support and reinforcement of the support. Instead of steel joints, Maillart shaped the cross-like elastic slab support to take up the changing loads and stresses. By tapering it in the middle and inserting an ingenious armament, he gave the rigid slab the properties of a flexible joint and approached organic form.*

plicit in each of these fields similar elements have emerged which provide a creative impetus for both of them.

If the constructor, who necessarily proceeds from quite different considerations, finds he has to adopt substantially the same basic elements as the artist in order to solve his own technical problems, this signifies that in each case similar methods have informed optical imagination.

Contemporary artists continually reiterate the claim that their work forms part of Nature. This they explain as follows: "Modern art has reached the same results as modern science by entirely independent, intuitive steps. Like science it has resolved the shape of things into their basic elements with the object of reconstituting them in consonance with the universal laws of Nature." Now those forms in concrete which ignore former conventions in design are likewise the product of a process of "resolution into basic elements" (for a slab is an

277. MAILLART. Arve Bridge, 1936–37. *Supports and two of the box-like arches. Like archaic Greek idols, they stand in rows under the platform of the bridge.*

278. Dipylon Vase, seventh century B.C. *Detail. On archaic Dipylon vases the geometric abbreviations of human bodies are characterized by the triangular articulation of the hip joint. Maillart, on the other hand, is conceiving structural elements in approaching organic growth.*

irreducible element) that uses reconstruction as a means of attaining a more rational synthesis.

In this connection mention should be made of the "eggshell" concrete vaulting which Freyssinet used for some locomotive sheds he built at Bagneux, outside Paris, in 1929, though since then that particular branch of reinforced concrete engineering has produced forms of almost fantastic daring. On the same principle of using the slab as an active structural member, the

279. MOHOLY–NAGY. Painting, 1924.

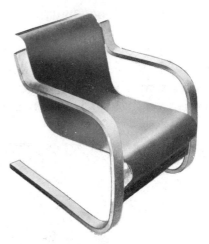

280. ALVAR AALTO. Armchair.

281. FREYSSINET. Locomotive sheds at Bagneux, near Paris, 1929. *Eggshell-thin reinforced slabs which can be bent like cardboard, change the former straight shed into a vault, providing excellent lighting.*

282. MAILLART. Cement Hall, Swiss National Exhibition, Zurich, 1939. *Two stiffening ribs end in two pairs of supports. A connecting gangway — as in Maillart's bridges — is an active part of the structure.*

466

Finnish architect, Alvar Aalto, has struck out an entirely new line in furniture design. He uses thin sheets of plywood, which, like the concrete slab, was formerly regarded as useless for purposes of structural support (*fig.* **280**).

In the community of method which now prevails in so many departments of human activity we may read a presage of far-reaching developments. The growth of this spontaneous identity of approach and its repercussions on society are being separately studied in every branch of knowledge. That there is a remarkable analogy between recent departures in philosophy, physics, literature, art, and music is a fact which has frequently been commented on. In the light of the particular case we have just examined, it is worth considering whether the field of structural engineering cannot be included as well. New methods are new tools for the creation of new types of reality. The greater the degree of identity in respect to what is fundamental to each of the creative spheres, and the closer the extent of their approximation to one another in terms of achievement, the sooner will the requisites for a new phase of culture be forthcoming.

A bridge is like a house. Each bridge and each house is a special case; each must be constructed and shaped according to the environment with which it must cope and the function it is to have.

Systems of bridges

As we have seen, Maillart conceived different systems for the construction of bridges. The stiffened arch, which is nowhere more beautifully realized than in the curved Schwandbach-Brücke (*figs.* **270, 271**) led to almost eggshell-thin members. Unfortunately, none of his later projects employing the stiffened arch ever saw execution. It is the most daring of his constructions, the least verifiable by calculation and the most opposed to the ruling taste.

Another system which he used for narrow and long spans with heavy loads is based on the principle of the continuous beam. This he further enhanced by hollowing out the heavy structure so that it gave an aspect of astonishing lightness. He built several very interesting smaller bridges in this way (for instance, the oblique river crossing at Gündlischwand, Berner

Oberland, 1937) but reached highest perfection in the bridge over the Rhône at Aire-la-Ville-Peney in 1937. Here the slablike column supports merge with the platform and the arches, which seem to be imbued with the elasticity of a steel spring and the suppleness of a willow branch. This bridge was never executed. A jury incapable of judgment rejected it.

From his early beginnings — about 1901 — to his last bridges, he developed the three-hinged arch with hollowed-out boxlike sections. He gave an elasticity to this type such as was previously known only in iron bridges. The Tavanasa bridge of 1905 (*fig.* **268**) was the first conceived out of a pure form. The Salginatobel bridge built in 1929–30 (*fig.* **269**) uses this system under daring conditions.

The section of the arch takes on a more and more precise U-sectioned form. In the bridge over the Thur, 1933 (*fig.* **273**), two arches are placed parallel to one another. The Arve bridge, 1936–37 (*fig.* **275**) uses three parallel U-sectioned arches, combining them with utmost skill and sensitivity with the elastic supports. The repetitive use of standardized elements is of great economical advantage, for the same scaffolding and shuttering can be used several times. From the viewpoint of aesthetics, the reëmployment of identical elements is even more decisive.

In Maillart's last bridges, the problems to be solved become more complicated but conversely the solutions more simple. The bridge over the Simme built in 1940 (*figs.* **286, 288**) and the bridge near Lachen (*fig.* **284**) completed in 1940 after his death are his solution to the problem of an oblique crossing. The bridge near Lachen with its twin arches forms a highway overpass on the Zurich-Arlberg railway line where highway and tracks intersect at an acute angle. Maillart used parallel U-shaped girders here as in the Thur and Arve bridges. According to the needs of this situation, the abutments and the arches start at different levels and one behind the other. Maillart was awarded this last contract because he was able to produce a design for this unusual situation within a few days, faster than any of his competitors.

In the Simme bridge, 1940 (*fig.* **288**) Maillart reaches his highest degree of simplification. The girders meet in the

283. MAILLART. Cement Hall, Swiss National Exhibition, Zurich, 1939. *Parabolic barrel vault of extreme thinness (six centimeters) touches the unsolved vaulting problem of our period. A sturdy construction and yet hovering over the earth like a silken balloon ready to rise. Span of the vault, sixteen meters; height of the vault, twelve meters.*

center like a pair of knives. The question cannot be wholly dismissed: Was this the limit? What would the next step have been?

Some hints, if only very fragmentary, should be given on the relation of Maillart's constructional methods with practical achievements and their aesthetic impact.

284. MAILLART. Bridge at Lachen, 1940. *Span, 40 meters; width, 8 meters; system, three-hinged arch. The bridge forms a highway crossing over the railway line from Zurich to Arlberg. Highway and tracks cross at acute angles. The independently constructed box-sectioned arches start at different levels and one behind the other, thus solving the problem of the oblique crossing. This bridge was finished after Maillart's death.*

285. MAILLART. Bridge at Lachen. *The joint of the arch.*

286. MAILLART. Bridge over the Simme, Berner Oberland, 1940. *Span, 32 meters; width, 7.9 meters; system, three-hinged arch of two hollow rib girders. This bridge shows the highest degree of simplification. A straight line of enormous strength springs from the abutment up to the center pin. The girders meet in the center like a pair of knives. Nothing is left of the traditional arch. (Compare the girders of the Galerie des Machines, p. 269.)*

287. MAILLART. Bridge at Lachen, 1940.

288. MAILLART. Bridge over the Simme, 1940.

Together with the lowering of the height of the arch between center pin and abutment goes the new shaping of the arch. The bridge over the Salginatobel (1929–30) still clings to the continuous masonry arch (*fig.* **269**) even if the construction is completely revolutionized. The bridge over the Thur (1933) shows how reinforcement of this type leads from the curved masonry arch to the pointed arch (*fig.* **273**). In the bridge over the Simme (1940), a straight line of enormous strength springs from the abutment to the center hinge (*fig.* **288**). It is as if one could see the unbent reinforcing rods embedded in the concrete. Nothing is left of the traditional arch; the ultimate simplification seems to have been reached.

Maillart had a particular sensitivity, an almost intuitive understanding of the forces which act upon a structure. He felt, like a dowser discovering the course of subterranean waters, movements and forces running through it and tried to form it as the artist tries to reveal emotions through irrational curves. Steel rods and concrete were not dead materials to him.

What he formed out of an artifact — ferroconcrete — was an organism in which every particle throbs with life. He never permitted dead masses or excess weight where shrinkage-cracks easily develop. He hollowed out his girders, reduced the dimensions of supports to the utmost.

This requires an imaginative, flexible mind in close contact with nature, and not the bookeeper's mentality of the mere calculator. Against such as these and their academic representatives, Maillart waged a lifelong struggle.

Every part of a construction had its active role. Even an aqueduct crossing a valley (Châtelard, Canton Valais, 1925–26) assumes under his hand an astonishing shape that strikes the senses immediately without the explanation that in this case the water conduit is formed like the box girders of his bridges and the inclined supports are so conceived that they form with the bottom of the conduit the active parts of a vault.

Maillart's almost organic formations can be best understood by means of the various ways he treats supports and the changes they undergo in accordance with the conditions with which they must cope. We only direct attention to the unusual form of the articulated supports of the triple arch of the Arve bridge of 1936 (*fig.* **274**). Maillart simply said he did not employ steel joints as elastic supports for reasons of economy. Using only ferroconcrete, he shaped the cross-like elastic slab supports (*fig.* **275**) which stand, like archaic Greek idols (*figs.* **277, 278**), in double rows of three under the platform of the bridge. By tapering the supports in the middle and inserting an ingenious armament, he gave the rigid slab the properties of a flexible joint (*fig.* **276**).

The system of these bridges, in which all parts are active, keeps them in a state of continual tension. The inexplicable urge of this period to impart the highest tension to people, material, and things is symbolized in Maillart's work.

Toward the end of his life, Maillart was at last given an opportunity of expressing himself, without the constricting necessity of solving practical problems, in the pavilion of the Swiss Portland Cement Company at the Swiss national exhibition of 1939 (*fig.* **283**). Here he could reveal the art and elegance that a ferroconcrete structure can display. This hall was destined from the outset to be destroyed for the sake of experiments in tensile strength. And yet this mere "test-tube building" became a part of history.

The Cement Hall, 1939

A parabolic barrel vault of extreme thinness (six centimeters) — the back part of it slightly conical — touches the earth by two pairs of slender supports in the middle (*fig.* **284**). Ascending and encompassing the vault, they form two stiffening ribs which, together with the connecting gangway spanning the interval between them, are all that Maillart needed to produce a sturdy construction hovering over the earth like a silken balloon about to rise.

Kurt Schwitters, the Dadaist poet and painter, once remarked: "When an artist spits, it is art." In the hands of a great engineer, this pavilion, conceived only to combine strength and the utmost lightness, became at once a work of art.

This light and solid barrel vault could easily be thought of as a part of a civic center. Maillart touches unconsciously on

289. Japanese wooden bridge of the eighteenth century.

the unsolved vaulting problem of our period. With a very few exceptions — Le Corbusier, Aalto, and some others — the contemporary architect is rather hesitant as soon as he touches on the sphere of the ceiling, where he can let loose his imagination. The nineteenth-century genius gave form to the airy spans of the great exhibition buildings. But iron lattice girders are ephemeral in nature. The most brilliant halls have disappeared, and the Eiffel Tower will only stand as long as its rivets are continually checked and its structural members safeguarded from rust.

What will be the vault of our period in the great public buildings to come? Reinforced concrete and especially eggshell-thin slabs which can be bent like cardboard have both the buoyancy we like and the permanence we like. The slab with mesh reinforcement was used by Maillart and by Freyssinet (*figs.* **281, 282**) in the form of eggshells curved in one direction. It was employed in circular form in flattened domes for market halls in Algeciras, water tanks in the United States, and gambling casinos in Brazil.[9] The engineer Ove Arup, together

[9] "Shell Concrete Construction," Dr. K. Hajnal-Kónyi, in *Architects' Yearbook*, vol. II (London, 1947).

with the Architects' Coöperative Partnership, roofed an English factory building (1947–48) with nine concrete shells, nineteen thirty-seconds of an inch thick and curved in two directions.

All that is needed are architects who know how to stir the imagination of the engineer. The engineer is capable of fulfilling emotional needs just as he is capable of solving the most intricate practical problems. Maillart's Cement Hall points in this direction. He, as the humble servant of architects, constructed a very large number of buildings which do not reveal that he had anything to do with them. He never encountered an architect who fully knew how to integrate his genius. Where he was great, he was alone. Maillart is not an isolated case. It belongs to the unhappy constitution of this period that engineers like Maillart, sculptors like Brancusi, Arp, or Pevsner, painters like Picasso or Léger, had to create their works in isolation. Therefore this period produced fragments, worthy entities in themselves, but an orchestration in an encompassing whole was denied it.[10]

Afterword

Maillart's life was a continuous fight against economic pressures and public apathy. In 1912 he was called to Russia, where he constructed large factories and warehouses — most of which were Swiss investments — in Kharkov, Riga, Leningrad. After the revolution of 1917, he returned to his own country, penniless and heavily in debt to Swiss banks. In consequence he was never again able to have his own independent contracting firm.

Robert Maillart was born in 1872 and died in April 1940. He died at the age of sixty-eight; nevertheless one feels that it was too early and that his life work was not accomplished.

His bridges, immaterially spun in space, belong through their supreme sensitiveness to the purest expression that our period has been able to achieve.

---

[10] Since the death of Maillart much progress has been made in attempts to solve the contemporary vaulting problem, especially in the field of shell concrete: see the Introduction and *Architecture, You and Me* (Harvard University Press, 1958), the chapter on spatial imagination.

During his lifetime his country did not recognize his significance. He was often hampered and his intentions misunderstood, so that he did not give all that he might have given: a result of the difference between the advanced intellectual and the undeveloped emotional perception that most effectively prevents the organic development of our culture.

Like Brancusi, Maillart limited himself to a few forms and fundamental ideas which he never abandoned and which demanded a lifetime to be developed to their last crystalline shape. His main inventions, the bridge conceived as a single structural unit and the building conceived as a unit, were achieved before he was forty.

"Maillart's development in thirty years of research unfolds organically, springing from that inner power which enables every great artist or scientist to transcend the existing technical knowledge through his vision. One had only to talk with Maillart to realize at once that he was a man who had absolute confidence in his imagination. He often designed his bridges with a single curve on a scrap of paper while en route from his Zurich office to his Bern office. The specialist's simple calculations would have been too insufficient a guide toward new solutions where invention, in the fullest sense of the word, plays a more decisive part than calculation. It is significant of Maillart that he made calculation a servant and not a master. His bridges satisfy the feeling by the poetic expression which pervades them, and the mind by their delicate equipoise." [11]

Maillart's most important works, however, were nearly all accomplished during the last ten years of his life. As he advanced in age, his bridges became more daring in their aspect and more imbued with the vigor of youth.

[11] Since these lines were written in 1934 and two pages were devoted to a simple footbridge over a creek near Zurich (S. Giedion, "Nouveaux Ponts de Maillart," *Cahiers d'Art*, vol. IX, 1934, nos. 1–4), Maillart's name has acquired the weight denied him during his life and in his own country. The general public was introduced to his works through an exhibition initiated by the Museum of Modern Art, which commissioned us to assemble the material in Switzerland. For the first article on Maillart, see S. Giedion, "Maillart, Constructeurs des Planchers à Champignons," *Cahiers d'Art*, vol. V (1930), no. 3. For further information, see Max Bill, *Robert Maillart* (Zurich, 1949), a compilation of his work with pictures and drawings. Specialists may be directed to the excellent monographs of Professor M. Roš, Federal Institute of Technology, Zurich, for research on text reports of some of Maillart's bridges.

WALTER GROPIUS AND THE GERMAN DEVELOP-
MENT

Germany in the Nineteenth Century

Manual production methods are deeply rooted in the German temperament.

Hardly any European country has been subject to so rapid a sequence of disasters and successes as Germany, wedged as it is between East and West. Germany's high culture of the late medieval period was followed by a slow decline. In the seventeenth century the Thirty Years' War wrecked her material and political potential for more than a century. In the early nineteenth century Germany as a whole was pervaded by a depressing political reaction which expressed itself in bitter opposition to economic freedom in the development of commerce and industry.

Industrial liberty, proclaimed in France in 1791, was not adopted in Prussia until 1846. It did not come to the south of Germany until 1862. There was a great crisis in England during the second decade of the nineteenth century as a consequence of the change from hand to mechanized production. In France in 1835 hand weavers were declared to be "in the last spasms of agony." Gustav Schmoller, the economist, notes that this period in Germany witnessed an increase in the percentage of manual workers and a marked trend toward production by small artisans.

Belated industrialization of Germany

During the nineteenth century the number of power spindles in a country was an accurate index of its degree of industrialization. In the year 1865 there was one such spindle in Germany to three in France and eight in England. Other branches of industry showed parallel stages of development, including the steamship and the railroad, which, as Sombart says, entered Germany "on the crutches of English industry."

American industry was only in the first stages of its development in the first half of the nineteenth century. But, as later developments indicate, there was a fundamental difference between the two countries. From the start, the American spirit was orientated toward mechanized production.

Violent industrialization from 1870 on

But around 1870 a rapid transformation sets in and steadily gains speed. Germany, the country of the hand worker and the farmer, drives on with the aim of becoming not only an industrialized state but the leader of the industrial age.

This early indifference to the machine and the factory followed by a headlong acceptance had serious human and psychological consequences. The deep uncertainty that prevailed at this period in Germany is reflected in its architecture. Other countries were expanding, but their architecture shows nothing like so complete a loss of inner equilibrium and confusion with regard to fundamental principles as was seen in Germany. There was nothing that resembled William Morris' work in England during the sixties, nothing comparable to the Chicago school of 1880 or the Belgian movement in the nineties.

Increased efforts in applied arts after 1900

About 1900 there was another sudden change in Germany of quite a different kind. In the seventies there had been a great drive to catch up with the advance of industry; now there was the same kind of violent effort to overtake the developments in the realm of human feeling. It was at this time that Morris and Ruskin aroused the greatest admiration in Germany. Henri van de Velde was invited to exhibit there in 1897 and created a huge sensation. New movements sprang up in both Germany and Austria. For the next three decades Germany remained the country most hospitable to foreign ideas. The magnificent German edition of Frank Lloyd Wright's works that appeared in 1910 is only one among many instances of this receptivity. There were exhibitions by the advanced painters like those held in Brussels between 1880 and 1890, and the outstanding foreign architects were invited to build on an equal footing with their German colleagues.

New movements in architecture

In the late nineties the impulse for new movements in architecture came first from Austria, from Otto Wagner and even from Adolf Loos (1870–1933), whose work held more for the future than that of the overestimated Alfred Messel (1853–1909), whose huge Berlin department store — built at the same time as Berlage's Amsterdam Stock Exchange — had only local influence.

478

Peter Behrens (1868–1940) epitomizes German architecture at the start of the twentieth century. He rapidly became famous as a result of approaching the industrial plant as an architectonic problem. Behrens consciously transformed the factory into a dignified place of work. Despite the classical severity and the Cyclopean walls of his buildings, Behrens trained the eye to grasp the expressive forces concealed in such new materials as steel and glass, as his Berlin turbine factory of 1909 shows. The atelier of Peter Behrens was the most important in Germany. Mies van der Rohe, Gropius, and even Le Corbusier worked there, the latter for five months.[1]

Peter Behrens: industrial architecture

When a freshly industrialized Germany set out to make up lost ground in the realm of feeling, the effort produced several minor Renaissances in the courts of the small principalities. At Darmstadt, for example, in 1899 the Grossherzog Ludwig von Hessen attempted to revive the spirit of artistic creation by forming a colony of artists and fine craftsmen.[2] In 1920 the Grand Duke of Sachsen-Weimar called Henri van de Velde to his court. Numerous German Maecenases appeared. There was K. E. Osthaus, who gave van de Velde his first chance to build in Germany and commissioned sculptors like Georges Minne and Aristide Maillol to execute work for his gardens and his museum. Then there were leading industrialists like Emil Rathenau, the president of the A.E.G. (the General Electric Company), who in 1907 engaged Peter Behrens as artistic supervisor of everything from the trade-mark of the company to the design of street lamps and the erection of new plants. With this appointment the architect at last found his position recognized beside that of the engineer. The meaning of this should not be underestimated.

The Maecenas of the movement

All these endeavors of a country which had grown rich and self-consciously progressive during the past three decades

Deutsche Werkbund, 1907

---

[1] Le Corbusier's first, and now very rare, book is called, *Étude sur le mouvement d'art décoratif en Allemagne* (Chaux-de-Fonds, 1912). It was one of the first criticisms of the German movement.

[2] The houses which they produced for themselves (Peter Behrens' first house was one of them), together with their interior equipment and specimen works in the arts and crafts, were exhibited at the Mathildenhöhe, Darmstadt, in 1901. This was the first of those coöperative enterprises by German artists which were to prove so important in the future.

found their natural center in the Deutsche Werkbund, established in 1907.[3] Its chief aim was "the refinement of workmanship and the enhancement of the quality of production." Artist, workman, and industrialist were to collaborate in producing honest goods of artistic value.

The idea behind the Werkbund was not in itself a new one. Sir Henry Cole, one of the early English industrial reformers, founded "Art Manufacturers" in 1847 to "promote public taste" through "beauty applied to mechanical production." It was his efforts that led to the Great London Exhibition of 1851 and the Crystal Palace.[3a] The generation that followed William Morris made peace with industry and returned to Cole's line of attack with the formation of the arts and crafts guilds. In 1907, sixty years after the Art Manufacturers, the ground seemed to have been prepared for a final reconciliation: it seemed quite possible to bring art and industry into full collaboration.

The Werkbund; outlet for youthful talents in its exhibitions

The clash of opposed opinions marked the Werkbund almost from its inception. Throughout these controversies, however, the group worked steadily to create openings for youthful talents and found responsible roles for them at just the right moments. Both the rising generation and the generation that was at its height were represented in the Deutsche Werkbund's 1914 exhibition at Cologne. Next to works by Peter Behrens, Josef Hoffmann, and Henri van de Velde stood Bruno Taut's glass house and the office building by Walter Gropius, which was the work most discussed at the exhibition, and embodied the most seeds for future development.

Even after the war years and the period of inflation, the Werkbund was capable of actions that ensure it a place in history. The Weissenhof settlement of 1927 is evidence of the group's steady efforts to bring the creative forces of the period to realization. Germany was impoverished, and there was a shortage of materials, when the magnificent gesture was made of inviting creative artists from every country to erect buildings at Stuttgart.

[3] There is an excellent account of its founding in Heinrich Waentig's *Wirtschaft und Kunst* (Jena, 1909), pp. 292 ff.

[3a] For fuller treatment see *Mechanization Takes Command* (Oxford University Press, 1948).

At about the same time the architect Ernst May was called in Housing development to organize the housing development on the outskirts of Frankfort-on-Main. May worked with Haussmannean speed and energy; he was not fortunate enough, however, to be granted a seventeen-year period for his operations. After a few years the whole enterprise was cut short — a familiar happening in German history. While the work continued, May showed the open-mindedness which marked the Deutsche Werkbund by employing foreign architects, several Austrians and a Dutchman, Mart Stam.

In 1929 the government — through the Deutsche Werkbund — New prestige of the architect gave Mies van der Rohe full charge of the German pavilion at the Barcelona exhibition. In 1930 Walter Gropius was chosen to organize the first German exhibition at the Paris Salon since the war.

The Werkbund period witnessed a complete change in the status of the architect in Germany. In this period he ceased to be subservient to clients and contractors, as he is in so many countries even now. It was recognized that the architect had a part in forming the spirit of his times.

290. WALTER GROPIUS. Fagus works, 1911-13.

Walter Gropius

Walter Gropius [3b] entered upon his career in the Germany of the Werkbund period. After finishing his studies he worked in the office of Peter Behrens. This was from 1907 to 1910, when Behrens was engaged on the turbine plant of the General Electric Company in Berlin. Gropius at the same time took part in discussions at the newly founded Deutsche Werkbund, which helped to crystallize his ideas "as to what the essential nature of building ought to be." [4]

The Fagus works: a new architectonic language

The first large commission which Gropius received after opening his own offices was from the Fagus works. The shoe-last factory which he built for them at Alfeld a.d. Leine in 1911 was a sudden and unexpected statement of a new architectonic language. While he was with Behrens, Gropius had seen his turbine plant — at that time "the modern building *par excellence*" — take form. The moment he set to work for himself he dropped his master's classical solemnity entirely and made the new aims of architecture clearly apparent. In the Fagus works, Gropius brought together the accomplishments of the past fifteen years, and in doing so he furnished an incentive for that "honesty of thought and feeling" which he himself values. [5] The break between thinking and feeling which had been the bone-sickness of European architecture was healed.

Plane surfaces predominate in this factory. The glass and iron walls are joined cleanly at the corners without the intervention of piers (*fig.* **291**). Behrens bounded the glass walls of his famous Turbine Hall right and left with monumental cyclopean walls. These have disappeared with Gropius. His walls show that they are no longer supporters of the building, but simple curtains, protection against inclement weather, as Gropius put it. "The role of the walls [is] restricted to that of mere screens stretched between the upright columns of the framework to keep out rain, cold, and noise." It is "as a direct result of the growing preponderance of voids over solids" that "glass is assuming an ever greater structural importance." [6]

[3b] For a fuller treatment see S. Giedion, *Walter Gropius: Work and Teamwork* (New York, 1954).

[4] Walter Gropius, *The New Architecture and the Bauhaus* (London, 1937), p. 33.

[5] *Ibid.*, p. 17.   [6] *Ibid.*, pp. 22–23.

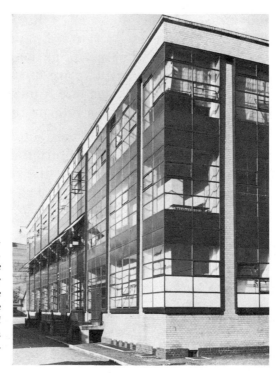

291. WALTER GROPIUS. Fagus works (shoe-last factory), Alfeld a.d. Leine, 1911. *The glass and iron walls are cleanly joined at the corners, without the intervention of piers. "The role of the walls [is] restricted to that of mere screens stretched between the upright columns of the framework."*

The American critic, Henry-Russell Hitchcock, is not likely to be challenged when he calls it "the most advanced piece of architecture built before the war." [7]   The hint of the theatrical in Behrens' work has disappeared. The new potentialities of iron, glass, and concrete, the cleaner treatment of the wall, the organic illumination of the interior are brought into a clearly thought-out balance. Regarded simply as a structure, the building is part of a tradition that reaches back to Eiffel's iron constructions of the late nineteenth century. The duality that marked that period has been overcome, however; architectonic and constructional means contribute equally to a unified expression. The walls are developed as planes, and conceived as sheer curtains between inner and outer space. This view of their function "naturally leads to a progressively bolder (i.e., wider) opening up of the wall surfaces, which allows rooms to be much better lit." [8]   The pillars are set behind the façade so that its curtain character is fully realized. It is undeniable that the way in which the volumes of the various

Balance between architectural and constructional means

---

[7] Catalogue of the Museum of Modern Art, *Modern Architecture* (New York, 1932), p. 57.   [8] Gropius, *The New Architecture*, p. 22.

buildings are freely juxtaposed foreshadows the scheme for the 1925 Bauhaus at Dessau. It is not only the façade which gives the factory its novel brightness; glass walls instead of the normal closed partitions are used in the offices. Behrens made a factory which was like a monument; Gropius gave it a simple and more humane interpretation.

The "Fabrik," Gropius' model factory and office building at the Werkbund's Cologne exhibition of 1914 (*fig.* **292**), had a covered terrace for dancing on the roof, a hall of machinery and open garages at the rear. It has, however, some architec-

292. WALTER GROPIUS.   Court elevation of the "Fabrik," Werkbund exhibition, Cologne, 1914. *Glass-walled offices and the covered terrace on the roof.*

tonic features which give it a new character. Before this, in the Fagus works, Gropius had discarded the normal stone enclosure of the staircase and replaced it by a shell of glass and iron. He repeated this practice in his Cologne building but handled it in an entirely new way. Here there were spiral staircases entirely encased in glass. They seem like a movement seized and immobilized in space (*fig.* **293**).

Our senses — slaves to habits built up during the centuries — automatically seek for the supports of projecting parts such as these staircases. The new conception of space, with its urge toward freely hovering parts and surfaces, leads one in exactly the contrary direction. It seeks the kind of aesthetic sensation that results when the relation between load and support is no longer traditionally obvious.

In the Gropius building at the Cologne exhibition (unfortunately destroyed by fire during the war years) it is notable that the roof was treated with the same care and skill that was devoted to other integral parts of the structure. The upper terraces provided space for the elevator and for dancing, with the whole area unified by a covered garden. Such details are never casual or accidental results; just because they outrun contemporary developments, they can only be created by minds unconsciously touched by the future.[9]

Germany after the First World War and the Bauhaus

All the vigorous efforts of the decade before the war ended in disillusionment. The arts and crafts movement was seen to have worked itself out. It had, indeed, done much to eliminate fashions that were carry-overs from the previous period, but improvements in furniture and reforms in household taste opened up no real outlet for continued future development. In the German movement, architecture was swallowed up by the applied arts. This in itself shows that the movement produced reforms but no new positive conceptions, since without a new conception there can be no new architecture. Solutions such as the Fagus works (1911–14) were isolated exceptions that could not make their influence felt at the moment.

A state of widespread uncertainty once more prevailed. This uncertainty was, so to speak, the working-capital — not the object of attack — of the expressionist movement. German expressionism had its beginnings previous to the war, continued to develop while the war lasted, and reached its height in the years immediately after the war. The movement eloquently states the grievances of mishandled humanity and indicts a tragic situation. But there is a fundamental dif-

Expressionism

---

[9] Contemporaries were rather undecided about the "Fabrik." Cf. the critique of Walter Gropius by Theodor Heuss in *Die Hilfe* (Berlin), July 2, 1914.

293. WALTER GROPIUS. Spiral staircase on corner of the "Fabrik," Cologne, 1914. *These staircases entirely enclosed in glass seem like movements seized and immobilized in space.*

ference between expressionism and other movements we have encountered — cubism, futurism, and the rest. Faustean outbursts against an inimical world and the cries of outraged humanity cannot create new levels of achievement. They remain transitory facts — however moving they may be — and not constituent ones.

The expressionist influence could not perform any service for architecture. Nevertheless it touched almost every German worker in the arts. Men who were later to do grimly serious work in housing developments abandoned themselves to a romantic mysticism, dreamed of fairy castles to stand on the peak of Monte Rosa. Others built concrete towers as flaccid as jellyfish.

This was the situation into which the Bauhaus came at its birth. The surviving ideals of the Werkbund proved its salvation: from the very beginning it set itself to unite art and industrial life and to find the keynote for a sound contemporary architecture. But even here, in the early productions of the Bauhaus and in works by Walter Gropius, traces of the literary, expressionistic approach appear. Expressionism infiltrated all German art.

Gropius was instinctively aware of the inadequacy of expressionism and of the need to escape from it. The war had left some vacancies on the staffs of the two schools at Weimar, the school of design and the school of applied arts. When Gropius united these schools to form the Bauhaus he tried to find teachers who had not worked in the field of applied arts. On the recommendation of Alma Mahler, he gave the basic design course — the first of its kind — to the young Swiss painter, Johannes Itten. Itten, while teaching in Vienna, had developed a completely new method for educating the tactile sense, the sense of color, and the sense of space and composition. It was this method of approach that baffled the public all through the Bauhaus period. The German sculptor Gerhard Marcks and the American-born Lyonel Feininger also came in with Itten at the beginning. Feininger was one of the few expressionists interested in problems of space.

Founding of the Bauhaus, 1919

The Swiss-German Paul Klee joined the staff in 1921. After this more and more men were recruited from the abstractionist groups: first Oskar Schlemmer, in 1921; then, in 1922, Wassily Kandinsky (who had been working on abstract compositions since 1911), and in 1923, L. Moholy-Nagy. The successive appointments of these men mark an ever stronger tendency toward the abstract movements and reflect the stages through which the Bauhaus passed.

Second stage in its evolution

Moholy-Nagy, a young Hungarian, was linked with the whole abstractionist movement by personal associations as well as through his own productions. His role in the Bauhaus has often been misunderstood. As editor of the Bauhaus books [10] he actively defended its ideas and gave the initiators of new movements in many countries the chance to address the Ger-

---

[10] Cf. *The Bauhaus, 1919–1928* (New York, 1938), pp. 222–223, edited by Herbert Bayer, Walter Gropius, and Ise Gropius. The bibliography by Beaumont Newhall embraces all the relevant literature on the subject. The book as a whole gives such an excellent account of the details of the Bauhaus development that there is no need in this discussion to retrace the same ground. Since then several documented histories of the Bauhaus have been brought out, for instance by H. Winkler (Cologne, 1962).

294. WALTER GROPIUS. Deutsche Werkbund exhibition, Paris, 1930. *Club lounge shown in cut-away section of a slablike many-storied apartment house.*

man public directly. Besides this, he helped through his own activities to overcome the lingering remnants of romantic mysticism.

Third stage The third stage in the development of the Bauhaus, bringing it into closer contact with industry, came about when it moved from Weimar to Dessau. At that time the Bauhaus showed its powers of self-renewal by adding to its staff from the groups of its former students. Among those who became masters in the school were Josef Albers, Herbert Bayer (typography), and Marcel Breuer.

The Bauhaus was soon well known all over Europe in those circles where the elements of a contemporary art were being sought — the Dutch "Stijl" group, for example. Theo van Doesburg himself came to Weimar in 1922 but, for various reasons, never acted as one of the Bauhaus teachers. The Stijl group's influence on the Bauhaus — underrated and overrated with about equal frequency — was on the side of the formal approach to aesthetic problems, of their accent on basic elements and basic relations.

As far as public opinion was concerned, all the Bauhaus leaders were taken, in spite of their actual differences, as advocates of one artistic doctrine, a doctrine which was as cordially detested by the expressionists as it was by the conventional and the academic. Political divisions were likewise forgotten: Gropius and the Bauhaus came under attack by Left and Right wing elements equally. According to Leftist critics, "no art school, however good, could be anything but an anachronism at this time" (1928). Critics of the Right, seeing the Bauhaus program of education as only so many unrelated activities, and judging them from either the academic or the arts and crafts point of view, could see no sense at all to the venture.

The work of the Bauhaus can be grasped only when the conception behind modern painting has been understood. Without an understanding of the feeling which has developed out of the new sense for space and the new interest in textures and plain surfaces, the studies of the Bauhaus fall to pieces.

The École Polytechnique of 1797 was dedicated to the fusion of science and life. At the Bauhaus under Gropius the effort was made to unite art and industry, art and daily life, using architecture as the intermediary. Now that it is possible to see the whole Bauhaus institution in its historical relationships, we recognize what an important outlet it was for the German gift of teaching and organizing. The principles of contemporary art were there for the first time translated into the field of education. Dispersed tendencies were brought together and concentrated.[11] This treatment of the Bauhaus has been lim-

---

[11] Very early in his career Gropius saw that the exhibition could serve as an instrument for just such a coördination of new tendencies and conceptions. He wanted to use the exhibition systematically as a means for presenting ideas — that is, with all its features adjusted to one general point of view. He worked in this direction until 1928 at the Bauhaus and, later, again with his old associates at the Bauhaus —Moholy-Nagy, Breuer, Bayer, and others. Their collaborative efforts developed a new type of exhibition in which every modern technique of display was called into service.

At the 1930 exhibition of the Salon des Artistes Décorateurs in Paris, the Werkbund was invited to participate. This was the first official foreign exhibition since the war to admit

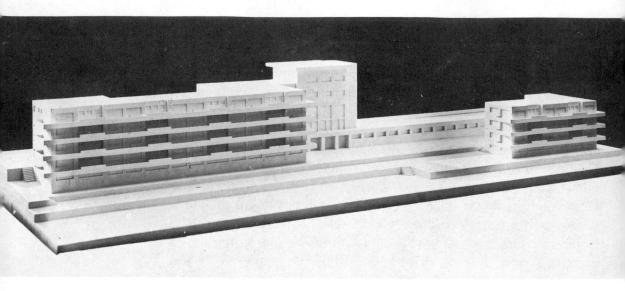

295. WALTER GROPIUS. Project for an international academy of philosophical studies, 1924. *This advanced scheme was produced two years before the Bauhaus, which is foreshadowed in its open planning. Meant for the university town of Erlangen, it would have combined dormitories and common rooms. The idea of such an academy was typical of the internationalist spirit which prevailed in Germany during this period.*

ited to those of its aspects which have a bearing on our constant concern: the way in which this period has moved toward consciousness of itself. The vital and difficult development of the Bauhaus reflects that process in the circumscribed realm of education as no other institution of the period does.

The establishment of practical connections between industry and the Bauhaus and the manner in which these relations functioned fall outside our subject. We can only note how a system of education based upon fundamental conceptions of our period and conducted by genuinely creative artists supplied industry with a variety of models for its products. Experimental handiwork in the Bauhaus shops led to articles of

German entries. Gropius and Breuer showed a club lounge interior mounted in a section of a slablike modern apartment block (fig. 294) designed by Gropius. By this time the old animosities had subsided, and the French critics greeted the display with surprise and admiration. For many of them it was the first revelation of what had been accomplished in Germany during the post-war years.

Exhibitions in which Gropius participated are: World's Exhibition, Antwerp, 1912 (interior); Werkbund Exhibition, Cologne, 1914 (the "Fabrik," series of interior rooms; officers' quarters for warships, automobile bodies); Werkbund Exhibition, Paris, 1930, Building Exhibition, Berlin, 1931 (scheme for a many-storied apartment block, with Schawinsky); Berlin Exhibition, 1933 (display in nonferrous metals, with Joost Schmidt).

industry which were reproduced all over the world: lighting fixtures, carpets, fabrics, and the famous tubular steel furniture by Marcel Breuer. Foreign manufacturers began to seek Bauhaus-trained supervisors of their productions.

The Bauhaus Buildings at Dessau, 1926

The building program for the new school at Dessau had to meet many different requirements. There was first the Bauhaus — the School of Design — itself; then the school of the city of Dessau for continuation courses in the trades; finally, combination studio and dwelling quarters for the students had to be provided. A dining hall, a stage, administration rooms, and a private studio for Gropius were also necessary. The instructors were given houses, also designed by Gropius, in a small pine wood. The architect's chief aim was to produce a clear separation of each of these functions from the others, at the same time not isolating them but bringing them together into efficient interrelation.

The chief accents fall on the Bauhaus, the nucleus of the whole school (*fig.* **296**). The Bauhaus combines "laboratories of design" with exhibition spaces, classrooms, and lecture halls. The laboratories of design were devoted to such various activities as cabinetmaking, theatrical crafts, dyeing, weaving, printing, wall coverings, and metalworking. On the third floor the lecture halls and the laboratories for metalworking and wall painting could be thrown together to make a single room. The Bauhaus is enclosed by the famous glass curtains. The section containing the pupils' studio-dormitory rooms rises six stories. The twenty-eight rooms it contains require the hyphenated title because each is intended not only for the student's residence but for his private work as well. Each has a small balcony, a concrete slab which juts out into open space. These slabs, hovering close to the massive wall, give the building its singular and exciting aspect. The students' building connects directly with the School of Design through a one-story wing. The wing ingeniously combines an assembly hall, the dining hall, and the stage of the school. These rooms can be thrown open to form a single hall accessible from the "aula," or main entrance hall of the whole school.

The building program

491

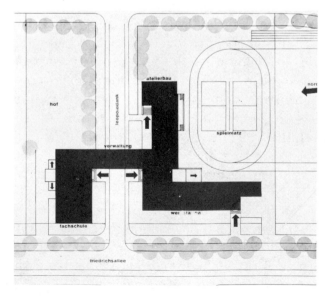

296. WALTER GRO-
PIUS. The Bauhaus,
Dessau, 1926. *Air view.*
This air view shows how
the different units blend
together. The eye cannot
sum up such a complex
at one glance.

297. WALTER GRO-
PIUS. The Bauhaus,
Dessau, 1926. *Plot plan.*
This complex reaches
out over the ground and
expands into a kind of
pinwheel with three
hooked arms.

A separate wing was reserved for the Dessau trade school. A short two-story bridge, supported by four pillars and crossing an intervening street, connects it with the School of Design. This *passerelle* or connecting bridge was reserved for administration rooms, meeting places for the masters' and students' councils, the architectural department, and the private atelier of Gropius.

The Bauhaus has a skeleton of reinforced concrete. Because of the German building ordinances, the supporting pillars are much heavier than they would have been in France or Switzerland. The continuous glass curtain is brought into abrupt juxtaposition with the horizontal ribbons of white curtain wall at the top and bottom of the building. An aerial photograph shows them plainly for what they are: mere ribbons, supporting nothing. In a bird's-eye view the whole cube seems like two immense horizontal planes floating over the ground.

Significance of the glass curtain

The glass curtain is not the limited and marked-off transparent area which Eiffel had already exploited in the 1878 exhibition: it flows smoothly around the building, the corners showing no vertical supporting or binding members. As in the Fagus works, the pillars from which it hangs are set behind the glass, making the curtain a specimen of pure cantilever construction. The glass curtain is simply folded about the corners of the building; in other words, the glass walls blend into each other at just the point where the human eye expects to encounter guaranteed support for the load of the building (*fig.* **299**).

Two major endeavors of modern architecture are fulfilled here, not as unconscious outgrowths of advances in engineering but as the conscious realization of an artist's intent; there is the hovering, vertical grouping of planes which satisfies our feeling for a relational space, and there is the extensive transparency that permits interior and exterior to be seen simultaneously, *en face* and *en profile*, like Picasso's "L'Arlésienne" of 1911–12 (*fig.* **298**): variety of levels of reference, or of points of reference, and simultaneity — the conception of space-time, in short. In this building Gropius goes far beyond anything that might be regarded as an achievement in construction alone.

Picasso and Gropius

298. PICASSO. "L'Arlésienne," 1911–12. *Oil.* "*In the head may be seen the cubist device of simultaneity —
showing two aspects of a single object at the same time, in this case the profile and the full face. The transparency of overlapping planes is also characteristic*" (*Catalogue of the Picasso Exhibition, Museum of Modern Art,
New York, 1939, p. 77*).

494

299. WALTER GROPIUS. The Bauhaus, Dessau, 1926. *Corner of the workshop wing. In this case it is the interior and the exterior of a building which are presented simultaneously. The extensive transparent areas, by dematerializing the corners, permit the hovering relations of planes and the kind of "overlapping" which appears in contemporary painting.*

The glass curtain wall is famous, but the really important function of the Bauhaus was fulfilled by it as a unit. When it was erected in 1926 it showed how the new space conception could be used to organize a great building complex; nothing comparable to this had until then been achieved in contemporary architecture.

There is no doubt that Frank Lloyd Wright, in the first decades of this century, worked with hovering vertical and horizontal planes in his houses. In this Chicago period he also realized open planning in some of his large houses — the Martin house in Buffalo (1904), for example, and the Coonley house at River Forest (1908). Their ground plans are extended and complicated, and the different parts are sometimes connected by bridges. But these wings are strongly attached to the ground, reach out over the plot like the exploratory tentacles of some earth-bound animal. They do not hover over the ground, and they embody no wish to do so. The whole treatment of the walls — their sudden structural changes, their overhanging eaves, their complicated relief — indicates this. This may explain why Wright is somewhat repelled by what has been done in Europe since his appearance.

By 1926 a new generation had set to work in architecture. They were in contact both with the artistic discoveries that had been made since 1910 and with the new methods and materials of construction. They brought these two formerly separate realms together and out of their conjunction developed what we know as contemporary architecture. The generation of Le Corbusier, Gropius, Mies van der Rohe, and the others knew the work of the artistic explorers and the new spatial feelings which they had discovered. Finally they were able to select from the accumulated developments in engineering just the means that were needed to give architectonic expression to this new space sense.

The Bauhaus complex is an arrangement of cubes, one juxtaposed against another — cubes differing in size, material, and location. The aim is not to anchor them to the ground but to have them float or hover upon the site. This is the reason for the winglike connecting bridges and the liberal use of glass. The glass was called in for its dematerializing quality; the

496

previous generation had used it either for practical purposes or (in private houses) had stained or painted it.

These cubes are juxtaposed and interrelated. Indeed, they interpenetrate each other so subtly and intimately that the boundaries of the various volumes cannot be sharply picked out. The views from the air show how thoroughly each is blended into a unified composition. The eye cannot sum up this complex at one view; it is necessary to go around it on all sides, to see it from above as well as from below. This means new dimensions for the artistic imagination, an unprecedented many-sidedness.

New organization of volumes

The ground plan lacks all tendency to contract inward upon itself; it expands, on the contrary, and reaches out over the ground. In outline it resembles one of those fireworks called "pinwheels," with three hooked arms extending from a center (*fig.* **297**). The impression one receives from it is similar to that produced by the glassed staircase in Gropius' exhibition building of 1914: it suggests a movement in space that has been seized and held.

The Bauhaus was the only large building of its date which was so complete a crystallization of the new space conception. Its appearance is in a way testimony to the irrational course of history. Germany in the second half of the nineteenth century showed a greater loss of architectonic honesty than any other country. But it was in this very country, after less than thirty years of effort, that the way was opened to new levels of accomplishment in architecture.

Architectural Aims

Gropius is happiest when he is planning on a large scale; he is the architect of buildings for whole social groups — factories, offices, schools, theaters of new types.[12] It was natural that he

Buildings for social groups

---

[12] His *Totaltheater,* for example, is completely adjusted to the new space conceptions. The stage is no longer a fixed focal point for every perspective in the body of the theater as it had been since Renaissance and Baroque times. It is placed in the middle of the building and fitted for circular and vertical movement, so that a many-sided spectacle is presented. Cf. W. Gropius, *Theaterbau* (Rome, 1934).

should take part in the building that went on in the twenties, when Germany set out to make up its shortage of middle- and working-class dwellings. Gropius built a large number of such apartments and housing colonies — in Berlin, Dessau, Frankfort-on-Main, Karlsruhe, and elsewhere. His most interesting work in this field was a scheme for a government institute for housing research.[13] The colony was eventually built, but not as Gropius had proposed. We shall discuss later on, in dealing with the new scale in city planning, the sort of slablike block unit which Gropius worked with in this scheme.

Designs in other fields: their advanced character

The fact that so many of his works — even those of his youth — have retained all their original freshness is evidence of Gropius' creative force. This holds true not only for his architectural productions — the Fagus works, for example — but for his work in other fields as well. Gropius designed a Diesel locomotive as far back as 1913. On a carefully studied functional basis he arrived at an artistic solution that was astonishingly advanced. He produced, in fact, a design which two decades later would have been recognized as "streamlined." [14] His 1932 memorial at Jena to those who fell in the Revolution — a composition of cement planes and prisms — was completely contemporary in design. Unfortunately it was destroyed by the Nazis when they came into power.

The fact that a man's work had kept its contemporaneous character for two or three decades would have required no special comment in a period where thought and feeling moved in parallel channels. It is far from being a matter of course in periods like ours, however. Among us such sureness of production is — unfortunately — possessed by few artists.

Gropius, like many German artists, has a strong and solid rather than a quick imagination. But, working very quietly, he arrives at new and startling conclusions. Albrecht Dürer's ponderous figures lack the grace of the Venetian school; nevertheless, Dürer's conceptions are characterized by an inherent depth.

---

[13] The Reichsforschungsgesellschaft.

[14] Illustrated by S. Giedion, *Walter Gropius* (Paris, 1931).

WALTER GROPIUS IN AMERICA

What effect have his American surroundings had on Gropius, and how has Gropius influenced his American environment? There are delicate mutual reactions which obviously can only be very imperfectly gauged. Before attempting even the most summary analysis we shall have to consider a more general question: the significance of the post-1930 emigration from Europe to America.

The Significance of the Post-1930 Emigration

This emigration was the outcome of political pressure, but it was of an entirely different nature either from that of the European intellectuals driven into exile after 1848 or the mass exodus of peasants and artisans about 1860. At those periods America was still an only half-formed country. Wide stretches of its territory and many professional fields were just being opened up. Whoever went to America in those days became an American citizen almost automatically, and could acquire land either as a free gift or for a purely nominal price. But those who migrated in the 1930's were confronted with quite another situation; America was now believed to be settled and was defended by entry quotas; newcomers were regarded as aliens, whether they became American citizens or not. All the same, the influence of this emigration may in the long run prove to be deeper and more far-reaching than those of 1848 and the 1860's. For this did not consist of representatives of politics, business, or unskilled labor, but of representatives of cultural life — the most advanced scientists, humanists, and artists, who during the thirties had a direct impact in every domain of science and culture, from modern aesthetics to nuclear physics.

There are moments in the lives of nations when, like certain plants, they require extraneous fertilization in order to achieve a further phase of their cultural evolution. Just as, after the artistic exhaustion which followed the Gothic development, Italian artists of the Renaissance were called to France to incite a new development, so America, after a preponderant role of business, needed a new spiritual orientation. The laws of chance made this need coincide with the exodus of many of the best European minds during the 1930's.

State of American architecture around 1930

After the structural forthrightness of the first Chicago School during the eighties, after Louis Sullivan's outstanding purity of architectonic expression and Frank Lloyd Wright's exciting example around 1900, the spirit of American architecture had degenerated into a mercantile classicism. The impulse to shake free from this disastrous development had to be initiated from outside. The time came in the late thirties.

As early as the 1920's a few modern-minded European architects had settled in the United States. It was at this time that Richard J. Neutra, for example, started his hard fight for contemporary architecture in Southern California, after earlier endeavors of Frank Lloyd Wright, Greene & Greene, and others had been submerged by sham Spanish imitations. In the twenties, American universities and similar institutions were all in the hands of representatives of the Académie des Beaux Arts. The modern spirit was excluded everywhere. But in the late thirties some far-sighted men in leading institutions felt the necessity of inviting men such as Walter Gropius, Marcel Breuer, Mies van der Rohe, Moholy-Nagy, and later on, Alvar Aalto, to teach in America.

That the United States, unlike certain other countries, should have decided to employ some of Europe's most creative architects says much for that nation's intuitive sagacity. These appointments provided the rather devious retrospective means by which Americans were at last enabled to recognize their own pioneers. Even the American Institute of Architects began to reconsider its attitude toward Frank Lloyd Wright and awarded him its gold medal on his eightieth birthday in 1948. This recalls inevitably the honors with which the French Academy eventually loaded Ingres after having embittered his whole active career as a painter.

Walter Gropius and the American Scene

What did America do for Gropius and what has Gropius done for America? To begin with, there are definite points of resemblance to the functional type of American architecture in Gropius' own work, evidence of which can be found as far back in his career as the international competition for the Chicago Tribune Building in 1922. Though at that time Gropius did not know of the work of the Chicago School of 1890, the project he submitted was imbued with the selfsame spirit. Had his project been carried out instead of the pseudo-Gothic design that was chosen, it would be regarded today as a natural continuation of the Chicago School.

As it was, every rational design was laughed out of court, although there were names such as Duiker, Lönberg-Holm, and Bruno Taut among the other European architects who took part. In the library of Harvard University's Graduate School of Design there is a satirical pamphlet, issued by the "Celestial Jury" (1923), in which Gropius' design is referred to as that of "the man who invented the mouse-trap."

There were other points, too, in which, quite early, Gropius had shown a certain affinity with American building technique and its large-scale production and assembly. In 1909 — during the time he worked in the office of Peter Behrens — he laid before the German industrialist Emil Rathenau "A Plan for Forming a Company to Undertake the Construction of Dwellings with Standardized Component Parts." Gropius said at the end of this unpublished twenty-eight-page proposal, "It becomes today economically and technically possible to satisfy the justified demands of the client for individualized treatment of his dwelling by the use of the infinite possibilities for combination of these variable parts." Standardized component parts

Thus in 1910 Walter Gropius perceived the pivotal problem, which forty years later has not yet been completely solved, of the part mechanization has to play in the mass production of houses. This problem consists in the reconciliation of individual needs with mechanical production to produce a solution that can satisfy varying human requirements.

As is well known, industry, trying first to mass-produce identical houses, like automobiles, had to learn the hard way that houses, unlike automobiles, demand respect for individual flexibility and that all that industry can do is to find out the best

501

means of creating parts to be assembled in such ways that the necessary diversity may be guaranteed.

Since 1942, Konrad Wachsmann in collaboration with Gropius developed a new system of prefabricated houses (the "general panel system") based on Gropius' work with prefabricated corrugated-copper houses for Hirsch Kupfer, near Berlin, in 1931. The beveled edges of the frame were done there first and then taken over for General Panel. Its standardized wooden slabs or panels combine individual planning and architectural freedom with modern industrial methods.

Architectural Activity

Gropius' house in Lincoln, 1938

At the same time as he inaugurated his architectural teaching in America, Walter Gropius started to build himself a home at Lincoln, some twenty miles from Cambridge, Massachusetts. When I was staying with him in the autumn of 1938 crowds of visitors used to come over every weekend, and often on weekdays as well, to see the newly finished "modern house" (*fig.* **300**); for up till then not a single example could be found within a radius of upwards of a hundred miles.

Yet neither its flat roof, its screened porch (though here designed as an extension of the dining room, protruding from the house to catch eastern and western breezes during the hot and humid summers), its vernacular weather-boarding (in which, however, the boards were laid vertically instead of in the traditional horizontal manner), nor its large windows could be said to mark any notable divergence from the local New England building idiom.

Several country houses in the same area followed, all of which, like Gropius' own home, were designed in partnership with Marcel Breuer. Breuer's hand can be felt in the particularly charming one-room Wayland cottage (1940) which hovers over the ground like a butterfly (*fig.* **301**). There were larger houses, too, less successful in design, which had to be planned for clients with exaggerated personal requirements.

The defense housing colony of New Kensington, near Pittsburgh, built in 1941 for the employees of an aluminum factory, caused quite a belated commotion in the Pennsylvania newspapers. The attacks in the local press must have reminded

300. WALTER GROPIUS and MARCEL BREUER. Gropius' own house in Lincoln, Massachusetts, 1938. *View from the south and ground plan. This was the first modern house to be built in the vicinity of Boston.*

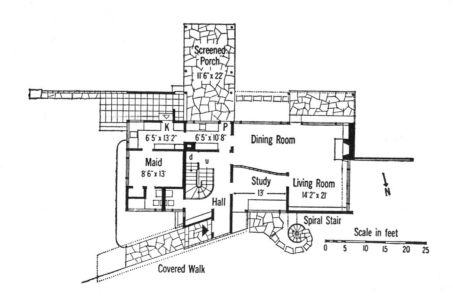

Screened Porch. 11'6" x 22'

K 6'5" x 13'2"   P 6'5" x 10'8"   Dining Room

Maid 8'6" x 13'   d u

Study 13'   Living Room 14'2" x 21'

N

Hall   Spiral Stair

Scale in feet
0 5 10 15 20 25

Covered Walk

503

Gropius of those aroused by his Törten Siedlung at Dessau more than two decades earlier.

Differing European and American views on academic teaching

European architects who emigrate to the United States are surprised that important jobs are nearly always placed in the hands of large firms with staffs running into hundreds; and that small architects' offices, such as they were accustomed to at home, have a hard struggle to keep going at all.

Another difference they find is that in Europe a teacher of architecture usually has to acquire a reputation in the field before being called to a chair, while in America a professor of architecture has been regarded until lately as someone estranged from reality, and best kept away from actual building activity, the teaching of architecture being regarded as a career in itself.

That Mies van der Rohe and Gropius did not accept this frustrating role was not the least of their accomplishments in bettering the standard of architectural training in America. All of us are convinced that an academic teacher can have a real influence on his students only as long as he is creative himself. To young people who are in a state of spiritual flux the close contact with a personality who is himself in a creative mood is the best means to liberate their own creative capacities.

When Gropius and Marcel Breuer entered the competition for Wheaton College in 1938 — their first contribution to American college architecture — conditions were not ripe for them. No trustee could have been persuaded to vote the necessary funds. The consuming itch for representationalism still prevailed in the design of university dormitories. Yet this was just the time when it began to break down and a year later, in 1939, it was possible for Mies van der Rohe to be commissioned to design the new campus buildings for the Illinois Institute of Technology. In 1947 Aalto was able to persuade the trustees of the Massachusetts Institute of Technology to allow him to carry out his revolutionary design for his dormitory on the Charles River, and in 1949 Gropius was entrusted with the building of the Harvard Graduate Center for "America's oldest and most respected educational institution."[1]

---

[1] "Harvard Builds a Graduate Yard," *Architectural Forum, the Magazine of Building*, December 1950, pp. 62–71.

301. WALTER GROPIUS and MARCEL BREUER. House in Wayland, Massachusetts, 1940. *This little house for an elderly couple is embedded in old pine trees.*

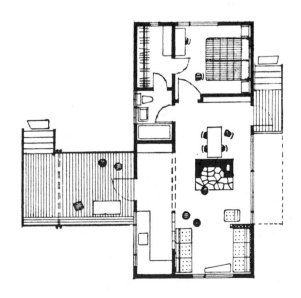

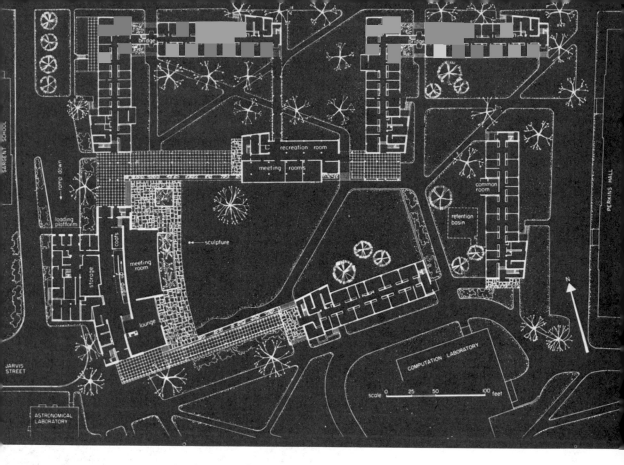

302. Graduate Center, Harvard University, 1949–50. *Plan of the whole complex, including the Commons.*

Although it was customary for undergraduate students to live in university-built dormitories, it was unusual, at that time, for the university to provide shelter for the graduate students. The Harvard Graduate Center and Aalto's building for the Massachusetts Institute of Technology were, however, dormitories for graduates; and in 1962–63, Harvard built a large housing complex for 500 married students, designed by José Luis Sert as three 28-story towers in combination with lower buildings that, for the first time, created an interlocking urbanistic entity (*fig.* **528**).

All his life, Gropius felt the need to work closely with others. In 1945 he formed an association with several young American architects called The Architects' Collaborative.[2] His early

---

[2] The Architects' Collaborative in 1945: Jean Bodman Fletcher, Norman Fletcher, Walter Gropius, John C. Harkness, Sarah Harkness, Robert S. McMillan, Louis A. McMillen, Benjamin Thompson.

303. Graduate Center, Harvard University. *The Harkness Commons building, with passageways. In the background are some of the dormitory buildings.*

works, like the Fagus Factory (1911), or the factory for the Cologne Werkbund exhibition (1914), also bore the names of his collaborators: Adolph Meyer, who died early, then — in America — Marcel Breuer, and, after their parting, the working team of TAC.

The Harvard Graduate Center was built in an extremely short time, 1949–50, by TAC (The Architects' Collaborative). The funds available were rather limited compared to those used for former students' quarters or even for Aalto's new M.I.T. dormitory. This is not the only reason for the disappearance of a palatial type of building; it is also because another aspect of life is developing. Greater simplicity and deeper spiritual demands are to be found in the post-war generation.

The dormitories for 575 students are spread informally. No enclosures separate them from the outside. All of the three-

304. Graduate Center, Harvard University. *View of the Harkness Commons, with a passageway to one of the dormitories in the foreground.*

and four-story buildings are of reinforced concrete. Yellowish bricks, such as Gropius has liked ever since his Fagus works of 1911, form their curtain walls. Covered passageways connect the different buildings. Their long horizontals and slim, widely separated columns impart movement and smoothness. There is also a certain interplay with different horizontal planes: the flat-roofed three- and four-story dormitories, the two-story Commons, and the sunken garden before it.

Commons
Building

The Commons Building forms the social center for graduate student life at Harvard. Two-story structure, steel frame, limestone facing, large glass areas. It is delightful to observe how the carefully planned organization of this building gives an architectonic impetus to the whole structure.

Unusually placed on the second floor are the dining rooms and kitchen, which serves 1200 meals at a time. A cantilevered ferroconcrete ramp, forming a kind of backbone within the structure, leads directly to the cafeteria counters. The dining area is divided into four units to avoid the impression of mass feeding.

508

305. Graduate Center, Harvard University. Interior of Harkness Commons, with wooden reliefs by Hans Arp. *It was a courageous experiment to invite creative artists — Hans Arp, Joan Miró, Josef Albers, and others — to reënforce the emotional content of the Commons building. Contacts between planner and artist are as important for future development as air conditioning,*

The ground floor, with its wide glass areas, serves as a social gathering place and the larger of its two lounges can easily be converted into a meeting hall.

One thing should not be forgotten, that in spite of the rather limited means at their disposal, Gropius insisted that contemporary art should be present in the Commons Building. It was not an easy problem to solve.

Commons Building and contemporary art

For one and a half centuries contemporary art and the public have lost contact. Belatedly and only after generations, the public responded. The banishment of creative art from public life had another effect: it estranged artists and architects from the habit of working together. This is the situation today.

It needed courage around 1920 to invite the most advanced painters to join the staff of a state institution like the Bauhaus. And the same intrepidity was necessary in 1949 to introduce

509

the work of modern artists [3] within a university; not in the form of an exhibition, but as a daily companion to the student's life.

At the Sixth CIAM Congress, at Bridgewater, England, in 1947, in which Gropius took part, the problem of aesthetics came to the fore and especially the question, is mutual coöperation between architect, painter, and sculptor possible? Everybody knew that this coöperation was not easy to accomplish because artists and architects had so long been separated by the circumstances. In the Commons Building it can sometimes be felt that the two did not work together from the beginning. In order to strengthen the emotional and symbolic content of community buildings the integration of art and architecture has again become an urgent demand. The Commons Building is a bold step toward this goal.

The TAC Harvard Graduate Center and the Aalto M.I.T. Dormitory are very different, just as Ingres and Delacroix are different in their means of expression. Which is to be preferred depends on the personal approach and the personal likes and dislikes of the individual; but one thing can be regarded as certain; the future will not forget that two distinguished institutions in the same city gave contemporary architecture a chance to mold itself into upgrowing generations.

Gropius as Educator

What predestined Gropius to become a teacher is that trait in his nature which makes him ready to listen to others and give them their full due. He might not have the temperament, or the eruptive inventiveness of other leading figures, but no one in the architectural movement possesses the far-sighted philosophical approach which enables him to perceive problems at a distance and correlate them within a broad framework.

Born teacher and organizer though Gropius is, much of his success in both capacities lies in his power to see his problems

---

[3] Mural paintings for the dining hall by Joan Miró, later replaced by a new one, also by Miró, on enameled tiles; wood reliefs by Hans Arp; tile mural accompanying the ramp by Herbert Bayer; a brick relief by Josef Albers; steel pylon by Richard Lippold in front of the Commons; world maps by Gyorgy Kepes in the dormitory lounges.

from every side. There is another quality he possesses: his mind is the reverse of rigid. It has nothing in common with the hidebound inflexibility of those sterile natures whose dim instinct of self-protection invariably makes them negate anything that might disturb the even tenor of their lives. Gropius is always prepared to consult and learn from others when he feels they have something of value to impart. He allows himself much time for his fellow man. His willingness to understand the minds of others liberates the creative capacity of his students and wins him friends.

He knows and likes the human side of life. This is the secret of his ability as a coördinator of diverging minds; it was quite the same whether he was dealing with the manifold personalities of his Bauhaus period, in the CIAM (Congrès Internationaux d'Architecture Moderne), where there is also no lack of individual opinions, with the Harvard students, or finally with the team of architects with whom he works.

That the Bauhaus managed to survive from 1919 until 1928 under his direction, during what were the most crucial years for the development of the new architecture, can only be ascribed to an act of faith which might be compared to building a house while one raging storm after another kept blowing away the mortar before it had time to set. And this miracle of tenacity was accomplished in a Germany crippled by inflation, where, under the mask of resurgent nationalism, the advent of the future Nazi state was ominously heralded.

It has often been said that the Bauhaus rationalized the teaching of modern art by a pedantic bottling of its various manifestations into neatly labeled compartments. But Gropius had something completely different in mind when he founded the Bauhaus in 1919. His leading idea then was: "The Bauhaus strives to coördinate all creative efforts in art into a new unity." In 1923 in its first large publication, *Staatliches Bauhaus in Weimar 1919–1923*, the idea was further evolved: "The guiding principle of the Bauhaus was the idea of creating a new unity of the welding together of many 'arts' and movements: a unity having its basis in Man himself and significant only as a living organism."

In autumn 1947, speaking at the Sixth CIAM Congress at Bridgewater, England, after ten years of having directed the work for the master's degree in architecture at Harvard, Gropius summed up his experience in this field, and what he had to say was the natural outgrowth of the concepts of his youth. And it was not only relevant for the training of the architect but for the reform of educational methods as a whole:

"In architectural education the teaching of a method of approach is more important than the teaching of skills. . . . The integration of the whole range of knowledge and experience is of the greatest importance right from the start; only then will the totality of aspect make sense in the student's mind. . . . Such an educational approach would draw the student into a creative effort to integrate simultaneously design, construction, and economy of any given task with its social ends."

There are certain highly skilled mechanics in the Detroit automobile factories who work behind protective glass screens. It is their job to make the jigs and tooling which later on will be used for turning out millions of component parts needed for next year's models. In much the same way, a little body of picked architectural students is now being trained in some of the leading American universities and technical institutes to leave its impress on the life of the nation in the immediate future.

Later Development

When Walter Gropius was seventy he said, "I am still building practically nothing." When he was eighty, he saw himself laden with prizes, honors, and so many commissions that they could scarcely be accomplished. The same fate has befallen almost all pioneers of contemporary architecture.

Frequently our period has allowed itself to be overtaken by reality. Its decision makers are seldom prepared for eventualities. Usually they are incapable of recognizing early enough which solutions bear within them the seeds of future development. In the United States since the fifties a wholly unexpected urge developed for urban renewal, without anyone dar-

512

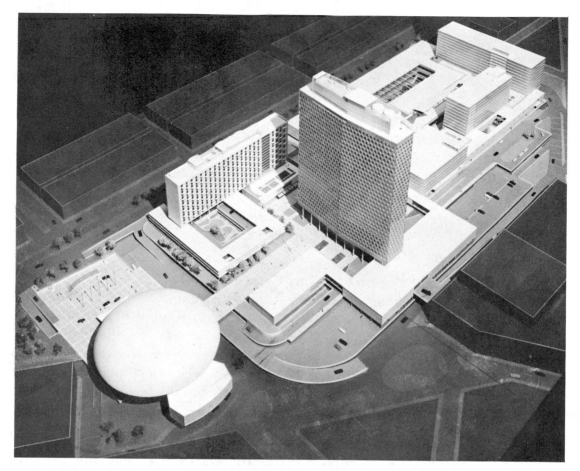

306. WALTER GROPIUS. Project for Back Bay Center, Boston, 1953. *A well organized complex dominated by the high-rise office block; balanced relationships between buildings of different heights with different functions. A wide pedestrian bridge links the Center with a convention hall. If this project had been implemented it would have been the finest American urban center.*

ing to say that this would require new solutions. Prototypes that could give three-dimensional reality to new ideas were not fully developed. They existed only on paper and in small models that remained unrealized.

One project that, had it been realized, could have served as prototype for a new city center was the Back Bay Center for Boston, 1953 (*fig.* **306**). It was designed by a group of university professors including Gropius. It is a sign of Gropius' temperament that he can work on a project as part of a team and yet in the final design the hand of the master can be felt.

Boston Back Bay Center, 1953

The Back Bay Center is a well articulated complex. The largest office building dominates the grouping but does not oppress it. Its façades meet at an obtuse angle to mitigate its volume and massivity, as in Le Corbusier's design for a tall office building for Algiers (1934) and in Gropius' later Pan American Building in New York. But in New York this immense high-rise building stands alone, flanked by haphazard structures. In Boston the office building stands as the dominant structure of a well coordinated complex of buildings with different functions. A wide pedestrian bridge links the Center to a large convention hall. In the middle of a congested, traffic-ridden metropolis, this center would have been a pedestrian's paradise.

The Boston Back Bay Center falls into the category of projects whose importance was recognized too late. Short-sighted politicians prevented its realization with the threat of impossibly heavy taxation. Then, on the same site over the freight yards of the Boston and Albany railroad — a site whose potential was first recognized by a class of Harvard architectural students in a project that provided the impetus for this urbanistic leap forward — rose the Prudential Center, a purely profit-making structure of no urbanistic interest.

Since its inception in 1945, the work of TAC has grown greatly. In 1957 it undertook the tremendous project of Baghdad University, beset by local difficulties in building construction and dramatic shifts in the political structure of the country. There was also the Pan American Building (1958–63) rising high over Grand Central Station in New York. Though its size gave rise to heated controversy, its structural sensitivity cannot be denied. In 1962 Gropius was asked to prepare a master plan for a sector for fifty thousand people in West Berlin: a commission such as the struggling, combative Gropius of 1930 could never have dreamt of. This sector bears his name — Gropiustown.

American Embassy in Athens, 1956–61

Only one building from the 1953–64 period is selected here for detailed comment: the American Embassy in Athens. In it

514

Walter Gropius' hand is particularly evident. In the Fagus factory (1911), Walter Gropius had introduced several definitive elements of contemporary architecture and presented the first uncompromising manifestation of the non-bearing glass curtain wall. Transparency was raised to monumentality in the upper stories of the Dessau Bauhaus (1926). In the embassy in Athens this approach, passed over for half a century, is again followed. Both transparency and the glass walls are retained but they are integrated with the organization of the whole building. Around the square embassy run free-standing, marble-clad columns. The cornice projects hoveringly, casting a shadow, but leaving a wide slit open as an air vent, so that the accumulated heat can escape upward.

What can be seen at first sight is that an embassy, whose business obliges it to house many secrets, here presents a friendly and welcoming appearance. One is drawn through the open colonnade to an inner court also surrounded by columns like those outside (*fig.* **310**). This inner court is a patio perforated on two sides and thus directly linked to the outer space.

The embassy is placed on a rise beside a main thoroughfare. Steps, landings, and low railings direct one into the inner court and up to a glass wall through which one enters the embassy. The cube-shaped structure has no specially emphasized façade. The same elements occur on all four sides: the surrounding columns, the projecting cornice and wide air vent, and the recessive glass walls. The two main entrances are only spatially emphasized: one, the pedestrian entrance from the main thoroughfare, by steps and landings (*fig.* **307**); the other, the official driveway entrance (*fig.* **309**), by its high level and by a large hovering canopy which runs inward under the building.

This building expresses the outcome of a general development since 1911 which is not confined to Walter Gropius. It is expressed not in a negative approach but in pressing forward solutions to once-opened problems: the relation between enclosure and perforation, between differentiation and a more distinct repetition of single parts, and the ability of the architect to integrate all these elements into a spiritual entity.

307. WALTER GROPIUS. American Embassy, Athens, 1956–61. *The building is raised on a platform. The pedestrian entrance from the main road leads directly up a flight of steps into the interior court. A line of white marble above the black marble of the supporting wall shows the level of the court and of the automobile entrance.*

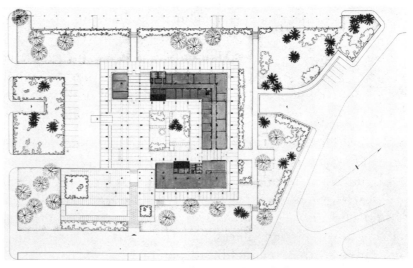

308. American Embassy, Athens, 1956–61. *Ground plan.*

309. American Embassy, Athens, 1956–61. *Automobile entrance above which hovers a long projecting canopy.*

310. American Embassy, Athens, 1956–61. *The perforated interior court. The architectural structure, interior and exterior, is identical on all four sides: continuous squared columns, projecting cornice, wide air vent, set-back glass walls. The photograph shows the degree to which the interior court is opened up and the direct relationship between the interior and the exterior.*

311. The young Le Corbusier at La Chaux-de-Fonds.

LE CORBUSIER AND THE MEANS OF ARCHITEC-TONIC EXPRESSION

Le Corbusier (Charles Edouard Jeanneret) was born in 1887 in the watchmaking town of La Chaux-de-Fonds in the Swiss Jura Mountains.[1] The Jeannerets had lived there since the fourteenth century. The family trace their descent from the

---

[1] It was in this region that the astonishing automaton — the writing doll (fig. 86) — was produced.

518

Albigenses, that heretical sect from the south of France that was hunted down and forcibly expelled from the country.

Just as Le Corbusier's handwriting appears even in the stained-glass windows of the chapel at Ronchamps, so Le Corbusier from very early days inserted his personal life and experiences in his writings. In his book *L'Art décoratif d'aujourd'hui* (Paris, 1925) is a chapter entitled "Confession" which gives an intimate insight into his youth. He describes how his father, an enthusiastic mountain climber, took him up to a summit of the Jura Mountains: "We were frequently on the peaks. The immense horizon was a customary experience" (p. 197). Much later he reasserted this impression when he demanded: the horizon must be captured. In connection with Ronchamps, not very far from the Jura Mountains, he spoke of an *architecture acoustique*. Here one may note that his mother was a pianist. Le Corbusier was very close to her, as is touchingly witnessed in his charming little book, *Une petite maison* (Zurich, 1954).

Le Corbusier's father was a designer of watch dials. Le Corbusier also learned this trade. He always wore a watch whose face he had engraved himself. When he was thirteen and a half he entered the trade school of La Chaux-de-Fonds. There he found a teacher, L'Eplatenier, who opened his eyes. Le Corbusier never forgot that it was this man who awoke in him a recognition of masterpieces in art, who brought him close to architecture, who led him to the direct observation of life, and who aroused in him the impulse to make sketches everywhere and of everything.

In his work, Le Corbusier showed the instinctive prescience of genius by turning up wherever new things were being done, or wherever a stimulating relationship to a bygone era could be established. From 1909 to 1910 he was in Paris, learning to use ferroconcrete in Perret's atelier. At Berlin he worked in the studio of Peter Behrens. His first published book — an examination and criticism of the German industrial art movement — was a product of this experience.[2] He saw Vienna and the Wiener Werkstätte, but made his excuses when Josef

Relations to his contemporaries

---

[2] *Étude sur le mouvement d'art décoratif en Allemagne* (Chaux-de-Fonds, 1912).

Hoffman (Otto Wagner's best-known pupil) asked him to come and work with him.

Instead Le Corbusier set out — with empty pockets — on a long voyage, *le voyage utile*, as he called it. From Paris he journeyed through the Balkans to Asia Minor and Greece, then on to Rome and back to Paris. From the white houses indigenous to Mediterranean culture, from the Acropolis of Athens, from the city of Istanbul, and from St. Peter's in Rome, he derived just the assistance he needed for his later development. It was in effect a voyage of discovery — a grand tour — through the source countries of western civilization.

This immersion in past periods and cultures exerted a decisive influence on Le Corbusier's entire work. He was able to see the relation of the structures of a specific period to the period's contemporary life, both seen and unseen, openly expressed and striving for expression.

Yet another influence must be mentioned: Le Corbusier's contact with (and share in) modern painting. Contemporary painting was at the high point of its development in 1917, the year Le Corbusier finally returned to Paris. He had the advantage not merely of living there at this time but of being himself a painter.

Le Corbusier recorded in his " Confessions" how he wandered through the museums and what he was searching for. He was not so much interested in works of the old masters as in works of primitive and prehistoric art — woven carpets and carved idols — such as the objects André Malraux presented ten years later in his *Musée imaginaire.*

Our specialized period rarely produces a combination of painter and architect in the same person. Le Corbusier was one of the exceptions; in his scheme of daily work the morning was devoted to painting, the afternoon to architecture. Architectural creations came easily to him, but he continued always to struggle with painting. The foundation of his work in both

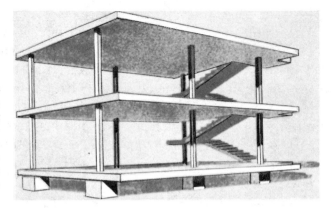

312. LE CORBU-SIER. Ferroconcrete skeleton for a dwelling house, 1915. *Le Corbusier was able to transmute the concrete skeleton developed by the engineer into an architectural means.*

fields was his conception of space. Architecture and painting were merely two different instruments through which he expressed the same conception.

The spirit of Le Corbusier's houses shows an absolute identity with the spirit that animates modern painting. The floating transparency achieved in the works of modern painters finds its echo in Le Corbusier's own paintings (*fig.* **313**). He himself assured us in his *Peinture moderne* [3] that he had deliberately chosen the most uninteresting of objects — bottles, drinking glasses, and the like — so that attention would not stray away from the actual painting. A historian is not likely to view this choice as an accident, however. He sees in it a preference for floating, transparent objects whose mass and outlines flow into each other in a *mariage des contours* that leads us from Le Corbusier's pictures to his architecture (*fig.* **314**).

Interrelations between his architecture and modern painting

Around 1910 Picasso and Braque, as the consequence of a new conception of space, exhibited the interiors and exteriors of objects simultaneously. In architecture Le Corbusier developed, on the same principle, the interpenetration of inner and outer space. We have already observed gropings toward such an interpenetration in the seventeenth-century buildings of Francesco Borromini. But this interpenetration of space at large and space-particles could have further development only in an age whose science and art both perceived space as essentially many-sided and dynamic.

[3] Amedée Ozenfant and Le Corbusier (Paris, 1925).

Le Corbusier took ferroconcrete as the instrument for the expression in architecture of his ideas.[4] In this he joined the French tradition, continuing the work of Auguste Perret and Tony Garnier. It was only in France that architects could use ferroconcrete unrestrictedly and without hesitation. Building legislators in Germany and England distrusted elegant constructions in reinforced concrete and insisted upon an unnecessary bulkiness. The French had always sought for lightness and precision in their buildings, and they made corresponding laws.

313. LE CORBUSIER. "Still Life," 1924. *Oil. Like the cubists, Le Corbusier and Ozenfant were greatly interested in commonplace objects and in the problems of transparency. The "mariage des contours" between the different objects and outlines in this painting points ahead to the interpenetrations of inner and outer space which Le Corbusier achieved later in his buildings.*

The real starting point of LeCorbusier's career was a drawing dated 1915 (*fig.* **312**). It shows nothing but six reinforced

---

[4] Thanks to the early initiative of the Zurich publisher Dr. Hans Girsberger, and to the loyal care taken by the architect Willy Boesiger, Le Corbusier's works since 1910 have been set out in *Le Corbusier, Œuvre complète.* seven volumes (with slight variations in title), published in Zurich in 1929, 1934, 1938, 1949, 1953, 1957, and 1965.

concrete pillars and three horizontal slabs which are connected by a mere hint of a staircase. Le Corbusier was able — as no one before him had been — to transmute the concrete skeleton developed by the engineer into a means of architectonic expression. He knew how to bring out the secret affinity that existed between ferroconcrete construction and the human needs and cravings that were just coming to the surface.

To create houses of unprecedented lightness and to carry still further the kind of "open planning" which Frank Lloyd Wright

314. LE CORBUSIER and P. JEANNERET. Settlement houses at Pessac, near Bordeaux, 1926. *In this early experimental work, Le Corbusier played with screens, volumes, light, shadow, and color. Soon to be followed by solutions of great plastic sureness.*

had begun, Le Corbusier used those properties of the supporting framework of reinforced concrete which make the disposition of the inner walls a matter of choice.

The problem of the dwelling was the unequivocal center of Le Corbusier's early work, both theoretical and practical. His first house, built in the Swiss Jura in 1916, was externally of conventional form. It already showed, however, the reinforced concrete skeleton which appeared in all its successors. The skeleton was actually turned to the purposes of housing.

Le Corbusier laid down five points of liaison between contemporary architecture and contemporary construction:

1. *The pillar*, which is to be left free to rise through the open space of a dwelling.

Such a use of the pillar had been made early in the nineteenth century by John Nash. Henri Labrouste in 1843 had also used a free-standing cast-iron pillar in one of the rooms of his Bibliothèque Sainte-Geneviève. Le Corbusier used the free pillar with a difference, however: through the girders of the framework it takes up all the load in the structure and leaves the walls with nothing to support.[5] This leads directly to Le Corbusier's second principle.

2. *The functional independence of skeleton and wall*, in the case not only of the outer walls but of the inner partitions also.

William Le Baron Jenney, in the first true skeleton construction, his Leiter Building of 1889 (Chicago), also took advantage of the complete freedom this type of framework building permitted in the disposition of the nonsupporting inner walls. Victor Horta, in his house in the Rue de Turin (1893), and Perret, in his house in the Rue Franklin (1903), gave impetus to the flexible treatment of the ground plan which the mutual independence of the separate stories made possible.

3. *Le plan libre.* Le Corbusier converted the ferroconcrete skeleton from a technical device into an aesthetic means. Le Corbusier used the partition walls to model the interior space of the house in the most varied manner, employing curved staircases and curving or flat partition walls for both functional and expressive purposes. The same means allowed him to hollow out large portions of the house, and to bring about interpenetrations of outer and inner space which are unfamiliar and daring.

This whole treatment, the completely free and individualized organization of separate stories, is what is meant by "open

---

[5] The machine shop which Walter Gropius built at the Fagus works in 1914 also placed the steel columns behind the outer wall.

planning" or *le plan libre*. By now the difference between the open planning of Frank Lloyd Wright and that of European architects should be apparent. The work of the latter was based upon the new conception of space as essentially many-sided which grew out of cubism.

4. *The free façade*, which is a direct consequence of skeleton construction.

5. *The roof terrace*. Frank Lloyd Wright's houses demand that we go around them if we wish to understand their formation. Now a house can be looked at from above or below; in a sense it presents a surface that opens on the sky. The flat roof is a recognition of a spatial extension of the house. It was used by Le Corbusier for single family houses in his early period, in the twenties and thirties. It was later developed more widely, as in the plastically modeled roof top of the Unité d'Habitation in Marseille, 1947–52 (*fig.* **326**).

The Villa Savoie, 1928–30

Since 1922, when he first began to build regularly, Le Corbusier made use of and developed these five principles.[6] The experience gained in the construction of several private homes enabled him to use them in his work in more and more clarified form. They appear at their purest, perhaps, in his Villa Savoie, built at Poissy in 1928–30.

All Le Corbusier's houses attack the same problem. He was always endeavoring to open up the house, to create new possibilities for connections between its interior and exterior and within the interior itself. We want rooms which can be thrown open or enclosed at will, rooms whose outer partitions fall away when we wish. Briefly, it is a question of achieving dwellings of a sort which, up to then, had been beyond the reach of conception and execution alike. The armature construction was here in secret alliance with our half-realized desires; it anticipated them, in fact.

Previously, Le Corbusier's houses had been built on rather cramped plots, in more or less close proximity to their neigh- The site

[6] Cf. S. Giedion, "Le Corbusier et l'architecture contemporaine," *Cahiers d'art*, V (Paris, 1930), 205–215.

315. LE CORBUSIER and P. JEANNERET. Villa Savoie at Poissy, 1928–30.

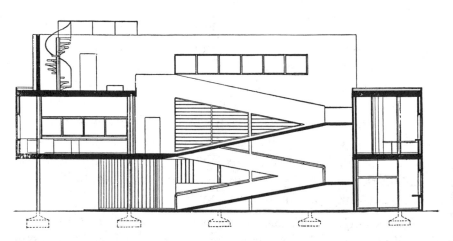

316. LE CORBUSIER and P. JEANNERET. Villa Savoie, 1928–30. *Cross section. The hollowing out of the house from above and from below is accomplished with astonishing sureness.*

526

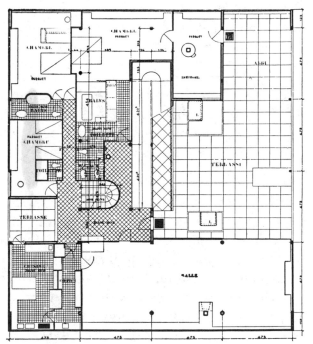

317. LE CORBU–
SIER and P. JEAN–
NERET. Villa Savoie,
1928–30. *View of ter-
race and roof garden,
and ground plan. Large
glass areas of the living
room are directed toward
the great terrace, which
gives the landscape as
well as the sky only in
silhouette. The ramp
leads from the first to
the second floor inside
the house and from the
second floor to the roof
garden outside.*

bors. The site of the Savoie house, on the contrary, was completely isolated (*fig.* **315**).

This attempt to renew our connections with nature raises the same fundamental questions wherever we build, by the sea-shore, in the mountains, or — as in this case — on the undulating expanses of the Seine valley just outside Paris.

At one period in his development Frank Lloyd Wright used to employ the smallest crevices in the rocks to help bind his houses still more closely to the earth. In the Savoie house Le Corbusier did exactly the opposite. The city-dweller for whom it was designed wanted to look out over the countryside rather than to be set down among trees and meadows. He wanted to enjoy the view, the breezes, and the sun — to experience that unhurried natural freedom which his work deprived him of. This is another instance of two eternally opposed responses to nature: a contemporary reflection of the difference between the Greek temple, sharply outlined against its background, and the medieval town, attached like a plant to the site on which it stands.

The structure   This house is a cube elevated on pillars. The cube part is not a solid mass; it is hollowed out on both the southeast and southwest sides so that when the sun comes up the light floods the whole interior instead of merely skimming the outer wall.

The entrance hall is on the northwest, but in coming in from the road one has to go all around the south side of the house to reach it. Of course there is really no façade and no back or front, since the house is open on every side.

The living room — five meters by fourteen — has horizontally sliding windows on two sides. The third wall (facing onto the terrace) is glass from floor to ceiling for some two-thirds of its length (*fig.* **317**). Half of this glass partition can be slid back by an easily manipulated lever. As a result, the room can be arranged quite freely, while the occupant is brought into connection with both the interior and the outdoors. The surrounding landscape, however, never appears in its full sweep. It is always shown in segments — framed, as it were — not only in the interior rooms but also on the terrace.

The ramp in the Savoie house is in two sections (*fig.* **316**): one wing is inside; the other wing continues along an outer wall to the roof garden. Besides the ramp, there is a spiral staircase which leads from the ground to the roof.

The use of a ramp as a means of linking different horizontal levels with interior and exterior spaces can be followed in Le Corbusier's work up to his latest buildings. In the Capitol of Chandigarh it appears in both the High Court of Justice and the Secretariat. In the Visual Arts Center of Harvard University (1963) the ramp perforates straight through the building (*fig.* **330**).

It is impossible to comprehend the Savoie house by a view from a single point; quite literally, it is a construction in space-time. The body of the house has been hollowed out in every direction: from above and below, within and without. A cross section at any point shows inner and outer space penetrating each other inextricably.

Borromini had been on the verge of achieving the interpenetration of inner and outer space in some of his late baroque churches. This interpenetration was first realized in our period, through the methods of modern engineering, with the Eiffel Tower of 1889. Then, in the late twenties, it became possible to achieve it in a dwelling. This possibility was latent in the skeleton system of construction, but the skeleton had to be used as Le Corbusier used it: in the service of a new conception of space. That is what he meant when he defined architecture as *construction spirituelle*.

The neglect of the Villa Savoie is unfortunately typical of the fate of many of Le Corbusier's buildings, and not only of his. One has only to remember the fate of the Dessau Bauhaus, which was treated disgracefully by both the Nazis and the Communists, and the Frank Lloyd Wright Robie house. The Villa Savoie was used as a hayloft during the German occupation and was severely damaged. In 1959 it was taken over by the municipality of Poissy, which planned to demolish it and erect a school in its place. At the last moment it was saved by the Minister André Malraux and placed under protection as a scheduled monument. Like the Maison La Roche, it is now part of the *Fondation Le Corbusier*, which receives all proceeds from the sale of Le Corbusier's writings and paintings.

The League of Nations Competition, 1927: Contemporary Architecture Comes to the Front

The 1927 international competition for the League of Nations Palace at Geneva is one of the most illuminating episodes in the history of contemporary architecture. For the first time present-day architects challenged the routine of the Academy in a field which it had dominated for generations, the design of monumentally impressive state buildings. The Academy won this particular engagement, but its victory injured the prestige of its methods.

The conventional routines showed themselves incapable of producing architectonic solutions to problems of modern organization. The proof of that helplessness did much to break down popular resistance to modern treatments.

It was plain from the start that, among the 337 projects submitted, one — the work of Le Corbusier and Pierre Jeanneret — was peculiarly important and significant. Later developments verified this first judgment.

What made it important? It unexpectedly forced high officials from everywhere in Europe to consider seriously a kind of architecture which they had always dismissed as aesthetic trifling. For decades there had been an established style for the stately official building — an international style that hardly varied from country to country. Custom had made its validity seem guaranteed for all time, and the official element automatically turned to it when the matter of their Geneva setting came up. The scheme that came to the forefront, however, shockingly disregarded the stylistic approach in order to tackle specific problems.

Program   The idea of a league of nations is one which we encounter time and again in history. Its realization, however — the actual establishment of a neutral center where representatives of every country might meet to maintain the equilibrium of the world — was a completely new thing and brought a highly

530

complex institution into being. Its varied functions required a division of its headquarters into three main parts: a secretariat, where the daily work of its administration could be carried on; a meeting place for committees of various sorts whose sessions occurred intermittently (the *Conseil* and the *Grandes Commissions*); and a hall for the yearly sitting of the *Assemblée générale*. Besides this, a great library was needed in the whole complex.

The outstanding fact about the scheme submitted by Le Corbusier and Jeanneret [7] is that they found the most compact and best-conceived solution to these needs (*fig.* **318**).[8]

Le Corbusier's scheme

The Secretariat (*fig.* **321**), the great administration building near the entrance to the grounds, was given a slender wing which paralleled the lake. The rows of horizontally sliding windows gave every clerk or typist an unimpeded view over water and mountains. A roof garden was available for rest periods. The building had a ferroconcrete skeleton and seemed to hover above its site on supporting pillars set back of the curtain walls. Le Corbusier had used the same treatment, a short time before and on a smaller scale, in his Villa Cook at Boulogne-sur-Seine.

The great Assembly Building was moved forward to the lake front. Two huge expanses of glass made up its side walls. The Grande Salle des Assemblées (*fig.* **319**), meant for twenty-six hundred auditors, was designed with the needs of a large audience as the determining factors. It had to be possible to hear and see perfectly from every one of its seats. To ensure this, the ceiling was given a nearly parabolic curvature. This was on the advice of the specialist, Gustave Lyon.[9] But the ceiling is not simply introduced into the design as an acoustical aid:

---

[7] Cf. Le Corbusier, *Une Maison, un palais* (Paris, 1928). Here the architect himself explains what he was aiming at in this scheme.

[8] At the suggestion of the Friends of Modern Architecture — an association connected with the International Congress for Modern Architecture (CIAM) — Le Corbusier's plans for the palace of the League of Nations were saved and purchased by the University of Zurich in 1939. The great view of the palace (fig. 318) hangs near the mathematics seminar of the University of Zurich. The other seventeen plans are preserved in the archives and are always available for study.

[9] Lyon had already constructed the Salle Pleyel at Paris. Le Corbusier's hall was designed before the loud-speaker came into use and simplified the problem of hearing. Such methods may be called for again in the future, however. We can reasonably expect a revived demand on the part of the public for the natural tones of the human voice, unaltered by electrical transmission.

it is taken up into and influences the whole form of the hall. Le Corbusier converts what was offered simply as a technical expedient into aesthetic means. Le Corbusier went a step further in his project for the United Nations building in New York, 1947. There he included the floor in the total curvature of the space. This would have been the most inspiring interior space of our period if its realization had not been made impossible by certain political interests. The later development of the hall by others shows no trace of Le Corbusier's inspired sketch; it is merely an enormous igloo.

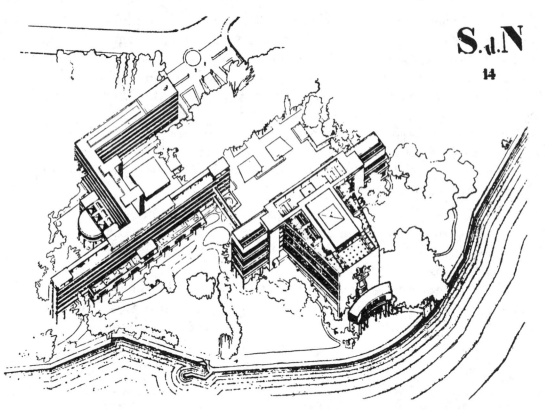

S.d.N

14

318. LE CORBUSIER and P. JEANNERET. League of Nations Palace, Geneva, 1927. *The first contemporary project for a monumental state building to gain serious attention from the public and the official element. Open planning in ferroconcrete achieved an efficient solution to a complex and variegated set of demands.*

In the treatment of the ceiling Le Corbusier unconsciously followed the example of earlier men. Thus Davioud in the seventies used a parabolic ceiling in a project for a theater of a capacity of five thousand. The Adler and Sullivan Auditorium

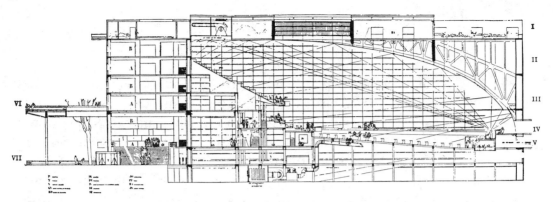

319. LE CORBUSIER and P. JEANNERET.   League of Nations Palace, 1927. *Cross section of the Grande Salle.   The ceiling has the form of an acoustic shell with polished surfaces; it is hung from bridge girders in the roof.   (The same problem was met and solved by Adler and Sullivan in their Chicago Auditorium of 1887.)   Le Corbusier takes a technical device and converts it into an aesthetic expression.*

320. LE CORBUSIER and P. JEANNERET. League of Nations Palace, 1927. *Sheltered, platform-like entrance. The loading platform has been purified in line and transformed into architecture with a classic sureness, just as the traffic ramp was in the Villa Savoie.*

of 1887 in Chicago — the finest assembly hall of its period —
is similarly modeled by considerations of acoustics.

Le Corbusier's plans show a thoroughly considered treatment
of the traffic problem. The problem was acute when the
General Assembly was in session, and it had to be possible to
move great streams of cars in short order. The rear entrance
of the Assembly Building accordingly took its form from an
everyday solution to the same difficulty — the sheltered load-

321.   LE CORBUSIER and P. JEANNERET.   League of Nations Palace, 1927. *Administration Building (Secrétariat général), rear view.*

ing platform set between two transit lines (*fig.* **320**). But once
again a purely utilitarian development is transmuted into an
expressive means. The development of such a means of expression can be seen thirty years later in the transformation
of the architectonic articulation of the flat platform roof of the
League of Nations project into the upward curving concave
shell that rises majestically above the façade of the Secretariat
Building at Chandigarh (*fig.* VII).

In the requirements of the Secretariat simply as an office building, in the need for making it possible to hear from every bench in the Grand Salle, in the traffic problems that arose at general sessions — in the needs of life, that is — Le Corbusier and Jeanneret found incentives to artistic creation.

But it was exactly those requirements which proved stumbling blocks to the architects who adopted the familiar monumental routine. The requirements of a complex new social organism like the League of Nations could not be met by schemes whose general outline was determined in advance by the need for a certain type of impressive external appearance. Everything was smothered by the ostentatious exterior, as unsuitable here as plate armor for a man driving a car. And an architecture which cannot mold itself to the needs of its own time has lost its vital force.

Program evaded academic solution

The conventionally monumental schemes broke down in another respect. At Versailles, where a great building complex was first juxtaposed to nature, unlimited space was available, and the absolute will behind this endeavor stamped its own imprint upon the surrounding landscape. At Geneva the site was strictly limited. Moreover, in this period we no longer desire to *forcer la nature:* we seek to preserve it intact and to bring it and our buildings into harmonious unity. This the academic schemes were unable to do; they found no way of avoiding extensive terracing of the site, which destroyed its natural contours and left the huge bulk of the Palace perched upon a ridiculously small pediment of lawn.

The Le Corbusier-Jeanneret project would have preserved the integrity of the plot. The flexibly arranged Assembly Building, the narrow Secretariat, the Library, and the elevated passageways connecting all three achieved a perfect adjustment to the actual site.

Means developed during previous years are here brought together in the solution of a purely contemporary social problem. The plane surfaces which a long period of development had brought to a position of dominance are joined with the new lightness and charm achieved by construction. The result is a kind of informality and flexibility such as had been attained years earlier in the ground plan of the house. A building complex is evolved which goes beyond Renaissance conceptions of space and cannot be grasped by a view from any one point. In its entirety the Palace realizes the new conception of space-time.

A confusion of architectural languages

The projects that were entered in the 1927 international competition permit an exceptionally wide survey of the state of architecture at that time. All the architectural fashions of the late nineteenth century are represented, together with all the experimental developments in contemporary architecture.

The adherents of the Academy submitted beautifully executed schemes which treated the Palace as if it were a *prix de Rome* problem worked out in the quiet of the Villa Medici. From the northern countries and from Germany there came either smooth and placidly decorative projects or Faustean expressionistic sketches in soft charcoal. The work from Italy and from eastern Europe featured cupolas or mosque-like edifices — one of which had no fewer than twenty interior light wells. And from various countries the most radical experimentalists sent plans — not always ripe for execution — of structures imbued with Russian constructivism or of dream fantasies in glass.

Although no other designs for the League of Nations building had the clear-sighted rightness of Le Corbusier's plans, there were other very considerable entries, such as those submitted by Hannes Meyer and Hans Wittwer, R. J. Neutra, E. Mendelsohn, and the Polish group Prezens. The catalogue of the projects published by the awarders is even more instructive than the catalogue of the competition for the Chicago Tribune mentioned earlier. It demonstrates that the lowest mass standards guided the judgment of designs. The jury had to thread its way through a confusion of crosscurrents, a confusion that was reflected in its own composition.

Divisions among the jurors

In fact, the state of architecture in each of the European countries appeared in its choice of a distinguished man to represent it on the jury. Those countries which had witnessed genuine struggles for a new architecture sent men who had stood in the midst of the fighting. The Dutch sent H. P. Ber-

536

lage; the Austrians, Josef Hoffmann; the Belgians, Victor Horta. Switzerland was represented by Karl Moser, the man whose efforts brought about the present high standard of architectural education in that country.

The opposition, not only on the jury but in political circles, came from countries which the thirty-year war for a new architecture had scarcely touched — countries like England and France, where the new movements had no influence upon the public or upon state functionaries. The English juror was Sir John Burnett; the French was M. Lemaresquier, one of the heads of the Académie. He was the most active and influential member of the academic party. It was he who prevented the consideration of Le Corbusier's project on the trivial ground that he had submitted blueprints instead of original drawings. Lemaresquier was supported by Aristide Briand, the French president of the Council of the League of Nations, and an inflexible opponent of contemporary architecture.

Berlage, Hoffmann, and Moser made up the group favoring the choice of a work in the modern spirit; with the support of Horta they would have constituted a clear majority. And there was an intimate connection between Baron Horta's early productions and the work of the younger architects. His house in the Rue de Turin of 1893 and his Maison du Peuple of 1897 had signaled the whole of Europe to abandon methods that were in opposition to the times. For all that, Horta joined the advocates of the conventions and made it impossible for a nonacademic project to be selected for execution. Le Corbusier's project was one of these. The task of making the final choice was passed on to the diplomatic arm.

The jury finally reached a verdict by awarding nine first prizes *ex aequo*. Not unreasonably, some of the diplomats regarded this action as an evasion of duty on the part of the jury. As a last compromise, the creators of four schemes in the established international monumental style were selected to collaborate in a final version.[10]

---

[10] Further complications arose when a new and larger site was made available for the Palace. In the effort to satisfy the daily needs of the League while at the same time retaining a majestic interior, several plans were drawn up. In the end it was found that

A new type of social organization, such as the League of Nations, could not acquire a meaningful physical setting by incorporating elements borrowed from Le Corbusier's project in a formally academic architectural complex. In consequence the Palace of the League of Nations has proved almost unusable. This principle holds good for architecture, and perhaps also for politics. In 1927 the following comment appeared under my name in the Berlin journal *Bauwelt* (p. 1096): "A League of Nations building that ties itself to the ghosts of history is likely to become a haunt of ghosts."

We have paid particular attention to the League of Nations Palace because it served as the general public's first introduction to contemporary architecture. The same year also marked its introduction to modern solutions of the housing problem. It was in 1927 that the Deutsche Werkbund put Mies van der Rohe in complete charge of the Weissenhof settlement at Stuttgart. Mies van der Rohe entrusted the design of the houses to those architects from all over Europe who had been most active in the new developments. The elimination of Le Corbusier's project for the League of Nations was one of the reasons for founding the CIAM in 1928.

The Centrosoyus, Moscow

Le Corbusier's Geneva plan remained a project, but the principles embodied in it were partially realized in the Centrosoyus at Moscow (1928–34). The erection of the Centrosoyus — now the Ministry of Light Industry — was retarded partly by the requirements of the Five-Year Plan and partly by the emergence of an architectural reaction. It was one of the last modern structures erected in Russia.

Le Corbusier's design for the Palace of the Soviets (1931) fell within the period of Stalinist reaction. With the ceiling of the great hall suspended on wire cables from a parabolic curve (*fig.* **433**), it was Le Corbusier's boldest accomplishment up to that time. In 1931 the realization of this project or any of the other contemporary schemes, such as those by Gropius and

the only possible solution was to follow Le Corbusier's general layout. This general arrangement the architects treated in a spirit of routine that shows in their use of colorless academic shapes to produce a formal exterior appearance. In 1937, ten years after the competition was held, the building was opened and put into service. Everyone, from typists to diplomats, agreed that it was a failure.

538

Breuer and by the sculptor Gabo, was no longer conceivable in the U.S.S.R.

Large Constructions and Architectural Aims

In Paris, at about the same time, two large constructions by Le Corbusier appeared in quick succession: the Salvation Army hospice (1929–33) and the Swiss Pavilion of the University City (1931–33). Both show additions to Le Corbusier's equipment of aesthetic means.

The pavilion of the Swiss dormitory is one of Le Corbusier's freest and most imaginative creations. The whole building is supported by immense ferroconcrete pillars which run deep into the soil to the underlying rock. One side of the building consists of the glass curtain wall of the studios; the other is modeled carefully in a curved wall of rugged stone. To the best of our knowledge this was the first time that the curved wall again came into use in modern architecture (*fig.* **322**).[11]

But what strikes one from the very first as extraordinary is the molding of volumes and space in the entrance hall. Although the room at his disposal was relatively limited, the imagination of the architect has created a space that is living, free, and vast. In the inventiveness it displays it is comparable to the work of the great periods. It is significant that the means employed are apparently very simple: the exact placement of the staircase and the unexpected undulations in the walls (the principle of the *plan libre*).

Le Corbusier's writings — ranging in subject from painting to city planning — have had as much influence as his buildings, not only in Europe and the United States but in Latin America as well. Le Corbusier's literary connections were not even restricted to the arts. The articles in the periodical *L'Esprit nouveau* which Jeanneret (Le Corbusier) and Ozenfant published during the years 1919–25 deal with developments in every field which had a formative influence upon the thought of the period.

Le Corbusier as a writer

---

[11] For further illustrations see *Le Corbusier, Œuvre complète, 1929-1934*, vol. II (Zurich, 1934), with introduction by Sigfried Giedion.

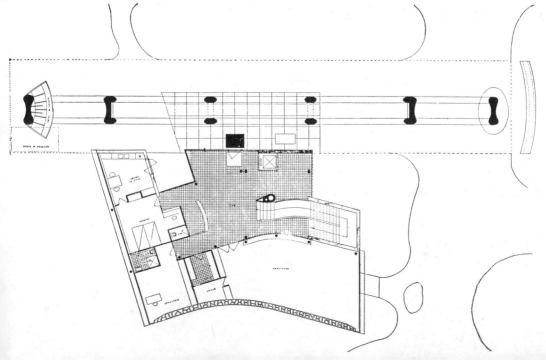

Le Corbusier had two great gifts: he could reduce a complicated problem to astonishingly simple basic elements, and he could summarize those results in formulas of lapidary clearness. But however summary the manner of treatment might be, basic concepts and principles were never lost sight of. The first three chapters of Le Corbusier's *Vers une architecture* [12] cannot be ignored in any study of our time. In turning "les yeux qui ne voient pas" to the beauty of "les autos, les avions, les paquebots" he pointed out the bridge between the engineer and the architect. At the same time he found enchanting words for the beauty of the Parthenon.

On what does Le Corbusier's achievement rest? His constructions do not show Auguste Perret's precise engineering, and his houses do not match J. J. P. Oud's infinitely painstaking attention to detail. Le Corbusier approached the house with a seismographic delicacy of perception and freed it from its inherited ponderousness. It was his aim to incorporate in the house the floating counterbalance of forces, the lightness and openness, which nineteenth-century iron construction succeeded in expressing in abstract terms. He showed us how to model all the surfaces of a house — above and below as well as at the sides, a tendency that approaches the sculptural modeling of a volume on all sides around 1960.

The elements Le Corbusier used are often to be found ready to hand in industry. The pillars on which his houses are poised occur in many warehouses; the elongated window — *fenêtre en longueur* — is a familiar consequence of methods of construction used in factories. The loading platform which he incorporated in state buildings and the ramps he employed in some of his houses for an interpenetration of inner and outer space are used in many French railway stations (for example, the Gare Montparnasse).

Le Corbusier lifted these elements out of their everyday existence and changed them as the painters changed scraps of

[12] Originally published in *L'Esprit nouveau*, 1920.

←
322. LE CORBUSIER and P. JEAN-NERET. Swiss dormitory in the Cité Universitaire, Paris, 1930–32.

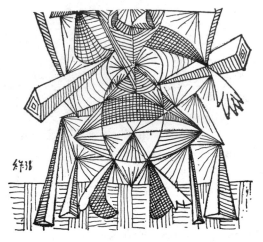

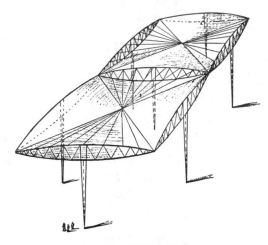

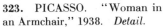

323. PICASSO. "Woman in
an Armchair," 1938. *Detail.*

324. LE CORBUSIER. Project for
exhibition at Liège, 1937.

paper into art. He fused these elements on the basis of our
spatial conception into a new architectonic language.

Social Imagination

Between 1938 and 1953 small structures and one-family houses
played no important role in Le Corbusier's development:
during this period he became more and more the creator of
large-scale designs.[13]

These projects coincided with general signs of a new humanization of urban life on the horizon. Man is no longer satisfied
to remain a mere onlooker, whether at a football game or a
television screen. His spontaneous reactions can be seen in
every part of the world during moments in which the passive
spectator has become transformed into an active participant.[14]
There is a world-wide trend toward creating centers of social
activity, and this calls for far more from the architect than
just technical capacity. His task today is infinitely more
complicated than that of his predecessors at the time when
Versailles was built. They had but to give concrete form to
an exact program placed before them by a clearly stratified

[13] For detailed information see *Le Corbusier, Œuvre complète*, vol. IV (Zurich, 1949) and
vol. V (Zurich, 1953).

[14] S. Giedion, "The Humanisation of Urban Life," in *CIAM, The Heart of the City*,
edited by Tyrwhitt, Rogers, Sert (New York, 1952).

society. Today the architect has to anticipate needs and to solve problems that exist only half consciously in the crowd. This involves a great responsibility. The architect has to have the rare gift of a peculiar sensitivity that we would like to term *social imagination*.

This is the aspect of Le Corbusier's work between 1938 and 1953 which will here be evaluated.

Le Corbusier cast the net of his vision over the chaos of the contemporary metropolis.[15] In his plans he cut thoroughfares through vested interests, demolishing whole quarters and raising them anew. Reality does not easily permit the realization of such radical operations, yet many of these plans — such as the second master plan for Algiers, 1942 [16] — will have more significance for future planners than the usual piecemeal rehabilitation.

Three landmarks stand out from Le Corbusier's work between 1938 and 1952. All of them are related to farsighted plans: The Core of St. Dié, 1945, the Unité d'Habitation, Marseille, 1947–52, and the Capitol of Chandigarh, India, since 1951.

St. Dié

The civic center of St. Dié [17] displays in a masterly way a new kind of spatial relationship. The different buildings are designed and placed in such a way that each emanates its own spatial atmosphere and yet bears a close relationship to the whole core. The area is perforated by volumes of widely different shape that continually fill in or hollow out the space like contemporary sculptures.

People walking around or sitting in the cafe that forms a corner of the square would have a continuously changing spatial experience. Theater, museum, administration center, all are freely placed in space, and the eye can even glimpse the distant old cathedral and on the opposite bank of the river green-girdled factories, *les usines vertes*, as Le Corbusier called

---

[15] S. Giedion, *A Decade of Contemporary Architecture* (Zurich, 1951), p. 201; e.g. Buenos Aires, 1938, and pilot plan for Bogotá with J. L. Sert and P. L. Wiener, 1949–50; *Le Corbusier, Œuvre complète*, V, 142–147.

[16] See *Le Corbusier, Œuvre complète*, IV, 44–65. The story of this scheme has been told by Le Corbusier himself in a small booklet *Poésie sur Alger* (Paris, 1950), with most charming sketches.

[17] *Le Corbusier, Œuvre complète*, IV, 132–139.

them. Medieval Italy knew how to place volumes in space: in the Piazza del Duomo in Pisa the cathedral, baptistry, campanile, and *camposanto* give an exciting display of volumes in space. The modest unrealized scheme of St. Dié develops a different spatial conception. The relationship in the medieval period was the relationship of formally closed volumes. Today we are moving toward a more dynamic conception of space, created by solids and voids.

The whole area of the core of St. Dié is reserved exclusively for pedestrians and this, but not only this, relates it to the Greek Agora. St. Dié, for the first time in our period, would have presented a crystallization of community life which could have equaled the Greek meeting place. All political parties of the small French city of St. Dié, including those of the extreme left, incited by the academicians, shouted so effectively against the scheme that Le Corbusier's core was condemned to remain on paper.

Architecture cannot be confined to those buildings that have been erected. Architecture is a part of life and architecture is a part of art. As a part of life it is more dependent than any other form of art upon the will of the public; upon their desire to see or not to see a scheme come into being. In architecture the standard of values of the client is as important as the standards of the builder.

If in the time of the Parthenon, the Pantheon, Chartres, or St. Peter's the taste of those who had power to order the erection of public buildings had been as weak and debased as it is today, none of them would ever have been built. They were daring experiments, all of them.

The Unité d'Habitation, 1947–52

One of the few instances where social imagination has been given three dimensional expression is the "Unité d'Habitation," 1947–52 — the residential unit — on the Boulevard Michelet in the outskirts of Marseille. The Marseillais call it simply "Maison Le Corbusier." That this daring building could be successfully completed during five difficult postwar years is due to the courage of M. Claudius Petit, the French

Minister of Reconstruction, who defended it to the very last against violent attacks, and who on the opening day in October 1952 decorated Le Corbusier with the Legion of Honor upon the roof of the Unité d'Habitation.

The housing problem begins to take on a wider meaning. Both architect and planner are now working to rebuild the broken relationship between the individual and the collective spheres.

The boldness of the Unité d'Habitation does not consist in housing some 1600 people under one roof or even in providing twenty-three different types for its 337 apartments varying from one room up to dwellings for "families with eight children." Its boldness consists in its social implementation. The most interesting experiment in this residential unit was to take the shopping center from the ground and from the street and to place it on the central floor of the building itself. From outside, this central shopping street — *la rue marchande* — can be immediately identified by its two-story louvers. These, together with the vertical rows of square staircase windows in the middle of the block, vitalize and give scale to the whole front. The shopping street includes shops for groceries, vegetables, meat and fish, laundry and cleaning services, hairdresser and beauty shop, newspaper stand, post-office, cafeteria, and hotel rooms. On the seventeenth floor is placed the nursery for 150 children. A ramp leads directly to the roof terrace with its rest room on pilotis, its shallow pool, and some charming installations for the children, who are encouraged to decorate the walls with their own murals.

The other part of the 24 × 165 meter roof terrace is designed for social activities of the adults. There is an area for gymnastics, partly open and partly covered, and, at the north end of the building, a large slab which acts as a protection against the strong north wind — the *Mistral* — and also as a background for open-air theatrical performances. On July 26th 1953, when CIAM celebrated its twenty-fifth anniversary on the roof terrace of the Unité d'Habitation, it looked like a painting of Paolo Veronese, for all the different levels were filled with people, and architecture was vibrant with life.

325. LE CORBUSIER. Unité d'Habitation, Marseille, 1947–52. *Detail.*

The features that make the Unité d'Habitation so rare an architectural spectacle are its plastic qualities. In the hands of Robert Maillart, reinforced concrete lost its rigidity and became almost an organic skeleton, where every particle throbbed with life. In the hands of Le Corbusier the amorphous material of crude concrete — *béton brut* — assumed the features of natural rock. He did not smooth away the marks and hazards of the form work and the defects of bad craftsmanship which, as Le Corbusier stated in his opening address, "shout at one from all parts of the structure." The use of the

326. LE CORBUSIER. Unité d'Habitation, Marseille, 1947–52. *View, and cross sections.*

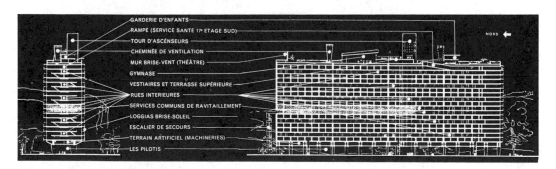

GARDERIE D'ENFANTS
RAMPE (SERVICE SANTE 17ᵉ ETAGE SUD)
TOUR D'ASCÉNSEURS
CHEMINÉE DE VENTILATION
MUR BRISE-VENT (THÉÂTRE)
GYMNASE
VESTIAIRES ET TERRASSE SUPÉRIEURE
RUES INTERIEURES
SERVICES COMMUNS DE RAVITAILLEMENT
LOGGIAS BRISE-SOLEIL
ESCALIER DE SECOURS
TERRAIN ARTIFICIEL (MACHINERIES)
LES PILOTIS

NORD

natural imprints of wooden boards to vitalize a concrete surface was far from new, yet it had never been used so consistently to give ferroconcrete the properties of "a natural material of the same rank as stone, wood or terra cotta." Le Corbusier continued: "It seems to be really possible to consider concrete as a reconstructed stone worthy of being exposed in its natural state." [18] In England, a few years later, there arose an architectural trend calling itself "the new brutalism" that took this approach as its starting point.

---

[18] *Le Corbusier, Œuvre complète*, V, 191.

The rough concrete surface is employed wherever it can strengthen plastic intentions, as in the herring-bone pattern of the huge supporting pilotis, left by the narrow boards that composed their wooden form work. On the roof the rough surfaces of the ventilator shafts and elevator tower, on which every change in the strong Mediterranean light plays with a peculiar intensity, help to transform these utilitarian objects into exciting plastic elements.

Strong, pure colors are used in this building, but Le Corbusier, the painter, refrained from using any colors directly upon the façade. He painted the side walls of the balconies red, green, yellow, but not the front. In this way they are made to gleam like vivid colors through gauze. Bright color is also used in all the artificially lit *rue-intérieures* and serves to lighten the dimness of these long corridors.

Site The Unité d'Habitation rises beside the road which leads to the Riviera and faces east and west. Each two-story apartment looks to both sides. To the east their view embraces an arena of the limestone mountains that can be found everywhere in Provence. To the west lie the blue waters of the Mediterranean; while directly below the eye can rest on tree tops interspersed with red-tiled southern roofs. If Cézanne was able to seize the soul of Provence in his pictures, Le Corbusier knew how to capture it within an architectural frame.

Le Corbusier, as well as everybody else, knew that the Unité d'Habitation was a daring experiment both in the plastic sense and even more in the sphere of social imagination. Even after its successful opening in the fall of 1952 the French government remained skeptical and dared not even to take the risk of renting the apartments and shops but demanded that they be sold outright, loading any risk upon the shoulders of the inhabitants and shopkeepers.

Yet there is no longer any doubt that this building has had an enormous influence in shaping the mind of the younger generation. It has also helped to liberate the mind of the architect and planner from the conception of housing as a simple addition of single units and to expand it to the wider frame of the human habitat.

548

Chandigarh

The foundation of new towns is a sign of vitality and of an enterprising courage. New towns are often related to higher living standards or to the promise of them. This was the case during the Gothic period, when new towns suddenly sprang up in central and western Europe. The same phenomenon occurred during the last century in the United States, foreshadowing its industrial hegemony.

Toward the middle of the twentieth century we are witnessing the decentralization of western culture. New energy radiates from its former fringes: Finland, Brazil, Colombia, Venezuela, Canada, to name only some areas of the centers of a new vitality. Countries which have long been slumbering begin to awake and to become active participants in an evolution which is encompassing the entire world. In this process spirits of East and West are meeting together.

In the foreword to the Japanese translation of this book we tried to give some hint of this development: "Western civilization is actually in a state of transition. Experience is slowly showing us that the rationalist and exclusively materialistic attitude upon which the latest phase of western civilization has been grounded is insufficient. Full realization of this fact leads us slowly towards a new hybrid development."

This meeting of East and West may explain why India — through the understanding of its leader Pandit Nehru — could choose a western architect for the new Capitol of Chandigarh. Yet there is also another reason. This is an inherent trend in contemporary architecture toward satisfying cosmic and terrestrial conditions and the habits which have developed naturally out of them. This explains why the forms of Brazilian architecture and Aalto's work in Finland, though so different, are both imbued with the spirit of the age. Both are regional contributions to a universal architectural conception. This attempt to meet cosmic, terrestrial and regional conditions may be termed the new regional approach. This is the method of the best contemporary architects and is fully developed in Le Corbusier's boldest architectural adventure: the Capitol of Chandigarh.

New regional approach

549

327. LE CORBUSIER. The High Court of Justice, Chandigarh, completed in March 1956.

When the Punjab was divided in 1947 between Pakistan and India, the ancient capital Lahore was attached to Pakistan. A new capital became necessary for the East Punjab with its twelve and a half million inhabitants. On a sloping plateau at the foot of the Himalayas a superb site was discovered in 1950 through airplane reconnaissance by E. L. Varma, an eminent Indian government engineer.

The new capital city was called Chandigarh after a village on the site. When complete, it will house half a million people. The first section is for a population of 150,000. Le Corbusier made the operative master plan of the city, with its many walled units, each 800 × 1,200 meters.[19] The development of these units, each surrounded by major traffic streets, was directed by Pierre Jeanneret, who continued to work in Chandigarh until his death. For the first years he was joined by Jane Drew and Maxwell Fry. The plans were carried out by a staff of Indian architects and engineers.

[19] See *Le Corbusier, Œuvre complète*, V, 128–159. The first master plan, less regular in form, was designed by Albert Mayer and Matthew Nowiczky, 1949–50. See Otto Königsberger, "New Towns in India," *Town Planning Review*, XXIII, 116 (1952).

328. LE CORBUSIER. The High Court of Justice, Chandigarh, completed in 1956. *The building is reflected in a large pool. The arcade below the butterfly roof gives the whole building something of the delicacy of Indian architecture. The perforated wall of the arcade and the downward slope of the roof serve as a natural ventilating system, permitting air to pass freely through the building, and also serve to express contemporary tendencies.*

A town planner, an architect, an artist, a sculptor, and a man with the grasp of a poet surveyed a wide empty space at the foot of the Himalayas. These five were united in one person. This is the spot where the Capitol of Chandigarh now stands. There is nothing more thrilling for the truly creative mind than to turn a dream into reality here on this myth-soaked soil. To achieve this, it may be worthwhile to have accepted a lifetime of humiliations.

We can follow line by line in Le Corbusier's sketch-book how the vision of the new Capitol crystallized, how it became a mighty monument in which, for the first time, eastern and western thought flowed into each other without a break. Western calculation, shell concrete vaulting and a butterfly roof of huge size which are normally associated with locomotive sheds and station platforms, here change under our very eyes into some dream-building of the East (*fig.* **328**).

The program for the Capitol consists of a House of Parliament, a building for the Ministries (the Secretariat), and the High Court of Justice. The Governor's Palace, in which a huge upward-curving concrete roof was used for the first time, unfortunately remains unbuilt.[20] The Secretariat (*fig.* **VII**) was completed in 1956. It was followed by the Parliament Building, whose assembly hall takes the form of an upright hyperboloid, its upper part projecting far beyond the horizontal roof. The entry to the Parliament Building, on the south side, is formed by a mighty free-standing, upward-curving shell supported on pillars (*fig.* **VII**). The High Court of Justice, with its seven chambers, was completed in 1956. Its enormous butterfly roof provides an umbrella of reinforced concrete against tropical sun and monsoon rains, which last from July to October. The huge sloping eaves stretch far out from the building. Parabolic shell vaults stiffen the structure and span the wide open entrance hall, which reaches up to the full height of the building. In this strange Palace of Justice modern techniques comply with cosmic conditions, with the country and with the habits of its people.

What astonishes the European eye is the large distances between the buildings. But there will be no dead surfaces between them. The sculptor in Le Corbusier took the opportunity to mold the enormous surface by varying levels, large pools, green lawns, single trees, artificial hills made of surplus material; and also by symbolic representations of the harmonic spiral, the daily path of the sun and other such. A dominant symbol will be the "open hand," planned to be seen from everywhere and to "turn on ball bearings like a weathercock." [21] The impress of the human hand placed upon the rock was the first artistic utterance of man. This symbol is still alive in India, and at the marriage feast friends leave the red stamp of their hands — red is the color of good luck — on the white walls of the bridal pair.

---

[20] *Le Corbusier, Œuvre complète*, V, 154.

[21] See *Le Corbusier, Œuvre complète*, V, 150, 151.

A monument in the form of an enormous hand can be found earlier in the work of Le Corbusier. It was then an aggressive and menacing hand. Now under an eastern sky it has quieted down like the hand of Buddha.

E. L. Varma, who discovered the site of Chandigarh, has given the Indian response to this symbol in a letter to Le Corbusier:

"We have a word, *Ram Bharosa*, which indicates deep faith in the ultimate — faith born of the surrender of the will to the Ultimate Source of Knowledge, service without reward and much more. I live in that faith and feel happy in the vision of the new city which is so safe and so secure in its creation in your hands.

"We are humble people. No guns to brandish, no atomic energy to kill. Your philosophy of 'Open Hand' will appeal to India in its entirety. What you are giving to India and what we are taking from your open hand, I pray, may become a source of new inspiration in our architectural and city planning. We may on our side, when you come here next, be able to show you the spiritual heights to which some of the individuals have attained. Ours is a philosophy of open hand. Maybe Chandigarh becomes the center of new thought."

Later Work

The 1953–64 period brought Le Corbusier recognition and the realization of many of his large schemes. It had taken a long time before he could build his first project, the Unité d'Habitation in Marseille. He had to wait till he was sixty years old. Then commissions multiplied, just as with the other pioneers. He had to refuse commissions that during the years of his ripe manhood he would have pursued in vain.

One of the principal reasons for this is that Le Corbusier never relinquished holding in his own hand the entire development of a project — just like a painter or a sculptor. It was for him quite unthinkable to operate an "architectural factory" with a hundred or more assistants. Like Picasso he remained a Bohemian and lived frugally. He continued to use the same drab studio he had had since his early days (at 35 Rue de Sèvres), with its cramped drafting room and four or five as-

329. LE CORBUSIER. Pilgrimage Chapel of Notre Dame du Haut, Ronchamps, 1955. *The aspirations of contemporary architecture are concentrated in this single building: a restrengthening of the sculptural approach to the handling of volumes is linked to the hollowing out of space, within and without.*

sistants. Often the working drawings for projects had to be made elsewhere.

We have to wait before it is possible to evaluate the complete significance of Le Corbusier's work. We need historical perspective in order to make a final assessment of his buildings. However, the unity of his work is already clear, even though the outward appearances of his early and late work seem so different. A cubist painting by Picasso around 1912 is very different from his "Guernica" (1937), a painting that gave lasting form to a moment in time (*fig.* **266**) — and also very different from his later female figures. The same is true of Le Corbusier's early and late work. Like Picasso, Le Corbusier had antennae that sensed coming changes. The Pilgrimage Chapel at Ronchamps, 1955 (*fig.* **329**), is outwardly very different from the Villa Savoie, 1928–30; and the Dominican Priory of La Tourette near Lyons, 1960, is very different from the La Roche house in Auteuil, 1923–24.

What does this mean?

Le Corbusier's development mirrors the unfolding of our period — an unfolding that first centered on an awareness of the possibilities that lay dormant in the new sources of strength. Le Corbusier, like Gropius and Mies van der Rohe, each in his own way, found this development led to a desire for the inter-penetration of interior and exterior space. How Le Corbusier's development coincides with that of contemporary architecture is discussed in the introduction to this book: volumes in space, sculptural tendencies, architecture and sculpture, the vaulting problem, the revitalization of the wall.

The Villa Savoie, 1928–30 (*figs.* **315–317**), represents the peak of Le Corbusier's early period, and at the same time contains elements of the period to come. It is a cube standing on a wide plain. But the cube has been hollowed out, made transparent, and raised aloft on supports. These supports are a prelude to the huge reinforced concrete pillars of the Swiss student dormitory in the Cité Universitaire of Paris, which stand in the open, supporting the whole building mass. The free-standing concrete walls on the roof terrace of the Villa Savoie, with their lightness and curvature, are an introduction to the play of volumes on the roof of the Unité d'Habitation at Marseille (1947–52).

The Philips Pavilion at the Brussels Worlds Fair (1958) was a hyperbolic-parabolic sheath. Upon the curving walls of the dark, cave-like interior a film was projected every twenty minutes, a poem of mankind by Le Corbusier accompanied by electronic music by Varese. There were other hyperbolic-parabolic constructions at the Brussels exhibition, but they lacked the inner tension of the Philips Pavilion. It was a source of inspiration for other buildings such as Kenzo Tange's bold steel wire stadium for the Olympic Games in Tokyo, 1964 (*fig.* **VI**).

In addition came buildings such as the Pilgrimage Chapel of Ronchamps, 1955 (*figs.* **V, 329**) [22] and the Dominican Priory of La Tourette near Lyons (1960), that outwardly completely changed the conventional plans of a pilgrimage church and a priory.

---

[22] For a description of its inauguration on June 25, 1955, see S. Giedion, *Architecture, You and Me.*

330. LE CORBUSIER. The Carpenter Center for Visual Arts, Harvard University, 1963. *General view of the building from Prescott Street. The ramp starts at the height of the second floor from a platform that roofs over the library book stacks of the neighboring Fogg Museum of Fine Arts.*

The Carpenter Center for Visual Arts, Harvard University, 1963

The Visual Arts Center, which would be better called the Center for Visual Education, is designed for students whose normal courses — law, economics, medicine, chemistry, theology, philosophy and so forth — have nothing to do with the creative arts. At the beginning of their studies, in their first years in college, the Center should open their eyes and teach them to see. This is an electronic age, when visual understanding is constantly growing in strength in comparison to the written word. Seeing cannot be understood merely from the aspect of optics. It is more of a psychic manifestation. This is

332. *Third floor plan showing penetration of the ramp: above, Quincy Street; below, Prescott Street.* →

331. *General view from Quincy Street. The ramp. To the right, the elevator tower. To the left, the projecting studio for two-dimensional studies.*

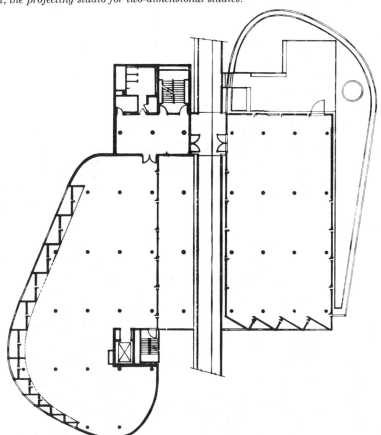

where the function of art and its means of expression come to the fore.

The Arts Center is squeezed between the University's Fogg Art Museum and the Faculty Club. The search to obtain a more open site to give the building greater room to breathe was fruitless. Thus the Center lies between two buildings and between two streets, Prescott Street and Quincy Street, with no possibility to radiate its sculptural strength.

The building consists of a central cube with curving bays that reach out to the two streets. The elevator shaft projects above the building. An outstanding feature is the S-shaped ramp which begins at both streets and tunnels through the third story of the building (*fig.* **330**). It presents a symbol of the bridge to the outer world that the Center is intended to create.

In Le Corbusier's work, ramps appear early as links between two levels, as in the marvelous interpenetration of inner and outer space of the Villa Savoie, 1928–30 (*fig.* **316**). The immediate predecessor of the Carpenter Center is the ramp of an industrial office building in Ahmedabad, 1954. As at Harvard the entry ramp is for pedestrians only, but at Ahmedabad it runs straight into the building, without curving and without penetrating through it.

The origin of the Center

Some years ago the design of an art center was given as a thesis problem in the Harvard Graduate School of Design. A student named Alfred H. Carpenter was particularly impressed by the problem. A year later he appeared at Harvard and presented the dean of the Graduate School of Design, José Luis Sert, with a check for one and a half million dollars, in the name of his father, to build a Harvard Art Center. The dean recommended that Le Corbusier be commissioned as the architect. It was the first and last commission that Le Corbusier received from the United States after his disappointing experiences with the United Nations building in New York.

Le Corbusier came only once to Harvard to examine the site and situation before he started to sketch out a design. The exact time of his arrival had not been announced; nevertheless, the entire school of architecture was at the airport to greet him. The students objected to the secrecy of the visit and took a friendly revenge. All around the walls of Robinson Hall, the center of the Graduate School of Design, rough charcoal drawings appeared, depicting a group of American Indians on the warpath tracking down signs of Le Corbusier's presence. Finally, they showed him discovered in the form of the famous Modular man, with upraised hand and a large hole through his navel; the form that Le Corbusier had used to establish his system of proportions. This was the start.

The creation of an institute for visual studies within the framework of a great university presented many difficult problems in its planning and still more in its implementation, since it dealt with the creation of a prototype. These difficulties arise from the structure of our society, from the cutting off of relations between the intellectual and emotional spheres of life — between scholarly development and artistic expression — a separation that has existed for more than a century and a half. This disastrous rift between thinking and feeling now has to be overcome.

Purpose of visual studies

We have no example of how to operate an institution that has set itself the goal of reinstating an uninterrupted relationship between thinking and feeling. Without the active participation of the most important representatives of different faculties this is not possible. The basic question is the same for all faculties: "What relations exist between my discipline and art?" We can be sure that the basis of these relationships given by the different disciplines would certainly not be the same, especially as the structures of the various sciences are so very different.

The term "Visual Arts" can easily be misunderstood. The goal is by no means to practice dilettantish painting or sculpture. All efforts should be bent to developing an emotional sensitivity and powers of artistic judgment.

A routine program, such as can fairly easily be proposed for a physics or chemical institute, does not exist for this kind of center. Thus, Le Corbusier was given no detailed instructions about programing of spaces. He was simply asked to create the maximum amount of flexible space. This involved the danger of designing the interior like a warehouse. Both the

The plan

333. The Carpenter Center for Visual Arts, Harvard University, 1963. *The studio for three-dimensional studies projects forward (see plan, fig. 332). The ramp is visible in the distance, below it on the right.*

sunlit and shadow sides of the resulting space were clear to me when in the spring of 1964 I held lectures and seminars in the Center.

The basement of the building was designed to be used as a luxurious setting for photographic and cinematic research, naturally including a projection room, which must now also be used as a lecture hall. The absence of a real lecture hall is very noticeable.

The second and third floors, with their curving walls, are used as studios (*fig.* **334**). The fourth floor, in my view, has not yet acquired its final form. If the relationship with other faculties is to be brought to life, many more seminar rooms must be created as well as a small specialized library, and also space where students and professors can talk together. Indeed, if the

334. *The studio for two-dimensional studies.*

Center is to achieve its goal it must fulfill an intellectual and scientific function.   On the fifth floor is a magnificent sculptor's studio (*fig.* **335**).

Somehow Le Corbusier was aware of the understandable incompleteness of the program.   Below the sculptural forward thrust of the working studios, under the pilotis, is a hollow space that can be vitalized only with difficulty.   Had a lecture hall been included in the program, Le Corbusier, the master of

335. *The studio of the sculptor Mirko, artistic head of the Center.*

shaping interior space, would doubtless have found a marvelous way to incorporate it into the volume of the building.

Behind us lies the tragic history of the nineteenth century, when art ceased to be the key to reality. Only when the best representatives of the faculties are convinced that a close relation between art — between psychic seeing — and science is today vitally necessary can a center of this kind succeed in its aim to educate — or just to bring an awareness to — future leaders for their later functions in life.

Bridge between thinking and feeling

The problem is anchored deep in the heart of our period. It is a long way from the specialization of today to the reinstatement of a universal viewpoint, in the absence of which any true culture is unthinkable. It lies in the incorporation into science of the realm of emotion as it is expressed in art. Happily, this need is strongly advocated not only by historians and philosophers but also by scientists. In his book *Der Mensch und die Naturwissenschaftliche Erkenntnis* (Man and the Knowledge of Natural Sciences) Professor Heitler, atomic physicist at the University of Zurich, attacks his own discipline. He affirms that the qualitative must enter alongside purely quantitative research in physics. In other words, the human factor must be included. Werner Heisenberg and the British biologist C. H. Waddington are also not afraid of including findings from the realm of art in their scholarly views of the world.

The humanization of scientific research desired by a modern physicist is just what the new Carpenter Center should move toward. It is the task of this new institution to throw a bridge across the chasm between methods of thinking and methods of feeling.

To prepare for this, a seminar of professors from different faculties was proposed, to be attended by major personalities such as Kenneth Galbraith (economics), Arthur Maass (government), David Riesman (behavioral sciences), I. A. Richards (poet and critic), José Luis Sert (architect and planner), Gyorgy Kepes (an artist who has studied optical phenomena since Bauhaus days), as well as a philosopher, a pathologist, an anatomist, a musicologist, and the faculty of the Carpenter Center.

562

At a meeting on April 30, 1964, I presented two themes for their discussion: "How can a relationship be established between the different faculties and the Carpenter Center?" and "How can the aesthetic judgment of the students be sharpened?" Everyone recognized the possibilities as well as the practical difficulties. To give one example, the anatomist pointed out that students found it very difficult to distinguish longitudinal from transverse sections under the electron microscope.

The Carpenter Center is an attempt to penetrate the unknown. If this attempt is to succeed, it needs the active and interested cooperation of the different faculties and a head for whom modern art is a living part of his being, and who also possesses intellectual and scientific insight.

Le Corbusier and His Clients

Le Corbusier epitomizes why we have again and again to reiterate what a heavy burden we have inherited from the nineteenth century, a period when the real specialists in the realm of feeling — painters, architects, sculptors — were banished from the stage of life. Their clients — people who held power — proved incapable of recognizing those who possessed the creativity and imagination to give form to the eternally changing stream of life and thus to find an answer to the inner needs of the contemporary situation. The reason for this inability lies in the discrepancy between the clients' highly developed methods of thinking and their retarded methods of feeling. The mistaken views of clients are certainly not always owing to bad will or the interests of particular cliques. Clients are unable to recognize instinctively those who carry the germs of the future and are thus able to solve new problems because their judgment often remains generations behind.

The tragic note that sounded throughout the life of Le Corbusier was the note of obstruction. He was a man who bore a message and cried it aloud only to be pushed aside again and again. He was obliged to see others achieve what he had proposed.

The exploration of a synthesis of the elements of complex problems was in his blood: from the problem of proportions to the urbanistic assembly of complex structures for world organizations — the League of Nations, the United Nations, UNESCO. In the case of the League of Nations building in Geneva (1927), it was French political intrigues that annihilated his scheme though, in the end, his rivals were obliged to imitate the organization of his site plan (see pp. 537–538).

In the case of the United Nations building in New York (1947), twenty years after the Geneva competition, the situation was completely different. The United Nations had learned something from the maneuvers of its predecessors. It abstained from an international competition and selected ten architects from different countries, of which Le Corbusier from France, Sven Markelius from Sweden, and Oscar Niemeyer from Brazil —all long-time members of CIAM—were the best known. The summer of 1947 saw them all amicably working at their drawing boards in the same room. Each contributed his part to the whole: thus Markelius designed a large housing settlement for the United Nations staff on the far side of the East River, which bordered the United Nations site. Finally, they singled out Project 23A, Le Corbusier's project, as the one to recommend for execution.

It was natural that an American had been appointed chairman of the ten — the architect Wallace K. Harrison. He had worked on the Rockefeller Center and was known as a good administrator and a reliable architect: in addition he was related to the Rockefeller family. What more could one want?

What happened? Harrison alone was named Planning Director of Project 23A. In the eyes of the client the ten had fulfilled their contract, and Harrison opened his own "UN Headquarters Planning Office." This marked the end of the happy period of the affair, which had had such a friendly and hopeful beginning.

In the twenty years since the unhappy League of Nations competition, the power of the French *Académie des Beaux Arts* had declined and Harrison was himself close to modern artists and architects. It was thus certainly not artistic opposition, but more personal ambition on the part of Harrison to build the United Nations Headquarters alone and have it associated with his name. It would have been a farsighted act if Harrison had followed objective principles and had had the modesty to make Le Corbusier a partner in the architectural office after the ten had singled out Project 23A as the one to be followed in structure and in plan. He did this in the case of the Rockefeller Center with Raymond Hood, who stood head and shoulders above the other partners and whose features the Center undoubtedly bears.

Nothing of the sort occurred. The erection of a building that should be the symbol of a future world government required the hand of a genius. Harrison put his feet in the shoes of a genius — that is, he took the outer form of Le Corbusier's sketch — but the shoes proved far too big for him: he was not able to fill them.

When the building was nearing its completion, the editor of a New York architectural journal asked for my opinion of it. I went through the whole complex with him and Harrison. But I declined to publish my opinion at that time. Among other things, I wanted first to see the building in action. However, my judgment then was no different than it is today. The great assembly hall presents a shattering helplessness as to how to handle the great space. I was further astonished, when I stood on the roof of the slab-like Secretariat block with its technical apparatus, to see that the architect could not find another way to organize it than to hide it behind an ornamental concrete screen seven stories high. It is not necessary to go into further detail to show that the United Nations building did not become the masterpiece conceived by Le Corbusier.

When things went wrong, Le Corbusier had neither the stoical calm of Mies van der Rohe nor the friendly attitude of Alvar Aalto. Le Corbusier, obsessed by his message, did his utmost to combat the injustice inflicted on him by those in power, but his efforts only made matters worse.

The third and most bitter blow was the political handling of the UNESCO building, the cultural center of the United Nations in Paris. No one would have been so qualified as Le Corbusier to design an international cultural center in the city of Paris that he loved: a structure that would spring directly from the stones of Paris and possess at the same time a universal character. This time Le Corbusier was put aside by the client in the most abrupt way. At the first meeting to deal with the choice of architects for the UNESCO building, Brazil's permanent delegate to UNESCO, Carnero, rose and emphasized that Le Corbusier was the only architect that came into question. On that, Jacobs, the representative of the United States State Department, sprang up and issued a veto with the one word: "Impossible." Unfortunately, Brazil's voice had not much influence in this case and Le Corbusier was ruled out. One must not forget that the United States paid the lion's share of the costs of the building.

To neutralize him completely, Le Corbusier was elected a member of the committee of five to choose the architect for the UNESCO building. The other members were Gropius, Markelius, Ernesto N. Rogers, and Eero Saarinen, all friends and long-time participants in CIAM. Undoubtedly Le Corbusier made their lives somewhat difficult by his hopeless endeavors somehow to take part in the building. With the best will his friends could do nothing to help him.

Le Corbusier's voice was often not listened to. Nothing hurt him so deeply as this diplomatic precaution to obviate from the beginning any risk that he might undertake the UNESCO building. Paris was the city in which he had battled throughout a lifetime. But the *Académie des Beaux Arts* and shrewd academic architects still ruled in the official circles of Paris. To them, Le Corbusier was just as nonexistent as modern art, the glory of France. In Le Corbusier's hands a building far surpassing the limited imagination of French officialdom could at last have risen in the heart of Paris.

It is further depressing to note that Switzerland determinedly overlooked the only architectural genius ever to arise from Swiss soil.

The client, it seems, is as important as the architect. He possesses the power. He decides. But what can one do when his ideals and emotional outlook are generations behind? The

566

average politician, fully absorbed in his specialized aims, has only very exceptionally an interest or even an awareness of architecture.

All his friends and colleagues knew that it wasn't easy to work with Le Corbusier. As soon as he encountered opposition or intrigue in the outside world, he lost both tactics and psychology. And yet, among the circle of his friends he was never rigid. I had plenty of experience of this during the many years of our collaboration in CIAM. He came to the first congress at the Château of La Sarraz in 1928 with his proposal for our manifesto already in print. This was plucked apart, sentence by sentence (particularly by the young Swiss and Dutch), until finally with the agreement of everyone — including Le Corbusier — the document that became the Manifesto of La Sarraz was produced.

None of the really great buildings — the Parthenon; the mortuary temple of Queen Hatshepsut (that marvel of cooperation between client and architect); and St. Peter's in its various stages with Bramante, Raphael, and Michelangelo — would ever have been built if client and architect had not been on the same level of emotional development; nor would the buildings have arisen if second or third rate talents had been chosen to design them, as has been the rule in both the nineteenth and the twentieth centuries.

It was certainly not easy to work with Le Corbusier. But as soon as he had a client who understood him (because the client experienced parallel feelings within himself), Le Corbusier was able to work hand in hand with him and come to a remarkable result. This was so with the Unité d'Habitation at Marseille, whose implementation was supported by Claudius Petit. Claudius Petit, then Minister of Reconstruction, and a former leader of the French Resistance, was by profession a cabinetmaker, who showed his visitors with pride the model of a sinuous miniature commode that had marked the end of his apprenticeship. He had always the courage to back Le Corbusier against furious attacks from the press, architectural organizations, and others.

336. Part of a letter from Le Corbusier to S. Giedion written in Chandigarh on December 9, 1952.

The Pilgrimage Chapel of Ronchamps came into being thanks to the Dominican Father Couturier. In his own fashion he knew how to dispel the grave doubts of the Church.

The great problem of today's clients in the Western World — their shortsightedness, their lack of confidence and inner security — becomes clear when we turn to Chandigarh. Neither Paris nor New York brought itself to give Le Corbusier a major commission. This came from a technically under-developed and poor country, and it required a first-ranking statesman such as Nehru to give Le Corbusier a commission that could kindle his genius and keep him from being pushed aside by the ambitions of smaller rivals.

In the life of Le Corbusier it was not the architect but the client who failed. It is no wonder that the problem of the client dogged him constantly. This, like everything else with him, demanded graphic expression. From Chandigarh he sent me a letter (December 9, 1952) with a drawing (*fig.* **336**). It reported a talk with Ernesto N. Rogers, the well-known Italian architect: Rogers stated "that I am a genius and I asserted that I am an ass. I have therefore posed the question by this drawing." Beneath the drawing he wrote, "Does the genius support the ass or does the ass support the genius?"

The Priory of Ste. Marie de la Tourette, 1960

Long before Le Corbusier undertook the Pilgrimage Chapel of Ronchamps or the Priory of La Tourette he was deeply pre-occupied with the problem of the church and the mystic quality of its space. Once, years before he ever had a commission to build a church, I asked him how he imagined a modern, sacred space, and he told me he would let a tall tower rise from the center and erect a series of cruciform concrete beams, one above the other, so that the upward-looking eye would appear to reach out into infinity.

By the time he became entrusted with the construction of church buildings, he felt his position was strong enough for him to design them on the basis of his own personal architectural vocabulary. Three structures bear witness to this: the Pilgrimage Chapel of Ronchamps, 1955; the Priory of La Tourette, 1960; and the projected church for Firminy, designed 1963. Each differs greatly in its structure, yet each is permeated with the same artistic spirit. This spirit is perhaps most pronounced in the Priory of La Tourette at Eveux-sur-l'Arbesle near Lyons, where he considered the church and the complex of monastic buildings as two distinct elements. The three-sided monastic complex is spatially separated from its fourth side — the church.[23]

At the suggestion of the Dominican Father Couturier, Le Corbusier visited the Cistercian abbey of Le Thoronet in Provence, which had been abandoned since the French Revolution. This abbey of the end of the twelfth century has as concentrated a ground plan as La Tourette, with a three-sided monastic building confronting its church. The monastic buildings of Le Thoronet have also a roof promenade, which no doubt strengthened Le Corbusier's idea of incorporating an ambulatory roof terrace in the Priory of La Tourette (*fig.* **337**).

Le Corbusier ends his preface to a publication on the monastery of Le Thoronet by voicing his respect for the past, "Light and

[23] Jean Petit's publication *Un couvent de Le Corbusier* (Paris, 1964) contains letters from the actual instigator of the project, Father Couturier, and from Le Corbusier, as well as extracts from the building records which give one an insight into the building's gradual formation.

337. LE CORBUSIER. Priory of Ste. Marie de la Tourette, 1960. *Air view. The church and the horseshoe-shaped monastery complex are spatially separatea.*

338. La Tourette. *View of the south and west wings of the monastery. On the lower two stories the common room and refectory; on the third story, studies. The bottom three floors have vertically organized glass surfaces, as in Chandigarh, but not so strongly emphasized. Above them are two floors of the friars' cells. On the left is the rear wall of the church with the projecting housing for the organ.*

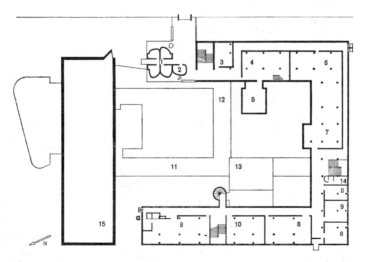

339. La Tourette. *Ground plan.*

shade are the loudspeakers of this architecture of truth, tranquillity, and strength. Nothing further could add to it. In these days of 'crude concrete' let us greet, bless and salute, as we go on our way, so wonderful an encounter."[24]

An extensive property had been presented to the Dominicans and Le Corbusier was free to decide the exact position for the priory. He chose a site beside a wood, with a wide view down the slope and across the river valley: an old manor house still stands near the entrance, shielded by trees.

The monastic buildings   Seldom did Le Corbusier employ such force of expression and such a range of variety in every detail as in La Tourette. There is a continuous interplay of strictly geometrical and

[24] Rayner Heppenstall, *Architecture of Truth* (London, 1957).

340. La Tourette. *East side of the monastery and the friars' promenade. The unostentatious main entrance to the monastery can be seen. From it one looks directly into the interior court.*

572

341. La Tourette. *View into the interior court. The pyramid covers the square oratory, which seems to hover above two thin cross walls. A light vent projects from the left of the pyramid. In the background, pilotis (as in the Villa Savoie, 1928–30) free the building from the ground. Atop the pilotis are rectangular glass walls of different colors, above them two stories of cells, and finally the wall higher than a man that surrounds the ambulatory roof terrace.*

organically curving lines. In the monastic complex, rigid verticals divide the large windows of the community room but the spaces between them change constantly. The projecting loggias of the two upper stories have specially treated surface texture on the exterior and horizontal window slits in the interior. Below these slits are three rows of rectangular window openings, differently arranged on each story. Le Corbusier's adventurous imagination is well shown in the church block, where two sloping walls rise at one end of its flat roof, and support an asymmetrically projecting box that constitutes the bell tower.

342. La Tourette. *The long north side of the church block. Its asymmetrical bell tower is composed of a box poised on two tilted slabs. In the foreground is the low crypt with its variously organized light funnels. Shadows are cast on the crypt walls by round projections that contain the ends of structural reinforcing rods.*

343. La Tourette. *The bell tower from the ambulatory roof entrance.*

344. La Tourette. *Interior of the crypt. The floor is stepped. A series of rectangular walls of different colors, at different heights and at different angles to one another, confronts a continuous curving wall surface: a juxtaposition of geometric and organic elements. The altars stand on steps next to one another, without separating walls.*

Within the court, an oratory for private prayers, standing on two cross walls, is placed in direct relationship to the library (*fig.* **341**). Its helm is an elongated pyramid, reminiscent of the funerary monument of Cestius in Rome, which Le Corbusier had sketched on his early journey through Italy. Light enters through narrow vertical slits near the corners of the walls of the oratory itself and a lighting funnel projects from the rear wall of the sloping pyramid.

Externally, the monastic building is held together by the two projecting upper stories which house one hundred cells for the friars. As was Le Corbusier's later custom, the building's austerity is relaxed and enlivened in the lower stories by the narrowing and widening of the intervals between the uprights of its continuous glass wall.

This is but a brief summary of the building. It says nothing of the special qualities of an architecture intended for a monastic community, concentrated upon the inner life. In seeming contrast to this, the whole building breathes a fervent vitality.

Everyone must be astonished that the customarily indispensable cloister is absent from the court of La Tourette; instead, the court is occupied by sculpturally roofed passages and stairways. The cloister is absent because the complex is mostly raised upon pilotis, which prevent the austere enclosure demanded by a cloister. The use of these pilotis, which are of different heights on each of the sides, made it possible to leave the slope of the hillside untouched. The hillside, on its original level. rises right into the courtyard. Its steep slope is evened out by building three stories on the hillside and four on the valley side, so that the two projecting upper stories are on the same level.

Undoubtedly Le Corbusier intended the continuous flat roof, bounded by walls higher than a man, to serve instead of the customary ground floor cloister as an area for ambulatory meditation (*fig.* **337**). The view here is concentrated on the infinity of the heavens. But this direct confrontation with the sky, to which Le Corbusier continually returned, seems not to have found favor with the friars, for one seldom finds them on

344a. Stele at the neolithic monumental "Tomb of the Giants" in Sardinia.

344b. LE CORBUSIER. Pilgrimage Chapel of Notre Dame du Haut, Ronchamps, 1955. *View from the west. A Mexican architect, R. Barragan, pointed out the secret affinity of the tower of Ronchamps with a prehistoric cult structure in Sardinia.*

the roof. They prefer to meditate in the woods. Grass already grows upon the roof of La Tourette (*fig.* **343**).

Three large round openings, blue, red, and white, give light from above to the low crypt adjacent to the main church. The three funnels on the roof which provide this light (*fig.* **342**) are tilted in different directions, so that the intensity of each of the three colors varies throught the hours of the day. The side altars for reading mass stand next to one another, raised on steps but without intervening partitions. The walls behind the

The priory church

577

altars do not extend up to the ceiling, and the colored light from the circular openings hovers over them, partly extending into the main church. These walls are of different heights, are placed at different angles to one another, and are painted red, blue, and yellow. Opposite them stands a curving wall, again showing an interplay of geometric and organic forms (*fig.* **344**).

For Le Corbusier an organic form has a mythic connotation which cannot be confined within a logical analogy. He always looked for the experiences of former times in his travels and he was equally interested in crystalline Greek forms and in the forms of Roman vaults or Islamic and Gothic architecture. His search for inner similarities had nothing to do with art history: it embraced the experiences of the entire architectural development. It is no accident that the tower of Ronchamps has been compared with a primitive cult structure (*figs.* **344a, 344b**).

The interior of the main church of La Tourette is a pure and crystalline space. Down the center of the floor a slender black line (of asphalt) runs from the steps of the high altar to the layman's altar. The organ projects outward from the rear wall (*fig.* **337**); within there is only a square black cloth, which hides it from all eyes. In contrast to the colored light that enters from low horizontal windows along both sides of the church, white light streams through a narrow horizontal slit at the very top of the end wall, which rises unbroken almost to the ceiling. White light also pours from a square opening in the roof.

The Legacy of Le Corbusier

The end:
August 27, 1965

True creative force can never be suppressed. It is a natural force, stronger than the personal ego. But there is also the human being, the man who suffers when not permitted to realize the powers he feels within himself. A profound bitterness was etched into Le Corbusier's features, and his insistence on self-defense and solitude bear witness to it. It was his fate to be obstructed and misunderstood in the realization of his work, always to be mistrusted and pushed aside.

In his last years, Le Corbusier was constantly preoccupied with thoughts of death. This was the reason for his many meticulous written statements regarding the *Fondation Le Corbusier*. His words in his last publication give an insight into

345. Le Corbusier's studio on Cap St. Martin. *In a letter dated April 15, 1954, Le Corbusier wrote, " 15 meters from my cabin, I have built myself a site-worker's hut [baraque de chantier] 4 meters by 2 meters. I live like a happy monk . . ."*

the bitterness in his heart: "When I have re-entered some celestial sphere . . . the No-men will still be in the ascendant: always against!"[25]

In the summer of 1965, Le Corbusier was in Venice to receive the commission for his hospital there. He had always been happy to communicate with young people, and I recall the gaiety with which he had responded to the students at Harvard University a few years earlier. But here in Venice (as reported in *Time*) he almost thrust the students from him, asking, "Qu'est ce que vous voulez vous d'une ruine?"

---

[25] *Mise au point* (Editions Forces-Vives, 1966), p. 14: "Lorsque j'aurai rejoint quelques zones célestes . . . Messieurs les Non, vous serez toujours a l'affut, toujours contre."

At the moment of Le Corbusier's death, the *Fondation Le Corbusier* was set up in Paris to look after the future of his projects, and to maintain the Villa Savoie and the Maison La Roche in Auteuil. Unfortunately the opportunity was not taken to include his studio at 35 Rue de Sèvres, the place with which his work was most personally connected.

The Le Corbusier Center in Zurich, 1967

Le Corbusier's last building (designed 1964, construction started 1966) stands in Zurich. Thanks to private initiative, this city was given a fine site on the lake of Zurich for the erection of a building to house Le Corbusier's works of art: paintings, sculptures, tapestries and also, one hopes, his architectural plans and models, since one cannot leave out the most important works of a genius like Le Corbusier. It is essentially the *synthesis of the arts* that was expressed so strongly in everything he created. "So far as I can see, Le Corbusier is the only architect of our time for whom there are sufficient grounds to say that he had an all-embracing genius: as architect, painter and urbanist with the vision of a poet. In earlier times, painters were occasionally creators of architectural forms: Raphael's name is also known as an architect, Michelangelo was the conceiver of the dome of St. Peter's, Bramante, foremost an architect, was also an interesting painter. Each possessed an all-embracing genius which is renewed in Le Corbusier." [26] Like the men of the Renaissance, Le Corbusier mastered all three media.

This century has been a period of great timidity in the collaboration of architects and painters. Le Corbusier did not allow his friend, Fernand Léger, to paint one of the walls of the Unité d'Habitation at Marseille. This refusal grew from an earlier incident. When he himself was offered a contract to paint a permanent mural on the wall of his Swiss Pavilion in the University City of Paris, he declined it and, instead, mounted a large photo-montage on the wall. It was only many years later, when the photo-montage had become faded, that Le Corbusier took up his original contract and consented to paint a large mural on the wall. Apart from this he painted murals only on the walls of a few of his friends' houses in the

---

[26] S. Giedion, Foreword to the "Catalogue of the Exhibition" of Le Corbusier's work (Zurich Art Gallery, 1957), p. 6.

country, such as the Badovici house at Cap St. Martin. He permitted no murals in the Esprit Nouveau exhibition in Paris, 1925, but only a few framed pictures by Fernand Léger and himself, as well as some sculptures by Jacques Lipchitz.

The Le Corbusier Center on the lake of Zurich was deliberately designed to include a small dwelling for the donor as well as the Le Corbusier collection. Although Le Corbusier planned it entirely of prefabricated parts, the ground plan is completely free because of the nature of the prefabricated parts. The roof consists of two similar funnel-shaped elements juxtaposed, one pointing downward, the other upward (*fig.* **346**). The roof was brought to the building site in parts and assembled there (*fig.* **347**). Its weight rests on four rectangular steel supports, and slender rods keep the ends in equilibrium (*fig.* **348**). The interior is a single space which can be divided at will, independent of the construction. This idea had lain in Le Corbusier's mind ever since he devised a pavilion for the Liège Exhibition, 1937 (*fig.* **324**), consisting of two square roofs supported from the outside so that the interior was entirely free.

The Zurich pavilion was built only after Le Corbusier's death. Its use of prefabricated elements to form a completely free ground plan is especially significant in this late work; here Le Corbusier used standardized parts to create individual forms instead of uniform repetitions. Le Corbusier did not stand apart from his period. Younger architects, such as Jørn Utzon, were also grappling with the problem of the free and imaginative use of prefabricated elements.

The pencil was snatched from Le Corbusier's hand. One glance in the seventh volume of his *Œuvre complète* (1957–65) gives some idea of the many projects in widely different stages that were waiting to be realized: the tragedy of work left incomplete. Almost all these projects show a much looser disposition of the individual buildings of each complex, but the planning achieves a close interaction of the buildings with the organism of the city. This interaction in the relation of the building volumes to one another has been apparent in Le Corbusier's work ever since his unrealized project for the center of St. Dié in 1945. However, in these new plans there is an even

Unfinished work

581

stronger integration of the project with the total art form. The rhythm of every road is related to the whole highway system; the usual rigidly curving traffic lanes are given a new vitality and their curves have a sensuous allure. This is not unimportant since the highway, despite its two-dimensionality, binds the whole complex together like mortar in a wall.

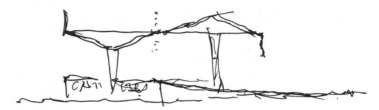

346. LE CORBUSIER. Le Corbusier Center, Zurich, 1967. *From this sketch, it is clear that a fully free interior space is envisaged. This idea had lain in Le Corbusier's mind since the Liège Exhibition of 1937 (fig. 324).*

347. Le Corbusier Center, Zurich, 1967. *Raising the roof. The roof was brought to the site in prefabricated parts and assembled there. It consists of two identical parts, one with the center thrusting upward, the other with it sinking downward. In this picture half of the roof is being raised; the other half still lies on the ground.*

348. Le Corbusier Center, Zurich, 1967. *The roof and its prefabricated supports. The slender end supports take only the vertical stress of the roof. Wind thrusts are absorbed by the larger box-shaped columns.*

The Electronic Center for Olivetti (designed 1962) is one of the most typical of Le Corbusier's last projects (*fig.* **349**). It is on the highway from Milan to Turin and consists of a marvelous mingling of tall, rectangular buildings (housing the research center); low, organic, kidney-shaped structures; and the curving outlines of the parking places. Everywhere one observes a desire to move toward the organic — the desire that has recently suddenly erupted everywhere like a clarion call — but here it is always held in check by the discipline of architectural form. The whole is a bolder interplay of open and closed forms than had yet been attempted and shows how someone like Le Corbusier, saturated with the insight of a painter, was able to sense instinctively the wavelength of his period, and with the greatest sensitivity interpret it in his own work.

There are other projects that kindle the imagination, such as his plans for the center of Berlin (*fig.* **517**) or for a great Museum of the Twentieth Century in Paris, among others.

583

349. LE CORBUSIER.   Model of the Olivetti Electronic Center at Rho-Milan, designed in 1962.

A project that will be realized is his Venice hospital, designed 1964–65.   The Academy of Architecture in Venice has taken over the responsibility for this, working with two of Le Corbusier's collaborators.   At no point does this hospital overtop the dwellings surrounding it.   Le Corbusier had the instinct to enter into the character of a specific region — a sensitivity that never descended to imitation.   On the limited building site of the project Le Corbusier combined his abiding interest in concentration with the tendencies of the youngest generation of architects.

Paul Rudolph, the American architect, expressed the significance of Le Corbusier in a single sentence: "Le Corbusier was the only 20th Century revolutionary who grew beyond his own revolution to expand the art of architecture to such dimensions that there is a clear direction for the foreseeable future." [27]

In Le Corbusier, architecture lost a great leader.

[27] *Progressive Architecture*, November 1965, p. 199.

What will be the influence of Le Corbusier on the coming generation?

From the beginning to the end of his life Le Corbusier had a double role: as an inventive artist and as a fighter. The reason for his double role is today apparent. His position as a fighter was the direct outcome of the nineteenth century's tragic rift between its advanced scientific thinking and a reactionary romantic feeling that continued to live on in the mind of the people and the authorities. Le Corbusier was forced to be simultaneously a creative artist and a protagonist for his ideas.

Le Corbusier's strength lies in his architectural force. This grew out of a common emotional background in painting and sculpture. One of Le Corbusier's main functions was to inaugurate once again the role of contemporary expression in architecture. Yet it would be completely wrong to regard Le Corbusier as an isolated figure. The creation of contemporary architecture had its roots in many other personalities such as Gropius, Mies van der Rohe, the Stijl Group in Holland. But Le Corbusier's unique historical function lies in the fact that he was simultaneously a painter, an architect, and a poet.

The architect of today has to open his eyes more widely than the architect of the Renaissance. He has to fulfill both the human and artistic demands of a much wider circle, extending from the private home to agglomerations of people, while making use of new materials, taking advantage of standardization, and considering even such matters as the general control of traffic. Just as important as the solution of structural problems is the creation of breathing spaces. The human habitat needs more and more breathing space for the private life of its inhabitants since the business areas outside the home are becoming more and more congested.

Architects from Frank Lloyd Wright to Le Corbusier continually demanded more breathing space for the people. Wright always spoke about "organic architecture," combining freely organized buildings with the surrounding nature. Le Corbusier gave no direct name to what he wanted but expressed it by cosmic symbols, representations of the course of the sun (such as he wanted to do in the monument for Chandigarh). Perhaps the strongest architectural expression of this feeling is the roof terrace of his monastery at La Tourette, bordered on both sides by walls about two meters high, so that one cannot see the landscape but only the sky. We are not accustomed to this kind of cosmic orientation.

Le Corbusier's spirit as a creative artist and a protagonist is still alive today. I see Le Corbusier more and more as an opponent of certain developments in the architecture of the generation (especially in France and England) that is forming big clusters of houses pinched together into a compact whole, which come more and more to resemble machines that do not need breathing spaces, and which completely neglect the needs of a human habitat. These architects disregard the close relationship between man and nature stressed from Wright to Le Corbusier — a relationship which demands continuation!

Le Corbusier's influence on leading architects all over the world is inestimable. Though these each follow their own line, they have developed Le Corbusier's fundamental drive to unite architectural and plastic expression. At the same time, Le Corbusier has often been simply imitated by others who have copied his pilotis, his houses, his churches. Thus we can understand why many young architects reject the work of all their predecessors and want to start from something absolutely different to express their own right of existence.

This leads us to a final question regarding Le Corbusier's work. Will architecture pursue a completely mechanical development or will it respond to the continuity of human demand common to all the high civilizations since antiquity, and recognized in our period by all the great architects from Frank Lloyd Wright to Le Corbusier? This demand was always to link man and nature and to do this always with the help of the newly invented technical possibilities of each age.

MIES VAN DER ROHE AND THE
INTEGRITY OF FORM

350. PETER DE HOOCH. Mother and Child, c. 1650. *Dutch interiors with their crystal-clear atmosphere have an inner affinity with Piet Mondrian as well as with Mies van der Rohe's balancing of plane surfaces.*

Mies van der Rohe grew up in Aachen, a residence of Charlemagne, the oldest center of German civilization. The town lies close to the Dutch border, and many of its inhabitants possess the calm, phlegmatic nature of the Netherlanders. This is not obtuseness, but rather a shield against the outer world — a withdrawal into an inner concentration. At least this is the way it is with Mies van der Rohe.

At all events, his work is closer akin to the Dutch than that of any other German architect. How these qualities are reflected in his buildings will be traced in the following pages. The spirit of Dutch seventeenth-century "interiors" with their crystal-clear atmosphere and precisely framed walls and openings (*fig.* **350**), have an inner affinity with Mies van der Rohe's balancing of plane surfaces.

The correct placing of brick upon brick and stone upon stone was known to Mies van der Rohe from childhood in his father's workshop. His fanaticism for pure form and the great care with which he uses materials are probably derived from these early experiences.[1]

But these are merely general preliminary conditions. How does Mies van der Rohe's work stand in relation to his own period?

The Elements of Mies van der Rohe's Architecture

The secret of every creative architectural development is based mainly on three factors: a client with an instinct for quality; a master who, by his own work and personality, knows how to awaken the creative possibilities of a younger generation; and the existence of a rising generation, able to select the best place to provide the right nourishment for their needs.

Peter Behrens and Mies van der Rohe

In this instance, the client was Emil Rathenau, president of the General Electric Company of Berlin; the master was Peter Behrens; and the rising generation that found their way to Peter Behrens at this important moment included Mies van der Rohe, Gropius, and — for a short time as a visitor — Le Corbusier. Peter Behrens' atelier was the only one in Germany where this younger generation could find what it needed. Peter Behrens' turbine factory of 1909 showed that materials such as glass and iron possessed within them a secret strength of expression that could be brought out as soon as an artist understood how to develop their means and possibilities. Between this building of 1909 and the buildings of the forties lies the gulf created by the new conception of space. Nevertheless, the factories of Peter Behrens provided firmer foundations for Mies van der Rohe's means of expression than the country houses of the romantic German classicist Karl Friedrich Schinkel (1781–1840) or of Berlage, who, around 1900, brought the smooth wall surface back into European architecture.

---

[1] For further details see Philip C. Johnson, *Mies van der Rohe* (New York: Museum of Modern Art, 1947), with passages from the artist's writing and bibliography.

588

In 1910 Frank Lloyd Wright came into the European field of vision. During the time that Walter Gropius and Mies van der Rohe were working with Peter Behrens, the exhibition of Frank Lloyd Wright's work was shown in Berlin. "We young architects found ourselves in painful inner discord. The work of this great master presented an architectural world of unexpected force, clarity of language and disconcerting richness of form," Mies van der Rohe wrote much later. Frank Lloyd Wright in Berlin, 1910

The openness of the Wright ground plan, which grew out in all directions like a spreading plant (*fig.* **243**), and Wright's tendency to conceive the entire house as one flowing space brought the European architects to a sudden realization of their own stiffness. The man from the prairie taught them to return to living forms.

Among the elements of Mies van der Rohe's later work we can recognize the care in handling new materials that Peter Behrens had shown, and also the free ground plan of Frank Lloyd Wright's houses. The Fagus factory that Gropius was to build in the following year (1911) gives evidence of the altered outlook of the younger generation. Glass and iron were no longer enclosed by massive walls. They joined directly together at the corners, with effortless ease (*fig.* **291**).

Just as in Mies van der Rohe's well-known studies for glass skyscrapers between 1919 and 1921 [2] and in his scheme for a large office building in 1922,[3] artistic expression was given to the fact that the skeleton lies within the building or, as Mies

---

[2] These studies began in 1919 with a competition scheme for an office building in the Friedrichstrasse of Berlin. They should not be considered in isolation. In the office building for the Friedrichstrasse, while Mies van der Rohe's treatment of materials and the pureness of his form is far ahead of his competitors, his indented ground plan still reflects the expressionistic tendency of German architecture in the twenties. In the Dutch journal *Wendingen*, volume III, Series 5 (Amsterdam, 1923), there is an interesting article by H. Th. Wijdeveld and Dr. A. Behne on the romanticism of the skyscraper motif that was then sweeping through Europe. Here one becomes aware of the relationship as well as the difference between Mies van der Rohe's scheme and those by Hans Poelzig, Hugo Häring, and others.

[3] Johnson, *Mies van der Rohe*, p. 31.

van der Rohe puts it: "Columns and girders eliminate bearing walls. This is skin and bone construction."

The Stijl movement

A third impetus for Mies van der Rohe's creative development came from Holland. Around 1920 no other country was producing as many interesting developments in the field of housing as the Netherlands. The decisive outlet for expressing the new architectural vocabulary was neither in factories nor in retail stores, but in the human domain of the dwelling house and the housing group.[4]

It is therefore understandable that, following upon all the good work that was realized as well as some misguided efforts of the so-called Amsterdam school, Theo van Doesburg set forward an ideal clearing and purification program in his journal *Stijl* (1917).[5] The exhibition of the Stijl Group (painting, sculpture, and architecture) that was designed by Theo van Doesburg together with C. van Eesteren and G. Rietveld at Léonce Rosenberg's gallery in Paris (October 1923) exerted a great influence upon the leading talents such as Le Corbusier and Mies van der Rohe, particularly through its models and presentation of architectural material. This exhibition showed that the steps toward Frank Lloyd Wright's perception of the house as a flowing space bounded by vertical and horizontal planes had been fully taken and understood (*fig.* **81**).

Country Houses, 1923

Mies van der Rohe's studies for two country houses (1923), one in brick and one in concrete (*figs.* **351, 352, 354**) are of

[4] No other country in 1920 could parallel J. J. P. Oud's workers' housing project in Rotterdam, Ir. J. B. van Loghem's Rosehaghe settlement in Haarlem (1920) and his concrete Watergraafsmeer houses in Amsterdam (1922), Jan Wil's Papaverhof dwellings in the Hague (1919–21), or, with reservations, M. de Klerk's apartment houses in Amsterdam between 1914 and 1923 (fig. 432) and W. M. Dudock's work in Hilversum around 1920. The sole forerunner was Robert van t'Hoff's concrete single-family houses in Huisterheide (1914–15).

[5] See above, pp. 442–443, and also J. J. P. Oud, *Hollandische Architektur*, Bauhausbücher Nr. 10, ed. by Walter Gropius and L. Moholy-Nagy (Munich, 1925); Ir. J. B. van Loghem, *Holland Built To Live In* (Amsterdam, 1932). Both books are written by leading architects and therefore particularly interesting in their selection of materials.

[6] Published first in *G*, Number II (Berlin, September 1923). This is a journal edited by Mies van der Rohe, Richter, and Graff, of which three numbers appeared. Its contents come near to *Stijl* and *Esprit Nouveau*.

inestimable importance for the development of modern architecture. The analytical spirit of Theo van Doesburg had enabled him to show by means of his transparent architectural drawings that the conception of the house as a self-contained cube had lost its meaning. In these two studies, Mies van der Rohe gives this conception a clear and concentrated artistic expression.

Under Mies van der Rohe's orderly hand the planes become assembly points for material and structure — plate glass, ferro-concrete, and, soon afterward, marble. Even more clearly than in the *Stijl* studies, these country houses of Mies van der Rohe give a realizable form to the floating character of the elements that make up the house. This is the period during which Le Corbusier built his La Roche house at Auteuil and G. Rietveld his stylized house at Utrecht (1924). Planes protruding from within the house do not halt at the outer walls, as with van Doesburg, but spread out into the landscape like the sails of a windmill. At the same time, the surface elements have become assembly points for the structural elements. Transparency is achieved by penetration through long window strips surmounted by a hovering roof slab (*fig.* **354**). All these elements, which are not individual inventions, are brought together with a masterly artistic control.[7]

In the houses Mies van der Rohe actually built about this time, he was unable to realize the daring that he had developed in his paper studies. His visions became a reality for the first time in his exhibition pavilion in Barcelona in 1929 (*fig.* **353**). With unsurpassed precision he used pure surfaces of precious materials as elements of the new space conception. Perhaps his most famous house is the Tugendhat House [8] in Brno, Czechoslovakia (1930), which achieves extreme generosity in its flowing interpenetration of space. Even so, one does not get away from the feeling of being exposed to an aquarium-like existence.

---

[7] In the introduction to R. J. Neutra's *Buildings and Projects* (Zurich, 1951), we have attempted to develop further the great influence which the unrealized schemes of both the Stijl Group and Mies van der Rohe had upon R. J. Neutra's own development.

[8] Johnson, pp. 76–86.

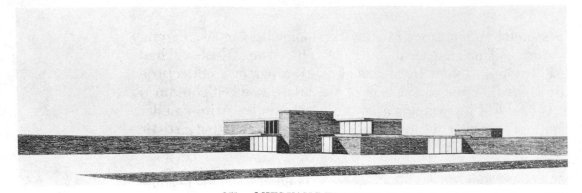

351. MIES VAN DER ROHE. Project of a brick country house, 1923.

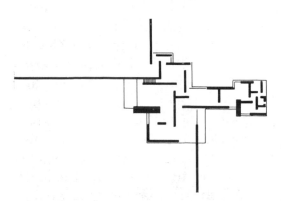

352. MIES VAN DER ROHE.
Brick   country   house,   1923.
Ground plan. *Planes protruding
from within the house do not halt
at the outer walls, but spread out
into the landscape like the sails of
a windmill.*

353. MIES VAN DER ROHE. German pavilion at the International Exhibition,
Barcelona, 1929. *Here his visions became a reality for the first time. With unsurpassed
precision he used pure surfaces of precious materials as elements of the new space conception.*

592

354. MIES VAN DER ROHE. Project of a concrete house, 1923. *The plane sur-faces have become assembly points for the structural elements. Transparency is achieved by penetration through long windowstrips, surmounted by a hovering roof slab.*

355. MIES VAN DER ROHE. Country house for a bachelor, Berlin Building Exhi-bition, 1931. *In the center of the great exhibition hall, Mies van der Rohe erected one of his glass-walled single-story houses. One of the last modern manifestations before the collapse of German culture.*

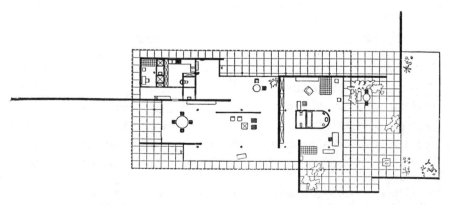

356. MIES VAN DER ROHE. Country house for a bachelor. Ground plan. *The same trends are shown as in the brick country house, 1923. Planes protruding from within the house, as well as the flowing space of the interior, become reality.*

In 1931, when the Brownshirts were already filling the streets of Berlin and the country was in a state of crisis — five million unemployed, breakdown of industry in all fields, market difficulties of all kinds — a building exhibition on a grand scale was opened. In it the creative forces of Germany worked together. It was the last time. Walter Gropius, L. Moholy-Nagy, and Herbert Bayer of the Bauhaus, who were commissioned by the Coöperative Housing Society, attempted to show the public, with all the power of modern display techniques and artistic eloquence, what should be done to achieve a human approach to the housing problem.

In the center of the great exhibition hall, undisturbed by all the excitement, Mies van der Rohe erected a glass-walled single-story house with fine interiors, apparently for a bachelor, in which without any compromise he proceeded to develop the unity of space, plane, and structure which lay so near to his heart (*figs.* **355, 356**).[9]

Neither the propaganda appeal to the masses nor architectural achievement was able to have the slightest effect, however. Developments had to move in another direction.

In Germany, the architectural contribution was made in a terribly short time. The opportunity existed for only a very few years. No one who was present at the opening of the Weissenhofsiedlung in Stuttgart in 1927 could have foreseen that only five years later all would be over.

The Weissenhof Housing Settlement, Stuttgart, 1927

There was a moment in the middle of the twenties when the clear primary colors used by Picasso, Braque, Léger, and other modern painters seemed to radiate an optimism that had not been present before and was not to occur again. Once the war and the inflation had been overcome, it seemed that a new period was about to dawn in which the upsurge of a new way

---

[9] There were also family houses by the Berlin architects Luckhardt and Marcel Breuer, and a hall by Walter Gropius for one of his multi-story apartment houses. See Peiro Bottoni, "Berlin 1931," *Rassegna d'Architettura*, 15 September 1931.

of life, new art, and a new architecture could no longer be held under.

Germany was at this time more aware of the outside world than ever before. The *Avantgarde* were dragged out from their seclusion and plunged into active life. This explains the founding of the Bauhaus by Walter Gropius (1919) together with painters such as Paul Klee, W. Kandinsky, and Moholy-Nagy, as well as the appointment of Mies van der Rohe as first vice-president of the Deutscher Werkbund.[10]

The Weissenhof Housing Settlement at Stuttgart (*figs.* **357, 358**), which the Werkbund had entrusted to Mies van der Rohe, is perhaps the clearest indication of the change that had taken place within the all-too-thin layer of the elite. Invitations were issued, in the most generous manner, to young architects from other nations to execute their own buildings. From Holland came J. J. P. Oud and Mart Stam, both of whom built row houses following the custom of their own country. From France came Le Corbusier, who erected his two most-discussed houses on pillars. From Belgium came Victor Bourgeois. The young Swiss architects were given one of the flats in Mies van der Rohe's apartment home. At one end of the settlement, Peter Behrens, the veteran German architect, built his fortress-like apartment block; and around and between, the German and Austrian architects established their single-family dwellings — Walter Gropius, Bruno Taut, Scharoun, Rading, Hilbersheimer, Doecker, J. Frank, and others. No one who lived through these opening days will forget the optimism and the moral support produced by this event — achieved against apparently inflexible opposition.

A few paragraphs written in 1927 [11] may convey a more immediate impression:

"The exhibition certainly gave us an insight into actual life. We believe that it has extraordinary significance because it has brought new methods of construction out from the secluded

---

[10] See pp. 479–480.

[11] S. Giedion, "L'Exposition du Werkbund à Stuttgart 1927," and "La Cité du Weissenhof," in *Architecture Vivante* (Paris, 1928).

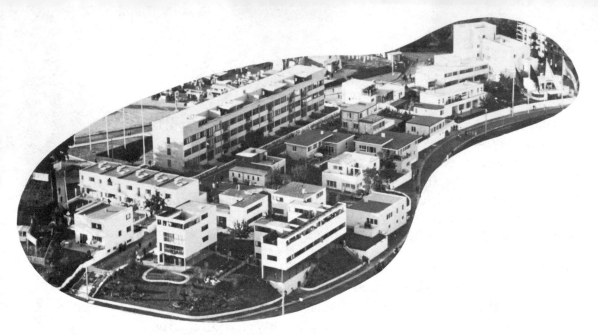

357. Weissenhof settlement, Stuttgart, 1927. *In the foreground, Le Corbusier's two houses with roof gardens; to the left, J. J. P. Oud's row houses and Mies van der Rohe's apartment houses; to the rear, Peter Behrens' apartment house with tower; the two-story row houses in front of it are by Mart Stam.*

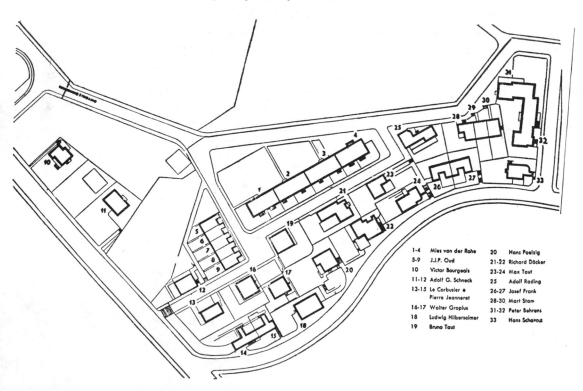

1-4	Mies van der Rohe	20	Hans Poelzig
5-9	J.J.P. Oud	21-22	Richard Döcker
10	Victor Bourgeois	23-24	Max Taut
11-12	Adolf G. Schneck	25	Adolf Rading
13-15	Le Corbusier e Pierre Jeanneret	26-27	Josef Frank
		28-30	Mart Stam
16-17	Walter Gropius	31-32	Peter Behrens
18	Ludwig Hilberseimer	33	Hans Scharoun
19	Bruno Taut		

358. Weissenhof settlement, Stuttgart, 1927. Plan. *This settlement marks the moment when contemporary architects from different countries had an opportunity to show for the first time, not by words but by building together upon the same site, that a new approach to the housing problem had been developed.*

359. Weissenhof settlement, Stuttgart, 1927. *Mies van der Rohe's special contribution was the first adaptation of the steel skeleton to meet new needs in the housing problem. His large Chicago apartments are here foreshadowed.*

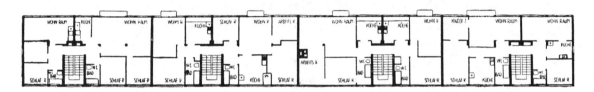

360. Ground plan of the second floor. *Each floor had a different plan. The apartment to the left leaves the steel columns passing freely through the room.*

361. Steel skeleton of Mies van der Rohe's apartment house.

laboratory of the *Avantgarde* and caused them to be put into operation on a broad scale. The new architecture . . . can never develop soundly without the active participation of the masses. Of course, the problems that have to be solved are not posed by any conscious expression of the masses. For many reasons their conscious mind is always ready to say 'No' to new artistic experiences. But if the unconscious mind is once directed into a new path, then the laboratory product will be broadened and adapted to meet the needs of real life. The Stuttgart exhibition appears to us as the nucleus of such a process, and herein lies its importance.

"The Weissenhof Housing Settlement gives evidence of two great changes: the change from handicraft methods of construction to industrialization, and the premonition of a new way of life.

"Mies van der Rohe's original plan was to interlock the house-plots so that a unified relationship could be created and the green areas would flow into one another. This plan unfortunately could not be realized for commercial reasons. Even so it is possible to experience how relationship and order are created by the level unassertive surfaces of flat roofs in places that would otherwise have been utterly chaotic. In flat towns, such as the Hague, one can observe how the flat roofs create wide interconnecting bands.

Mies van der Rohe's steel-framed apartment house

"The Weissenhof Housing Settlement is dominated by Mies van der Rohe's steel-framed apartment house (*figs*. **359, 360, 361**). Even the apartment house, which today usually takes the form of a palace or a castle, is here transformed into a more loosely articulated structure. The steel frame permits one to eliminate all rigid inner and outer walls. For the outside, an insulated filling wall with a half-brick thickness is sufficient, and the inner walls can be disposed according to the liking of the tenants, in whatever manner they choose. The wide and continuous window strips are the only limiting factors. These window strips are wide and continuous in order to enable good light to penetrate as deeply as possible into the building. The problem of the apartment house is today (1927) even further from solution than that of the single-family house.

Mies van der Rohe's steel skeleton shows a possible way of unraveling this problem.

"Many architectural critics found the continuous steel supports that ran freely through the houses of Mies van der Rohe and Le Corbusier very unsightly. It seems that it is especially difficult for the architect to free himself from the appearance of traditional structural methods in which the walls were the bearing members of the house. It is fundamentally organic to our present-day conceptions of space that complete expression is given to the inner construction of our houses. The continuous steel support is definitely not an aesthetic focal point. It may be allowed to run quietly through the space. Just as the columns of ancient architecture give the onlooker a feeling of security by means of their ordered play of load and support, so the continuous steel or concrete shaft gives today's onlooker an impression of a powerful energy that flows uniformly through the house. The free-standing visible column is thus given a new expressive quality apart from its constructive objectivity. Here is continuous energy at work: nothing in our life remains an isolated experience; everything stands in a many-sided interrelationship — within, without, above, below!

"Mies van der Rohe has followed the possibilities of his building through to the utmost detail. Plywood walls that can be screwed onto the ceilings enable the occupier to alter the disposition of his space at will. Doorless connections between rooms. One is continually amazed at the amount of space that this method makes possible within an area of 70 square meters (750 square feet). It acts upon us as a necessary stimulant — an impetus that can set industry into motion."

The Weissenhof Housing Settlement was, at the same time, a living manifesto of rational planning and organization of the house interior. We have described elsewhere how the general public was here, for the first time, introduced to the organization of work and space within the kitchen as well as to the cantilever tubular chair as developed by Mies van der Rohe and at the same time by Mart Stam.[12]

---

[12] *Mechanization Takes Command*, pp. 523–526, 493–503.

362. MIES VAN DER ROHE. Model of the campus of Illinois Institute of Technology, showing all proposed buildings. *(1) Athletic field; (2) Gymnasium and swimming pool; (3) Field house; (4) Alumni Memorial Hall; (5) Metallurgical and chemical engineering; (6) AAR research building; (7) Library and administration; (8) Chemistry; (9) Liberal studies; (10) Mechanical engineering; (11) Civil engineering and mechanics; (12) Laboratory building; (13) Laboratory building; (14) Electrical engineering and physics; (15) Student Union and auditorium; (16) Architecture and applied arts; (17) ARF research and administration; (18) Institute of Gas Technology; (19) Research laboratory; (20) Research laboratory; (21) Metal research; (22) ARF engineering research; (23) ARF engineering research; (24) Heating and power plant; (25) ARF engineering research.*

363. MIES VAN DER ROHE. Administration Building, 1944. *The pureness of form, juxtaposition of different structures, sensitivity of proportion, and discipline of outline — all previously indicated in his country house of 1923 — are here fully developed.*

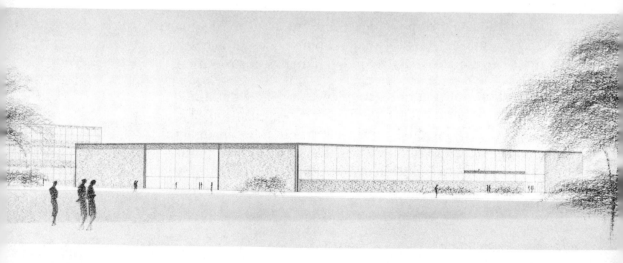

600

364. MIES VAN DER ROHE. Chemical Engineering and Metallurgy Building, 1949. *Northwest view.*

The Illinois Institute of Technology, 1939 ——

Scarcely anything is so much wasted today as creative energy in the field of the arts. This waste is aggravated by the fact that the dictatorships of our time — themselves without any awareness of contemporary art — detest everything which is not strictly reactionary in its means of expression.

If Mies van der Rohe, who — as we noted at the start — is well endowed with patience and tranquillity, had not been invited to Chicago in 1938, what would have become of him? The subsequent fate of German architects and architecture — one of the most depressing spectacles of our time — gives sufficient answer.

Now his tall apartment houses spring up in the most beautiful parts of Chicago and he has been working since 1939 on the buildings for the Illinois Institute of Technology.[13] Usually an

[13] For details see Hugo Weber, "Mies van der Rohe in Chicago," *Bauen und Wohnen*, No. 9 (Zurich, 1951), an excellent survey of the work of Mies van der Rohe.

365. MIES VAN DER ROHE. Minerals and Metal Research Building, 1943. South view. *The module of twenty-four feet as a basis for the planning of the whole campus, together with a careful balance within the plane surfaces, is evident in the south-front view of this laboratory.*

American building is completely amortised within this period. It would seem thus that Mies van der Rohe has somehow been able to transfer his own inborn patience to the American board of trustees.

The spatial disposition of the twenty-four buildings can be best understood when one looks back upon Mies van der Rohe's design for a country house in 1923. There the new relationship between the different fragments of the walls induced a feeling of an all-penetrating oneness of space. The same is true of the buildings for the Chicago campus. The twenty-four buildings stand in a rectilinear relationship to one another like that of the walls of the earlier project. At the same time, they are so disposed that an all-embracing space is created though not visible at one glance — a space that can only be slowly perceived by including the dimension of time, that is, by movement (*fig.* **362**).

Like an Egyptian sculptor working on a bas-relief, Mies van der Rohe stretches a network of squared coördinates across all the buildings on his campus. His module is 24 feet (*fig.* **365**). Without one's realizing it, this module is imprinted upon the spectator at every step.

Mies van der Rohe, with Le Corbusier, is among the very few architects who are again deliberately cultivating proportional relationships in their work. Both do this in the Pythagorean sense in which measurements are not merely measurements but possess qualitative as well as quantitative properties.

Proportions

Care in handling proportions is allied with care in handling materials. The buildings for the Illinois Institute of Technology display none of the walls of onyx and columns of chromium of Mies van der Rohe's earlier period. But proportion, structure, and material are here related to one another with an even greater finesse.

The side walls of a laboratory or a factory, with their exposed skeletons of steelwork and brick infilling, are usually disregarded secondary factors, but with Mies van der Rohe they are transformed into elements of the highest artistic value.

This may not all be apparent to the casual observer. All the same, it is certain that — even without one's knowledge — an ordered environment of this sort has its effect upon one. Just as the Weissenhof housing settlement in 1927 was a manifesto which greatly influenced subsequent development, so the buildings of this Chicago campus make an appeal for greater artistic integrity in architecture.

High-rise Apartments

In 1949, thirty years after his early skyscraper studies, Mies van der Rohe was building tall apartment blocks along Lake Michigan. One of these, the Promontory Apartments, stands in South Chicago, not far from the buildings shown in figure **513**. The view from the great glass windows over the limitless

Promontory Apartments, 1949

366. MIES VAN DER ROHE. Promontory Apartments, Chicago, 1949. East front. Detail of the entrance side. *Great care has been given to incorporate the ferroconcrete skeleton into the artistic expression of the façade. The photograph shows the distinct setback of the joists which grow slimmer as they gain height. This accentuation of the pillars together with the well-calculated setback of the window areas and filling walls is typical of Mies van der Rohe's integrating hand.*

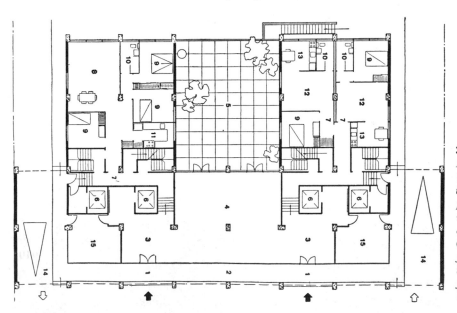

367. Promontory Apartments, 1949. *The U-shaped ground plan together with the free planning of each floor was first used in Chicago office buildings (compare fig. 176); then for housing in the twenties, and toward 1950 for large apartment houses.*

604

368. Promontory Apartments, 1949. East front. *This apartment house is situated in the South Side of Chicago, very near those in fig. 513. The windows overlook the broad expanse of Lake Michigan and the occupants enjoy a feeling of individual existence and contact with air and nature much greater than they can have in row houses on a side street.*

lake is overwhelming. Twenty-two stories. Ferroconcrete skeleton. U-shaped ground plan, as in Holabird and Roche's Marquette Building, Chicago, 1894 (*fig.* **230**). The Promontory Apartments actually consist of two units joined as one, each containing its own elevators and stairway. The detailing is monastic in its austerity (*figs.* **366, 369**).

369. Promontory Apartments, 1949. *View from the lobby dividing the symmetrically built wings. Here too, the treatment of detail and proportion has a very stimulating effect.*

The hand of Mies van der Rohe can be felt in the ground plan of each of the apartments (*fig.* **367**) and particularly in the treatment of the façade (*fig.* **368**). These soaring ferroconcrete verticals, set back four times in their height, are handled with an extraordinary sensitivity and give a musical articulation to the whole façade.[14] A comparison of this façade with the immense columns that hold up Le Corbusier's Unité d'Habitation at Marseille, 1947–52 (*fig.* **325**), demonstrates the widely different ways in which ferroconcrete was then being used.

Lake Shore Apartments, 1951

None of Mies van der Rohe's buildings has had such an immediate influence upon his American contemporaries as his two largest and most radical apartment houses at 860 Lake Shore Drive, Chicago (1951; *figs.* **370, 371**). The Lake Shore Apartments consist of two volumes — two high-rise buildings

[14] The following were connected with the Promontory Apartments: Associated Architects, Pace Associates and Mies van der Rohe; Consulting Architects, Holsman and Klekamp; Engineer, Frank J. Kornacker.

— placed in a reciprocal relation such as Mies often repeated later, for example, in the Commonwealth Apartments, 1956. Since then such "twin buildings" have become fashionable in the United States — even to a point of distortion (for instance, Yamasaki's International Trade Center in New York). In the Lake Shore Apartments — as in his Farnsworth House at Plano, Illinois (1950) — integrity of form has become the supreme law to which everything else is subordinated. With uncompromising strength the architect permits not the slightest deviation from the clear-cut plane surfaces of the glass parallelepipeds. Each detail seems to remind the spectator: Architecture is discipline; architecture is an artifact!

Mies van der Rohe's skyscraper apartments revive — after a dismal interval — the tradition of the Chicago School of the 1880's. In them a strange symbiosis has come about: an understanding between the creative powers of an artist and the gigantic organization of modern building industrialization.

Art and high mechanization

Around 1880 Adler and Sullivan could themselves assume complete responsibility for erecting their buildings as could, naturally, the engineer and building contractor, William Le Baron Jenney. Today this is no longer possible. The list of those responsible for the erection of a major building is even longer than the list of those collaborating in a major film. But, just as whether the movie is good or bad depends on the intensity of the chief director, so the quality of a building depends on the capabilities of its form-giving architect. He has to give it that imponderable quality that can be called its architectural expression. That the American building industry — in rare cases — has put its trust in an artist and not just a stereotyped architect is a sign that a synthesis between art and high mechanization is possible. Once the creative architect knows how to play upon the stupendous keyboard of mechanization we need not feel troubled about the future of architecture.

Office Buildings

Mies van der Rohe's work in America increased greatly from the early fifties on. In particular, he designed several important office buildings.   It took another decade for his work to become recognized in Germany, but by the early sixties he was accepted by all sides: by German industrial barons (the Friedrich Krupp office building in Essen) and by German officialdom (the project for the Twentieth Century Gallery in Berlin).

Among the New York skyscrapers, the dignified bronze Seagram Office Building (1958) on Park Avenue with its generous forecourt holds a special position of dignity.

During the sixties Chicago fell much less into the trend of playboy architecture than New York.   Several large office buildings were erected for the state and the city in this period. It was almost as though the local genius of the earlier Chicago School had been resurrected.

The Federal Center in Chicago, 1963   Mies van der Rohe designed the large Federal Center complex situated in the Chicago Loop, right in the heart of the city. It includes the Court House, the Federal Office Building, designed by one of his students, and the Central Post Office (*fig.* **372**).   The space available for this Center, which was

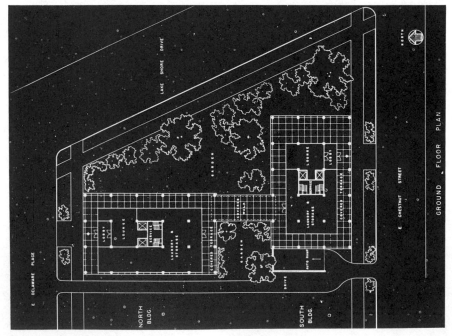

370.   MIES VAN DER ROHE.   Lake Shore Drive Apartments, 1951.   Plan.   *One of the most advanced examples of building by assembling prefabricated parts.*

371. MIES VAN DER ROHE. Lake Shore Drive Apartments, 1951. *The use of glass may here have reached its zenith, unless industry creates the technical means for adjusting the different qualities of light without the use of curtains.*

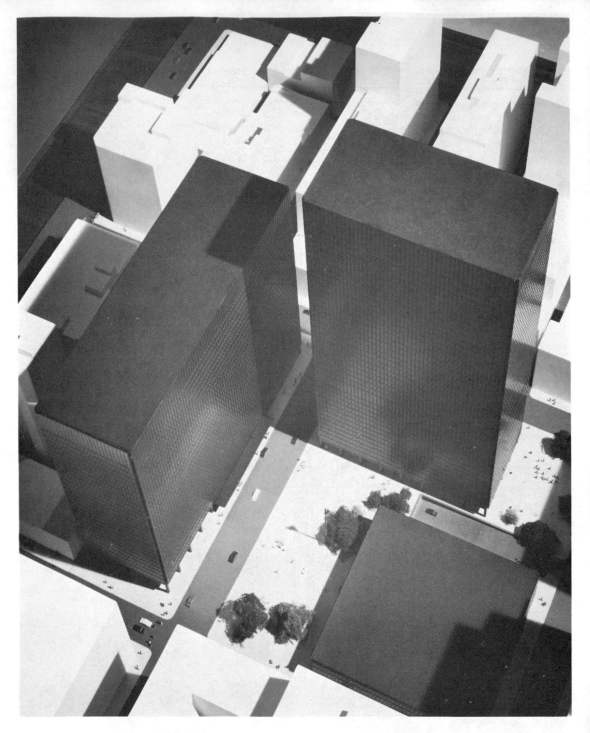

372. MIES VAN DER ROHE. Federal Center, Chicago, 1963. *Model. Left, 30-story Court House; center, 45-story Federal Office Building. Each building has one floor reserved for a staff restaurant. The single-story Central Post Office on the right is a typical undivided interior space, 60 meters square. Despite the narrow checkerboard of the street system that reduced the available space to the minimum, the architect has succeeded in creating an interplay of volumes within the limitations of the site.*

610

reduced to the minimum by the narrow checkerboard of Chicago's street system, permitted no interplay of large volumes in space. However, one can observe from the model how, even under these conditions, Mies van der Rohe was able to bring about an interrelation of the three structures: Court House, Federal Office Building and the lower Central Post Office.

Of all Mies van der Rohe's later buildings, the office building for the Bacardi rum factory in Mexico (1961) possesses the most sublime architectonic instrumentation. It lies in open country on the way from Mexico City to Teotihuacán, the holy city of the Aztecs (*fig.* **373**).

Here Mies van der Rohe developed his methods of approach still further. The exterior: emphasized columns, glass surfaces to the front and to the set-back ground floor (*fig.* **378**). The interior: one single flowing space. This was achieved by an extremely subtle knowledge of how to arrive at perfection through the smallest alterations of position and proportion. One thing is most striking: the conscious emphasis on the relation between horizontal planes, an emphasis which often appears in Mies van der Rohe's later work (*fig.* **376**).

The forerunner of this Mexican building was a single-story office for the same firm in Cuba (1958), whose heavily coffered concrete ceiling hovers above the floor. Its eight tapering concrete columns make their junction with the ceiling about fifteen meters from the corners, so that the projecting horizontal plane seems to float in space. A similar relation between horizontal planes appears in this two-story Bacardi building in Mexico, where stress is laid on the wide encircling travertine floor that in one place reaches out from the building (*fig.* **378**).

The hovering relation between the horizontal planes of ceiling and floor is strengthened by one, seemingly simple, device: there are no columns at the corners. Instead they are set far back from the short end walls, so that — in its own way — the ceiling projects freely forward (*fig.* **376**). Thus the relation between the plane surface of the floor and the ceiling is given full strength of expression. In Jørn Utzon's work the horizontal plane comes even more strongly into the foreground as a constituent element of contemporary architecture.

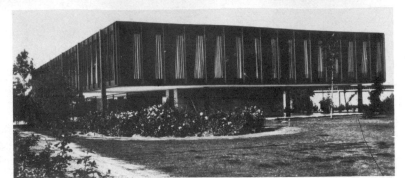

373. MIES VAN DER ROHE. Bacardi Office Building, Mexico, 1961. *General view of the building with its set-back columns and projecting upper floor.*

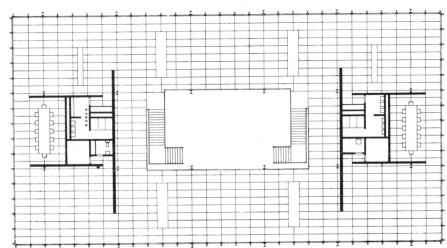

374. Bacardi Office Building, Mexico, 1961. *Plan of the upper story. The working rooms are along the long sides. Two cross walls of cedarwood stand freely in space, separating the meeting rooms from the main space.*

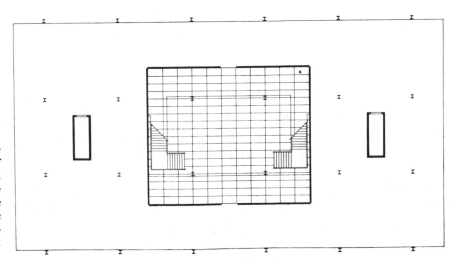

375. Bacardi Office Building, Mexico, 1961. *Ground floor plan. The patio-like character of the large open room in the center strengthens the flow of the "single space." The set-back columns show the projecting roof at either end.*

612

376. Bacardi Office Building, Mexico, 1961. *The floating relation between ceiling and floor is emphasized by setting back the columns so that the upper story projects forward.*

377. Bacardi Office Building, Mexico, 1961. *Relation between the surfaces of floor and ceiling. Unfortunately, planting has been concentrated at the corners and will, in a few years, diminish the crystal clarity of the building.*

378. Bacardi Office Building, Mexico, 1961. *The hovering relation of the horizontal surfaces of floor and ceiling is stressed at the entrance where the travertine floor flows outward in a wide stream.*

379. MIES VAN DER ROHE. Project for Twentieth Century Gallery, Berlin, 1963. *Model. In this museum the relation between horizontal surfaces is carried further by introducing three levels: roof, raised platform, and street. As in the Bacardi Office Building, Cuba, 1958, the columns are placed far from the corners and the glass walls are set back.*

The tinted glass of the upper story makes it appear opaque from the outside and transparent from within. This strengthens the interplay of the strong black steel verticals with the lightness of the whole building.

In the interior Mies van der Rohe again follows the principle of forming a single flowing space as he had done from the Tugendhat house at Brno (1930) to the Farnsworth House near Chicago (1950). The glass enclosed space, although roofed, operates like a patio (*fig.* **375**). The space for the secretarial staff is organized along both sides of the surrounding gallery. At the narrow ends the meeting rooms are demarcated by walls of cedarwood. Light stairways lead from the open ground floor to the work spaces on the upper story (*fig.* **374**).

Closely related to the Bacardi Building in Cuba is Mies van der Rohe's project for the Twentieth Century Gallery in Berlin, 1963 (*fig.* **379**). Here too the columns are placed far back from the corners; this, together with setting back the

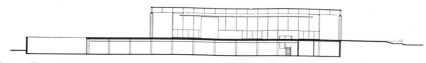

380. Twentieth Century Gallery, Berlin, 1963. *East-west section. To the far left, the sculpture court. The permanent collection was to have been housed below the raised platform and temporary exhibitions shown on the ground floor.*

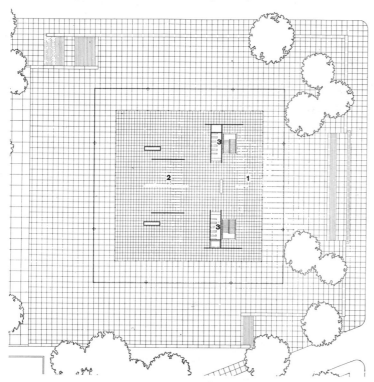

381. Twentieth Century Gallery, Berlin, 1963. *Plan of the upper story for temporary exhibitions.*

glass walls, strengthens the hovering relation between the different levels of roof, platform, and street. The building was designed to stand on a raised level (*fig.* **379**), which as the section shows (*fig.* **380**), contains a basement housing the main collection. The glazed hall on the entry level would hold only temporary exhibitions (*fig.* **381**).

On the Integrity of Form

There exist different types of creative spirits. Some conceive what they are destined to contribute to human culture once and for all at an early stage. Descartes perceived his philosophic system, as he has said himself, during the course of a single night. He elaborated it, but he never changed its structure.

There are other creative spirits who cannot be pinned down to what they thought in their youth, but who are continuously developing, continually in movement, throughout the span of their lives. Goethe is the prototype for this kind of eternally changing and developing spirit.

Mies van der Rohe and Le Corbusier

Confining our outlook to contemporary architecture, similar differences appear: Le Corbusier's development, for instance, undoubtedly reflects the second type; Le Corbusier pushed the sculptural approach still further, while, at the same time (in the sense of the third space conception) he sought to bring about a new balance between interior and exterior space. Mies van der Rohe belongs to those who, at an early stage, conceive what their temperaments will elaborate throughout their lives.

The conquest of pure form

From the moment in the early twenties when Mies van der Rohe realized the possibilities of artistic expression in the combination of glass walls and a steel skeleton, he felt impelled to develop this approach further, using continually more refined methods. Without the touch of a magic wand, these two industrially produced materials — steel and glass — sink back into their natural state: an amorphous mass. Their transformation to an acme of artistic refinement comes about from a hypersensitive adjustment of details: the most minute changes in proportions. Mies van der Rohe has always held "an organic principle" in mind: "We desire an order which gives everything its rightful place and we desire everything to have what is right for it according to its own nature."

It is understandable that he has required wooden models of the details of supports and their connections to be built in his studio to a scale of 1:1. The linkage of flat surfaces with the skeleton must be examined for the first hint of a reduction in intensity. In Mies van der Rohe's studio, in April 1964, I saw on a drawing board the squared modular grid of the Berlin Twentieth Century Gallery at a scale of 1:5 and a three-dimensional model of one of the supports with a cross-like section.

616

His persistent desire to vitalize space drove him to an ever more intensive architectonic expression. He did not rest till he had subdued all forms to the utmost purity. He holds ever more strongly to one of the constituent elements of contemporary architecture, the plane surface, which he likes to use in its smoothest and most transparent form — the glass sheet. This continuous pressure for the conquest of pure form has been accompanied by an ever stricter renunciation of all that seemed to the architect hampering or nonessential. It is this demand for the absolute that lies behind Mies van der Rohe's often deliberately misinterpreted saying: "Less is more." Mies van der Rohe's exclusiveness has had the greatest influence upon American architecture, although he is as impossible to imitate as Piet Mondrian.

He makes no distinction between his approach to a single-story dwelling, two-story buildings, or multi-story apartments. The attitude of the perfectionist controls the dimensioning of all surfaces, outlines, and details. Volumes are reduced to their simplest form. An increasing architectonic refinement can be observed from his Promontory Apartments, 1949, to the black skeleton of the Lake Shore Apartments, 1951, and the light, almost immaterial, aluminum ribs of the Commonwealth Apartments, 1956.

Mies van der Rohe's strict discipline has had a deep moral influence upon contemporary American architecture. Without it, it is possible that Eero Saarinen's delicately organized complex for the General Motors Technical Center (Detroit, 1951), would never have arisen in its present form; nor one of New York's purest skyscrapers, the twenty-four-story Lever House (Park Avenue, 1952). To create the socially welcoming plaza of the Lever House, Gordon Bunschaft of the firm of Skidmore, Owings, and Merrill removed an area of exceedingly valuable urban land from the money market and made it freely available for the use of New York pedestrians.

If later an investigation is made as to which of the architects of our period have best understood how to link a continuously flowing interior space with the shaping of precisely limited forms, Mies van der Rohe will appear as the clearest exponent of the inherent volition of our period.

ALVAR AALTO:
IRRATIONALITY AND STANDARDIZATION

Aalto is the strongest exponent of the combination of standardization with irrationality, so that standardization is no longer master but servant. The moral force behind the development of architecture in recent decades has had one supreme concern: to reëstablish a union between life and architecture. Aalto is the youngest of those architects who have created the present-day vocabulary.

Union between Life and Architecture

Earlier, Frank Lloyd Wright evolved a language of forms, direct, as it would seem, from the prairie. His private houses of about 1900 emphasized the human aspect and stood in complete contrast to the skyscrapers the young Wright had watched as they grew.

The road that Europe had to take to free itself from the devaluated architectural language of the ruling taste proved to be a much more difficult one. There architectural expression had become so debased that it could no longer follow any direct path. The curative process could only succeed if one pruned away everything so that there remained only the healthy base bearing the insignia of the period — a steel and concrete skeleton.

Another factor in the cleansing process was the elimination of the pseudo-individuality admired so much by the wealthy classes around the turn of the century. This work demanded a firm program and an emphasis on function. When Walter Gropius put forward a new means of architectural expression in Europe about 1913, he could not begin directly with the home; he had to begin by confining himself to frame structures, factories, and exhibition buildings.

Around 1920 Le Corbusier shaped the house on the basis of a new space conception. His points of departure were the ferroconcrete skeleton and the means of artistic expression that had developed since cubism. A sensitive understanding of construction techniques and an unerring functional analysis of problems were essential for the health of the new movement.

At the same time, through the work of the *Stijl* group, Holland contributed theories of artistic fundamentals as well as practical solutions. This movement centered around Theo van Doesburg, Mondrian, Rietveld, van Eesteren, and others. J. J. P. Oud expressed its social concepts in the workers' quarters that he built from 1919 onwards, in which the marriage of function and aesthetics is handled in a masterly fashion.

These means of expression and their elements — standardization, new methods of construction, and, above all, a new space conception — had developed so far by 1930 that an architectural language already lay at the disposal of anyone capable of using it.

The Complementarity of the Differentiated and the Primitive

About 1930 Alvar Aalto's name began to be known outside Finland. What part was he to play?

At this time, painters like Joan Miró and Paul Klee, whose work is closely bound to the organic and the irrational, were coming to the fore. A similar event was about to happen in architecture.

As early as 1925, in Le Corbusier's Pavillon de l'Esprit Nouveau in Paris, natural objects — stones, shells, and grotesque roots — lay alongside mechanically formed objects which have acquired a perfect standard type through man's long experience with them, such as everyday drinking glasses, wine bottles, or laboratory equipment. It seems today to be requisite that we should live both with objects shaped by man and with objects of organic growth.

We have seen how the new architecture had first to develop out of those elements that had remained sound: iron construction and ferroconcrete. But by about 1930 the new means of expression had been attained. Now it was possible to strive for further development and to dare the leap from the rational-functional to the irrational-organic. This need already lay concealed within the functional conception. To avoid misunderstanding, let it be stated that this development toward the organic in no way approximates the German reaction of the 1930's that carried on the ruling taste of the nineteenth century under the sign of the swastika. The feeling for mass production and for standardization has not been discarded at all, only now we have at hand not only the necessary techniques but also perhaps an insight into the use of these from a human standpoint.

Alongside iron and ferroconcrete construction, the ancient material, wood, came again to the fore. By 1930 it appeared that wood had been squeezed by manufacturers of all its potentialities. It seemed as though the constellation under which Aalto was born predestined him to look with new eyes upon this material which has become so closely linked with his name. He is as near to organic chemistry as he is to the artistic principles of our period.

Finland is with Aalto wherever he goes. It provides him with that inner source of energy which always flows through his work. It is as Spain is to Picasso or Ireland to James Joyce. Part of the essence of present-day art is that its true representatives originate in a definite human environment and their work is not created in a vacuum. But it is also part of its essence that barriers between space and time, barriers between countries, and barriers between future and past are torn down, and with a bold sweep our own period, the whole world, and the whole of history are embraced. Georges Braque expresses this in a Bergsonian manner in his sketchbook: "L'avenir est la projection du passé, conditionée par le présent." [1]

Perhaps later periods will observe that one of our good qualities was our endeavor to combine the technical with the

---

[1] *Cahier de Georges Braque 1917–1947* (Paris, 1948).

primeval. This same phenomenon appears in all the arts: out of forgotten strata of consciousness the elements of primitive man which are dormant in us are again brought to light, and at the same time unity is sought with the present day.

Aalto is restless. He does not always remain in the pine and birch forests of Finland. First he made contact with the continent; since 1939 he has stood with one foot in America. His nature leads him to come into contact with whatever the place and the period have to offer for the forces of artistic development. In addition, he has had personal friendships with such artists as Fernand Léger, Hans Arp, and Brancusi. He recognizes modern art as a great reservoir which, though often invisible, provides the decisive power for his own creativeness. One senses this in his sanatorium, in his factories, in his Viipuri Library, as well as in the simplest schemes that he sketches on the wall.

When Aalto was in the United States in 1939, building the Finnish Pavilion for the New York World's Fair, he and I were once sitting together with Brancusi, the sculptor. Brancusi had been telling of some work that he had done for an Indian Maharajah when Aalto suddenly exclaimed, "I see now, Brancusi! You stand at the crossroads of Asia and Europe!" Finland is also at the crossroads of East and West, but for the moment we would only stress the fact that many remnants of primeval and medieval times still remain alive there and intermingle with modern civilization. This double nature is instilled in Aalto too, and gives creative tension to his work.

Finnish Architecture before 1930

Finland is one of the countries that were longest covered with glaciers. Civilization, as it traveled over the earth, always reached this country very late — from the neolithic period onward to this century. Often eastern and western influences have intermingled here.

Of all the countries of Europe, Finland is in many respects one of the most peculiar. Its people have never risen to imperial-

382. Finland, transportation of wood. *After drying in the forests, the logs start a year-long journey over lakes and rivers down to the sea, where they are converted into pulp at cellulose plants.*

istic power and splendor, like the Vikings of Norway in early days, the Danes in medieval times, or the Swedes in the seventeenth century. For hundreds of years, Finland formed a part of Sweden, till Napoleon delivered it, in a moment of rage, to the Russians. Each of the rulers left his imprint on the country; but not one of the invaders could really curb the people. The only way to get along with the Finns was to treat them in a friendly manner and, as far as possible, to leave them undisturbed. This has remained true throughout Finland's whole history. It is a unique mixture of smoothness and friendliness, with an imperturbable firmness in the depths of their soul, that makes up the strength of these people.

Finland, covered with its network of lakes and forests, suggests in its structure the days of the Creation, when water and earth were first separated. It is a country of vast dimensions and solitudes: although ten times the size of Switzerland, it contains only the same number of inhabitants. Copper, timber, water — these are its principal resources. Finland is favored in that its ten thousands of lakes are connected in four or five systems and have outlets to the sea, not to the frozen north as in Russia, but to the west and to the south.

Finland's chief raw material is wood. The trees are felled in the north during the summer season. After drying in the forests for six months, they start a year-long journey over lakes and rivers, hundreds of miles, down to the sea. There in large cellulose plants at the rivers' mouths they are converted into pulp (*fig.* **382**).

Shortly before the first world war, Central Europe and Scandinavia, including Finland, all experienced a period of prosperity. It was the result of long years of peace. The efforts that Finland made at this time to establish a strong architectural expression of its own were immediately noticeable.[2]

Lars Sonck, a man of over eighty when I met him in the autumn of 1948 at a luncheon in the Liberal Club of Helsinki, was doubtless the strongest personality among the older Finnish architects. Himself resembling a block of unhewn granite, he built the best churches of the whole Art Nouveau movement in the first decade of this century. Their expressive directness and the manner in which granite, concrete, and space are treated still immediately capture the onlooker of today.[3]

Long before Eliel Saarinen left Finland for America, he was known outside his own country for his railway station in Helsinki (1906–14). In this celebrated building it is very easy to be reminded of South German influences; but, just like its architect, it is more elegant and flexible than its prototypes.

J. S. Sirén's House of Parliament in Helsinki, built in the late twenties, is an example of Swedish classicism (especially that of Ivar Tengboom and his circle); yet from this building there does not emanate that over-perfumed flavor which makes

---

[2] *Architecture in Finland* (Helsinki, 1932), published by the Finlands Architektfoerbund, is the only book which gives an insight into Finnish development up to that time.

[3] Perhaps we are considering his rough granite church in Tampere, the Finnish Manchester, more than the Kallio Kirk (1908), a kind of landmark in Helsinki.

383. ALVAR AALTO. Pavilion for an exhibition of forestry and agriculture in the village of Lapua, North Finland. *Exterior. This structure of unhewn logs seems rather a palisade fortress against Indians than an exhibition building for forestry and agriculture. Built in 1938 in a Northern Finnish forest, it shows in its roughness that Aalto had not become conventional through his contact with Western Europe. More delicate versions of this kind of vertical articulation appear frequently in Aalto's work (International Exhibitions at Paris, 1937, and New York, 1939).*

384. ALVAR AALTO. Pavilion for an exhibition of forestry and agriculture in the village of Lapua, North Finland. *Interior.*

385.   ALVAR AALTO.   Orchestra platform for the 700-year Jubilee of Turku, 1929.

Oestberg's Town Hall in Stockholm unsupportable after a time.

Aalto's First Buildings

Alvar Aalto's active life coincides with the most consistently agitated period of Finland's existence. First came liberation, followed by only a short span of undisturbed freedom, and then two wars. By normal reasoning, either of these should have been sufficient to wipe out Finland once and for all. After these catastrophes very little money remained for the rebuilding of the damaged instruments of production. Housing had to be reduced to the utmost, and there were no funds at all for town halls, museums, civic centers, and other such signs of financial prosperity. Great public buildings will not be found in Aalto's early work, and such schemes as the sanatorium at Paimio, the factory complex of Sunila, the luxury of Mairea, were created during the short period before Finland's two great fights for its very existence.

In Finland, architects and foresters have a much higher social standing than in other countries, and they form a kind of aristocracy, to which Alvar Aalto's forebears (who were foresters) belonged. Aalto himself was brought up in a village, Alajarvi, close to the northwestern end of the most densely populated region of Finland. He had an early start in his career, and while still a student at the Institute of Technology in Helsinki he built his first house, for his parents, in Alajarvi. He built his first church in 1922 near Jyväskylä.

In these early days, Aalto had much to do with several Finnish exhibitions, but only one of these temporary buildings shall be mentioned here: the Orchestra Platform in the exhibition that celebrated the 700-year Jubilee of the founding of Finland's old capital of Turku (Åbo). This slightly curved wooden sound box (*fig.* **385**), reduced to the utmost in all its parts and delicately outlined, works, together with the inclined orchestra floor, to assure perfect sound transmission, and reveals simultaneously its plastic flexibility. It was conceived at the same time that Aalto was marrying ceiling and wall in his Viipuri lecture hall.

In the mid-twenties, three young Finnish architects began work: Aalto, Bryggman, and Huttunen. They all used the ferroconcrete skeleton in the way that had been developed in France and elsewhere. It is difficult to distinguish their artistic handwriting at the time when Huttunen built his excellent flour mills, Bryggman his hotels, chapels, and insurance offices, and Aalto his first large block for an Agricultural Cooperative, containing offices, flats, and a theater for 600 persons. This was in 1928, in Turku, where Aalto had opened his own office.

Then, in 1928–30, came the office building for the *Turun-Sanomat* in Turku, the first of Aalto's buildings to become known outside Finland. Here can already be seen a coalition of western technique with an artistic language all his own: the ferroconcrete skeleton, bands of horizontal windows, roof terrace, and, especially, the mushroom ceiling of the subterranean hall that houses the printing press. The tapered columns of this skylight-illuminated hall, with their sensuous

626

386.   ALVAR AALTO.   *Turun-Sanomat* building, Turku, Printing room, 1928–30.

387.   ALVAR AALTO.   Building for the *Turun-Sanomat*, Exterior, 1928–30.

627

388. ALVAR AALTO. Tuberculosis Sanatorium, Paimio, South Finland, 1929–33. *Rest hall on top of patients' wing.*

one-sided mushroom capitals, show Aalto's hand at its best (*figs.* **386, 387**).

Before Aalto was thirty he had been commissioned to execute the Agricultural Coöperative, the *Turun-Sanomat* building, the Viipuri Library, the sanatorium at Paimio — all of them as a result of winning competitions. These facts are mentioned more to give an insight into Finland's atmosphere than to give proof of Aalto's genius. Had Aalto grown up in one of the other democratic countries, Switzerland for example, or the United States, he could never, as early as 1929, have been given first prize for a scheme such as the sanatorium at Paimio. His wings would have been broken before he had flown, or would have been crushed by compromises. Nothing reveals more clearly the spiritual leadership of a country than the capacity of its administration to recognize the best talents right from the start, and to trust them.

Paimio: The Sanatorium, 1929–33

As far as we can see, there are three institutional buildings inseparably linked to the rise of contemporary architecture: the Bauhaus at Dessau by Walter Gropius (1926); the project for the League of Nations Palace at Geneva by Le Corbusier (1927); and Alvar Aalto's sanatorium at Paimio (1929–33) in the southwest part of Finland, not far from the former capital Turku.

This institution is a medium-sized tuberculosis sanatorium with accommodation for about 290 patients. The main building, an unbroken line of six stories, is oriented to the south-southwest; the solarium with its cantilevered balconies adjoins it at a slight angle (*fig.* **389**). At the end of 1928, when Aalto won the competition for this public sanatorium, courage was needed to rest the solarium on a single row of ferroconcrete pillars, to close it at the back with one flat wall, and to let seven rows of balconies protrude in an unbroken line. In a sanatorium we have been accustomed to conceive room and balcony as a single unit, to allow the patient direct access to the open air. There are no balconies connected with the rooms at Paimio. But this separation between room and balcony is intentional. Physicians considered it as a very important factor in the rest cure that patients be brought together in small groups — according to their own choice, their own preference. To avoid the impression of endless rows of patients, small partition walls have been introduced so that the patients can be divided up into these small groups (*fig.* **390**). The top floor is used as a rest hall and runs the whole length of the building (*fig.* **388**). At the point where the main building and the rest hall intersect, Aalto links them together by giving the shelter an undulating curve. From the lounge chairs one can look into the tops of near-by fir trees and see the forests beyond them. But Aalto also planted pine trees in tubs along the balconies, to soften the concrete planes.

The human side also comes into consideration in the basic layout of the individual rooms. This is made clearly evident by the position of the electric light near the bed, by the oval-shaped plywood doors of the small closet, by the simple ar-

389. ALVAR AALTO. Tuberculosis Sanatorium, Paimio, 1929–33. *View of the entrance.*

rangement at the window to provide fresh air without causing drafts, by the specially designed wash basins which permit a noiseless flow of water, and by the early use of ceiling heating. These illustrate the minute elaboration of details.

Set at a right angle to the main building which houses the patients is a short wing with staircases and elevators which

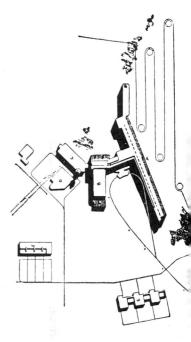

391. ALVAR AALTO. Tuberculosis Sanatorium, Paimio, 1929–33. *Ground plan.*

390. ALVAR AALTO. Tuberculosis Sanatorium, Paimio, 1929–33. *View of the patients' rooms and rest hall.*

forms the link to the dining and social rooms. Slightly lower wings for clinic and administration and still lower sections for kitchen, laundry, and power station radiate therefrom (*fig.* **391**). Farther off and separated from the complex are houses for the doctors and resident staff (*fig.* **391**). Aalto's town-planning principles can already be recognized in the loose-knit layout of this whole complex.

Wherever you stand, new aspects enrich the space–time conception of this complex. Each of the walls has its own existence and is formed according to the function of the rooms behind it, but all are modeled and related to each other by a strong plastic vision. At the time of its construction no building in the northern countries could compare with the sanatorium at Paimio in its purity of form and boldness of conception. As in Le Corbusier's League of Nations Palace, as in the Bauhaus, the various parts are fully integrated — like the organs of a body — each having its distinct functions and yet being inseparable from the others. Only by encompassing the whole compound can one perceive its space–time planning and its relation with earth and woods.

The Undulating Wall

Viipuri Library   One of the few buildings in which Aalto could freely express himself was the Viipuri Library, built with difficulty between 1927 and 1934. It was damaged in the first Russo-Finnish war and almost razed to the ground in the following conflict. It consisted of the library proper, which had carefully constructed circular overhead lights, and an unusually shaped lecture hall with a spacious connecting vestibule.[4]

Aalto's treatment of the undulating wooden ceiling of the lecture hall is of great historical importance. The architect today appears nowhere so hesitant as in the region of the ceiling, above the reach of everyday functions. Here, to a large extent, the architect has freedom of expression. Since the Roman Pantheon, the vault — the ceiling — has always been the place for the expression of the symbolic power of the period.

Alvar Aalto is, like Le Corbusier, one of the few architects who in our times has tried anew to attack the vaulting problem in a way peculiar to this period.[5] In the intimate hall of the

---

[4] For a complete description see Alfred Roth, *The New Architecture* (Zurich, 1940), pp. 181–194.

[5] E.g., Le Corbusier's original plan for the large assembly hall of the United Nations building (New York, 1947), which linked ceiling, wall, and floor by consecutive yet segmented parts.

392. ALVAR AALTO. Viipuri Library, 1927–34. *Undulating ceiling of the lecture hall.*

Viipuri Library the irrational curves of the ceiling glide through space like the serpentine lines of a Miró painting (*fig.* 392). From the floor behind the speaker, narrow strips of redwood sweep upward, curving irrationally along the glass wall. Of course, the architect himself can prove, with meticulous acoustic diagrams, that the undulating form he gave the ceiling enables sound to reach the human ear more perfectly. Here, therefore, scientific reasoning and artistic imagination have merged to free architecture from that rigidity which is today an ever-present menace.

Aalto treated the walls of his Finnish Pavilion with even greater freedom. This was without doubt the most daring piece of architecture in the New York World's Fair of 1939: an inclined wooden screen three stories high embraces the interior space in a freely drawn curve. The screen consists of three sections, each cantilevered over the other; at the same time the whole structure leans forward, intensifying thereby the impression of continuous movement. A series of vertical ribs and the rhythm of their changing shadows animate the surface of the huge screen (*fig.* 393).

Finnish Pavilion
New York, 1939

633

393. ALVAR AALTO. Finnish Pavilion, World's Fair, New York, 1939. *Undulating wall in the interior.*

394. Finnish lakes and forests, Aulenko.

395. ALVAR AALTO. Finnish Pavilion, World's Fair, New York, 1939. *Ground plan.*

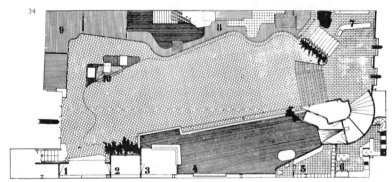

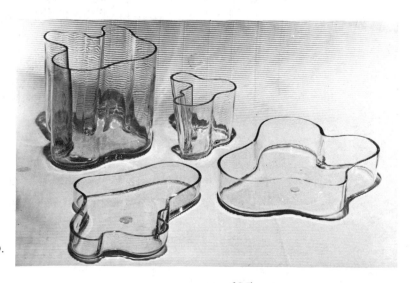

396. ALVAR AALTO. Glass vases.

Each detail has a well-reasoned explanation. In the technique of poster display, the undulating surface provides more space for large photographs; the forward tilting brings the uppermost pictures closer to the angle of vision; the series of vertical ribs thrusts the photographs forward; the cantilever of the upper stories, which so intensifies the impression of hovering movement, provides room for a concentrated display of objects.

The outstanding feature is the new modeling of inner space that is involved in this experiment, which to many still appears rude and almost barbaric (*fig.* **395**). But there is no doubt that the Finnish Pavilion stood in the main line of development and, like every integral work, displayed elements of both the past and the future.

Dormitory M.I.T., 1947 Having given flexibility to the ceiling and to partition walls, Aalto then attacks the outer wall in his Dormitory for the Massachusetts Institute of Technology (Cambridge, 1947).

The sober program of a dormitory is given a new interpretation. All means are employed in the attempt to avoid the ant-hill atmosphere often emanated by such buildings. Aalto gives the individual his personal rights through a great variety of means: by the way he arranges the staircases, by the blending of spaces, by alternating the capacity, form, and arrangement of the bedrooms. He dares to free the façade in an undulating wall so that, as he explains, every student has a clear view of the Charles River without being made aware of the large expanse of the building (*fig.* **397**).

The large student dormitories of Harvard along the Charles River were mostly built in the style of English country houses of the eighteenth century. One lives well in them even though they perhaps impose upon the college students too much of a feudal manner of behavior that is in strong contrast to the contemporary way of life to which most of them are accustomed.

Aalto's dormitory changes this approach. Inside, its unplastered brick walls are rough and the bedrooms and workrooms of the students are as small as possible without destroying the vitality of the atmosphere. The same goes for the common rooms. It is interesting how Aalto equips the almost

397. ALVAR AALTO. Dormitory (Baker House), Massachusetts Institute of Technology, 1947–49. *Air view.*

square dining room with his typical circular skylights. He is not afraid simply to attach the dining room to the undulating façade of the building. The space itself has the two levels that are characteristic of Aalto (*fig.* **401**), as in the Viipuri Library and other, later buildings. The unconventional way in which he lets the long lines of the staircase structure project plastically from the rear façade shows Aalto's independent attitude (*fig.* **402**). As soon as one steps into the entrance one sees through the whole transparent building.

The Harkness Center built by Walter Gropius for the graduate students of Harvard University overcomes the weightiness of the early student dormitories in quite a different way. Gropius kept the complex low so as to organize it around an open court. José Luis Sert adopted yet another way in his large complex on the Charles River for five hundred married Harvard students, 1963–64. Here there is an interplay between three strongly articulated 22-story towers and other differentiated low and higher buildings.

Aalto's attempt to free architecture from the threat of rigidity continues what Le Corbusier had attempted in the curved walls of the Swiss Pavilion in the Cité Universitaire (Paris, 1930–32), and in his project for Algiers (1931). As we have pointed out earlier, these continue the tradition of the undulat-

637

398. ALVAR AALTO.
M.I.T. Dormitory,
1947–49. *Charles River
front, with projecting
lounge and dining
hall.*

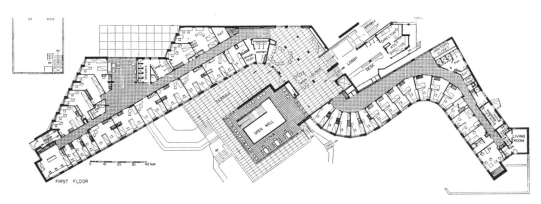

FIRST FLOOR

400. M.I.T. Dormitory. *Lounge with terrace, and basement dining hall.*

401. M.I.T. Dormitory. *Balcony lounge and stairway to dining room. Note the circular skylights — a typical Aalto detail.*

402. M.I.T. Dormitory. *View from athletic field, showing entrance and projecting staircases.*

ing wall as a means of modulating space from Francesco Borromini's façade of San Carlo alle Quattro Fontane, 1662–67 (*fig.* **82**), to the serpentine windings of English crescents in the late eighteenth century (*fig.* **83**).

Aalto's endeavor to imbue things with an almost organic flexibility has another source: the nature of his country. As Joan

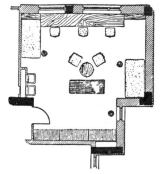

403.   ALVAR   AALTO.
M.I.T. Dormitory. *Three-man study, with bunks to save space. Unplastered brick walls.*

Miró is rooted in the Catalan landscape, as the cubists transmitted the experiences — tables, glasses, bottles, newspapers — of a Parisian café into a new conception of space, so Aalto found a direct incentive in the curved contours of the Finnish lakes, shaped with astonishing smoothness by nature itself and set in high relief by forest masses pressing on all sides down to the water's edge (*figs.* **394, 396**).

Sunila: Factory and Landscape, 1937–39

One of Aalto's main activities in Finland is industrial planning, from the factory itself to the resettlement of whole industrial areas. This was the case in the Vuoksi river valley development (1947), where the left bank, annexed by the Russians, had to be abandoned, and all industry, settlements, and community centers transplanted and a new road system laid out.

Aalto has built several cellulose factories [6] and sawmills.[7] Theirs are not the grand dimensions of American industrial plants, nor the elegant luxury of the van Nelle factory in Rotterdam (1927). Yet Aalto knows how to raise a plant from a purely professional instrument up to a piece of architecture in which the site, the use of different materials, and the organization of volumes in space are given as much attention as the production line. Nowhere is this more apparent than in Sunila (1937–39).

Sunila, with a yearly output of 80,000 tons of cellulose sheets, was built jointly by five Finnish wood concerns. Good factories are taken for granted today. But Sunila is not merely a factory. It is a complex of homogeneous living zones and production areas. The living quarters were started before the factory itself and are strewn around in the fir forest, together with their *saunas* and laundries (*fig.* **407**).

Sunila stands on an island in a small bay. Its aspect is defined by the long horizontality of the warehouse, extending along the seashore (*fig.* **405**), and the vertical accents of the different coördinated buildings of the plant. The inclined diagonals of the conveyors, leading to and from the storage towers, aggressively penetrate the whole complex.

Aalto took care that the rounded granite rocks on which the factory stands were not blasted to the level of the shore (*fig.* **404**). He knew how to use the contrast between the massiveness of these granite rocks on the one hand and the delicate steel structure of the row of pylons which support the conveyor and the different texture of the flat brick walls on the other.

Sunila has a most perfect production line. In the interior there are immense containers, boilers and digesters. There are pipe tunnels through which fluids and wood pulp flow, and a large machine for drying cellulose standing isolated in a spacious

---

[6] For instance, the Toppila pulp mills at Oulu (1933), where the suggestive form of the flake bins is not completely mastered.

[7] Sawmills, with their flat boarded walls, generally recall the lifelessness of barracks. In Aalto's Warkhaus sawmill (1947), the usual dreariness of a sawmill is imbued with vitality just by the use of carefully profiled round timber and by giving the wall a lively contour.

404. ALVAR AALTO. Sunila, 1937–39. *Conveyors, factory, and granite blocks.*

405. ALVAR AALTO. Sunila, 1937–39. *Warehouse, conveyors.*

406. ALVAR AALTO. Sunila, 1937–39. *View toward the open sea.*

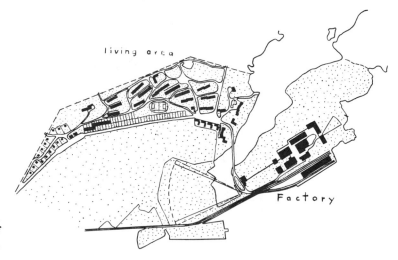

living area

Factory

407. ALVAR AALTO. Sunila, 1937–39. *Plan of factory and living quarters.*

643

408.   ALVAR AALTO.   Mairea, 1938–39.   *Exterior.*

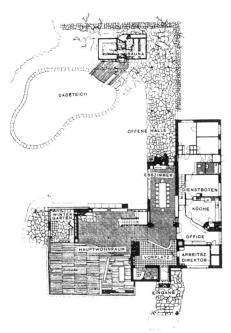

409.   ALVAR AALTO. Mairea, 1938–39.
Ground plan.

644

hall. But no men are visible. Only forty-five men are required to supervise the daily transformation of 30,000 logs into wood pulp; but more than three thousand men work in the forests to keep the plant supplied. No one is to be seen on the stairways connecting the different levels or in the numerous halls. There is an atmosphere like that in Captain Nemo's *Nautilus* in *Twenty Thousand Leagues under the Sea*. The problem of the production line here reaches a perfect solution. Here no human being is misused to become an adjunct to a machine.

One stands finally on the top level, on the flat roof-terrace of the high brick-clad storage building, from which the material, obeying the law of gravity, is conducted into the production process. Below radiates the organism of the factory, the large covered flake conveyor mounts almost to the terrace, and the eye passing over the granite rocks meets the Finnish landscape (*fig.* **406**): water, water, trees, and a vast expanse of space.

Close to the shore is an island of logs which have been floated down the river from distances of hundreds of miles. A cable crane picks them out to feed the machines. Ships wait in the bay to carry the brown cellulose sheets overseas. It is a Faustian prospect.

Mairea, 1938–39

Aalto's genius cannot be apprehended in a single piece of furniture, a living room, or a house. These must be seen together with his large-scale planning and the structure of the country. In Finland in these unsettled times there has been no opportunity for one-family houses and luxury villas. Aalto built a small house for himself and a larger one for his friend Gullichsen, president of one of the Finnish wood concerns. Gullichsen's house, named "Mairea" in honor of his wife, was built in 1938–39 in a clearing hewn out of the pine forest on the crown of a hill not far from the coast. Behind the house are a garden and a swimming pool with a group of gray silver willows in the background. It is a large mansion, yet it is intimate.

Mairea is a house poured, as it were, from a single crucible, for architect and client worked together, as in the eighteenth century. They had the same will and the same inclinations, a rather rare coincidence in this period when the architect has to spend most of his energy convincing a hesitating client in whom the last century still lingers. Moreover, nothing leads the modern architect farther astray than building for a client of large financial means, whose main concern it is to invent extravagant needs and an endless series of superfluous gadgets.

Even one accustomed to judge immediately the qualities of a building will not easily comprehend the architectural instrumentation of Mairea. It is architectural chamber music which demands the strictest attention to perceive the subtleties in the resolution of its motifs and intentions — and especially to grasp fully the handling of space and the extraordinary handling of materials. The broad windows permit the interpenetration of inner and outer space; the forest seems to enter the house and find its concomitant echo in the slender wooden poles employed there.

The use of textures

The spatial organization can perhaps be experienced to a certain extent from illustrations. It is otherwise with the use of the many materials and the lyricism which results from their juxtaposition. This is already apparent from the outside. The rough-hewn slabs of black slate beneath the window — whose texture it is impossible to recognize in the illustration (*fig.* **408**) — are combined with the warm brown of the teakwood shutters and the yellow band of birch of the parapet running above.

The interior has a more delicate use of texture. In conjunction with the spatial accentuation, the vestibule has large tiles of a curious brown, set diagonally — tiles used normally for the restoration of churches. In contrast to these, smaller reddish tiles cover the floor of the drawing room with the heavy Finnish fireplace and continue into the dining room, placed at right angles in the other wing. The four steps leading from the vestibule to the slightly raised level of the rooms opening from it are of a wood with a strikingly lucid quality. I asked Aalto later what kind of wood he had used here. It is rather rarely used, he said — a kind of white beech, the same as that used

646

410. ALVAR AALTO. Mairea, 1938–39. *View toward the Finnish fireplace and drawing room.*

for the small strip which runs around the hull of a yacht. To indicate that the different parts of the main living room blend into each other, the tile zones merge with the wooden floor in an undulating curve.

A subtle juxtaposition of materials appears everywhere. The shiny twin columns of the living quarters are of an ebony black which is relieved by small bands of wickerwork, placed at varying heights around the columns, sometimes individually wrapped, sometimes bound together (*fig.* **410**). The large Finnish fireplace (Finnish because it follows the old tradition of the country of building the hearth about on table level) has cantilevered granite shelves above the floor level so that one may stretch out along them. In contrast to the American custom, the granite blocks are not continued in the surrounding wall, which is left white and smooth. One has to observe very precisely to apprehend the textual effect of the contiguous wall of roughly whitewashed brick.

647

This use of different textures has the same meaning as the use of the rocaille in the eighteenth century; it helps to modulate spaces in flux.

Spatial organization It is the spatial organization which interests us most here. You enter the vestibule. The undulating wall of eye-level height that faces you gives a hint of other rooms to the right. Four steps lead to the level of the main living room, which unfolds in different directions. Diagonally in the background expands the area of the fireplace, and, on stepping toward it, you are drawn, diagonally again, into the depth of the large music room with its black wicker-clad columns and generously dimensioned windows. Only the library is granted complete privacy.

The moment you are on the level of the main living room, the slender poles arranged at irregular intervals on both sides of the wooden staircase captivate you by the way they separate it and yet permit space to penetrate. Incidentally, it is often the manner in which the staircase is integrated into the spatial organization of a house that betrays the architect's capacity for handling space. In this case, the light wooden staircase flows into the main room, announces the existence of other rooms and yet preserves its own identity. It is treated like a transparent sculpture (*figs.* **411, 412**).

In this house a rare thing has been achieved; the feeling of an uninterrupted flow of space throughout the house is never lost, and yet the feeling of intimacy is preserved, wherever you are.

Organic Town Planning

Town planning is only another term for integration. In this heyday of narrow-minded specialization, nothing is more difficult than to conceive or to build up a whole from a number of different parts.

The ability to integrate is normally developed toward the end of a period, when it is at its cultural peak. This is particularly true in relation to town planning.

We are now at the beginning of a period; yet, it is already necessary for us to possess those qualities that normally develop much later. As far as I know, this situation is unique. But it exists, and we must act accordingly. We are confronted here and now with the necessity of finding a solution to the complex problems of the city, although specialists are still sharply discussing what kind of city it should be. Let us not forget the present situation: that our imagination begins to freeze as soon as problems of integration are involved.

What is Aalto's contribution in the field of town planning? The same qualities which enliven his buildings are even more

411. ALVAR AALTO. Mairea, 1938–39. *Details of the staircase.*

412. ALVAR AALTO. Mairea, 1938–39. *Staircase, drawing room.*

obvious in his planning schemes. With the same freedom that he has employed to loosen up the structure of walls and ceilings, he loosens up the rigid framework of the human settlement. Rows of houses scattered in all directions seem to have been strewn by the wind, and yet they are held together by an invisible force, like filings in a magnetic field.

In the layout of Sunila, 1937–39 (*fig.* **407**), Alvar Aalto's approach to town planning is already manifest. The whole sequence of his later schemes will reflect the same principles.

Sunila, 1937–39

These may be briefly described as establishing an equipoise between the primary demands for a human environment: an equipoise between the living area, the center of production, and nature.

To secure the right of the individual to privacy, to a simple community life, and to the most intimate contact with the earth is today the preoccupation of every planner. This aim is no longer original. Today these demands have become a matter of course. What is still lacking is their realization.

We will not easily find, as early as 1937, many achievements like Sunila, where both the production area and the living area have been conceived in such a way that each has been given its necessary rights without disturbing the other. The grasp of a town planner can be felt in the layout of one-family houses upon the narrowest strip of the available land; in the grouping of row houses freely in the forest; in the slight variations of the engineers' row houses, which lie nearer to the waterfront and are arranged in a slight curve, to ensure the utmost privacy for each dwelling. It goes without saying that the necessary social facilities (especially several *saunas* — communal bathing houses) are located at strategic intervals.

Aalto's integrated approach enables him to have the structural completion of the whole community in his mind, even when he begins with only the first few cells. For some years after 1944 he worked with other architects on the solution of the large-scale problem of the reconstruction of Rovaniemi, the principal town of Finnish Lapland, which was completely destroyed at the end of the second Russo-Finnish war. This plan was never implemented. The time was not ripe.

Experimental town, 1940

In his scheme for "An Experimental Town" which Aalto published in 1940, he had already indicated how he would synchronize, from the very beginning, the simultaneous growth of the single house, the town, and the processes of production (*fig.* **413**). Taking an area of hilly woodland scattered with lakes, so typical of the Finnish landscape, he laid out the various types of dwellings in the freest possible way. The terraced houses (f) circle about the hilltops in amoebic spirals, so that the structure of the landscape breaks through;

650

413. ALVAR AALTO. Project for an experimental town, 1940.

the apartment houses (e) are turned at a slight angle one to another and sited at right angles to the slope of the hillside; the wood infiltrates into the area of the one-family houses (d); public buildings, schools, and sports grounds (b, c) are close to every part of the town, though each is laid out to its own advantage. The standardized and the irrational here flow together, as in all Aalto's works.

In 1940, this scheme was only a scrap of paper, designed for the students of M.I.T. When I was in Finland in the fall of 1948, the Finnish government had just granted the necessary funds for the erection of several such experimental towns in Finland but their implementation was delayed.

But by 1938, Aalto had already planned Kauttua. Well hidden, in a narrow valley cut by a creek and about three to four hours' drive from Turku, lies a paper mill called Kauttua. On the opposite side of the valley, Aalto built, amidst the forest, a row of workers' houses. These climb the steep hillside in four great steps (*fig.* **415**). The flat roof-terrace of one house forms the large veranda of the next. It may well be that Aalto remembered the peasant houses on the Greek isles. Here, too, the children play on their neighbor's roof — something that is only possible in countries where people do not immediately become anxious if they have to share something. As on the Greek island of Santorin, the houses of Kauttua use the natural slope to avoid the expense of staircases (*fig.* **416**). In their form and shape they express man's relation to the soil from which he springs.

Only one row of houses has been built, owing to lack of money and materials. The matter of real importance here is not this single row of houses, but the realization of the whole plan, one of the best proposals for the shaping of a rural settlement (*fig.* **414**). Four rows of these terraced houses had been planned, each placed so that the natural forms of the slope are perfectly utilized. The brow of the hill is, as Frank Lloyd Wright liked to see it, untouched. Connected with these units, there are a school and a small community center, and, further down the slope, close to the river, a steam bath, the *sauna*, built as usual together with the communal laundry — the first facility to be erected. This corresponds to an old habit of the Finns, to start the small bath hut before building the dwelling. This early plan of continuous houses following the slope of a hill came into general use in the next decade with increasingly complicated forms.

Oulu, 1943

Rapids rush through the city of Oulu, situated at the mouth of the river Oulu in northwestern Finland. An architectural problem here had to be solved: How could one make full use of the water power without destroying the beauty of the marshy islands that lie at the mouth of the river? Aalto wanted to create a Venetian-style development (*fig.* **417**) by taking the hundreds of thousands of cubic meters of stone and rubble resulting from excavation of a canal and the necessary dredging of the river and using this material to enlarge the islands and to raise their ground level a few inches.

The islands nearest to the power plant were to support the dwelling quarters of the workers. An administrative civic center and a sports center were to be created on the desolate

414. ALVAR AALTO.
Kauttua. *Ground plan.*

416. ALVAR AALTO. Kauttua.
*Terraced houses showing entrances on
different levels.*

415. ALVAR AALTO.
Kauttua. *Terraced houses.*

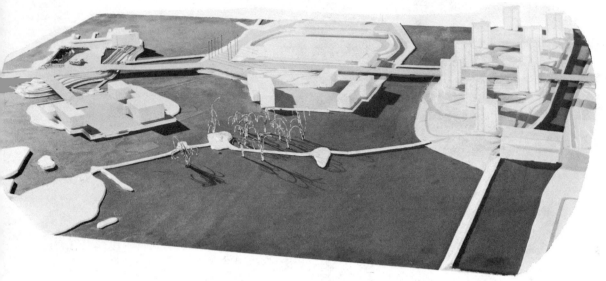

417. ALVAR AALTO. Oulu, 1943. *Model.*

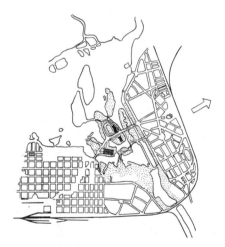

418. ALVAR AALTO. Oulu, 1943.
The city with the new civic centers.

islands that face the open water. A large highway would connect all with the two parts of the existing city of Oulu (*fig.* **418**). In front of the public center, a number of fountains would spring, geyser-like, from the surface of the water. This plan was also not implemented, and in 1962 a new competition was held in which Aalto did not take part.

Decentralization The northern countries have taken the lead in decentralizing their universities and technical institutes to meet their needs for expansion. Finland was in the vanguard. The Helsinki Institute of Technology has been rebuilt in the forests of

654

Otaniemi, ten kilometers from the city. The plan, coordinated with a new highway network, was made by Aalto in 1955 and building started in 1962.

Civic and Cultural Centers

One of Aalto's most perfect schemes — a Sports and Cultural Center for Vienna (won in competition, 1953) — has unfortunately not been built. Its main building for 25,000 people, which could serve as sports arena, concert hall, and exhibition hall, had a concave ceiling and slanting walls at front and back (*figs.* **419, 420**).

Only fragments were built of Aalto's general plan for a village on the little island of Saynätsalo about three hundred kilometers north of Helsinki, across from the island where Aalto built his summer house, Muuratsalo. This civic complex standing in a pine wood represents the first three-dimensional realization of a fully planned community center (*fig.* **421**). Its planning goes back to 1945, but building was not begun until 1950. This complex was Aalto's first community center to be erected. It contains the Council House with its offices on three sides of a raised court facing a small library. Below them, on the ground level, are shops and dwellings.

Saynätsalo,
1950–52

This project, with its different levels, is dominated by the Council Chamber. The construction of its wooden ceiling as a radiating focus served to evoke Aalto's plastic imagination — it is like the spokes of an opened umbrella.

The most interesting aspect of this complex is its use of two different levels. Aalto created the upper level from excavation materials, organizing the buildings one above the other. The Council Chamber, meeting rooms, and library lie one upon the other, opening onto a raised patio split open on two sides leading to stairways: one with polygonal projecting steps bordered by stone risers. Grass grows on the steps — intentionally. Later Aalto was to emphasize the relations between two levels even more strongly.

Saynätsalo was the start. In the next decade realizations followed unusually rapidly on an increasingly larger scale. By

Seinäjoki,
1960

419. ALVAR AALTO. Sports and Cultural Center, Vienna, 1953. *The building for simultaneous operations is a roofed sports arena accommodating 25,000 that can also serve as a concert hall and an exhibition hall. The suspended roof also covers a row of smaller halls. The large room has a concave suspended roof and walls that slope inward.*

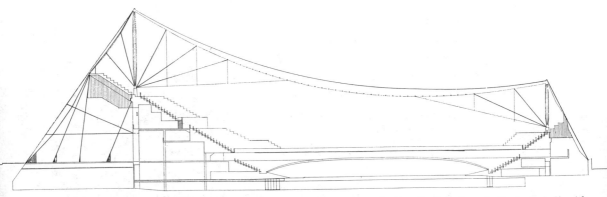

420. Sports and Cultural Center, Vienna, 1953. *Section through the large hall with suspended roof and tension members.*

656

1960 it had become possible to erect a complete community center in the rural district of Seinäjoki, five hundred kilometers north of Helsinki. This is dominated by the Council House (*fig.* **424**), its upper chamber set back to emphasize its volume. The exterior walls are clad with dark-colored glazed enamel bricks, like those Aalto had used in 1955 on the interior walls of the Pensions Office in Helsinki.

Although the Council House is the dominating element, the whole complex is a group form containing the library whose outstretched wing lies parallel to the Council House, and a small theater (*fig.* **422**). These buildings do not surround an enclosed space; instead they are held together by the relations of their three volumes. Like the Saynätsalo patio, the open area is slit open at the sides so that the space flows freely through it.

The element of space construction which underlines most strongly the relations between volumes and space is the stairway, which rises from the earth like the spread-out base of a truncated pyramid (*fig.* **423**). The part played by the stairway in the total complex is much clearer than it appears in the model (*fig.* **422**), where it seems to be made of stone. In reality, instead of being smooth curving steps, the treads are held by wooden planks and are overgrown with grass, like the surface of the plaza. Only one narrow paved path traverses both plaza and stairway.

Is it after all a stairway? There would never be such a large crowd of people to give a rational justification for its dimensions. It is there because it must be there. It is a fourth element whose stratifications give an added emphasis to the interrelation of the volumes. Such a plan would have contributed to the glory of any Greek agora.

A broad road separates this civic and cultural center from the religious center, which with its church and community house forms a second plaza.

Aalto started relatively late to erect large buildings in the center of the capital; the first was the Government Pensions Office (1952–56). To bring a human note into this office

Helsinki Civic Center, 1964 ——

657

421. ALVAR AALTO. Saynätsalo, designed 1945, built 1950–52. *Saynätsalo was the first of Aalto's community centers to be built: in addition to administrative offices it included a small library (right), shops, and dwellings. The use of two levels is especially interesting. Aalto created the upper one from the excavation materials. The steps lead to a patio split open on two sides.*

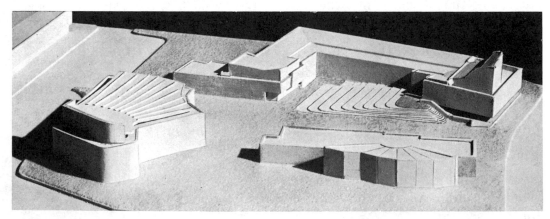

422. ALVAR AALTO. Seinäjoki, construction started 1960. *The community center of the small town of Seinäjoki, 500 kilometers north of Helsinki. To the right, the Council House with wide steps. At the time of the model the steps were designed to be made of stone. In the right foreground is the library, left, a theater. Off the photograph to the right is the religious center. As at Saynätsalo, the area between the buildings is split open.*

658

423. Seinäjoki Council House, construction started 1960. *As at Saynätsalo, the steps are built up from the excavation debris, like the base of a pyramid, and are overgrown with grass. Only a small path is paved. In the background the religious center is visible.*

424. Seinäjoki Council House, construction started 1960. *The façade is dominated by glazed enamel elements.*

425. ALVAR AALTO. Helsinki Civic Center, design started 1958, building started 1964. *Instead of being in the center of the city, it radiates out from it, between water and sloping hills. In a dynamic rhythm, museum, concert hall, and other buildings stretch out along an existing park. The treatment of the traffic lines is particularly important. An existing highway runs behind the new center and is linked to a new one run on the far side of the water.*

building he used dark glazed porcelain elements to clad the interior walls, sometimes only in bands, sometimes completely covering the walls. (He used this motif time and again, almost as in a symphony). It took some time before these elements appeared on the outer walls. In the auditorium (which serves as a concert hall and opera house) of the Helsinki Civic Center (designed in 1958; building begun in 1964), Aalto used small square bricks which easily followed the great curve of its rear wall. This is the largest auditorium in Helsinki and its vaulted ceiling has proved to be acoustically excellent.

660

Aalto's new civic center for the capital focusing on this auditorium is not situated in the middle of the city. It radiates out from the city on open land gently sloping toward the water. Again Aalto avoids an enclosed square. Auditorium, theater, museum, and other buildings flow through an existing park in a dynamic stream (*fig.* **425**).

Despite its extrusion from the city, the Helsinki Civic Center retains contact with the existing National Museum and Olympic Stadium. (The capital of Chandigarh is also, in another way, separated from the body of the city.) The new buildings extend partly over the water. The plan provides for generous underground parking; an existing highway runs behind the center, and a new one will be built along the opposite bank of the water. A few kilometers away, deliberately separated from the civic center, will arise a business center with restaurants, radio station, and television building.

This project is on an unusually generous scale when one recalls that the Technological Institute with all its branches is being decentralized at the same time. The enterprise is astonishing for a small country of only five million inhabitants. No other country in Europe can be compared to Finland in the general quality of its architectural development.

Furniture in Standard Units

In Alvar Aalto's opinion, a house is not only a far more complicated organ than an automobile; there is also a real difference between an object which one may live in for a generation and a vehicle of transport which one may conveniently exchange every second season. Furthermore, no two sites are the same. Above all, the house reaches too far into the psychic to admit of total mass fabrication.

Only elements of it should be standardized: doors, windows, mechanical equipment, and constructional members, whether they consist of skeleton or panel. The important matter is that architectural freedom should be preserved. The standardized elements should awaken, not destroy, architectural vision.

Both house and furniture today are composed of machine-made parts. The comparison can be taken no further, however. The type house, the prefabricated house, kills the phantasy of the architect and administers a deathblow to organic town planning. But furniture is predestined to be conceived in standardized types. I have discussed this question at length elsewhere,[8] yet I cannot close these remarks upon Aalto without mentioning his stimulation of furniture design in the middle thirties. The cause lies once again in his integration of the regional element with the latest mechanical processes and his full awareness of contemporary means of expression. The substance which he took in his hands and made flexible, as he had made walls, ceilings, and town planning flexible, was that organic material wood.

The constituent element of Aalto's furniture, like the slab in a bridge by Maillart or the plane surface in a modern painting, is a sheet of plywood. Aalto received the impetus for his first experiments when he had to furnish the Paimio sanatorium from top to bottom in 1929. Here can be found the first mass-produced plywood chairs, consisting of a ribbon-like wood frame, within which is suspended the undulated plywood seat (*fig.* **280**). About 1935, Aalto dared to do away with the closed plywood frame and built the chair as a free cantilever, a construction that, till then, had only been expected of steel.

Like all those who succeed in taking the plunge into the unknown, Aalto possesses the gift of seeing things as freshly as though they had never been touched before. This is the kind of talent that is urgently needed today, to discover an emotional equivalent that may rescue us from drowning in the flood of technical processes that is being poured over us.

Aalto announced a new development in the manufacture of furniture. By a special suction process it is possible for wood to acquire such suppleness and flexibility that the architect may twist it and turn it as he pleases. Further, chemists have found a method of forming a cable-like structure from a number of small rod-like pieces of wood tapered at both ends — "wood macaroni" Aalto calls them. A physician, on

[8] *Mechanization Takes Command* (Oxford University Press, 1948).

seeing them, was at once reminded of certain organisms within the large intestine.

The Rococo developed the greatest mastery and finesse in wood carving. The skeleton of the chair was then reduced to astonishing slenderness and shaped in elegant forms. Today, entirely new possibilities have been opened up through the aid of chemical changes. We wonder whether this chemical processing will be assimilated emotionally.

Aalto as Architect

If one were to try to sum up the distinguishing marks of Aalto's work and to assess his position in the constellation of the pioneers of the modern movement, one would arrive at something like the following. As we have said before, in the decisive period of the late twenties, three buildings came to the fore: the Bauhaus of Walter Gropius (1926), Le Corbusier's project for the League of Nations (1927), and Aalto's tuberculosis sanatorium at Paimio (1929–33). Aalto, although working in distant Finland, stepped very early into the front rank of contemporary architects.

Like Gropius and Le Corbusier, Aalto was very early convinced that a building could not stand as an isolated object of art, but must form part of a greater complex. This conviction was early embodied in his sanatorium at Paimio (1929–33), whose wings — different in height from the main building and radiating out in different directions — avoid any rectangular enclosure.

At the same time, Aalto, like Le Corbusier, desired to create a simultaneity of inner and outer space. To bring about this unity, he often modeled a shell-like vault over the interior of a building and emphasized its plastic volume on the exterior — a phenomenon particularly interesting to our period.

Aalto is wedded neither to the right angle nor to the cube. He is one of those architects who have worked unswervingly to create a flexible wall and to intensify its architectonic properties. The stages of this process can be hinted at in Aalto's case as follows: first came the astounding boldness of the

The flexible wall

663

wooden ceiling of the lecture room at Viipuri (*fig.* **392**), rising in waves from the floor, up and over the space. The Finnish Pavilion of the Paris World's Fair, 1937, had steeply sloping and rounded wall surfaces superimposed on one another, strengthened with wood cladding. In the Finnish Pavilion at the New York World's Fair, 1939, Aalto curved the walls, which also slanted inward. In the M.I.T. dormitory, 1947 (*fig.* **398**), the whole façade was brought into a swinging curve. He pursued this line steadily in apartment houses (in Bremen, 1958); private houses, like the Mairea house; and public buildings like the Pensions Office and Civic Center in Helsinki, the Opera House at Essen (the nearest in grandeur to his Viennese project), and the Seinäjoki Council House.

Relations between horizontal surfaces

The establishment of relations between horizontal surfaces — working with different levels — is one of the long neglected elements of architecture. One can notice in almost every competition how inept most architects have become at working with different levels and using their varieties of tension to strengthen architectural expression.

Aalto stressed the relation between horizontal surfaces in the undulating ceiling of the Viipuri Library (1927–34), where he deliberately enlarged the space of the reading gallery. This relationship was emphasized more strongly in the library of the Wolfsburg Cultural Center (1959–62). In the dining hall of his M.I.T. dormitory (*fig.* **400**) Aalto did the opposite: he hollowed out the floor. Out of doors, we find Aalto working with several artificially created ground levels at the Saynätsalo community center (*fig.* **421**) and, even more subtly, in the Seinäjoki community center (*fig.* **422**).

In Denmark he designed the museum at Aalborg (building was started in 1964) with well studied lighting in the interior and, on the exterior, amphitheater-like terraced steps up the hillside, designed for the display of sculpture.

Town planning

From the beginning Aalto was very interested in town planning. A flexible organic element runs through all his planning: from his project for an experimental town, 1940 (*fig.* **413**) to the Seinäjoki community center, 1960 (*figs.* **423, 424**). It also appears in his flowing, outstretched civic center for Helsinki, with its well-organized relationship both to the structure of the landscape and to the traffic routes (*fig.* **425**).

Aalto embodies the type of architect who can take regional features and translate them into a universal language without ever losing their individual flavor. Regional roots and a world-wide orientation do not conflict in those artists who are sensitive to the mood of our period.

It has been said of Hans Arp, whose art is close to that of Aalto, that his shapes and forms never even momentarily slipped into modishness, but instead were deeply rooted in the eternal verities of mankind. This can also be said of Aalto.

The Human Side

One cannot speak about Aalto the architect without speaking about Aalto the man. People are at least as important to him as architecture. Aalto is interested in every human being, in each of their particular desires and experiences, no matter where they come from or to what social class they belong. He draws incentive and stimulation from contact with men of varied callings, much as James Joyce did. Indeed, Aalto cannot set foot outside his door without becoming involved in some human episode. He approaches people directly and without inhibitions, in the same way that he approaches the organic material wood.

When Aalto first appeared, unknown to the rest of us, within the circle of the newly formed CIAM, in Frankfurt in 1929, he did not talk about his buildings but instead told us of a delicate adventure that had befallen him at nine o'clock that morning, on his way from the station to the hotel. In 1933, when he was traveling from Finland to the Athens Congress by plane, rail, and automobile, to take part in the formulation of the Charte d'Athènes, the long conversations that he had on his journey were of the greatest interest to him. Accompanying him on his journey through the Balkans was his grandmother, who had a plaster cast and whom he had to assist from train to train.

Aalto came to America for the first time in 1939 to build the Finnish Pavilion at the New York World's Fair. His English vocabulary was far from extensive, yet he lectured to the jaded public of the Museum of Modern Art in New York. The way that he stood there, the way in which he was able to express what he had to say with his fragmentary vocabulary and a few "okay's," captivated his audience from the start.

Aalto's call to a professorship at the Massachusetts Institute of Technology was a natural consequence of his personality, the success of the Finnish Pavilion, and the approval accorded to his furniture. Thus Walter Gropius and Alvar Aalto were at work in the same town.

Aalto then divided his time and his work between the rebuilding of Finland and his American professorship. The dormitory that he erected for M.I.T. was a particularly bold undertaking when one considers that American college architecture had traditionally been decked with pseudo-gothic or colonial forms.

Aalto's relationship with man in his completeness cannot be defined on a rational basis. His personality radiates in direct contact. But, when he is gone, there does not seem to be any possible means of contact with him. It is probable that he has never carried on a regular mail correspondence in his life. However, immediately he appears, his tales, flavored by a whimsical understanding of human situations, and the radiance of his whole being, make it seem as though he had only left the day before.

There are certain architects whose work develops almost of itself. Aalto's work is of a different kind. Each line tells of his close contact with human destiny. This may be one of the reasons why his architecture encounters less difficulty in overcoming the resistance of the common man than that of others of his contemporaries.

I agree with Ernst Cassirer, the philosopher, who, in his last work,[9] demands so fervently that history should be written only with an intimate knowledge of the human side.

---

[9] E. Cassirer, *An Essay on Man* (New Haven, 1944), p. 181.

All Aalto's exhibitions and his work up to 1949 were signed "Aino and Alvar Aalto." It was not a gesture of chivalry that induced him to place the name of his wife before his own. This marriage was as singular as everything else related to him. Its steadfastness was based upon common sharing of all struggles and successes ever since their joint student days. But its real secret lay more likely in a profound reciprocation of human contrasts. Aalto is restless, effervescent, incalculable. Aino was thorough, persevering, and contained. Sometimes it is a good thing when a volcano is encircled by a quietly flowing stream.

Though Aino Aalto died on January 13, 1949, her name will always be connected with the work of Alvar Aalto. He always put her name before his own, but Aino herself always insisted, "I am not creative, Alvar is the creative one." This is not the moment to determine the extent of Aino's influence on Aalto's production. But we know that she had her quiet say as an architect at all stages of his work and life. She never appeared in the foreground or admitted what had really been designed by her. She was always at work behind the scenes, as when I last saw her in the fall of 1948: by day, director of Artek, the corporation engaged in the designing and manufacture of Aalto's furniture; in the evening, hostess at a dinner party for Finland's intellectual elite, sitting relaxed in a white gown among her guests, quiet as the Finnish lakes and forests from which she had sprung.

The, for Aalto, inseparable connection between productivity and human relations explains why his closest working partners were women. First it was Aino. Then, some years after her death, Aalto married the young Elissa, who had formerly worked in the studio. She has a quite different nature from Aino, a mixture of absolute femininity and intensive activity: the daughter of a general who prevented the isolation of Finland from Sweden in 1939. Elissa's active strength is seldom outwardly apparent; one exception is when she undertook responsibility for Louis Carré's large house in Bazoches. On the other hand she knows well that Aalto always needs human company, and so she steadfastly accompanies him on his unpredictable journeys, wherever they may lead him.

JØRN UTZON AND THE THIRD GENERATION

We have before us the work of three generations of men concerned with building up the architecture of this century. There are differences between these generations, but what is significant is that, while being true to itself, none has felt it necessary to renounce its forebears, and each has thus been able to carry further what the earlier generation had begun. In the fifties the third generation of architects came into action. How do they stand in relation to the development since the twenties?

The social orientation is pushed further: a more conscious regard for the anonymous client.

Open-ended planning: the incorporation of changing conditions as a positive element of the plan.

Incorporation of traffic as a positive element of urban planning.

Greater carefulness in handling the existing situation, so that an interplay can arise between architecture and environment, each intensifying the other.

An emphasis upon the architectural use of horizontal planes and different levels. More forceful use of artificial platforms as urbanistic elements.

A stronger relation to the past; not expressed in forms but in the sense of an inner relationship and a desire for continuity.

Further strengthening of sculptural tendencies in architecture. A freer relationship between inner and outer space and between volumes in space.

The right of expression above pure function.

Relations to the Past

The relation to the past, the desire to make contact with the past, now expresses itself in a special manner, quite differently

668

from the way it appeared in the second generation, especially the second generation in America. It is not concerned with playing with historic details torn from their context.

The rejection of yesterday was understandable at the beginning of contemporary architecture, in order to regain self-awareness. Le Corbusier is the sole pioneer who never broke off a contact with the past. The situation has now long since quieted down and one can feel again the living forces of the past, the reservoir of human experience.

Relations with the past can be both positive and negative. In the United States a series of well-known architects of the middle generation has tried to incorporate isolated details and stylistic fragments into their buildings as decorative features. But this selection does not lead to a relationship to tradition or to the past. It leads only to a decadent architecture that delights the public and the press, since it reminds them of the only half-buried ideals of the nineteenth century. From a formal adoption of details it moves further to a decadent imitation of space relationships which have no contact with contemporary society nor with contemporary space conceptions. A typical example is the Lincoln Center in New York.

Pseudo-relations to the past

The relation of the third generation to the past is expressed differently. It appears in its attitude toward anonymous structures which are everywhere living bonds with the past. The older generation — with certain exceptions — was indifferent to anonymous architecture. It is quite different with the third generation. Wherever one goes one finds a reawakening of the desire to live in a wider span of time; this generation is revolted by the wanton destruction of old buildings in a period of high prosperity.

The third generation

This is linked to something else: a different attitude toward the single building. A recurrent theme in the projects of the younger generation is that they are not centered upon an individual building, that their essence lies in an interplay of different buildings; just as in Greece on the acropolis, or in the agora of Athens. Archeologists have long since called the relationships on the acropolis or in the agora "group design."

This approach now appears in Japanese urban planning even more than in the West.

The attitude of the third generation to the past is not to saw out details from their original context. It is more an inner affinity, a spiritual recognition of what, out of the abundance of architectonic knowledge, is related to the present time and is, in a certain sense, able to strengthen our inner security.

The attitude to the past of Utzon's generation differs from that of the historian, at least from that of those historians who lack an inner relation to the contemporary scene. The architect is little interested in when or by whom a certain building was erected. His questions are rather: *What* did the builder want to achieve and *how* did he solve his problems? In other words, the architect is concerned with searching through previous architectonic knowledge, so that he can immediately confront contemporary architectural aims with those of a former period. Travel gives the best possibility for such immediate questioning.

The approach to the past always revolves around the same question: How did man in another time under other circumstances solve certain problems, and what were they? The buildings of primitive peoples are often closer to the architect of today than those of later cultures. So it is understandable that a ruin may sometimes express the essentials more immediately than a completely organized palace. This means, among other things, that an instinct is alert to penetrate the historic atmosphere of a city and, in a certain sense, its *genius loci*, without submerging itself in the space conception or details of the past period.

426. Temple at Uxmal (Yucatan) with various levels and monumental stairways. *The attitude of the third generation of contemporary architects to the past is concerned with the question of how certain problems were solved by men in other times and under other circumstances. In the broad horizontal platforms on different levels and the monumental stairways of Mayan architecture, Utzon discovered elements that had long lain slumbering in his own consciousness.*

427. Reconstruction of the temple at Uxmal. *It gives a better impression of the disposition of the temple's wide terraces and immense stairways.*

428. JØRN UTZON. Steps rising up to the foyer of the Sydney Opera House.

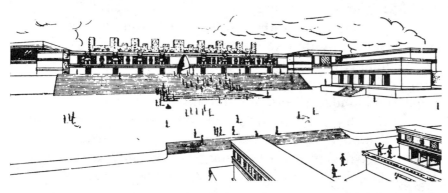

We select the figure of Jørn Utzon, since in him several sensitive characteristics of the third generation are sharply delineated. Jørn Utzon was born in 1918 and grew up in Denmark. At the Royal Academy of Art in Copenhagen he came under the influence of the excellent historian and town planner Steen Eiler Rasmussen, who sought from the very beginning to widen Utzon's powers of perception. In 1945 he studied with Alvar Aalto and Gunner Asplund. He regarded them as his Nordic teachers and later developed their tendencies further. For a short time Utzon had his own practice. In 1948 he met Fernand Léger and Le Corbusier in Paris, but above all he came in contact with the sculptor Henri Laurens. From him Utzon learned how one builds forms in the air, and how to express suspension and ascension.

Le Corbusier, almost alone in the first generation, visited ethnological museums and around 1910 toured Europe and Asia Minor. Utzon, like many of his contemporaries, pressed on to a more direct review on a world scale. In 1948 he went to Morocco. What most interested him there was the unity of village and landscape brought about by their identical material — earth. This created an unbroken sculptural unity between the environment and the up to ten-story housing. When Utzon later designed his housing projects, such as Kingo and Fredensborg, with unified walls of yellow brick, he had in mind the unity of primitive structures.

In 1949 a scholarship took him first to the United States and then to Mexico. He spent a short time with Frank Lloyd Wright in Taliesin West and Taliesin East. He came in contact with Mies van der Rohe. In Mexico he was impressed by the Mayan and Aztec architecture. In their sanctuaries he recognized something that had long slumbered within him: wide horizontal planes as a constituent element of architectural expression (*figs.* **426, 427**).

On his return to Denmark, Utzon entered numerous competitions. He was not so much concerned about their terms and conditions; he was interested only in the problems to be solved. Little was built. His compatriots had long been accustomed only to gentle and smiling forms, such as helped Danish furniture to its world renown. Almost the only things he built were the sixty-three Kingo Houses near Elsinore (1956), and a smaller housing project near Fredensborg, 1962 (*figs.* **442, 443, 444**).

In 1957 he was surprised to find he had won the competition for the Sydney Opera House in Australia. It was a great act of Eero Saarinen (who died in mid-career) that he recognized at once the world significance of Utzon's entry and pressed with all his energy for Utzon to receive the first prize and execution of the building. When Saarinen looked through the projects that had already been eliminated from the competition, he found Utzon's scheme among them. He returned to the jury with it and said, "Gentlemen, this is the first prize."

After 1957 Utzon found opportunities to visit China, Nepal, India, and Japan, and to experience the varieties of their cultures. He noticed differences between Chinese and Japanese architecture. In Japan measurements were taken with a flexible cord and not with a stiff rod as in China, and he noticed the effect this had upon their architecture.

Strange encounters led remote themes to come close to aims dormant in his own creativity. In Peking he chanced to meet Professor Liang, who had made a collection of ancient Chinese building laws from before 800 A.D. and had translated them into modern Chinese in seven volumes. These described prefabricated building systems developed in great detail, not, as today, only in their dimensions, but in every possible combination and with great care for their symbolic content.

In March 1963, Utzon went to Sydney to oversee the difficult construction of his opera house. In 1964 he won first prize for a new building for the Zurich theater.

The Horizontal Plane as a Constituent Element

The relation of a building to the horizontal plane came about at the beginning of architecture, with the forerunners of the ziggurats of Sumer. The first volume of *The Eternal Present, The Beginnings of Architecture* (New York, 1964), follows this development in Mesopotamia, as well as in Egypt. One sees there, again and again, the relationships of horizontal planes on a grand scale: in the Old Kingdom, the relation of the high desert plateau, on which stand the pyramids of Giza, to the low lying plain of arable land; in the architectonic summit of the New Kingdom, the cosmic embedding of the three horizontal terraces of Queen Hatshepsut's mortuary temple at Deir-el-Bahari.

The emotional content of the plane is only recovered with the advent of cubism. In the forefront stands the relationship of

429. JØRN UTZON. Sketch of a Japanese house. *Utzon has drawn only the roofs and platforms. He says, "This Japanese platform is like a table top, and you do not walk on a table top."*

vertical planes. The third generation now places the *horizontal* plane in the foreground as a constituent element of their architecture. Both of the foregoing generations were also conscious of its architectonic significance, but more in the sense of linking different levels.

Le Corbusier uses it in the form of the ramps of the Villa Savoie (1928–30), in the great structures of Chandigarh, and in the ramp of the Carpenter Center for Visual Arts at Harvard (1963), where it has become a definite architectural element.

Among the second generation it is Alvar Aalto who, from the start — ever since his library at Viipuri (1927–34) has used the

674

relations of horizontal levels as a form-giving element. Enough has been said of how this has penetrated his entire work and how he — very early — built up different artificial levels and used them to dramatize the architectonic expression of his structure (Saynätsalo Council House, 1950–52).

The incorporation of the horizontal plane as a constituent element has acted almost like a new discovery among the third generation. As we have said, Jørn Utzon was inspired by the great scale of the terraced buildings of the Aztecs and Mayas (*figs.* **426, 427**). In the late culture of Mexico, around 1000 A.D., he found a confirmation of something that had always slumbered within him. Several years later, in the article "Platforms and Plateaus," he refers to horizontal planes as a means of architectonic expression as follows: "The platform as an architectural element is a fascinating feature. I first fell in love with it in Mexico on a study trip in 1949, where I found many variations both in size and idea of the platform . . . A great strength radiates from them." [1] Everywhere Utzon felt

Zodiac, X (1959), 114.

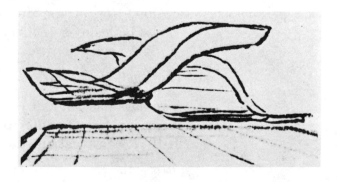

675

the horizontal plane — the platform — to be "the backbone of architectural compositions";[2] in Greece, in the Middle East, and in India.

When he wishes to show the nature of the Japanese house in a drawing (*fig.* **429**), he draws the roof hovering above the floor, without including the transparent walls. "The floor in a traditional Japanese house is a delicate, bridge-like platform. This Japanese platform is like a table top, and you do not walk on a table top. It is a piece of furniture."[3]

When he draws clouds over the sea, he notices the sharp horizontal line of the water and above it the apparently horizontal level of the vaulting clouds (*fig.* **430**). This is a prefiguration of the vaults of his opera house and hints at the meaning that he gives to them. He perceives them as hovering over the horizontal structure and only touching the earth at one point (*fig.* **431**).

Further, the building itself stands on a definite platform. "The idea has been to let the platform cut through like a knife, and separate primary and secondary function completely. On top of the platform the spectators receive the completed work of art and beneath the platform every preparation for it takes place."[4]

Manmade horizontal level The use of the platform, an artificially constructed ground, runs through all the work of this generation. It can be found everywhere where efforts are made to rescue the pedestrian from a chaotic intermingling with automobiles and trucks: in the plan for North Amsterdam, 1963, by Bakema, van den Broek, and van Eyck; in the plan for a sector of Tokyo (*fig.* **526**) by Fumihiko Maki — among the youngest of the rising generation — or in the different platforms with which Kenzo Tange builds over the bay of Tokyo (*figs.* **524**, **525**).

The Right of Expression: The Vaults of the Sydney Opera House

A remarkable amount of opposition manifested itself against the series of great vaults for the Sydney Opera House (designed in 1957, construction started in 1963). This did not, by any

---

[2] *Ibid.*, p. 115.   [3] *Ibid.*, p. 116.   [4] *Ibid.*, p. 117.

means, come only from people who consider anything different from what has been customary to be a personal affront.

It is not usual to have a series of ten vaults that rise one behind the other up to sixty meters and overshadow the building both front and back. The most widespread objection is that these shells, which come together in a ridge, are quite arbitrary, as no relation exists between the inner and outer space, and even the high, rectangular stage is arched over by the wing of a huge vault (*fig.* **I**).

This objection gives rise to a basic question. A question that our period must again answer and decide, a question of conscience. Are we prepared to go beyond the purely functional and tangible as earlier periods did in order to enhance the force of expression?

Beyond the purely functional

The "shells," as Jørn Utzon calls his staggered vaults, are superfluous if one recognizes only the functional in architecture, so far as this can be tested by a direct material coherence between cause and effect. After half a century of development, contemporary architecture demands something more than this. The autonomous right of expression must again assert itself in building, over and above the purely utilitarian.

We are fully aware that at the present moment only a master hand can dare to manifest the independence of expression from function. In the hands of minor talents this can only lead to sliding off the rails.

In two grandiose private publications (65 × 40 cm.), Utzon gives some insight into the origins and development of his creative approach. In the first publication, 1958, whose cover shows the silhouette of the Sydney Opera House on a red ground, the staff of specialists is given opportunity to express itself. For today's complex buildings, a staff of specialists — structural engineers, acoustic experts, heating experts, stage construction experts — is taken for granted. In the end they usually vanish anonymously behind the work of the architect. In this publication, Utzon presents their tasks with their separate working drawings and explanations. Through these the outsider gets a rare glimpse into the mosaic of contemporary teamwork.

The second large publication, 1962, has no text and consists simply of a series of masterly drawings. Its cover shows the graphic calculations determining the shell vaults as elements of a sphere. Within the book the architectural development of the building is presented step by step, especially the contrapuntal interplay of the interior ceilings and the external shells.

A section (*fig.* **432**) through the small hall shows clearly how the curving ceiling plays contrapuntally against the shells, which climb up in sequence to the third and largest, rising high above the stage. They are closed from the outside by glass curtain walls: not vertical, but fanning inward like the wings of a bat. The shells are so organized that the cords linking their vertex and their base each spring from the same point in space (*fig.* **438**). From this ideal point the vaults radiate out front and back. Though the eye cannot check this directly, it realizes that an inner order exists.

Jørn Utzon, like others of the better architects of the third generation, possesses a double gift: he is able to have direct contact with the cosmic elements of nature and the past and also complete control of contemporary methods of industrialized production — especially prefabrication. As a result he is able to detach prefabrication from its purely mechanistic attributes and bring it nearer to the organic.

This is apparent in the flexible glass walls that hang from the shell vaults of the Sydney Opera House and serve as a link between the soaring shells and the horizontal level of the earth. To Utzon, a vertical glass wall gives the impression of a load-bearing element. He has therefore transformed its abstract verticality into a dynamic flexible form, made up of separate glass panes, each one overlapping the one below, as in a greenhouse (*fig.* **436**).

Utzon has said that this solution was inspired partly by the organic-dynamic movements of a bird's wing (*fig.* **437**) and partly by the many connections of an automatic telephone which, when correctly assembled, enable one to "dial anywhere."

Utzon ultimately took the sphere as his starting point: the sphere which Plato describes as the most perfect and unified body since all points on its surface lie at the same distance from its center. It is the only regular form that appears as sculpture in the earliest primeval art. Saturated with symbolism, it became the monumental starting point of Byzantine architecture.

Utzon did not want to use the enclosed form of a dome. He uses only segments of the sphere in which both the ever constant and the ever changing are inherent, expressed by the rising sequence of the shells of the opera house, one behind the other. Whether we like it or not, the fragment is a mark — a symbol — of our period.

One day Utzon sent me from Australia three wooden balls, from which he had sliced the different segments of his vaults (*fig.* **435**). These show that the curves of his vaults are far from being arbitrary.

It was essential to retain the hovering expression. Yet architecture has to be built and demands that a metaphysical idea be made practical and workable. Utzon is in the core of the present period. Although he has absorbed the past, he thinks in the realistic categories of the practitioner. This means that, to him, the rational production of prefabricated parts and the full use of constructive possibilities hidden within the form of the sphere cannot be detached from a metaphysical background.

Thanks to these wooden spheres, whose surface lies always at the same distance from their center, Utzon could renounce complicated scaffoldings and substitute a single, movable formwork. Age-old methods thus find a place in developing the complicated vaults of our period. We know from Choisy that the Egyptians of the New Kingdom (the Ramasseum at Thebes) constructed their barrel vaults (built up with courses of unburnt bricks) with the help of a movable formwork.

In a letter dated June 1963, Utzon tells how spatial geometry, as he calls his method, enabled him to arrive at "a construction of prefabricated elements using only movable formwork without any of the heavy scaffolding usual for shell concrete

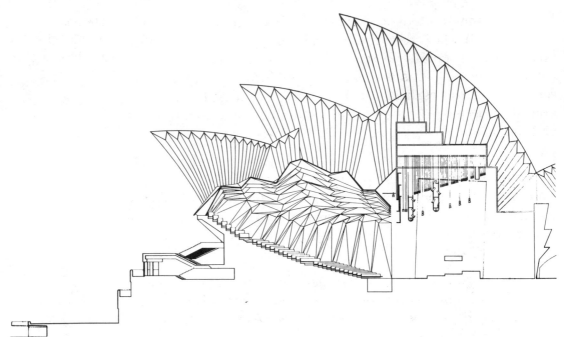

432. JØRN UTZON. Sydney Opera House, 1957. *Section through the small hall showing its wooden ceiling suspended freely from the roof. In the background the great shells rise from behind the stage. "The character, the style, has developed from a series of shapes in combination, all with the characteristics of water, waves — waves within waves — the wave that breaks, foams, etc. In my thought, I mould the invisible space with geometrically defined shapes in combinations and when I have established the void I want, I freeze the situation in my mind. Because I have moulded space with geometrically defined shapes, the whole enclosure of the void is fully defined and the surface of the enclosure is divisible in a number of similar elements. These similar elements can be mass produced — and when their relationship has been clarified they can be assembled like a big jig-saw puzzle in space."* (Jørn Utzon, in Zodiac, XIV, 1965.)

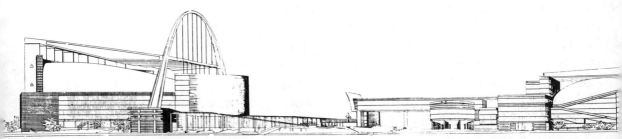

433. LE CORBUSIER. Project for the Palace of the Soviets, 1931. *The ceiling of the great hall was to be suspended on wire cables hung from a great parabolic concrete arch that thrust itself high into the open air. This was the most advanced of Le Corbusier's projects of that period. Utzon acknowledged that it had given him the idea for his hanging ceiling and free vaults.*

680

434. JØRN UTZON. Determining the forms of the shell vaults on the basis of a sphere. *The regular surface of a sphere proved the simplest basis for determining the construction of prefabricated elements that could be built up to form the vaults.*

construction." The use of segments of a sphere also simplified the working drawings: "As a result of my spherical system I can give all dimensions their true size because I inscribe on the sphere great circles that intersect at the North Pole [*fig.* 434]. I have thus come to a solution that is as simple as cutting up an orange into small identical pieces." Utzon re-

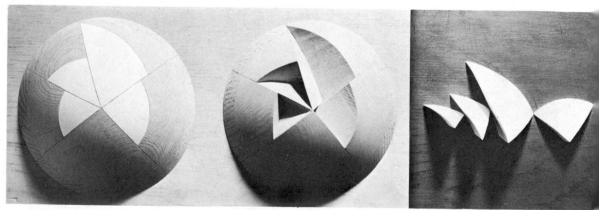

435. JØRN UTZON. A wooden ball showing the way Utzon cut out the different segments of the vaults "as easily as slicing up an orange."

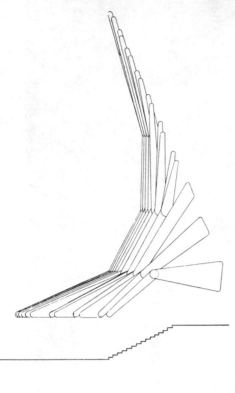

436. JØRN UTZON. Drawing of the flexible, fan-like glass curtain walls that hang within the great shell vaults of the Sydney Opera House, 1957.

437. Photograph of the wings of a skua gull in flight.

438. Sydney Opera House, 1957. *The sails of the shell vaults all meet at a single point.*

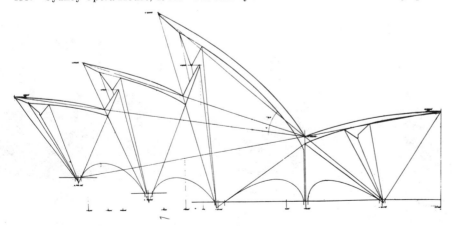

ferred to the shells of Saarinen's TWA building in the Kennedy Airport as an example of how difficult the representation of vertical and horizontal sections through complicated curves can become. These drawings had to be calculated by a computer.

On the front cover of the second volume on the opera house, 1962, Utzon shows the mathematical development of the vaults from a sphere and, on the back, his first quick sketches of its form. These show the two poles around which everything turns: an immediate record of the imagination and its practical development.

Interlocking of expression and prefabrication

This was not an easy road.

The shells were first drawn as the imagination envisaged them. Ove Arup, a Danish engineer who has long lived in England where he has acted as a sympathetic defender of contemporary architecture, undertook the task of finding a way to construct the shells. His office did their best but could find no solution and had to give up.

439. Sydney Opera House, 1957. *Ground plan showing the two halls, one seating 3500 people, the other 1200.*

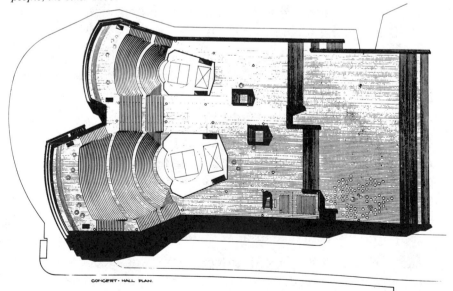

CONCERT· HALL PLAN.

The solution was reached in Utzon's own office between May and October 1961, when he turned from the two-dimensionality of the drawing board to three-dimensional representation. Utzon arrived at the final form of his shells, he says, just as Le Corbusier arrived at the idea of his "Domino" house, 1914 (*fig.* **312**), composed of several supports and horizontal concrete slabs.

As a result it was possible to construct the high shells from prefabricated elements, made partly on the building site and partly in Sweden and put together into ribs, which were then tied together in steel shoes.

Why all this? Why this expenditure of time and money? For nothing more than the right of expression that the imagination demands. The unyielding tenacity with which this right of expression was upheld opens a new chapter in contemporary architecture.

The interpenetration of artistic volition and the laws of matter is at the root of all artistic creation. It is methods of construction that have changed with time.

Ceilings and vaults

People have objected to the lack of a "functional" relationship between the ceiling and the vaults of the opera house. But the suspended wooden ceiling has quite a different function from the vaults, which attract the audience of 5,000 into the hall not along a single axis but like bees to a flower.

The light ceiling, as planned, is freely suspended, its curved surface made up of prefabricated wooden boards with complicated, acoustically derived profiles, also fabricated with the help of a geometric form, based this time on the cylinder.

The idea of a hanging ceiling, as stated by Utzon in one of our talks, went back to Le Corbusier's project for the Palace of the Soviets, 1931, though there it was expressed in a quite different and more primitive manner. Le Corbusier's ceiling of the great hall was suspended by steel cables fastened to a high rising parabolic concrete arch (*fig.* **433**).

What happened in spring 1966

In the spring of 1966, a new government was elected that set up a committee of six consultants under the official government architect. Utzon was asked to be one of the consultants.

684

What then happened is best documented in the "New South Wales Parliamentary Debates," March 9, 1966 (pp. 4,008, 4,019–4,032).

The parliamentary debate on the Opera House opened with an extremely courageous defense of the Utzon scheme by Mr. Ryan, former Minister of Public Works and Utzon's client for six years: "This project is of such magnitude and importance that it is regrettable that it has already been dragged down to the level of political controversy . . . It is a project that has established a new principle in architecture and new engineering techniques that have excited the interest of professional people throughout the world. It is an undertaking of which this country can be, is, and certainly will be very proud, if it is completed as originally designed . . . I say this with full knowledge of the fact that for six years I was the Minister in charge of this great project" (p. 4,019).

Utzon had found that existing experience in acoustics was insufficient for his project. To be sure of the result he needed to build and test a prototype of the acoustic ceiling. "I had," said Mr. Ryan, "the experience of seeing the difficulties of this problem revealed in a striking way at the Lincoln Centre in New York. The Philharmonic Hall, the first unit of the complex to be completed has an acoustic ceiling that was rebuilt three times at a cost of over $1,000,000 because in the first instance not enough attention had been given to experimentation" (p. 4,024). "The Sydney Opera House is not a costly building by comparison with others — £4,400 a seat as against approximately £5,500 for the Lincoln Centre" (p. 4,031).

The case of the Sydney Opera House is highly significant. In earlier years an architect of genius had been eliminated before he was engaged. As noted, this happened to Le Corbusier in 1927 when, as a result of intrigues, other people were called upon to build the League of Nations in Geneva; a similar situation developed when an American architect took over Le Corbusier's sketch of the United Nations Building in New York. Everybody can judge the results.

In the case of the Sydney Opera House the situation was different. Through the influence of some farsighted jurors,

Jørn Utzon won first prize in the competition for the Sydney Opera House. But when he had nearly finished the project, another political party came into power and decided to hand over completion of Utzon's highly individualized building to a committee whose task was to cheapen it and simplify all details.

The curved wooden acoustic ceiling is to disappear (*fig.* **432**) as a consequence of Utzon's demand for a prototype test model. Utzon is certainly not alone in requiring acoustic experiments before a major building is erected; such experiments were needed for the Symphonic Hall in Berlin and, as Mr. Ryan commented, for the Lincoln Center in New York. The sensitive curves of the protecting glass walls of the shells (*fig.* **436**) are to be flattened.

Such major changes should arouse profound protest in every architect who feels a responsibility toward his work. A building being erected in every detail according to a pre-arranged program cannot have its program changed at the last minute, when the building is already nearing completion.

What has happened? The great hall, designed from the beginning as the opera house, is suddenly changed into a concert hall and a movie theater. Its stage machinery is thrown out and its beautiful plywood mullions will be replaced by concrete. The small hall (*fig.* **432**) will now become the opera house. These are only some of the projected changes.

The role of the historian

The verdict of the historian is very different from that of the politician. It is a moral duty for the historian to stand up for the real qualities of one of the most outstanding works of this period.

From Finland to Italy there is today a general trend in architecture to develop simultaneously sculptural qualities and interior space. In his Philharmonic Hall in Berlin (1956), with its excellent interior, Hans Scharoun showed that different methods are needed to give a building both a spatial and a plastic expression. He worked with sculptural models — not two-dimensional drawings — in an atelier next to the building site, just as Gaudi had done. Even so Scharoun did not fully succeed in creating both a plastic volume and a fine interior space.   How difficult this is can be seen in Le Corbusier's Pilgrimage Chapel of Ronchamps and in Utzon's Sydney Opera House.

Architecture has always had close contact with the proportions of geometry, regardless of its different forms: the pyramids, the Parthenon, the Pantheon.   This has held true for highly geometric forms and for highly organic ones (as in the late baroque) and it is still valid for contemporary architecture. A comparison, for example, of the expressionistic drawings of Finsterlin with the organic shapes Utzon created leaves one with no doubt that they represent two quite different trends. The real secret of Utzon's Sydney Opera House is its obedience to the eternal architectural law: the close relations of architecture and geometry.

The historian needs to bring forward yet another aspect that should not be forgotten: differences have always existed between the exterior and the interior of a monumental building. The most famous example is Hadrian's Pantheon in Rome (early in the first century), the starting point for all subsequent domed architecture.   The cupola with its graduated cofferings appears from within to indicate the construction system; however, it is only a façade supported by the actual construction system of arches and columns.   The innovation in the Pantheon is that arches and columns were used to build a vaulted ceiling instead of a vertical wall, as in the Colosseum. Even there, the bold construction uprights embodied in the staircases were formerly covered with reliefs.

Although Utzon's approach to interior and exterior appears very different, it is not essentially so in principle.   He unites, in a new manner, two separate intentions.   The exterior of his building with its marvelous vaulting shells projecting forward from its unique site creates a vivid symbol for the incoming ships and for the entire city.   Beneath these wings he has inserted the functional interior of an opera house and a concert hall.

What is so devastating in the new decisions about the Sydney Opera House?   This is the first time in our period that the architect's intentions — based on the explicit demands of the original client — have been changed by another government because of a dilettantish misunderstanding. This involves something that should deeply offend the architectural profession. The architect has to be regarded as an artist. It shows crass irresponsibility to change the program of a masterpiece when it is already almost complete.

It is understandable that Utzon resigned and went back to Denmark.

The building as a totality

One must see the Sydney Opera House as a totality, and above all, how it fulfills its human purpose. Its only goal is to prepare the audience for a festival.

Whoever visits the theater at Delphi in Greece, high above the sanctuaries, must first experience a long slow climb up the winding sacred way. In the theater itself he first experiences the full majesty of the landscape. On a smaller scale, something similar is attempted at Sydney. The leisurely and dignified approach ascends to different levels by steps as wide as those of the monuments of the Aztecs or the Mayas (*fig.* **428**). As Utzon says, "The building has the possibility of opening all halls and foyers during the intervals, so that the audience when moving through the foyers can have a full sensation of the hanging shells which command a wide view over the harbor." Eero Saarinen recognized from the beginning that the Sydney Opera House would be one of the great buildings of our period.

Empathy with the Situation: The Zurich Theater, 1964

One of the traits of the third generation is a strong feeling for landscape and the architectural environment. Environment and architecture should be interlocked as intensively as possible. In Sydney this meant correlating a high-rise building with a cosmic expanse of sea and sky.

In June 1964, Jørn Utzon won first prize in a competition for the Zurich Theater (*fig.* **440**). The situation there was totally different from that in Sydney. In Zurich it meant incorporating a new building within a fixed and static environment and simultaneously creating a definite urbanistic accent, creating

688

the focus for an extensive district of closely packed teaching institutions — high school, university, technical institute, medical school, and numerous others. At present any such focal point is lacking. This area ends in an open square crossed by traffic lines and bordered by one of the most important through roads: a miserable green patch with a public lavatory and kiosk stands in the middle of it. On the axis of this modest square rises Karl Moser's noble art gallery (1910). Toward the mountain and far in the background is a high school (1839) in the good tradition of Schinkel's Building Academy in Berlin. In the green area between them, the new theater is intended to bind this scattered neighborhood together and to give it some dignity.

How can this be achieved by a single building?

A fluid is never tangible. It flows between the fingers and then, at a certain temperature, through the action of energy, it suddenly acquires form and shape. Something similar happens in city planning.

This situation is not limited to the special case of a particular piece of land in a city of half a million people. It is symptomatic of a period when, wherever one looks, in the most different circumstances, one finds fragments of a lost sense of community trying to glue themselves together again. In the case of Zurich it is apparent that the need is not so much for immense, new structures as for the healing of a wounded situation.

To work in an existing situation is only justified when no compromise of architectural purity is involved. The problem in Zurich was not, as in Sydney, to stretch out antennae into the cosmos. In Zurich it was a matter of entering the puritanical atmosphere of the city without loss of artistic vision. Utzon's building rises up the slope in delicately graduated horizontal levels: "a flat, relief-like carpet of building with a structured roof," stated the competition jury. The sculptural roofs step gradually up the hill with their almost organically shaped folds, such as exist also in the lower part of the Sydney Opera House. Their varied profile is due to considerations of statics arising from the unusually wide spans. In

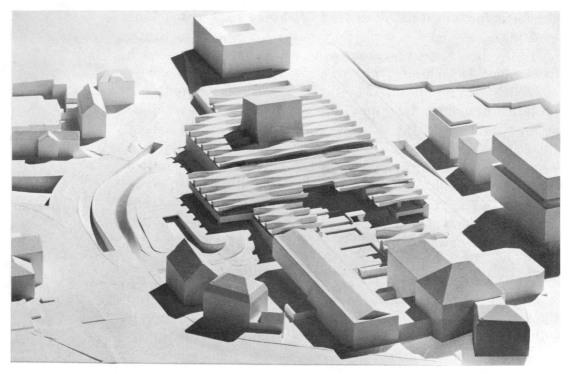

440.   JØRN UTZON.   Model of the Zurich Theater, 1964.   *It grows up the slope in a series of stepped horizontal planes.   The result is a flat, relief-like carpet of buildings with a structured roofscape (as stated by the competition jury).*

441.   Zurich Theater, 1964.   Elevational view of model.   *The beams, which have an almost organic form, permit extraordinarily wide spans and a significant reduction of columns: the result is a very flexible organization of interior space.*

690

Zurich these folds appear decisively upon the upper surface (*fig.* 441). The wide spans not only permit a freer development of the interior space; they also emanate an inner elasticity — an expressive sense of movement — like the structures of Robert Maillart. Their form gives a structural backbone to the entire building.

The foyer, its horizontal planes adapted to the smaller scale, has stairs developed across its entire width, as in Sydney. These produce the opening scene where, as Utzon says, "The spectator becomes an actor." The drawing-in of the audience is not accomplished here by soaring vaults but by "an entry way developed in depth" (in the words of the competition jury).

Whether one likes it or not, Utzon worked neither in Sydney nor in Zurich with a variable stage. This was partly owing to the conditions of the architectural program. In both places he created the theatrical space like an amphitheater, "as a deepened shell" (Utzon's phrase).

In his combination of empathy with a given situation and an unrelenting maintenance of his own expression, Utzon is not alone among his generation. For instance, there is the horizontally layered City Theater of Helsinki (1959), where Timo Penttila (then only twenty-eight years old) cut the stage area partly out of the living rock.

It can be observed that the Zurich project is not fully elaborated in all details and that, thanks to the wide spanning beams, the theater needs only a minimum of supports. This means that the development of the building will have great flexibility.

It is no accident that every detail of the building is not fixed. In city planning, which comes most strongly under the pressure of the explosive population increase, there is an increasing tendency to plan so that, despite dynamic development, it will not be necessary to destroy what has already been built.

The same tendency appears in many large buildings. The buildings of the Philadelphia architect, Louis Kahn, are famous for being designed so that extensions can take place without disrupting the original conception. Le Corbusier developed this idea first in his study for a museum of contemporary art, 1931, with its continuous, unbounded spiral formation. In the case of Utzon the boundaries of his buildings are firmly established: their flexibility lies in the development of their interior space.

The linking of constancy and change as a single complementary entity and not as irreconcilable opposites comes ever more strongly into consciousness.

Sympathy with the Anonymous Client

The relation between the individual and the collective spheres is a problem which has preoccupied generations but whose solution becomes increasingly urgent. Very few have succeeded in expressing this relation in architectural form. Among Utzon's buildings in Denmark there were two housing projects: the sixty-three Kingo Houses near Elsinore (1956) and a smaller project for Danes returning from abroad, near Fredensborg, fifty kilometers north of Copenhagen (*figs.* **442, 443, 444**). Both show great sensitivity in their site planning. The placing of the houses willingly responds to slight changes in the slope of the land. They are linked together like the scales on a butterfly's wing, while the flexible plan of the individual houses makes full allowance for individual privacy.

The houses of both projects are based on the frequently employed L-shaped ground plan, but used in an individual manner. They are disposed on the site so that they share the minimum length of common wall (*fig.* **444**). This is made possible by forming each house into a square with its own open court. Should not one really call this court a patio since it is the private open space of the house?

The detailing of the Fredensborg project shows that Utzon knows how to model space. He cut a rectangle from each garden wall so that the landscape, the garden-like exterior space, can flow freely into the private zones (*fig.* **443**). In surgery everything depends upon the sureness of the cut; it is the same with the architect. Instead of a small scale landscape of minuscule gardens the site displays a spacious gen-

692

442. JØRN UTZON. Fredensborg housing near Copenhagen, 1962. *View of the flexible rows of single-
family dwellings from the community house. Utzon
created a visual relationship between private and public
areas simply by cutting rectangular wedges from the walls
bounding the houses.*

443. Fredensborg housing, 1962. *View of a dwelling
across the rectangular opening.*

444. Plan of Fredensborg housing settlement, 1962. *The community house is
at the head of the long loop to the left.*

erosity. The same kind of thinking, though formulated quite differently, resulted in the common gardens of the Bloomsbury Squares of London in the first half of the nineteenth century.

Steen Eiler Rasmussen, Utzon's teacher at the Copenhagen Academy of Architecture, once told me that he had a great regard for Utzon since he possessed a two-fold ability: he could give a spatial solution to monumental projects with fully mechanized means and to social projects with the simplest possible means.

Imagination and Implementation

In his own personality Utzon mirrors our period in all its complexity. In architecture Utzon stands for the right of expression as the supreme law, as it has always been supreme for all creative spirits.

Jørn Utzon combines a rare power of spatial imagination with the ability to express this graphically. Behind this imaginative power stands a primary impulse to depart from the two-dimensionality of the drawing board and come to three-dimensional sculptural forms. Thus full-scale models play an important role in his work. In Mies van der Rohe's studio there is a wooden model of his steel profiles at a scale of 1:1, so that he can check the behavior of their dimensions. As stated, Utzon went further and required three-dimensional confirmation of the spatial behavior of his shell vaults.

The primacy of expression must always be achieved through the contemporary technical possibilities. This implies something more: the machine has to be subordinated to the creative process, not the creative process to the machine. Rationality of construction in the nineteenth century was the only refuge to which the creative core of architecture could flee. Today something quite different is needed. Industrial production is all powerful. It tyrannically imposes its purely mechanistic standardization on every sector, not least on architecture.

For the first and the second generations the way to bring their imagination to implementation was hard enough, but it was less complex than today. For the third generation creative imagination is inextricably bound up with the industrial production of all structural elements. The machine must be so guided that its products are not based solely upon rationalistic considerations.

It is said that the ancient architecture of Japan was based upon an attitude of mind — upon a philosophy — and it was this attitude that influenced technical production, and not techniques that influenced architecture. Today we possess no vitalizing philosophy that can influence everything.

In its place we have something else — however vague it may appear — an attitude toward humanity. This is the problem around which all now turns. Production must no longer be based solely on a mechanistic outlook; the machine must be guided in such a way that its products stem directly from a human point of view, fundamentally growing out of a humanistic atmosphere, as they did previously through their direct contact with the human hand. Everything centers on the use of today's powers of production to restore the imagination to its earlier freedom. Freedom in this sense means to transform the prefabrication of building components so that, in the house, all detailing from foundations to roof can have a wide range of flexibility; and, in monumental building, even the most complex forms can be solved by contemporary methods.

The vaults of the Sydney Opera House in their formation and in their meaning are symptomatic.

THE INTERNATIONAL CONGRESSES FOR MODERN ARCHITECTURE (CIAM) AND THE FORMATION OF CONTEMPORARY ARCHITECTURE

The International Congresses for Modern Architecture (Congrès Internationaux d'Architecture Moderne — CIAM) were not founded to protect the rights of the profession — that is the task of the large official architectural organizations. The purpose of CIAM was to establish contemporary architecture's right to existence against the antagonistic forces of official architectural circles, who controlled the major building enterprises. The aim of CIAM was to deal with problems that could not be solved by the single individual. This was approximately the definition Le Corbusier gave of CIAM's purpose.

In February 1928, I received a letter from Madame Hélène de Mandrot, telling me that she was about to visit Zurich. The purpose of this visit was to arrange for a meeting of architects connected with this new movement at her château of La Sarraz, a few kilometers north of the lake of Geneva in the canton of Vaud. Madame de Mandrot had already spoken of this possibility with Le Corbusier and other friends (P. Chareau, G. Guevrekian, and others) in Paris. The term "congress" was to be employed in its original sense of "working together." It would be a congress of collaboration, not a congress in which each would report on his own specific field.

Three circumstances favored an international union of young architects. One was the initiative of Hélène de Mandrot, who had founded the *Maison des Artistes* and had already held a meeting of young painters. She now invited young architects from Belgium, Germany, France, Holland, Italy, Austria, Spain, and Switzerland to meet at this neutral spot in the center of Europe.

The second was the scandal that had resulted from the competition for the League of Nations building at Geneva. Le Corbusier had been awarded the first prize *ex aequo:* his project was, in every way, superior to the others. As a result of intrigues by a professor of the Paris *Académie des Beaux Arts*, Aristide Briand, the most influential politician in the League of Nations, declared he would accept only a building in academic style. Thus the prize was not granted to Le Corbusier and a wall was thrown up against contemporary architecture. It seemed imperative to create a new organization — CIAM — to assert freedom of architectural conception and support it whenever necessary so that there could be no repetition of the Geneva affair.

Third, and the reason that proved decisive, was the need to provide for helplessly isolated architects in various countries an ideological basis and professional support that would enable them to tackle special problems and to defend their approach.

At the first congress in La Sarraz, 1928, a small international group, not without lively discussion, formulated the manifesto that first laid down the bases of contemporary architecture. At the end of the congress Le Corbusier produced a long drawing and spread it on the walls of the Gothic chapel where the medieval lords of the estate are buried. The drawing is reproduced in the first volume of Le Corbusier's collected works.[1] It depicted in diagrammatic form the course CIAM should follow. At that time it was absurdly Utopian to expect that the forces of contemporary architecture would one day overcome the opposition of officialdom and be admitted to the citadel of the state.

The Manifesto of La Sarraz

At this congress, Professor Karl Moser of Zurich, the noted teacher and architect, was elected first president of CIAM.

The second congress was held at Frankfort in 1929 at the invitation of Ernest May, then head of that city's Department of Housing, Planning, and Building. On the walls of his offices, members' drawings, all on the same scale, were presented on the theme: "Low Income Housing." (These drawings were subsequently reproduced in *Die Wohnung für das Existenz-minimum*, issued by J. Hoffman, Stuttgart, 1930.) This system of using the same scale and the same techniques of presentation became the rule for all CIAM congresses, so that the

Low income housing

---

[1] *Le Corbusier, Œuvre complète* (Zurich, 1937), I, 175.

subjects under discussion could be immediately compared with one another.

At this congress, Walter Gropius, Alvar Aalto, and José Luis Sert made their first appearance in CIAM.

Rational
methods of
site planning

The third congress was held in Brussels in 1930 on the initiative of Victor Bourgeois: its theme was "Rational Methods of Site Planning" (publication: *Rationelle Bebauungsweisen*, J. Hoffman, Stuttgart, 1930). The actual topic of discussion — then a burning question — was the relative merits of laying out areas with row houses, walk-ups, and high-rise apartments. All the speakers — Walter Gropius, Le Corbusier, R. J. Neutra, among others — were obliged to address themselves to this theme.

Cornell van Eesteren, the young head of the Amsterdam Office for City Planning, was elected president because Professor Karl Moser wished to hand over his position to a younger man. The election of a city planner instead of an architect showed the future direction CIAM would take.

A cabled invitation from the highest official of the Housing and Building Association of the U.S.S.R. to hold the fourth congress in Moscow was accepted.

The Athens
Charter

At the end of 1932, C. van Eesteren and I were invited to attend a preparatory meeting in Moscow that lasted ten days. The program of the fourth congress was settled with mutual friendliness and the date fixed for June 1933. This congress was planned on the largest scale. If it had been held in Moscow it would have been of immense significance since Russia was so greatly interested in city planning. But a few months later the news came from Moscow that the congress had been postponed. We immediately understood the reason for this measure: the *Avantgarde* had no place in Stalin's Russia.

Since all the congress material had already been prepared, I called an emergency meeting in Le Corbusier's studio in the Rue de Sèvres, Paris. What should be done? Marcel Breuer proposed that the congress should be held on a ship. Le Corbusier telephoned at once to the director of a Greek shipping company whom he knew. As a result the fourth congress was held on the "Patris II" sailing between Marseille and Athens, and in Athens itself.

The Brussels congress had shown that interest centered on a study of city planning. C. van Eesteren, on the basis of his experience in Amsterdam, had the task of developing and distributing three sample plans using standardized symbols and methods of presentation:

1. A land-use plan using symbols to show areas mainly devoted to residential, industrial, and recreational uses.
2. The traffic network.
3. The relation between the city and its region.

All plans shown at the fourth congress were based on these examples derived from the city plan of Amsterdam, and each used the same symbols and was drawn to the same scale. Thus their different problems could be seen at a glance.

The purpose of these drawings was to give an insight into the comparative structure of small and large cities — an insight which simply did not exist up to that time. Thirty-three cities were analyzed (including London, Paris, Berlin, Detroit, Los Angeles, Athens, Rome, Warsaw, Madrid, and Zurich). Their main functions — living, working, recreation, circulation — could at once be recognized and compared.

This was the longest, most exciting, and most fruitful of the CIAM congresses. Excellent studies had been prepared. It was possible for the groups to make analytical comparisons of the thirty-three cities and, on this basis, to lay down the principles of contemporary city planning in the Athens Charter (Charte d'Athènes).

Wells Coates made his first appearance at this congress as organizer of an English group of CIAM. With us were a number of interested painters, poets, and art historians — such as Fernand Léger, Moholy-Nagy, Guéguin, Christian Zervos, and Jean Badovici — who effectively cleared the atmosphere of dry professionalism.

J. L. Sert brought together the results of the fourth congress in a comprehensive book, *Can Our Cities Survive?* (Harvard University Press, 1942). The complete text of the Athens

Charter was published in French as *La Charte d'Athènes* (Paris, 1943), with an introduction by Jean Giraudoux. It was republished in 1957 by Jean Petit, Paris. The complete English text is in *Ekistics*, XVI (October 1963), 263–267.

In the shadow of dark years ahead the fifth congress met in Paris in 1937. The theme was "Housing and Recreation" — a theme that is not yet resolved. Le Corbusier assembled its documents under the title *Logis et Loisirs* (Paris, 1938). It was intended to hold the sixth congress in 1939 in the United States, where, in 1937, Walter Gropius and Marcel Breuer had been invited to work at Harvard University and Moholy-Nagy at Chicago. One year later, I also was invited to Harvard.

Then came the war and the sixth congress was postponed ten years. During the war the different CIAM groups were separated from one another, but they carried on their work independently. In New York Lönberg-Holm, Walter Gropius, Richard J. Neutra, José Luis Sert, and I, with Stamo Papadaki and a few other friends, formed the "CIAM Chapter for Relief and Post-War Planning" (R. J. Neutra was the president). In the Netherlands, members of CIAM met secretly throughout the Occupation to prepare for the rebuilding of Rotterdam, which later proceeded according to their recommendations. In England, the Modern Architectural Research Group — MARS, the name the English CIAM group had adopted — rose to the fore: its members took leading roles in the development of post-war city plans and the preparation of new planning legislation.

A decade of new architecture

It was the MARS group who in 1947 organized the sixth congress at the small town of Bridgwater in southwest England. After the ten years that had passed since the last congress it was necessary to reformulate the goals of CIAM and to renew broken contacts.

The usual CIAM custom was broken. The works of individual members of the different CIAM groups were displayed to explain the situation in their countries. As the Argentinian delegate Ferrari-Hardoy said, the congress was astounded to find how the "development of an idea" had followed parallel lines in the completely separated groups. *A Decade of New*

700

Architecture, by S. Giedion (Zurich, 1951), resulted from this congress.

In Bridgwater the question of aesthetics was broached for the first time. Until then it had been avoided. Two approaches could be distinguished. The MARS group, led by J. M. Richards, held that the question should be approached from the view of the "man in the street." Hans Arp and I concentrated on the relationship between architect, painter, and sculptor. A short account of the ensuing discussion appears in my book *Architecture, You and Me* (Harvard University Press, 1958), pp. 70–78.

At this congress, José Luis Sert was elected president.

The seventh congress was organized by the Italian group and held in Bergamo in 1949. The selection of subjects for presentation at this congress was left completely open. It was only stipulated that they should be presented within the format of the "CIAM Grid" [2] developed by the French group ASCORAL (Assemblée de Constructeurs pour une Rénovation Architecturale) and Le Corbusier, and later published as a special supplement by *Architecture d'Aujourd'hui* in 1949.

The CIAM Grid and the problem of aesthetics

All groups brought analyses of different urbanistic problems in the form of the Grid. These analyses were examined in turn. Problems of the development of new towns and of new community centers were particularly stressed.

The problem of aesthetics, apparently so far removed from this analytical approach, gave rise to heated discussion. Following a Polish recommendation to adopt the Stalinist approach to art, long smoldering differences came to light as positions were taken on the relation between art and the views of the "man in the street." This discussion is also summarized in *Architecture, You and Me* (pp. 79–80).

The eighth congress was again organized by the MARS group and was held at Hoddesdon, near London, in 1951. The four

The heart of the city

---

[2] The CIAM Grid took the form of a matrix with living, working, recreation, and circulation as the main heads, along the side; and along the top, a series of heads including region, building volume, aesthetics, economic and social considerations, legislation, etc. Material was displayed in the appropriate positions. (It was not necessary to fill in all the squares.)

notions of living, working, recreation, and circulation that were the basis of the Athens Charter had proved useful for the first analysis of a city. But it now appeared that something more was needed to grasp the spirit of a city. The theme, "The Heart of the City," had been proposed by the English group.

This congress heralded the final period of CIAM, in which it would concentrate more and more on social aspects of urban planning: first in the formation of the city center and, in the following congresses, on the human habitat.

One of the points most stressed in the eighth congress, the rights of the pedestrian (la royauté du pieton) has now become one of the chief points of city planning in the rehabilitation of city centers. The first sketches of Chandigarh were shown at this congress. The results of this congress, edited by J. Tyrwhitt, J. L. Sert, and E. N. Rogers, were published under the title *The Heart of the City* (London and Milan, 1952).

The human habitat

The ninth congress was organized by ASCORAL and held in Aix-en-Provence in 1953 on the theme: "The Human Habitat." To the zoologist, the word "habitat" means the natural area in which an animal lives and procreates; to the botanist, the area in which a particular plant flourishes. In addition habitat can be defined as the area best suited to meet the inborn and future needs of man. This congress considered the extensions of man's living quarters (logement prolongé) outside the four walls of the dwelling and attempted to gain insight into the many-sided relationships between members of a family and members of a community.

CIAM was an *avantgarde* movement, and in the art world *avantgarde* movements normally have only a short span of life. CIAM was already twenty-five years old. The founders of CIAM, who were still leading the movement, now had large-scale projects on their hands and heavy demands on their time. They wanted to hand over leadership to the younger generation, but their retirement was not accepted at this point. However, the organization of the tenth congress was entrusted to Team X, a group of younger architects, who would carry out the preparations with the cooperation of the older leaders. J. B. Bakema was appointed head of this team.

702

Team X, who were to prepare the transition from the older to the younger generation, had prepared the method of representation of work at the tenth congress, held in Dubrovnik in 1956.

The task of the congress was to outline the form of the Charte de l'Habitat, which would specify the spatial relations of the individual within the family, taking into consideration the cycle of human life; his relations with the community; his needs for quiet and seclusion; his needs for contact with nature. The isolated individual of today should be transformed from a passive on-looker to an active participant in community life. The political aspect is only one part of the problem.

In place of the usual terms — village, city, metropolis — Le Corbusier proposed a general expression: "the human agglomeration." Present agglomerations, in their continuous change and continuous growth, are something quite different from former cities. In the emerging habitat there can be no self-sufficient settlements, but instead of an amorphous sprawl there could be what the congress termed "urban constellations."

J. L. Sert and his colleagues at Harvard University were entrusted with the formulation of the Charte de l'Habitat. It was never written, not only because of the strenuous schedule of a large American university, but also because, in the absence of the many polyphonic voices of a congress, such a document could not be brought into being. But what had already been arrived at could and should be set down.

In Dubrovnik the entire former leadership of CIAM resigned, and a proposal was made that the old name "CIAM" should be dropped so that the new leaders could start afresh. This proposal was unfortunately not accepted.

At the final session of CIAM a letter from Le Corbusier to the younger generation was read: "Messieurs, Amis, attention au tournant!"

CIAM came into existence at the same moment as the first large buildings of contemporary architecture. The main influence of CIAM was to strengthen the convictions of its

The influence of CIAM

members. Because they believed so strongly in what they were doing, CIAM's members were willing to undertake large-scale projects without pay. CIAM never had any financial resources. It was an assembly of individualists who tried to establish a common basis. Step by step they worked to penetrate unsolved problems, using the tool of comparative analysis: studies using the same symbols and drawn to the same scale. It was one of the unwritten laws of CIAM that participants should not display their own individual work so that criticism of each other's projects would not divert them from the general theme of the congress. It was typical of the spirit of CIAM that the great pioneers of the modern movement also submitted to this discipline.

CIAM was led by its officiers, J. L. Sert, president; Walter Gropius and Le Corbusier, vice presidents; S. Giedion, secretary-general; and delegates from twenty-two countries. Some of the most prominent delegates were: Belgium, Victor Bourgeois and L. von Stynen; Brazil, A. E. Reidy and O. Niemeyer; Germany, Ernest May, Hugo Häring, W. Hebebrand, and H. Scharoun; England, Maxwell Fry, J. M. Richards, P. Smithson, and W. Howell; France, G. Candilis, J. Preuvé, and E. Parent; Netherlands, C. van Eesteren, B. Merkelbach, A. van Eyck, and R. B. Bakema; Italy, E. N. Rogers, L. B. Belgiogoso, I. Gardella, E. Peresutti, and G. Terragni; Japan, K. Maekawa, Kenzo Tange, and J. Sakakura; Poland, S. H. Syrkus and J. Soltan; Sweden, S. Markelius and G. Seidenblad; Switzerland, W. Moser, M. E. Haefeli, R. Steiger, and A. Roth; United States, R. J. Neutra, Moholy-Nagy, Marcel Breuer, and K. Lönberg-Holm.

CIAM called whoever had talent to collaborate whether his name was already made or not. As a result, almost all creative architects took an active part in the CIAM congresses. CIAM started near the beginning of the movement in a moment of crisis, and CIAM ended at a moment of great prosperity, when contemporary architecture had prevailed.

Architecture a moral problem
Architecture has long ceased to be the concern of passive and businesslike specialists who built precisely what their clients demanded. It has gained the courage to deal actively with life, to help mold it. It starts with intimately vital questions,

704

inquiring into the needs of the child, the woman, and the man. It asks, "What kind of life are you leading? Are we responsible for the conditions you have to put up with? How must we plan — not just in the case of houses, but clear through to regional areas — so that you may have a life worthy of the name?"

When we go to the bottom of questions like these, we see that contemporary architecture takes its start in a *moral* problem. Architecture has emerged from the realm of narrow specialization. And by taking off his specialists's blinders, the architect has greatly extended his influence. Architecture is a highly complex activity; it works in the boundary area halfway between the regions of aesthetic feeling and practical doing. But this is just the reason why we look to it to give us the kind of surroundings that will express the life of our period.

Modern painters have enlarged our visual experience by working with relations between objects which we had never taken cognizance of in our ordinary, half-automatic seeing. Contemporary architects have been just as willing to anticipate public understanding. They too have refused to wait until they could be sure of universal approbation for their work. Following an impulse which was half ethical, half artistic, they have sought to provide our life with its corresponding shell or framework. And where contemporary architecture has been allowed to provide a new setting for contemporary life, this new setting has acted in its turn upon the life from which it springs. The new atmosphere has led to change and development in the conceptions of the people who live in it.

In the past (and to some extent even now) really creative art has met with resistance from a public whose conceptual development had outdistanced its emotional growth. The fight which contemporary architecture had to wage to establish itself was due to just this gap between thinking and feeling. That fight would never have succeeded if architecture had waited for other branches of knowledge to arrive at a coordinated and universal outlook. Builders, sociologists, economists, political theorists — none of these have as yet fulfilled all their aims. Meanwhile the architects have worked with whatever means were at hand — sometimes very primitive ones, with which completely satisfactory solutions were impossible — to establish the contours of a new kind of life.

Universal trends
and local problems Many different countries have contributed to the development which we have been discussing. It would be interesting to observe the spread of the new movements, through Holland, France, Germany, Sweden, England, and elsewhere; to see what direction was taken in each of these countries and the special dangers which each involves; to note the influence of environment and tradition upon the solution of architectural problems. Such local differences have a more than superficial importance. Those countries which accepted contemporary architecture as a kind of universal coinage — a collection of particular shapes which retained their full value wherever they were transplanted — invited architectural bankruptcy. Modern architecture is something more than a universally applicable means of decoration. It is too much the product of our whole period not to exhibit some universal tendencies, but, on the other hand, it is too much concerned with problems of actual living to ignore local differences in needs, customs, and materials. Finland, under the leadership of Alvar Aalto, has shown how contributions can be made to architecture universally through solutions adapted to the specific conditions of their native setting.

PART **VII** **CITY PLANNING IN THE NINETEENTH CENTURY**

Early Nineteenth Century

Once again we must turn back to the nineteenth century. We can appreciate what is required in the sphere of town planning today only if we understand how the present situation has come about.

A universal attitude basic to town planning

If a universal attitude is needed anywhere at all in architecture, it is in town planning. In the absence of a wide survey, a far-sighted point of view, there can be no urban order. Periods incapable of arriving at a consistent outlook on the world are also incapable of carrying out the kind of town planning that goes beyond mere patchwork. Armies of specialists are no help when what is missing is a universal attitude covering the whole of life.

Reign of the specialist in nineteenth-century town planning

On the contrary, specialists who lack a universal attitude are incapable of grasping real relationships. Valuable and precise as their work may be, its results will be limited and out of balance — perhaps even harmful, since one task is overstressed at the expense of others. Periods which depend on specialists are incapable of successful town planning. What happens in such times is something like the case of a man who reads a book with such extreme exactitude that he never manages to get beyond the first ten pages. He loses the meaning of the whole in attending to the details. The situation nowadays is an analogous one. In spite of the existence of many conscientious town-planning associations and of specialists trained in the planning and administration of towns, there prevails a shocking lack of direction and an inability to remove the most obvious inconveniences.

This penalty cannot be evaded since for a hundred years there has been almost nothing but chaos in town planning. Regulations alone can offer no solution, for the regulations also bear the stamp of the men who make them. A new universal vision is needed.

It would be unreasonable to expect new solutions to town-planning problems from a period like the nineteenth century. A century that (especially in its later period) was dominated by the spirit of laissez-faire and under the rule of specialists was no time for town planning, which by its very nature must result from broad vision and foresight.

There is no doubt that the charm of many individual forms of living of the last century will be more and more fully recognized in the near future. But this coming revaluation will not include town planning.

Our interest in town planning can be reduced to three questions: Was the highly developed late baroque art of town planning continued during the nineteenth century? What arose to take its place afterwards? Finally, what new solutions has the twentieth century to offer?

In times when there is a universal vision resting on a long and solid tradition, town planning is taken as a matter of course. We have considered some eighteenth-century solutions which were interesting for their farsightedness and for the feeling for space which they manifest. Many plans of an amazingly high quality are the work of anonymous architects, even of speculators. It is important to notice that solutions which come out of universal vision of the eighteenth century still remain valid long after the death of the society — or the ideal of a society — for which they were formulated, and after changes in circumstance which the designers could never have foreseen. But when the vision of a period is predominately influenced by specialists, the solutions arrived at do not even satisfy the needs of the time.

Late baroque town planning: summary

The late baroque showed a magnificent power of dominating outer space. This period was thoroughly aware of the different relationships between one building and another and between buildings and nature: between constructions and organic life.

The social life from which baroque town planning sprang limited its attention to connections between palatial residences and the spatial treatment of beautiful plazas in the great towns.

Late baroque town planning is the expression of two absolutisms: the first produced by the Counter Reformation, the second by monarchy. All great constructions of the period were built for the Church, for the king, or for those who helped them to rule.

The lodgings of the common people did not enter into these schemes; they were not thought of as presenting any problem. The people formed the invisible foundation and support of the state; everything that was newly built was intended, without question, for the ruling class. People of great experience and wide vision — like Vauban, Louis XIV's great military engineer — saw the dangers of a system which put such burdens upon the people. But Vauban's *Projet d'une dixième royale* (1707) [1] cost him the monarch's favor by its assertion that "what is wrongly called the dregs of the people" merited the "celestial king's" serious attention. "This mass is . . . very important," Vauban continued, "in view of its numbers and the services it renders to the state." The system itself inevitably dictated the rejection of Vauban's main proposal that the nobility and clergy should be taxed (to the extent of one-tenth of their incomes) as well as the people.

Thus it came about that a great town, as far as the mass of the people was concerned, was simply a crowd of houses, neglected in every respect. On the other hand, historical justice forces us to state that great towns in the eighteenth century in no way played the part they did in the nineteenth. The eighteenth-century city lay outside the interest and attention of the chief forces in the period. After the departure of Louis XIV for Versailles, town planning was entirely neglected except in so far as it concerned the building of *places* and great avenues of communication.

Everything that affected the people was either abandoned to disorder or arranged merely provisionally. The confusion and filth, the neglected approaches to the houses, and even the tragicomedy of the city-dweller's longing for flowers and greenery appear in an etching of 1786 (*fig. 445*). The etching, *Pot de fleurs*, is from Mercier's *Tableau de Paris*, a book which so fascinated Diderot that he described it as "pensé dans la rue et écrit sur la borne." The illustration shows the ordinary houses of Paris and the misfortune of one of the fifth-story tenants who has just seen his aerial garden tumble into the

---

[1] Published in 1708 in London under the title, "A project for the Royal Tythe: or General Tax; . . . by the famous Monsieur Vauban."

445.   MERCIER.   *Etching from Tableau de Paris, 1786.*

dirty disorder below.   But such houses were sparsely populated and cannot be compared with the crowded slums created by the nineteenth century.

During the century between Versailles (1668–84) and Lansdowne Crescent in Bath (1794) [2] residences came to be placed in direct contact with nature. This direct contact belonged first to the monarch, next to the nobility, then to anonymous wealthy citizens.   The increased stress in the eighteenth century upon the connection of the dwelling with nature may be laid in large part to the trend of the times toward Rousseau's cult of the "natural man."

Contact with nature of late baroque residences

---

[2] See p. 157.

446. Tuileries, gardens laid out by Lenôtre. *Engraving by Mariette. The avenue of trees to the right still exists, and now borders the Rue de Rivoli along one side.*

Space is necessary if houses face greenery. Such space was impossible in the old walled towns, but in the seventeenth century Vauban moved the defenses of Paris much farther out in order to protect the city against new developments in armaments. It was this which permitted the eighteenth-century *places* to grow up in Paris.

It will be recalled that, in the north and south alike, baroque architects of the second half of the eighteenth century took pains to preserve the association of architecture and greenery. This new phase of town planning continued and was extended for a long while in the nineteenth century. Because in any period town planning is the last department of architecture to acquire a form, the association of architecture and greenery was maintained until the influence of industrialization seriously altered the daily life of the nineteenth century. However, the industrial towns that grew up around slums from the very start show no trace of this tradition.

447. Rue de Rivoli, Paris, c. 1825. *The part of the Rue de Rivoli first built by Percier and Fontaine for Napoleon 1, looking toward the Place de la Concorde. Its single row of houses facing across the roadway onto greenery inspired the Regent, later George IV of England, to develop the Regent's Park terraces shortly thereafter.*

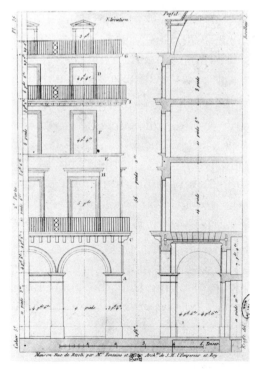

448. PERCIER and **FONTAINE.** Elevation of a house on the Rue de Rivoli, 1806. *This charming and unified façade is a basis for Haussmann's boulevards half a century later. Shops are hidden behind the arcades. Thus this street of Napoleon I has already, in germ at least, that mixture of residence and business functions which the English avoided.*

Late baroque
tradition in the
Rue de Rivoli
(1801)

When Napoleon I commissioned Percier and Fontaine, the founders of the Empire style, to design the Rue de Rivoli, the main outlines of the design were already established by existing conditions.

The Rue de Rivoli of Napoleon I, still the most beautiful street in Paris, is not a *rue corridor*. It has only *one* wall, and this faces upon the gardens of the Tuileries and, what is more important, upon an avenue of trees. This avenue had been laid out under Louis XIV (as an eighteenth-century engraving by Mariette plainly shows), and at first bordered the royal stables (*fig.* 446). These stables occupied the site upon which the Rue de Rivoli was built.

The Place de la Concorde, where the Rue de Rivoli begins, was built under Louis XV and Louis XVI, and the bridge over the Seine was built just at the beginning of the Revolution, in 1790.

Louis XIV laid out the park, Louis XV the square, and Napoleon the street. It was quite typical of the building programs of the period that Napoleon should have commanded a street to be built (this was at the time of his consulate, in 1801). The street was intended for the rich bourgeoisie and offered them a view of the former royal gardens.

In marked contrast to the English practice of making business and residential streets entirely separate, the Rue de Rivoli was both in one.[3] Continuous pillared arcades protected shoppers from the weather and at the same time prevented the shop fronts from diminishing the dignity of the street. Placards and grocers' shops were excluded. These arcades continue the tradition of the seventeenth-century Place des Vosges.

In working out their new task Percier and Fontaine used a form which is as neutral as it is appealing (*fig.* 448). It goes without saying that the whole house was treated as a repeating unit. To preserve the total effect of the street, there are but few accents. The pillared arches of the ground floor are in

---

[3] This separation appears in the Bloomsbury section of London, built up around the same time.

714

449. Rue de Rivoli, view toward the Louvre, 1840.

strict alignment; the balconies of the first, third, and attic floors are continuous; the walls are smooth-surfaced.

The Rue de Rivoli of the time of Napoleon I is a part of the late baroque tradition (*fig.* **447**). Its single row of houses permits as free an outlook as the brothers Adam provided for the occupants of their splendid Adelphi Terrace, built in 1768, overlooking the banks of the Thames. The Rue de Rivoli, at this stage of its development, inspired John Nash and his employer, the Prince Regent, in their plans for laying out Regent's Park and its terraces.

The various continuations of the Rue de Rivoli — the last completed as a part of Haussmann's *percement de Paris* — changed its whole character and made it over into one of those "endless streets" born out of the nineteenth century (*fig.* **449**).

THE DOMINANCE OF GREENERY: THE LONDON SQUARES

In the garden squares of London we have for the first time since the Middle Ages the outward appearance of a city determined by the building activities of the upper middle classes. These classes created a residential style as self-confident as it is lasting. Like the Flemish towns of the fifteenth century, these London squares of the early nineteenth century will bear witness for generations to the sureness with which the middle classes set about providing a framework for their lives, unless these squares are destroyed by insensate building.

To understand the true nature of their development we must first of all remember the English preoccupation with the idea of comfort, especially the Englishman's insistence upon comfort in the home, all the way from the comfortable chair before the fire to the undisturbed privacy of the individual house. This strong urge toward *bienséance* does not appear for the first time in the eighteenth century. To see how far back it goes and how early it influenced the organization of his dwelling, one need only compare the spacious settings and arrangement of early English manor houses with their Continental counterparts. It is to this desire for comfort and privacy that the garden squares of London owe their particular pattern. Indeed, if the development of London may be said to follow any rule, it is unwritten — like so many of those English laws that carry most weight — and derives from the democratic insistence that a man shall not be disturbed in his private life. The rule runs roughly as follows: The residential quarters of a city should, as far as possible, merge into greenery. They should be inconspicuous.

London's irrational growth

London developed with an almost total disregard for definite axes. Its growth was at the mercy of the divisive influences of the great landowners, of the Crown, the nobility, the Church. Its lack of guiding axes such as those which make Paris so easy to survey makes it almost impossible to orient oneself. On the other hand, the numerous small districts into which London resolves itself act as refuges from the sheer immensity of a city which has outgrown the human scale.

716

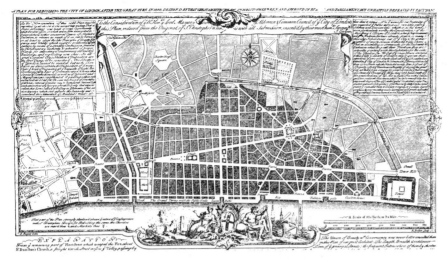

450.　WREN.　Plan for the reconstruction of London, 1666.

Rejection of
Wren's plan, 1666

The comprehensive unity sought by the baroque was not acceptable to seventeenth-century England. The coördinated plan of Christopher Wren for the general rebuilding of London following the great fire of 1666 was rejected by Charles II after only three days' consideration (*fig.* **450**). And this just at the time when Bernini was laying out the Piazza in front of St. Peter's, and Le Nôtre the gardens of Versailles! The sweep of Wren's scheme — half baroque, half Renaissance in character — was too thoroughgoing to permit its execution,[1] but for a reason more fundamental than the one usually given. The popular belief is that Wren's plan was not used because it was impossible to reach agreements with the owners of a half-dozen burned-over sites through which Wren's axes inconveniently ran. But it was not merely a complicated question of ownership which blocked the laying out of axes in the Renaissance or baroque manner; there was also an inner repugnance to them. This same repugnance operated to prevent any systematically related arrangement of terraces, squares, and streets in those areas where it could have been most easily

---

[1] London was self-governing and independent of the Crown. Neither Wren nor any other architect would have thought of using the Continental idea of organizing London around the Royal Palace. Wren's intended point of accent — almost in the Renaissance manner — was the center of the city, at the Stock Exchange. All his lines of force radiated outward from that point to penetrate the whole body of London. St. Paul's stood near the town gates, at the confluence of two main arteries; in the same fashion, two decades later, Rainaldi placed twin churches facing the Piazza del Popolo.

achieved — within the great estates. The Crown and the Duke of Bedford ignored such schemes in the Covent Garden district; the Earl of Southampton did likewise in Bloomsbury. The way in which these squares are irrationally scattered over a site, separated and yet not quite cut off from each other, is like the pattern of an Oriental carpet or a painting by Paul Klee.

451. Queen Square, Bloomsbury, London, 1812. *Around 1800 the open spaces in the middle of the London squares were laid out with freely planted trees and lawns, the beginning of that luxuriant greenery which natural growth brought in due course of time. "Queen Square, situated to the eastward of Bloomsbury Square, is a handsome area, surrounded on three sides by good houses, having an extensive garden in the center. . . . The north side formerly commanded fine views of Hampstead and Highgate." ("Ackermann's Repository of Arts," September 1812.)*

Nature of a square   "The square," according to a *Dictionary of Architecture* published in 1887, "is a piece of land in which is an enclosed garden, surrounded by a public roadway, giving access to the houses on each side of it." For all its brevity, this definition is an excellent statement of the nature of the London squares.

It very properly begins with the "piece of land"; next it stresses as an essential feature the enclosed garden (enclosed because it is only for the tenants, who all have keys); last of all, it mentions the houses which invariably surround it. It does not specify the shape of the square, which may be four-sided, three-sided, regular or irregular. There is no rule requiring that the square must bear any specific relation to neighboring squares, *places*, streets, or crescents.

The London squares of the seventeenth and eighteenth century have great significance for the town planner. In them for the first time the countryside was built upon without being obliterated beneath masses of stone and networks of streets. As living flesh gleams warmly through sheer material, so the one-time gardens of the Duke of Bedford still disclose themselves beneath the residential developments of Bloomsbury with which they have been overlaid. Modern architects often boast of the attention they pay to trees; indeed, they sometimes build a house around one. In the best of the London squares a whole district is composed architecturally around the existing countryside. Herein lies the prescience of the squares.

The main constituent of all the London squares is a central garden of grass and plane trees (*fig.* 451). When newly planted, the rows of plane trees did not achieve the effect of a secluded, romantic garden which they were intended later to produce. Such a picture required the existence of a wall of greenery, which, grateful both to eyes and to lungs, had also the advantage of ensuring privacy from one's neighbors. Each square garden was treated as a unit, just as the houses were. There was no ridiculous breaking up into small allotments but wide expanses where the residents might stretch themselves out on the grass on sunny days or play tennis on the green lawns in front of their own houses. And all this within five minutes' walk of the surging traffic of Tottenham Court Road or Oxford Street.

Central garden

At the start, some of these areas were by no means gardens. "Originally these open spaces were neither so aesthetically pleasing nor so healthful as they might have been, owing to the fact that it was the inevitable fate of open ground in every European city of the seventeenth century to become a dumping place for filth of all kinds. This was prevented only when the inhabitants of squares applied for powers to enclose, clean, and beautify them; St. James's Square, in 1726, was one of the first to seek such permission." [2]

Houses serial and inconspicuous

The architecture of the houses around these squares is also affected by the unwritten rule that residential quarters shall be as inconspicuous as possible. They are arranged serially in apposition, a treatment which was used for more than half a

452. Grosvenor Square, Mayfair, in the early eighteenth century. "*The square is a piece of land in which is an enclosed garden, surrounded by a public roadway, giving access to the houses on each side of it.*"

century in the newly erected parts of London without ever becoming either tiresome or antiquated. Everything is avoided that might obtrude; there are simply smooth, continuous surfaces with as little subdivision as possible. The building material — brick, without stucco — is admirably suited to con-

---

[2] W. R. Davidge, "The Planning of London," *Journal of the Royal Institute of British Architects*, March 10, 1934, p. 433.

ditions. Plain brick, instead of suffering from the dampness and fog of London, becomes mellowed and dignified with the passage of time, like a well-smoked meerschaum pipe. Paint is used sparingly, and only in places where weather cannot harm it and where it can be easily renewed: on the inside of window casements, along the narrow moldings at the entrances, and on the pediments of the houses. Nash's use of stucco in Park Crescent, London (begun in 1812), showed a

453. Square in the Bloomsbury district, built c. 1825. *Even though Bloomsbury was originally a suburb, the separation of traffic and residential quarters was carefully observed. The result is that even today, only a step from the most congested London traffic, the houses are intimately and directly related to their pleasure grounds.*

Continental influence which departed somewhat from the main tradition.

How did the London squares originate? An answer to this question will help us understand better their architectural inheritance. The desire for green spaces within London reaches back to Gothic times. In the fifteenth century the court of Lincoln's Inn was laid out as a lawn and converted into walks.

Origin of London squares

721

At the same time a piece of land outside the town, Moorfields, was being used by the inhabitants as a recreation ground for archery and other sports. As early as the seventeenth century, the most important of the popular parks, Hyde Park — far out of London, and the property of the Crown — was opened to the public.[3]

It was in the seventeenth century also that the first squares were built. They originated in the desire of various noble landowners to build up portions of their estates. These constructions followed the baroque pattern of *places* rather than streets. About 1630 the Earl of Bedford gave over seven acres of his land to building purposes. The result was the first London square: Covent Garden. It has often been pointed out that this first square — never quite completed, by the way — resembles the Place des Vosges in Paris (1612). Both are typical seventeenth-century *places*, rectangular, and with arcades running through the ground floor of the houses. As a matter of course they were open to the public and devoid of lawn or trees. The application to them and other such spaces of the name "piazza" clearly shows a recognition of their Italian origin.

The Earl of Bedford's example was soon followed by the Earl of Leicester. Leicester Square, in front of Leicester House, was laid out by him on the same principles in 1635. It is a business center today and has been totally disfigured. In 1665 the Earl of Southampton "was building a noble square or piazza, a little town," [4] which became a fashionable quarter. This later became Bloomsbury Square. Several other squares followed: Soho Square in 1681, St. James's Square in 1684, and Grosvenor Square (Mayfair) in 1695 (*figs.* **452, 454**).

From this brief account the pertinent point emerges that as early as the late seventeenth century London, unlike Paris, was becoming attractive for residences of the upper classes. Furthermore, the London squares were separate, widely scattered areas like the French and Italian *places*.

---

[3] Steen Eiler Rasmussen, *London, the Unique City* (New York, 1937), pp. 86, 92.

[4] *The Builder*, July 28, 1855, p. 349.

There was increased building activity during the eighteenth century. About fifteen squares in all appear to have come into existence during this century.[5] To some extent this activity was devoted to completing the seventeenth-century squares. Thus Grosvenor and Hanover squares were completed in 1720, and Berkeley Square around 1730. Then building took another spurt just as the century began its last quarter: the Adelphi Terrace on the banks of the Thames was built by the brothers Adam around 1770, Manchester Square in 1774, Bed-

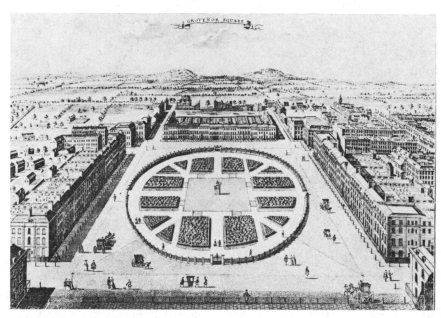

454. Grosvenor Square, London, begun in 1695. *An eighteenth-century square set in the midst of open fields with the enclosed area laid out as a formal garden. The gardens behind the houses stretch out into the fields.*

ford Square in 1775, Portland Place in 1778, and Fitzroy Place in 1790. The greatest activity went on in Bath from about 1730 — the time of the emergence of the elder Wood — until the construction of the Royal Crescent in 1767. What is important at Bath is the interrelations between the various squares and crescents, relations so much more subtle than the purely axial ones employed in French town planning. Such carefully thought-out relationships were arrived at in London toward the end of the eighteenth century.

[5] *The Report of the Royal Commission on London Squares* (London, 1928).

THE GARDEN SQUARES OF BLOOMSBURY

That harmonious interrelation of squares, *places*, and crescents upon which alone rests London's claim to a high level of urban planning came about during the years between 1775 and 1850.[1] On such sites as Bloomsbury, well-ordered spaces of every shape — oblong, circular, square, elliptical — accumulated to form a new and composite organism. In them the late baroque inheritance was carried on in a completely native manner, perfectly adapted to the conditions peculiar to London.

Bloomsbury's human scale The development of Bloomsbury occupied more than a century and a half, approximately from the time Louis XIV began planning the removal of his court to Versailles down to the rise of great industrial cities like Manchester. It is the one known instance over such a long period of urban development to a constantly increasing perfection. As an architectural composition, Bloomsbury is, in its way, fully the equal of such widely different organizations as the monumental baroque squares before St. Peter's and, later on, the Place de la Concorde. Though there is no doubt that both these, playing with the whole orchestra of monumental voices, are much more impressive, the Bloomsbury district can take its place beside them. For although it employs shapes of an anonymous and humble character, these shapes have a timeless validity, and the way in which they were successively added together to form ever-larger units — *places*, squares, terraces — produced a district which for its human treatment remains unsurpassed to this day.

Bloomsbury is all of a piece, a simple and democratic fabric in which any touch of the monumental is a violation. The comparatively small mansions of the Bedfords and Montagues, around which it grew up, were no intrusion upon this unity, but the building of the British Museum early in the nineteenth century introduced an element harshly out of scale. Today the huge buildings of the University of London and other office

[1] *The Report of the Royal Commission on London Squares* (1928) places the building peak between 1800 and 1850: "The activity in the development of the squares reaches its height in the early part of the nineteenth century. By 1850 practically all the well-known squares were completed" (p. 11).

724

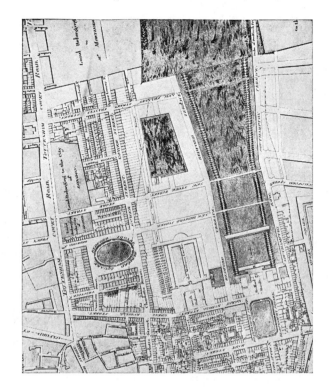

455. Bloomsbury at the end of the eighteenth century. *Part of a 1795 map. This shows the original boundaries of the district just before the period of its greatest development, when it was still largely composed of estates of the Duke of Bedford.*

456. Bloomsbury in 1828. *Map of James Wyld, engraved by N. R. Hewitt. The whole plan follows late baroque tradition in emphasizing the squares, but they are laid out flexibly and informally. In their careful yet irrational planning they resemble the pattern of an Oriental carpet or a painting by Paul Klee more than any rigid French axes.*

buildings have largely destroyed the old Bloomsbury scale. The dominant three-hundred-foot tower thrusts itself upward like an explosion, shattering forever the serenity and cohesion of the district lying below.

However, the tower does serve one good purpose. It affords a unique vantage point from which to survey Bloomsbury and trace the pattern of its squares. Laid out so that there are no extended vistas, their relationship to each other is not discernible from any one of them. Only from above is it possible to see the balanced proportion between building and open space, a balance so nicely maintained as to give every resident an equal sense both of his privacy and his freedom (*fig.* **457**).

Boundaries of Bloomsbury
: The great thoroughfares that bound Bloomsbury are also easily distinguished from the tower — Holborn and New Oxford streets on the south, and Tottenham Court on the west; Bloomsbury itself stretches away to the east, to the gardens of Gray's Inn and the squares beyond, until it fades out of sight in the distance. The original boundaries of the district, as shown on a map of 1795 (*fig.* **455**),[2] were Tottenham Court Road, New Road, Southampton Row, and Holborn Street. This map defines Bloomsbury just before the period of its greatest development, when it was still largely composed of the estates of the Duke of Bedford, with Bedford Square as the most conspicuous architectural organization.

Bloomsbury Square (1667)
: The beginnings of the Bloomsbury district date back to Restoration times. Southampton Square — later called Bloomsbury Square — was laid out in 1667 by the Earl of Southampton along the axis of Bedford House, his town mansion in Bloomsbury. Bedford House, with its *cour d'honneur* and extensive grounds and gardens, dominated the square. Thus the houses and the green but treeless areas of Bloomsbury Square were dependent, like any French *place* or Italian *piazza*, on a noble residence. Bedford House was still standing when new and greatly increased building activity began in the late eighteenth century.

---

[2] University of London, *The Bloomsbury Site* (c. 1933), a pamphlet by Eliza Jeffries Davis. Cf. also *London Topographical Record*, XVII, 78 ff.

457. Bloomsbury: air view of Russell, Bedford, Bloomsbury, and adjacent squares. *Only from above is it possible to see the balance between buildings and open spaces and the relationship of the squares to each other.*

The first of the new squares was Bedford Square. It was located at some distance from the gardens of Bedford House and on an axis at right angles to Bloomsbury Square. On the 1795 map it appears isolated and treeless and completely independent of its surroundings. Executed about 1775, this noble square, with its oval enclosure, is one of the few associated with the name of an architect — in this instance, Thomas Leverton.[3] Montague House, the town mansion of a family related to the Bedfords, also appears on the map of 1795. It resembled Bedford House and had, like it, a *cour d'honneur*. In 1753 the British Museum was housed in it.

Thus at the end of the eighteenth century, Bloomsbury had three points of accent: Bloomsbury Square, Bedford Square, and the British Museum with its gardens.

The third and decisive stage in the evolution of Bloomsbury occupies the first quarter of the nineteenth century. The fifth

Bedford Square
(1775)

Bedford Place
(1800)

[3] Even this attribution has been questioned. See John Summerson, *Journal of the Royal Institute of British Architects*, March 6, 1939, p. 440.

458. Bedford Place, from Bloomsbury Square to Russell square, begun in 1800. *This street, lined by houses the neutral architecture of which is the result of an old and highly refined tradition, is not a long extended street in the Continental sense but a short connecting link between two places.*

Duke of Bedford pulled down his house in Bloomsbury Square in 1800; its groves and avenues fell with it. On the site arose Bedford Place with its magnificently coördinated houses (*fig.* **458**). What was left of the gardens was also turned over to residential development; the largest and most lordly of the squares, Russell Square, was really the very heart of the gardens cut out and preserved intact in the midst of its new buildings.

The Duke did not undertake these projects himself. Instead he leased his lands to James Burton, a speculator and builder, who planned, designed, and executed Russell Square (1800–14) [4] and at the same time carried out work on several streets that open off that square — Keppel Street, Montague Place,

[4] These dates are the result of John Summerson's research. Earlier sources — for example, Henry Clutton, "The Squares of London," *Builder*, July 28, 1855, p. 349 — give the date as 1804.

and Southampton Row. Burton constantly pushed farther eastward, always striving to evolve appropriate dispositions of large open spaces.[5] He planted the land behind the houses on Bedford Place, which runs between Bloomsbury and Russell squares, with lawns and shrubbery. The result was particularly pleasing, for the low mews or stables behind the houses did not obstruct the view, and the openings at the ends of the rows of houses linked the parallel areas of greenery so that there were no closed blocks.

After 1820 Burton's work in this district was taken over by Thomas Cubitt (1788–1855). "He was thirty-two and already famous in the building world for his great workshops in Gray's Inn Road where he was doing what had never been done before — employing all the trades on a permanent collective basis. To keep his organisation going he took land and built wherever a good opportunity occurred."[6] Cubitt completed Torrington Square in 1827,[7] using a greatly elongated quadrangular pattern which, although it maintained sufficient distance for privacy between the opposite rows of houses, wasted no land. The intentions of its unknown architect are shown by a map of 1828, only one year after its completion, on which already there is indicated a row of trees planted along the middle axis of the enclosure (*fig.* **456**). This central garden has remained till today one of the most attractive in the district.[8]

Thomas Cubitt

In every particular Bloomsbury is imbued with the architectural tradition of the eighteenth century. The delicacy and

Single-family house the basic unit

---

[5] The segmented North and South crescents and Alfred Place (the broad connecting link between them) represent some of the solutions at which he arrived.

[6] Summerson, *Journal of the Royal Institute of British Architects*, March 6, 1939, p. 442.

[7] According to Summerson. According to Davis (*London Topographical Record*, XVII, 92), it was completed in 1829.

[8] Cubitt was a pioneer in the construction of great building units, one of the few contractors to undertake works on a large scale and carry them through successfully. But it is perhaps of more interest that, although he was essentially a builder of streets, squares, and *places* in the late baroque tradition, he had nevertheless a definite connection with the new potentialities. In 1839 he became a member of the Institution of Civil Engineers. One of his two contributions to its proceedings was a paper entitled, "Experiments on the Strength of Cast-Iron Girders." Toward the end of his life, when the Crystal Palace Exhibition was being undertaken with doubtful success, Cubitt did everything possible to promote it and was among those who offered to guarantee the necessary funds.

imagination which marked its town planning are here continued and very graciously united with the naturalistic landscape gardening of the early nineteenth century. The basic unit is the single-family house. The dwellings were intended for the professional upper middle class, for the lawyers and judges of Gray's Inn near-by, for writers and others of similar intellectual pursuits. The rows of houses are treated like the garden squares, as homogeneous units. Here again is the exercise of a wise distinction between what must be private and what is best held in common.

The architecture has that timelessness, that independence of fashion, so often found in farmhouses. Yet every detail of these buildings has refinement, from their apparently paper-thin slate or cast-iron balconies to the graceful sweep of their interior staircases. Sometimes the balcony is overhung with a small canopy which is carried on slim, cast-iron trellis work so delicate that it is more like the veining of a leaf than a design in metal.

The ground plan of the individual houses follows late eighteenth-century practice. At the core of the house is a stairway rising in spaciously curved flights through the entire height of the building to a skylight. This arrangement, first employed by the brothers Adam in their Adelphi Terrace (begun in 1768), leaves the exterior walls unblocked. Thus every room receives direct outside light. The rooms themselves are perfectly proportioned, being neither too large nor too small. It must be affirmed that their dimensions are human.

The location of the servants' quarters in the basement where they are exposed to the dust of the street has often been thought callous. Certainly it is a defect in planning. Even so, it is more humane than the Continental use of cramped attic stories.

Mews The light-well, used later on with disastrous effect by Continental speculators, is in these houses happily avoided. Ample space both at front and back gives every room, whether opening on the back yard or on the street, its full amount of light. And the location of the stables and coachmen's quarters in one-story buildings (mews) at some distance to the rear of the

730

459. Bloomsbury district, Woburn Square, row of houses. c. 1825–30.

houses removes any possible obstruction to openness of view. This combination of tall houses and low mews back of the gardens appeared as early as the late sixteenth century. Up to the sixties of the nineteenth, two of these combinations were often paired, creating twice the ordinary amount of space between the backs of two rows of houses. Occupying the wide distance between the houses was a double row of carriage houses forming a mews, or service street exclusively for the private carriages and coaches.

These London quarters condense and continue architectural experience going back to Renaissance times. Nevertheless, they were as much the products of building speculation as those later Continental residential blocks which brought chaos into the structure of the city. The difference was one of control. The contractors active during the reconstruction of Paris had to build façades according to Haussmann's requirements, but that was all. What lay behind was subject to no real con-

Controlled development

460. Kensington, London, 1830–40. Air view. *Though comparatively modest in area, the squares of Kensington show a fine freedom of planning and the achievement of new organic shapes toward the end of the development.*

trol, and they adopted the quickest means to the largest profits. In their hands buildings became part façade and part light-well. In London a much more careful control was exercised by the great landowners on whose estates the buildings were erected. These owners were accustomed to reckoning in terms of hundreds of years. The land and everything on it usually reverted to them in not more than ninety-nine years. Knowing very well that estates could be destructively exploited, they retained in their leases control over the utilization of the ground, and their trustees had the power to undertake maintenance work in cases of neglect.

Wandering through London, one frequently comes upon squares built between 1830 and 1860 in the most diverse and unexpected parts of the town.[9] Some of these almost unknown places (for example, Lloyd Square of about 1840) were laid out for people of small means; though simpler in execution than those of Bloomsbury, they too were treated in a manner that adapted them to human living.[10] Others, like the squares of South Kensington, are also comparatively modest in area, but show a fine freedom of planning and achievement of new organic shapes (*fig.* **460**). All of them, whatever their location and proportions, are the products of a town planning which strives for a plastic modeling of space. They continue the eighteenth-century tradition of towns like Bath and Edinburgh. They achieve a unity at once charming and reassuring, and demonstrate the vitality which can be introduced into the structure of a city through the laying out of quite freely formed complexes.

There is an obvious degeneration in the treatment of the houses after 1860, particularly in their architectonic features. The hitherto discreet front becomes loud; the windows are overloaded with detail; the whole house disintegrates into separate and conflicting parts. In addition, other influences were at work. The uniformly treated square was being supplanted by the semidetached suburban house with its miniature garden. Also growing up along the great roads were settlements consisting of endless rows of tiny houses, like boxes, merging without distinction into other settlements. Devastating in themselves, they are the ruin of all comprehensive town-planning schemes.

---

[9] In 1858 *Building News* was still able to announce new work: "At present there are ten new squares in actual progress in the suburbs of London." It lists Kensington Square, Leinster Square, Bayswater Square, with its "first-class dwelling houses," Princes Square, and Norfolk Square. All these are in Bayswater and Paddington. (*Building News*, May 7, 1858, p. 479.)

[10] See Christopher Hussey, "Georgian London, the Lesser-Known Squares," *Country Life*, LXXXV (January 28 and March 4, 1939), 91–94, 224–225.

LARGE–SCALE HOUSING DEVELOPMENT: REGENT'S PARK

During the last stages of the development of Bloomsbury, John Nash was commissioned to design a scheme of buildings and gardens for what was then Marylebone Park, a large, irregularly shaped tract of meadow land belonging to the Crown at the north edge of London. The Regent wished it developed for residential purposes, but not crowded with buildings. He particularly desired the creation of a large new park accessible to the inhabitants of the city. Nash drew up his first plan in 1812 (*fig.* **464**); after some modification and delay, the project was carried out during the twenties. The result was Regent's Park and its terraces.

In making his plan Nash "declared his aims to be threefold: firstly, to assure the greatest possible revenue to the Crown; secondly, to add to the beauty of the Metropolis; and thirdly, to study the health and convenience of the public." [1] His work was another essay in the free disposition of large building complexes facing nature. It followed not so much the example of the London squares as that line which begins with Versailles and continues through the Bath crescents and the arrangement of some other English towns.

Regent's Park lies along the axis of the Adams' Portland Place (1778). Connecting it and Portland Place with Piccadilly Circus in the heart of London is Regent Street, also Nash's work. This imposing London business street was built around 1820, being finished just as the Regent's Park terraces were begun. The two are the English counterpart of Napoleon's Rue de Rivoli. Nash had started his Park Crescent in 1812 (*fig.* **461**) at the end of Portland Place. The time, however, was not yet ripe; Napoleon was still unbeaten, commercial conditions were unsettled, bankruptcies were frequent. But by 1825 everything had been set straight, and a new wealthy class had sprung up.

It was for this new class that the Regent's Park residences were intended. An opulent and anonymous class who had been

---

[1] W. R. Davidge, "The Planning of London," *Journal of the Royal Institute of British Architects*, March 10, 1934, p. 443.

461. JOHN NASH. Park Crescent, London, begun in 1812. *The individual houses are treated as parts of a unit, organized in a single semicircular block behind a façade of a unified design. Park Crescent was the beginning of the large-scale housing development of Regent's Park.*

made rich by industry, the development of trade with the colonies, or the exploitation of English victories in the field,[2] they were quite able to afford the magnificent houses which Nash designed for them. In 1825, almost overnight, there appeared long rows of terraces which, starting from Park Crescent, embrace Regent's Park like a pair of giant lobster claws. Set well back from the road encircling the park, most of the houses are on raised plots with the ground between them and the road terraced to separate them from it. They face directly on the park, which they overlook without dominating.

In Park Crescent the individual houses are once again treated as parts of a unit — a unit often consisting of fifty separate houses (*fig.* **462**). But this regard for the effect of the whole does not achieve the completely neutral result attained in

---

[2] It is said that observers sent by the London financiers followed all Wellington's campaigns and reported everything of importance by carrier pigeon.

Bloomsbury. The terraces of tall and narrow houses were consciously conceived with an accent on monumentality. They remind one of the Royal Crescent at Bath, but in their pilastered central portions they already reveal the seeds of late nineteenth-century form.

Boldness in treating outer space

Definitely more important to us than the actual execution of park and terraces is Nash's original plan of 1812, which unfortunately was not carried out. For in that plan are shown a boldness of imagination and a daring treatment of outer space which are highly significant today. The simple sketch of it which appears in Summerson's biography proves the origi-

462. JOHN NASH. Large-scale housing adjacent to Regent's Park.

nality and sweep of Nash's thought.[3]. Its boldness of conception is illustrated by several striking details.

For one thing, Nash planned to erect two huge semicircular crescents in the north of the park, which would have stood like two enormous half-cylinders in the midst of a sea of greenery. He also wanted to place a double circle in the center of the park. The houses of its concentric rings were to face in opposite directions, those of one inward, those of the other outward.[4] But even more interesting is his proposal to enclose

[3] John Summerson, *John Nash, Architect to George IV* (London, 1935), p. 113.

[4] Summerson discovered that the huge double circle was not entirely original with Nash. He found in a scheme of 1794 what "was obviously the prototype for Nash's plan" (*Journal of the Royal Institute of British Architects*, vol. XLVI, March 6, 1939, pp. 444–445). This was the work of quite obscure architects — more evidence that town planning was as much within the reach of everyone at this period as industrialized design is now.

463.   JOHN NASH.   A terrace of Regent's Park.

464.   JOHN NASH.   First project of the housing development in Regent's Park, 1812. *This plan, which was not carried out as designed, is an essay in the free disposition of large building complexes in open spaces.   It followed not so much the example of the London squares as that trend which begins with Versailles and continues through the Bath crescents and the arrangement of some other English towns, and has its continuation in our period.*

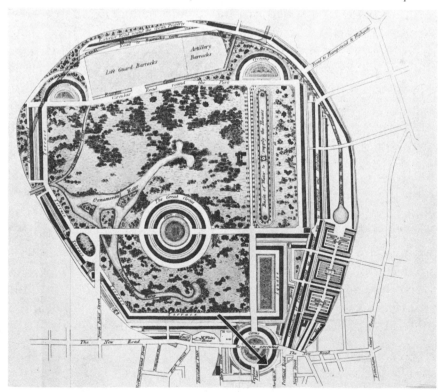

465. View of Birmingham, 1850. *The squares of Bloomsbury do not give a picture of what happened during the first half of the nineteenth century to other English cities which endured the full impact of mechanization. Its devastating effect on the urban pattern appears in this bird's-eye view of Birmingham. Living quarters and industry are inextricably mixed; back yards are choked with chimneys and factories.*

the eastern side of the park with a series of terraces. He planned to push great complexes of buildings into the park, with a liberty of disposition that would be daring even today. At the southeast corner, supporting the main entrance,[5] an open square, intended by Nash to be larger than Russell Square, joined with the open space of the park. Near the short upper arm of this square he placed a long building, parallel to it and receding still further, and at right angles to that a single unit which, quite asymmetrically, extended half the length of the park. (See *fig.* **464**).

Such an organization of exterior space, with advancing and receding complexes which cannot be embraced in a single glance, was never actually realized during this period. However, the free disposition of large building units in contact with nature that appears in this first plan of Nash's was a premonition of twentieth-century ventures. Just as Francesco Borromini in the late seventeenth century extended building frontiers by seeking to accomplish an interpenetration of inner and outer space, so Nash in this project approached in the

---

[5] On Nash's plan the main entrance lies at the south of the park, as it does today. It was given the form of a circle which led into Portland Place. Only the southern half — Park Crescent (1812–19) — was completed.

realm of town planning that freedom of spatial organization which has since been explored on an even larger scale.

We have seen that the fundamental requirement for town planning is the maintenance of one controlling authority, with no dispersion among independent owners of control over the ground. But it is perhaps as important for this controlling authority to possess an instinct for town planning. In the twentieth century enormous blocks of residential or business premises have been thrust into the beautiful late baroque squares — Berkeley Square, for example — destroying everything. Business is not alone the offender. The University of London has steadily reduced the noblest district of the city to insignificance. Thanks partly to Continental, partly to American influences, London seems to have lost that instinct for scale which was responsible for Bloomsbury.

THE STREET BECOMES DOMINANT: THE TRANSFORMATION OF PARIS, 1853–68

The London squares antedate the railroad; the transformation of Paris, on the other hand, took place during the feverish middle years of the railway age. The London squares were designed primarily to be lived in, with busy thoroughfares excluded. Thus the traffic of London — at this period a city three times as big as Paris — circled the Bloomsbury district at a distance, and the same thing was true of many other sections of the town. Residential quarters were kept intact and systematically isolated from traffic routes.

Contrast between London and Paris

The situation in the Paris of Napoleon III was quite different. One element dominated all others: the street, the "cannon-shot boulevard," seemingly without an end. The great town of the latter half of the nineteenth century, the metropolis of the industrial era, suddenly took its typical form in Paris between 1850 and 1870. In no other city of this period did the changes consequent upon the development of industry proceed with such impetus.

Alterations begun
by Napoleon III

A large map of Paris hung on the wall of Napoleon III's study at Saint-Cloud. With his own hand — "his own august hand," Haussmann prefers to say — he plotted on it the alterations he intended to make in the city. These proposed alterations were marked out in red, blue, and green, in descending order of urgency. For the most part, those sketched in green were never executed.

The original plan and all but one of the copies made of it were lost in a fire. The surviving copy was found in the library of the castle in Berlin by a French historian.[1] This had been presented to the King of Prussia by Napoleon III on the occasion of the German monarch's visit to the Paris Exhibition of 1867 — the apogee of the Second Empire. It is not quite identical with the original, as certain works — the extension of the Rue de Rivoli, for example — are prematurely shown as existing (*fig.* 466). Nevertheless it gives an idea of the vast amount of town planning that was compressed within the short span of seventeen years.

Motives for
this work

At first sight, the thick lines crisscrossing through the dense confusion of houses in the center of the city suggest not so much town planning as the layout of a trench defense system for some difficult piece of terrain. And in fact it was a kind of trench system, erected with an internal foe in mind. According to a French authority,[2] during the quarter century between 1827 and 1852 the streets and alleys of Paris had seen barricades thrown up on nine separate occasions. This called for drastic remedies, and wide, unbroken lines of streets were the best means of controlling incipient riots.

But since history refuses to progess in straight lines or in accordance with rational schemes, these streets and boulevards of the Second Empire never proved of service in its defense.

---

[1] André Morizet, *Du vieux Paris au Paris moderne* (Paris, 1932), p. 130.

[2] Morizet, p. 133.

466. Map of Paris by Napoleon III. *The Emperor's own project for the transformation of Paris.* →

The enemy which overthrew Napoleon came from elsewhere than the interior of his capital city.

Industry and the growth of cities

The rapid growth of big cities — the increase in their number as well as the violent expansion of their populations — is the outstanding phenomenon of nineteenth-century urbanism. It was in the second half of the century, just when there was the greatest uncertainty about how life should be organized to meet new conditions, that the major part of this growth took place. This speed and uncertainty were responsible for the heaviest tasks that confronted town planners of the next period. We have already argued that the social disorder which was so clearly reflected in the mid-century town planning was connected to the break between methods of thinking and methods of feeling during the period.

The increase in the numbers of cities and the size of their populations and the spread of industry are interrelated events. Thus the evolution of London into a great nineteenth-century city precedes the similar change in Paris by, roughly, a half century. The same interval lies between the industrialization of England and the industrialization of France.

Paris under Louis-Philippe

As a consequence of the French Revolution the population of Paris fell off by a hundred thousand. But, following this first decrease, the population doubled between 1801 and 1808, rising from a half million to more than one million. During the eighteen years of Louis-Philippe's reign, a total of only forty-one and a half million francs was spent on street undertakings for Paris. This averaged somewhat less than half a million dollars per year. Over the same interval — 1831 to 1848 — the population grew from three-quarters to more than one million.

Rambuteau, a forerunner of Haussmann

The guiding formula of Count Rambuteau, prefect under Louis-Philippe, was to give the Parisians water, air, and shade — "donner aux Parisiens de l'eau, de l'air, de l'ombre." He cannot be said to have been entirely successful in his endeavors, since at the end of them twenty thousand water-carriers still patrolled the streets of Paris — and they still depended on the Seine to supply their stock in trade. In general the achievements of this Burgundian nobleman have not been given a very high rating. A French historian regards

742

him as a half-ridiculous figure who conducted his work in petty-bourgeois fashion, never undertaking anything which threatened to exceed the amount of spare cash on hand.[3] On the other hand, an English authority regards him as the forerunner of Haussmann, one who anticipated him as a maker of modern Paris.[4]

Rambuteau (earlier a prefect under the first Napoleon) was in fact a most amiable person. Tactful and considerate, possessed of a social conscience and regard for his fellows, Rambuteau genuinely loved nature. As prefect of the Swiss Department of Valais under Napoleon I, he imported the vintage grapes of Burgundy to these valleys, so favorable to their growth. In exchange he gave Burgundy the pine trees of the Valais district. During the fifteen years of his prefecture in the Department of the Seine (terminated by the collapse of the July Monarchy) he leveled and paved the Boulevard Saint-Denis and the Boulevard des Bonnes Nouvelles, carefully planting them with trees, giving them their present aspect.

Rambuteau worked untiringly to humanize institutions for the unfortunate — prisoners, the sick, the insane, and the destitute. His name remains associated with the model prison of Mazas, the hospital of Lariboisière, and the Salpêtrière, whose barbarous methods and equipment for treating the insane were changed on his initiative. He founded playgrounds, and placed public benches in the squares and public parks, where before his time there had been only chairs for hire.

In short, Rambuteau was neither ridiculous nor the maker of modern Paris: he was as typical of the July Monarchy as Haussmann was of the Second Empire. Achievements on a grand scale are possible only under regimes that demand them and seek out the proper instruments for the work. Under Louis-Philippe, Haussmann would have remained a provincial prefect all his life, and would never have found an opening for his talents.

---

[3] Morizet, pp. 104 ff.

[4] O. F. Abbott, "A Maker of Modern Paris," *Contemporary Review* (London), no. 873 (September 1938), pp. 350–356.

The "Trois Réseaux" of Eugène Haussmann

Paris the first
city to conform to
the industrial age

Time after time, in many different fields, Paris had been the center of Europe. The guiding spirit of every age is crystallized in its monuments — from the Sainte-Chapelle to the Rue de Rivoli. But this splendid heritage was set in the midst of a thoroughly disorganized city, each monument surrounded and isolated by a tangle of streets. The herculean efforts of Georges-Eugène Haussmann (1809–91), Préfet de la Seine under Napoleon III, drastically altered this situation. It was his desire to provide a splendid framework for the great traditions preserved in Paris. At the same time he wished to make Paris the first great city of the industrial age.

We have already mentioned the fact that Napoleon III had outlined the transformation of Paris before Haussmann was called in. He had even begun actual operations on some of his projects: the extension of the Rue de Rivoli, the Boulevard de Strasbourg (whose starting point, the Gare de l'Est, was in process of construction), the preparatory work on the Bois de Boulogne, and the erection of the Grandes Halles (for which there had been a demand since the late thirties).[5]

Napoleon's
unsuccessful
beginnings

Napoleon was none too successful with these undertakings, however. He proposed, for example, to lead a river through the Bois de Boulogne, in the style of London's Hyde Park. When Haussmann arrived on the scene, the bed for this new river had already been dug, under the direction of an old *jardinier-paysagiste* who had worked on the estates of Napoleon's father. Haussmann discovered that the water would have had to run uphill in one section. The old gardener "avait commis une erreur, sinon un complet oubli de nivellement." [6] There was nothing for it but to substitute two lakes on different levels for the projected river. A similar neglect of the elementary rules of surveying in the extension of the Rue de Rivoli led to serious difficulties later on. The start on the great markets was more encouraging. We have already recorded that the first stone pavilion had to be torn down.

---

[5] Cf. the account of Horeau's design, p. 231.

[6] Georges-Eugène Haussmann, *Mémoires* (Paris, 1890–93), III. 122.

Napoleon III behaved in these matters as he did in politics: he drew up great schemes, but when serious difficulties arose he tried to twist his way through by making numerous petty concessions. This instinctive attempt to bargain his way out at the cheapest price had undermined his regime from the beginning. Thus Napoleon allowed Haussmann to rule Paris while things went smoothly, but as soon as he became a political storm center, Napoleon to all intents and purposes abandoned him. Without Haussmann's energy and determination, the transformation of Paris would never have been carried through — certainly not in the short space of seventeen years.

Between 1853 and 1869 Haussmann expended some two and one-half billions of francs on "extraordinary expenses," about forty times what had been spent under Louis-Philippe. Easily the largest portion — nearly one and one-half billions — was spent on street construction and on the demolition necessitated by the decision to run new streets through closely packed quarters. Paris in Haussmann's time was adapted to the totally changed conditions of the nineteenth century (*fig.* **467**).

Haussmann's aims

The fundamental aims behind Haussmann's schemes — communicated by him to the city council as he began his duties — are strongly colored by the fear of street fighting.[7] The latest outbreak of such rioting had occurred in 1852, shortly before his appointment.

The first of these aims was "to disencumber the large buildings, palaces, and barracks in such a way as to make them more pleasing to the eye, afford easier access on days of celebration, and a simplified defense on days of riot."

The second fundamental principle aimed at "the amelioration of the state of health of the town through the systematic destruction of infected alleyways and centers of epidemics." The central part of Paris was littered with these dreadful alleys. Many of them (including the one in which Gérard de Nerval, the romantic poet, hanged himself) were photographed by Atget.[8] Haussmann never really succeeded in cleaning up these areas, and the middle of Paris remained in bad condition.

---

[7] This policy is summarized in E. M. Bouillat, *Georges-Eugène Haussmann* (Paris, 1901), pp. 8–9.

[8] One of the early photographers.

467. The transformation of Paris by Haussmann. *Map by Alphand.*

The third point was "to assure the public peace by the creation of large boulevards which will permit the circulation not only of air and light but also of troops. Thus by an ingenious combination the lot of the people will be improved, and they will be rendered less disposed to revolt." This point shows very clearly why the Second Empire took such pains to build wide streets.

Haussmann's fourth principle was "to facilitate circulation to and from railway stations by means of penetrating lines which will lead travelers straight to the centers of commerce and pleasure, and will prevent delay, congestion, and accidents." Here the traffic problem was the main consideration.

Haussmann's *réseaux*

Haussmann's operations were conducted in three sections — *en trois réseaux*, to use his own terms. These *réseaux* do not constitute topographical units; the "first," "second," and "third" refer to different methods of financing. Thus works forming parts of the third *réseau* might be located in the areas of the first or second and might be completed before these were.[9]

9 Haussmann, *op. cit.*, III, 55.

746

The first *réseau* was in full swing when Haussmann took office. It was financed, without any difficulties, by the state and the city of Paris jointly, under the act for the *prolongement* of the Rue de Rivoli (1849). The chief work under this act was the extension of the Rue de Rivoli from the Place de la Concorde to the Bastille. This operation, which provided for cross-town, east to west communication in Paris, was carried out in the years 1854–55.

Haussmann began with the Rue de Rivoli. Demolition and construction went on piece by piece, first as far as the Pavilion de Marsan, then to the Louvre. Forty-seven houses were pulled down, then twenty more, then a group of one hundred seventy-two (to clear the Palais-Royal and the Louvre on both sides of the Rue de Rivoli). If we also consider in this connection the entirely new market halls (*fig.* **131**) which were constructed near by, it may be said that a new district and not merely a new street was organized.[10]

Extension of the Rue de Rivoli (1853–54)

The Rue de Rivoli was next carried to the Hôtel de Ville — the starting point of all Parisian revolts. The confusion of narrow streets in front of the Hôtel de Ville was cleared away; on their site appeared the Place du Châtelet (*fig.* **469**), soon to connect with the Boulevard Sébastopol (1858).

The first *réseau* also included the transformation of the Bois de Boulogne into a place of recreation for the elegant world. In connection with this were also built the Longchamp race track and the magnificent approach to the Bois de Boulogne, the Avenue de l'Impératrice, today the Avenue Foch (*fig.* **471**). Haussmann was responsible for its great width of nearly four hundred feet, three times as wide as its architect had proposed.

Bois de Boulogne

In the second *réseau* the city was required to provide the greater part (three-quarters) of the cost. A decree of March 18, 1858, authorized the state to pay the remaining fraction, provided that the total amount did not exceed a hundred and eighty million francs, and that all the work was finished within ten years. This particular piece of legislation became known as "the decree of the hundred and eighty millions."

The second *réseau*

[10] Cf. pp. 230 ff.

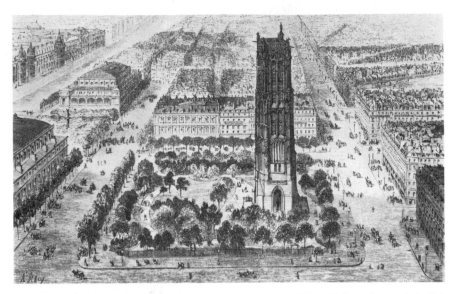

468. Square de la Tour Saint-Jacques, 1855. *One of Napoleon III's endeavors to imitate the London squares. The great difference is that it is set in the midst of traffic.*

With the second *réseau* north to south communications received further extension: Haussmann led the Boulevard Sébastopol across the Seine to the Île de la Cité and the Latin Quarter on the Left Bank. From there it was continued as the Boulevard Saint-Michel (*fig.* 470). The extension transformed the Île de la Cité into an administrative center. The adaptation of the Bois de Vincennes (1860) — the eastern counterpart of the Bois de Boulogne — to a park for the working class was financed under the same arrangements. Another of the works in this *réseau* was the *percement de l'est*. This interlacing of working-class quarters with wide, straight roads — *à plan voyant* — proceeded from 1858 onward, and was more carefully carried out here than in any other district. By it the last likelihood of really dangerous rioting was removed. As a result of this clearance, the Hôtel de Ville seems almost to float in space, but it remains isolated and unrelated to its neighbors. The Napoleon Barracks were erected next to the Hôtel to ensure its safety.

The final stage was the extension of the Rue de Rivoli decided upon in 1854. Crosswise communication in Paris was achieved by this extension. It connected those points where the political regime was most sensitive — the Hôtel de Ville

469. Place du Châtelet.

and the Louvre — and formed the first of those streets reaching interminably into the distance which were soon to determine the picture of Paris.

The route of east-west communication — the Rue de Rivoli — joined the north-south route, the Boulevard Sébastopol, which was Haussmann's prolongation of Napoleon's Boulevard de Strasbourg. All this work by which *la grande croisée* of Paris was achieved had to be carried on in a densely populated section.

Haussmann now turned to what he called the *Westend du nouveau Paris*. In spite of the strongest resistance, the Boulevard Malesherbes was cut through from the Madeleine. This work involved the demolition of several luxurious houses which had been built quite recently, in the time of Louis-Philippe. This final part of the second *réseau* was opened with great pomp and ceremony on the fourteenth of August, 1861.

Haussmann took this opportunity to complain that the moment he interfered with the "habits of the people who have been favored by fortune" he found himself assailed by a storm of complaints. He observed, rather pointedly, that the merchants, shopkeepers, and workmen had borne with great pa-

470. Boulevard Saint-Michel, 1869.

tience the "highly penalizing removals" made necessary by the work on the Boulevard Sébastopol.

The incorporation of the suburbs

The second *réseau* was affected by a development of great moment — the decree of June 16, 1859, which incorporated the surburbs into the city of Paris. The area of Paris was thereby increased by more than half. The incorporation was essential for the future, but it seriously handicapped Haussmann's immediate calculations and set him his most extensive task. Eighteen communities spread out about Paris had to be incorporated, with all their chaotic agglomerations of buildings and their neglected street systems. Great additional expense could not be avoided; the budget estimate was exceeded by a hundred and sixty million francs. Napoleon and Haussmann did not stop at simple incorporation. Although the expression did not exist at the time, Haussmann arrived at the notion of regional planning. According to his *Mémoires*, he wanted to make the entire Department of Seine-et-Oise a single unit. This would ensure control over the small outer communities and thus over the course of development of the great city.

Attempted belt of greenery; defeat of the project

A belt of greenery was to be created all around Paris, following the line of its fortifications. The project adopted by the Emperor in June 1859 used the land attached to these forti-

750

471. Avenue de l'Impératrice (Avenue Foch), 1862. *The great width (nearly four hundred feet) of the approach to the Bois de Boulogne was insisted upon by Haussmann. His architect's original version was only a third as wide.*

fications as well as a strip two hundred and fifty meters wide that lay beyond them. This latter area was subject to military restrictions and had greatly depreciated in value as a consequence. The Emperor wished to transform this land into a boulevard and to provide "vast plantations" with walks for the residents of the new faubourgs and of the contiguous communities. The belt would have completely encircled the city, connecting its two great parks in the east and west, the Bois de Boulogne and the Bois de Vincennes.

But when Napoleon left for the Italian battle front his own *Conseil d'État* found opportunity to defeat his intentions. Haussmann, the implacable enemy of all shortsighted politicians, gives this account of what happened: The president of the council, M. Baroche, "a bourgeois full of the narrow and hidebound ideas of the Parisian middle class and opposed at heart to our great works," fought and defeated the whole project.[11]

Paris never got its belt of greenery. After his return from Italy Napoleon hoped to find a chance to repair this shortsightedness, but he never did. Public parks in this area would have prevented the erection of rows of seven- and eight-story tene-

[11] Haussmann, *op. cit.*, II, 233.

ments. These enormous buildings — magnificent slums, in effect — stand in the way of replanning Paris even more than the original fortifications would have.

The third *réseau* The third *réseau* had to be supported in its entirety by the city: the deputies wanted nothing more to do with the building or the financing of Paris. Haussmann was left standing alone. In financing these works he had to manipulate the machinery

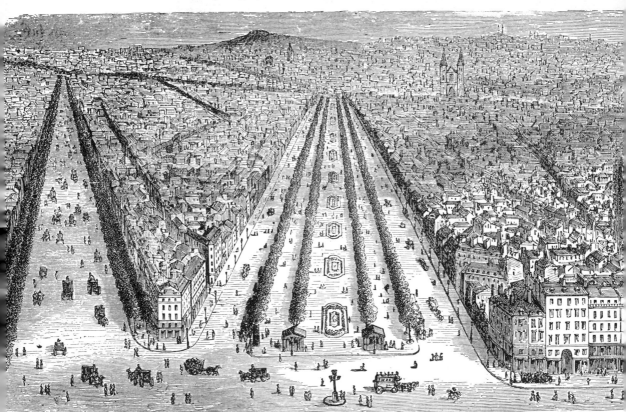

472. Boulevard Richard-Lenoir, 1861–63. *Planned by Haussmann to cover an old canal. Behind the regular and endless street fronts a tremendous disorder is crammed, as though in a closet.*

of credit singlehanded. It was these financial operations (the whole cost of the third *réseau* had not yet been raised when he left his post) which enabled the deputies to bring about his downfall.

Haussmann's operations over a seventeen-year period had called for eight hundred million francs in excess of normal expenditures. The sum had been raised without creating any new taxes or increasing the old ones. And was not Paris becoming more prosperous daily? Its population was growing at an unheard-of rate: within a bare two decades it had almost doubled. The five or six hundred million francs beyond what was actually on hand would certainly be found. The cost of the work could be paid off through annuities based on the increasing revenues of the city. Nothing was involved except time.

Two parks — Montsouris in the south and the Buttes-Chaumont in the north — were created by the third *réseau*. Both were conversions of useless and neglected areas. The Buttes-Chaumont was an abandoned quarry: it became a popular park.

The suburbs needed more and more streets. Streets leading out from Paris were extended, and new crosswise roads were made. In this manner the budget for the suburbs increased to double the amount estimated.

Haussmann pressed rapidly on with the development of Paris as though he knew there was no time to be wasted. To the west was a field for new town planning. The old toll barriers marked the western edge of the city; beyond them stretched the open country. The Champs-Élysées led up to the toll barriers. Just behind them stood the Arc de Triomphe de l'Étoile in its circular *place*. From the thirties on, the Champs-Élysées was one of the places where all Parisians with any claim to smartness were expected to make an appearance.

Creation of the Champs-Élysées district

Haussmann could work with a free hand in this district. There was open land for the twelve avenues which he led out from the Place de l'Étoile; no demolition was necessary. His enemies accused him of running these avenues out into the open country and destroying the grainfields of Passy. But once more Haussmann's foresight was justified; the Paris of 1900 was to stand on this area.

The interconnection of the various streets that pierced Paris greatly occupied Haussmann. Thus he insisted that the Rue Lafayette should reach a length of five kilometers so that it might lead travelers from the north and east railway stations to the Opéra and the Grands Boulevards in the heart of the city.

Rue Lafayette

The Avenue Napoléon, now the Avenue de l'Opéra, is his master work in town planning. Besides being a magnificent street in itself, it functions as a traffic bridge between several main thoroughfares. Through this avenue, the Rue de Rivoli and the opposite bank of the Seine achieve direct contact with the Grands Boulevards and the northern parts of the city.

None of Haussmann's schemes appeared so foolish to his contemporaries as this comparatively short street. So far as they could see, it could only serve to connect the Théâtre Français with the Opéra — and who could possibly want to attend both on the same evening? Actually, if it were not for this street, the circulation of twentieth-century traffic in Paris would be impossible (*fig.* **473**).

Haussmann built only the beginning and the end of this thoroughfare. Between the two sprawled a network of streets which was not cleared away until much later. The whole length of the Avenue de l'Opéra was only opened to traffic in 1879. This was under the Third Republic, long after Haussmann had left office.

If one were to select a specific monument to Haussmann and to that Second Empire in which he believed so thoroughly, it would be this avenue and its opera house. The grand staircase of the Opéra never served its original purpose, never furnished a background for the gliding train of the Empress Eugénie. Designed in 1861, when the Second Empire was at its zenith, the Opéra was not completed until 1875. It remains, nevertheless, the purest expression of the transitory glories of the Second Empire.

Squares, Boulevards, Gardens, and Plants

We have observed the interrelations since the seventeenth century between groups of buildings and nature, and since the eighteenth century between squares and greenery. It is true that in the transformation of Paris other questions are in the foreground, but we must not overlook the great efforts made to save the city from becoming simply a vast acreage of asphalt and masses of stone. In discussing this work it is necessary to distinguish between the layout of squares with their gardens and the old and new parks and pleasure grounds.

As a refugee in London, Louis Napoleon was much impressed by the English squares and parks. When he came to power, he desired to provide his capital with similar open green spaces — immense romantic parks and squares planted with trees and shrubs. Both were unknown in Paris. From the point of view of town planning, too, the squares of Paris differed from those of London in one important respect: the London squares were isolated from traffic, whereas those in Paris were no more than the enlargement of streets. For example, the Place des Arts-et-Métiers was a broadening of the Boulevard Sébastopol; that around the Tour Saint-Jaques (*fig.* **468**), of the Rue de Rivoli. The houses were placed in straight, continuous lines along the streets, permitting no free spaces apart from sidewalks and trafficways.[12] It was inevitable that the small parks created out of these squares, quite unlike those of London, should be set amidst the noise and dust of traffic.

No innovation in urban planning was more generally imitated in the years immediately following than this arrangement of squares filled with greenery in the midst of traffic. Especially pleasing and completely new was the fact that they were open to the general public. W. Robinson, the English landscape gardener, whose books had great influence on English landscape gardening, expressed the contemporary reaction to one bit of Haussmann's work: "The first thing that strikes the visitor in this square is its freshness, perfect keeping, and the number of people who are seated in it, reading, working, or playing." He also recognized the social significance of squares created for and open to the public: "but while we still persist in keeping the squares for a few privileged persons, and usually without the faintest trace of any but the very poorest plant ornament, they make them as open as our parks and decorate them with a variety and richness of vegetation."[13]

---

[12] The evils inherent in the "block system" of houses were recognized about two decades later by the critic of straight-line thoroughfares, Camillo Sitte, in *City Planning According to Artistic Principles*, trans. George and Christiane Collins (New York, 1965), p. 179; originally published as *Der Städtebau nach seinen künstlerischen Grundsätzen* (Vienna, 1889).

[13] W. Robinson, *The Parks, Promenades, and Gardens of Paris* (London, 1869), pp. 82, 85.

756

473. Avenue de l'Opéra, from the Opéra to the Louvre and the Rue de Rivoli. *Haussmann's masterpiece, carried through against great opposition. Few people could see how necessary it would be later on as a traffic bridge.*
←

474. Grand staircase of the Tuileries. Imperial Ball, 1860.

"Boulevard" means literally a walk on the walls of a fortified town, the word going back to the German *Bollwerk* (bulwark). The first boulevard in Paris was opened by Louis XIV in 1670 and extended from the Porte Saint-Denis to the Bastille, occupying the site of the ancient walls leveled by Vauban. These boulevards were formal footways, designed like gardens for the *promeneur* — not, like Haussmann's boulevards of the nineteenth century, intended as roads for heavy traffic.

"If not already the brightest, airiest, and most beautiful of all cities, Paris is in a fair way to become so; and the greatest part of her beauty is due to her gardens and her trees." Such was the impression on Robinson of the Paris of the new boulevards at the height of their splendor (1869), and he continued: "What would the new boulevards of white stone be without the softening and refreshing aid of those long lanes of well-cared-for trees that everywhere rise around the buildings, helping them somewhat as the grass does the buttercups? . . . In Paris, public gardening assumes an importance which it does

Boulevards

757

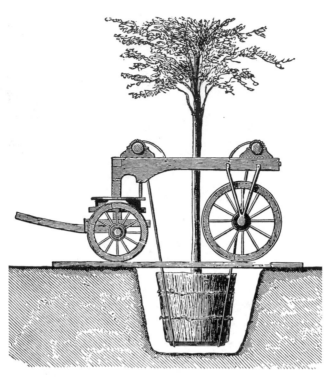

475. Tree-lifting machine for transplanting full-grown trees. *Through the use of such contrivances, thirty-year-old trees sprang up along the boulevards overnight.*

476. Place de la Concorde and Champs-Élysées. Air view, 1855.

477. Hardy subtropical plants: Wigandia. *These huge-leaved and impressive plants which Alphand introduced stood out at great distances.*

not possess with us. . . . It follows the street builders with trees, turns the little squares into gardens unsurpassed for good taste and beauty . . . presents to the eye of the poorest workman every charm of vegetation." [14]

The speed with which these boulevards were created was amazing. They seemed to come into being overnight — great thoroughfares lined with thirty-year-old trees in full leaf. Indeed, "the chief gardeners and the city architects were often called upon to extemporize shady avenues in a few days." [15] They were able to accomplish such extraordinary tasks by the use of a tree-lifting machine which they invented, a cart by which in a simple and ingenious way they were able to transplant trees as much as thirty feet high (*fig.* **475**).

[14] Robinson, *op. cit.*, pp. 1, 2.   [15] Édouard André, quoted by Robinson, *op. cit.*, p. 551.

Like the squares with their greenery, these tree-lined streets leading to the heart of the city were accepted and copied everywhere. But they represented a solution of the problem which forced town planning to take a very dangerous direction that had no future.

The parks   The great range of Haussmann's talent as an organizer is still evident today in the system of parks which he created on a large scale and in the grand manner. They derived from that

478.   Bois de Boulogne, 1853–58.

class of English landscape gardens which imitated nature, often with romantic aim, encompassing within their limits miniature mountains, valleys, lakes, and brooks. Their function was to give Paris the lungs that it lacked. They were designed for the *promeneur*, for the workman on his day off, the Sunday stroller, who was thus enabled to take the air along their broad paths like a seigneur walking in contemplation through his estate. Their wide vistas and the massing of their herbage were made to be looked at and enjoyed. And into these parks were introduced plants which had not previously appeared in public gardens.

Types of new plants   As a result, the old masters of gardening, the English, now came to Paris to learn how "a new aspect of vegetation" could also be given to English gardens. These new plants were hardy subtropical species (*fig.* 477) which Jean Alphand and his collaborators discovered and brought to Europe in the greatest variety. They were large, vigorous, and easily grown. Some of them attained a height of ten or twelve feet (*Centaurus babylonius*); others, like pampas grass (*Gynerium argentium*), were remarkable for the "rapid vigor and great size of their herbaceous vegetations," or, like a type of the common

479. Bois de Vincennes, from Plateau de Gravelles, 1857–64.

tobacco (*Nicotiana macrophylla*), were "readily raised from seeds and [grew] luxuriously in rich soil." [16] Their enormous leaves and the grandeur of their aspect could be perceived from greater distances than usual, so that they were not lost when planted in spacious lawns.[17]

The two great parks in the west and east of Paris, the Bois de Boulogne (1853–58; *fig.* 478) and the Bois de Vincennes (1857–64; *fig.* 479), look on the map of Paris like the two lungs of the city. If Haussmann's idea had been carried out properly, they

Parks for *promeneurs*

---

[16] Cf. W. Robinson, *op. cit.*, chapter on "Subtropical Plants for the Flower Garden," pp. 182 ff., and chap. XI, "Hardy Plants for the Subtropical Garden," p. 210.

[17] Herein lies the principal reason for their choice by Alphand and his gardeners, and for their general use in European gardens up to the beginning of this century. Then they seem to have been forgotten until recently, when their charm and vigorous growth again commended them.

would have been connected with one another by a wide green belt around the girdle of fortifications. Each park contains about two thousand acres. To them, besides previously existing parks which were reorganized, must be added the Parc Monceau in the center of Paris, the charming Parc Montsouris in the south, and in the north the Buttes-Chaumont for the laboring classes. In keeping with the taste of the period, they were laid out on the most extensive scale as leisure grounds for the *promeneur*. The next step in development was not reached until more than three decades later, when parks for the *promeneur* gave way to a playground system, as in the south parks of Chicago.

The City as a Technical Problem

Haussmann stands as a symbol of the nineteenth-century faith in production.

It took Borromini nearly thirty years to erect a small church, and even then it was not quite complete. Louis XIV spent a lifetime building Versailles, despite the fact that he had all the resources of France at his disposal. In seventeen years, by a mixture of determination and foresight, Haussmann created the great nineteenth-century city. The speed of the work reflects the tempo and enterprise of the industrial expansion which gave rise to it.

Subordinate role of the architect

To solve the problems connected with the city of the industrial age, Haussmann brought together the first precisely coördinated staff of technicians.[18] He could rely on very little assistance from the quarters from which one might expect it to come. There were no town planners at that date and the architects were of singularly little help. They could not even adjust themselves to the scale of his projects; on many occasions he had to send their work back and insist upon its extension. He remarked that the Second Empire was unfortunate in not producing a single artist equal to the problems of the *temps nouveaux*. Haussmann seems to have resigned himself to this. The official Bureau of Architects with its staff of

---

[18] Haussmann gave a lively account of the way this staff was built up in his *Mémoires*, vol. VII, chaps. IV, VIII, IX, XI, XIV–XVI.

academicians and celebrities was the one department which he left almost undisturbed when he took over the administration. His problems were too novel and too extensive for these men to handle; as Henri Labrouste had already noted, their training left them completely out of touch with their own period. This detachment from reality had gone so far that they could no longer even figure the costs of their own projects. "As artists . . . [they] had little concern for expenses. I might add that in general they possessed neither the knowledge required for drawing up an estimate nor the careful and detailed attention which is needed for checking a bill." [19] Estimates and bills alike had to be referred to two special commissions which Haussmann created for this purpose. Such architects could have no understanding of the new and pressingly practical problems which town planning involved. They were trained only to design single buildings, for erection on sites pointed out by someone else.

Haussmann had to look in other fields for his helpers, and in any case buildings were for him only the *décor de la vie*. From the beginning he looked on his work as a technical problem of urban services and carried his real difficulties to the engineers, his closest collaborators. Most of these men were relatively unknown when he engaged them, but he was very astute in his choice, and his assistants grew up with him and with the work. Haussmann had been prefect of the Yonne and later of Bordeaux; he knew the able men in these southern districts and looked for his helpers there. Belgrand, for many years a subordinate engineer in a small provincial town, constructed in a faultless manner the enormous sewer system of Paris and the aqueducts which, for the first time in its history, provided Paris with an adequate water supply, drawn from the reservoirs of the Yonne and the Dhuis. Belgrand was of the inventor type; "a man of genius," he was always "modifying his original ideas in some respect or other." As engineer-in-chief and inspector-general of the bridges and highways department "he took upon himself all the work connected with the projects which he had most at heart, even though he had his choice of the most competent collaborators." This trait, Haussmann

Haussmann's staff of "unknowns"

---

[19] Haussmann, *op. cit.*, III, 511.

remarked, was "no doubt due to his long service in the inferior grades." [20]

An engineer creates the Paris park system

To replace Napoleon's *jardinier-paysagiste* (whom he had dismissed after the fiasco in the Bois de Boulogne) Haussmann found a *jardinier-ingénieur* — Jean Alphand. Haussmann had known him in Bordeaux, where he had been an engineer in the bridge and highway service, and recognized him as a technician who possessed "le sentiment de l'art." Made head of the Service des Promenades et Plantations, Alphand transformed the old leisure grounds in Paris and laid out new ones: the Bois de Boulogne, the Bois de Vincennes, the Champs-Élysées, the Parc Monceau, the Buttes-Chaumont, and the Parc Montsouris. These kidney-shaped systems of walks in Paris reflect his workmanship.

Haussmann provided Alphand with — as he put it — "a right and left hand" for his work: Davioud and Barillet-Deschamps. Davioud, a young architect (later, in 1878, the builder of the Trocadéro), had one of the rare clear heads in his profession, owing in part, perhaps, to his long training under Alphand. Barillet-Deschamps, an excellent horticulturist, remained comparatively obscure (in marked contrast to Alphand, who later became head of the service, and was made *commissaire général* of the 1889 exhibition).[21]

A surveyor takes charge of the *Plan de Paris*

Haussmann had found an engineer and a landscape gardener; he still needed a man to plot the lines of the streets which he proposed to cut through the body of Paris. This time he found his collaborator among the specialists employed by the city: Deschamps, its chief surveyor. Haussmann thought enough of his work to say afterwards that "le Plan de Paris, c'était M. Deschamps." When the suburban zone was annexed in 1859, Haussmann created a new municipal service, the Direction du Plan de Paris, and made Deschamps its chief. Deschamps and his assistants in this service constituted the general staff for the planning as a whole and were largely responsible for its outcome.

[20] Haussman, *op. cit.*, III, 118–119.
[21] It was Barillet who selected the plants that decorate the various public gardens in Paris.

764

These three departments — the Service des Eaux et des Égouts, the Service des Promenades et Plantations, and the one just named — were Haussmann's chief instruments for his work. This would not have been possible elsewhere, since only France had an institution, the École Polytechnique, that was systematically training engineers with an unexcelled theoretical background. The first transformation of a great city to adjust it to the changes brought by industry was carried through by engineers.

Haussmann's Use of Modern Methods of Finance

The technical aspects of town planning had never before been so systematically and precisely organized. It was also necessary for Haussmann to attempt a similar control over the complex machinery of credit and finance. Parliament (both the parties of the Left and the Right) opposed his program and so did the landowners (whose privileges the regime was pledged to support). In these circumstances it took a real mastery of the complications of finance, as well as extraordinary adeptness on Haussmann's part, to push the scheme through. Because of rises in values owing to work he had already accomplished, Haussmann had repeatedly to find new sources of credit.

In the course of these manipulations Haussmann endeavored to persuade the legislative bodies concerned that the budget of a nation must find a place for "extraordinary expenditures" which — when managed with intelligence — can have the remarkable effect of enriching rather than impoverishing the country. This was his *théorie des dépenses productives* — theory of productive expenditure. His point was that some expenditures which are not strictly necessary can be justified because they lead to "a general increase in revenue," and he went on to observe that "these 'productive expenditures' which ordinarily meet with economic censure" can really be incurred with little risk, "since they are optional, and are less trouble to cut down again than the others" [22]

"Productive expenditure"

---

[22] Haussmann, *op. cit.*, II, 265.

Haussmann ruled Paris from its city hall, the Hôtel de Ville. His city council was appointed by Napoleon and was not, as Haussmann put it, subject to "the accident of the vote." After a decree granting him one hundred and eighty million francs in 1858, he established a fund for public works in Paris — *la caisse des travaux de Paris* — which was under his own control. This *caisse* was the financial instrument that made his huge operations possible. But the Cour des Comptes still rendered final judgment on all revenue and expenditure. The members of this board had been appointed under Louis-Philippe. In 1868 they reported adversely on a loan made directly to Haussmann by the Crédit Mobilier. Half a year later (March 1869), this report made Haussmann's expenditures in excess of budgeted amounts [23] the subject of debate in the Chamber of Deputies.

Haussmann frankly admitted that the *caisse des travaux* had been made to carry an entirely unauthorized debt of a hundred and fifty-nine million francs, but promised that such high-handed practices would be abandoned. In spite of the violent opposition of Adolphe Thiers, the Chamber passed the laws needed to regularize this affair, and the Senate confirmed them by a vote of 110 to 1.[24] But the *caisse des travaux* was liquidated. This meant the curtailment of Haussmann's liberty of action and the beginning of his downfall. He did not resign, since he hoped to find other ways of continuing his work. However, political developments were against him. The new elections were a triumph for the Republicans, and the Emperor, trying to maintain his regime, took as his prime minister Émile Ollivier, a man who proposed to "concilier l'empire et le libéralisme."

Haussmann, the dictator of the Hôtel de Ville, saw quite clearly the mendacity of *l'Empire libéral:* "L'Empire Parlementaire, ah! oui. C'est celui-là que je repoussais de toutes mes convictions, auquel j'entendais ne participer en rien, tant

---

[23] The budget for the first *réseau* was exceeded by seventy million francs, the second by two hundred and thirty million francs, and the third by a hundred and eighty million francs. Haussmann's virtues as a town planner — the ability to carry projects through in the shortest possible time and to build them up to the proper grand dimensions — had financial consequences.

[24] There is an excellent account of the episode in Morizet, *op. cit.*, p. 298.

je sentais qu'il allait nous mener fatalement aux abîmes!" [25]
Napoleon III permitted Haussmann's power to decline, and in
January 1870 he resigned his place in the Hôtel de Ville. The
same year saw the end of the Second Empire.

The bourgeoisie overthrew Haussmann, in spite of the fact
that he had protected that class better than any of his predecessors. Even the Commission for Expropriation which fixed
the compensation for houses that had to be demolished was
made up of house-owners. One of Maxime du Camp's anec-
dotes sums up the situation: when he asked a certain *nouveau
riche* how he had arrived at his present prosperous state, the
man replied simply, "I was expropriated."

The bourgeoisie, however, could not forgive Haussmann for
disturbing their peace. What he achieved was accomplished
against the will of the majority.

The Basic Unit of the Street

To obtain an insight into Haussmann's Paris let us take a
typical apartment house, and see how it was occupied.

Boulevard Sébastopol, 1860: an apartment house (*figs.* **480, 481**)
of normal type with shops on the ground floor, a mezzanine
floor, three main floors, and two attic floors. The three main
floors have the same plan. They are apartments intended for
upper middle-class tenants. The three-windowed bedroom for
Monsieur and Madame takes up the space at the corner. To
its left is the living room, to the right the dining room. Further
along to the right are the other bedrooms. There is a nursery
which receives almost no light. The kitchen and the servant's
room look onto a narrow light-well.

An apartment house and its sociological background

These narrow light-wells are an evil characteristic of Continental dwelling houses of this period, and for years afterward.

The attic floors are the most densely overcrowded parts of the
building. Here bed is placed next to bed, in the most confined

---

[25] Haussmann, *op. cit.*, II, 537. "Ah yes! The parliamentary empire! That is just
what I have rejected with all my convictions and determined to have no part in; I was
convinced that it would infallibly lead us into disaster."

480. Apartments on the Boulevard Sébastopol, Paris, 1860. *Façade and section. Typical apartment house of the period (shops on ground floor, middle-class apartments above them, servants' quarters in attic). The basic unit of Haussmann's street. It exhibits an intermingling of functions which had been possible earlier but would not work in an industrial age.*

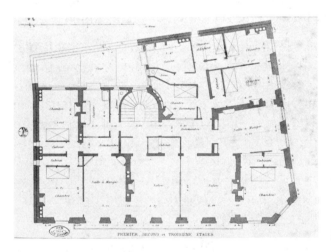

481. Apartment house on the Boulevard Sébastopol, 1860. *Plan of second, third, and fourth floors.*

space possible, for the accommodation of servants, night lodgers, and the lower classes generally.

The uniform façade of this apartment house of 1860 covers a unit in which the most diversified functions of daily living swirl together. Business takes over the ground floor, and often encroaches on the mezzanine, in workrooms connected with the various establishments. The three main floors are given over to apartments for the well-to-do. The attic floors are congested slums.

In earlier times the association of production with dwelling quarters was quite natural, but this connection could not be carried over into large towns. Such apartment houses artificially bring together functions which, in an industrial society, should be kept strictly separate. It is absurd in an age of industrial production to permit residence, labor, and traffic to intermingle. It is not merely the endless streets that are inhuman but also the units that go up beside them.

Haussmann is not alone to blame for this mixture. The same phenomenon appears in all countries. Behind it lies a failure that is peculiar to the nineteenth century, a marked inability to control the available resources.

It is true that there are fine houses which offer excellent rooms and the best of locations to the more prosperous. But just as poison gas does not stop outside the window, so a general sense of disorder cannot be avoided in these luxurious dwellings. They stand in the midst of airless routes of heavy traffic, cut off from natural surroundings and exposed to every noise and disturbance.

If in an industrial age the various functions of daily life cannot be clearly separated, that fact alone spells the death sentence of the great city.

Haussmann showed his sagacity in refusing to allow any tricks to be played with façades. Simply and without discussion, he spread a uniform façade over the whole of Paris. It featured high French windows, with accents provided by lines of cast-iron balconies like those used in the Rue de Rivoli under Napoleon I. In the unobtrusive Renaissance shapes of a pleasantly neutral nature that he employed, one can still feel a last touch of the unity that had marked baroque architecture. Their neutral façades and general uniformity make Haussmann's enormous projects of rebuilding better than any others executed in or after the fifties of the nineteenth century.

The Scale of the Street

Haussmann's reorganization of Paris demonstrates the French fondness for the *culte de l'axe*. Wherever possible, he tried to introduce "grand prospects," usually without success.[26] The great length of the streets causes a building put at the head of a boulevard to be soon lost in the blue distance. Thus the Gare de l'Est, where the Boulevard Sébastopol originates, sinks from its dominating position long before one reaches the end of this thoroughfare. The streets themselves, not squares or single buildings, dominate the scene. These Parisian streets were sometimes as much as three miles long. This was a new phenomenon in the history of architecture. (Several decades later, in Los Angeles, city streets were to extend for more than thirty miles.)

The boulevard developed out of the baroque avenue. The baroque idea was to have long avenues of trees unrelated to houses. In the nineteenth century this idea was taken up and transmuted. It reappeared in the form of endless tree-lined streets bordered by uniform apartment houses.

Miscellaneous building activity

We are tempted to forget that during these seventeen years Paris was also sprinkled with buildings of the most various types: great exhibition halls, churches, schools, markets, the Bibliothèque Nationale, and so on.[27] Although these include many buildings which cannot be overlooked in the history of nineteenth-century architecture, they tend to be overlooked because the new picture was dominated by the street.

Two units of scale for the street: the *promeneur* vs. the vehicle

To most of his contemporaries Haussmann seemed a dangerous *démolisseur*, a man who was mortgaging the future of the city and a financier who was inclined to play fast and loose with the law. All his projects were repugnant to "common sense" — with the exception of the work on the Rue de Rivoli, which had been under consideration from the time of Napoleon I. If he had confined himself to enlarging streets already in existence, there would have been no objections. But when he cut new ones he disturbed the settled scheme of

---

[26] Haussmann, *op. cit.*

[27] Haussmann cited an impressive list of buildings put up during his transformation of Paris. See *Mémoires*, II, 524–528.

things and showed a lack of respect for the rights of property. With these new developments "on tombe dans ce que j'appelle la fantaisie, on est dans l'imaginaire et on marche vers la ruine financière." [28] So stated Haussmann's bitterest opponent, the historian Adolphe Thiers, whose political career began under Louis-Philippe and — unlike Haussmann's — continued after 1870 under the Third Republic.

Regarding the organization of the city mainly as a technical problem, Haussmann concentrated primarily on the problems of traffic and transportation — this before the railway age and long before automobiles had added to the burdens of city streets. His contemporaries, lacking his vision, could not understand Haussmann's passion for new lines of communication through the center of the city, and even into the suburbs, where no such counterrevolutionary measures were needed. "Pour les promeneurs," Thiers inquired, "quelle nécessité avait-il d'aller de la Madeleine à l'Étoile par la voie la plus courte? Mais les promeneurs, au contraire, veulent allonger leur promenade et c'est pour cela qu'ils font trois ou quatre fois le tour d'une même allée." [29]

This remark reveals unconsciously the grounds for Thiers's criticisms. The town planning he understood worked from the point of view of the *promeneur;* Haussmann's started from the demands of an industrial age. The first result of approaching the planning of a city as a large-scale transportation problem is the endless street, the street that stretches beyond the range of the eye.

Haussmann's preoccupation with traffic tended to force the residential problem into the background. His boulevards dismembered the city. That housing was definitely a secondary consideration is depicted in the etchings which illustrate Alphand's large publication, *Les Promenades de Paris* (Paris, 1867–73). The Boulevard Richard-Lenoir (*fig.* **472**), for ex-

Traffic receives primary consideration

---

[28] "We fall into what I call fantasy, we are in the realm of the imaginary and on the march toward financial ruin." Quoted in Morizet, *op. cit.,* p. 297.

[29] "Do people out walking need to go from the Madeleine to the Étoile by the *shortest* route? On the contrary; *promeneurs* want to prolong their walks. That's the reason they will take three or four turns up and down the same street." Quoted in Morizet, *op. cit.,* p. 297.

ample, shows a wide highway, its center strip covered with lawns and planted with trees; but behind the uniform façades of its apartment houses is concealed the most appalling disorder.[30] The street dominated Alphand's bird's-eye view of the city; all houses which do not front on it were obviously allowed to spring up in a huddled confusion. Haussmann used the uniform façade as a kind of closet door behind which all the disorder could be crammed. All other aspects of the life of the city were sacrificed to the problem of traffic.

One can now recognize easily enough the mistake involved in considering only the problem of transportation and ignoring the residential problems. But at the stage of social and industrial development that existed in Haussmann's day not even the beginnings of a solution to housing problems in great cities had been found.

Difficulties in the aesthetic evaluation of Haussmann's work

Haussmann's later critics have concerned themselves mainly with an aesthetic evaluation of his work. This is obviously a difficult undertaking, and it is not made any easier by comparing his "merely straight and convenient" [31] thoroughfares with "rhythmically articulated aesthetic compositions" by Renaissance masters. Haussmann himself was devoted to the *culte de l'axe*, but the enormous scale of his work made certain things impossible. The street cannot have "organic unity . . . as part of a dominant building" when it is required to serve as an artery for huge volumes of cross-town traffic. To criticize Haussmann for breaking with Mansard and Le Nôtre is to ignore his transformation of Paris.

It is true that "the wall of houses around the Place de l'Étoile is so broken that one hardly feels it as circular," [32] and that, indeed, it "has no right to be called a 'place' in the sense of the word established by the French architects of the seventeenth and eighteenth centuries." But this is no more than a dispute about definitions. And in any event this is not a failure peculiar to or even characteristic of Haussmann's planning.

[30] Haussmann planned the Boulevard Richard-Lenoir (1861–63) to cover a canal. The avenue of trees is planted above the "roof" of the canal.

[31] This and the following quotations are taken from Elbert Peets, "Famous Town Planners: Haussmann," *Town Planning Review*, XII, no. 3 (June 1927), 187–188.

[32] Haussmann himself saw this defect in the work of his architect and planted tall trees before the small houses, which were completely out of scale.

Badly organized squares, reflecting a general loss of the baroque ability to model space, were common in the nineteenth century.[33]   London was the exception.

Haussmann's work was done at a time when architecture was in a very unsettled state.   The best he could hope for — and at the time it was a considerable achievement — was to give his street fronts the most neutral character possible.   No one in his day, or later in the century, managed to equal the sure and inoffensive neutrality of his uniform Paris façades.   Finally, any aesthetic judgment of Haussmann's work is bound to place undue emphasis upon the transitory facts that appear in it.   Granted that everything has "a silk-hat slickness" and reflects the artistic standards of "the bank-president and the midinette," but this does not touch the main issue.   Haussmann was in fact the first man to view the great city — the capital with millions of inhabitants — as a technical problem.   Hence his distant relations with architects and his close collaboration with expert technicians.

Haussmann's Foresight: His Influence

Haussmann made extraordinary strides toward the solution of urban traffic problems, strides far in advance of the actual needs of his time.   Almost a generation after Haussmann's death at the age of eighty-two, the influx of automobiles made this problem still much more urgent and complex.

Haussmann's work anticipates the future in another respect; every great town planner has been driven — at whatever cost to himself — to attempt undertakings that only the future could justify.   The Prefét de la Seine was no exception, and he ran into disaster through schemes whose intentions went beyond the current desires of the populace.   Haussmann's work on the incorporation of the *banlieue*, the suburban zone of Paris, was just such a *coup de génie*.

Anticipates development of the suburbs

This enterprise, begun, as we have noted, under the Second Empire, was still incomplete when Haussmann left the Hôtel de Ville.   His intention was to give the great mass of the people a chance to live outside the city.   It was, however, an

---

[33] This point is discussed with reference to some German squares in the author's *Spätbarocker und romantischer Klassizismus* (Munich, 1922).

undertaking whose extent could not be estimated in advance.[34] Haussmann's "illegal borrowings" from the *caisse des travaux* were being used to finance work in the suburbs whose scope constantly widened. His critics, who acknowledged only the scale of the *promeneur*, could not have been expected to understand Haussmann's plans, intended as they were for generations yet unborn. They could not have foreseen that these roads, carried clear over the horizon, would prove to be the most "productive" of all the prefect's "expenditures," and would open up the future living space of Paris.

It was useless for Haussmann to point out that in the years during which this network of suburban streets was being developed the population of the zone rose from 258,000 to 368,000. Since Haussmann's time, the population of Paris has increased seventy per cent, the population of the suburbs eight hundred per cent.[35] This trend of growth in the area surrounding Paris has justified his schemes to an extent even he could not have foreseen. The same phenomenon has occurred around most other large cities.

The later expansion of Paris

The subsequent peripheral expansion of Paris proceeded without a hint of order. No one had the power either to carry Haussmann's plans further or to adjust them to the growing need for a careful separation of residential and industrial areas. The inability of the declining century to master and give form to its life gave rise to a chaotic mixture of villages suddenly inflated into cities and tiny houses and new industrial centers scattered at random over the countryside.[36]

---

[34] The final cost was over three hundred and sixty million francs — a hundred and sixty million more than had been allotted for this purpose.

[35] *The Columbia Encyclopedia*, 1964.

[36] See *Les Banlieues urbaines* (Paris, 1920) by Henri Sellier, Conseiller général de la Seine. Sellier gives a true picture of how immense agglomerations of high tenement houses were built along unpaved village roads, often without sewers, in the midst of old peasant houses, and soon became thickly populated slums, entirely lacking in sanitary facilities.

The result, as Professor Duguet revealed in his reports to the Commission of Hygiene, was a shocking death rate from tuberculosis in the Department of the Seine. For every hundred people dying of tuberculosis in the rest of France, a hundred and fifty died in the Department of the Seine. (See *Revue des deux mondes*, July 15, 1923, p. 444.)

The chaotic growth of American cities since the sixties has often been attributed to a lack of tradition. Yet in the *banlieue* of Paris, a city with a history of twenty centuries, a similar disorganization occurred. The reasons in both cases were the same.

The wide scope of Haussmann's activities was not owing solely to the autocratic powers given him by the regime of which he was so firm an adherent. He belonged to a generation — that *génération forte*, as he himself called it — which showed extreme initiative in all fields, and an irrepressible urge to do things which had never been accomplished before.

Haussmann's enemies referred to him derisively as the *Louis quatorze municipal*. There was more truth in this than his contemporaries recognized. To be sure, his work lacked the unity of conception which underlay the great projects of Louis XIV. They show the split personality of the nineteenth century with its almost inextricable mingling of constituent and transitory facts. On the one hand there is foresight and energy; on the other, dangerous expedients which reflect the uncertainty of Haussmann's period.

But the huge scale of Haussmann's work is genuinely overwhelming. He dared to change the entire aspect of a great city, a city which had been revered for hundreds of years as the center of the civilized world. To build a new Paris — attacking all aspects of the problem simultaneously — was an operation still unequaled in scale. The indomitable courage of the Préfet de la Seine has also remained unequaled. Haussmann allowed no group to block his schemes: in his transformation of Paris he cut directly into the body of the city.

Haussmann's direct influence was immense. In almost every other country where industrialization developed later, one encounters details imitated from his transformation of Paris, particularly from the accomplishments of the first *réseau*. Few such cities are without a main street directed toward the axis of the central station, like the Boulevard Sébastopol and the Gare de l'Est. The Parisian boulevards echo in monumental streets built up along the lines of razed fortifications. But it was only details which were imitated. No one arose with Haussmann's power to attempt a general attack upon the new problem of the city.

Haussmann's influence

PART **VIII** **CITY PLANNING AS A HUMAN PROBLEM**

The Late Nineteenth Century

From 1870 on, the great cities developed continuously toward what they are today — unserviceable instruments. No one knows when this tremendous waste of time and health will be stopped, when this pointless assault on human nerves will end, when this failure to achieve a dignified standard of life will be remedied.

Cities cannot simply be discarded, like worn-out machinery; they play too large a part in our destiny. But by now it is plain that the life which they have abused is increasingly exacting its revenge, and that this fundamentally provisional and feverish institution must soon be brought within narrower limits. Whether the work will be done by intelligence or by brute disaster cannot be foreseen.

Unsuccessful attempts at change and reform have been going on for a long time. As early as 1883 the Society of Arts — the body which organized the Great Exhibition in London in 1851 — offered twelve hundred pounds in prize awards for essays on the best ways of rebuilding central London and housing its poor.

Camillo Sitte's return to the city of the Middle Ages (1889)

On the Continent there was an early reaction against the degenerate and omnipresent imitations of Haussmann's work. In 1889 the Viennese town planner Camillo Sitte (1843–1903) — like the handicrafters of four decades earlier — suggested that the remedy was to be found in a return to methods of the medieval period.[1] Sitte saw in the organic growth of the medieval town a way of humanizing the contemporary city. He made sensitive analyses of these towns — northern and southern, Roman, Gothic, Renaissance, and baroque. He was interested in the successful organization of open spaces expressed in their layout. He found this in the way streets flow into squares in a medieval town, in the relations between the market square and the church or town hall, and in the free and well-pondered equilibrium of all parts of these urban organisms.

[1] See the English edition of Camillo Sitte's *Der Städtebau* (Vienna, 1889), *City Planning According to Artistic Principles*, trans. George and Christiane Collins (New York, 1965).

778

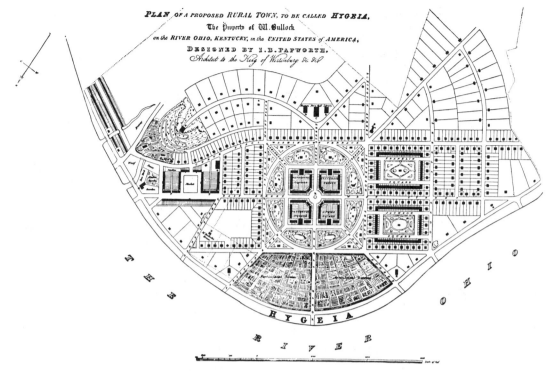

482. J. B. PAPWORTH. Scheme for "Rural Town" on the banks of the Ohio River, "Hygeia," 1827.

Camillo Sitte felt, as everyone must, that the laws of town building are summed up in Aristotle's laconic statement: Towns should be built so as to protect their inhabitants and at the same time make them happy.

Most of us nowadays share Sitte's further conviction that the artistic problems raised by urban development are fully as important as the technical ones.

Camillo Sitte's intentions were of the best. He sought to overcome the monotony and the artistic lifelessness of the typical late nineteenth-century city. Its defects he saw very clearly, but the measures he suggested to correct them were no more than palliatives. Clearing the centers of squares and placing all statues and monuments at the corners, locating gardens in the courtyards of apartment blocks instead of in busy public places, building high walls to isolate public parks from street noises — all these were superficial reforms.

779

Such proposals show the extent to which the town planner had lost contact with his period. He had become a kind of troubadour, ineffectually pitting his medieval songs against the din of modern industry.

In the late nineteenth century the urbanist, like the popular painter, lost himself in the composition of idylls. Neither was able to work on the scale that was necessary. Life moved on along a different track.

What attitude did really creative artists around 1900 — men like Wagner, Garnier, and Berlage — take toward the problems of urbanism? The answers may give us some insight into how much mastery over town planning was possible at this period.

Otto Wagner's faith in the big city

Otto Wagner (1841–1918) belonged to a generation which had retained the hopeful attitude of the nineteenth century toward industry. He could never have imagined that the time would come when the great city — then at the full tide of its growth — would find its prosperity seriously threatened.

Wagner began formulating his ideas when Sitte's influence was at its peak. The garden city had just been advanced as the solution to the urban residential problem. From the very beginning Wagner recognized that the garden city could not solve the housing problem of the major cities. Much later, popular opinion was forced to acknowledge that Wagner was right.

The architectonic vision and energy apparent in so much of Wagner's work seemed overcome by a sort of paralysis when he entered the field of town planning. In an endeavor to avoid the usual haphazard and chaotic urban development, Wagner drew up detailed plans for a whole quarter in Vienna (*fig.* **483**).[2] His scheme provided for a sizable open area in the middle — "a center for air" — but the layout as a whole was rigidly formal and a great deal more static than Haussmann's arrangements in Paris. The dominant unit of his design was the enclosed, five-story apartment block, the basic element in

---

[2] Cf. Otto Wagner, *Die Groszstadt, eine Studie über diese* (Vienna, n.d.). These studies date back to the nineties.

483. OTTO WAGNER. Scheme for a district center in Vienna, c. 1910.

almost every large Continental city of the time. Wagner
could not seem to devise any alternative to this kind of planning. In the late nineteenth century it appeared that town
planning had exhausted all its possibilities and that no new
solutions could be reached. The ability to organize space in
accordance with actual problems had been lost.

But there did arise in this period the realization that the needs
of its inhabitants ought to govern the planning of the modern
city. Otto Wagner was among the first to see this clearly. His
chief interest was the creation of a healthful environment for
the average man. He was one of the earliest to recognize that a
great city embraces many different types of people, each type
requiring a different kind of dwelling. He realized too that
the residential needs of the average city-dweller changed with
his circumstances.

Wagner called for community ownership of those areas which
would be required for the future growth of the city. Only by
that means could the city regulate land prices and maintain
control over its own development. (Amsterdam had already
adopted this system.)

Wagner perceived very clearly what was responsible for the diseased state of the big city: "The expansion of cities can no longer — as in the past — be abandoned to blind chance, with artistic influences regarded as superficial and the development of great towns left to detestable usury."

More than thirty years later, at its congress in Athens in 1933,[3] the CIAM laid down the same requirements (in less violent language):

"It is of the utmost urgency that each town establish an urban program, and that it create the laws necessary for its realization."

Ebenezer Howard and the Garden City

The idea of the garden city was advanced as a panacea for the many dwelling problems of the late nineteenth century. The essence of the plan was that the community should control the ground, and that all profits through increases in the value of the land should be returned to the community in order to discourage speculation of any sort.

The idea of the garden city as it was formulated by Ebenezer Howard is quite different from the forms the idea took in actual practice. Howard's book, *Tomorrow, a Peaceful Path to Real Reform*, first appeared in 1898. As the title indicates, it was no mean achievement at which Howard aimed. He aspired to nothing less than the abolition of the evils of the industrial revolution, the elimination of slums and overcrowded industrial districts. All this was to be accomplished without arousing the antagonism of any group, even the landlords. He expected to create new forms of public wealth through a complete transvaluation of values, without even waiting till some party sympathetic to his views was in power.[4]

One is reminded of Frank Lloyd Wright's "Broadacre City" when one reads in Ebenezer Howard of the migration of an industrial population into the country, the colonization of the

---

[3] See pp. 698–700.

[4] Dugald Macfayden, *Sir Ebenezer Howard and the Town Planning Movement* (Manchester, 1933), p. 29.

land, and the setting down of factories in an unspoiled landscape.

Ebenezer Howard was an expert stenographer working in the London courts when the idea of the garden city came to him. That was in 1898, and he had just finished reading Bellamy's *Looking Backward*, published not long before in America, which a friend had lent him. He responded to the book with such enthusiasm that he immediately set to work to promote its publication in England. This book presented a graphic picture of the whole American nation organized on coöperative principles, and in reflecting on it Howard "was led to put forward proposals of his own for testing out Bellamy's principles, though on a very much smaller scale — in brief, to build by private enterprise an entirely new town, industrial, residential, and agricultural." [5]

Origin

This was how the garden-city idea got its start. It grew out of the same soil as the general problem of a coöperatively organized society.

Howard conceived of his city as a set of concentric circles. The center consists of a group of civic buildings grouped about a common. Midway between the center and the outermost circle is a circular grand avenue, four hundred feet in width, with trees and greenery. The outermost circle is an agricultural belt. An area set aside for manufacturing is anticipated. In a circular park at the center stand the larger public buildings, each in its own ample grounds: town hall, concert and lecture hall, theater, library, and so on. The "Crystal Palace" encircles the central park and recreation ground. It consists of a glass arcade, opening on the park; within it manufactured goods may be exposed for sale. One part of it is used as a winter garden, a place of resort in bad weather.[6] The fundamental idea of this scheme — which, as Howard noted, is a diagram only, the plan necessarily depending on the site selected — had been developed in the Renaissance. It has since been repeated under many different forms, and other proposals made in the early nineteenth century do not differ markedly from Howard's conceptions.

Howard's scheme

[5] Macfayden, p. 20.

[6] Ebenezer Howard, *Garden Cities of Tomorrow* (London, 1899), p. 23.

As early as 1827 proposals were made by the English architect J. B. Papworth for what he called "rural-towns." [7] Hygeia (*fig.* **482**), a settlement that was never brought into being, was to be on the Ohio River in Kentucky. He conceived of it as having community buildings in the center, with broad areas given over to gardening and with zoning regulations. The whole conception was very close to the late baroque urban tradition of John Nash.

It is often said that Howard treated his idyllic garden city as an isolated phenomenon unrelated to reality. He knew quite well, however, that overcrowded cities had "done their work" and that the great cities of the future would have to be constructed on another pattern.

He remarked at the end of his *Tomorrow* that "a simpler problem must first be solved. One small Garden City must be built as a working model and then a group of cities. . . . These tasks done, and done well, the reconstruction of London must inevitably follow. . . ."

Failure of the garden-city idea

But execution and idea were, as is so often the case, quite different. No "Crystal Palace" in a garden city ever appeared.[8] For half a century, the most that resulted was the creation of new suburban settlements by coöperative societies and the introduction of better architectural schemes.[9] For the most part the idea degenerated into the building of conglomerations of small houses in small gardens until it was partially revived in the British New Towns movement of the late forties and fifties.

It is easy to see why the original idea of the garden city, "where town and country are married," was doomed to failure. No partial solution is possible; only preconceived and inte-

---

[7] Much of Cheltenham remains as a memorial to his powers as a town planner. Cf. R. P. Ross Williamson, "John Buonarroti Papworth, Architect to the King of Wurtemburg," *Architectural Review*, vol. LXXIX, 1936. Cf. also R. G. Thwaites, *Early Western Travels, 1748–1846* (Cleveland, 1904–07), vol. XIX, map preceding Bullock's "Sketch of a Journey through the Western States of North America."

[8] The first model, Letchworth, in 1903, failed to attract much over half of its intended population.

[9] For example, the scheme of Peter Behrens in 1918; Vreewyke's garden city at Rotterdam; Radburn, N. J. in 1929, with segregation of automobile traffic; and Neubühl near Zurich in 1932.

grated planning on a scale embracing the whole structure of modern life in all its ramifications can accomplish the task which Ebenezer Howard had in mind.

Patrick Geddes and Arturo Soria y Mata

If one turns over the pages of the standard handbooks on city planning of 1900 to 1920, one is astonished to see that nineteenth-century drawing-board methods are still followed unchanged and even repeated like recipes. One finds routine studies of how to determine the dimensions of long and cross sections of traffic streets and "avenues," or how open spaces can be inserted into a sea of masonry. Officialdom seemed to be blind to the total disorder of the situation.

In a period of transition city-planning specialists appeared helpless. They could function when directives were provided, but they were incapable of inventing new directives. Only the unblinkered eyes of a few outsiders brought the disorder of city planning to public consciousness and laid the foundations for a new orientation. Four are listed here.

Ebenezer Howard, who cleared the way for the humanization of the environment through his advocation of the garden city, was a parliamentary stenographer. Sant' Elia, whose futuristic city-planning studies made him a complete visionary in the eyes of the professionals, was nevertheless the first to present traffic as a constituent element of the urban structure.

In addition, both a biologist and a highway engineer prepared decisive directives for the new orientation of city planning. With almost prophetic vision they were prepared to wait for a far distant time when their ideas would finally become reality. They were the Scottish biologist and student of Huxley, Patrick Geddes (1854–1932), and the Spanish highway engineer, Arturo Soria y Mata (1844–1920).

Patrick Geddes looked at human agglomerations with the eyes of a biologist interested in the phenomena of life — all life. The new edition of his best known book, *Cities in Evolution*,[10]

Patrick Geddes: unity of city and region

---

[10] First published in 1915; revised edition, edited by Jaqueline Tyrwhitt, published in London, 1949.

includes an extract from Geddes' famous "Cities Exhibition," in which he displayed pictorially the organic development of cities and elaborated his main theme: the city is inseparable from the landscape in which it is set and can only be understood in terms of its geographic situation, its climatic and meteorological facts, its economic bases, and its historic heritage. One sentence from the introduction to this exhibition can best explain how Geddes read a city plan: "Town plans are thus no mere diagrams; they are a system of hieroglyphics in which man has written the history of civilization, and the more tangled their apparent confusion, the more we may be rewarded in deciphering it." [11]

Lewis Mumford, who modestly describes himself as a "true disciple" of Patrick Geddes, but who naturally developed his ideas further, has included in his book, *The Condition of Man*, several of Patrick Geddes' finest thoughts. One finds there how Geddes considered sociology as evolving from biology and used this idea to show the development of the city.[12] Geddes, a Scot who lived in the "Outlook Tower" in Edinburgh and spent many years in India developing a rich and subtle practice of city planning, was simultaneously provincial and cosmopolitan, a type only really recognized a generation after his death. When one reads Mumford's words, "Geddes' Scotland encompassed Europe and his Europe encompassed the World," it is difficult not to think of a passage in James Joyce's *Portrait of the Artist as a Young Man* in which Joyce — Stephen Daedalus — identifies his own position: moving out from the strictly localized situation of the individual to cover Ireland, Europe, the world, the universe.

Soria y Mata: the linear city

The highway engineer, Arturo Soria y Mata, started out from a totally different point of view. He was a practical man. In 1882, a time when the electrified street railway exercised an almost hypnotic charm, he recognized transportation as an element of the highest importance for city planning. His starting point was the street railway track. On both sides of this track he set housing and industry.

---

[11] Patrick Geddes, *Cities in Evolution*, rev. ed. (London, 1949), p. 170.

[12] Lewis Mumford, *The Condition of Man* (New York, 1944), pp. 382–390.

786

Soria y Mata saw the realization of his dreams, on a modest scale, in a suburb of Madrid. It was not until the thirties that his linear-city idea was taken further, in Russia. Le Corbusier adopted the linear-city notion in his plan for St. Dié's development alongside an expressway. However, the trend of the linear city came into real prominence only in the sixties, with the development of a continuous urbanized area — such as from Boston to Washington: a development that is not without its dangers.

Tony Garnier's Cité Industrielle, 1901–04

In 1898 a young man named Tony Garnier was installed in the Villa Medici as the current holder of the *grand prix de Rome*. At about the same time Frank Lloyd Wright was building his early houses in the suburbs of Chicago, and Ebenezer Howard was vigorously urging his garden-city scheme. To satisfy the prize requirements, Garnier sent the Academy in Paris a reconstruction of the plan of Tusculum, Cicero's home. As with Henri Labrouste before him, however, the work he did on his own account was of a different character. This holder of the *prix de Rome* set himself the task of planning a complete town — not merely its general layout, but all the rooms of every building. His Cité Industrielle was intended for some thirty-five thousand inhabitants (*fig.* **484**).

First example of contemporary town planning

According to Garnier, the general layout was exhibited in 1901, and the detailed plan in 1904. It was not until 1917, however, that Garnier's ideas were published (in a limited edition).[13] The great influence of this book was not restricted to France; it was circulated from hand to hand wherever new solutions were being sought.

Garnier had taken a great step forward in treating a whole town without losing himself in masses of detail, as many of his contemporaries did. His designs for houses, schools, railway stations, and hospitals likewise represented a great advance.

Architecture begins in construction and ends in town planning; Garnier's work is based on both. His Cité Industrielle grew

---

[13] Garnier, *Étude pour la construction des villes* (Paris, 1917).

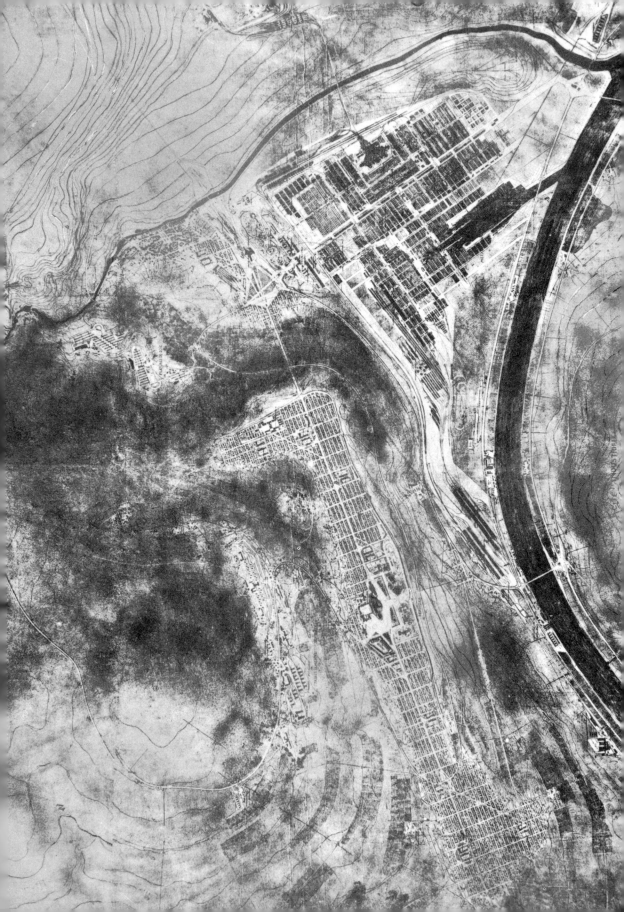

out of a broad understanding of social requirements. The balance of its layout is not destroyed by overconcentration on single issues, such as specialized problems of traffic or the more or less specialized problems of housing that absorbed the advocates of the garden city. Garnier sought for an organic interrelationship between all the functions of his town.

Ferroconcrete was the material Garnier chose for his constructions. Its potentialities were just beginning to be appreciated around 1900, especially by the traditionally alert French constructors. It was quite natural that it should fascinate a young architect, even an "ancien pensionnaire de l'Académie française à Rome." With ferroconcrete Garnier could realize more adequately than with any other material his intention of providing an appropriate frame for industry, public services, and the life of the average man.

> Ferroconcrete Garnier's primary material

In the plans for the Cité Industrielle there is a clear separation of all the different functions of the town: work, residence, leisure, and transport. Industry is cut off from the town proper by a green belt, as it was later in the Russian schemes for linear cities, based on Soria y Mata's much more radical ideas. Tony Garnier's large medical complex is located on a protected site on the slope of an outlying hill and is oriented toward the south.

> Clear distinction between different functions

The middle of Garnier's elongated town is reserved for a civic center, a high school district, and very complete and elaborate athletic fields.[14] This sports area adjoins open country, which gives it room to expand and a fine view as well.

Main-line railway traffic enters the city terminal (*fig.* **201**) through a subway. (This terminal, like some other buildings in the Cité Industrielle, is extraordinarily advanced for its date; its simple and functional exterior is genuinely revolutionary.) Garnier even includes a speedway, or racetrack for cars, as well as testing grounds for *moteurs d'aviation*.

---

[14] This is rather curious; at that time the French paid little attention to sports.

←

484. TONY GARNIER. Cité Industrielle, 1901–04.
General map. Designed for 35,000 inhabitants.

The town site is subdivided into elongated lots, running east and west to facilitate proper orientation of the rooms in the houses. These lots — the basic units of the Cité — are thirty by a hundred and fifty meters. Such long plots give a new aspect to the town and represent an extreme departure from the centralized Renaissance type of layout. Unconsciously the basic principle of the linear city is here carried out — at least in part.

485. TONY GARNIER. Cité Industrielle, 1901–04. *Houses and gardens. Most traffic is routed away from the houses. An attempt is made to solve the residential problem through the use of low houses set in communal gardens.*

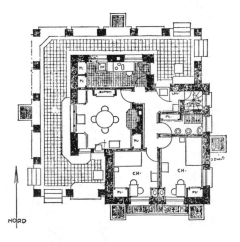

486. TONY GARNIER. Cité Industrielle, 1901–04. *Plan of a dwelling unit; terraces.*

Urbanists of a generation later adopted a similar arrangement to avoid the *rue corridor* and to isolate residential sections from heavy traffic routes. Garnier was quite aware of what he was doing: "On traverse la ville indépendamment des rues" (*fig.* **485**).[15] In the Cité Industrielle the closed blocks and light-wells of Haussmann's time are completely eliminated. There are open communal spaces between all Garnier's low

487. TONY GARNIER. Cité Industrielle, 1901–04. *A school, with open terraces and covered verandah. An attempt is made to blend the surrounding open spaces with the houses to form a neighborhood unit.*

housing blocks (many with roof terraces) on the main thoroughfares.

Each individual dwelling has a large central living room and small but well-organized bedrooms, bath, and kitchen (*fig.* **486**). The open areas between the houses are filled with greenery. The schools, low and open in their planning (*fig.* **487**), are distributed throughout the town, adding their lawns and shrubbery to the green areas around the houses. New suburbs of Amsterdam were later developed along similar lines.

---

[15] This is not to be taken with complete literalness, but it would have held true for the small volume of traffic in 1900. Germs of later solutions are certainly present in Garnier's layout.

488. TONY GARNIER. Cité Industrielle, 1901–04. *Ferroconcrete houses with open staircases and roof gardens.* *Through the use of ferroconcrete, Garnier arrived at solutions which would later reappear.*

Tony Garnier was attracted to the classical, as the modeling of his buildings shows. He broke away from this attachment, however, in many of the details of his Cité Industrielle. Its houses, with their terraces and the gardens on their flat roofs (*fig.* **488**), are a sound combination of modern construction and the old tradition of the Mediterranean culture.

Parts of Garnier's scheme were later realized at Lyons, where he built hospitals, stockyards, athletic stadia, and a residential district.[16]

Garnier's plan clearly separated the different functions of the city: work, housing, traffic, and recreation. Garnier allotted each its own space so that a future expansion of any one of them would leave the others undisturbed. His long residential blocks with their greenery were planned to form neighborhood units with their own schools and all necessary services. His drawings for every building, complete down to the last details of construction and layout, often foreshadow future developments to an astonishing degree. Garnier's main material, ferroconcrete, was employed to arrive at new solutions for his schools, railway stations, sanatoriums, and residences.

---

[16] See Garnier, *Les Grands Travaux de la ville de Lyon* (Paris, 1924).

489. LE CORBUSIER. Settlement at Pessac, near Bordeaux, 1926.

The Cité Industrielle directly influenced many of the men who have contributed most to the city planning of the future. This influence is understandable, since Garnier's scheme contained the germs of contemporary methods. Developments often take unpredictable courses: the lost instinct for town planning was recaptured by a young *pensionnaire de l'Académie à Rome*.

AMSTERDAM AND THE REBIRTH OF TOWN PLANNING

We turned to London to gain an insight into the state of town planning between 1800 and 1850. Our example for the years between 1850 and 1870 was Paris, and for the period between 1900 and the thirties it is Amsterdam. There are other cities where, over a short interval, a more rapid advance occurred — for example, Frankfort on the Main in the late twenties. And in some respects building activity was more extensive in Rotterdam, though it was sometimes carried on without coördination. It was at Rotterdam (after 1919) that J. J. P. Oud built his carefully planned apartments for lower income groups, and that van Tijen experimented (after 1930) with tall slablike apartment houses to come closer to the special requirements of a modern European city.

But Amsterdam is one of the few cities of our times that
shows a continuous tradition in town planning, unbroken
since 1900. This uninterrupted building activity is particularly
important for our purposes, since it affords us a view over a
long period of development and eliminates the necessity of
collecting different examples from all corners of the world.
Amsterdam is thus the city best adapted to a study of the
main currents working through the period.

Town planning in Amsterdam operated within the realm of
what was really possible. There were no erratic developments,
no Utopian enterprises, but a steady progress. The method
behind the work might be called analytic. It admirably
suited the temperament of the Dutch, who disliked daring
speculations like those that went on in England around 1820.
Both progress and mistakes were made by slow stages at
Amsterdam.

For a long time the population of Amsterdam had remained
stable, but in 1875 it began to rise steeply. This rise followed
the opening of a canal which gave Amsterdam an outlet into
the North Sea. Between 1875 and 1900 the population
doubled, and in the interval between 1900 and 1920 there was
another increase of almost fifty per cent. It was in this second
period (barring the war years) that tremendous building activity took place.

For what classes were these buildings raised? The early London squares and crescents were for the gentry and the richest
members of the middle class. The middle classes were the chief
objects of Hausmann's boulevard-building in Paris — with
the poor often crowded into slumlike apartments on the top
floors of the buildings. In Amsterdam building activity was
carried on in the service of the lower middle class and the
working people.

Traveling in Holland during the twenties one encountered
brand-new housing settlements in every part of the country —
variable in quality, but all marked by clean brick surfaces, big
windows, and a visible intention of giving the Dutch scene the
imprint of the best contemporary architecture. Nowhere else

was modern architecture given such an opportunity to change the whole face of a country.

The impetus for this entire development came from the Dutch Housing Act of 1901. "This enactment," to quote from the Harvard City Planning Studies, "is perhaps the most comprehensive single piece of legislation ever to be adopted in this field. Its eleven chapters provide the essentials of a complete attack upon the national housing problems. Some amendments have been made since its passage, but the basic structure of the law remains and is the authority for the greatest part of all governmental intervention in housing in the Netherlands." [1] The act required every town of ten thousand or more inhabitants to draw up a scheme governing its future expansion. Detailed as well as general plans were required, and the general plan had to be revised every ten years. The process of expropriation was also regulated by the act, and was made easier for the cities to carry through.

Impetus furnished by Dutch Housing Act of 1901

This act came just when the northern countries were entering upon a new stage in the treatment of the housing problem. Up to this time, ideal dwellings for the lower class family had often been displayed at the great exhibitions, but had never formed a recognized part of building activity. The Dutch Housing Act of 1901 was shrewdly drawn to encourage constructions for the use of people of small means.

The city becomes a landowner

Coöperatively organized building societies received building credits on very easy terms from the state, the credits being guaranteed by the community. Thus the whole tendency of the act was to make the city a decisive influence upon all building activity. At the same time Amsterdam made intensive (though not always successful) efforts to constitute itself a great landowner by acquiring land for its housing settlements before speculation forced up prices. And, like the nobles who were the landlords in London, the city of Amsterdam leased the ground instead of selling it.

---

[1] Richard Ratcliff, in Mabel U. Walker's *Urban Blight and Slums* (Cambridge, 1938), p. 398 (vol. XII of Harvard City Planning Studies). Ratcliff examines the effect upon slums and blighted areas of construction standards, housing and population surveys, closure and demolition of unfit structures, expropriation, town planning, slum clearance and redevelopment, financial assistance by municipalities and by the state, etc.

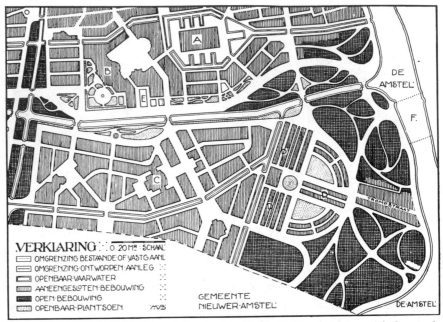

490. H. P. BERLAGE. Plan of Amsterdam South, 1902. *A mixture of influences is evident here, along with the uncertainty that accompanied Berlage's attempt to break with old formulas.*

Many cities have attempted to use a similar land policy. Amsterdam, however, actually succeeded in building whole districts which were homogeneous and met the demands of the community. Building contractors were forced to submit to the judgments of what was called a "commission for beauty," which saw to it that uniform façades were erected. This commission formed the basis for the building activities of de Klerk and the other architects of the Amsterdam school in the twenties.

Land tenure and the character of the façade were pretty thoroughly controlled by the community; regulations governing ground plans were not set up until later.

H. P. Berlage's Plans for Amsterdam South

First plan, 1902   Besides the 1901 ordinances, individual creative forces were at work in Amsterdam to bring about a kind of city planning that broke loose from routine. Such energies were not confined to this Dutch city; they could have been found elsewhere as

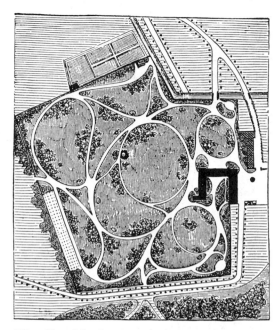

491. French landscape gardening, 1869. *The kidney-shaped windings of the paths are recalled in Berlage's 1902 plan for the Amsterdam South district.*

well. There was, for example, Otto Wagner in Vienna, who was conducting a long, bitter, and ultimately unsuccessful fight with the city administration. Amsterdam, by contrast, afforded remarkable freedom to a private architect of real genius by handing over the development of the Amsterdam South district to Hendrik Petrus Berlage (*fig.* 490). Berlage drew up his first plans for this development in 1902. The Stock Exchange Building which was to make his name the center of discussion in all parts of Europe was just then nearing completion.

Berlage assumed the responsibility for laying out a whole residential district — Amsterdam South — in complete independence of the city officials and the Department of Public Works. The results form an ideal test case for our purposes: nowhere could we gain a better insight into the level of town planning at that period, and the actual limits of what could be accomplished. Conclusions drawn from the Berlage development also apply very closely to architecture.

Berlage's schemes reflect the central difficulty at that date: the inability to arrive at new means of expression in the solutions offered for the problems peculiar to the times. In the 1902 plans particularly (and to some extent even in the later version of 1915) we sense the struggle involved in Berlage's attempted break with the formulae of previous decades, his spasmodic efforts to attain modes of expression suited to his purpose — the humanizing of the residential district.

When one recognizes that an eminent architect such as Berlage could not free himself from the overriding power of stereotyped preconceptions, one can understand the situation of routine official city planning in 1900. This is the reason that Berlage's plans for Amsterdam South will be considered in some detail.

Romantic character of the plan

At first glance Berlage's 1902 drawings suggest a diagram of the convolutions of the brain more than the layout of a city. The oval windings of the streets embody curves which are familiar in Haussmann's public parks of the sixties (*fig.* **491**). These outlines are quite in keeping with the generally romantic character of Berlage's first plan.

Another influence shaping the layout was a horror of the forced and artificial axis, and of the whole gridiron system. Camillo Sitte's sermons had made it seem that the remedy for this cheerless aspect was a return to the medieval town, with its natural patterns of growth.

The specific problem was to construct a residential quarter for middle and working class tenancy; essentially it was a problem in housing. But how could dwellings be brought close together without becoming sources of mutual annoyance? Berlage's concern with this question is evident in every line of his work, and with it a horror of relapsing into the cruel and banal solutions that guided average practice.

Uncertainty revealed in it

Actually, a real solution of this difficulty was impossible at the moment. Though the garden-city idea had been advanced a few years earlier, Berlage had perhaps not heard of it. It was, at any rate, irrelevant to his task: he was planning a district which was expected to be rather densely populated. In this period of uncertainty as to the direction town planning should take, Berlage fell back on the Renaissance system, in which every major street axis is dominated by some prominent public building. The dwelling houses which should have given each section its character are thereby reduced to a mere back-

798

drop. And the centers of force which they frame — markets, theaters, auditoriums — are located quite arbitrarily. They form an artificial backbone upon which the whole scheme is pegged out, and the way in which they are brought into relation with each other (by patching or building out) suggests a jigsaw puzzle. Finally, the residences themselves are not well oriented to human needs; they are not even properly related to the play of sunshine.

This example may serve to show that in 1900 even the most progressive minds tended toward an artificial monumentality — artificial or pseudo because it was used to hide the uncertainty and perplexity with which the organization of a town was approached, even when carte blanche had been given to the planner.

Berlage's second scheme for the Amsterdam South region, made in 1915 (*fig.* 492), merely provided a general framework for its development. This time the city asked only for a plan which would cover the broad aspects of any later expansion, without specifying details of execution. These could be filled in to satisfy whatever necessities should arise. Berlage was still given a free hand in his work, and the site was unobstructed meadow land, cut only by some small irrigation canals. Second plan, 1915

Berlage's original map for this area (a beautifully executed drawing) was hung in the office of the Department of Public Works at Amsterdam. One's first and decisive impression is derived from the network of streets which appears upon it.

This network is so dominant that at a casual glance one would suppose the plan to deal with a business center rather than a quiet residential quarter occupying undeveloped land on the outskirts of town. The most prominent feature is the enormous Y formed by three streets which lead up from the bank of the Amstel River. The backbone of the 1915 layout is the Amstellaan Boulevard, unusually wide for Holland, which forms the base of the Y.

The Amsterdam South district — especially around the Amstellaan (*fig.* 493) — was built up by the so-called Amsterdam school some years after World War I. Before his early death, the leader of this group, de Klerk, played a major part in the

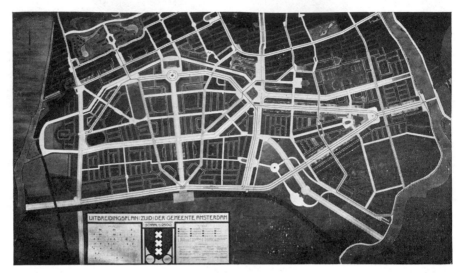

492. H. P. BERLAGE. Final plan for Amsterdam South, 1915.

work (*fig.* **496**). During the twenties this section with its uniform façades was the best-known example of the possibility of making a residential area both attractive and well-adapted to human living.

The street humanized

The Amstellaan does not owe its unusual width and the trees and greenery down its center to any attempt at traffic control. Nor did it — like the Boulevard Richard-Lenoir in Paris (1861–63) — come about as the covering for a canal or any other break in the ground (*fig.* **494**). Its landscaping was something more than a tasteful screen for the light shafts and ventilation ducts required to keep the old canal under the Boulevard Richard-Lenoir operable. Width and greenery were both intended to produce a better living space, to give more air and freedom to the residents (*fig.* **495**). And its façades are not used like the doors of a closet to hold in a tangle of houses jammed together behind them. To the rear of the houses fronting on the Amstellaan are spacious courtyards, planted with lawns and shrubs. [2] The 1915 plan as a whole, however, was not preceded by sufficient research into the housing requirements of the Amsterdam South area.[3]

---

[2] It was J. J. P. Oud who, in his Tusschendiyken settlement (1919), first used the interior courtyard as a means of humanizing apartment blocks.

[3] Later architects pointed out that this plan — as was usual at the time — pays little regard to traffic needs. Thus a main artery (Rijn Straat) crosses the Amstellaan just before the latter opens out into a square.

493.   Amsterdam South, North and South Amstellaan in the thirties.   *Air view.*

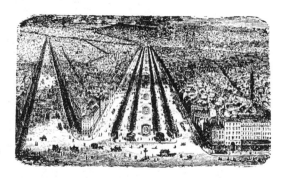

494.   Boulevard Richard-Lenoir, 1861–63.

Though it is doubtful whether Berlage was familiar with the garden-city movement in 1902, he flatly rejected it in 1915. He wrote then that the residential apartment block was the only serviceable expedient; pending the development of an original style in architecture which would be capable — as in earlier periods — of binding together all the individual houses. Building authorities should regulate streets or parts of streets instead of single dwellings, so that the streets' unity would include the residences that were parts of them. "The building of dwellings is becoming a work of mass production. The block building must be used again, and to an even greater extent than formerly, to provide a solution." [4]

Berlage's opposition to the garden city

---

[4] The remarks are from the foreword to his 1915 scheme, "Memorie van Toelichting." *Gemeenteblad van Amsterdam*, March 9, 1915.

495. Amsterdam South, the Amstellaan. *This was one of the first projects in which the street was dealt with as a unit. It remains, however, essentially the street of the nineteenth century, though considerably humanized and with garden areas behind the houses.*

496. Amsterdam South, the Amstellaan. *Apartment houses by de Klerk, 1923. This district was built up by the Amsterdam school, especially by its leader, de Klerk.*

Berlage's reaction not only against the dismal street frontages common at the time but also against the romantic ideal of the garden city is easily understandable. In his plans for the district he proposes as remedies the employment of a unified surface and an arrangement that is quiet and unemphatic. These are precisely the qualities we find in his Stock Exchange Building. But at the same time his historical position is made quite plain. The demand for the erection of whole streets with unified fronts is a demand for the reinstatement of Haussmann's neutral façade. In effect, Berlage was trying to regain a historical level which had passed for good. This attempt, however, left the atmosphere cleared for new developments.

The streets throughout the Amsterdam South sector are wide and extensively planted with flowers and trees, handled with the great pains that the Dutch take in their gardening. This scheme is much more human and dignified than the nightmarish town planning of the preceding decades. But this plan, like architecture in the years before 1900, still failed to arrive at a genuinely contemporary expression based on a new conception of life. It succeeded only in reforming the streets and weakening their dominance of the total layout. They remain streets bordered by residences, and that kind of street is not the solution to the problems of living in a great city. This is not to deny that the district possesses a marked grandeur; no one can tour the Amsterdam South region without feeling it. And nowhere else on the Continent at this period was greenery brought so graciously into combination with uniform rows of buildings.

Berlage displayed the courage needed to formulate a genuinely impressive system of streets and to conceive a whole district of a city as a unit. Individualized house façades disappeared, and uniform street walls — treated as surfaces — took their place. These walls, despite their monumental and much-censured treatment at the street corners, never completely surrender their plane effect.

When we look back at the Amstellaan from the point of view of later developments, we perceive that it belongs in the main line of nineteenth-century town planning: the street dominates the whole. The Amstellaan, moreover, is representative of the whole scheme; there is reform but no new conception. [5]

---

[5] Berlage had a great influence upon the development and increase of town planning in Holland. He himself planned extensive projects for several Dutch cities: The Hague

The General Extension Plan of Amsterdam, 1934

The general extension plan of Amsterdam, 1934, was a collective achievement carried out by the Department of Public Works. It represented the close-knit collaboration of an entire staff of specialists. The layout of the scheme as a whole shows signs of an approach similar to that of contemporary art in its response to the world today.[6]

Our main concern is the way in which our age is becoming conscious of its own nature, and we have therefore largely avoided technical detail. But it is impossible to understand the tendencies at work in the inner structure of the Amsterdam extension plan unless we know the problems that had to be solved by this scheme.

The general plan (*fig.* **497**) for the future development of the city, prepared by the Department of Public Works,[7] was based on a careful correlation of all those factors which determine the social make-up of a community. All measures proposed had their foundation in figures that come under the heading of vital statistics: birth and death rates, immigration and emigration totals, etc. Statistics more difficult to obtain also entered the planning: calculations of the number of people who could make their living in the district, the rate and direction of population changes, and forecasts of the probable course of the business cycle.

(1908), Rotterdam (1914), and Utrecht (1921). He was responsible for the execution of some squares of a monumental character — Mercatorplain in Rotterdam, for example. See the article by K. P. de Bazel in *Dr. H. P. Berlage en zihn werk* (Rotterdam, 1916), a symposium produced in honor of Berlage's sixtieth birthday.

[6] See the two volumes published by the Amsterdam Department of Public Works, November 1934: *Algemeen uitbreidingsplan*. A complete understanding of the scheme and the methods employed in it can be derived from this publication and the maps which illustrate it. These volumes should be in the hands of every town planner.

For short references in English, see *Town Planning Review* (Liverpool), vol. XVII, no. 1 (June 1936), and *Architectural Review* (London), vol. LXXXIII (June 1938), "A New Plan for Amsterdam," by Arthur Korn.

[7] Ordered by the city, prepared by this public department, and approved as the master plan for the extension by the Amsterdam City Council. Research, planning, and execution were in the same hands. The situation was vastly different in some other cities: New York, for example, where the extensive 1929 regional survey of New York and its environs was supported by a group of civic-minded private citizens and had no official character.

497. Master plan for Amsterdam South, 1934. *An extension plan based upon coördi-nated scientific research. It was intended to be flexible and to lay down the general outlines for the city's expansion, not to be taken as a rigid scheme.*

Vital statistics and livelihood statistics	From a consideration of all these factors it was concluded that population growth in Amsterdam would eventually cease, though it would continue to increase throughout the century, up to the 900,000 or 1,000,000 mark.[8] Accordingly, the plan for the extension of Amsterdam was based on the supposition that 250,000 additional inhabitants would have to be accommodated between 1934 and the close of the century.
Extent of the plan	The expansion was directed westwards, toward open land which required years of preparation to make it fit for building purposes. The key area was the western edge of the harbor, and the big industrial plants that lie beyond the docks. The southern part of the development was a residential area for workers employed around the dockyards and in the neighboring industrial plants. At the time there was not sufficient accommodation for these people within reasonable proximity of their places of work. This quarter extends to the limits of Berlage's Amsterdam South district of 1915.
Distribution of greenery	The general extension plan did not destroy the rural belt around the city. The market gardeners on its outskirts were not dispossessed, and the natural aspect of the Amstel's banks on the southern boundary was preserved.

In the southwest, great parks — planned with extreme care — were developed. (One, the magnificent Amsterdam Bosch, has an area of 2,135 acres, about that of Haussmann's Bois de Boulogne.) This park system took up land unsuitable for building purposes and converted it into wooded areas.

The recreational needs of the population were studied in detail. It was found that people make little use of any parks farther than a quarter of a mile from their homes. The maximum distance between any two parks was therefore limited to a half mile. Such planning is consciously proportioned to the human scale, to the scale of the *promeneur*. It moves in the direction of those "playgrounds at the doorstep" which Le Corbusier proclaimed as one of the fundamental requirements in town planning.

---

[8] See D. T. J. Delfgaauw, "A Study of the Future Growth of Population in Amsterdam," *Journal of the Town Planning Institute* (London), February 1933, pp. 79–80. (In 1960 the population was around 870,000.)

From the aesthetic point of view, this planning is important because of its new town structure. The formerly unbroken spread of dense masses of houses is everywhere broken up by strips of greenery of various dimensions.

The accommodation of 250,000 additional inhabitants was planned to be carried out by building successive units comprising ten thousand dwellings (*fig.* **498**). Each dwelling provided, on the average, for three and one-half inhabitants.

Major unit of ten thousand dwellings

Methods of forecasting the future needs and composition of its population were developed very early in Holland. As far back as 1920, the city of Rotterdam used a carefully differentiated method for accurately determining not only the number of dwellings needed but the kinds of people who would occupy them and the sort of dwellings each would require.[9]

The decision to provide for three and a half tenants per unit-dwelling in the Amsterdam extensions was the result of this sort of research. The planning authority knew what different categories of tenants had to be housed, as well as their various needs, and the proportion of each type in the population as a whole.

The composition of a major unit of ten thousand dwellings reflected these varying needs. The majority (sixty-five hundred) had two rooms and a kitchen; fifteen hundred had three rooms, eleven hundred four rooms. Four hundred and fifty were designed for families with six children, and two hundred and sixty were especially designed to meet the needs of older people.

The actual building of these major units was carried out by private enterprise and by coöperative societies alike. The city, however, exercised control over the ground plan and the façade, and determined where houses of a given type — two, three, or four rooms, etc. — were to be located. Both private contractors and coöperative societies had to build on a site approved by the city as maintaining the organic unity of the whole unit of ten thousand dwellings.

Municipal control over site, ground plan, and façade

Town planning must be controlled by the needs of the people who, on the basis of preliminary researches, will make up the

Row-housing basic

---

[9] See T. K. van Lohuizen, *Zwei Jahre Wohnungs-Statistik in Rotterdam* (Berlin, 1922).

807

population of a district. In the Amsterdam extension plan four-story houses in continuous rows predominated. These rows, made up of individual apartments with a volume of two hundred cubic meters, were left open at the ends, not formed into closed blocks (*fig.* **498**). High buildings, houses of eight stories, were rare at this time.[10] Single-story houses facing south were planned for the use of elderly people, following an old Dutch tradition. The differences in height, location, and spaces between the housing types established unexpected inter-relations in the layout.

Execution of the extension plan: "Het Westen"

It will help us to gain a notion of the special character of this work if we study some of its smaller units rather carefully. How does such a theoretical study work when put into active practice?

We shall take a small part of the Amsterdam West region, with its various building complexes and the school at their southern edge.[11] In this quarter the extension plan called for residential blocks of three and four stories (*fig.* **499**). The architects (different men were responsible for the various blocks) proposed an open layout, at right angles to the traffic thoroughfare (*fig.* **501**). They oriented the blocks in such a way that space was left in the south, at their open ends, for the smaller residences of the elderly. This scheme was perfectly adapted to the general layout, whose effect is intensified by the better orientation of the buildings. It is one of the chief advantages of a flexible general layout that it can easily be brought into harmony with changed circumstances.

This project, which provided seven hundred apartments for low-income classes, was erected by several coöperative building societies. One of them, the "Het Westen" society, built a group of two hundred and eight apartments designed by the architects Merkelbach and Karsten in 1937 (*fig.* **500**).

The unit of the single dwelling

The architects desired to offer the tenants the greatest possible amount of comfort (*fig.* **502**). The living room was given

---

[10] Van Tijen's experience with them at Rotterdam revealed that they did not suit Dutch habits, and this discouraged their use.

[11] For a detailed account, see *Tijdschrift voor volkshuisvesting en stedebouw* (Amsterdam). vol. XVIII, no. 9 (September 1937).

498. Amsterdam, master plan, district Bosch en Lommer, with detail of model, 1938. *A single unit of the general extension plan. Designed for 35,000 inhabitants. The neighborhood unit shown in the model makes the most economical use of open spaces and greenery.*

broad French windows at the front, so that the house could be thrown wide open in the summer time, and to facilitate moving. The coöperative societies maintain the gardens and play areas. The whole project gives an impression that the apartments were designed to meet actual demands. That this was recognized was clear from the sixteen hundred applications that poured in for the two hundred and eight apartments when they were opened.

Interrelations of Housing and Activities of Private Life

Housing must offer something more than privacy. It must provide for access to parks, playgrounds, schools, recreation centers, stores, and places of business. Such needs have always been recognized, but the problems they pose have usually been solved separately and not within a comprehensive system. Until then town planning had not dealt in any carefully preconceived way with the interrelations between residence and the other activities. In the Amsterdam West development the chaotic methods of the late nineteenth century were discarded and provision made in advance for such activities, and for their complex interrelations. And the preliminary research and calculation resulted in a flexible plan that could be changed when necessity arose.

The task of the town planner is to avoid mutual interferences in the various functions of a section, uniting or separating them as the case may require. Thus he will separate traffic arteries from residential streets, which may be closed to through traffic and serve only the housing. He will concentrate stores in one area and avoid a random dispersion of working places. Schools, playgrounds, and athletic fields will be so related to the rows of houses that greenery will penetrate the body of the town to the greatest extent compatible with its economic life.

Planning such as this results in an alteration of the structure of the city. The ground plan of the modern house has been made flexible and informal: the layout of the modern town tends in the same direction.

Caution in planning the extension

In Holland all measures toward this end have had to be carried through with great caution. Land is very expensive and

810

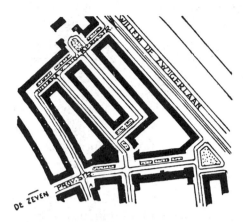

499. Master plan of Amsterdam West, proposal for "Het Westen." *Such proposals do not have to be followed exactly. The architect is permitted certain liberties in developing his scheme, provided it remains in harmony with the larger unit.*
←

500. MERKELBACH and KARSTEN. Low-cost housing settlement, Amsterdam West ("Het Westen"), 1937. *An element in the 1934 plan as executed.* ↓

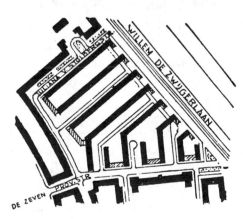

501. Changes of the master plan by the executive architects of "Het Westen."

502. MERKELBACH and KARSTEN. Low-cost housing settlement, "Het Westen." *Apartment with living room, two bedrooms for parents and children, kitchen, balcony, and shower. The Dutch have succeeded in reconciling very low rentals with a high standard of living. The means employed can be traced back to the careful utilization of the available space in J. J. P. Oud's early apartment blocks in Rotterdam (1919).*

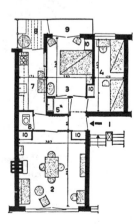

must be used with strictest economy: pile foundations have to be driven for every house; an elaborate engineering service has to be maintained; and greenery and open areas require years of preparatory work. All these factors contribute to raise the price of land.

In addition, rental rates are fixed at extremely low levels. In this situation there is no room for free flights of genius; advance is possible only by one careful step after another.

Dutch experience in such developments is scrupulously collated and checked with that of contemporary architects in other countries. The town-planning authority is a clearinghouse for such data, which are carefully studied and which guide the layout of the city. Practice has continued to justify the measures these experts adopted.

It has sometimes been objected that houses in Amsterdam are too closely massed together, that more open space and greater individual freedom are needed. The scheme as a whole, however, operates under circumstances which put a freer layout beyond the power of the planner. As one of the Amsterdam officials remarked, "It is not really the architect who makes these plans — it is society."

The technical and the human approach

The kind of technical staff needed for large-scale urban developments was first brought together by Haussmann in the fifties for his transformation of Paris. Since then the tasks such staffs must deal with have changed. It is not merely engineering works in the service of the population as a whole that are needed — streets, traffic arteries, parks, sewer systems, aqueducts, etc. — but ways to facilitate an integrated life for each individual citizen. The focal point of later developments was the individual and the interrelation of his activities with the total life of the city.

The scheme for the extension of Amsterdam presupposed a continuance of the city's growth. And the project for humanizing the city was joined to the belief that all population increases would be included in an expansion of the limits of the city. No satellite towns were projected. Units of ten thousand dwellings and some thirty-five thousand inhabitants would continue to be joined onto the existing city for as long as its growth persisted.

In the steady process of realizing this scheme, only conditions actually in force — and those which calculation established as most probable in the near future — could be taken into consideration. All measures adopted have been justified by the later course of events. Life has filled out and diversified the original plan in the way a river occupies and shapes its bed.

It may be that the range of the popular Dutch traffic vehicle — the bicycle — constituted a basic unit of scale for the extension plan, and it might, therefore, prove unsuited to other countries. Even if this were true the value of what has been achieved at Amsterdam remains undiminished. It is the methods employed in these developments and not their specific successes which are important. There are cities ten times as large as Amsterdam — cities like London and New York — which are still far behind it in methods of planning. Attempts are still being made to restore the sick bodies of these immense towns by operations performed on isolated subsections. Slum areas are selected here and there, re-housing is carried through — and the existing disorder in the city as a whole is simply increased. Research and statistics are not enough in themselves. They must be backed by vision, by a general understanding of the course of development today's cities must take.

The plan of Amsterdam involves no attempt at clearing out slums in the center of the city: it establishes a new town on its outskirts. And the freedom and flexibility of the scheme are not hopelessly constricted by the *rue corridor* or the gridiron system. The conception of space-time — the basis for a contemporary town planning — can already be felt in the 1934 extension plan for Amsterdam.

PART **IX** SPACE–TIME IN CITY PLANNING

Contemporary Attitude toward Town Planning

What is the general attitude of the contemporary town planner? What does he seek to achieve? From what concepts does he proceed to his work? Questions such as these are of the utmost importance in any consideration of our subject. For town planning is first and foremost a human issue: its problems are by no means exclusively technical and economic. It can never be carried on satisfactorily without a clear understanding of the contemporary conception of life.

Town planning and contemporary life

Nowhere else in architecture do we encounter the influence of the prevailing outlook so strongly as in town planning. Very little town planning can be expressed in shapes and structure; often its participation in a given project can only be felt, an adumbration without explicit accent. But even when not visibly defined, it acts to unite the organism which is a town, much as the hidden skeleton of steel supports the modern building. Whenever town planning lacks such organic integrity, it must fall back upon artificial expedients, just as a building of faulty design requires buttresses.

In the future the town planner will need to advance further and further beyond the limits of the purely technical. The reconquest of the unity of human life is nowhere more urgent than in his work. Representative of contemporary attitudes is the Dutchman C. van Eesteren,[1] who, as chief architect of the city of Amsterdam, conducted its general extension plan from 1929 to 1960. From his conversation we may gain a personal insight into the mind of the town planner.

Van Eesteren's idea of the town planner

The town planner, as van Eesteren sees him, is not concerned primarily with architecture. Nor does he believe that the town is essentially either an object of financial speculation or, as in the Russian formula, one of the instruments of production. He seeks to discover how the town came into being and how it has reached its present stage of growth. He wants to know

---

[1] Van Eesteren, who was trained as an architect, decided very early to concentrate upon town planning. He used a traveling scholarship to establish contacts with the leading European artists. As we have already noted, he collaborated with Theo van Doesburg; as a young man, his training under such modern architects as the members of the Stijl group laid the foundations for his later development.

as much as he can of the site (a matter of peculiar importance in Holland) and of its relations to the surrounding region and the country as a whole. Above all, he studies the different categories of people who have to be accommodated, each according to his manner of life; he finds out whether they are young or old, married or single, with few or many children. He must consider where these people work, the routes traffic must take, the distance there should be between residential and industrial sections. He must also establish a control of the relation between the communications of the city and its living quarters. He thinks no longer in linear terms of street and axis, but in terms of population densities. His approach to the town is conditioned by this population ration, which in the Amsterdam extension plan, for example, was allowed to range between 110 and 550 inhabitants per hectare.

The task of the town planner is to form plans on the basis of widespread inquiries, so that they are adjusted to existing conditions and, as far as possible, to those of the future. But he must not adopt a rigid and definitive system; he must handle each section in such a way that unforeseen changes can be met. There must be a vital and mutual relation between the desired goal and the existing reality, between wishes and facts. Moreover, he must not attempt to force the functions of residence, work, and leisure into conformity with tight and final arrangements; he must make only generalized distributions, leaving their ultimate shape to the interplay of circumstances. Yet these arrangements cannot be left to develop haphazardly; his aim must be to find the forms best suited to every special condition. The town planner must know what functions have to be provided for; his task is to create a whole out of the existing potentialities and conditions.

Flexibility of contemporary town planning

The foundation of town planning is our contemporary conception of life; without it order cannot be brought into the enormous mass of factual material that confronts the planner. This conception of life is molded and expressed in many different ways. Modern traffic, for example, educates and sharpens our sense of space. City-dwellers moving across congested avenues seem almost to know what is taking place behind them. This kind of spatio-temporal awareness was

Conception of life the foundation of planning

unknown in baroque times; it may be a case of the redevelopment of a primitive sense.

The plan of a modern town must be developed in a more complicated way and take account of a tighter net of relations than ever before. Paper planning in two dimensions — the method of the last century — will not suffice, nor will the three-dimensional planning of the baroque. The contemporary planner must take a different approach. A town plan must bring all constituent elements into a measured and living balance. When the planner is seeking, for instance, the proper location of a cemetery or a market hall, he must be able to go over his plan with almost tactile perceptiveness, sensing the contrasting character of its districts as plainly as though they were velvet or emery beneath his fingers.

In the modern city — only fragments of which have been realized so far — there exist interrelationships which are more than merely spatial. These subtle values are the elements on which the charm of the city and the proper coördination of the various functions of the community depend. No element — even the technical and industrial ones — can be allowed to dominate at the expense of the others. Technical and industrial factors should not complicate development (as in the nineteenth century), but should help to overcome difficulties. In this manner the town may pass from a static condition to the free equilibrium of an organism.

DESTRUCTION OR TRANSFORMATION?

Reasons for
structural change

Again and again we have tried to point out how in the various domains of construction, painting, and architecture — all independent each of the other — there has arisen a certain identity of method. We have observed that contemporary architecture can be explained in terms either of functions or of sociological patterns. But such explanations are not enough. They are intellectual only; they do not comprehend and reveal the quality of feeling which underlies contemporary architecture. It is the same with town planning. Cities have always, in every period, been essentially agglomerations of social,

818

political, and economic interests. Consequently, changes in urban structure have been difficult to realize. Sometimes, as we well know, they have been forced by independent processes exerting pressure from the outside. For example, the evolution in warfare and arms which rendered older cities helpless against attack forced changes in their structure for the sake of protection.[1]

The contemporary city is more profoundly menaced in all countries and without exception — not by any outside danger, but from within, by an evil shaping within itself. This is the evil of the machine. Because of the confusion of its different functions, its growing mechanization, the omnipresence and anarchy of the motorcar, the city is at the mercy of industrial machines. If it is to be saved, its structure must change. This change, forced by mechanization just as in other days it was forced by implements of war, is inevitable, whether it comes through insight or through catastrophe. The city must be changed or it will perish, and our civilization with it.

However, here, as when discussing construction and architecture, we wish to deal with the formation of the city in so far as it is emotionally conditioned, to look for the interrelations between its structure and the form-giving tendencies of our time. Resistance to changes in urban structure springs not only from private interests but also from emotional sources. Complete freedom in the development of an area is not enough in itself. Even in countries where the authority of the state over land use is absolute, planning still proceeds according to nineteenth-century ideas unless those in power are moved by later artistic conceptions.

The question arises whether the large city as it has been inherited from the nineteenth century, with its chaotic intermingling of functions, should not be allowed to die. One

Future of the city

---

[1] Lewis Mumford's *The Culture of Cities* (New York, 1938), so far as it is concerned with the change of the structure of the city, is based on social, political, and economic developments, and points out especially the influence of arms and defense on the growth of the city, as does his later work, *The City in History* (New York, 1963).

A volume prepared under the auspices of the International Congress for Modern Architecture (*Can Our Cities Survive?* edited by J. L. Sert, Harvard University Press, 1942) contains a general analytical survey of the conditions of life in the cities of today based on the principle formulated by leading town planners of eighteen different countries.

opinion is that the metropolis cannot be saved and must be broken up; the other that, instead of being destroyed, the city must be transformed in accordance with the structure and genius of our times.

Proposals for decentralization

Several suggestions have been made as to how the break-up of the city is to be accomplished. Differing as they do in details, it is significant that they possess one tendency in common — an urge toward the organic, which has become increasingly strong in our time as a kind of self-protection against the evils of civilization. The difference between these proposals lies in how this organic development may be realized.

One suggestion is that instead of concentrating the population in gigantic blown-up agglomerations, the whole country should be colonized in small tracts of one or two acres. Such a decentralization would change us from city dwellers to country dwellers living on an independent mechanized farm unit which would maintain a balance between rural and industrial occupation. This is the complete and conscious destruction of the idea of the city. It also undermines to a large extent that differentiation in occupations which has been the basis of our civilization, for it makes the small, self-sufficient landowner predominant. Such schemes go back to the doctrines of Charles Fourier, the most thoroughgoing of the French utopian economists, who, in opposition to the existing industrial system, wanted to achieve the fullest development of human nature by the creation of a social and organic life in which each individual could find his greatest satisfaction. He envisioned such a life as a decentralized society in which agriculture would be the staple industry. Since Fourier developed his ideas in the twenties of the nineteenth century, many social thinkers have followed him in an effort to deal with the evils produced by industrialization. Frank Lloyd Wright, with his "Broadacre City," was one of the most vocal among the twentieth-century theorists. He based his program, as he himself admitted, on the ideas and experiments of Ralph Borsodi.[2]

---

[2] An economic consultant who realized his program of decentralization or "distributism" by means of small-owner units and mechanized home production (small tractors, small-scale labor-saving machines, etc.), first in Dayton, Ohio, and after 1935 in Bayard Lane, near Suffern, N. Y., only an hour's drive from New York City. See John Chamberlain, "Blueprints for a New Society: Borsodi and the Chesterbelloc," *New Republic*,

There is no doubt that self-sufficient units have a proper place in economic life, but there is also no doubt that this primitive form of society cannot replace that differentiated organization which, whatever the political system, is basic to our culture. It would change the country into a forlorn hybrid, something neither rural nor yet urban, but with the limitations of both. In any case, a proposal to parcel the inhabitants out in small communities, with agriculture the staple industry, is completely out of scale with the problems which today demand solution.

The opposing point of view — that the city must be transformed but need not be destroyed — likewise holds that men cannot be separated from nature, and consequently that the city cannot continue to exist in its present form. But it immediately points out that the city is more than a contemporary and passing phenomenon. It is a product of many differentiated cultures, in many different periods. Thus the question of its life or death cannot be settled simply on the basis of present-day experience or conditions. The city cannot be damned to extinction merely because it has been misused since industrialization or because its whole structure has been rendered impotent by the intrusion of a technical invention, the motorcar. The question has to be considered from a broader view and extended into other queries: Are cities connected with every sort of society and civilization? Did urban agglomerations simply arise, first for defense and later for production, or is the institution of the city a profound need of man himself? Are cities a temporary phenomenon, a stage in development, the difficulties of which we have to overcome by means of mechanical inventions, radio, television, the motorcar, and the like? Or are they an eternal phenomenon based on the contact of man with man despite the interference of mechanization?

Transformation of the city

Those who hold that the present state of the metropolis is inhuman and cannot continue are preëminently right. The only

January 1, 1940. Borsodi's book, *This Ugly Civilization* (New York, 1929), is an attack upon the entire factory and industrial system. In his *Flight from the City* (New York, 1933) Borsodi tells of his experience with the self-sufficient small community, which performs all functions from canning food to making cloth.

question is whether this means the end of the city as such. Can the unworkable disorder of today's giant cities be eliminated without destroying the institution itself? Those who believe that the city has been a component of every succeeding human civilization see its existence menaced if its whole structure cannot be brought into harmony with the needs and requirements of present-day life. Clearly, small means are of no aid; they serve merely — and in this Frank Lloyd Wright was quite correct — to prolong its existence artificially without offering any real hope of recovery. Nothing positive can be accomplished by sowing the streets with more and more traffic lights or by clearing slums and simply erecting new buildings on the same sites. Destroying all the slums in existence will not make the city any less unworkable than it is today.

When Haussmann undertook the transformation of Paris, he slashed into the body of the city — as a contemporary expressed it — with saber strokes. Cleanly he drew the blade, cutting keen, straight thoroughfares through the congested districts, solving his traffic problems by single daring thrusts. In our period even more heroic operations are necessary. The first thing to do is to abolish the *rue corridor* with its rigid lines of buildings and its intermingling of traffic, pedestrians, and residences. The fundamental constitution of the contemporary city requires the restoration of liberty to all three — to traffic, to pedestrians, and to residential and industrial quarters. This can be accomplished only by separating them. Haussmann's endless streets belonged not only in their architectural features but also in their very conception to the artistic vision born of the Renaissance: optical perspective. Today we must deal with the city from a new aspect, dictated by the advent of the automobile, based on technical considerations, and belonging to the artistic vision born out of our period — space-time.

The residential structure   Cities have to be modeled around human needs. Human rights must be restored. From our architectural inheritance comes the tradition of placing large groups of buildings in natural surroundings, a tradition that extends from the Versailles of Louis XIV to the London squares. In Haussmann's Paris of 1850 functions of traffic and housing were intermingled, in contrast to the London squares, where it was wisely remembered that in his residence man needs quietude and the companionship of growing things. Contemporary architecture and city planning revive the old demand that men should not be separated from the great outdoors, from nature.

How is this to be accomplished? How can we realize the eternal law of urban life, that cities must be more than masses of stone, that they must be joined to the living soil, either by their small scale, as in the Middle Ages, or by an intermingling with greenery, as in the late baroque?

In our brief outline of the attitude of the contemporary town planner, we stated as a fundamental requirement that town planning must consider the prevailing conception of life and its expression through contemporary artistic means. An overriding unity unconsciously underlies all technical, engineering, social, and aesthetic problems.

THE NEW SCALE IN CITY PLANNING

The American Parkway in the Thirties

We found that in the nineteenth century construction was ahead of architecture in expressing, often unconsciously, the true constituent forces of the period. The engineer has often been nearer to future developments than the town planner, who has too frequently been concerned exclusively with the reorganization of the body of the city itself. The American parkways as they developed in the early nineteen twenties and thirties — coincident, by the way, with the flowering of contemporary architecture in Europe — revealed in their whole treatment the fact that they were one of the elements of the contemporary town, one of those born out of the vision of our period.

The definition of "parkway" has never been exactly established.[1] The "definite legal definition of a parkway," as

What is a parkway?

---

[1] Professor Hubbard commented on this confusion of definition in his *Parkways and Land Values* (Cambridge, 1937), vol. XI of Harvard City Planning Studies: "What is a parkway? How does it differ from a boulevard or an avenue, or a highway beautified with trees? These terms . . . have been so loosely applied and have crystallized by custom as

H. V. Hubbard pointed out, "is an attenuated park with a road through it. That is, a parkway is primarily for traffic, but mostly or exclusively for pleasure traffic." [2] In this sense the parkway is not new.[3] But considered in relation to the contemporary city, the modern parkway, as developed in America in the early thirties, is clearly different from that of the normal legal definition. As an element of the future town it restored the rights both of traffic and of the pedestrian; it harmonized the functions of both; in separating them definitely from one another, it gave full freedom to each. Out of this separation came the fundamental law of the parkway — that there must be unobstructed freedom of movement, a flow of traffic maintained evenly at all points without interruption or interference. To secure this steady flow, no direct crossing was permitted, nor had the owners of abutting property the right of direct access: at intersections the conflicting or converging lines were organized separately through the use of overpasses and cloverleaves of connecting roads. It is interesting to note that, whether by tradition or coincidence, the earliest parkways were created in the same area as the large parkway systems of the thirties — in New York. About 1858,[4] America's great landscape architect, the elder Olmsted, in his plan for Central Park in New York provided underpasses for vehicular cross traffic, cutting his roadbed through rock (*fig. 503*).

Parkway and terrain

Up to this point the parkway may be said to be identical with the European *autostrade*, the highway without grades. But it was not, like certain Continental highways, laid out for military purposes, driven rigidly through the country in danger-

---

the names of such different things in different places, that nothing but specific local knowledge will make it safe to apply to a 'parkway' in one town what has been learned about a parkway in any other town" (p. xii).

[2] *Ibid.*, p. xii.

[3] The green belt by which Haussmann intended in the sixties to surround Paris and to connect the Bois de Boulogne and the Bois de Vincennes, the boulevards linking the south park system in Chicago in the early nineties, the layout of park-like drives in Minneapolis by Professor Cleveland in 1883 — all these belong in the category of parkways. The device of passing one road under another to avoid the confusion of cross traffic, commonly applied to railways and even to overcrossing streets, was an established practice in the nineteenth century.

[4] *Third Annual Report of the Board of Commissioners of the Central Park* (New York, 1860).

824

ously straight lines. Nor was it, like a railway, built to provide the most direct and rapid transit. Instead it humanized the highway by carefully following and utilizing the terrain, rising and falling with the contours of the earth, merging completely into the landscape.[5] The road was laid into the countryside, grooved into it between gentle green slopes blending so naturally into the contiguous land that the eye cannot distinguish between what is nature and what the contribution of the landscape architect. In the middle, separating the opposing movements of traffic, were garden strips, widening and contracting as the course of the road required. Sometimes the traffic lanes flowed together in approaching a bridge, joined as they passed under, and then separated again, drawing apart to restore the landscaped spaced between them. Air views show the great sweep of these early highways, the beauty of their alignment, the graceful sequence of their curves, but only at the wheel of the automobile could one feel what they really meant — the liberation from unexpected light signals and cross traffic, and the freedom of uninterrupted forward motion, without the inhuman pressure of endlessly straight lines pushing one on to dangerous speeds. Confidence was given the driver by the way the road fitted into the earth between its sloping sides and by the dividing green and wooded strips which afforded protection against the hazards of contrary traffic. Yet he was held to a reasonable speed limit by the adaptation of the roadbed to the structure of the country, by its rise and fall, the smooth swing of its curves, its clear open runs before creeping under a cross highway or bridge. Freedom was given to both the driver and car. Riding up and down the long sweeping grades produced an exhilarating dual feeling, one of being connected with the soil and yet of hovering just above it, a feeling like nothing else so much as sliding swiftly on skis through untouched snow down the sides of high mountains (*figs.* **504, 505**).[6]

---

[5] It is probably no accident that several branches of the first complete parkway system in Westchester County (1913–25), just north of New York City, followed the courses of rivers. See Jay Downer, "Principles of Westchester's Parkway System," *Civil Engineering*, IV (1934), 85; Stanley W. Abbott, "Ten Years of the Westchester County Park System," *Parks and Recreation*, XVI (March 1933), 307 ff.

[6] The Merritt Parkway, continuing the Hutchinson River Parkway from New York through Connecticut, opened 1939, is a masterpiece of organic layout. The State High-

503. F. L. OLMSTED. Overpass in Central Park, New York City, 1858. *This early employment of the overpass by Olmsted, the great American landscape architect, had little influence. Only the traffic confusion of recent times has forced its adoption.*

In other sections the parkways, in technical contrast, crossed rivers and islands by great links of bridges with broad drives leading up to them (*fig.* **506**). These bridges, their mounting drives, and the modern sculpture of numberless single or triple cloverleaves proved that the possibilities of a great scale were inherent in our period. As with many other creations born out of the spirit of this age, the meaning and beauty of the parkway cannot be grasped from a single point of observation, as was possible when from a window of the château of Versailles the whole expanse of nature could be embraced in one view. It can be revealed only by movement, by going along in a steady flow as the rules of the traffic prescribe. The space-time feeling of our period can seldom be felt so keenly as when driving,

---

way Commissioner was authorized to undertake a layout of the route in 1931. Unfortunately, as in most other parkways, the architectonic detail used to embellish the overpasses is much below the high level of the scheme.

826

504. Merritt Parkway, Connecticut, 1939. *A masterpiece of organic layout exemplifying the arrangement of the parkway — adaptation of the roadbed to the structure of the country, careful alignment of traffic lanes, separation of vehicular from all pedestrian traffic, and overpasses at junctions.*

505. Merritt Park-
way, Connecticut,
with overpass.

506. Randall's Island, cloverleaf, with approach to Triborough Bridge, New York City, 1936. *Such bridges, with broad drives leading up to them and the modern sculpture of numberless single or triple cloverleaves, proved that the possibilities of a great scale were inherent in our period. Expressive of the space-time conception both in structure and handling of movement.*

507. "The Pretzel," intersection of Grand Central Parkway, Grand Central Parkway Extension, Union Turnpike, Interboro Parkway, and Queens Boulevard, New York City, 1936–37. *One of the most elaborate and highly organized solutions of the problem of division and crossing of arterial traffic in the thirties.*

508. West Side development, including Henry Hudson Parkway, 1934–37. *The parkways of the thirties could not penetrate the city, but could only go along its boundaries. Thus the Henry Hudson Parkway, leading down from the northern suburbs as a continuation of the Westchester park system, followed the Hudson River side of Manhattan almost to the tip of the island.*

the wheel under one's hand, up and down hills, beneath over-passes, up ramps, and over giant bridges.

It was Chicago that in the late eighties introduced the new potentialities in architecture. To New York in turn must go credit for the creation of the parkway. More than three hundred miles of parkways were constructed in the metropolitan area before World War II. At first they all ended at the outskirts of the city. One of them, the Henry Hudson Parkway (1934–37), a continuation of the Westchester park system, was extended for thirteen miles down the west side of Manhattan, almost to the tip of the island (*fig.* **508**). On the other side the Long Island system, of which the Northern State Parkway (1931–34) is the main artery, continued through open spaces, along and over rivers and through parks to the eastern entrances of Manhattan (*fig.* **507**).[7] From here the East River Drive runs beside the river to the southern tip of Manhattan where it meets the Hudson Parkway (*fig.* **508**). Thus, two parkways circumscribe the entire peninsula of Manhattan. These are the only routes that permit one to move faster than by using the subways from a point on the east or west of Manhattan to a point on the opposite side or from the Wall Street area to the southern tip of the peninsula. This great circumferential parkway with several new recreation centers and their linking highways constitutes the fore-runner of the city on a new scale.

But the problem of the city itself was scarcely touched. At that time the parkway ended where the massive body of the city began. It was not able to penetrate the city because the city remained an inflexible structure, tightly bound within itself and immovable. Robert Moses, then Commissioner of Parks of New York, who showed in his work for parks and parkways the enthusiasm and energy of Haussmann, pointed out that when his program was being carried through, "planners were producing one scheme after another for taking care of the traffic within the city limits," all of them to no effect. "Some were impractical, others over-elaborate, and others proposed such costly rights of way that they had to be tossed

The parkway and the city

---

[7] By the great Central Park extension (1937) and the Triborough Bridge (1936).

831

out of the window." [8] The parkway is not an isolated traffic lane independent of the organism of the city. It simply has a different scale from that of the existing city with its *rues corridors* and its rigid division into small blocks. Improvements in access to the city can accomplish very little. It is the actual structure of the city that must be changed.

Why can the parkway be called an element of the new form of the city? It fulfills a fundamental law of the nascent city: it separates the intermingled functions of vehicular and pedestrian traffic. At the same time it delivers a death blow to the notion that the highway is an isolated track running through the countryside but unrelated to it. It was conceived as part of its surroundings, as a part of nature. Perhaps most important of all, regulations govern all construction along its borders, limiting the number of gasoline service stations or restricting them to side roads, and prohibiting all residences, business houses, and factories.[9] Property owners have learned that their civil rights are not infringed when they are not allowed direct access to the parkway, and recognize its usefulness in a wider sense to them as well as to the community. Only when the same truth is recognized by the population at large will it be possible to attack the chaotic state of the cities. Finally, the parkway is the forerunner of the first necessity in the development of the future city: the abolition of the *rue corridor*. There is no longer any place for the city street with its heavy traffic running between rows of houses; it cannot possibly be permitted to persist. And the parkway was the first demonstration of a clear separation of traffic and housing. It looks ahead to the time when, after the necessary surgery has been performed, the artificially swollen city will be reduced to its normal size. The parkway was the forerunner of the urban highway which, properly designed and properly located, can weld the automobile and lines of traffic into the actual organism of the city, so that they are a constituent element of the whole. They can pass through the city as the early parkways

---

[8] Robert Moses, "The Comprehensive Parkway System of the New York Metropolitan Region," *Civil Engineering*, IX, no. 3 (March 1939), 160.

[9] The ribbon development of houses and factories erected along new highways, especially in England, has had a disastrous effect on the countryside.

passed through the landscape, as flexible and informal as the plan of the American home itself.

High-rise Buildings in Open Space

Both those who believe that the city will disappear and those who try to preserve it by changing its structure agree that the intricate disorder of the present day cannot continue, that man cannot live forever on asphalt. In Europe, the projects of those who were making creative efforts to find a solution for the problems of contemporary urbanism revealed a faith in the continued existence of the city. But they showed that, in order to achieve the placement of living quarters amidst greenery in densely populated districts, which is imperative, there must be a concentration of groups of high buildings standing in parks or, at any rate, in open spaces. Only by such means can the distances necessary for light and air between buildings be secured. Thus the basic principle on which these men worked was to condense large numbers of dwelling units into high buildings so as to gain free open spaces that could be used as gardens and recreation grounds.

There appeared in Germany during the early twenties proposals for slablike eight- to twelve-story residential blocks standing at considerable distances from one another, yet having at the same time a density of population equal to that of lower blocks placed close together on the same area.

Slablike housing units

This type (*fig.* **509**), which was first conceived by Walter Gropius and Marcel Breuer,[10] proved an important factor in changing the structure of the existing city. It involved breaking up the solid rows of houses along the street into units placed at right angles to the public road and parallel to each

---

[10] It was first introduced to the public in a scheme of Marcel Breuer's on the occasion of a competition in low-cost housing conducted by an architectural journal (*Bauwelt*, 1924). Such buildings became popular through the careful research and comparative studies of Walter Gropius, especially his work in the large competition for a low-cost housing project for three thousand dwellings at Haselhorst near Berlin in 1929. His entry showing three different projects — for low, medium, and high houses — won first prize, with its comparison by means of layouts and calculations of the respective effectiveness of each. He proved that the best conditions of light and economy of construction are achieved when the same number of dwelling units are built in twelve-story blocks rather than in two- or five-story units. Cf. Walter Gropius, "Das Ergebnis des Reichsforschungswettbewerbes," *Bauwelt*, 1929, no. 8, pp. 158 ff.

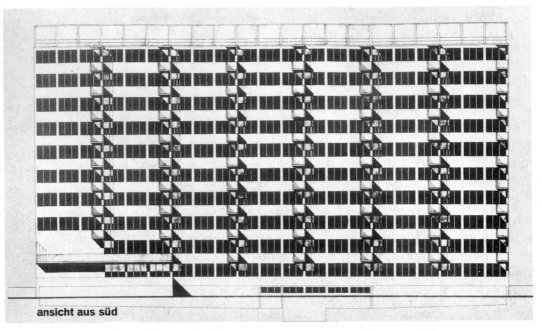

ansicht aus süd

509. WALTER GROPIUS. Slablike block units, 1930. *This type of slablike block was proposed in Germany about 1924 in parallel rows. These slablike blocks achieved more open space at the same density as the customary three- to five-story closely packed buildings.*

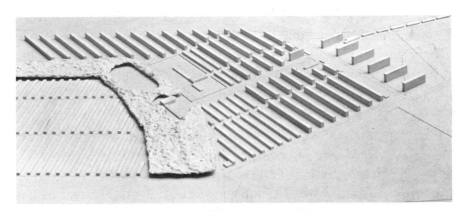

510. WALTER GROPIUS. Model for the settlement "Haselhorst," Berlin, 1929. *One of the studies in which slablike buildings were used in experimental form and to a limited extent. Such German layouts of the twenties had their effect on the extension plan of Amsterdam of 1934.*

other, facing onto landscaped areas between them. The first realization of this sort of slablike apartment house was built in Rotterdam about 1934, when the Dutch architect W. van Tijen built two blocks nine and ten stories high, for low-cost apartments of two and three rooms. These are located in

834

511. W. VAN TIJEN. The Plaslaan, Rotterdam, 1937–38. *Situated near parks and an artificial lake, this slablike unit was surrounded by a large amount of open space, foreshadowing the form of the city of the future.*

different parts of the outskirts of Rotterdam in districts where the existing buildings were not more than two or three stories high. The first one, the Bergpolder (1933–34), is a steel skeleton and was built in a densely populated district. The Plaslaan (1937–38; *fig.* **511**) was situated near parks and an artificial lake, surrounded by a large amount of open space, much as we imagine the town of the future could be. Such slablike buildings (*fig.* **510**) were also shown in the extension plan of Amsterdam (1934).

512. Apartment house at Highpoint, London, by the Tecton group, 1936–38. *To a certain extent similar to the slablike block unit, this building, on a luxurious scale, represents at the same time a return to the English tradition of placing large houses within extensive pleasure grounds.*

About the same time Le Corbusier used the slablike block for one of his most gracious and human town-planning schemes — the small colonial town of Nemours in Morocco, where the blocks are freely located on a slope. Similar slablike blocks were built on a luxurious scale in England at Highpoint, London (*fig.* **512**), by the Tecton group (1936–38). The Highpoint project recaptured the old English tradition of the house surrounded by and in immediate connection with a private park.

Such slender apartment buildings encountered great opposition at the time. The reason was that their form was expressive of a new space conception. For the first ten years, their light, open quality seemed very strange to a public accustomed to massive, earth-bound residential blocks.

Lacking the heavy massing of customary buildings, they appeared unsubstantial to people able to respond only to solid volumes. Thus they met an emotional resistance which was responsible for their slow acceptance. It is quite understandable that political opposition prevented Gropius' four high-rise slabs at Wannsee (Berlin, 1931) — with their roof terraces, restaurant, and terrace gardens on the seventh story — from being built.[11] If built, they would have shown the livability of this form of dwelling. In spirit they are the forerunners of Le Corbusier's Unité d'Habitation in Marseille (1947–52), though they lack his imaginative plastic handling.

When Gropius went to England in 1935 he worked with Maxwell Fry on an interesting project. An old estate belonging to the Duke of Gloucester, in the vicinity of Windsor Castle, was to be developed for housing. As usual, the preliminary plan had divided the estate up into small plots for single-family houses, quite destroying the "grand seigneur" aspect of the park-like landscape. As with the Wannsee project, Gropius' alternative high-rise project which preserved the free parkland remained on paper.[12]

By around 1960 the high-rise apartment slab had become accepted all over the world. In exceptional cases the tall buildings form a spatial relationship with lower blocks and thus become integrated into the urban scene. Their widespread distribution has meant however that they have usually been erected in isolation. Like the garden-city idea, they have led to a breaking up of the countryside.

Zigzag blocks (*maisons à redents*)

Another solution for the problem of highly populated districts — the use of zigzag blocks (*maisons à redents*) — was worked out by Le Corbusier. In 1922, his scheme for a "Contemporary City of 3,000,000" was exhibited in the Salon d'Automne in Paris. An adaptation of this project to Paris, the so-called Plan Voisin, was exhibited in his Pavillon de l'Esprit Nouveau in 1925, and the idea was further developed in his book *La Ville radieuse* (Bologne, 1935). In these schemes, *maisons à redents* — apartment slabs about a hundred and fifty feet high, with glass walls, and standing on pillars — zigzag across green areas. All schemes shared a clear separation

[11] See S. Giedion, *Gropius, Work and Teamwork* (New York, 1954), p. 81.
[12] *Ibid.*, pp. 206–207.

of traffic from pedestrians and of the residential sectors from the center of the city, which was composed of business offices in cruciform skyscrapers.

Le Corbusier designed schemes for the reorganization of cities all the way from Moscow and Stockholm to Rio de Janeiro, sometimes being magnificiently inspired by the site of a particular city — as, for example, Algiers, for which he proposed

513. Skyscraper apartment houses in open space near Lake Michigan, Chicago, c. 1929. *The baroque desire to surround the human dwelling with greenery is urgently desirable in our period. These high-rise apartments, built before the depression of 1929, have a view of Lake Michigan and are surrounded by open space.*

roads and buildings on a daring combination of levels utilizing the natural contours of the land.[13]   But always his thought swung back to Paris; again and again he returned to that city with radically new ideas.

Îlot insalubre, no. 6

In his project for Paris, 1937, Le Corbusier showed how the new scale of town planning could work in the reorganization of

[13] See pp. 159–161.

residential areas. Le Corbusier and Pierre Jeanneret concentrated on a section in the east of Paris in the Faubourg Saint-Antoine, designated by officials as an *îlot insalubre*,[14] an unhealthy area. Their plans united for the first time a solution of the traffic problem with a solution of slum clearance. Their scheme could have been realized immediately because it elim-

514. LE CORBUSIER. Skyscraper amidst greenery; project for Buenos Aires, 1929. *What in the case of the Chicago apartment houses was perhaps owing to local economic circumstances is here proposed as a principle.*

inated only the old street system within the boundaries of the section, replacing it by free-standing building groups of about the height of the early Chicago skyscrapers of the eighties.[15]

---

[14] Le Corbusier discussed his idea in *Des Canons des Munitions?* (Paris, 1938), pp. 67–82.

[15] Their height set the density of the district. The density Le Corbusier favored was about eight hundred persons per hectare, which seems rather too high for the city of the future. It may be observed that in most European projects of that period, especially in those of Le Corbusier, there persisted a belief that the existing level of population would remain the same, an optimism which is not in accordance with later observations.

These buildings were disposed freely in green spaces. Their long wings turned at angles according to the demands of the site and their orientation to the sun. At the end of our discussion of the London squares we referred to John Nash's unexecuted scheme of 1812 for the Regent's Park housing development, with its advancing and receding building groups which cannot be embraced in a single glance, as a premonition of twentieth-century developments. We had in mind projects like Le Corbusier's *îlot insalubre, no. 6* (*figs.* **515, 516**).

The large zigzag apartment buildings stand on pillars so that the ground is left free for the pedestrian. The open space rescued by this concentration of high buildings is used for landscaping, nurseries, cinemas, and sports. Even the twelve per cent of the ground covered by the buildings is available for recreation, and their flat roofs are also transformed into playgrounds and solaria such as he first realized magnificently in the Unité d'Habitation, 1947–52.

Unité
d'Habitation,
1947–52

The individual apartments are of various sizes. As in one of the rare projects of Frank Lloyd Wright for a skyscraper apartment building in 1929, they are duplex apartments, each two stories in height with an internal stairway. Room heights follow the old human scale of approximately seven feet which Le Corbusier found constant in rural houses all the way from Switzerland to the Greek islands. In other parts of the units the space is undivided, extending to its full height of fourteen feet.

The Unité d'Habitation is more complex than Le Corbusier's early project for the *îlot insalubre, no. 6*, since its apartments have a double orientation and are approached by a central corridor (*fig.* **326**). But the Unité still comes into the category of a high-rise slab. Since it was built, Le Corbusier erected a number of other unités such as those in Nantes-Résé, 1952–53, and Berlin, 1956–58. The sociologist P. Chombart de Lauwe has used the unités at Marseille and Nantes to make studies of the interrelationships between a building and its inhabitants.[16]

---

[16] P. Chombart de Lauwe, *Famille et Habitation*, 2 vols. (Paris, 1960).

515. LE CORBUSIER. Plan for "îlot insalubre, no. 6," 1937. *This large-scale slum clearance project, with its open spaces and concentration on slab-like buildings, was never realized.*

516. LE CORBUSIER. "Îlot insalubre, no. 6," zigzag apartment blocks.

Freedom for the Pedestrian

Though Le Corbusier's early projects for a city of high-rise apartment blocks may now appear unsympathetically uniform, two matters are highly significant. These tall slabs never grow along the borders of narrow city streets, but always stand as sculptural entities surrounded by free space. (It is possible that this freedom was in conscious opposition to the congested Manhattan skyscrapers of the same period.) The second important contribution of these early projects is the deliberate separation of pedestrian and vehicular traffic.

In his models of the Plan Voisin shown at the Paris Exhibition of 1925 and in his *îlot insalubre* plan for Paris of 1937, Le

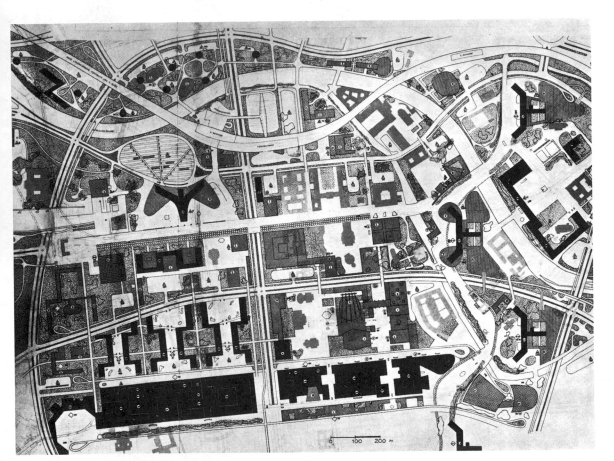

517. LE CORBUSIER. Entry in the international competition for replanning the center of Berlin, 1961. *The whole length of Unter den Linden becomes a pedestrian promenade.*

Corbusier showed all rapid traffic routes spanning the area on long viaducts. A quarter of a century later, in his entry for the international competition for the rebuilding of the center of Berlin, 1961, he also proposed an unhindered tract along the entire length of *Unter den Linden* (*fig.* **517**). But this time it was the pedestrians, not the cars, that were given the right of way under the open sky, undisturbed by the fumes and turmoil of rushing traffic.

Le Corbusier's 1937 dream of an elevated express highway running from east to west through Paris was too difficult to realize. This is not because it was too extreme. It was not so far ahead of its time as Haussmann's *percement* of the city; indeed, it was a parallel to Haussmann's projects, being simply an adjustment to later requirements. But circumstances had changed. It is a curious coincidence that the width of Le Corbusier's proposed expressway was the same (a hundred and twenty meters) as Haussmann's broadest street, the Avenue Foch, which, as we pointed out earlier, Haussmann had made three times as wide as the architect proposed. When Haussmann was transforming Paris, he once remarked bitterly that no architects were living to match the "temps nouveaux." In the Paris of almost a century later the situation seemed to be just the contrary: there were architects, but no directing officials equal as Haussmann was to the opportunities and needs of the period.

It rests with the instincts of the ruling class to select the right designers for major projects. Since the early nineteenth century the quality of those responsible for the government of cities and countries has sunk to dismally low levels. It is rare to find a man such as Claudius Petit who, when Minister of Reconstruction in France, was able to push through the erection of Le Corbusier's Unité d'Habitation in Marseille (which was conceived as an integrated element of a new residential quarter). When he became mayor of Firminy, in the center of France, Claudius Petit again called on Le Corbusier's services to prepare plans for the extension of this small industrial city. A stadium, with which Le Corbusier had wished to incorporate a youth hostel and a Unité d'Habitation had been built before Le Corbusier's death, the latter with parking for

three hundred cars, partly underground. Le Corbusier also designed a church (1963),[17] whose hyperparabolic form is reminiscent of the tower of the Chandigarh Parliament Building.

The use of a new and larger scale in town planning which would coincide with the scale of a parkway system is still an imperative necessity for the creation of the city of the future. This scale is closely connected with the space-time conception of our period.

The Civic Center: Rockefeller Center, 1931–39

The great cities of the future will contain civic centers, public places which, like the agora of Athens, the Roman forum, and the medieval cathedral square, will form a community focus and popular concourse. The first major civic center in which large buildings stand in a many-sided relationship to one another was the Rockefeller Center in New York, 1931–39, with later extensions (*fig.* **518**). The activities of the center are concentrated in high-rise buildings which express the highly differentiated requirements of contemporary social life. These buildings are freely disposed in space and enclose an open area, the Rockefeller Plaza, which is used as an ice-skating rink throughout the winter. Around 1940 such a development was a rare exception. When considering the new conceptions of our period we very seldom have the opportunity of referring to a completed building.

Rockefeller Center first consisted of a group of fourteen buildings in the heart of Manhattan between Fifth and Sixth avenues and Forty-eighth and Fifty-first streets. Its area of almost three city blocks (around twelve acres) was cut out from New York's checkerboard grid. Since then several other buildings have been added. All buildings are organized in

---

[17] See *Le Corbusier, Œuvre complète*, VII, 130–139.

←

518. Rockefeller Center, New York City, 1931–39. *Air view. The various buildings spread out like the vanes of a windmill from the highest (R.C.A. Building). Their slablike form represents a revolt against the former type of skyscraper which imitated a Gothic tower or an upward extension of the traditional four-story block, without considering new conditions and consequences.*

what was then a completely new and independent manner. It introduced for the first time into a contemporary city the larger scale of the parkways and other great engineering works. Its buildings were conceived as a coördinated unit and introduced new and original plastic elements.

Plastic elements of Rockefeller Center

First, let us consider what these plastic elements are and what they involve architecturally. In Chicago the office buildings of the eighties, with their fifteen to twenty stories, had dignity, strength, and scale. They were so organized as to provide light everywhere, often in an open plan with a U-shaped inner court.[18] The early New York skyscrapers had none of these qualities. They lacked scale, dignity, and strength, becoming simply towers rising to extreme heights. Louis Sullivan, who created some cf the purest examples of what should have been followed in later developments, pointed out that "the architecture of lower New York became hopelessly degraded in its pessimistic denial of our art and our civilization." Where the New York skyscrapers went astray was in the exaggerated use of high towers with an intricate mixture of pseudo-historical reminiscences and a ruthless disregard of their immediate surroundings, as well as of their effect on the entire structure of the city.

After passage of the New York zoning law of 1916, the chaotic state of building development was somewhat reduced by the use of the setback and the application of other zoning regulations, but fundamentally no real order was achieved until an entirely new architectonic form started to be explored: a structure adapted to the requirements of unusual height and its internal consequences. This change did not come about until nearly four decades after the birth of the skyscraper. How this new form developed step by step, in various cities, cannot be outlined here.[19] We can only note the emergence of the new form of the skyscraper in the R.C.A. Building of

---

[18] Cf. the ground plan of the Marquette Building (1891), fig. 230.

[19] Steps on the way to this overthrow of the tyranny of the tower, with its medieval echoes, are, for example, the Civic Opera House in Chicago (1928–29), by Graham, Probst, and White, three slablike wings, yet without any new spatial relationships; and the Daily News Building in Chicago, by Holabird and Root (1929), with its blunt, obtuse т-shaped plan in the upper stories.

846

519. The slablike skyscraper: R.C.A. Building, Rockefeller Center, New York, 1931–32. *Seventy stories and 850 feet high, this slab is based on the principle of 27 feet of lighting depth to give optimum working conditions around a core containing the elevators and service space.*

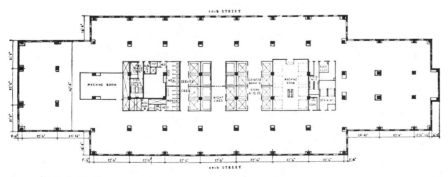

520. R.C.A. Building, Rockefeller Center. *Floor plan.*

1931–32 (*fig.* **519**), whose immediate forerunner was Raymond Hood's Daily Mail Building in New York, 1930.

"Its huge, broad, flat north and south fronts, its almost unbroken mass and its thinness," according to the *New York City Guide* of 1939, are the features that impelled observers to nickname it 'the Slab.'" [20]   This slab stands on its site like an immense upturned rectangle — a form impossible of realization in any other period.   The shape grew naturally from the purely technical and economic considerations of how to give normal lighting to every spot of usable space.   Raymond Hood explained the design thus: "Grouped in the center are the elevators, and the service facilities, and surrounding them on each floor we have stretched the 27 ft. of lighted space that experience has proved is the maximum to be allowed to provide adequate light and air to all parts of the building." [21]   The result — an immense slab born out of mathematical calculations for utilizing ground and space to the best advantage — is a form proper to our age.   It employs the same basic element as that used by a cubist painter in his hovering planes or by an engineer like Maillart in building bridges out of concrete slabs, all achieving solutions which would not have been possible with other means.   The skyscraper slab form is as significant and expressive for its period as the monolithic obelisk of Egypt and the Gothic cathedral tower were for their periods.

The walls   The walls of the R.C.A. Building rise up unbroken eight hundred and fifty feet.   In such a dimension the architectural form, when it is not spoiled by details inappropriate to the large scale, is not of decisive importance.   Its strength and power are expressed by the curtain walls, whose windows are reduced to mere grooves like ribbing in the texture of a fabric.

Even the staggered setbacks of the curtain walls were at least in part justified, as Hood explained, by practical considerations.   "We have," he said, "carried the principle [of providing light and air to all parts of the building] to its logical conclu-

---

[20] Federal Writers' Project, *New York City Guide* (New York, 1939), p. 336.

[21] Raymond Hood, "The Design of Rockefeller City," *Architectural Forum*, January 1932, p. 5.   Rockefeller Center was executed by three architectural firms: Reinhard & Hofmeister; Corbett, Harrison and MacMurray; Hood and Fouilloux.

848

sion. As each elevator shaft ended we cut the building back to maintain the same 27 feet from the core of the building to the exterior walls." [22] What was startling to the human mind was the idea that planes quite usual in the horizontal sense should be pulled into the vertical. It can be perceived that when great height is combined with the thinness of the structure, a certain feeling of hovering, of suspension, emanates from the surfaces — and, as a matter of fact, both the immense surfaces of the curtain walls and the whole skeleton move imperceptibly but flexibly in the wind.

Nothing new or significant can be observed in looking over a map of the site. The ground plan reveals nothing. The street gridiron runs through it, as everywhere else in the city. Even the first designs for grouping the buildings show no special approach; they were entirely conventional. Among the numerous preliminary studies made by different firms, one still shows an attempt to build up a sort of ideal pyramid composed of the five main buildings; in spatial terms this would have meant a centralized unit. However, the final project, even from the beginning, must have appeared somewhat aggressive and intriguing to eyes accustomed to former conceptions.[23] A celebrated designer of American Gothic churches attacked the scheme as being a conglomerate of "sprouting amorphous and cubicular mushrooms." Is not this curiously reminiscent of the protest of Charles Garnier, the builder of the Opéra in Paris, against the erection of the Eiffel Tower for the exhibition in 1889, in his conviction that this huge, hideous iron structure would destroy the skyline of Paris forever?

It is apparent that it was not through architectonic vision but through an effort to adjust design to changing necessities that the development gradually took its final shape — from the module of twenty-seven feet as optimum for well-lighted rooms to the organization of the volumes around the plazas,

---

[22] *Architectural Forum*, January 1932, p. 5.

[23] The scheme, whose architectural shape is far from being revolutionary, stirred up public opinion nevertheless. The newspaper columns of the *Herald-Tribune* and the *Times* were filled with discussions in the form both of editorials and of letters from readers. *Pencil Points* brought out an article with the headline, "The Functionalist Design for Radio City Has Aroused Public Indignation" (May 1931).

which for the first time expressed open planning on the new scale — which accomplished for town planning what the small Chicago houses of Frank Lloyd Wright in the nineties had accomplished for the free and open planning of the single house.[24]

The original fourteen buildings of Rockefeller Center are more closely grouped toward Sixth Avenue. Here is Radio City, with its enormous Music Hall, its Center Theater, and its slablike seventy-story R.C.A. Building, which contains the broadcasting studios. To the east, toward Fifth Avenue, the buildings are not so densely massed. Placed there are the lowest of the structures, the comparatively small six-story buildings dedicated to foreign nations. They stand with their narrow fronts lined up on the avenue, so that coming along the street from the north one gets the effect of a series of truncated structures behind which rise the higher units of the center. Standing a bit to one side is the forty-one-story International Building; and in the background, clearly separated from the lower buildings by the open space of the Plaza, rises the narrow slab of the R.C.A. Building. As one proceeds south, different dimensions in heights and depths are perceived, a succession of impressions like visual impulses recorded in time — the depth of the Plaza, the soaring reach of the R.C.A. Building, the narrow streets running through, and fragmentary glimpses of the broad side of another thirty-six-story building.

The actual arrangement and disposition of the buildings can be seen and grasped only from the air. An air-view picture reveals that the various high buildings are spread out in an open arrangement from the highest, the R.C.A. Building, like the vanes of a windmill, the different volumes so placed that their shadows fall as little as possible upon one another, some of them parallel to their neighbors, others at right angles. This is all quite rational, but the moment one begins moving in the midst of the buildings through Rockefeller Plaza, where the

---

[24] We cannot enter here into the history of Rockefeller Center, which started with the search of the Metropolitan Opera for a new home and which because of the depression of 1929 was changed into a radio and theatrical city-within-a-city. See Frederick Lewis Allen, "Radio City: Cultural Center?" *Harper's Magazine*, April 1932, and "Look at Rockefeller Center," *Harper's Magazine*, October 1938.

850

521. The towers of Asinelli and Garisenda, Bologna, thirteenth century. *These leaning towers of two noble families of Bologna are private patrician fortresses which though of great height can be embraced in a single view.*

three largest structures rise in different directions and to different heights, one becomes conscious of new and unaccustomed interrelations between them. They cannot be grasped from any single position or embraced in any single view. There becomes apparent a many-sidedness in these simple and enormous slabs which makes it impossible to bind them rationally together. Through the free orientation of the thirty-six-story slab to the south (completed in 1938), a decisive force of planes is brought into play, separated by air but combined unconsciously by the observing human eye. From these well-calculated masses one becomes aware of a new fantastic element inherent in the space-time conception of our period. The interrelations which the eye achieves between the different planes give their clearly circumscribed volumes an extraordinary new effect, somewhat like that of a rotating sphere of mirrored facets in a ballroom when the facets reflect whirling spots of light in all directions and in every dimension.

Such a great building complex presupposes not the single point of view of the Renaissance but the many-sided approach of

Space-Time and Rockefeller Center

851

522. Rockefeller Center. *Photomontage. Expressions of the new urban scale like Rocke-feller Center are forcefully conceived in space-time and cannot be embraced in a single view. To obtain a feeling for their interrelations the eye must function as in the high-speed photo-graphs of Edgerton.*

our own age. The difference can be indicated by comparing it with such thirteenth-century structures as the leaning towers of the two noble families of Asinelli and Garisenda in Bologna (*fig.* **521**). These private patrician fortresses rise magnificently into the sky, but they can be embraced at a single glance, in a single view.   There is no uncertainty in the observer concerning their relation to each other.   On the other hand, a view restricted to its central axis reveals none of the essential character of an organism like Rockefeller Center.   It possesses symmetries which are senseless in reference to the aesthetic significance of the whole.   The complex must be comprehended in terms of space and time analogous to what has been achieved in modern scientific research as well as in modern painting.

In Edgerton's stroboscopic studies, in which motion can be fixed and analyzed in arrested fractions of 1/100,000 of a second, a complete movement is shown separated into its successive components (*fig.* **523**).   At Rockefeller Center the human eye must function similarly (*fig.* **522**); it has to pick up each individual view singly and relate it to all others, combining them into a time sequence.   Only thus are we able to understand its grand play of volumes and surfaces and perceive its many-sided significance.

523.   EDGERTON. Speed photograph of golf stroke. *In Edgerton's stroboscopic studies in which motions can be fixed and analyzed in arrested fractions of 1/100,000 of a second, a whole movement is separated into its successive components, making possible comprehension in both space and time.*

Rockefeller Center houses many different activities. Leisure and entertainment, which were the initial motive in projecting the Center, are provided in Radio City, with its music hall, theaters, broadcasting studios, and night clubs; international trade is represented in the buildings on Fifth Avenue; journalism in the headquarters of the Associated Press, which gives its name to one of the buildings, as well as in the Time and Life Building. In addition there are a variety of other offices and establishments, an underground shopping center, and a six-story garage built into one of the structures (1939) with three of its stories below street level.

Obviously it can be objected that such a commercial composition does not constitute a civic center. It is a private enterprise arising from private initiative and carried out as a private speculation, based, as Raymond Hood said, on pure calculation of cost and return. What might have been a new home for the opera was changed by force of economic circumstances into the largest music hall in the world, where every night the world's longest line of shapely and well-trained girls' legs is on display. It may also be pointed out that, standing amid the chaos of midtown New York, Rockefeller Center is not surrounded by greenery but instead is confined by streets and traffic. Moreover, the Center dominates, indeed tyrannizes over, the entire vicinity — Fifth Avenue, the neighboring churches, all the surrounding buildings.

How then does it differ from the downtown district — from Wall Street and lower Broadway, which Louis Sullivan regarded as a center of infection, as "a plague spot of American architecture"?

The difference lies in one thing only: in the new scale of city planning inherent in Rockefeller Center, which relates to the scale of modern bridges and parkways.

When Rockefeller Center was projected, there was objection on the part of eminent critics to the increased congestion which would inevitably result from its location in the midst of the city. Proposals were therefore made to widen the street fifteen feet. This would have helped very little. What really needs to be changed is the entire structure of the city. The parkways and Rockefeller Center are small beginnings, isolated new growths in the immense body of New York, like new shoots on an old tree.

But it must not be forgotten that tiny new branches properly tended can change the whole shape and structure of a mature tree. Rockefeller Center was in advance of its period in the urban scale. What must change is not the Center but New York itself. Only when the whole city has adopted the new scale of its bridges and parkways will its civic centers stand amidst greenery. Until then Rockefeller Center will stand as a reminder that the structure of the city must be transformed, not just in the interest of single individuals but in the interest of the community as a whole.

New York combines intensive mechanization below and above ground, blighted areas directly in the shadow of the sky-scrapers of Manhattan, extreme fluctuations in the value of land, and rapid and disrupting changes in population. It has also a street system, completely inappropriate in scale, which cuts off the organic development of the city like an iron ring around a tree. The tree grows larger and larger, and the ring remains rigid and inflexible. It is no occasion for surprise when the city, like the tree, becomes completely deformed under these conditions. It may even be that the iron ring must burst or the tree die.

Yet with all these disadvantages New York in the thirties had the initiative to cope with some of the problems that have to be solved, to create leisure centers for the masses, parkway systems, and the skeleton of a civic center on an appropriate scale.

The hopeful upswing of the spirit of New York developers of the thirties in placing different volumes together in a spatial relationship is without equal in recent times and cannot there-fore be lightly brushed aside.

The United Nations building (1947) in its final form can only be considered a retrograde step. The Lincoln Center — that great cultural center of the sixties, with theater, opera house, concert hall, and several related institutions — is unfortunately a disappointing retreat to the customs of the late nineteenth century.

The Rockefeller Center's pioneering placement of different volumes in a new spatial relationship has remained unique. When, in the early sixties, there was a problem of massing together an even larger number of offices or apartments than before, these were, whenever possible, compressed into a single gigantic structure or into two isolated and exaggeratedly tall identical towers, such as the International Trade Center in New York. That complex is more akin to the sort of "exhibition architecture" that usually disappears at the end of six months.

Possibilites for the future and the danger of disaster are inextricably interwoven in the structure of New York, but its fundamental transformation will never be accomplished by the town planner alone. The contemporary city, as the most visible symbol of human interrelations, can only be built when the methods of human administration cease to be opposed to the developments in science and art which make men aware of undiscovered spheres.

CHANGING NOTIONS OF THE CITY

City and State

It is impossible to assess the problem of the contemporary city without briefly examining the changes in the structure of the city throughout history.

The notion of a relationship between city and state goes back to the first Mesopotamian city-states of the fourth and third millennia B.C. These were interdependent communities under priestly rule. The notion of the *polis* — the community of free men — arose during the last centuries B.C.; first in Ionia, then on the Greek mainland. With the *polis* came the agora, the first center for forming democratic public opinion. Here began the inseparable unity of city and state.

The city of Rome gave its name to the first world empire. The entire Roman empire consisted of a network of cities old and new.

The "free cities" of the Middle Ages, in contrast to those of Greece, were based on the rise of small, handicraft industries. The communal government of the city was extended to cover nearby food-producing villages. Thus in the Middle Ages the name of a city was often used for the region around it. Even today the names of Bern, Freiburg, Lucerne, and Zurich are used both for the cities and their surrounding areas — the cantons.

In the Renaissance the highest cultural development occurred in individualistic Italian city-states.

Surprisingly, the absolutism of the eighteenth century prepared the scene for what happened in the nineteenth century: the political regression of the city. The French Revolution went one step further; it did away with the guilds in the "Proclamation de la liberté du travail" (1791).

If we seek for the roots of our present difficulties, we find them in the nineteenth century. It was then that production for the international market weakened the original concept of the city, which had been based mainly on economic independence. However, the organic entity of the city had not yet been burst asunder by the automobile. Nor had incoming floods of people created mammoth cities.

The City: No Longer an Enclosed Organism

In the history of architecture, city planning — urban design — has been a late comer in every period. Usually several centuries were needed before a period became ripe enough to draw up city plans. City planning blossoms when the way of life of a period has become so self-evident that it can be immediately translated into plans.

The present situation is no exception to this rule. We are now neither at the peak nor near the end of our period. We stand at the beginning of the formation of a new tradition.

This moment of transition forces us into a new urbanistic organization on a scale without parallel in history.

Another fact characterizes the present situation: Europe is no longer the sole center of architectural development. The limits extend ever wider and wider. The problems of urbanization have become global and are not halted by any system of government. We are faced with a continued expansion of giant cities and a reduced rural population.

The notion of the city as a self-sufficient organism — as it had remained throughout history — has lost its validity. The simple solutions of earlier periods no longer apply to the complicated living requirements and related phenomena of contemporary urban life. Differentiation of occupations, industrial organization, and traffic demand a complex interrelationship of functions and a great increase of scale.

Far-reaching interrelations that have not as yet been successfully crystallized in plans have disrupted the traditional notion of the city. Continuous change and continuously extended frontiers destroy independent units and make the former terms — village, city, metropolis — useless. In 1953, at the CIAM congress in Aix-en-Provence, Le Corbusier proposed in place of these inadequate terms the designation: human agglomeration.

The structure of the urban organism has been changed more radically in recent years than ever before. What has happened since World War II was unforeseeable. Analogies with the end of World War I suggested the advent of unemployment, hunger, and serious crises. The opposite occurred: prosperity, shortage of workers, rising standards of living, together with a precipitant population increase. And in defiance of every logical anticipation the defeated countries — Japan and West Germany — made astonishing post-war advances.

Compared with the over ten million population agglomerations of New York, London, and Tokyo, Paris (with its suburbs) has had a relatively small increase. But the French provinces continually lose population to Paris. Like Stockholm in Sweden, Paris absorbs France even though the government tries to bring new life to the larger provincial cities and their regions and to stem the draining away of their population by granting them special privileges.

The unwieldy accumulation of population in one city in the heart of Europe — Paris — has led to a serious impoverishment of the countryside. This problem is far more serious in the Far East.

We have seen how one attempt after another was made to humanize the chaotic nineteenth-century metropolis, and how each proved disappointing: the garden city, the linear city, satellite cities, and, recently, the "new towns" — an experiment that has by no means come to an end. Great Britain, using government assistance, has since 1945 built twenty new towns at various distances from a major city. Sweden, Canada, Germany, France, and the Soviet Union have also founded new towns for widely varying numbers of inhabitants.

America was the slowest to follow this development. In the New Deal period of the thirties three "green belt cities" were started. There was also the unique experiment in Radburn, New Jersey (1929), where a new development was built in which the pedestrian was successfully isolated from vehicular traffic. It remained, at that time, an isolated experiment. However, by 1964 the United States had several new towns in the planning stages, each accommodating from 35,000 to 250,000 inhabitants.

The attempt to establish a satisfactory, intimate human environment by splitting up an area into "neighborhood units" for 2,000 to 5,000 people was not particularly successful. These units were said to be too small in scale for the purposes of redeveloping the city. A neighborhood unit did not meet the needs of the contemporary differentiated society. Placing an elementary school in the center of the unit did not necessarily correspond to the requirements of all inhabitants.

Continuity and Change

In human nature the tendency to change and the desire for continuity live side by side. In *The Beginnings of Art* (*The*

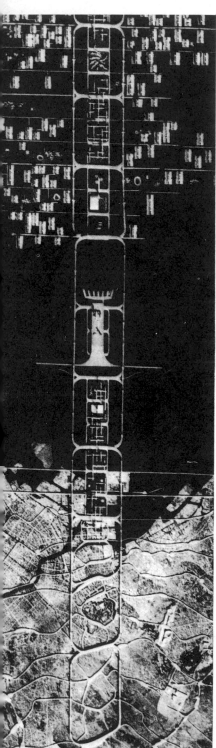

525. KENZO TANGE. Detail of the project for building over Tokyo Bay. *This project shows a combination of megastructure and group form. The megastructure consists of a continuous system of traffic lanes and other services on different levels; the group forms of large office buildings, often curved, sometimes boldly bridge the megastructure.*

←

524. KENZO TANGE. Project for building over Tokyo Bay, 1960. *The city would be extended lineally over the shallow bay. The huge megastructure of the central traffic system would be completed in four five-year plans.*

Eternal Present, vol. I), I have posed this problem in relation to art: What has been driven back into the unconscious in human nature and what must be reawakened for man to recover his inner equilibrium?

The problem is the same with the human habitat. Like life itself, it exists in a tension between continuity and change, one or the other of which is always in the foreground. Today relentless demands for change persist. These are symptoms that often occur during periods of transition.

All urban planning must become dynamic in consequence of this unprecedented flood of population to the metropolitan cities. The world population today is growing at a rate of about two per cent while the urban population grows at four per cent or more. We stand helpless in the face of this situation; the United Nations can do little more than place the "catastrophic perspective of the development" before the eyes of the world. It is now clear to everyone that this unparalleled population growth and the traffic chaos within the city organism indicate a completely different way of life and demand radical changes.

Proposals to handle the situation pile up endlessly — cities under the ground, cities hovering above the ground on steel scaffolding — proposals that would schematize the complex

526. FUMIHIKO MAKI. Project for rebuilding a section of Tokyo, 1964. *The principle that governs this, and many other projects of the youngest generation of architects, is the move away from self-contained individual buildings to a group form, in which the relation of the buildings to each other is stronger than any single structure. This example deals with a complex of department stores, other shops, and apartment houses connected with wide pedestrian ways.*

organism of the city more drastically even than the traditional two-dimensional checkerboard pattern. What is needed is a completely new attitude toward the structure of the city. The contemporary planner must be fully aware that he must simultaneously satisfy the most heterogeneous needs and create a "dynamic field" in which these forces are related to one another. In place of the rigid master plan proposed in the early years of the century a flexible "master program" is now being put forward, one that allows for changes and that leaves open-ended possibilities for the future. An example is the plan for the Free University in West Berlin by Candilis, Josic, and Woods, which creates only a framework and everywhere leaves openings for future developments.

At this time it is possible only to indicate how the demands for change can be met. All possibilities revolve around and penetrate one another. It is too early for a systematic presentation. Only an encompassing trend in which the whole development is involved can be given a name: open planning. The future will show in what forms this open planning can actually be realized; but we have already some fragmentary glimpses.

Spatial
organization

Urban planning has begun to move from two-dimensional to three-dimensional planning. By two-dimensional planning we mean the conception of the city built on a single level. The site of the city may be uneven — Rome, city of the seven hills, Greek and Italian hill towns — but in every case the city extended along the ground. Now two-dimensional planning gives place to three-dimensional. Jørn Utzon's emphasis on the relations of horizontal levels (*fig.* **428**) gives a hint in this direction. Urbanism has become the organization of horizontal levels below and above the ground.

Traffic as
a constituent
element of
city structure

The dynamism of traffic and the dynamism of change have unavoidably become as much a part of urban planning as the facts of nature. They must be integrated into the contemporary urban plan in a positive form-creating sense. History presents few prototypes of or analogies to this situation. It is the task of the most recent generation to solve the problem of reconciling simultaneous and conflicting functions. Two no-

862

tions start to emerge in the vocabulary of this generation: "megastructure" and "group form."

The megastructure consists of a large-scale structural framework encompassing many needs and functions. One of the first such megastructures was Kenzo Tange's project for building over the bay of Tokyo (*figs.* **524, 525**), whose different horizontal levels allow for an unhindered flow of traffic.[1]

Group form consists of the relations between buildings. The importance of the individual building is subordinated to the importance of the collective group form (*fig.* **526**). This is the description of the notion given by one of the word-makers of this generation — Fumihiko Maki, a Japanese architect who has studied at Harvard.[2] Maki has developed several projects for the renewal of sections of Tokyo. Kenzo Tange's project for building over Tokyo Bay combined both notions: group form and megastructure.

The Individual and Collective Spheres

The twin notions of individual liberty and communal order are inherent in every democracy. The right of the individual and the right of the community confront each other.

The balance between them has not yet been found. But a definite position has been taken by J. B. Bakema, an architect and planner in Rotterdam: "We must build individually for the anonymous client." With the Dutch CIAM group OPBOUW, he produced a series of projects for the Alexander Polder area near Rotterdam in the early fifties.[3] This settlement for 30,000 people was designed to give each inhabitant a feeling of individual existence.

In the simplest but most convincing manner, Jørn Utzon expressed the relations of the individual and collective spheres in

---

[1] For further details see *The Japan Architect*, April 1961; and Robin Boyd, *Kenzo Tange* (New York, 1962).

[2] Fumihiko Maki, *Investigations in Collective Form* (St. Louis: Washington University Press, 1964). The author and his friends present the notion in the essays, "Collective Form: Three Paradigms" and "Linkage in Collective Form."

[3] Illustrated in S. Giedion, *Architecture, You and Me* (Harvard University Press, 1958).

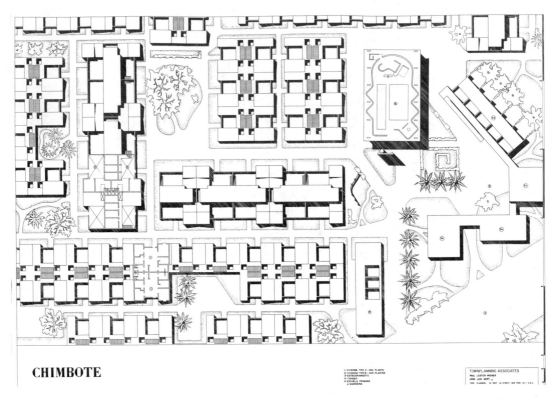

CHIMBOTE

527. J. L. SERT and P. L. WIENER. Project for a new mining town at Chimbote, Peru, 1949. *Various modest house types, each house with its small private sphere (patio), are organized within a wider public realm. The individual and the collective spheres are each given equal weight.*

his Danish housing settlement at Fredensborg, 1962 (*figs. 442–444*).

Definition of the spheres of the individual and the community is particularly important in the so-called developing countries, whose living standards are far below those of the western world. Even in new plans, the people are frequently housed in endless, identical, row-houses. J. L. Sert and P. L. Wiener's 1949 plan for Chimbote (a mining town in Peru on the Pacific Ocean) made a radical break with this practice. It included several very simple house types with individual patios, which are so organized that they everywhere frame small plaza-like spaces. Intimate private life and community life form an interlocking unity (*fig. 527*).

University dormitories are another area in which we can observe the interlocking of the individual and collective spheres. They have undergone great changes in type — from the early monastic assemblies of identical rooms within a single building to complex components of urban space. Aalto's dormitory for graduate students at the Massachusetts Institute of Technology (1947–49), with its undulating brick façade and varied layouts of the bedroom and study units, was still contained within one encompassing structure (*fig.* **397**). The Harkness Graduate Center by Walter Gropius (The Architects' Collaborative), 1949–50, had already spread out in a series of wings connected by passageways and opening directly to the outdoors (*fig.* **304**).

José Luis Sert's dormitories for married students at Harvard University, Peabody Terrace, 1964, marked a third step by being deliberately planned, from the start, to become an integral part of the city of Cambridge as soon as the slums which partly surrounded them were cleared. Sert's buildings form a strong contrast to the nearby Georgian style dormitories along the Charles River, whose high walls turn their backs upon the city while their open courts face the river.

Peabody Terrace, 1964

Peabody Terrace consists of a cluster of three high-rise buildings individually placed in different positions. They are combined with lower buildings of different heights, L-shaped or in single wings, so that open spaces of manifold forms can develop between them (*fig.* **528**). One of the difficulties of creating urbanistic groupings of residential buildings today is that we have no good intermediary between a three- or four-story walk-up and a ten-story elevator building. In this project the elevators of the high-rise towers fulfil a double function: they serve both the high-rise towers and the seven-story buildings, to which they are connected by bridges (*fig.* **530**). In this way an intermediate height structure is incorporated in the design without recourse to the inhuman five-story walk-up.

By this grouping of buildings of different heights the danger of an inhuman accumulation of housing for 1500 people on a rather limited site has been overcome, and only a third of the area is covered by buildings. Relations with the outside world

528. J. L. SERT. Peabody Terrace on the Charles River, 1964. *Air view showing differentiated building types. In the foreground is the parking garage, approached from Putnam Street.*

529. Peabody Terrace, 1964. *Plan. Memorial Drive, beside the Charles River, in the foreground and Putnam Avenue to the rear.*

530. Peabody Terrace, 1964. *Section through a twenty-one-story tower, showing by hatching the floors served by the elevator and the bridges to the adjacent seven-story block.*

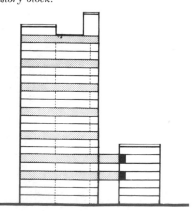

531. Peabody Terrace, 1964. *The central plaza.*

are carefully considered.   From Putnam Avenue one sees first
a row of three-story houses, similar in scale to the houses of
the surrounding area.   At right angles to these houses is
another low building, which steps up to form part of an L-
shaped apartment block connected to the central tower.
These buildings frame a green area with a tree planted in the
middle, whose fourth side is the wall of a garage for 350 cars
and a pedestrian promenade, with a double row of trees, which
runs right across the whole complex to the Memorial Drive
along the Charles River (*fig.* **528**).

Facing the river another L-shaped structure, freely related to
row-house units, forms a rectangular green space with a fountain, separated from the noisy Memorial Drive by a tall green

hedge which, by a happy chance, had existed previously and was carefully retained (*fig.* **529**).

Between these two groupings is a kind of central plaza (*fig.* **531**) around which all community functions take place, thus bringing this assembly of different dwelling units into a small but lively urban neighborhood.

Great care has been taken to define spaces at ground level, and yet not to create fully enclosed areas. Everywhere there are openings between or through buildings. The frequently criticized uniformity of contemporary residential buildings has been happily avoided. A unified complex has been created that is carefully calculated to allow for as much personal freedom and visual diversity as possible.

Sert's varied treatment of the façades shows one of the means of revitalizing the wall: breaking its uniform structure. This treatment has been employed ever since it first appeared in Le Corbusier's large unbuilt skyscraper for Algiers, 1931 (*fig.* **85**). It still seems strange to many people who have become accustomed to seeing walls only as massive volumes or glass curtains. The variations in the Peabody Terrace façades are never arbitrary. They follow rationally from the different orientations or aspects of the rooms — for example, the western ones, which face the Charles River, need careful protection from the sultry afternoon sun in summer.

Signs of Change and of Constancy

The demands placed on the city planner by continuous changes have given rise to a fanatical desire to design a city in which possibilities of change are woven into the plan and earlier buildings can remain when alterations or additions become necessary.

The use of change as a creative element is a problem that occupies several forward-thinking schools. For example, in the spring of 1964 the Master's Class in Urban Design at Harvard University (under F. Maki, J. Soltan, and J. Tyrwhitt) were set the problem: How can a new city for 50,000 people be built between Baltimore and Washington in such a way that its initial community structure will not be destroyed by its subsequent growth?

In the early stages of working toward a determined goal, one side of the problem is almost always overemphasized. In the case of group form, the accent has been laid on relations between individual buildings and their functions. Archaeologists speak of "group design" to describe the relation of the temples of the Acropolis of Athens to one another. Even the Parthenon is part of a group design, without this in any way weakening the perfection of its individual form. Strongly pronounced or complex relations between buildings do not mean that they must assume the insistent monumentality of buildings of the preceding century.

Beside frenzied change — child of our age — stands that other component of human nature: the desire for constancy. This shows itself behind the mask of growing demands for urban centers. The Capitol at Chandigarh (*fig.* **VII**), the Place of the Three Powers at Brasilia (*figs.* **III, IV**) are both no longer in the heart of the city, but at its head. The never-built Back Bay Center for Boston (*fig.* **306**), the community center of the little town of Seinäjoki (*fig.* **422**), and the large civic center for Helsinki (*fig.* **425**) are examples of countless efforts to design commercial centers so that they can substitute for the lacking community centers of our cities.

PART **X** IN CONCLUSION

All we have been able to do in this book is to select some
fragments that, pieced together, may give an image of our
period. Perhaps, at the present stage of our development, all
that is possible is to discern here and there at isolated points
what is going on under the surface. Certainly to have aspired
to any exhaustive or comprehensive treatment would have
been futile. The time for that is not yet ripe.

We have restricted our observations to architecture and its
interrelations. We have pointed out why architecture reflects
the inner tendencies of the time and therefore may properly
serve as a general index. We have regarded architecture as a
finite organism, isolating it, just as the scientist isolates certain phenomena to determine their interior processes. We have
not been interested in establishing any fixed or permanent
laws of architecture. Nor have we sought to chart closed
cycles of rise and fall or to determine whether such cycles repeat themselves in different cultures.

What has interested us throughout the periods we have observed has been the growth and change in the architectonic
organism and, especially, the development of those constituent
facts which form the substance of its true history. Only by
isolating architecture as an organism in itself, and by obtaining
in consequence understanding of its nature and growth, have
we been able to seek out and fix its relations to other and
cognate activities.

Before turning to other aspects, a basic question must be
posed: the relations between geometric and organic form —
between the rational and the irrational. Ever since Descartes,
the principle of rationality has held the upper hand. Descartes
unlocked the door to mechanization, even though it remained
closed for another century. The mechanization of the entire
world can be traced back to his thinking.

The world has now become aware of the impasse to which we
have been led through an overemphasis on purely rational
thought. We have again become conscious of the limits of logic
and rationality. We again realize that the principles of form
are based on more profound and significant elements than
rigid logic. We know that things are not simple, and that,

even when we wish to, we are unable to cut ourselves off abruptly from the whole of our past: it continues to live on in us.

What we have to do in the realm of architecture is to find a method of linking rationality with the organic in such a way that the organic becomes dominant and rationality is reduced to a menial position.

On the Limits of the Organic in Architecture

Where are the limits of the approach to the organic in architecture? No exact statement can be made. The limits of what comprises architecture cannot easily be drawn, although many definite positions can and have been held.

Architecture is an austere art that must obey harsh laws. This applies not only to the materials of which it is composed but also to the forms it adopts.

Architecture cannot have absolute freedom. It moves within certain limits which have, in each particular period, had the force of eternal laws. The nature of architecture is to find its fulfilment within the limits of these laws. However, relations between geometrical structure and organic form have run through architecture's development since the beginning. Geometrical structure was the basis of the first great architecture of stone: the pyramids, symbols of life eternal. Architecture then drew close to the geometric forms that Plato termed unchanging and universal.

Mankind has always felt itself drawn, in many different ways, each time starting anew, to the eternal stability of the square and the circle and their related bodies: the cube, the pyramid, the cylinder or half-cylinder (tholos, apse, vault), the globe or half-globe (cupola).

Architecture, when built, must create a unity from a number of different parts. One of the many ways to achieve the spatial relationships that transform an assembly of parts into a unity is through the use of a system of proportions or of a simple module — that is, by employing certain measurements that recur in all three dimensions.

The foundation of architecture is bound up with its relations to proportions and to geometrical forms. But architecture is not only geometrical structure. It is not solely dependent on eternal laws. It exists to serve man, who is as perishable as a plant. Thus architecture also bears certain human and plant-like traits.

The notion of the organic is anchored so deeply in the irrational unconscious that it is extremely difficult to define it at all precisely. Frank Lloyd Wright never put his notion of the organic clearly into words. His teacher Louis Sullivan — whose life span ran parallel with that of Antoni Gaudi — came close to it. Around 1900, in *Kindergarten Chats*, probably the most original book written by an architect, Sullivan stated that the organic is the "ten-fingered grasp of reality."

Antoni Gaudi (1852–1926) is the originator of the organic development of contemporary architecture. Gaudi combined the sure instinct of a sound constructor with an adventurous sculptural imagination. He absorbed an abundance of architectural legacies from his region: Gothic, Churuguerra-Baroque, Moorish Azulecho. At the same time he longed to express in his work a new sculptural modeling of architecture. But in the first decade of this century, the time was not yet ripe.

His precognative talent came out most strongly when he had the greatest freedom of expression, as in the Guell Park in Barcelona (1900–14). Irrational, sinuous planes gleam with the indestructible colors of majolica fragments. In his mosaics of broken pieces of glazed tiles he made use of the principle of *collage* more than a decade earlier than Picasso and Braque.

Le Corbusier was the first to open the eyes of others to Gaudi's talent, which he had recognized in 1928 when he was in Madrid in connection with the competition for the League of Nations building. Four years later, when the Council of CIAM met in Barcelona, a moment when most of us were stuck fast in the purely rational interpretation of architecture, Le Corbusier impressively brought Antoni Gaudi's artistic intensity to our attention. But, despite Gaudi's impetuous genius, the architecture of this century could not then follow his direction.

874

It had to complete the change-over to a new space conception — first made visible by the painters — and it was a decade after Gaudi had completed his final work before a new architectural generation felt able to reapproach the matter.

Politics and Architecture

We must also consider the relations between social development and architecture. These relations have often been too much simplified. Historical space has many dimensions. It is many-sided. It does not present the observer with a single point of reference from which to interpret its phenomena. Just as in modern physics, no exact causality, no exact determination, can be established. Identical causes do not inevitably lead to identical effects.

Modern physicists, when they attacked the Newtonian system, called this uncertainty between cause and effect "semi-causality." This semi-causality is as true for historical as for subatomic spheres. No definite rules, no simple causality, determines reciprocal dependence between political events and the human activities which explore thought and feeling. The irrational interferes.

No preëstablished point of view is possible. Works rich in constituent facts and works of the most pernicious influence have appeared under the same economic system. We have seen that speculators during the eighteenth and early nineteenth centuries were responsible for housing developments which achieved the highest in human and urban values. However, speculators in the later nineteenth century destroyed the very structure of our cities, engulfing them in hopeless living quarters which degraded human dignity.

In the same political system, at the same time, and in the same country, it is possible to produce both works full of power to invigorate the future and works of confusion and decadence. For example, during the eighties and nineties, speculators erected great office buildings and department stores in Chicago; but the quality of office buildings erected in New York at the same time, under the same economic conditions, made that city the "plague spot of American architecture."

We know that a unity of culture has existed in some periods when imagination and the external world flowed into one another. In those periods the spirit was not condemned to go its way alone, and reality did not mean only a struggle for existence. Those were the happy hours of mankind, but they have been rare and of tragic brevity. They occurred in Athens under Pericles, and in Rome during the lustrous reign of Augustus. But, for example, it is questioned among historians whether Augustus was formed by the great spirits who surrounded him (and who now represent the glory of Roman literature) or whether their creative power was called forth by his personal influence.

On the preconception of culture

It is in these short periods of unity of intellectual, emotional, and political culture, that life has been able to manifest such splendor as is possible to man. We cannot now aspire so high. We must proceed more humbly. Before demanding from a disorganized world such a unity of emotional, intellectual, and political culture, we must first understand how far the emotional and intellectual are today interrelated, how nearly we have approached that vital preconception of every culture: affinity between its methods of thinking and of feeling.

The sciences and the arts are activities which, by exploring the unknown in the human mind, directly enlarge man's consciousness. Every scientist, every artist, is part of a long line of tradition. However, only a creative spirit can go forward, beyond the limits of that tradition, to explore what until then no one has known, no one has seen, no one has felt. By means of intuition, imagination, mystical impulse — what you will — he is able to open up new spheres of the unconscious. These spheres are distinguished from the outer world in that their essential development takes place directly, personally, without interference from any external power. They develop only in liberty, for no command can open the way to the unexplored.

The creative spirit is also bound to the earth and to the social environment. It does not grow in air-tight cans. It is

876

affected by the primary impulses of hunger, love, and self-esteem. It is affected by good and bad conditions. Adverse conditions may kill creative effort before it reaches realization; favorable conditions may stimulate its sudden growth.

However, it is not so important to establish the conditions of creative growth today as to have an understanding of its real structure — that is, to become aware of *what kind of growth* is going on within the depths of our period. We cannot grasp the constitution of this growth without knowing what *methods of approach* underlie advances in the different realms of thought and feeling.

Here our insight is very limited. Barriers between the disciplines and the fact that people are educated to become submerged and confined by their special fields have resulted in a lack of interest in methodological principles; so much so that sometimes they cannot even be spelled out. Consequently, there has been practically no comparative study of methods in the different realms, whatever they may be, from biology to music. The methods of approach underlying creative research form an *écriture automatique*. They open the way to objective insight into its spirit by making plain how close the different disciplines are to the preconception of culture: an identity of methods.

A period's social and political development is fundamental to its structure and there is an extensive literature dealing with the influence of the social order on architecture and environment. However, we wish to emphasize still another factor whose influence on human life, though less obvious and easy to establish at a given time, reaches more deeply into the present state of culture: the influence of feeling.

Influence of feeling

The influence of feeling on practical decisions is often regarded as unimportant, but it inevitably permeates and underlies all human decisions. The chaos of our cities, from Soviet Russia to the United States, cannot be explained as a result of social and economic conditions alone. In the rebuilding of Moscow, in the slum clearance of New York, there is the same lack of scale, the same schism between retrogressive feeling and advanced technology. Actions are triggered by social and economic impulses, but every human act is affected, is formed unconsciously, by a specific emotional background. Without exception, every human being has both a mental and an emotional relation to his occupation, whether he be laborer, artisan, merchant, or scientist.

It is the same with politics and government. Every political system is operated by individuals whose actions reflect their mental and emotional equipment. The moment these come in conflict, the inner kernel of personality is split by the difference of level between our methods of thinking and of feeling. The result is the symbol of our period: the maladjusted man.

It is possible that before long this situation will be recognized everywhere, and the schism may then disappear. Until then it will continue to be much easier to promote the most difficult scientific theory than the simplest of new artistic means. Education is today directed toward intellectual specialization; the education of the emotions is neglected. Thinking is trained; feeling is left untrained.

Intellectually trained people are now able to follow the most difficult scientific research, but the same people are lost when faced with new artistic means that force an enlargement of their emotional response. The reason is that most of them have nothing equivalent to their mental training to rely upon in the world of feeling. Knowledge and feeling have been isolated from each other. So we arrive at the curious paradox that feeling has today become more difficult than thinking.

In periods of equilibrium between thinking and feeling no one needs to speak of the training of feeling. Though it goes its own way, it forms an inseparable unity with the act of thinking. Emotion is like liberty. When freedom exists, it is taken for granted, it is reflected in every action; no one thinks it necessary to mention it. But the moment freedom is suppressed, life is deprived of its tonic, its invigoration, and men become aware of its loss.

Science and art, in so far as they explore the unknown or anticipate the future, reflect the real level, the true being, of our age. They are the real moral forces; they will speak for us to later generations when the horrors of the external world of our period have faded away.

We may even go a step further. How can one explain the disorder in all spheres concerned with human relations? How explain disturbances involving the most elemental laws of human life? In addition to the many reasons always given for the present chaos, there is a fundamental one that is often forgotten: *factual knowledge has not been reabsorbed and humanized by an equivalent level of feeling.*

Reality, as mirrored in the organization of the external world, has the power to destroy every one of us. This reality, which crushes more people every day, and menaces our culture just as it has begun to be conscious of itself, cannot be identified with the true being of our period.

What is this menacing reality? It is opposed to the methods of approach employed by the creative forces of our time. Its energy and material power are expended on vain attempts to cope with the many-sided and complex problems of our period by means of a ruthless simplification.

In the nineteenth century the means of production were mechanized, and unrestricted production became an end in itself, bringing disorder into human relations. In the twentieth century the means of destruction were mechanized, and unrestricted power became an end in itself.

Architectural façades of the last century were erected in many diverse shapes and styles, but these styles were not used as statements of conviction. They functioned merely as curtains, disguising what was behind them. Similarly, mankind has today many diverse political systems. Most do not reveal — some even contradict — the continued urge toward the organic going on in the depths of the period. These political systems simply serve to disguise the fact that political power has become an end in itself.

Social disorder was delivered to us as an inheritance from the Industrial Revolution. To restore order in this unbalanced world, we must alter its social conditions. But history shows us that this is not sufficient. It would be a fundamental mistake to believe that socio-political change would itself cause today's maladjusted man, the product of a century-long rupture between thinking and feeling, to disappear. Unintegrated people are today multiplying everywhere and in every class, among employers and employed, among high and low. Their acts reflect their inner division.

At the end of the nineteenth century, one of the most impressive political thinkers of his period recognized one of our central problems when he demanded that the division of labor, the dominant fact of an industrial society, should be replaced by what he called "the integration of labor." "To integrate" means, according to the dictionary, "to make a whole out of different parts." Though such integration of labor is undoubtedly desirable, it would not be enough, for it would only be the treatment of a single symptom. At the base of everything is the individual man. It is he who must be integrated — integrated in his inner nature, without being brutalized, so that his emotional and intellectual outlets will no longer be kept apart by an insuperable difference of level. To bring this fact into consciousness and to try to overcome it is closely connected with the outstanding task of our period: to humanize — that is, to reabsorb emotionally — what has been created by the spirit. All talk about organizing and planning is in vain unless we first create again the whole man, unfractured in his methods of thinking and feeling.

We are still passing through the test period of our civilization. The existence of each of us is menaced. But at the same time, there is being revealed in different spheres of activity an affinity in methods of approach, which, though developed independently in each sphere, yet underlie all that is significant in our thinking and feeling. It seems as if, unconsciously and out of its own forces, our period were moving by a still unrealized process toward a cure of its fatal disease.

Some unpredictable event may change the situation, and all these isolated, drifting efforts may coalesce at once into an inner sureness. In this moment our period will master reality.

In a letter long believed to be apocryphal but now regarded as genuine, the philosopher Plato announced that no statement of his doctrines existed in his own hand and that he would never write one. Nevertheless, his doctrine, so he said, would never be lost. In the human soul, as a result of "being absorbed by these things and by being in permanent contact with them," it would suddenly arise, "as a fire is kindled by a leaping spark and blazes forth into a bright flame." We believe it is the same with the formation of our cultural consciousness. It may awake suddenly, but never unless we begin to become "absorbed by these things," never without a strong will for an inner change, and never without forward-looking preparation.

INDEX

INDEX

Aalto, Aino, 667

Aalto, Alvar, 417, 467, 500, 549, 618–667, 672; work for MIT, 504–506, 510, 636, 664, 666; relation to Finland, 620; early work, 625–628; Paimio Sanatorium, 629–632, 664; use of undulating wall, 631–639; Viipuri Library, 632–633, 663, 674; Finnish Pavilion, 633–636, 664; Sunila, 640–645, 649–650; Mairea, 645–648; town planning, 648–655; civic centers, 655–661, 664; furniture by, 661–663; significance of, 663–665; personality of, 665–667; in CIAM, 698

Abstractionism, 487

Académie des Beaux Arts, 500, 566

Adam, Robert and James, 150, 715, 723, 730; Portland Place, 734

Adams, W. J., 338

Adelphi Terrace, 715, 723, 730

Adler, Dankmar, 397, 607

Adler and Sullivan Auditorium, Chicago, 10, 372, 378, 532–533

Aesthetics, and modern architecture, 700–701

Agglomeration: defined, 703; proposed by Le Corbusier, 858

Ahmedabad, 558

Air conditioning, 421n

Albers, Josef, 488, 510n

Albert, Prince Consort, 249

Alberti, Leon Battista, 35–36, 45, 76, 112

Alphand, Jean, 285, 759; work with Haussmann, 764, 771

America: use of feroconcrete in, 325n, 327–328; at London Exhibition (1851), 336–338; tools, 339–341; furniture, 338, 341–342, 354–355; influence of industrial architecture in, 343; use of balloon frame, 346–354; use of plane surfaces, 355–363; development of dwelling house in, 398–400; post-1930 immigration to, 499–500; work of Gropius in, 499–517. *See also* Chicago; New York; St. Louis; Wright, Frank Lloyd

American architecture, elements of: balloon fame, 346–354; flat walls, 355–363; flexible ground plan, 363–368, 405; porch, 407–409. *See also* Chicago School; Mercantile classicism

Ammanati, Bartolomeo, 51

Amstellaan Blvd., 799–800; as nineteenth-century conception, 803

Amsterdam: town planning in, 27, 781, 791, 793–803; van Doesburg and van Eesteren house, 442–443; plan for North Amsterdam, 676; general extension plan for, 804–810; relation of housing to activities in, 810–813. *See also* Berlage, H. P.

Amsterdam Stock Exchange, 292, 309–313

Andreas, A. T., 353

Antonine Column, 98

Apartment house: in Paris, 328–330; in Chicago, 377–381; in Marseille, 544–548, 606, 840; Weissenhof settlement, 598; work of Mies van der Rohe, 603–607; in nineteenth-century Paris, 767–769; in Amsterdam, 808–810, 833; slab-like housing units, 833–837; zigzag blocks, 837–838

Apollinaire, Guillaume, 436

Arago, François, 15

Architects' Collaborative, the (TAC), 506–507, 514

Architecture: as organism, 19–23; as index of period, 19–20; continuity of evolution in, 21–23; construction as hidden force in, 24–25; and town planning, 25–27, 859–873; separation from engineering, 182–183, 763; and technology, 211–218; schism healed, 382, 618–619; role of modern, 704–706; and politics, 875; influence of feeling upon, 877–881. *See also* Engineering; Technology

Arnodin, 290

Arp, Hans, 416, 475, 510n, 621, 665, 701

Art: and science, 12–17, 182–183, 211, 430–431, 443, 562, 878–879; influence of École des Beaux-Arts, 212; functions of, 431–432; relation to public, 432–434; related to new types of construction, 450; related to modern architecture, 496–497; reunion with architecture, 509–510, 621. *See also* Feeling; Painting

Art nouveau: use in architecture, 302–304; outgrowth of work in iron, 322

Arts and crafts movement: in England, 298, 399; in Austria, 319–321, 399n; in Germany, 485

Arup, Ove, 474, 683

Ashbee, C. R., 298

Aspdin, Joseph, 324

Asplund, Gunner, 672

Assemblée de Constructeurs pour une

Rénovation Architecturale (ASCORAL), 701, 702
Austria: influence of Otto Wagner in, 318, 319, 478; influence of handicrafts, 319–321
Aztec architecture, 672, 675, 688

Back Bay Center, 513, 869
Badovici, Jean, 699
Baghdad University, 514
Bagnocavallo, 45
Bakema, J. B., 676; in CIAM, 702–703; builder in Rotterdam, 863
Balat, Alphonse, 306n
Balla, Giacomo, 445
Balloon frame, 346–354; principle of, 347–349; dependent on cheap nails, 350; and building of the West, 350–351; invention of, 351–354
Baltard, Victor, 230–231
Barcelona, Mies van der Rohe's pavilion at, 481, 591
Barillet-Deschamps, 764
Barnard, Henry, 338–339
Baroque: perspective of, 54, 109; in Rome, 75–106; universal outlook of, 107–109; late, 107–109; defined, 108; use of undulating wall, 110–113, 120; in South Germany, 127–133; in France, 133–141; town planning of, 709–710, 712; Rue de Rivoli, 714–715; avenues of, 770. See also Borromini; Guarini; Squares; Versailles
Barr, Alfred, 437
Bath, England: Royal Crescent, 147–149, 640, 723, 736; Lansdowne Crescent, 157–158; middle-class Versailles, 160; influence of, 734
Baudot, Anatole de, 271; Saint-Jean de Montmartre, 326–327
Bauhaus, the, 266, 486–497, 595; role of, 489–491, 511; buildings at Dessau, 491–497, 515, 529, 629, 663
Bayer, Herbert, 488, 510n, 594
Beams: cast-iron, 191, 192; rolled-iron, 195
Beardsley, Aubrey, 302
Bedford House, and Bloomsbury, 724–728
Bedford Place, 727, 728–729
Behrens, Peter, 318, 371, 595; atelier of, 479, 519, 588; contrasted with Gropius, 482–483
Belgrand, Eugène, 763
Bellamy, Edward, *Looking Backward*, 783
Bellangé, 176
Bellini, Jacopo, 62
Berkeley Square, 723, 739
Berlage, Hendrik Petrus, 115, 292, 309;

Amsterdam Exchange, 309–313, 357, 797; use of Romanesque by, 310, 314–315; influence of, 313, 315–316, 588; and F. L. Wright, 426; plan for Amsterdam South, 796–803; orientation toward the past, 803
Bernini, Giovanni Lorenzo, 65, 125; in France, 134, 137; Piazza Obliqua, 141–142, 717
Bertrand, Louis, 140
Bibliothèque Nationale, 222–228
Bloomsbury: Square, 722, 726; development of, 724–733
Boccioni, Umberto, 445
Bode, Wilhelm, 365–366
Bogardus, James, 195–200, 208, 255n; use of prefabricated parts by, 196, 236–237, 346; Harper and Bros. Bldg., 197; scheme for N.Y. World's Fair, 198–199, 290; as inventor, 199–200; elevator proposed by, 208
Boileau, L. A., 195; Bon Marché, 238–241; on transparent surfaces, 267
Bois de Boulogne, 744, 747, 761, 764
Bois de Vincennes, 761, 764
Bologna, fortresses in, 852–853
Bonnier, Louis, 327n
Bordino, Giovanni Francesco, 93
Borromini, Francesco, 110, 762; use of undulating wall by, 110–113, 120, 157, 640; San Carlo alle Quattro Fontane, 110–113, 143; rediscovery of, 111n; Sant' Ivo, 113–116; as sculptor, 117–120; connection with past, 121; forerunner of modern architecture, 155, 521, 529, 738
Borsodi, Ralph, 820
Boston: commercial buildings in, 234–235; Oak Hall, 235; granite warehouses, 359–360; Quincy Market, 359n; Back Bay Center, 513, 869.
Boulevard: defined, 757; in Paris, 757–759
Boulevard Richard-Lenoir, 771–772, 800
Boulevard Sébastopol, 748, 749
Boulton, Matthew, 191–192
Bourgeois, Victor, 316, 595, 698
Bourget, Paul, 381
Bowen, H., 353–354
Bramante, Donato, 36, 44, 76, 567, 580; Piazza Ducale, 48; Via Giulia, 57–58; use of stairways by, 62–64
Brancusi, Constantin, 475, 476, 621
Braque, Georges, 438, 443, 446, 521, 594, 620
Breuer, Marcel, 488, 500, 700; work with Gropius, 502, 504, 507, 539; high-rise buildings, 833n

891

204–206; in skyscraper, 206; Leiter Building, 382–383; Maison de Verre, 383; Carson, Pirie, and Scott Store, 389; as used by Le Corbusier, 529. *See also* Gropius; Mies van der Rohe

Skyscraper: forerunners of, 204–206; inventor of, 206–207; first built, 208; Chicago type, 846; new forms in New York, 846–849

Slab, concrete: Maillart's use of, 458–459, 547; sculpture of, related to painting, 461–463

Smeaton, John, 169, 323–324

Smirke, Sydney, 222

Snow, George Washington, 352–354

Soane, Sir John, 150

Social imagination: architect's need of, 542–543; Le Corbusier as example of, 543–553; of third generation of modern architects, 668; and urban planning, 702

Soho Square, 722

Sonck, Lars, 623

Soria y Mata, Arturo, 785

South Kensington, 158

Space: organization of in architecture, 23–24; new conceptions of, 26, 435–443; and perspective, 30, 435; Michelangelo's modeling of, 64–71; interpenetration of inner and outer, 117, 284, 436, 493, 521, 668; interrelated horizontals and verticals, 155; organized by Wright, 411; modern vs. classic, 435; and concept of simultaneity, 436, 445, 449; expressed by Bauhaus group, 496–497; medieval use of, 544; use of horizontal planes, 668, 672. *See also* Space-time

Space-time: concept of, 14, 430; and dissolution of perspective, 434–436; in cubism, 436, 444, 525; in futurism, 444; and modern cities, 822

Spanish Steps, 64, 95

Squares: in London, 27, 724–733, 739; planned by Sixtus V, 97–100; Piazza Obliqua, 141–142; in Paris, 142–143; interrelated, 143–147; Piazza del Popolo, 150–155; defined, 718–719

Stairway, Renaissance use of, 59–64

Stam, Mart, 481, 595, 599

Starrett, Theodore, 378

Statistics, in town planning, 816–818

Steel frame, 191–193; girders first used, 208n

Stephenson, Robert, 190; and Paine's bridge, 173–174

Stevens, Robert, 195

Stijl group, 413, 426, 442, 488, 585, 590, 619

Stone, as building material, 358–360

Stoss, Veit, 128

Street: treatment of in Renaissance, 57–59; plan by Sixtus for Rome, 93–99; becomes dominant, 739–754, 770–773, 803; Haussmann's plans for in Paris, 747–754; in Berlage's Amsterdam, 799, 803; *rue corridor* outgrown, 822, 832. *See also* Highway; Parkway

Sullivan, Louis, 239, 275, 309, 846, 854; Garrick Theatre, 10; Transportation Building, 275, 276; on Richardson, 361–362; on Jenney, 371; Carson, Pirie, Scott store, 388–390; style of, 390–391, 425; on Chicago World's Fair, 394, 395; Wright as apprentice to, 397, 398; as organic architect, 414–415, 874

Sunderland Bridge, 171–173

Sunila, 640–645

Surface, emphasis on: in painting, 462; in use of concrete slab, 463. *See also* Painting

Suspension bridges: by Seguin, 178; by Roebling, 178; Golden Gate, 179

Sweeney, J. J., 462

Sydney Opera House, 673, 676–688

Syrian architecture, 40

TAC, *see* Architects' Collaborative

Taliesin, 415–416

Tallmadge, Thomas, 391

Tange, Kenzo, 555, 676, 863

Tatlin, 117

Taut, Bruno, 480, 501, 595

Technology: schism between architecture and, 211–218; as incentive for new growth, 214–215. *See also* Architecture; Art; Science

Tecton group, 836

Telford, Thomas, 190, 218

Tengboom, Ivar, 623

Terrace, used by Le Corbusier, 525, 555

Théâtre-Français, iron roofing for, 175–176, 191

Thiers, Adolphe, 766, 771

Third generation of contemporary architects, characteristics of, 668; relation to past, 668–671; use of planes by, 674

Tijen, W. van, 793, 808n, 834

Time: as constituent fact, 436; new conception of, in art, 443–444; Edgerton's stroboscopic studies, 853. *See also* Space-time

Tokyo, plan for, 676

Tolnay, Charles de, 70

Tools, American, 339–341, 343

Karlsplatz station, 318, 322; Postal Savings Building, 318–319; solutions of urbanism, 780–782

Wall: as plane surface, 41, 311, 313, 318–319, 355–363; use of in Renaissance, 56–57; undulating, 110–113, 120, 158, 539, 638–639; Romanesque influence on, 314–315; as organized by Wright, 410; of glass, by Gropius, 482, 493; functional independence of, 524, 589–590; by Aalto, 632–639

Wanamaker Store, 238

Warehouses, 202, 237; Montgomery Ward, 327, 410; Leiter Building, 371, 373, 382–384

Warren, Clinton J., 378

Watt, James, 169, 200n, 208; iron framework for Salford cotton mill, 191–193

Webb, Philip, 398

Weber, Mrs. Heidi, 580

Weissenhof Housing Settlement, 538, 594–599

Werkbund, see Deutsche Werkbund

Whistler, J. A. M., 297

Wiener, P. L., 864

Wilkinson, John, 170, 174

Winckelmann, J. J., 432

Windows: influence of large displays on use of iron girders, 195; in commercial buildings, 202; the "Chicago window," 381, 387–388, 389, 392

Windsor chair, 354–355

Wittmer, Hans, 536

Wölfflin, Heinrich, 2, 3, 108

Women, influence on architecture, 134

Wood, John, 148, 723

"Woolworth Gothic," 391

Wren, Christopher, 717

Wright, Frank Lloyd, 26, 315, 316, 391, 478, 500, 781, 787, 840; use of simple brick wall, 357; flexible ground plan, 368, 405, 523, 525, 589; and mercantile classicism, 395–396, 425; place in American development, 396–400, 425, 585; Charnley house, 399, 409; cruciform plan, 400–405; Isabel Roberts house, 402–404; Suntop houses, 404–405; use of porch, 407–409; Robie house, 410, 417, 529; organization of space, 410–413; organic approach of, 414–417, 618, 874; Larkin Administration Building, 419–422; Johnson Wax Co. Building, 420, 422–424; influence of, 424–427, 589; late period, 427–428; compared with Gropius, 496; honored, 500; and Utzon, 672; on cities, 820, 822

Yamasaki, 607

Zervos, Christian, 699

Zorès, 195

Zurich Theater, 688–691